# A-Z NOTTINGHAM

C000098342

## CONTENTS

| | |
|---|---|
| Key to Map Pages | 2-3 |
| Large Scale City Centre | 4-5 |
| Map Pages | 6-81 |
| Postcode Map | 82-83 |

Road

Index
Villages, Stations, Hospitals etc.    86-128
and selected Places of Interest

## REFERENCE

| | | | |
|---|---|---|---|
| Motorway | **M1** | Car Park (selected) | P |
| A Road | A46 | Church or Chapel | † |
| B Road | B682 | Cycleway (selected) | |
| Dual Carriageway | | Fire Station | ■ |
| One-way Street<br>Traffic flow on A Roads is also indicated<br>by a heavy line on the driver's left. | | Hospital | H |
| | | House Numbers (A & B Roads Only) | 8  30 |
| Road Under Construction<br>Opening dates are correct at the time of publication | | Information Centre | 🄸 |
| Proposed Road | | National Grid Reference | ³45 |
| Restricted Access | | Park & Ride | Queen's Drive **P+R** |
| Pedestrianized Road | | Police Station | ▲ |
| Track & Footpath | | Post Office | ★ |
| Residential Walkway | | Safety Camera with Speed Limit<br>Fixed cameras and long term road work cameras.<br>Symbols do not indicate camera direction. | 30 |

Railway    Station — Level Crossing — Heritage Station — Tunnel

Toilet:
without facilities for the Disabled    ▽
with facilities for the Disabled    ▽
Disabled use only    ▽

Nottingham Express Transit (NET)
The boarding of NET trams at stops
may be limited to a single direction,
indicated by the arrow.    Stop

| | |
|---|---|
| Educational Establishment | ▢ |
| Hospital or Healthcare Building | ▢ |
| Built-up Area    ALMA ST. | Industrial Building | ▢ |
| Leisure or Recreational Facility | ▢ |
| Local Authority Boundary | Place of Interest | ▢ |
| Posttown Boundary | Public Building | ▢ |
| Postcode Boundary (within Posttown) | Shopping Centre or Market | ▢ |
| | Other Selected Buildings | ▢ |

Map Continuation ▲ 24    Large Scale City Centre ▲ 4

## SCALE

Map Pages 6-81
1:15,840  4 inches (10.16cm) to 1 mile  6.31cm to 1km
0    ¼    ½ Mile
0    250    500    750 Metres

Map Pages 4-5
1:7,920  8 inches (20.32cm) to 1 mile  12.63cm to 1km
0    ⅛    ¼ Mile
0    100    200    300    400 Metres

## Copyright of Geographers' A-Z Map Company Limited

Fairfield Road, Borough Green, Sevenoaks, Kent TN15 8PP
Telephone: 01732 781000 (Enquiries & Trade Sales)
01732 783422 (Retail Sales)
www.az.co.uk
Copyright © Geographers' A-Z Map Co. Ltd.
Edition 7  2013

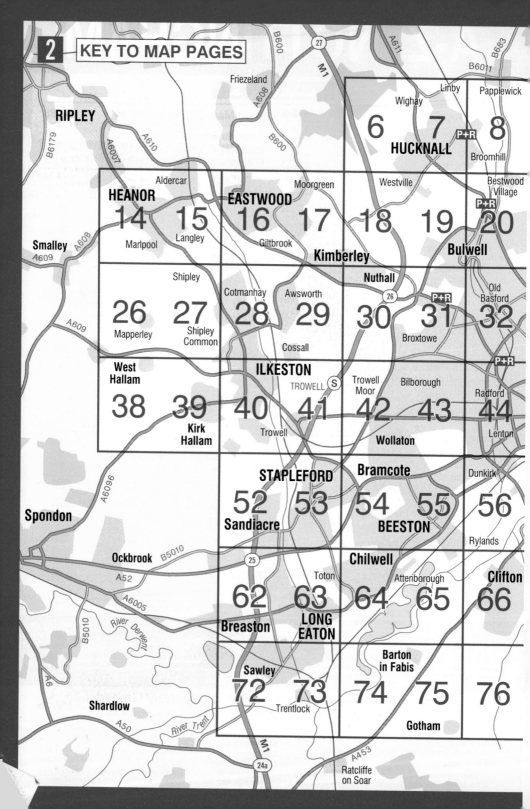

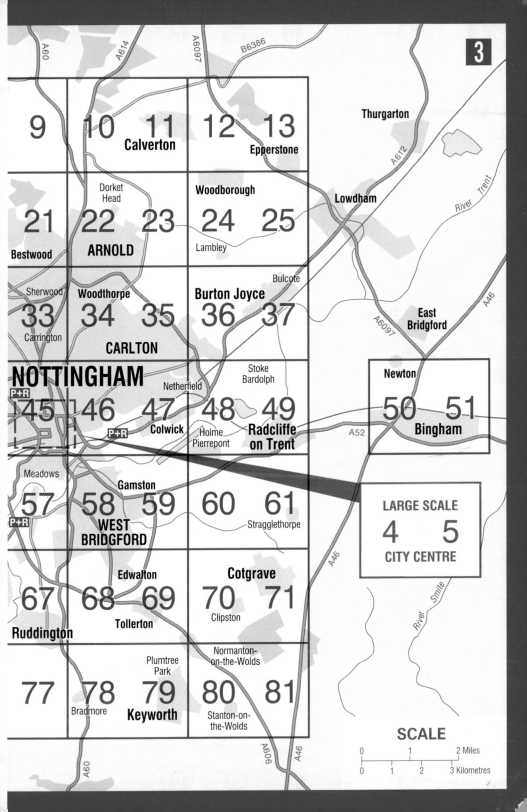

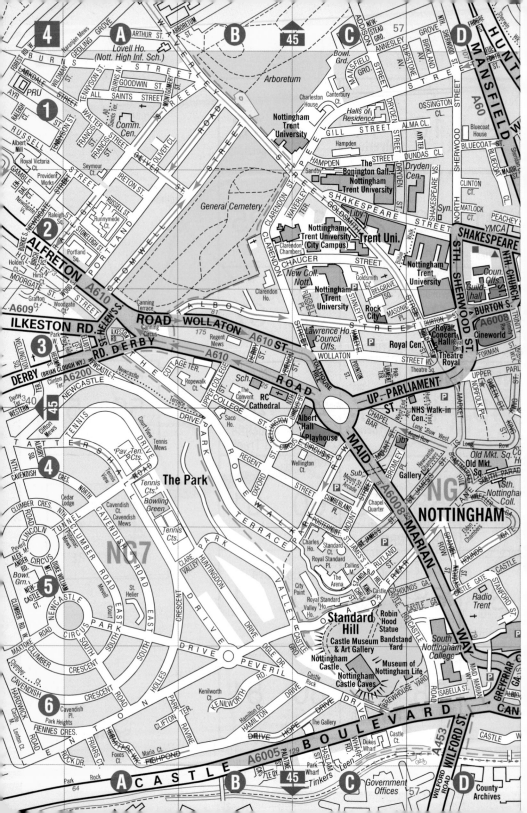

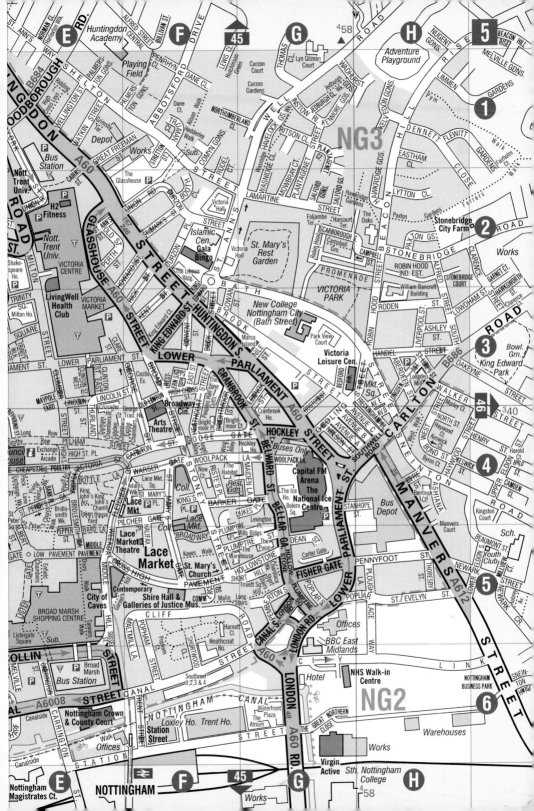

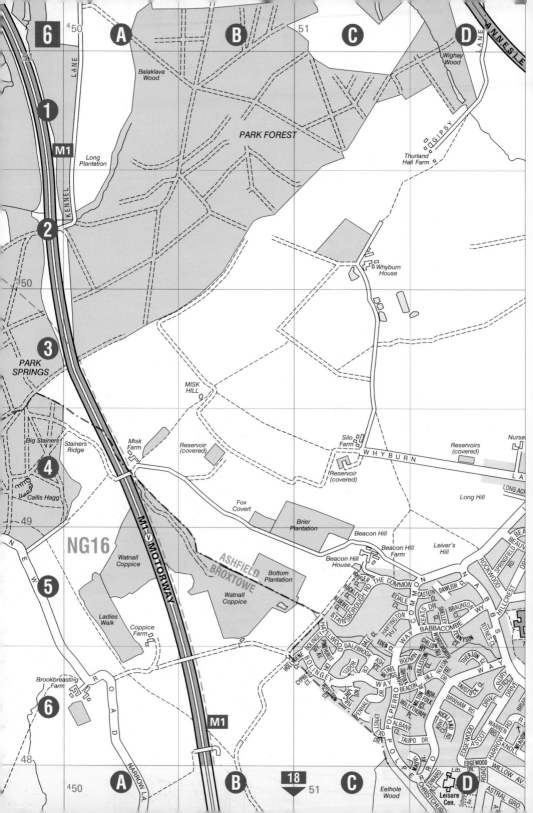

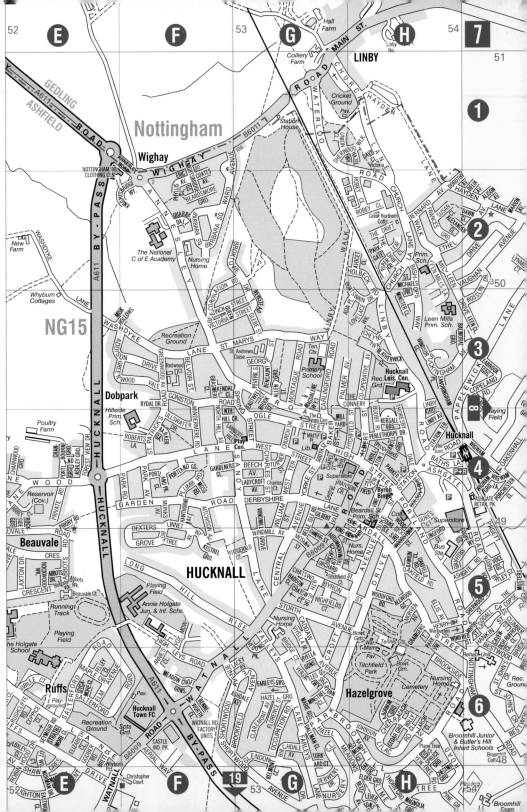

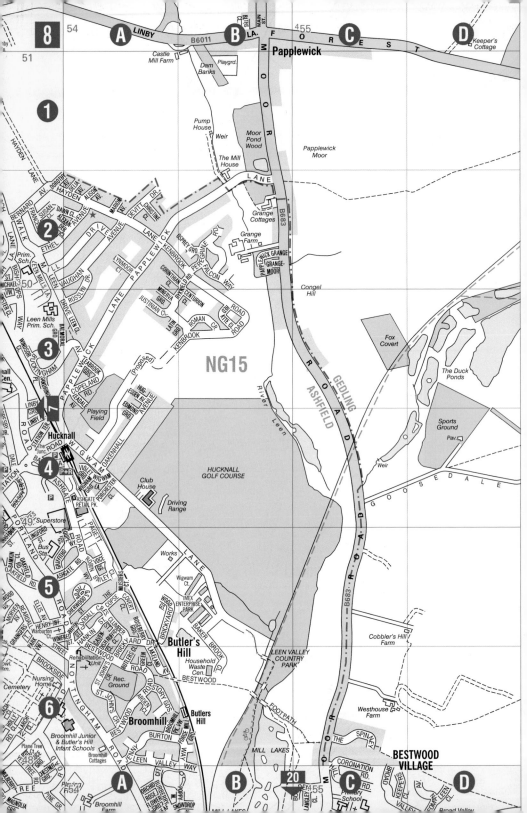

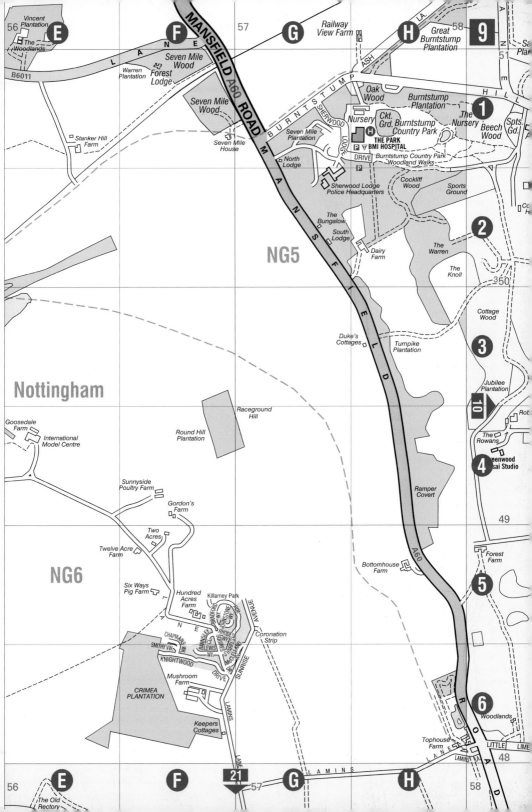

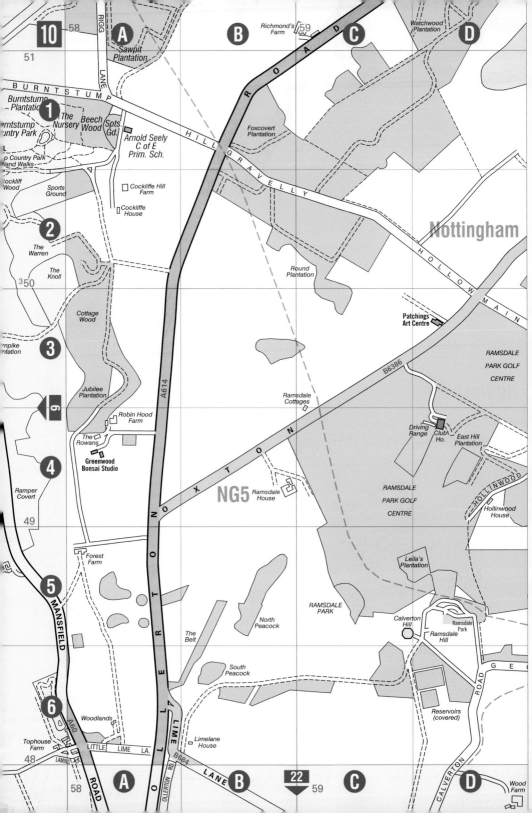

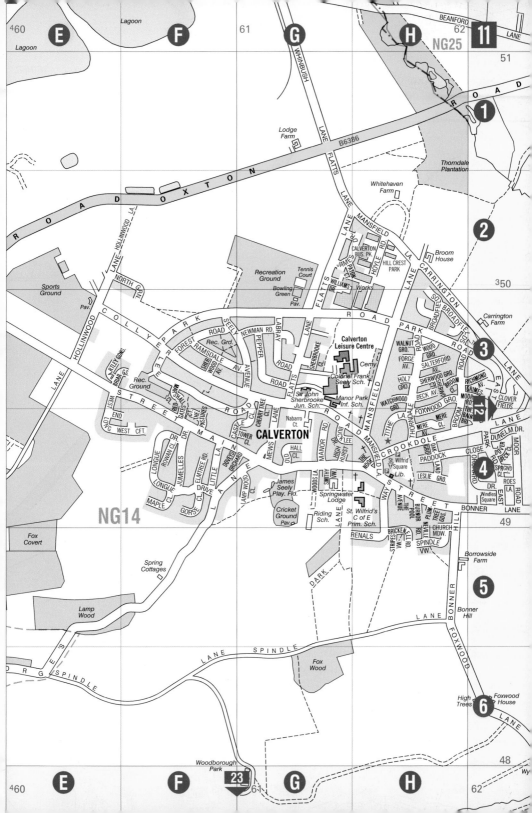

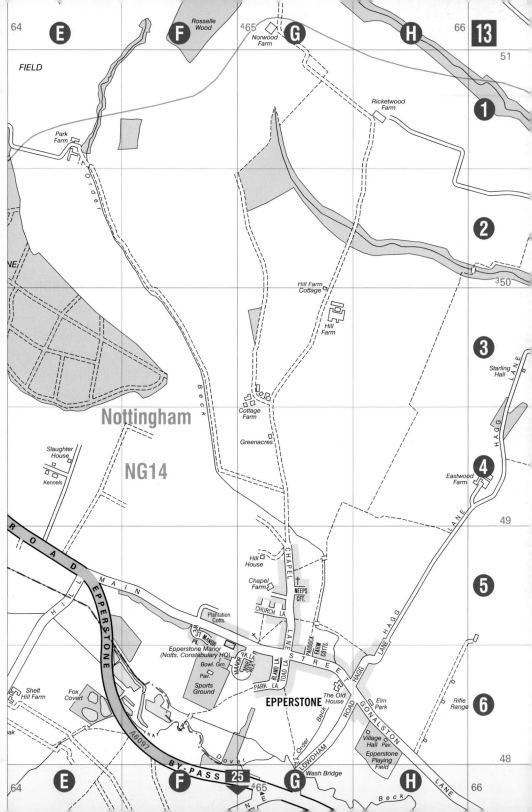

FIELD

Rosselle Wood

Norwood Farm

**1**

Ricketwood Farm

Park Farm

Order

**2**

350

Beck

Hill Farm Cottage

Hill Farm

**3**

Starling Hall

HAGG LANE

## Nottingham

Cottage Farm

Greenacres

Eastwood Farm

**4**

## NG14

Slaughter House

Kennels

LANE

49

Hill House

Chapel Farm

NEEPS CFT.

CHAPEL LANE

CHURCH LA.

**5**

ROAD

HILL

MAIN

EPPERSTONE

Plantation Cotts.

WEST MANOR PK.

Epperstone Manor (Notts. Constabulary HQ)

Bowl. Grn.

Pav.

Sports Ground

MANOR CT.

TOWN CT.

PK. LA.

BLIND LA.

TOAD LA.

PARK LA.

LANE STREET

PADDOCK FARM COTTS.

HAGG LANE

GONALSTON

Elm Park

Rifle Range

**6**

Shelt Hill Farm

Fox Covert

**EPPERSTONE**

The Old House

Beck

Order

LOWDHAM ROAD

Village Hall Pav.

Epperstone Playing Field

48

A6097

Dover

BY-PASS **25**

465

Wash Bridge

Beck

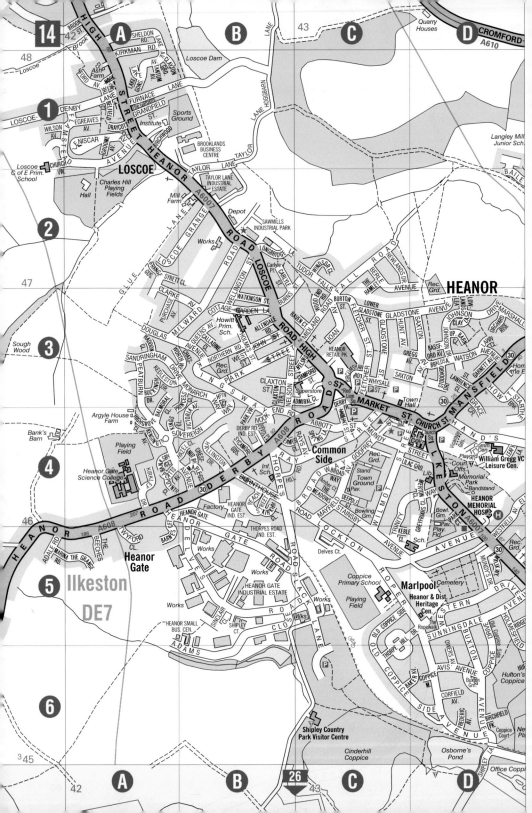

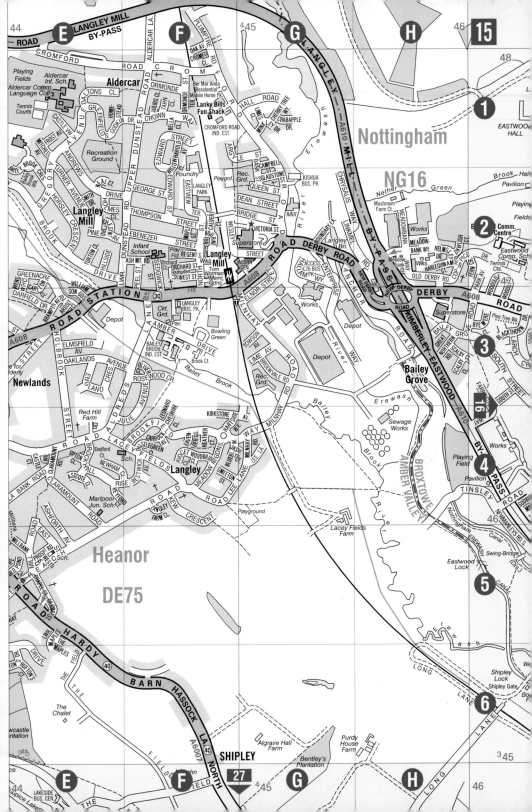

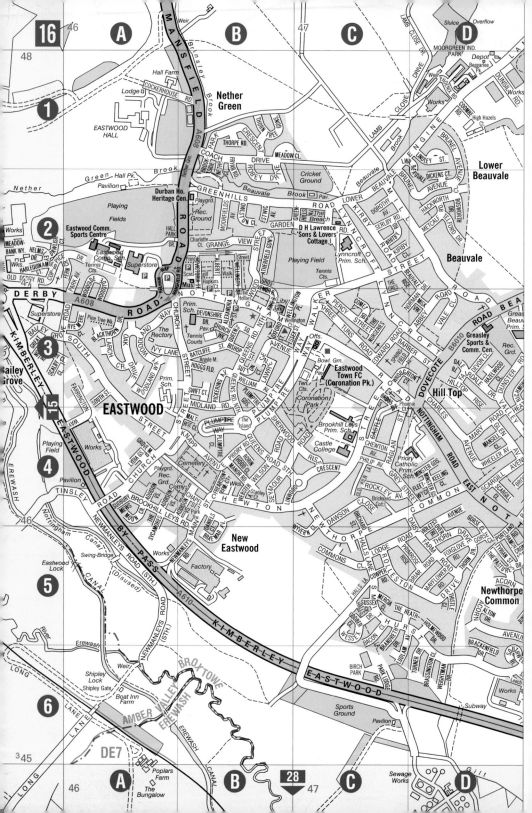

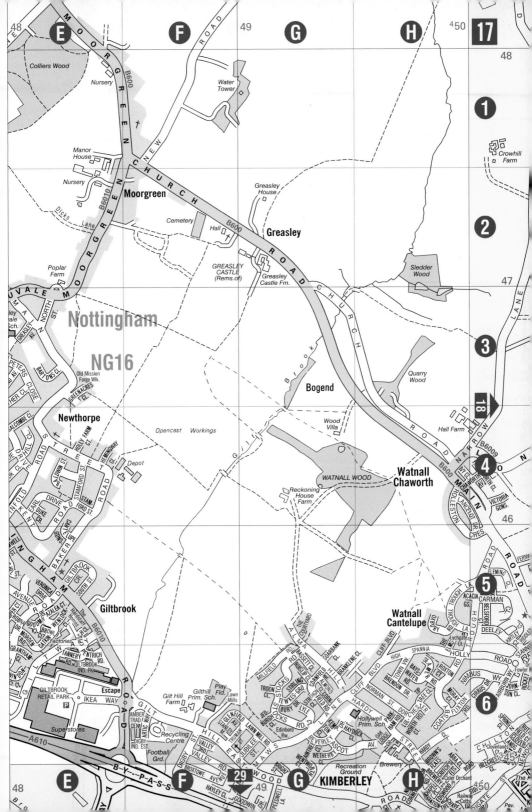

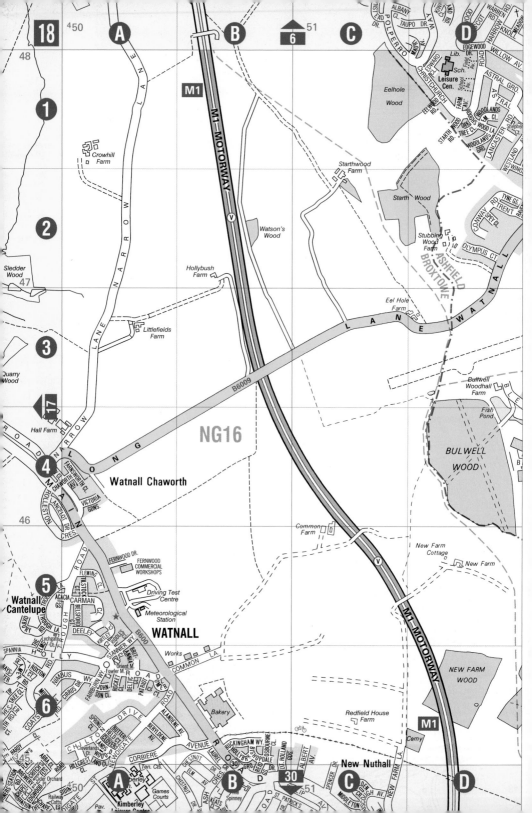

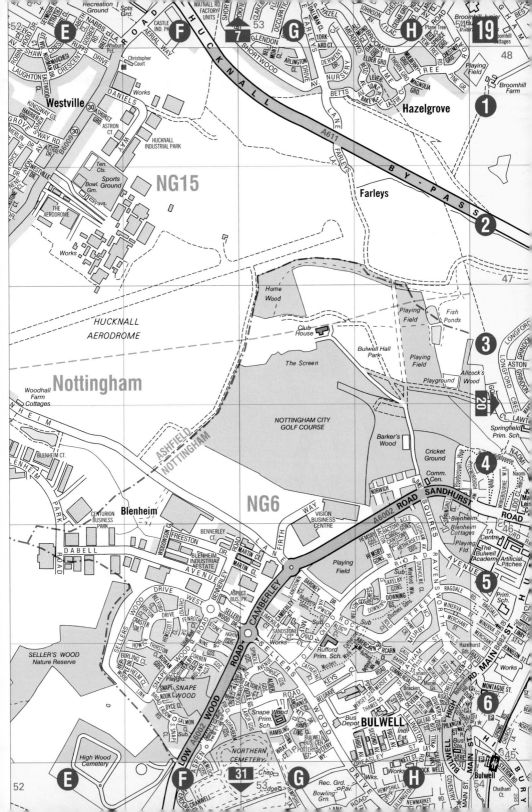

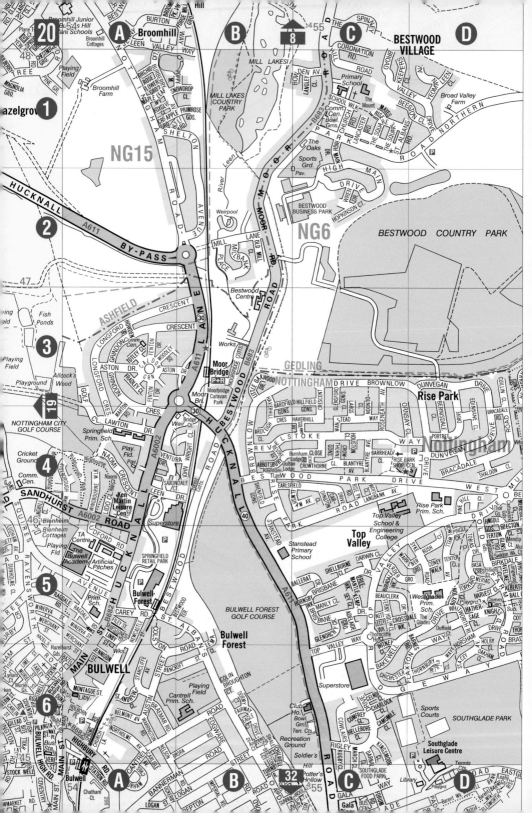

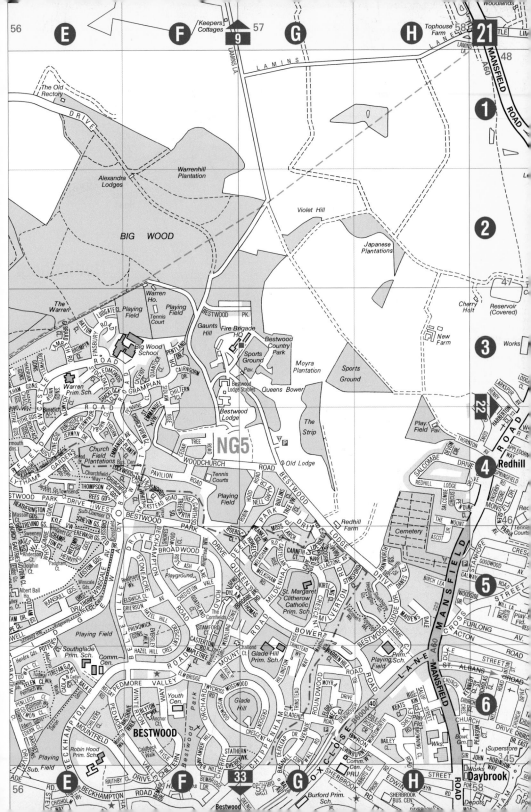

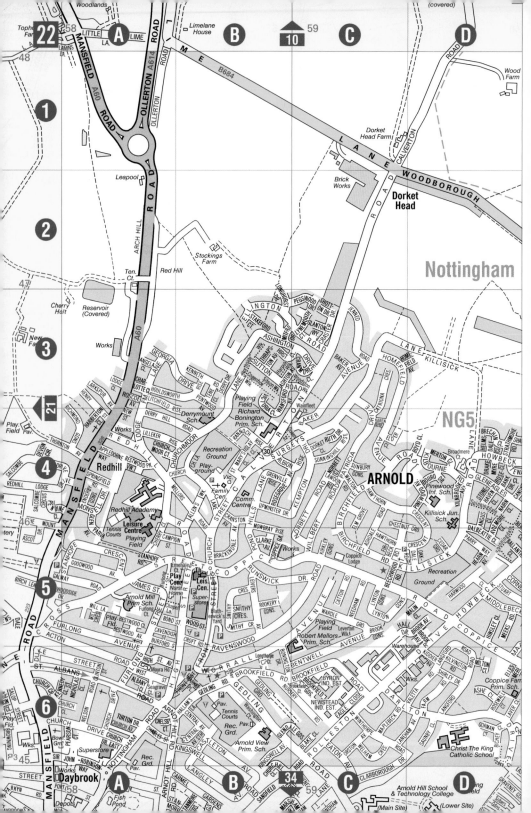

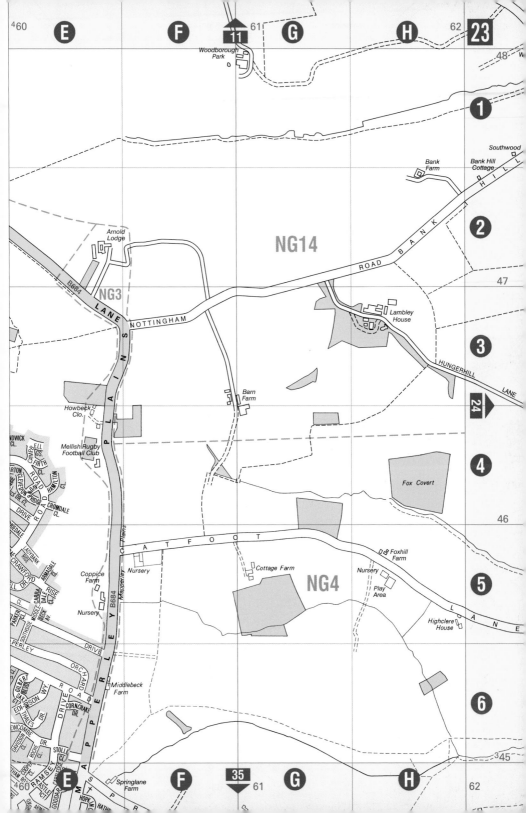

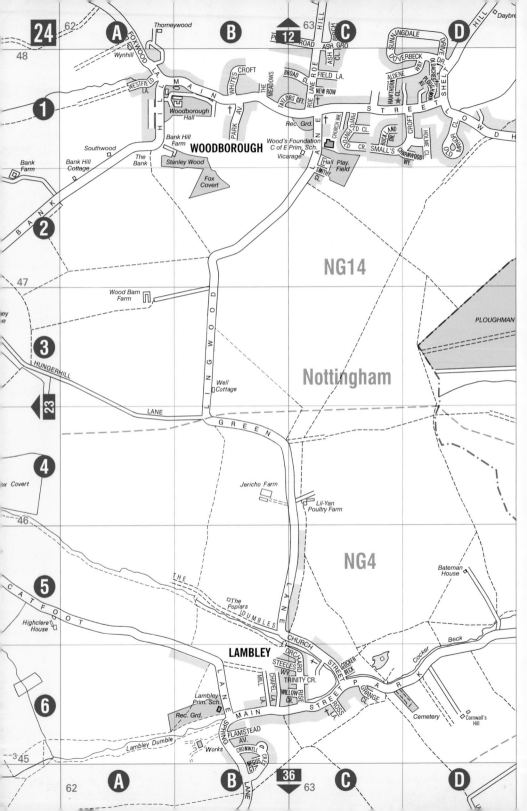

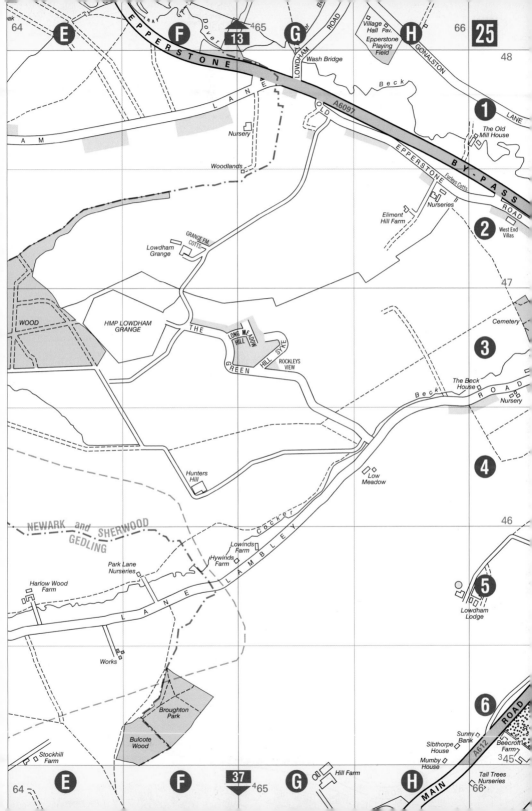

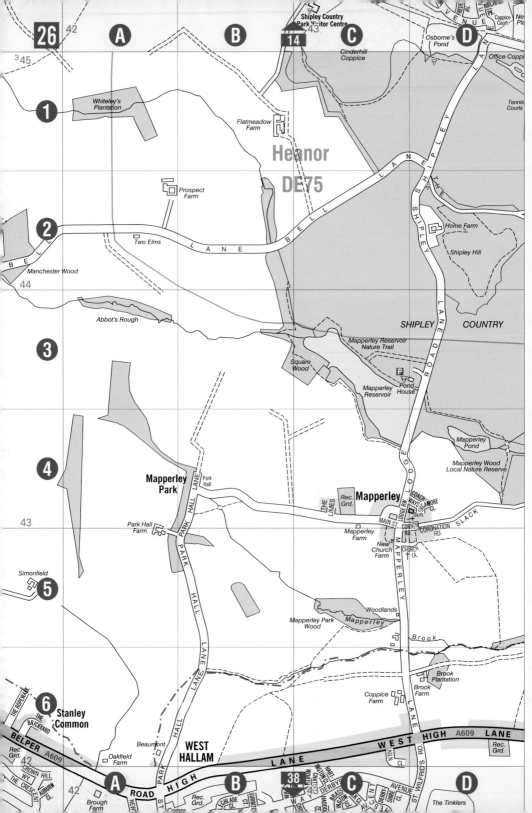

A    B    C    D

**Shipley Country Park Visitor Centre**

**14**

Cinderhill Coppice

Osborne's Pond

Office Coppi

New Pla

Coppice Court

**1**

Whiteley's Plantation

Tennis Courts

Flatmeadow Farm

**Heanor DE75**

Home Farm

Prospect Farm

Shipley Hill

**2**

Two Elms

LANE

BELL

BELL LANE

Manchester Wood

44

Abbot's Rough

**SHIPLEY COUNTRY**

Mapperley Reservoir Nature Trail

**3**

Square Wood

P

Pond House

Mapperley Reservoir

SHIPLEY LANE

SHIPLEY LANE

THE SHIPLEY

Mapperley Pond

**4**

Mapperley Park

Park Hall

PARK HALL LANE

Mapperley Wood Local Nature Reserve

43

THE LIMES

Rec. Grd.

**Mapperley**

COACH WAYS

SYCAMORE

Sch.

Park Hall Farm

Main St.

CORNTN RD.

CORONATION RD.

SLACK

MAPPERLEY

Mapperley Farm

New Church Farm

CHURCH

CHURCH LA.

LODGE ROW

**5**

Simonfield

Mapperley Park Wood

Woodlands

**Mapperley**

Brook

LANE

Brook Plantation

Brook Farm

**6**

**Stanley Common**

THE ROPEWALK

THE BRICKYARD

BELPER A609

Beaumont

**WEST HALLAM**

Coppice Farm

**WEST HIGH A609 LANE**

Rec. Grd.

Rec. Grd.

42

CROWN HILL WY.

THE CRESCENT

AUBURN CL.

Oakfield Farm

PARK HALL LANE

**ROAD HIGH LANE**

**38**

NEW ST.

Comm

Rec. Grd.

LECHLADE CL.

SUBTON CL.

DERBY

DERBY RD.

CHATSWTON

HARTINGTON

BRASSINGTON

AVENUE

DERBY

SHIRE CL.

ST. WILFRID'S RD.

NTH. CL.

CRESCENT

The Tinklers

A    B    C    D

42

Brough Farm

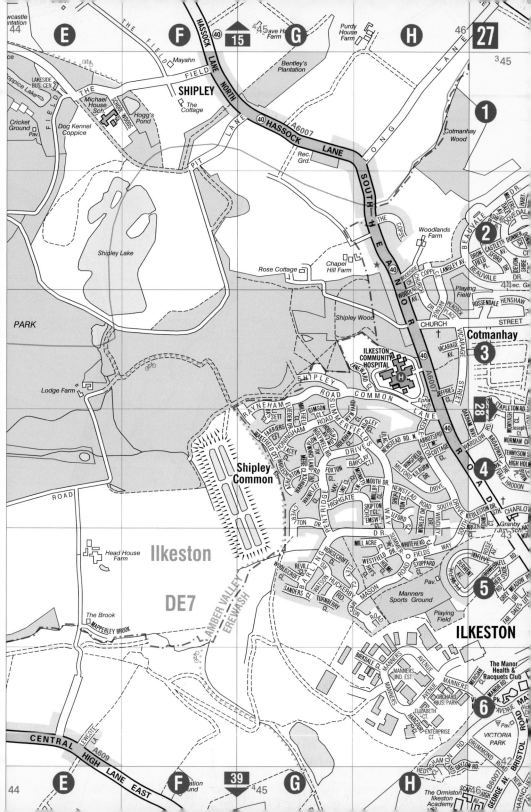

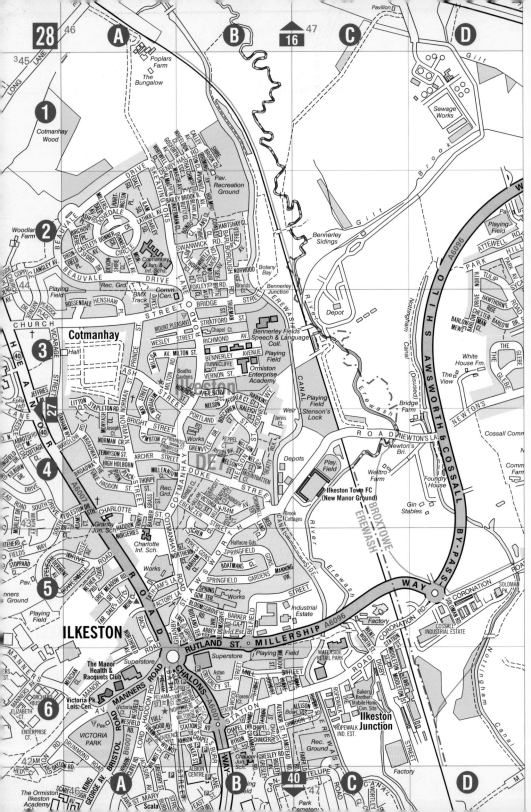

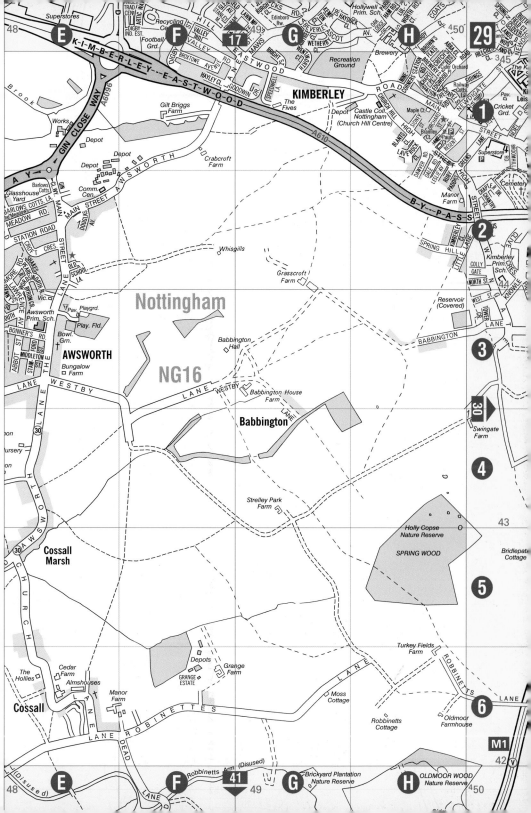

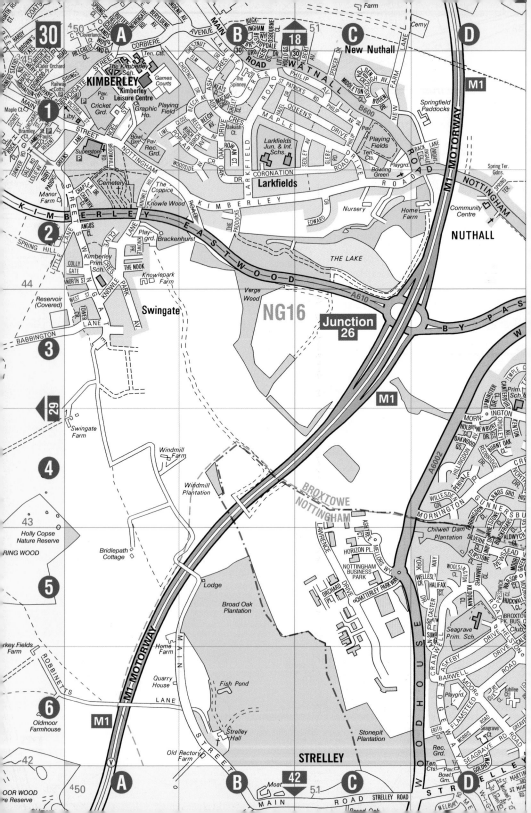

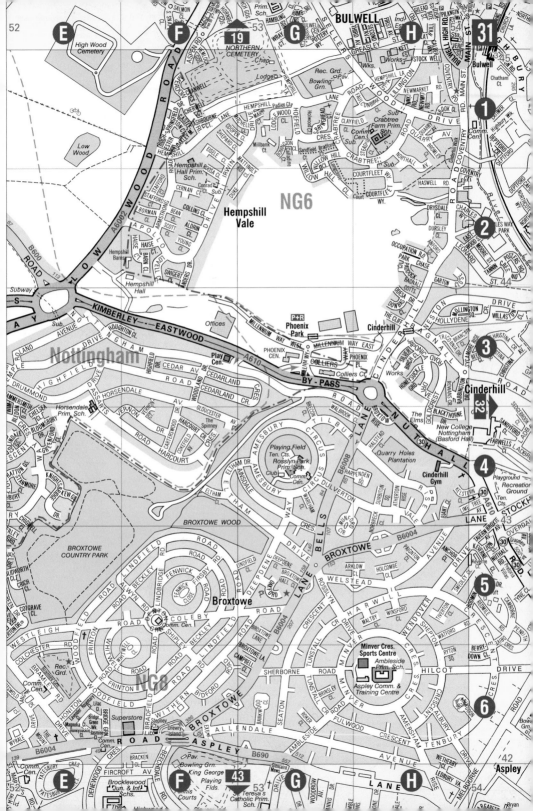

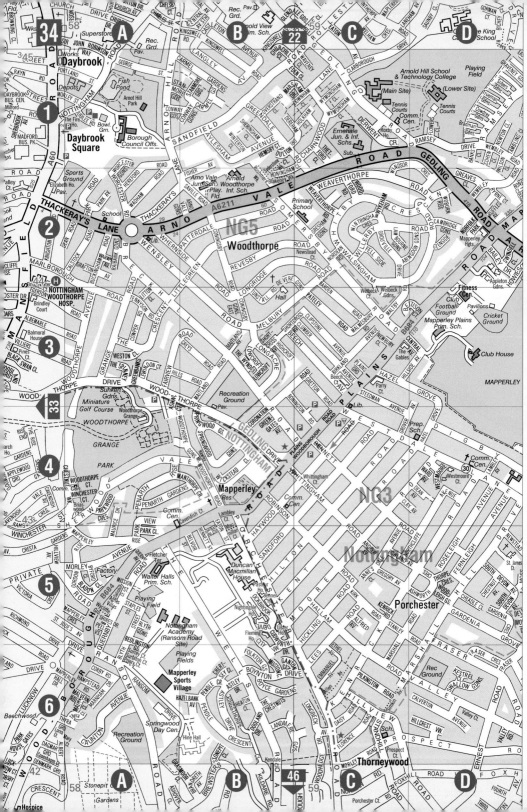

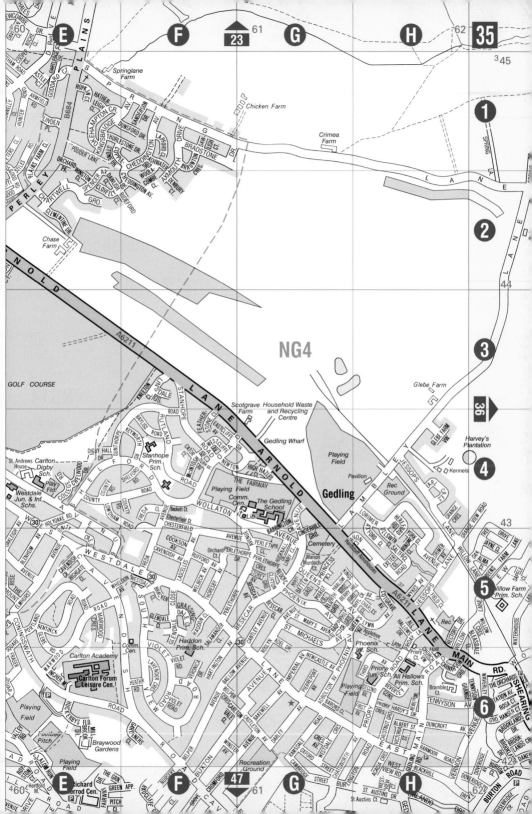

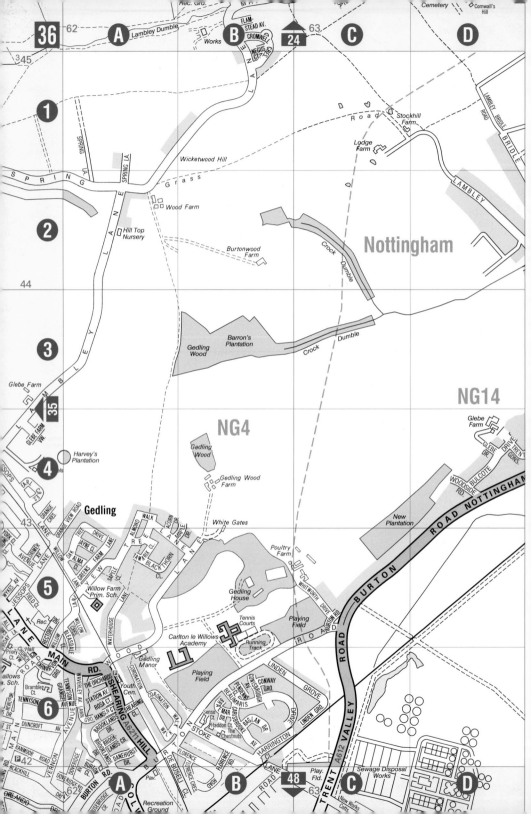

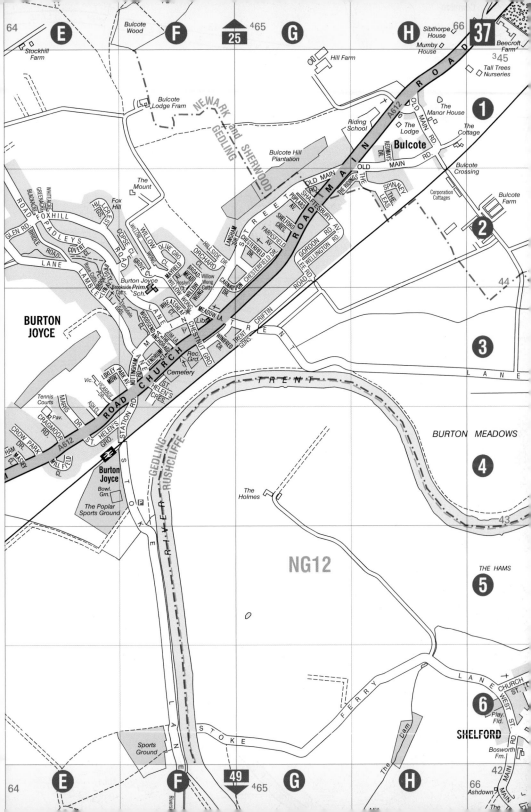

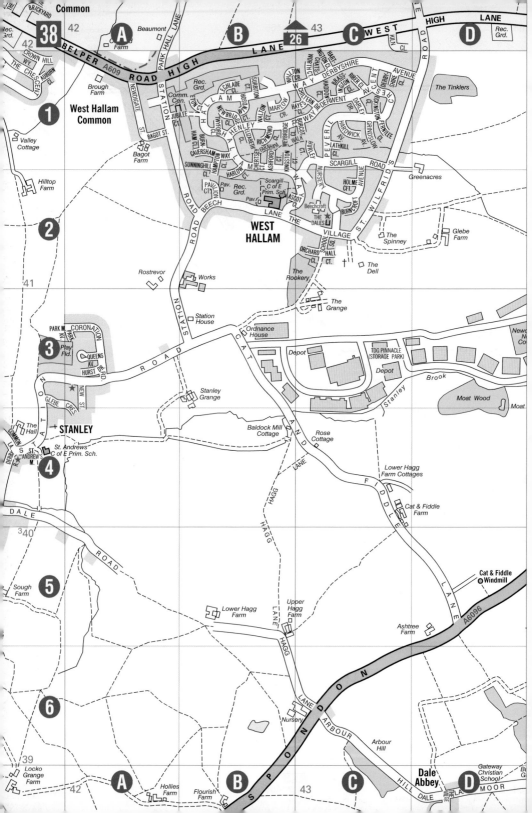

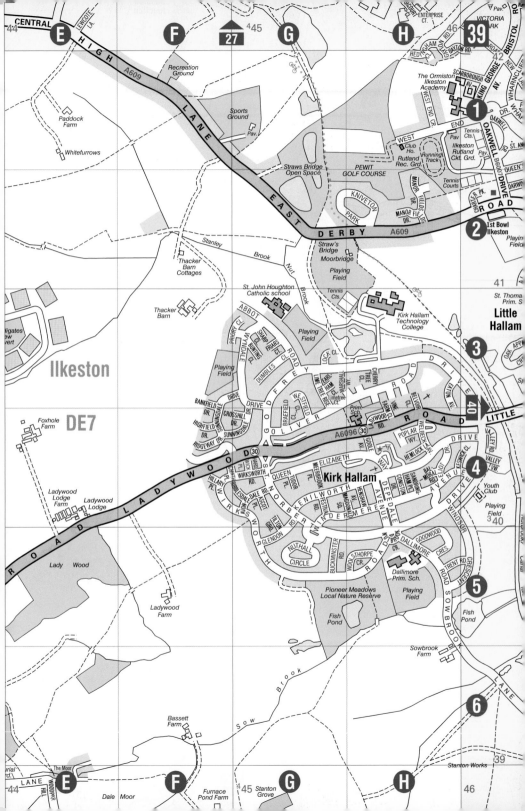

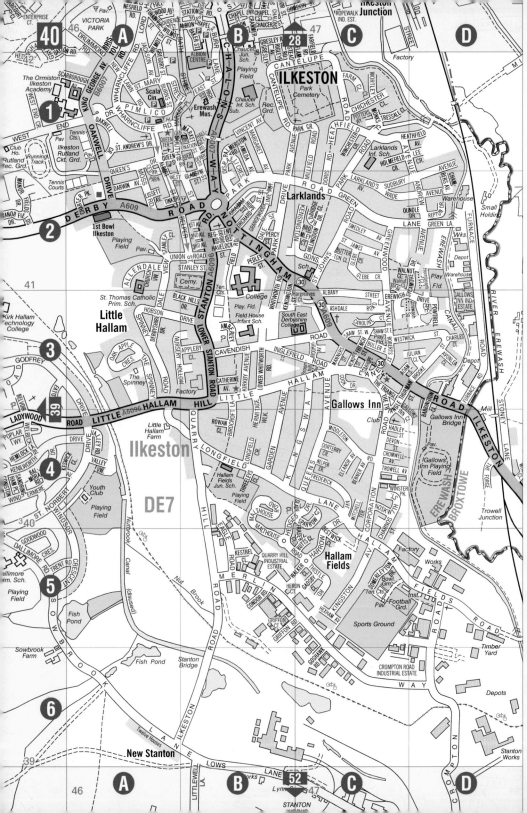

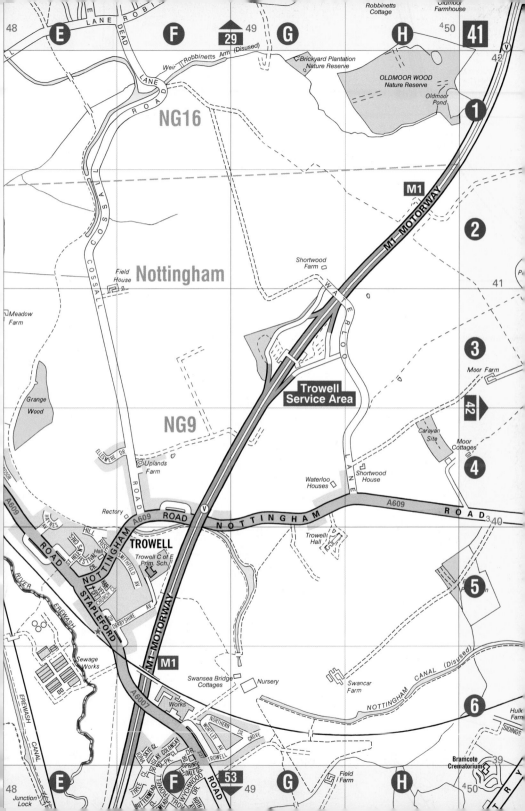

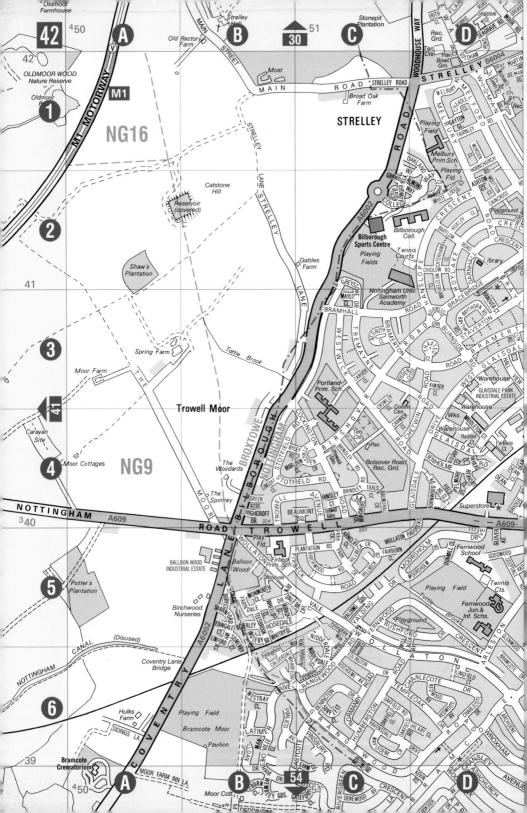

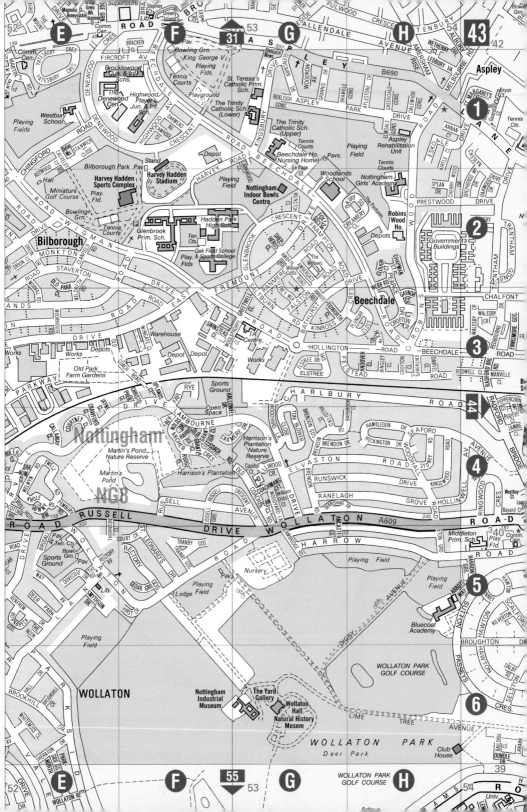

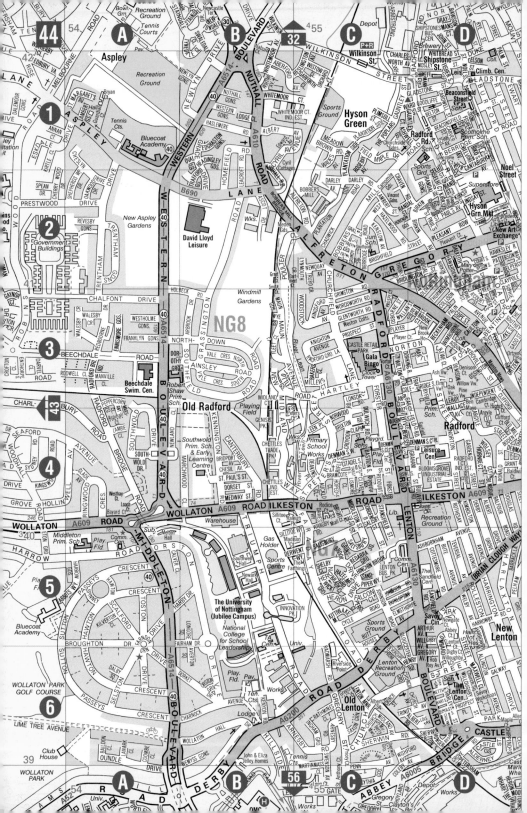

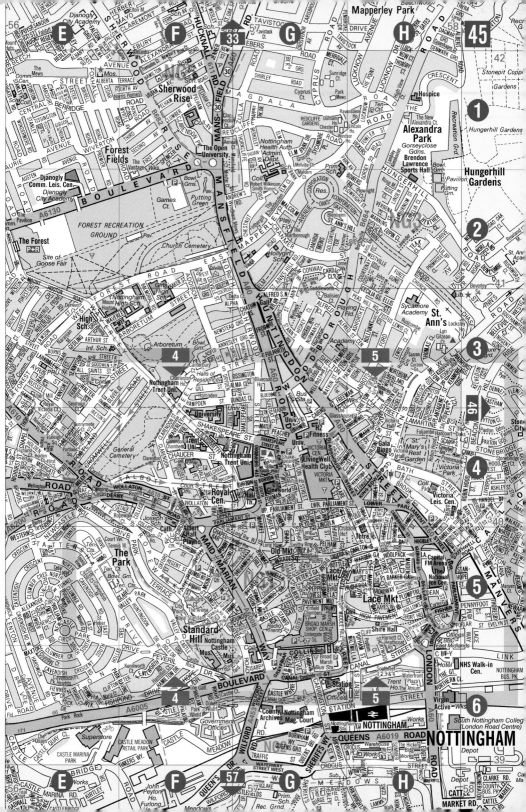

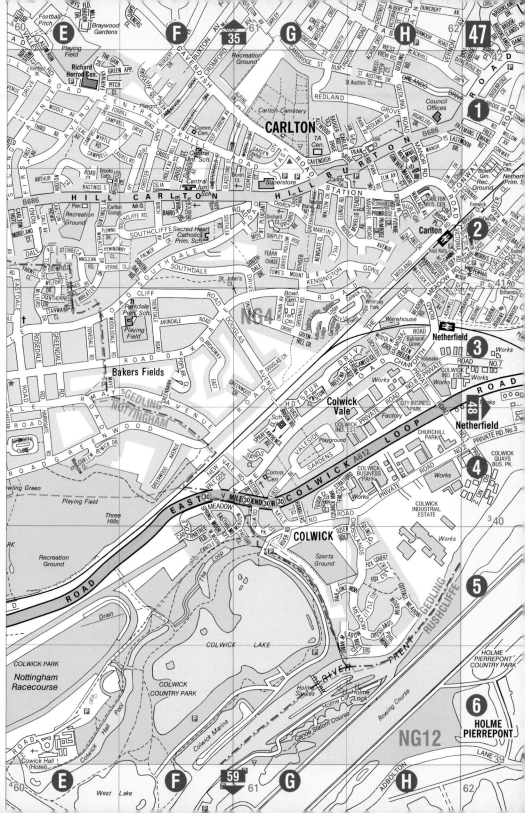

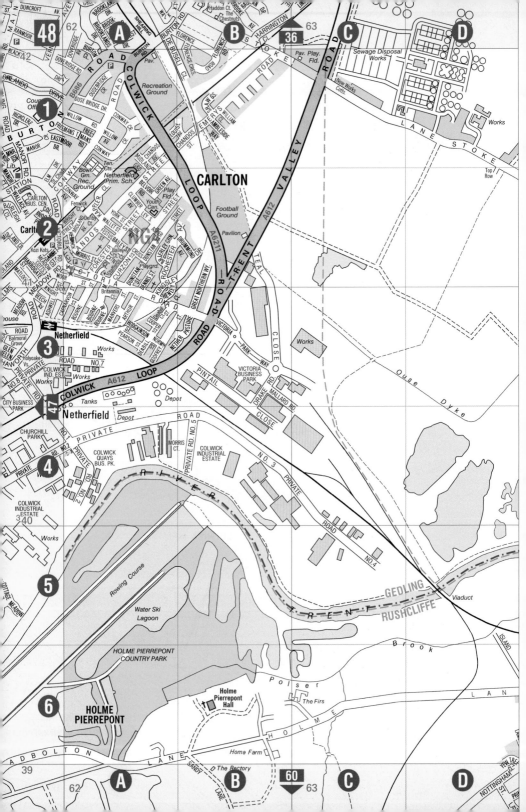

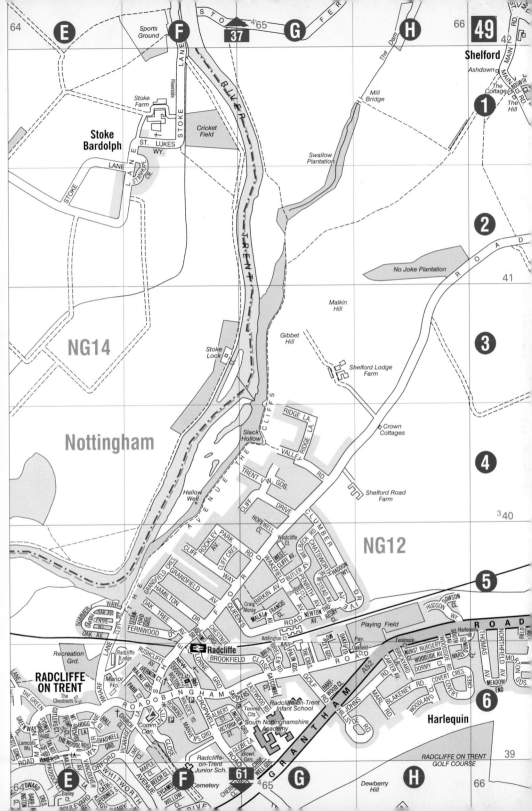

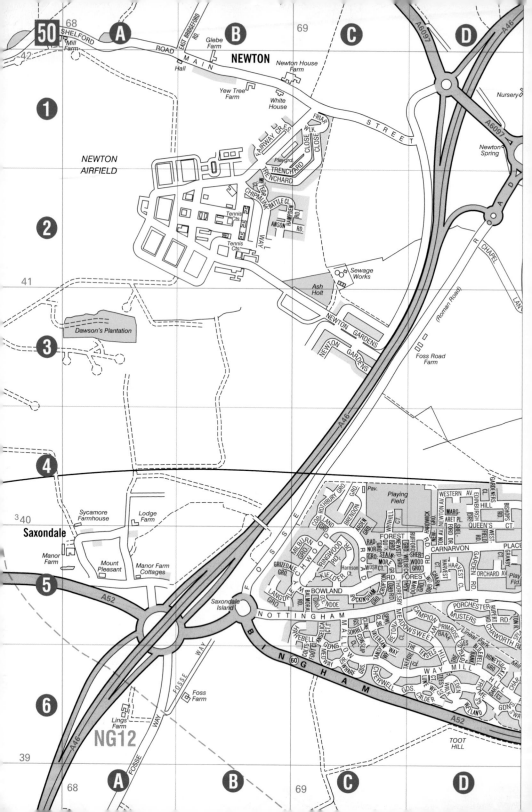

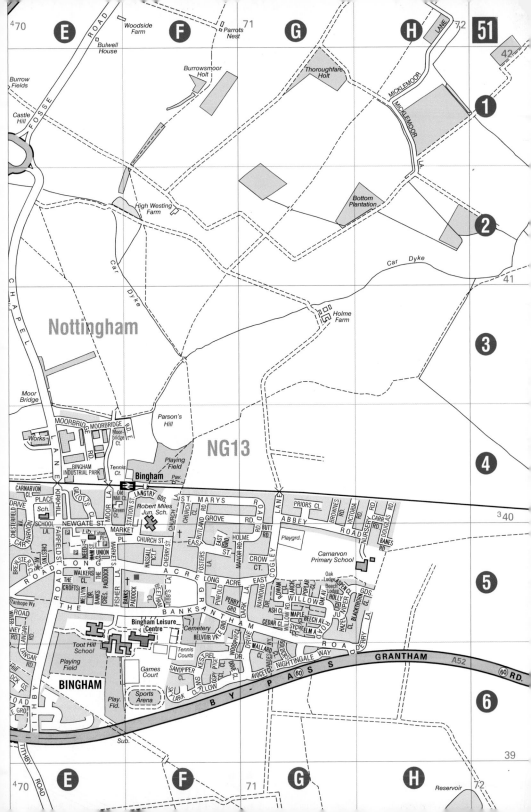

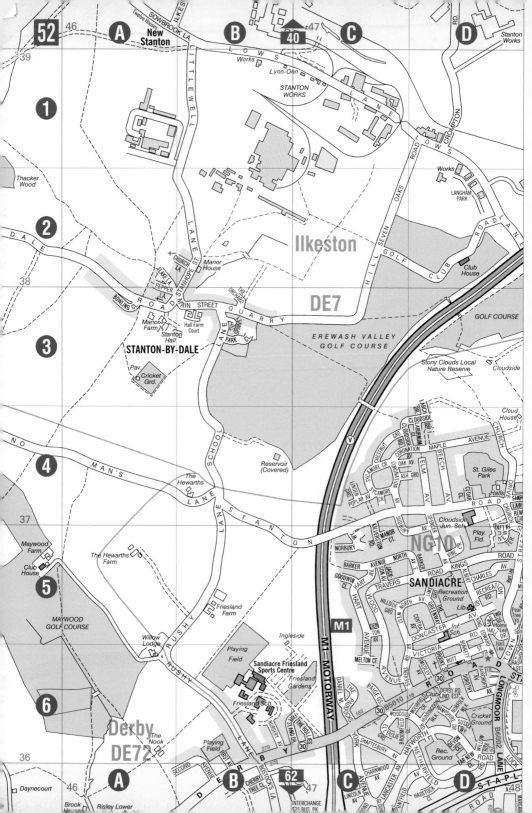

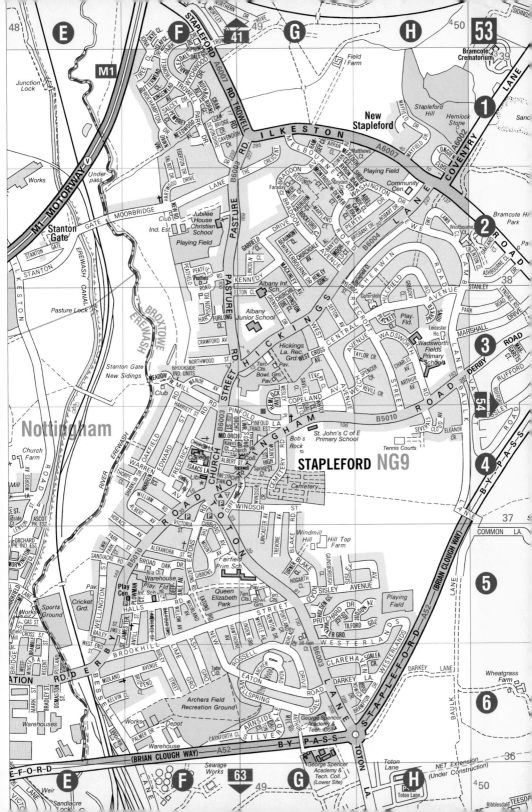

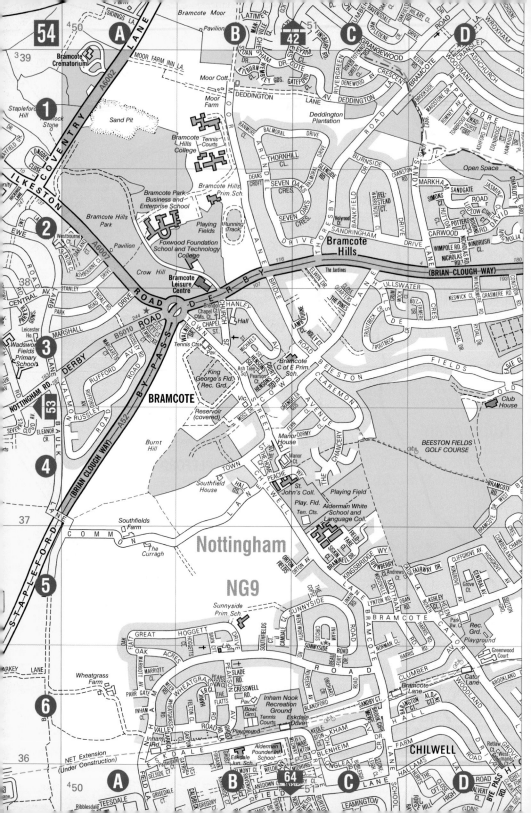

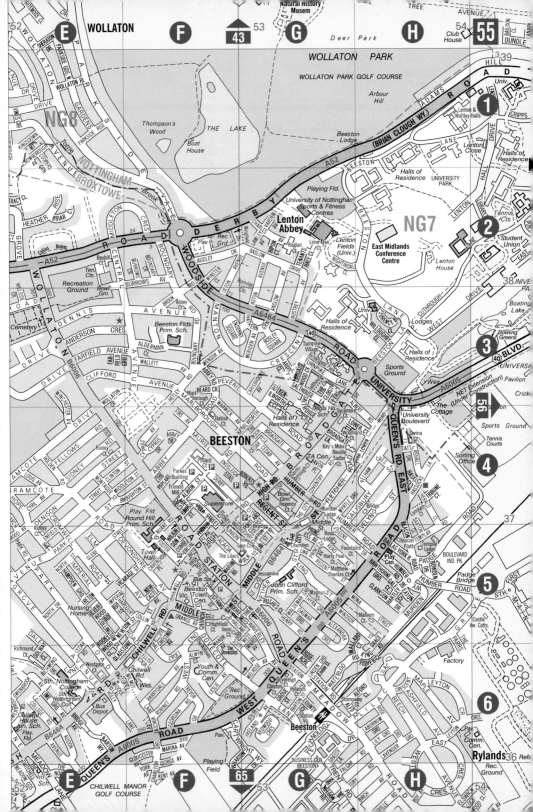

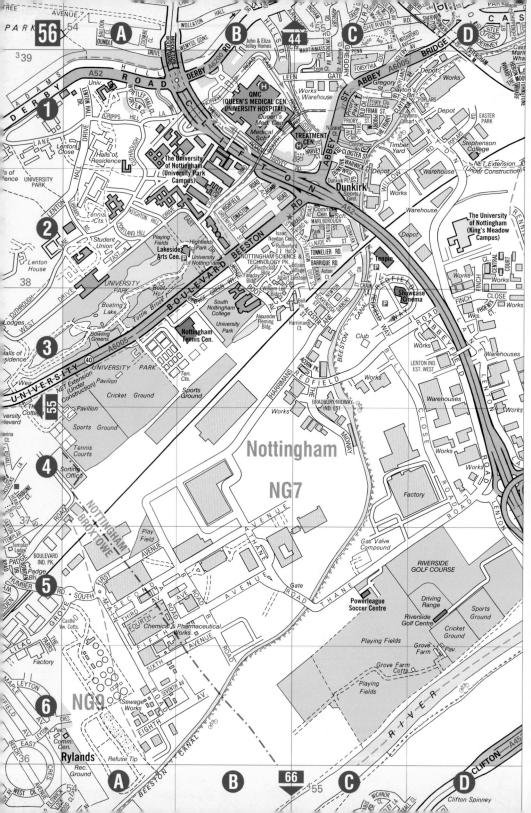

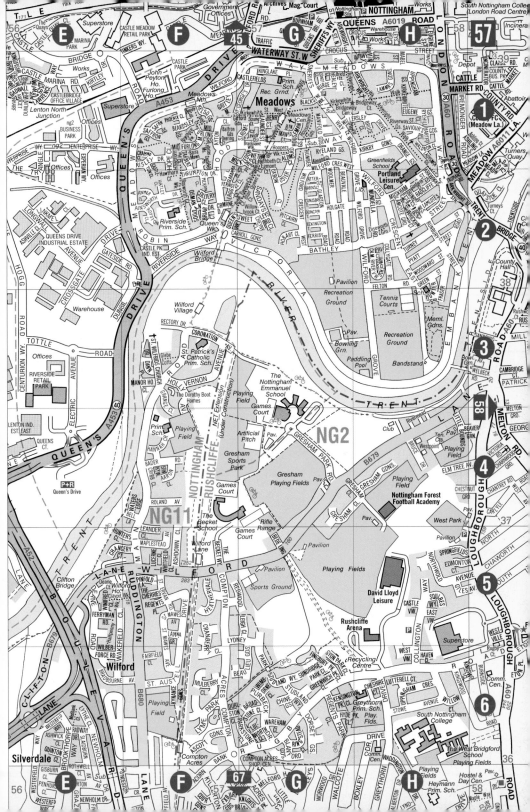

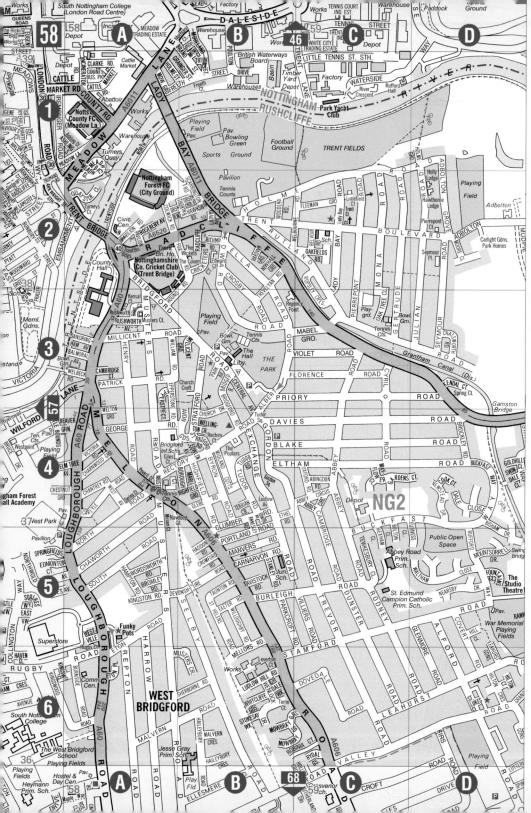

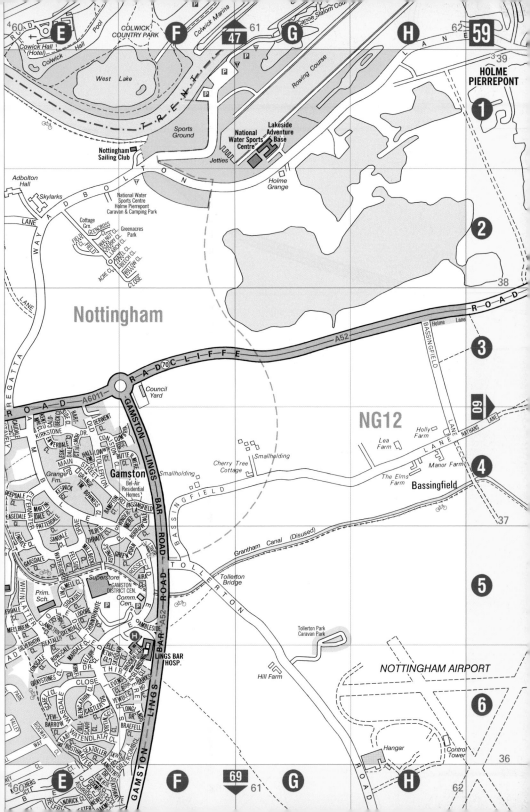

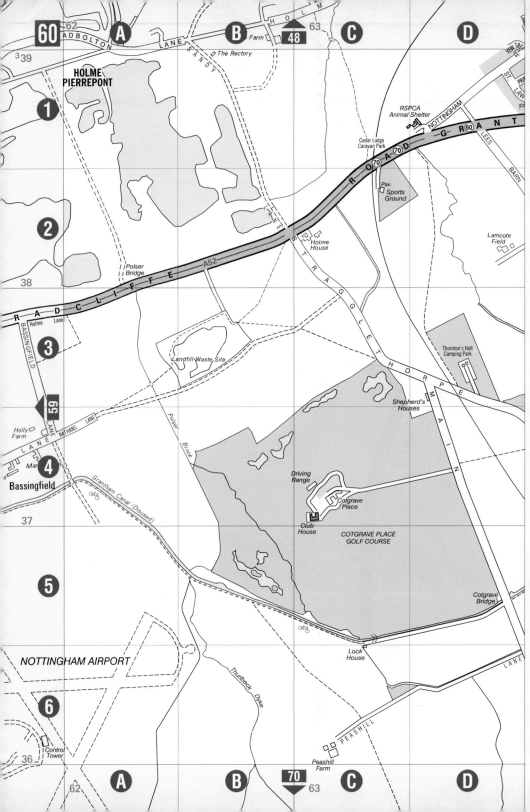

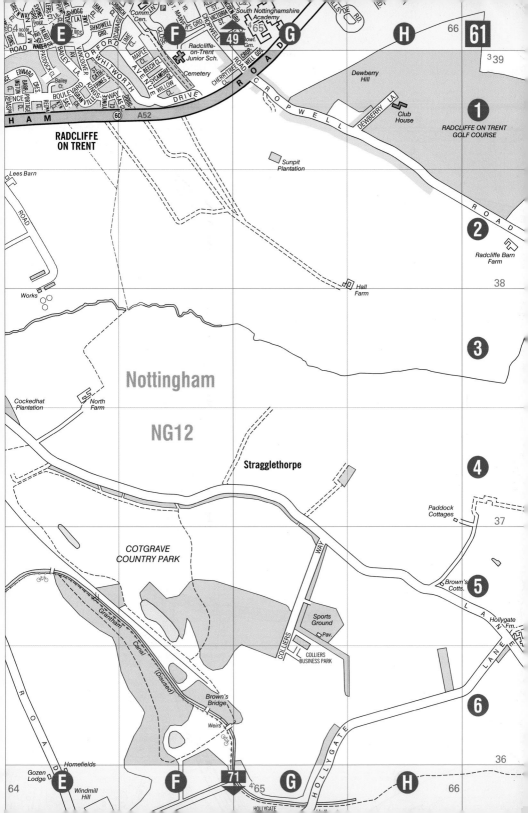

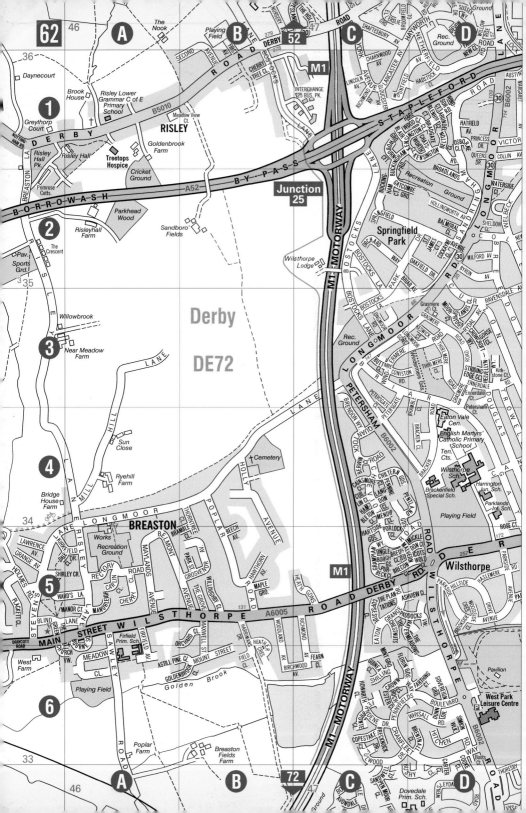

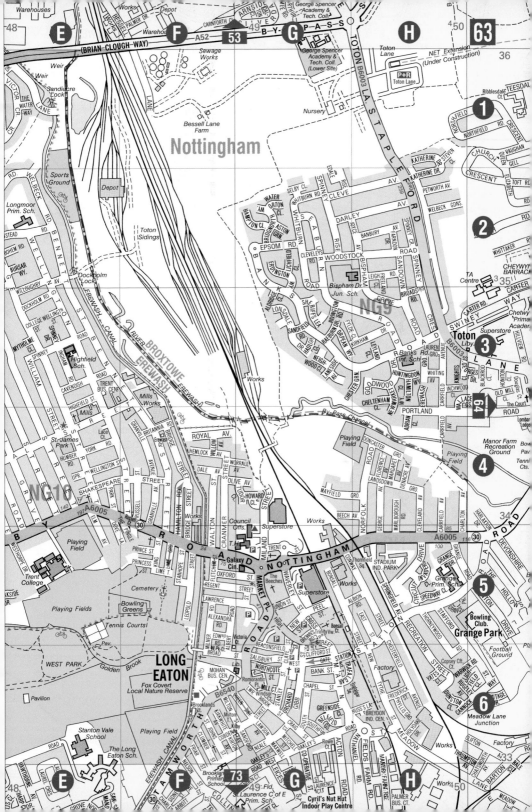

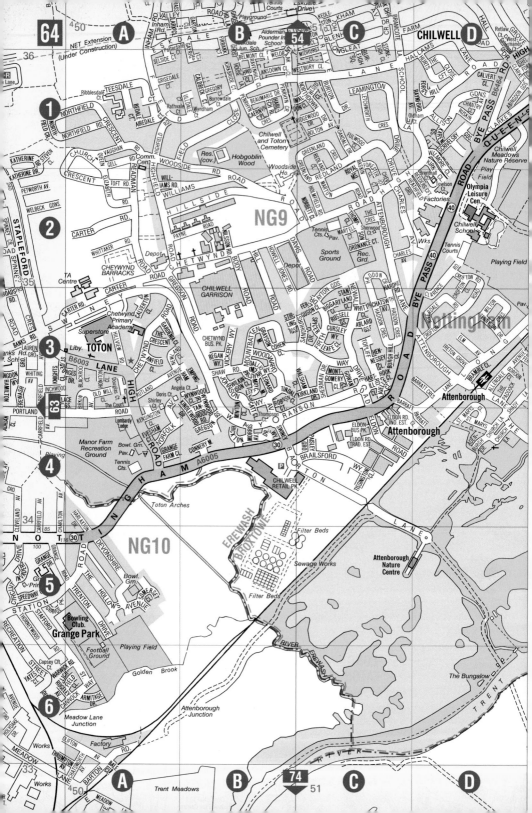

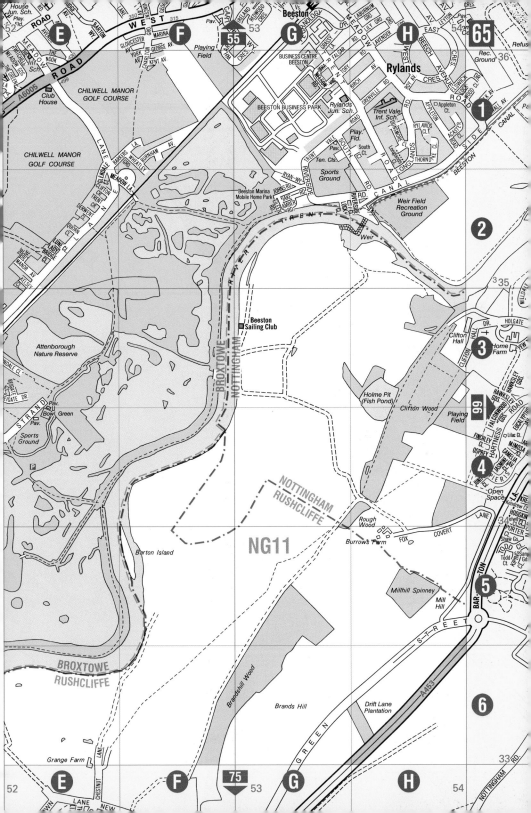

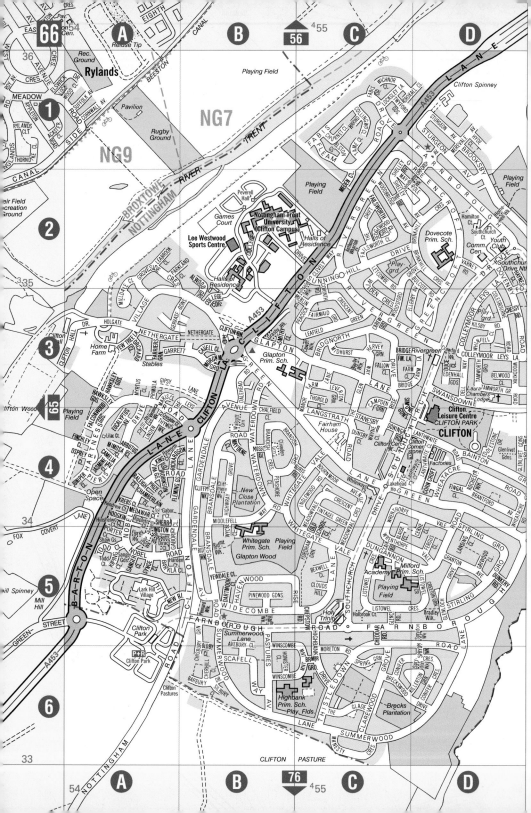

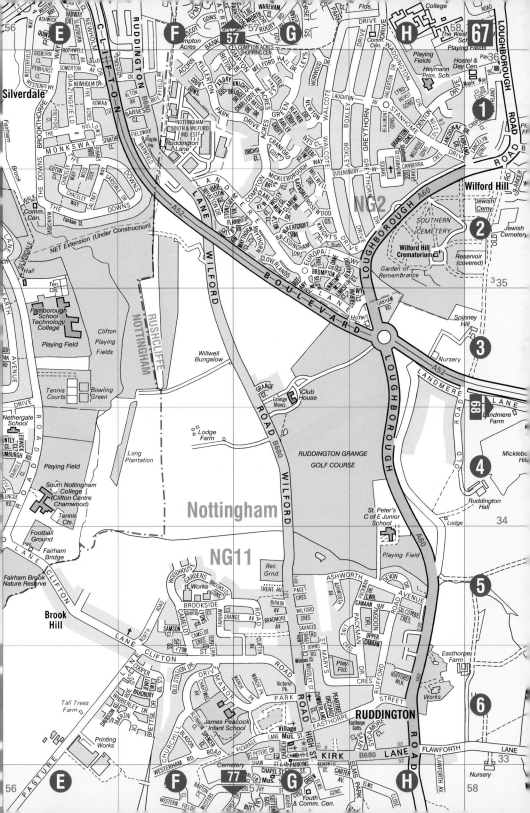

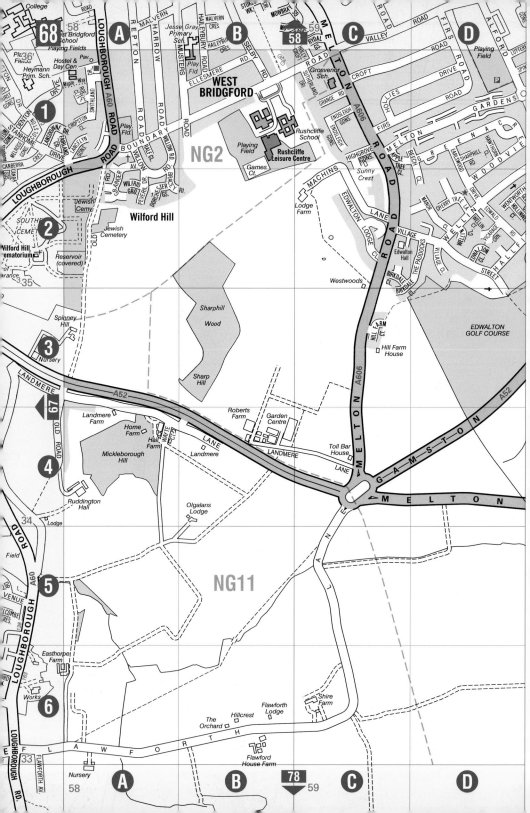

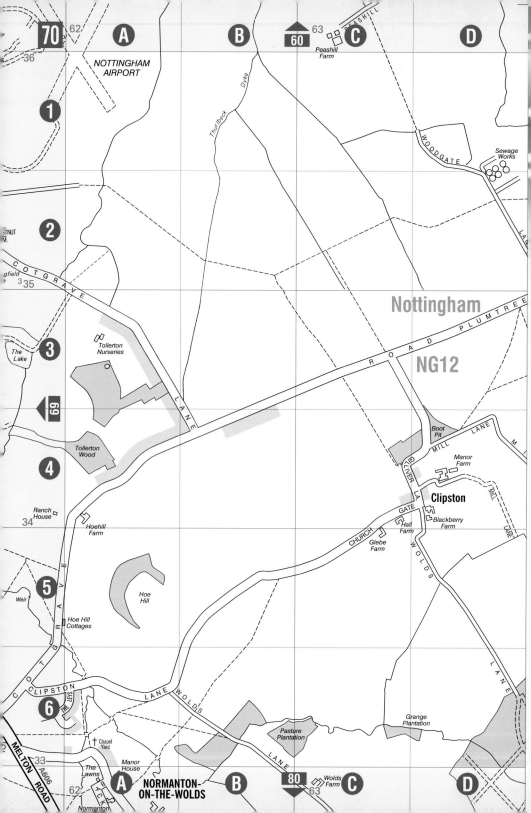

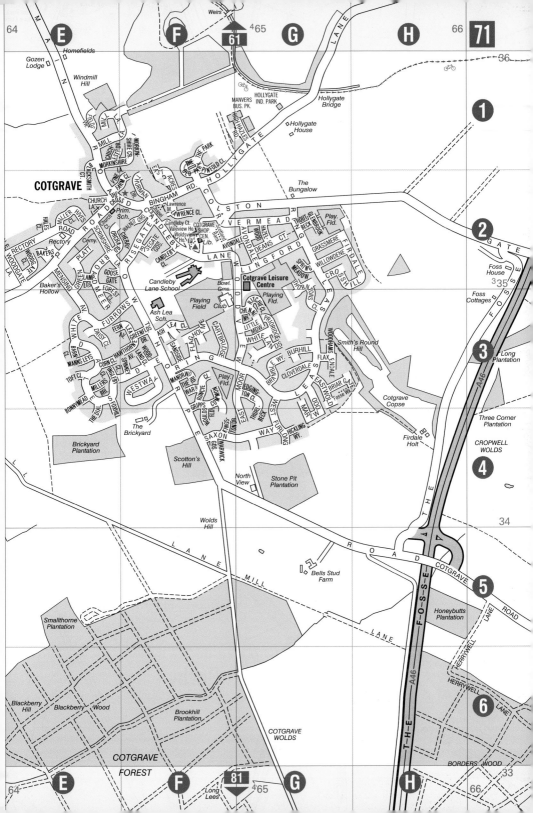

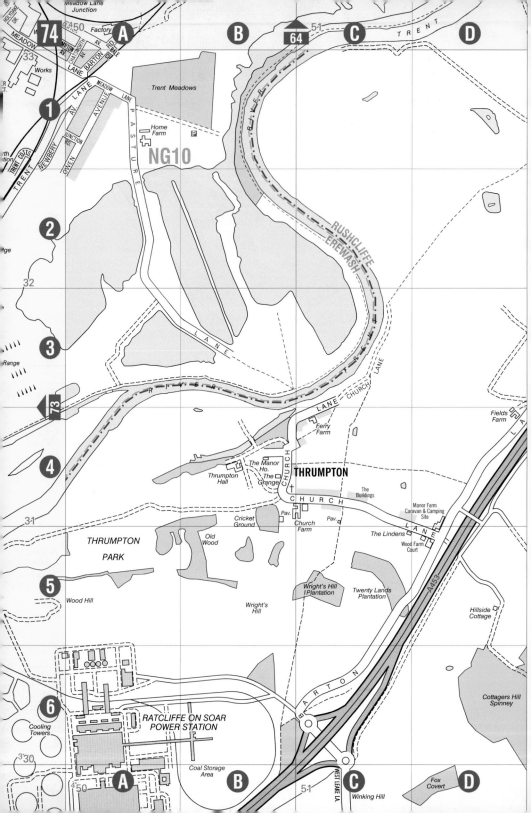

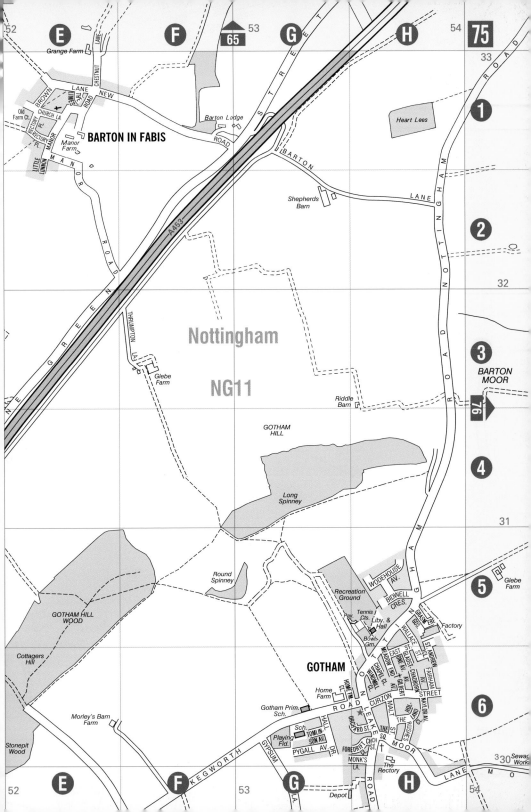

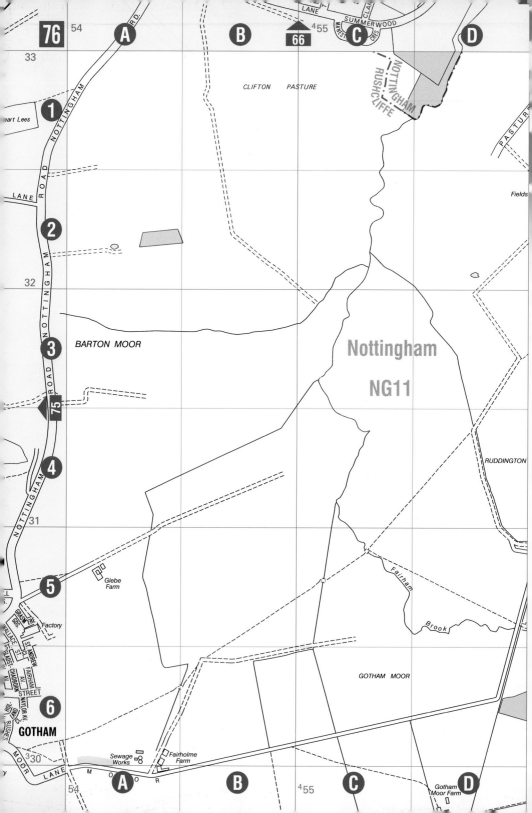

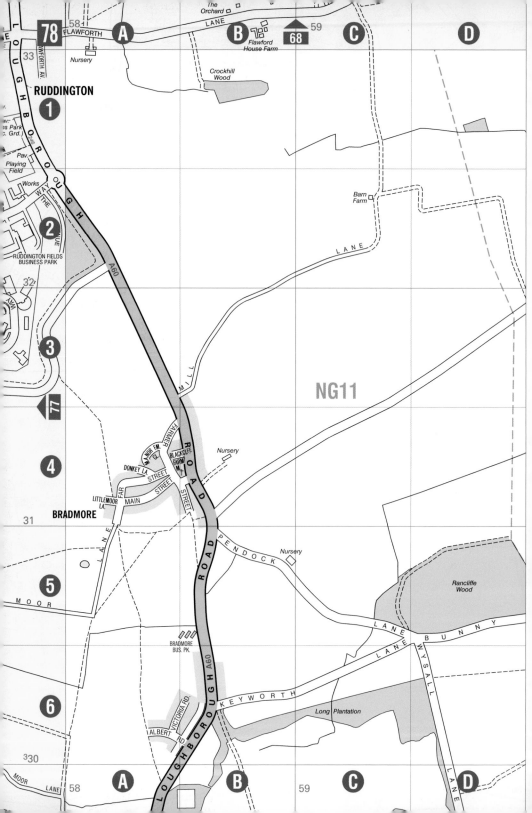

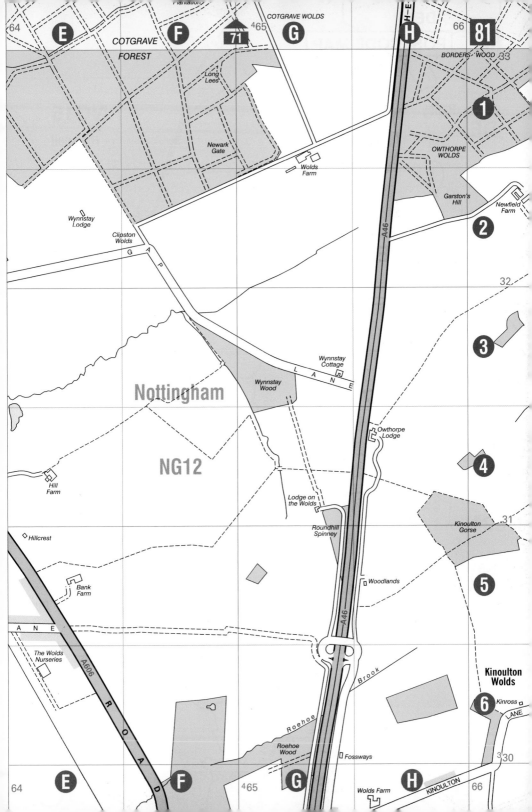

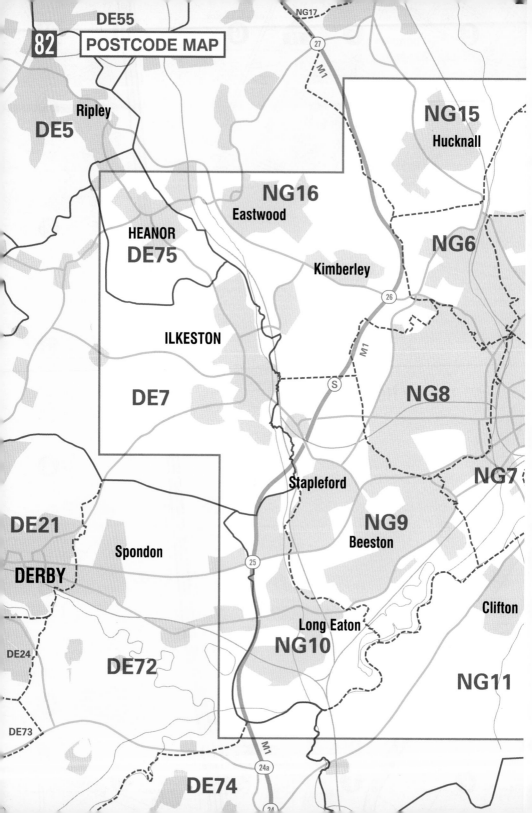

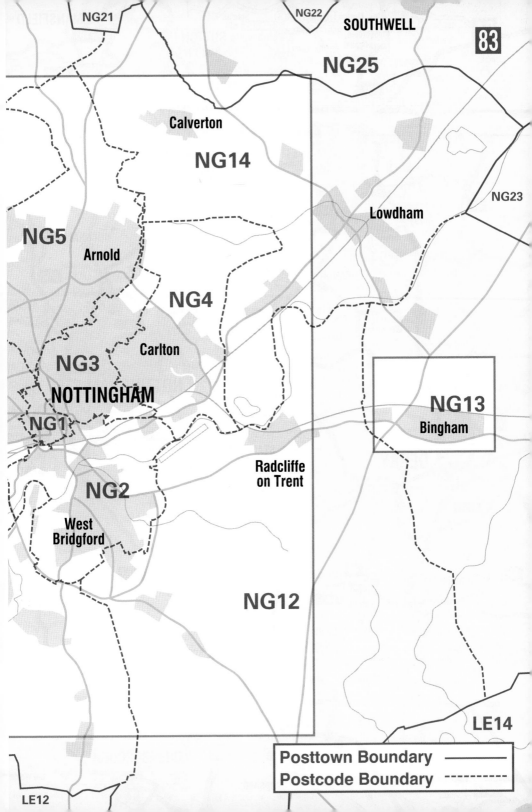

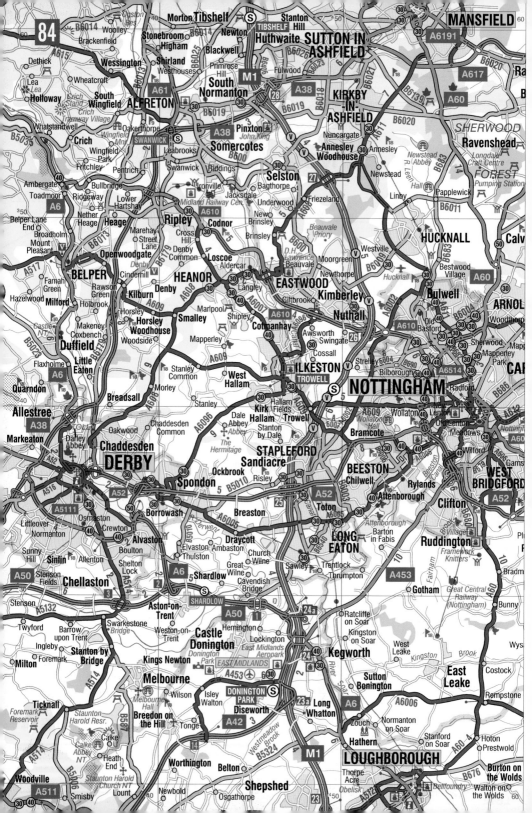

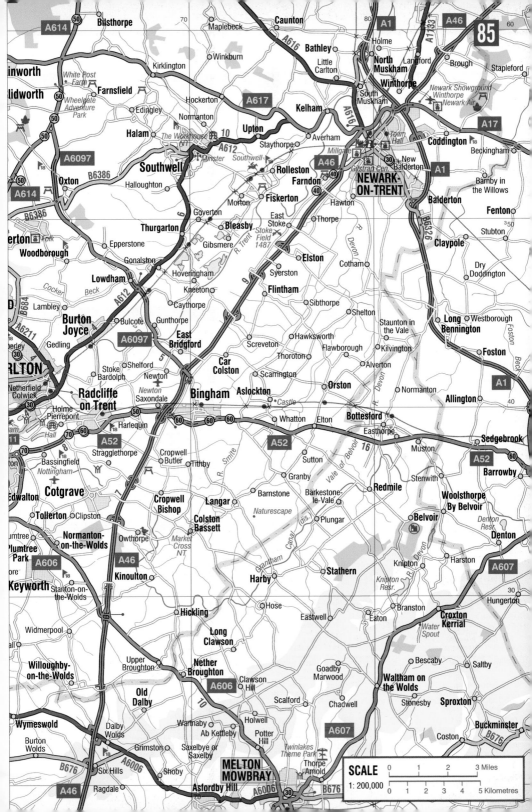

# INDEX

Including Streets, Places & Areas, Hospitals etc., Industrial Estates,
Selected Flats & Walkways, Service Areas, Stations and Selected Places of Interest.

## HOW TO USE THIS INDEX

1. Each street name is followed by its Postcode District, then by its Locality abbreviation(s) and then by its map reference;
e.g. **Abbey Bri.** NG7: Lent . . . .1C **56** is in the NG7 Postcode District and the Lenton Locality and is to be found in square 1C on page **56**.
The page number is shown in bold type.

2. A strict alphabetical order is followed in which Av., Rd., St., etc. (though abbreviated) are read in full and as part of the street name;
e.g. **Apple Tree Cl.** appears after **Appleton Rd.** but before **Appletree La.**

3. Streets and a selection of flats and walkways that cannot be shown on the mapping, appear in the index with the thoroughfare to which they are connected
shown in brackets; e.g. **Albion Ter.** DE7: Ilk . . . .6B **28** (off Northgate St.)

4. Addresses that are in more than one part are referred to as not continuous.

5. Places and areas are shown in the index in BLUE TYPE and the map reference is to the actual map square in which the town centre or area is located and
not to the place name shown on the map; e.g. **ARNOLD** . . . .6B **22**

6. An example of a selected place of interest is **DH Lawrence Birthplace Mus.** . . . .2B **16**

7. An example of a station is **Attenborough Station (Rail)** . . . .3D **64**. Included are Rail (Rail), Nottingham Express Transit (NET) and Park & Ride.
e.g. **Hucknall (Park & Ride)** . . . .4H **7**

8. Service Area names are shown in the index in BOLD CAPITAL TYPE; e.g. **TROWELL SERVICE AREA** . . . .3G **41**

9. An example of a Hospital, Hospice or selected Healthcare facility is **HEANOR MEMORIAL HOSPITAL** . . . .4D **14**

10. Map references for entries that appear on large scale pages **4** & **5** are shown first, with small scale map references shown in brackets;
e.g. **Abbotsford Dr.** NG3: Nott . . . .1F **5** (3H **45**)

## GENERAL ABBREVIATIONS

| | | |
|---|---|---|
| **All.** : Alley | **Fld.** : Field | **Pde.** : Parade |
| **App.** : Approach | **Flds.** : Fields | **Pk.** : Park |
| **Arc.** : Arcade | **Gdn.** : Garden | **Pas.** : Passage |
| **Av.** : Avenue | **Gdns.** : Gardens | **Pl.** : Place |
| **Blvd.** : Boulevard | **Ga.** : Gate | **Pct.** : Precinct |
| **Bri.** : Bridge | **Gt.** : Great | **Prom.** : Promenade |
| **Bldg.** : Building | **Grn.** : Green | **Res.** : Residential |
| **Bldgs.** : Buildings | **Gro.** : Grove | **Ri.** : Rise |
| **Bus.** : Business | **Hgts.** : Heights | **Rd.** : Road |
| **Cvn.** : Caravan | **Ho.** : House | **Shop.** : Shopping |
| **Cen.** : Centre | **Ind.** : Industrial | **Sth.** : South |
| **Chu.** : Church | **Info.** : Information | **Sq.** : Square |
| **Circ.** : Circle | **Intl.** : International | **St.** : Street |
| **Cir.** : Circus | **La.** : Lane | **Ter.** : Terrace |
| **Cl.** : Close | **Lit.** : Little | **Trad.** : Trading |
| **Comn.** : Common | **Lwr.** : Lower | **Up.** : Upper |
| **Cotts.** : Cottages | **Mnr.** : Manor | **Va.** : Vale |
| **Ct.** : Court | **Mkt.** : Market | **Vw.** : View |
| **Cres.** : Crescent | **Mdw.** : Meadow | **Vs.** : Villas |
| **Cft.** : Croft | **Mdws.** : Meadows | **Vis.** : Visitors |
| **Dr.** : Drive | **M.** : Mews | **Wlk.** : Walk |
| **E.** : East | **Mt.** : Mount | **W.** : West |
| **Emb.** : Embankment | **Mus.** : Museum | **Yd.** : Yard |
| **Ent.** : Enterprise | **Nth.** : North | |
| **Est.** : Estate | **No.** : Number | |

## LOCALITY ABBREVIATIONS

| | | |
|---|---|---|
| Ann : **Annesley** | Crop Bi : **Cropwell Bishop** | Lowd : **Lowdham** |
| Arn : **Arnold** | Crop Bu : **Cropwell Butler** | Mapp : **Mapperley** |
| Aspl : **Aspley** | D Ab : **Dale Abbey** | Mapp P : **Mapperley Park** |
| Atten : **Attenborough** | Dray : **Draycott** | Neth : **Netherfield** |
| Aws : **Awsworth** | East B : **East Bridgford** | Newth : **Newthorpe** |
| Babb : **Babbington** | Eastw : **Eastwood** | Newton : **Newton** |
| Bart F : **Barton in Fabis** | Edwal : **Edwalton** | Norm W : **Normanton-on-the-Wolds** |
| Basf : **Basford** | Epp : **Epperstone** | Nott : **Nottingham** |
| Bee : **Beeston** | Gam : **Gamston** | Nuth : **Nuthall** |
| Bestw : **Bestwood** | Ged : **Gedling** | Owt : **Owthorpe** |
| Bestw V : **Bestwood Village** | Gilt : **Giltbrook** | Oxt : **Oxton** |
| Bilb : **Bilborough** | Goth : **Gotham** | Pap : **Papplewick** |
| Bing : **Bingham** | Grea : **Greasley** | Plum : **Plumtree** |
| Bram : **Bramcote** | Hea : **Heanor** | Rad T : **Radcliffe on Trent** |
| Brea : **Breaston** | Hol P : **Holme Pierrepont** | Radf : **Radford** |
| Brins : **Brinsley** | Huck : **Hucknall** | Rat : **Ratcliffe on Soar** |
| Brox : **Broxtowe** | H Grn : **Hyson Green** | Redh : **Redhill** |
| Bulc : **Bulcote** | Ilk : **Ilkeston** | Ris : **Risley** |
| Bulw : **Bulwell** | Key : **Keyworth** | Rudd : **Ruddington** |
| Bunny : **Bunny** | Kimb : **Kimberley** | Sand : **Sandiacre** |
| Bur J : **Burton Joyce** | King : **Kingston on Soar** | Saxon : **Saxondale** |
| Calv : **Calverton** | Kin : **Kinoulton** | Shar : **Shardlow** |
| Car C : **Car Colston** | Kirk H : **Kirk Hallam** | Shel : **Shelford** |
| Carl : **Carlton** | Lamb : **Lambley** | Sher : **Sherwood** |
| Chil : **Chilwell** | Lang M : **Langley Mill** | Ship : **Shipley** |
| Cin : **Cinderhill** | Lent : **Lenton** | Smal : **Smalley** |
| Clif : **Clifton** | Lent A : **Lenton Abbey** | Sout : **Southwell** |
| C'ton : **Clipston** | Lin : **Linby** | Stan : **Stanley** |
| Colw : **Colwick** | Lock : **Lockington** | Stan C : **Stanley Common** |
| Coss : **Cossall** | Long E : **Long Eaton** | Stant D : **Stanton-by-Dale** |
| Cotg : **Cotgrave** | Los : **Loscoe** | Stant W : **Stanton-on-the-Wolds** |

1st Avenue—Anders Dr.

Stap : **Stapleford**
Stoke B : **Stoke Bardolph**
Stre : **Strelley**
Thru : **Thrumpton**
Toll : **Tollerton**
Top V : **Top Valley**
Toton : **Toton**
Trow : **Trowell**
Want : **Watnall**
West Br : **West Bridgford**
West H : **West Hallam**
Widm : **Widmerpool**
Wilf : **Wilford**
Woll : **Wollaton**
Woodbo : **Woodborough**
Woodt : **Woodthorpe**


**1st Avenue** DE7: Ilk 2B **40**
1st Bowl
Ilkeston 2A **40**
**2nd Avenue** DE7: Ilk 2B **40**
**3rd Avenue** DE7: Ilk 2B **40**

## A

**Aaron Cl.** NG11: Wilf 4F **57**
**Abba Cl.** NG16: Kimb 6H **17**
**Abbey Bri.** NG7: Lent 1C **56**
**Abbey Cir.** NG2: West Br 4C **58**
**Abbey Cl.** NG15: Huck 4E **7**
**Abbey Ct.** NG7: Lent 5D **44**
NG9: Bee 3F **55**
**Abbey Dr.** NG9: Bee 4F **55**
**Abbeyfield Rd.** NG7: Lent 3D **56**
**Abbey Gro.** NG3: Nott 2B **46**
**Abbey Rd.** NG2: West Br 4C **58**
NG9: Bee 3F **55**
NG13: Bing 4G **51**
NG16: Eastw 3D **16**
**Abbey St.** DE7: Ilk 5B **28**
NG7: Lent 1C **56**
**Abbot Cl.** NG12: Key 3G **79**
**Abbot Rd.** DE7: Kirk H 3G **39**
**Abbotsbury Cl.** NG5: Top V 4B **20**
**Abbots Cl.** NG5: Arn 1H **33**
**Abbots Dr.** NG15: Huck 5E **7**
**Abbotsford Dr.** NG3: Nott 1F **5** (3H **45**)
**Abbotsford M.** DE7: Ilk 4H **27**
**Abbots Rd.** NG15: Huck 5E **7**
**Abbot St.** NG16: Aws 3E **29**
**Abbots Wlk.** NG15: Huck 5E **7**
**Abbots Way** NG8: Woll 5H **43**
**Abbott St.** DE75: Hea 4C **14**
NG10: Long E 1F **73**
**Abercarn Cl.** NG6: Bulw 6H **19**
**Abercarn M.** NG6: Bulw 6H **19**
**Aberdeen St.** NG3: Nott 3H **5** (4A **46**)
**Aberford Av.** NG8: Basf 1B **44**
**Abingdon Dr.** NG11: Rudd 5H **67**
**Abingdon Gdns.** NG5: Woodt 2C **34**
NG9: Chil 1D **64**
**Abingdon Rd.** NG2: West Br 4C **58**
**Abingdon Sq.** NG8: Aspl 6H **31**
**Ablard Gdns.** NG9: Chil 3C **64**
**Acacia Cl.** NG15: Huck 6H **7**
**Acacia Cres.** NG4: Carl 1H **47**
**Acacia Gdns.** NG16: Want 5H **17**
**Acacia Wlk.** NG9: Bee 5F **55**
**Academy Cl.** NG6: Basf 4C **32**
**Acaster Cl.** NG9: Bee 1H **65**
**Access 26 Bus. Pk.** NG16: Lang M 2G **15**
**Acle Gdns.** NG6: Bulw 4H **19**
**Acorn Av.** NG16: Gilt 5D **16**
(not continuous)
**Acorn Bank** NG2: West Br 1F **67**
**Acorn Cen.** NG16: Lang M 2G **15**
**Acorn Dr.** NG4: Ged 4A **36**
**Acorn Pk.** NG7: Lent 3C **56**
**A'court St.** NG7: H Grn 3D **44**
**Acre Cl.** NG2: West Br 2E **59**
**Acton Av.** NG6: Basf 3B **32**
NG10: Long E 1G **73**
**Acton Cl.** NG10: Long E 1G **73**
**Acton Gro.** NG10: Long E 1G **73**
**Acton Rd.** NG5: Arn 5H **21**
NG10: Long E 6G **63**
**Acton Rd. Ind. Est.** NG10: Long E 1G **73**
(not continuous)
**Acton St.** NG10: Long E 1G **73**
**Adale Rd.** DE7: Smal 5A **14**
**Adams Cl.** DE75: Hea 6B **14**
**Adams Ct.** DE7: Ilk 4A **28**
**Adams Hill** NG7: Nott 1H **55**
NG12: Key 4H **79**
**Adam St.** DE7: Ilk 3C **40**
**Adams Wlk.** NG1: Nott 4F **5**
**Ada Pl.** NG15: Huck 3G **7**
**Adbolton Av.** NG4: Ged 6G **35**
**Adbolton Gro.** NG2: West Br 1D **58**
**Adbolton La.** NG2: West Br 2D **58**
NG12: Hol P 2E **59**
**Adbolton Lodge** NG4: Carl 3G **47**
**Adderley Cl.** NG5: Bestw 1E **33**
**Addington Ct.** NG12: Rad T 5G **49**
**Addington Rd.** NG7: Radf 3D **44**
**Addison Dr.** NG15: Huck 3E **7**
**Addison Rd.** NG4: Carl 1D **46**
**Addison St.** NG1: Nott 1C **4** (2F **45**)
**Addison Vs.** NG16: Eastw 4A **16**
(not continuous)
**Adelaide Cl.** NG9: Stap 2H **53**
**Adelaide Gro.** NG5: Top V 5C **20**
**Adel Dr.** NG4: Ged 5G **35**
**Adenburgh Dr.** NG9: Atten 4D **64**
**Admiral Cl.** DE75: Hea 3C **14**
**Adrian Cl.** NG9: Toton 4H **63**
**Aeneas Ct.** NG5: Sher 1F **45**
**Aerial Way** NG15: Huck 6F **7**
**Aerodrome, The** NG15: Huck 2E **19**
**Agnes Vs.** NG3: Mapp 5A **34**
**Aidan Gdns.** NG5: Top V 3E **21**
**Ainsdale Cres.** NG8: Cin 4G **31**
**Ainsley Rd.** NG8: Aspl 3B **44**
**Ainsworth Dr.** NG2: Nott 2F **57**
**Aintree Cl.** NG16: Kimb 6G **17**
**Aira Cl.** NG2: Gam 5F **59**
**Airedale Cl.** NG10: Long E 1C **72**
**Airedale Ct.** NG9: Chil 1A **64**
**Airedale Wlk.** NG8: Woll 6C **42**
**Aitchison Av.** NG15: Huck 4F **7**
**Alandene Av.** NG16: Want 6A **18**
**Albany Cl.** NG5: Arn 6A **22**
NG15: Huck 6C **6**
**Albany Ct.** NG9: Stap 2G **53**
**Albany Rd.** NG7: Basf 1E **45**
**Albany St.** DE7: Ilk 3C **40**
**Albemarle Rd.** NG5: Woodt 3H **33**
**Alberta Ter.** NG7: H Grn 1E **45**
**Albert Av.** NG4: Carl 2D **46**
NG8: Aspl 1B **44**
NG9: Stap 4F **53**
NG16: Nuth 1C **30**
**Albert Ball Cl.** NG5: Top V 5D **20**
**Albert Ball Ho.** NG5: Top V 5E **21**
**Albert Einstein Cen.**
NG7: Nott 2B **56**
**Albert Gro.** NG7: Lent, Radf 4D **44**
Albert Hall 4C **4** (5F **45**)
**Albert Mill** NG7: Radf 1A **4** (3E **45**)
**Albert Rd.** NG2: West Br 3B **58**
NG3: Nott 6H **33**
NG7: Lent 6D **44**
NG9: Bee 3G **55**
NG10: Long E 5F **63**
NG10: Sand 5D **52**
NG11: Bunny 6A **78**
**Albert Sq.** NG7: Lent 6C **44**
**Albert St.** DE7: Ilk 1A **40**
NG1: Nott 5E **5** (5G **45**)
NG4: Ged 6H **35**
NG9: Stap 4F **53**
NG12: Rad T 6F **49**
NG15: Huck 4H **7**
NG16: Eastw 2B **16**
**Albion Cen.** DE7: Ilk 1B **40**
**Albion Ri.** NG5: Arn 4B **22**
**Albion Rd.** NG10: Long E 5H **63**
**Albion St.** DE7: Ilk 6B **28**
NG1: Nott 6D **4** (6G **45**)
NG9: Bee 4F **55**
**Albion Ter.** *DE7: Ilk 6B 28*
*(off Northgate St.)*
**Albury Dr.** NG8: Aspl 6H **31**
**Albury Sq.** NG7: Nott 4A **4** (5E **45**)
**Alcester St.** NG7: Lent 3C **56**
**Aldene Ct.** NG9: Chil 6D **54**
**Aldene Way** NG14: Woodbo 1C **24**
ALDERCAR 1F **15**
**Aldercar La.** NG16: Lang M 1F **15**
**Alder Gdns.** NG6: Bulw 6G **19**
**Alderman Cl.** NG9: Bee 3F **55**
**Aldermens Cl.** NG2: Nott 1G **57**
**Alderney St.** NG7: Lent 6D **44**
**Alderton Rd.** NG5: Bestw 1G **33**
**Alder Way** NG12: Key 5A **80**
**Aldgate Cl.** NG6: Bulw 5G **19**
**Aldred's La** NG16: Lang M 4E **15**
**Aldreds La.** DE75: Hea 4E **15**
**Aldridge Cl.** NG9: Toton 3G **63**
**Aldrin Cl.** NG6: Bulw 2F **31**
**Aldworth Cl.** NG5: Bestw 1F **33**
**Aldwych Cl.** NG5: Arn 4E **21**
NG16: Nuth 5D **30**
**Alexander Cl.** NG15: Huck 2H **7**
**Alexander Fleming Bldg.** NG7: Nott 3B **56**
**Alexander Rd.** NG7: Nott 5A **4** (5E **45**)
**Alexandra Cres.** NG9: Bee 5G **55**
**Alexandra Gdns.** NG5: Sher 6F **33**
**Alexandra M.** NG5: Sher 1F **45**
ALEXANDRA PARK 1H **45**
**Alexandra Rd.** NG10: Long E 5F **63**
**Alexandra St.** NG5: Sher 1F **45**
NG9: Stap 5F **53**
NG16: Eastw 3B **16**
**Alford Cl.** NG9: Bee 6G **55**
**Alford Rd.** NG2: West Br 5D **58**
NG12: Edwal 5D **58**
**Alfred Av.** NG3: Mapp 5C **34**
**Alfred Cl.** NG3: Nott 3G **45**
**Alfred St. Central** NG3: Nott 1F **5** (3G **45**)
**Alfred St. Nth.** NG3: Nott 3G **45**
**Alfred St. Sth.** NG3: Nott 2H **5** (4A **46**)
**Alfreton Rd.** NG7: H Grn, Radf, Nott 2A **4** (2C **44**)
**Alison Av.** NG15: Huck 2A **8**
**Alison Wlk.** NG3: Nott 1F **5** (3H **45**)
**Allen Av.** NG3: Mapp 6C **34**
**Allendale** DE7: Ilk 2A **40**
**Allendale Av.** NG8: Aspl 6F **31**
NG9: Atten 3D **64**
**Allendale Rd.** DE75: Hea 3B **14**
**Allen Fld. Ct.** NG7: Lent 6D **44**
**Allen St.** NG15: Huck 3G **7**
**Allen's Wlk.** NG5: Arn 4B **22**
**All Hallows Dr.** NG4: Ged 5H **35**
**Allington Av.** NG7: Lent 6D **44**
**Allison Gdns.** DE7: Ilk 6C **28**
NG9: Chil 1D **64**
**All Saints St.** NG7: Radf 1A **4** (3E **45**)
**All Saints Ter.** NG7: Radf 1A **4** (3E **45**)
**Allwood Dr.** NG4: Carl 1G **47**
**Allwood Gdns.** NG15: Huck 5H **7**
**Alma Cl.** DE7: Ilk 2A **28**
NG1: Nott 1D **4** (3G **45**)
NG4: Ged 5A **36**
**Alma Hill** NG16: Kimb 5G **17**
**Alma Rd.** NG3: Nott 3B **46**
**Alma St.** NG7: Basf 1E **45**
**Almond Cl.** NG15: Huck 6H **7**
NG16: Kimb 6G **17**
**Almond Ct.** NG2: Nott 1G **57**
**Almond Wlk.** NG4: Ged 5A **36**
**Almond Way** NG8: Bilb 2D **42**
**Alnwick Cl.** NG6: Bulw 1B **32**
**Alpha Ter.** NG1: Nott 3F **45**
**Alpine Cres.** NG4: Carl 1G **47**
**Alpine St.** NG6: Basf 5C **32**
**Althorpe St.** NG7: Radf 4E **45**
**Alton Av.** NG11: Wilf 1F **67**
**Alton Cl.** NG2: West Br 2G **67**
**Alton Dr.** NG16: Gilt 5D **16**
**Alum Ct.** NG5: Top V 5D **20**
**Alvenor St.** DE7: Ilk 6B **28**
**Alverstone Rd.** NG3: Mapp P 6G **33**
**Alvey Ter.** NG7: Radf 4C **44**
**Alwood Gro.** NG11: Clif 2B **66**
**Alwyn Ct.** NG9: Bee 6F **55**
**Alwyn Rd.** NG8: Brox 5F **31**
**Alyth Ct.** NG6: Basf 4D **32**
**Amber Ct.** DE75: Hea 4C **14**
**Amber Dr.** NG16: Lang M 3F **15**
**Ambergate Rd.** NG8: Bilb 2G **43**
(not continuous)
**Amber Hill** NG5: Bestw 6F **21**
**Amberley Cl.** DE7: Ilk 3B **40**
**Amber Rd.** NG9: Bee 2G **65**
**Amber Trad. Cen.** NG16: Kimb 6F **17**
**Ambleside** NG2: Gam 4E **59**
**Ambleside Dr.** NG16: Eastw 2H **15**
**Ambleside Rd.** NG8: Aspl 6G **31**
**Ambleside Way** NG4: Ged 1B **48**
**Amersham Ri.** NG8: Aspl 6H **31**
**Amesbury Cir.** NG8: Cin 4G **31**
**Amilda Av.** DE7: Ilk 1B **40**
**Ampthill Ri.** NG5: Sher 3F **33**
**Ancaster Gdns.** NG8: Woll 4G **43**
**Anchorage, The** NG14: Bur J 3F **37**
**Anchor Cl.** NG8: Aspl 5H **31**
**Anchor Ct.** NG5: Bestw 6F **21**
**Anchor Rd.** NG16: Eastw 2G **15**
**Anders Dr.** NG6: Bulw 2F **31**

Anderson Ct. NG5: Top V . . . . . . . . . . . . .5E 21
Anderson Cres. NG5: Bee . . . . . . . . . . . .3E 55
Andover Cl. NG8: Bilb . . . . . . . . . . . . . . .3H 43
Andover Rd. NG5: Bestw . . . . . . . . . . . .1C 32
Andrew Av. DE7: Ilk . . . . . . . . . . . . . . .2D 40
   NG3: Mapp . . . . . . . . . . . . . . . . . .5C 34
Andrews Ct. NG5: Chil . . . . . . . . . . . . . .5C 54
Andrews Dr. NG16: Lang M . . . . . . . . . .1E 15
Anfield Cl. NG9: Toton . . . . . . . . . . . . . .3A 64
Anford Cl. NG6: Bulw . . . . . . . . . . . . . . .2H 31
Angela Cl. NG5: Arn . . . . . . . . . . . . . . . .3A 22
Angela Cl. NG9: Toton . . . . . . . . . . . . . .3A 64
Angel All. NG1: Nott . . . . . . . . . . . . .4F 5 (5A 46)
Angelica Ct. NG13: Bing . . . . . . . . . . . .5C 50
Angell Grn. NG11: Clif . . . . . . . . . . . . . .5A 66
Angel Row NG1: Nott . . . . . . . . . .4D 4 (5G 45)
Angletarn Cl. NG2: West Br . . . . . . . . . .5E 59
Angrave Cl. NG3: Nott . . . . . . . . . . . . . .2A 46
Angus Cl. NG5: Arn . . . . . . . . . . . . . . . .4D 22
   NG16: Kimb . . . . . . . . . . . . . . . . .2A 30
Anmer Cl. NG2: Nott . . . . . . . . . . . . . . .2F 57
Annan Cl. NG8: Aspl . . . . . . . . . . . . . . .1H 43
Anne's Cl. NG3: Mapp . . . . . . . . . . . . . .5C 34
Annesley Gro. NG1: Nott . . . . . . . .1C 4 (3F 45)
Annesley Rd. NG2: West Br . . . . . . . . . .4B 58
   NG15: Huck . . . . . . . . . . . . . . . . . .1D 6
Annies Cl. NG15: Huck . . . . . . . . . . . . . .6F 7
Anslow Av. NG9: Lent A . . . . . . . . . . . . .3G 55
Anson Rd. NG13: Newton . . . . . . . . . . . .2B 50
Anson Wlk. DE7: Ilk . . . . . . . . . . . . . . . .4B 28
Anstee Rd. NG10: Long E . . . . . . . . . . . .2E 73
Anstey Ri. NG3: Nott . . . . . . . . . . . . . . .4B 46
Anthony Wharton Ct. NG11: Clif . . . . . . .2C 66
Antill St. NG9: Stap . . . . . . . . . . . . . . . .5F 53
Apollo Dr. NG6: Bulw . . . . . . . . . . . . . . .2F 31
Appleby Cl. DE7: Ilk . . . . . . . . . . . . . . . .3B 40
Appledore Av. NG8: Woll . . . . . . . . . . . .1D 54
Appledorne Way NG5: Arn . . . . . . . . . . .4A 22
Appleton Cl. NG11: Clif . . . . . . . . . . . . .4A 66
Appleton Ct. NG9: Bee . . . . . . . . . . . . . .1H 65
Appleton Gdns. NG3: Mapp . . . . . . . . . .2D 34
Appleton Rd. NG9: Bee . . . . . . . . . . . . .1H 65
Apple Tree Cl. NG12: Edwal . . . . . . . . . .1C 68
Appletree La. NG4: Ged . . . . . . . . . . . . .5H 35
Apple Wlk. NG3: Nott . . . . . . . . . . . . . . .1C 46
Applewood Gro. NG5: Sher . . . . . . . . . . .4H 33
Arboretum St. NG1: Nott . . . . . . .1B 4 (3F 45)
Arbour Hill DE7: D Ab . . . . . . . . . . . . . .6C 38
Arbrook Dr. NG8: Aspl . . . . . . . . . . . . . .3B 44
Arbutus Cl. NG11: Clif . . . . . . . . . . . . . .4A 66
Archdale Rd. NG5: Bestw . . . . . . . . . . . .1G 33
Archer Cres. NG8: Woll . . . . . . . . . . . . . .4F 43
Archer Rd. NG9: Stap . . . . . . . . . . . . . . .6G 53
Archer St. DE7: Ilk . . . . . . . . . . . . . . . . .4A 28
Arch Hill NG5: Redh . . . . . . . . . . . . . . . .2A 22
Archway Ct. NG7: Radf . . . . . . . . . . . . . .3D 44
   (off Limpenny St.)
Arden Cl. NG9: Lent A . . . . . . . . . . . . . .3G 55
   NG15: Huck . . . . . . . . . . . . . . . . . .6A 8
Arden Gro. NG13: Bing . . . . . . . . . . . . . .4C 50
Ardleigh Cl. NG5: Top V . . . . . . . . . . . . .4B 20
Ardmore Cl. NG2: Nott . . . . . . . . . . . . . .6B 46
Ardsley Cl. DE75: Hea . . . . . . . . . . . . . .3E 15
Arena, The NG1: Nott . . . . . . . . . .5C 4 (5F 45)
Argyle Ct. NG7: Radf . . . . . . . . . . . . . . .4D 44
Argyle M. NG16: Eastw . . . . . . . . . . . . . .3B 16
Argyle St. NG7: Radf . . . . . . . . . . . . . . .4D 44
   NG16: Lang M . . . . . . . . . . . . . . . .1F 15
Aria Ct. NG9: Stap . . . . . . . . . . . . . . . . .5F 53
Ariel Cl. NG6: Basf . . . . . . . . . . . . . . . . .2D 32
Arkers Cl. NG6: Basf . . . . . . . . . . . . . . . .4B 32
Arklow Cl. NG8: Aspl . . . . . . . . . . . . . . .5G 31
Arkwright St. NG2: Nott . . . . . . . . . . . . .2H 57
Arkwright St. Nth. NG2: Nott . . . . . . . . . .6G 45
Arkwright St. Sth. NG2: Nott . . . . . . . . . .2H 57
Arkwright Wlk. NG2: Nott . . . . . . . . . . . .2H 57
   (not continuous)
Arleston Dr. NG8: Woll . . . . . . . . . . . . . .6D 42
Arlington Cl. NG15: Huck . . . . . . . . . . . .1G 19
Arlington Dr. NG3: Mapp P . . . . . . . . . . .6G 33
Armadale Cl. NG5: Arn . . . . . . . . . . . . . .5E 23
Armes Cl. DE7: Ilk . . . . . . . . . . . . . . . . .4B 28
Armfield Rd. NG5: Arn . . . . . . . . . . . . . .1E 35
Armitage Dr. NG10: Long E . . . . . . . . . . .6A 64
Armstrong Rd. NG6: Bulw . . . . . . . . . . . .2F 31
Armstrong Way NG7: Basf . . . . . . . . . . . .6C 32
Arncliff Cl. NG8: Woll . . . . . . . . . . . . . . .5C 42
Arndale Rd. NG5: Sher . . . . . . . . . . . . . .2G 33
Arne Ct. NG2: Nott . . . . . . . . . . . . . . . . .2G 57
Arnesby Rd. NG7: Lent . . . . . . . . . . . . . .6B 44
Arno Av. NG7: H Grn . . . . . . . . . . . . . . .1F 45
ARNOLD . . . . . . . . . . . . . . . . . . . . . . . .6B 22
Arnold Av. NG10: Long E . . . . . . . . . . . .3C 72
Arnold Cres. NG10: Long E . . . . . . . . . . .3C 72
Arnold La. NG3: Ged, Mapp . . . . . . . . . .2D 34
   NG4: Ged . . . . . . . . . . . . . . . . . . .4G 35
Arnold Leisure Cen. . . . . . . . . . . . . . . . .5B 22

Arnold Rd. NG5: Bestw . . . . . . . . . . . . . .3C 32
   NG6: Basf, Bestw . . . . . . . . . . . . . .3C 32
Arnos Gro. NG16: Nuth . . . . . . . . . . . . . .4D 30
Arnot Hill Pk. . . . . . . . . . . . . . . . . . . . . .1A 34
Arnot Hill Rd. NG5: Arn . . . . . . . . . . . . . .6A 22
Arnot Ho. NG4: Carl . . . . . . . . . . . . . . . .1G 47
   (off Foxhill Rd. E.)
Arno Vale Gdns. NG5: Woodt . . . . . . . . . .2B 34
Arno Vale Rd. NG5: Woodt . . . . . . . . . . .2A 34
Arnside Cl. NG9: Stap . . . . . . . . . . . . . . .6G 53
Arnside Cl. NG5: Bestw . . . . . . . . . . . . . .2F 33
Arnside Rd. NG5: Bestw . . . . . . . . . . . . .2E 33
A Road NG7: Nott . . . . . . . . . . . . . . . . .5A 56
Arran Cl. NG9: Stap . . . . . . . . . . . . . . . .1G 53
Arthur Av. NG7: Lent . . . . . . . . . . . . . . .5D 44
   NG9: Stap . . . . . . . . . . . . . . . . . . .3H 53
Arthur Cres. NG4: Carl . . . . . . . . . . . . . .2E 47
Arthur Mee Rd. NG9: Stap . . . . . . . . . . . .6G 53
Arthur St. NG4: Neth . . . . . . . . . . . . . . .3A 48
   NG7: Radf . . . . . . . . . . . . . . .1A 4 (3E 45)
Artic Way NG16: Kimb . . . . . . . . . . . . . . .6F 17
Arundel Cl. NG10: Sand . . . . . . . . . . . . .1D 62
Arundel Dr. NG9: Bram . . . . . . . . . . . . . .1B 54
Arundel St. NG7: Lent . . . . . . . . . . . . . . .4E 45
Ascot Av. NG16: Kimb . . . . . . . . . . . . . . .6G 17
Ascot Ct. DE7: West H . . . . . . . . . . . . . .2B 38
Ascot Dr. NG5: Redh . . . . . . . . . . . . . . .5H 21
   NG15: Huck . . . . . . . . . . . . . . . . . .6D 6
Ascot Pk. Est. NG10: Sand . . . . . . . . . . .4E 53
Ascot Pl. DE7: Kirk H . . . . . . . . . . . . . . .4G 39
Ascot Rd. NG8: Basf . . . . . . . . . . . . . . . .2B 44
Ascott Gdns. NG2: West Br . . . . . . . . . . .6F 57
Ashbourne Cl. NG9: Bram . . . . . . . . . . . .2A 54
Ashbourne Rd. NG6: Bulw . . . . . . . . . . . .1F 31
Ashbourne St. NG7: Lent . . . . . . . . . . . . .4E 45
Ashburnham Av. NG7: Lent . . . . . . . . . . .5D 44
Ashchurch Dr. NG8: Woll . . . . . . . . . . . . .1D 54
Ash Cl. NG13: Bing . . . . . . . . . . . . . . . . .5G 51
   NG14: Bur J . . . . . . . . . . . . . . . . . . .3E 37
   NG14: Woodbo . . . . . . . . . . . . . . . .1C 24
   NG15: Huck . . . . . . . . . . . . . . . . . .6C 6
Ash Ct. NG4: Carl . . . . . . . . . . . . . . . . . .2F 47
Ash Cres. NG16: Nuth . . . . . . . . . . . . . . .1B 30
Ashdale Av. NG15: Huck . . . . . . . . . . . . .6G 7
Ashdale Rd. DE7: Ilk . . . . . . . . . . . . . . . .3C 40
   NG3: Nott . . . . . . . . . . . . . . . . . . . .3D 46
   NG5: Arn . . . . . . . . . . . . . . . . . . . .5C 22
Ashdown Cl. NG11: Wilf . . . . . . . . . . . . . .5F 57
Ashdown Gro. NG13: Bing . . . . . . . . . . . .5D 50
Asher La. NG11: Rudd . . . . . . . . . . . . . . .1G 77
Ashfield Av. NG9: Bee . . . . . . . . . . . . . . .6H 55
Ashfield Rd. NG2: Nott . . . . . . . . . . . . . .5B 46
Ashford Ct. DE7: West H . . . . . . . . . . . . .1B 38
Ashford Pl. DE7: Ilk . . . . . . . . . . . . . . . . .2A 28
Ashford Ri. NG8: Woll . . . . . . . . . . . . . . .1D 54
Ashforth Av. DE75: Hea . . . . . . . . . . . . . .4E 15
Ashforth Bus. Cen. NG3: Nott . . . . . . . . .3H 45
   (off Ashforth St.)
Ashforth St. NG3: Nott . . . . . . . . . . . . . .3H 45
Ashgate Retail Pk. NG15: Huck . . . . . . . .4A 8
Ashgate Rd. NG15: Huck . . . . . . . . . . . . .4H 7
Ash Gro. NG9: Stap . . . . . . . . . . . . . . . . .6F 53
   NG10: Long E . . . . . . . . . . . . . . . . .1E 73
   NG10: Sand . . . . . . . . . . . . . . . . . .4C 52
   NG12: Key . . . . . . . . . . . . . . . . . . .5H 79
   NG14: Woodbo . . . . . . . . . . . . . . . .6C 12
Ashiana NG2: Nott . . . . . . . . . . . . .4H 5 (5A 46)
Ashington Dr. NG5: Arn . . . . . . . . . . . . . .3B 22
Ash La. NG15: Pap . . . . . . . . . . . . . . . . .1H 9
Ash Lea Cl. NG12: Cotg . . . . . . . . . . . . . .3F 71
Ashley Cl. NG3: Chil . . . . . . . . . . . . . . . .5D 54
Ashley Ct. NG9: Bee . . . . . . . . . . . . . . . .5E 55
Ashley Cres. NG12: Key . . . . . . . . . . . . . .4H 79
Ashley Gro. NG15: Huck . . . . . . . . . . . . .4E 7
Ashley Rd. NG12: Key . . . . . . . . . . . . . . .4G 79
Ashley St. NG3: Nott . . . . . . . . . . . .3H 5 (4A 46)
Ashling Ct. NG2: Nott . . . . . . . . . . . . . . .1A 58
Ashling St. NG2: Nott . . . . . . . . . . . . . . .1A 58
Ash Mount Rd. NG16: Lang M . . . . . . . . .2F 15
Ashness Cl. NG2: Gam . . . . . . . . . . . . . .5E 59
Ashover Cl. NG3: Nott . . . . . . . . . . . . . . .1A 46
Ashridge Way NG12: Edwal . . . . . . . . . . .1E 69
Ash St. DE7: Ilk . . . . . . . . . . . . . . . . . . .3A 28
Ashton Av. NG5: Arn . . . . . . . . . . . . . . . .3B 22
Ashton Ct. NG8: Bilb . . . . . . . . . . . . . . . .2D 42
Ash Tree Ct. NG8: Stre . . . . . . . . . . . . . .4C 30
Ash Tree Sq. NG9: Bram . . . . . . . . . . . . .3B 54
Ashurst Gro. NG15: Huck . . . . . . . . . . . . .1E 19
Ashview Cl. NG10: Long E . . . . . . . . . . . .5D 62
Ash Vs. NG7: Radf . . . . . . . . . . . . . . . . .3D 44
Ash Vw. NG5: Sher . . . . . . . . . . . . . . . . .6F 33
Ashville Cl. NG2: Nott . . . . . . . . . . . . . . .2E 57
Ashwater Dr. NG3: Mapp . . . . . . . . . . . . .1F 35
Ashwell Cl. NG5: Woodt . . . . . . . . . . . . . .3A 34
Ashwell Gdns. NG7: H Grn . . . . . . . . . . . .1C 44
Ashwell St. NG4: Neth . . . . . . . . . . . . . . .3H 47

Ashwick Cl. NG11: Wilf . . . . . . . . . . . . . .6E 57
Ashworth Av. NG11: Rudd . . . . . . . . . . . .5G 67
Ashworth Cl. NG3: Nott . . . . . . . . . . . . . .4E 47
Ashworth Cres. NG3: Mapp . . . . . . . . . . .5D 34
Askeby Dr. NG8: Stre . . . . . . . . . . . . . . .6D 30
Askham Ct. NG2: Gam . . . . . . . . . . . . . .4E 59
   (off Radcliffe Rd.)
Aslockton Dr. NG8: Aspl . . . . . . . . . . . . .5B 32
Aspect Bus. Pk. NG6: Bulw . . . . . . . . . . .5F 19
Aspen Cl. NG13: Bing . . . . . . . . . . . . . . .5G 51
Aspen Rd. NG6: Bulw . . . . . . . . . . . . . . .1F 31
Asper St. NG4: Neth . . . . . . . . . . . . . . . .2A 48
Aspinall Ct. NG8: Woll . . . . . . . . . . . . . . .4A 44
ASPLEY . . . . . . . . . . . . . . . . . . . . . . . . .1H 43
Aspley La. NG8: Aspl, Bilb . . . . . . . . . . . .6F 31
Aspley Pk. Dr. NG8: Bilb . . . . . . . . . . . . .1G 43
Aspley Pl. NG7: Radf . . . . . . . . . . . . . . .3D 44
Assarts Rd. NG16: Nuth . . . . . . . . . . . . . .3E 31
Astcote Cl. DE75: Hea . . . . . . . . . . . . . . .4E 15
Aster Rd. NG3: Nott . . . . . . . . . . . . . . . .2H 45
Astill Pine Cl. DE72: Brea . . . . . . . . . . . .6A 62
Astle Ct. NG5: Arn . . . . . . . . . . . . . . . . .1E 35
Astley Dr. NG3: Nott . . . . . . . . . . . . . . . .6B 34
Aston Av. NG9: Lent A . . . . . . . . . . . . . . .3G 55
Aston Cl. DE7: Ilk . . . . . . . . . . . . . . . . . .6B 28
   NG11: Rudd . . . . . . . . . . . . . . . . . .2C 56
Aston Dr. NG6: Bulw . . . . . . . . . . . . . . . .3A 20
Aston Grn. NG9: Toton . . . . . . . . . . . . . .2G 63
Astral Dr. NG15: Huck . . . . . . . . . . . . . . .1E 19
Astral Gro. NG15: Huck . . . . . . . . . . . . . .1D 18
   (not continuous)
Astrid Gdns. NG5: Bestw . . . . . . . . . . . . .1D 32
Astron Ct. NG15: Huck . . . . . . . . . . . . . .1E 19
Astwood Cl. NG8: Bilb . . . . . . . . . . . . . . .2E 43
Atherfield Gdns. NG16: Eastw . . . . . . . . .2B 16
Atherton Ri. NG8: Cin . . . . . . . . . . . . . . .4H 31
Atherton Rd. DE7: Ilk . . . . . . . . . . . . . . .4G 27
Athorpe Gro. NG6: Basf . . . . . . . . . . . . . .4C 32
Atrium, The NG2: Nott . . . . . . . . . .6G 5 (6H 45)
ATTENBOROUGH . . . . . . . . . . . . . . . . . .3D 64
Attenborough Cl. NG10: Long E . . . . . . . .2B 72
Attenborough La. NG9: Atten, Chil . . . . . .2C 64
   (not continuous)
Attenborough Nature Cen. . . . . . . . . . . . .5C 64
Attenborough Nature Reserve . . . . . . . . . .3E 65
Attenborough Station (Rail) . . . . . . . . . . .3D 64
Attercliffe Ter. NG2: Nott . . . . . . . . . . . . .2G 57
Attewell Rd. NG16: Aws . . . . . . . . . . . . . .2D 28
Aubrey Av. NG2: Nott . . . . . . . . . . .5H 5 (5A 46)
Aubrey Rd. NG5: Sher . . . . . . . . . . . . . . .5F 33
Auburn Cl. DE7: Stan C . . . . . . . . . . . . . .1A 38
Auckland Cl. NG7: Radf . . . . . . . . . . . . . .4C 44
Auckland Rd. NG15: Huck . . . . . . . . . . . .6D 6
Audley Cl. DE7: Ilk . . . . . . . . . . . . . . . . .4H 27
Audley Dr. NG9: Lent A . . . . . . . . . . . . . .2F 55
Audon Av. NG9: Chil . . . . . . . . . . . . . . . .6E 55
Augustine Gdns. NG5: Top V . . . . . . . . . .4E 21
Austen Av. NG7: H Grn . . . . . . . . . . . . . .2E 45
   NG10: Long E . . . . . . . . . . . . . . . . .2E 73
Austins Dr. NG10: Sand . . . . . . . . . . . . . .1D 62
Austin St. NG6: Bulw . . . . . . . . . . . . . . . .6A 20
Austrey Av. NG9: Lent A . . . . . . . . . . . . . .3G 55
Autumn Ct. NG15: Huck . . . . . . . . . . . . . .5G 7
Avalon Cl. NG6: Bulw . . . . . . . . . . . . . . .1C 32
Avebury Cl. NG11: Clif . . . . . . . . . . . . . . .5B 66
Aveline Cl. NG5: Top V . . . . . . . . . . . . . .5D 20
Avenue, The NG11: Rudd . . . . . . . . . . . . .2H 77
   NG12: Rad T . . . . . . . . . . . . . . . . . .5F 49
   NG14: Calv . . . . . . . . . . . . . . . . . . .4H 11
Avenue A NG1: Nott . . . . . . . . . . . .4G 5 (5H 45)
Avenue B NG1: Nott . . . . . . . . . . . .4G 5 (5H 45)
Avenue C NG1: Nott . . . . . . . . . . . .4H 5 (5A 46)
Avenue D NG1: Nott . . . . . . . . . . . .4H 5 (5A 46)
Avenue E NG1: Nott . . . . . . . . . . . .3H 5 (4A 46)
Averton Sq. NG8: Woll . . . . . . . . . . . . . . .6B 44
Aviemore Cl. NG5: Arn . . . . . . . . . . . . . . .4D 22
Avis Av. DE75: Hea . . . . . . . . . . . . . . . . .6D 14
Avocet Cl. DE75: Hea . . . . . . . . . . . . . . .4F 15
   NG13: Bing . . . . . . . . . . . . . . . . . . .6G 51
   NG15: Huck . . . . . . . . . . . . . . . . . .2H 7
Avocet Wharf NG7: Lent . . . . . . . . . . . . . .1E 57
Avon Av. NG15: Huck . . . . . . . . . . . . . . .2E 19
Avondale Cl. NG10: Long E . . . . . . . . . . .1C 72
Avondale Rd. DE7: Kirk H . . . . . . . . . . . . .4G 39
   NG4: Carl . . . . . . . . . . . . . . . . . . . .3F 47
Avon Gdns. NG2: West Br . . . . . . . . . . . .4B 58
Avonlea Cl. DE7: Ilk . . . . . . . . . . . . . . . . .3D 40
Avon Pl. NG9: Bee . . . . . . . . . . . . . . . . .4G 55
Avon Rd. NG3: Nott . . . . . . . . . . . . . . . .4D 46
   NG4: Ged . . . . . . . . . . . . . . . . . . . .5H 35
AWSWORTH . . . . . . . . . . . . . . . . . . . . . .2E 29
Awsworth & Cossall By-Pass
   NG16: Aws, Coss . . . . . . . . . . . . . . .3D 28
Awsworth La. NG16: Coss . . . . . . . . . . . .5E 29
   NG16: Kimb . . . . . . . . . . . . . . . . . .2F 29

Awsworth Rd. DE7: Ilk . . . . . . . . . . . . . . . .5B **28**
Axford Cl. NG4: Ged . . . . . . . . . . . . . . . . . . .5H **35**
Axmouth Dr. NG3: Mapp . . . . . . . . . . . . . . .2F **35**
Aylesham Av. NG5: Arn . . . . . . . . . . . . . . . .1B **34**
Aylestone Dr. NG8: Bilb . . . . . . . . . . . . . . .1H **43**
Ayr St. NG7: Radf . . . . . . . . . . . . . . .1A **4** (3E **45**)
Ayscough Av. NG16: Nuth . . . . . . . . . . . . . .1C **30**
Ayton Cl. NG2: Nott . . . . . . . . . . . . . . . . . . .1F **57**
Ayton Gdns. NG9: Chil . . . . . . . . . . . . . . . . .3C **64**
Azalea Ct. NG16: Gilt . . . . . . . . . . . . . . . . . .5E **17**

# B

Babbacombe Dr. NG5: Bestw . . . . . . . . . . . .1F **33**
Babbacombe Way NG15: Huck . . . . . . . . . . .5D **6**
BABBINGTON . . . . . . . . . . . . . . . . . . . . . . . . .3G **29**
Babbington Cl. DE7: Ilk . . . . . . . . . . . . . . . .3D **40**
Babbington Cres. NG4: Ged . . . . . . . . . . . . .5G **35**
Babbington Dr. NG6: Cin . . . . . . . . . . . . . . .3H **31**
Babbington La. NG16: Kimb . . . . . . . . . . . . .3H **29**
Babington Ct. NG9: Chil . . . . . . . . . . . . . . . .6C **54**
Back La. DE7: Ilk . . . . . . . . . . . . . . . . . . . . . .5A **28**
  NG12: Norm W . . . . . . . . . . . . . . . . . . . . .1A **80**
  NG16: Nuth . . . . . . . . . . . . . . . . . . . . . . . .1D **30**
Bacon Cl. NG16: Gilt . . . . . . . . . . . . . . . . . . .5C **16**
Bacton Av. NG6: Bulw . . . . . . . . . . . . . . . . .5H **19**
Bacton Gdns. NG6: Bulw . . . . . . . . . . . . . . .5H **19**
Baden Powell Rd. NG2: Nott . . . . . . . . . . . .5C **46**
Bader Rd. NG11: Wilf . . . . . . . . . . . . . . . . . .4F **57**
Badger Cl. NG4: Carl . . . . . . . . . . . . . . . . . .1G **47**
  NG15: Huck . . . . . . . . . . . . . . . . . . . . . . . .5C **6**
Bagnall Av. NG5: Arn . . . . . . . . . . . . . . . . . .1G **33**
Bagnall Cotts. NG6: Bulw . . . . . . . . . . . . . . .2H **31**
Bagnall Rd. NG6: Basf, Cin . . . . . . . . . . . . .3H **31**
Bagot St. DE7: West H . . . . . . . . . . . . . . . . .1A **38**
Bagthorpe Cl. NG5: Sher . . . . . . . . . . . . . . .4E **33**
Baildon Cl. NG8: Woll . . . . . . . . . . . . . . . . . .6A **44**
Bailey Brook Cres. NG16: Lang M . . . . . . . .2E **15**
Bailey Brook Dr. NG16: Lang M . . . . . . . . . .2D **14**
Bailey Brook Ind. Est.
  NG16: Lang M . . . . . . . . . . . . . . . . . . . . . .3F **15**
Bailey Brook Rd. DE7: Ilk . . . . . . . . . . . . . . .2A **28**
Bailey Brook Wlk. NG16: Lang M . . . . . . . . .2E **15**
Bailey Cl. NG5: Arn . . . . . . . . . . . . . . . . . . . .6H **21**
Bailey Ct. NG4: Neth . . . . . . . . . . . . . . . . . .5H **47**
  NG12: Rad T . . . . . . . . . . . . . . . . . . . . . . .1E **61**
Bailey Dr. NG3: Mapp . . . . . . . . . . . . . . . . .2D **34**
BAILEY GROVE . . . . . . . . . . . . . . . . . . . . . . .3H **15**
Bailey Gro. Rd. NG16: Eastw . . . . . . . . . . . .3H **15**
Bailey La. NG12: Rad T . . . . . . . . . . . . . . . . .1E **61**
Bailey St. NG4: Neth . . . . . . . . . . . . . . . . . .2A **48**
  NG6: Basf . . . . . . . . . . . . . . . . . . . . . . . . . .5C **32**
  NG9: Stap . . . . . . . . . . . . . . . . . . . . . . . . .5E **53**
Bainbridge, The NG14: Calv . . . . . . . . . . . . .4A **12**
Bainton Gro. NG11: Clif . . . . . . . . . . . . . . . .4D **66**
Baird-Parker Dr. NG4: Carl . . . . . . . . . . . . . .2F **47**
Baker Av. DE75: Hea . . . . . . . . . . . . . . . . . .6D **14**
  NG5: Arn . . . . . . . . . . . . . . . . . . . . . . . . . .4C **22**
Baker Brook Cl. NG15: Huck . . . . . . . . . . . . .5B **8**
Bakerdale Rd. NG3: Nott . . . . . . . . . . . . . . .3D **46**
Baker Rd. NG16: Gilt, Newth . . . . . . . . . . . .5E **17**
Bakers Brothers Mobile Home Caravan Site
  DE7: Ilk . . . . . . . . . . . . . . . . . . . . . . . . . . . .6C **28**
Bakers Cl. NG7: Radf . . . . . . . . . . . . . . . . . .3C **44**
  NG12: Cotg . . . . . . . . . . . . . . . . . . . . . . . .2E **71**
BAKERS FIELDS . . . . . . . . . . . . . . . . . . . . . .3D **46**
Baker St. DE7: Ilk . . . . . . . . . . . . . . . . . . . . .6B **28**
  NG1: Nott . . . . . . . . . . . . . . . . . . . . . . . . . .2F **45**
  NG15: Huck . . . . . . . . . . . . . . . . . . . . . . . .4G **7**
Bakewell Av. NG4: Carl . . . . . . . . . . . . . . . .6G **35**
Bakewell Dr. NG5: Top V . . . . . . . . . . . . . . .6C **20**
Bakewell La. NG15: Huck . . . . . . . . . . . . . . .1H **19**
Bakewell Rd. NG10: Long E . . . . . . . . . . . . .6D **62**
Bala Dr. NG5: Bestw . . . . . . . . . . . . . . . . . .6E **21**
Baldwin Ct. NG7: Radf . . . . . . . . . . . . . . . . .4D **44**
Baldwin St. NG7: Radf . . . . . . . . . . . . . . . . .4E **45**
  NG16: Newth . . . . . . . . . . . . . . . . . . . . . . .4E **17**
Bale Cl. NG10: Long E . . . . . . . . . . . . . . . . .1A **74**
Balfour Rd. NG7: Lent, Radf . . . . . . . . . . . . .4D **44**
  NG9: Stap . . . . . . . . . . . . . . . . . . . . . . . . .5F **53**
Balfron Gdns. NG2: Nott . . . . . . . . . . . . . . .1F **57**
Balisier Cl. NG3: Nott . . . . . . . . . . . . . . . . . .3G **45**
Ballantrae Cl. NG5: Arn . . . . . . . . . . . . . . . .5D **22**
Ballerat Cres. NG5: Top V . . . . . . . . . . . . . .5C **20**
Balloon Wood Ind. Est. NG9: Bram . . . . . . .5A **42**
Ball St. NG3: Nott . . . . . . . . . . . . . . . . . . . . .2B **46**
Balmoral Av. NG2: West Br . . . . . . . . . . . . . .3A **58**
Balmoral Cl. DE75: Hea . . . . . . . . . . . . . . . .4A **14**
  NG10: Sand . . . . . . . . . . . . . . . . . . . . . . . .2D **62**
Balmoral Cres. NG8: Woll . . . . . . . . . . . . . . .4C **42**
Balmoral Dr. NG9: Bram . . . . . . . . . . . . . . . .1B **54**
Balmoral Gro. NG4: Colw . . . . . . . . . . . . . . .3H **47**
  NG15: Huck . . . . . . . . . . . . . . . . . . . . . . . .3H **7**
Balmoral Ho. NG5: Woodt . . . . . . . . . . . . . .3H **33**
Balmoral Rd. DE7: Kirk H . . . . . . . . . . . . . . .4H **39**
  NG1: Nott . . . . . . . . . . . . . . . . . . . . . . . . . .3F **45**

Balmoral Rd. NG4: Colw . . . . . . . . . . . . . . . .3H **47**
  NG13: Bing . . . . . . . . . . . . . . . . . . . . . . . . .5C **50**
Balshaw Way NG9: Chil . . . . . . . . . . . . . . . .3B **64**
Bamkin Cl. NG15: Huck . . . . . . . . . . . . . . . .5H **7**
Bampton Ct. NG2: Gam . . . . . . . . . . . . . . . .4E **59**
Banbury Av. NG9: Toton . . . . . . . . . . . . . . . .2H **63**
Bancroft St. NG6: Bulw . . . . . . . . . . . . . . . .6A **20**
Bandstand Yard . . . . . . . . . . . . . . . . . . . . . . .5C **4**
Banes Rd. NG13: Bing . . . . . . . . . . . . . . . . .5H **51**
Bangor Wlk. NG3: Nott . . . . . . . . . . . . . . . . .2G **45**
Bankfield Dr. DE7: Kirk H . . . . . . . . . . . . . . .3F **39**
  NG9: Bram . . . . . . . . . . . . . . . . . . . . . . . . .2C **54**
Bank Hill NG14: Woodbo . . . . . . . . . . . . . . .2H **23**
Bank Pl. NG1: Nott . . . . . . . . . . . . . .4E **5** (5G **45**)
Banks, The NG13: Bing . . . . . . . . . . . . . . . .5E **51**
Banksburn Cl. DE75: Hea . . . . . . . . . . . . . . .4A **14**
Banks Cl. NG5: Arn . . . . . . . . . . . . . . . . . . . .1D **34**
Banks Cres. NG13: Bing . . . . . . . . . . . . . . . .5E **51**
Banksman Cl. NG3: Nott . . . . . . . . . . . . . . . .2B **46**
Banks Paddock NG13: Bing . . . . . . . . . . . . .5F **51**
Banks Rd. NG9: Toton . . . . . . . . . . . . . . . . .2G **63**
Bank St. NG10: Long E . . . . . . . . . . . . . . . . .6G **63**
  NG16: Lang M . . . . . . . . . . . . . . . . . . . . . .1G **15**
Banks Yd. NG6: Bulw . . . . . . . . . . . . . . . . . .6H **19**
  (off Main St.)
Bankwood Cl. NG8: Aspl . . . . . . . . . . . . . . .6G **31**
Bannerman Rd. NG6: Bulw . . . . . . . . . . . . . .1A **32**
Barbara Sq. NG15: Huck . . . . . . . . . . . . . . . .2F **7**
Barber Cl. DE7: Ilk . . . . . . . . . . . . . . . . . . . .4A **28**
Barber St. NG16: Eastw . . . . . . . . . . . . . . . .3C **16**
Barbrook Cl. NG8: Woll . . . . . . . . . . . . . . . .4H **43**
Barbury Dr. NG11: Clif . . . . . . . . . . . . . . . . .6B **66**
Barclay Ct. DE7: Ilk . . . . . . . . . . . . . . . . . . .4H **27**
Barden Rd. NG3: Mapp . . . . . . . . . . . . . . . .2C **34**
Bardfield Gdns. NG5: Top V . . . . . . . . . . . . .3B **20**
Bardney Dr. NG6: Bulw . . . . . . . . . . . . . . . . .5G **19**
Bardsey Gdns. NG5: Bestw . . . . . . . . . . . . . .6E **21**
Barent Cl. NG5: Bestw . . . . . . . . . . . . . . . . .1D **32**
Barent Wlk. NG5: Bestw . . . . . . . . . . . . . . . .1D **32**
Barker Av. E. NG10: Sand . . . . . . . . . . . . . . .5D **52**
Barker Av. Nth. NG10: Sand . . . . . . . . . . . . .5C **52**
Barker Ga. DE7: Ilk . . . . . . . . . . . . . . . . . . . .5B **28**
  NG1: Nott . . . . . . . . . . . . . . . . . .4F **5** (5H **45**)
  NG15: Huck . . . . . . . . . . . . . . . . . . . . . . . .4F **7**
Barkers La. NG9: Chil . . . . . . . . . . . . . . . . . .1F **65**
Barkla Cl. NG11: Clif . . . . . . . . . . . . . . . . . .5A **66**
Bar La. NG6: Basf . . . . . . . . . . . . . . . . . . . . .5A **32**
  NG8: Aspl . . . . . . . . . . . . . . . . . . . . . . . . . .5A **32**
Bar La. Ind. Pk. NG6: Basf . . . . . . . . . . . . . .5B **32**
Barlborough Rd. DE7: Ilk . . . . . . . . . . . . . . .2B **28**
Barley Cft. NG2: West Br . . . . . . . . . . . . . . .5D **58**
Barleydale Dr. NG9: Trow . . . . . . . . . . . . . . .1F **53**
Barleylands NG11: Rudd . . . . . . . . . . . . . . .1G **77**
Barling Dr. DE7: Ilk . . . . . . . . . . . . . . . . . . . .5G **27**
Barlock Rd. NG6: Basf . . . . . . . . . . . . . . . . .3C **32**
Barlow Dr. Nth. NG16: Aws . . . . . . . . . . . . . .3D **28**
Barlow Dr. Sth. NG16: Aws . . . . . . . . . . . . . .3D **28**
Barlows Cotts. NG16: Aws . . . . . . . . . . . . . .2E **29**
Barlows Cotts. La.
  NG16: Aws . . . . . . . . . . . . . . . . . . . . . . . . .2E **29**
Barnby Wlk. NG5: Sher . . . . . . . . . . . . . . . . .2G **33**
Barn Cl. NG6: Bulw . . . . . . . . . . . . . . . . . . . .2F **31**
  NG10: Long E . . . . . . . . . . . . . . . . . . . . . . .2E **73**
  NG12: Cotg . . . . . . . . . . . . . . . . . . . . . . . .3E **71**
Barn Cft. NG9: Chil . . . . . . . . . . . . . . . . . . . .5B **54**
Barndale Cl. NG2: West Br . . . . . . . . . . . . . .2G **67**
Barnes Cl. NG11: Wilf . . . . . . . . . . . . . . . . . .1F **67**
Barnes Cft. DE75: Hea . . . . . . . . . . . . . . . . .5A **14**
Barnes Rd. NG5: Top V . . . . . . . . . . . . . . . .5D **20**
Barnet Rd. NG3: Nott . . . . . . . . . . . . . . . . . .2D **46**
Barnett Ct. NG12: Key . . . . . . . . . . . . . . . . .4G **79**
Barnfield NG11: Wilf . . . . . . . . . . . . . . . . . . .1F **67**
Barnsley Cl. NG6: Bestw V . . . . . . . . . . . . . .5F **9**
Barnsley Ter. NG2: Nott . . . . . . . . . . . . . . . .2G **57**
Barnston Rd. NG2: Nott . . . . . . . . . . . . . . . .4B **46**
Barnum Cl. NG8: Woll . . . . . . . . . . . . . . . . . .4E **43**
Barons Cl. NG4: Ged . . . . . . . . . . . . . . . . . .6G **35**
Barrack La. NG7: Nott . . . . . . . . . . . . . . . . .5D **44**
Barra M. NG2: Nott . . . . . . . . . . . . . . . . . . . .1F **57**
Barratt Cres. NG9: Atten . . . . . . . . . . . . . . . .3D **64**
Barratt La. NG9: Atten . . . . . . . . . . . . . . . . .3C **64**
Barrhead Cl. NG5: Top V . . . . . . . . . . . . . . .4C **20**
Barrington Cl. NG12: Rad T . . . . . . . . . . . . . .1E **61**
Barrique Rd. NG7: Lent . . . . . . . . . . . . . . . . .2C **56**
Barrow Slade NG12: Key . . . . . . . . . . . . . . .5G **79**
Barrydale Av. NG9: Bee . . . . . . . . . . . . . . . .6F **55**
Barry St. NG6: Bulw . . . . . . . . . . . . . . . . . . .6H **19**
Bartley Gdns. NG14: Calv . . . . . . . . . . . . . . .3E **11**
Bartlow Rd. NG8: Bilb . . . . . . . . . . . . . . . . . .2D **42**
Barton Cl. NG11: Rudd . . . . . . . . . . . . . . . . .1F **77**
BARTON IN FABIS . . . . . . . . . . . . . . . . . . . .1E **75**
Barton La. NG9: Atten, Chil . . . . . . . . . . . . .4B **64**
  NG11: Bart F . . . . . . . . . . . . . . . . . . . . . . .1G **75**
  NG11: Clif . . . . . . . . . . . . . . . . . . . . . . . . . .5A **66**
  NG11: Rat, Thru . . . . . . . . . . . . . . . . . . . . .6C **74**
Barton Rd. NG10: Long E . . . . . . . . . . . . . . .1A **74**

Bartons Cl. NG16: Newth . . . . . . . . . . . . . . .3E **17**
Barton St. NG9: Bee . . . . . . . . . . . . . . . . . . .6G **55**
Barton Way NG9: Chil . . . . . . . . . . . . . . . . . .6E **55**
Barwell Dr. NG8: Stre . . . . . . . . . . . . . . . . . .6D **30**
Basa Cres. NG5: Top V . . . . . . . . . . . . . . . . .5D **20**
Basford Rd. NG6: Basf . . . . . . . . . . . . . . . . .6B **32**
Basford Stop (NET) . . . . . . . . . . . . . . . . . . . .4C **32**
Baskin La. NG9: Chil . . . . . . . . . . . . . . . . . . .1C **64**
Baslow Av. NG4: Carl . . . . . . . . . . . . . . . . . .6F **35**
Baslow Cl. NG10: Long E . . . . . . . . . . . . . . .2C **72**
Baslow Dr. NG9: Lent A . . . . . . . . . . . . . . . .2G **55**
Bassett Cl. DE7: Ilk . . . . . . . . . . . . . . . . . . . .4G **27**
  NG16: Kimb . . . . . . . . . . . . . . . . . . . . . . . .6G **17**
Bassford Av. DE75: Hea . . . . . . . . . . . . . . . .3D **14**
BASSINGFIELD . . . . . . . . . . . . . . . . . . . . . . .4H **59**
Bassingfield La. NG2: Gam . . . . . . . . . . . . . .4F **59**
  (not continuous)
  NG12: Rad T . . . . . . . . . . . . . . . . . . . . . . .3H **59**
Bastion St. NG7: Radf . . . . . . . . . . . . . . . . .4C **44**
Bateman Gdns. NG7: H Grn . . . . . . . . . . . . .2D **44**
Bathley St. NG2: Nott . . . . . . . . . . . . . . . . . .2G **57**
Baths La. NG15: Huck . . . . . . . . . . . . . . . . . .4H **7**
Bath St. DE7: Ilk . . . . . . . . . . . . . . . . . . . . . .6A **28**
  NG1: Nott . . . . . . . . . . . . . . . . . . .2F **5** (4H **45**)
Bathurst Dr. NG8: Bilb . . . . . . . . . . . . . . . . .3G **43**
Battle Cl. NG13: Newton . . . . . . . . . . . . . . . .2B **50**
Baulk La. NG9: Stap . . . . . . . . . . . . . . . . . . .3H **53**
Bawtry Wlk. NG3: Nott . . . . . . . . . . . . . . . . .3B **46**
Bayard Ct. NG8: Woll . . . . . . . . . . . . . . . . . .4A **44**
Bayliss Rd. NG4: Ged . . . . . . . . . . . . . . . . . .4F **35**
Bayswater Rd. NG16: Kimb . . . . . . . . . . . . .6H **17**
Baythorn Rd. NG8: Bilb . . . . . . . . . . . . . . . .3D **42**
Beacon Flatts NG9: Bee . . . . . . . . . . . . . . . .5H **55**
Beacon Hill Dr. NG15: Huck . . . . . . . . . . . . .6C **6**
Beacon Hill Ri. NG3: Nott . . . . . . . .2H **5** (4A **46**)
Beacon Rd. NG9: Bee . . . . . . . . . . . . . . . . . .5H **55**
Beaconsfield St. NG7: H Grn . . . . . . . . . . . .1D **44**
  NG10: Long E . . . . . . . . . . . . . . . . . . . . . . .6G **63**
Beaconsfield Street Stop (NET) . . . . . . . . . .1D **44**
Bean Cl. NG6: Bulw . . . . . . . . . . . . . . . . . . .2F **31**
Beanford La. NG25: Oxt . . . . . . . . . . . . . . . .1H **11**
Beardall St. NG15: Huck . . . . . . . . . . . . . . . .4H **7**
Beardsall Rd. NG7: Lent . . . . . . . . . . . . . . . .5C **44**
  (off Faraday Rd.)
Beardsley Gdns. NG2: Nott . . . . . . . . . . . . . .1F **57**
Beardsmore Gro. NG15: Huck . . . . . . . . . . . .2F **7**
Beastmarket Hill NG1: Nott . . . . . . . .4D **4** (5G **45**)
Beatty Wlk. DE7: Ilk . . . . . . . . . . . . . . . . . . .4B **28**
Beauclerk Dr. NG5: Top V . . . . . . . . . . . . . .5C **20**
Beaufort Ct. NG2: West Br . . . . . . . . . . . . . .2G **67**
Beaufort Dr. NG9: Chil . . . . . . . . . . . . . . . . .6C **54**
Beaulieu Gdns. NG2: West Br . . . . . . . . . . . .6G **57**
Beaumaris Dr. NG4: Ged . . . . . . . . . . . . . . . .6B **36**
  NG9: Chil . . . . . . . . . . . . . . . . . . . . . . . . . .1B **64**
Beaumont Cl. NG9: Stap . . . . . . . . . . . . . . . .2G **53**
  NG12: Key . . . . . . . . . . . . . . . . . . . . . . . . .3G **79**
Beaumont Gdns. NG2: West Br . . . . . . . . . .1H **67**
Beaumont Sq. NG8: Woll . . . . . . . . . . . . . . .4B **42**
Beaumont St. NG2: Nott . . . . . . . . . .5H **5** (5A **46**)
BEAUVALE
  NG15 . . . . . . . . . . . . . . . . . . . . . . . . . . . . . .5E **7**
  NG16 . . . . . . . . . . . . . . . . . . . . . . . . . . . . . .2D **16**
Beauvale NG16: Newth . . . . . . . . . . . . . . . .3D **16**
Beauvale Cl. NG15: Huck . . . . . . . . . . . . . . .5E **7**
Beauvale Cres. NG15: Huck . . . . . . . . . . . . .5D **6**
Beauvale Dr. DE7: Ilk . . . . . . . . . . . . . . . . . .2H **27**
Beauvale Ri. NG16: Eastw . . . . . . . . . . . . . . .2D **16**
Beauvale Rd. NG2: Nott . . . . . . . . . . . . . . . .2G **57**
  NG15: Huck . . . . . . . . . . . . . . . . . . . . . . . .5D **6**
Beaver Grn. NG2: West Br . . . . . . . . . . . . . .4H **57**
Beck Av. NG14: Calv . . . . . . . . . . . . . . . . . . .3H **11**
Beckenham Rd. NG7: Radf . . . . . . . . . . . . . .3D **44**
Beckett Ct. NG4: Ged . . . . . . . . . . . . . . . . . .4F **35**
Becket Way, The NG2: West Br . . . . . . . . . . .5F **57**
Beckford Rd. NG2: Nott . . . . . . . . . . . . . . . .6B **46**
Beckhampton Rd. NG5: Bestw . . . . . . . . . . .5F **21**
Beckley Rd. NG8: Brox . . . . . . . . . . . . . . . . .5F **31**
Beckside NG2: West Br . . . . . . . . . . . . . . . . .1E **69**
Beck St. NG1: Nott . . . . . . . . . . . . . .3F **5** (4H **45**)
  NG4: Carl . . . . . . . . . . . . . . . . . . . . . . . . . .1F **47**
Bedale Ct. NG9: Chil . . . . . . . . . . . . . . . . . . .1A **64**
Bedale Rd. NG5: Sher . . . . . . . . . . . . . . . . . .2G **33**
Bedarra Gro. NG7: Lent . . . . . . . . . . . . . . . .5C **44**
Bede Ling NG2: West Br . . . . . . . . . . . . . . . .5G **57**
Bedford Ct. NG7: H Grn . . . . . . . . . . . . . . . .1D **44**
  NG9: Stap . . . . . . . . . . . . . . . . . . . . . . . . .2G **53**
Bedford Gro. NG6: Bulw . . . . . . . . . . . . . . . .2B **32**
Bedford Row NG1: Nott . . . . . . . . . .3G **5** (4H **45**)
Bedlington Gdns. NG3: Mapp . . . . . . . . . . . .5A **34**
Beckham Av. NG9: Bee . . . . . . . . . . . . . . . . .3B **46**
Beech Av. DE72: Brea . . . . . . . . . . . . . . . . . .5B **62**
  NG3: Mapp . . . . . . . . . . . . . . . . . . . . . . . . .3B **34**
  NG4: Neth . . . . . . . . . . . . . . . . . . . . . . . . . .3H **47**
  NG7: Basf . . . . . . . . . . . . . . . . . . . . . . . . . .1E **45**
  NG9: Bee . . . . . . . . . . . . . . . . . . . . . . . . . .6H **55**
  NG10: Long E . . . . . . . . . . . . . . . . . . . . . . .4G **63**
  NG10: Sand . . . . . . . . . . . . . . . . . . . . . . . .4D **52**

Beech Av. NG12: Key .................5H 79
NG13: Bing ........................5G 51
NG15: Huck .........................4G 7
NG16: Nuth ........................1B 30
Beech Cl. NG2: West Br .............2F 59
NG6: Cin ..........................3A 32
NG12: Edwal .......................1D 68
NG12: Rad T .......................1F 61
Beech Ct. NG3: Mapp ...............3C 34
Beechcroft DE7: West H .............2C 38
BEECHDALE ..........................3G 43
Beechdale Rd. NG8: Aspl, Bilb .....6F 31
Beechdale Swimming Cen. ...........3A 44
Beeches, The DE7: Smal ............5A 14
NG3: Nott .........................1C 46
NG10: Long E ......................5G 63
Beech La. DE7: West H .............2B 38
Beech Lodge NG13: Bing ............5G 51
Beechwood Rd. NG5: Arn ............5C 22
BEESTON ............................4G 55
Beeston Bus. Pk. NG9: Bee .........1G 65
Beeston Cl. NG9: Bestw V ..........1C 20
Beeston Ct. NG6: Bulw .............6B 20
Beeston Flds. Dr. NG9: Bee, Bram ..3C 54
Beeston Fields Golf Course .........3D 54
Beeston La. NG7: Nott .............2H 55
Beeston Marina Mobile Home Pk.
NG9: Atten ........................2G 65
Beeston Rd. NG7: Nott .............2B 56
Beeston Sailing Club ...............3G 65
Beeston Station (Rail) .............6G 55
Beetham Cl. NG13: Bing ............5F 51
Beggarlee Pk. NG16: Newth .........1D 16
Bel-Air Res. Homes NG2: Gam .......4F 59
Belconnen Av. NG5: Bestw ..........2D 32
Beldover Ho. NG7: Lent ............5C 44
(off Faraday Rd.)
Belfield Ct. DE75: Los ............1A 14
Belfield Gdns. NG10: Long E .......6G 63
Belfield St. DE7: Ilk .............5B 28
Belford Cl. NG6: Bulw .............5F 19
Belfry Way NG12: Edwal ............1E 69
Belgrave M. NG2: West Br ..........2G 67
Belgrave Rd. NG6: Bulw ............6A 6
Belgrave Sq. NG1: Nott .......3C 4 (4F 45)
Bella Cl. NG16: Lang M ............1F 15
Bellar Ga. NG1: Nott ........4G 5 (5H 45)
Belle Isle Rd. NG15: Huck .........5G 7
Belleville Dr. NG5: Bestw .........6F 21
Bellevue Ct. NG3: Nott ............3A 46
Bell Ho. NG7: Nott ................3C 56
Bell La. DE7: Smal ................2A 26
DE75: Ship ........................2C 26
NG11: Wilf ........................4F 57
Bells La. NG8: Cin ................5G 31
Bell St. NG4: Carl ................1F 47
Belmont Av. DE72: Brea ............5A 62
NG6: Bulw .........................6A 20
Belmont Cl. NG9: Chil .............1B 64
NG15: Huck ........................1G 19
Belmore Gdns. NG8: Bilb ...........4D 42
Belper Av. NG4: Carl ..............6F 35
Belper Cres. NG4: Carl ............6F 35
Belper Rd. DE7: Stan C, West H ....6A 26
NG7: H Grn ........................2D 44
Belper St. DE7: Ilk ...............2B 40
Belsay Rd. NG5: Bestw .............6E 21
Belsford Cl. NG16: Want ...........5A 18
Belton Cl. NG10: Sand .............1D 62
Belton Dr. NG2: West Br ...........1F 67
Belton St. NG7: H Grn .............1D 44
Belvedere Av. NG7: H Grn ..........1D 44
Belvedere Cl. NG12: Key ...........3G 79
NG10: Long E ......................2G 73
Belvoir Cl. DE7: Kirk H ...........3H 39
Belvoir Hill NG2: Nott ............5B 46
Belvoir Lodge NG4: Carl ...........3G 47
Belvoir Rd. NG2: West Br ..........2C 58
NG4: Neth .........................2A 48
Belvoir St. NG3: Mapp .............5B 34
NG15: Huck ........................3F 7
Belvoir Ter. NG2: Nott ............5B 46
Belvoir Va. Gro. NG13: Bing .......5F 51
Belward St. NG1: Nott .......4G 5 (5H 45)
Belwood Cl. NG11: Clif ............3D 66
Bembridge Ct. NG9: Bram ..........3A 54
Bembridge Dr. NG5: Bestw ..........1F 33
(not continuous)
Bencault Gro. NG15: Huck ..........3G 7
Bendigo La. NG2: Nott .............6C 46
Benedict Ct. NG5: Top V ...........4E 21
Benington Dr. NG8: Woll ...........6C 42
Ben Mayo Ct. NG7: Radf ............3D 44
Benner Av. DE7: Ilk ...............4C 40
Bennerley Av. DE7: Ilk ............3B 28
Bennerley Ct. NG6: Bulw ...........5F 19
Bennerley Rd. NG6: Bulw ...........5F 19

Bennett Rd. NG3: Mapp .............4C 34
Bennett St. NG3: Mapp .............5B 34
NG10: Long E ......................2E 63
NG10: Sand ........................6D 52
Benneworth Cl. NG15: Huck .........6F 7
Ben St. NG7: Radf .................3D 44
Bentinck Av. NG12: Toll ...........4F 69
Bentinck Ct. NG2: Nott ............4H 5
Bentinck Rd. NG4: Carl ............5E 35
NG7: H Grn, Radf ..................3D 44
Bentinck St. NG15: Huck ...........3F 7
Bentley Av. NG3: Nott .............3C 46
Bentwell Av. NG5: Arn .............6C 22
Beresford Dr. DE7: Ilk ............2A 28
Beresford Rd. NG10: Long E ........2C 72
Beresford St. NG7: Radf ...........4C 44
Berkeley Av. NG3: Mapp P ..........1G 45
NG10: Long E ......................1E 73
Berkeley Ct. NG5: Sher ............6G 33
Berle Av. DE75: Hea ...............2C 14
Ber Mar Anda Res. Mobile Home Pk.
NG6: Lang M .......................1F 15
Bernard Av. NG15: Huck ............2H 7
Bernard St. NG5: Sher .............6F 33
Bernard Ter. NG5: Sher ............6F 33
Bernisdale Cl. NG5: Top V .........4D 20
Berridge Rd. NG7: H Grn ...........1E 45
Berridge Rd. Central NG7: H Grn ...1D 44
Berridge Rd. W. NG7: H Grn ........2C 44
Berriedale Cl. NG5: Arn ...........4D 22
Berrydown Cl. NG8: Aspl ...........6A 32
Berry Hill Gro. NG4: Ged ..........5G 35
Berwick Cl. NG6: Bestw ............1G 33
Berwin Cl. NG10: Long E ...........4C 62
Beryldene Av. NG7: Want ...........6A 18
Besecar Av. NG4: Ged ..............5G 35
Besecar Cl. NG4: Ged ..............5G 35
Bessell La. NG9: Stap .............6E 53
Bestwick Av. DE75: Hea ............4F 15
Bestwick Cl. DE7: Ilk .............5C 40
BESTWOOD ...........................6F 21
Bestwood Av. NG5: Arn .............5A 22
Bestwood Bus. Pk.
NG6: Bestw V ......................2C 20
Bestwood Cl. NG5: Arn .............5A 22
Bestwood Country Pk. ..............2C 20
Bestwood Footpath NG6: Bestw V ....6B 8
NG15: Bestw V, Huck ...............6B 8
Bestwood Lodge Dr. NG5: Arn .......4G 21
Bestwood Lodge Stables
NG5: Arn ..........................3F 21
Bestwood Pk. NG5: Arn .............3F 21
Bestwood Pk. Dr. NG5: Top V .......4F 21
Bestwood Pk. Dr. W. NG5: Top V ....4B 20
Bestwood Pk. Vw. NG5: Arn .........4A 22
Bestwood Rd. NG6: Bulw ............5A 20
NG15: Huck ........................6A 8
Bestwood Swimming Pool ...........1F 33
Bestwood Ter. NG6: Bulw ...........5A 20
BESTWOOD VILLAGE ..................1C 20
Bethel Gdns. NG15: Huck ...........6C 6
Bethnal Wlk. NG6: Bulw ............6H 19
Betony Cl. NG13: Bing .............5C 50
Betts Av. NG15: Huck ..............1G 19
Betula Cl. NG11: Clif .............4A 66
Bevel St. NG7: H Grn ..............2D 44
Beverley Cl. NG8: Woll ............5B 42
Beverley Dr. NG16: Kimb ...........6G 17
Beverley Gdns. NG4: Ged ...........6H 35
Beverley Sq. NG3: Nott ............2A 46
Bewcastle Rd. NG5: Arn, Top V .....4E 21
Bewick Dr. NG3: Nott ..............4E 47
Bexhill Ct. NG9: Bee ..............2E 55
Bexleigh Gdns. NG8: Bilb ..........1G 43
Bexon Ct. NG4: Carl ...............2G 47
Bexwell Cl. NG11: Clif ............5C 66
Biant Cl. NG8: Cin ................4H 31
Bideford Cl. NG3: Mapp ............2F 35
Bidford Rd. NG8: Brox .............6F 31
Bidwell Cres. NG11: Goth ..........5H 75
Biggart Cl. NG9: Chil .............3C 64
Biko Sq. NG7: H Grn ...............1D 44
Bilberry Wlk. NG3: Nott ...........3A 46
Bilbie Wlk. NG1: Nott .......2C 4 (4F 45)
BILBOROUGH .........................2E 43
Bilborough Rd. NG8: Stre ..........4B 42
Bilborough Sports Cen. ............2C 42
Bilby Gdns. NG3: Nott .............4B 46
Billesdon Dr. NG5: Sher ...........3D 32
Billingham Ho. NG5: Sher ..........6F 33
BINGHAM ............................5E 51
Bingham By-Pass
NG13: Bing ........................5B 50
Bingham Ind. Pk. NG13: Bing .......4E 51
Bingham Leisure Cen. ..............5F 51

Bingham Rd. NG5: Sher .............5G 33
NG12: Cotg ........................2F 71
(not continuous)
NG12: Rad T .......................6F 49
Bingham Station (Rail) ............4F 51
Bingley Cl. NG8: Bilb .............3H 43
Birch Av. DE7: Ilk ................2C 40
NG4: Carl .........................2F 47
NG9: Bee ..........................1H 65
NG16: Nuth ........................1B 30
Birch Cl. NG16: Nuth ..............1B 30
Birchdale Av. NG15: Huck ..........6G 7
Birchfield Pk. DE75: Hea ..........6D 14
Birchfield Rd. NG5: Arn ...........4C 22
Birch Lea NG5: Redh ...............5H 21
Birchover Pl. DE7: Ilk ............2A 28
Birchover Rd. NG8: Bilb ...........4C 42
Birch Pk. NG7: Newth ..............6C 16
Birch Pas. NG7: Radf ..........2A 4 (4E 45)
Birch Ri. NG14: Woodbo ............6C 12
Birch Wlk. NG5: Sher ..............4H 33
Birchwood Ct. DE75: Los ...........1A 14
Birchwood Av. DE72: Brea ..........6B 62
NG10: Long E ......................1E 73
Birchwood Rd. NG8: Woll ...........5C 42
Bircumshaw Rd. DE75: Hea ..........3C 14
Birdcroft La. DE7: Ilk ............4B 40
Birdsall Av. NG8: Woll ............5E 43
Birkdale Cl. DE7: Ilk .............6H 27
NG12: Edwal .......................2C 68
Birkdale Way NG5: Top V ...........5D 20
Birkin Av. NG7: H Grn .............2D 44
NG9: Toton ........................3A 64
NG11: Rudd ........................5G 67
NG12: Rad T .......................5G 49
Birkland Av. NG1: Nott .......1D 4 (3G 45)
NG3: Mapp .........................3C 34
Birley St. NG9: Stap ..............6F 53
Birling Cl. NG6: Bulw .............6F 19
Birrell Rd. NG7: H Grn ............1E 45
Bisham Dr. NG2: West Br ...........4D 58
Bishopdale Cl. NG10: Long E .......1C 72
Bishopdale Dr. NG16: Want .........6B 18
Bishops Cl. NG12: Key .............3G 79
Bishops Dr. NG13: Bing ............4D 50
Bishop St. NG16: Eastw ............3B 16
Bishops Way NG15: Huck ............2H 7
Bispham Dr. NG9: Toton ............2H 63
Blackacre NG14: Bur J .............2E 37
Blackburn Pl. DE7: Ilk ............4A 28
Blackburn Way NG5: Bestw ..........2E 33
Blackcliffe Farm M. NG11: Rudd ....5A 66
Blackett's Wlk. NG11: Clif ........5A 66
Blackfriars Cl. NG16: Nuth ........5D 30
Blackhill Dr. NG4: Carl ...........1H 47
Black Hills Dr. DE7: Ilk ..........3A 40
Blackrod Cl. NG9: Toton ...........3A 64
Blacksmith Ct. NG12: Cotg .........1E 71
Blacksmiths Cl. NG15: Pap .........1B 8
Blackstone Wlk. NG2: Nott .........1G 57
Black Swan Cl. NG5: Sher ..........3H 33
Blackthorn Cl. NG4: Ged ...........5A 36
NG13: Bing ........................5G 51
Blackthorn Dr. NG16: Eastw ........3A 16
Blackthorne Dr. NG6: Cin ..........4H 31
Blackwell Av. DE7: Ilk ............2B 28
Bladon Cl. NG3: Mapp .............5A 34
Bladon Rd. NG11: Rudd .............6F 67
Blair Ct. NG2: Nott ...............2G 57
Blair Gro. NG10: Sand .............1C 62
Blaise Cl. NG11: Clif .............5C 66
Blake Cl. NG5: Arn ................6C 22
Blake Ct. NG10: Long E ............2D 72
Blakeney Ho. NG7: H Grn ...........2D 44
(off St Paul's Av.)
Blakeney Rd. NG12: Rad T ..........6H 49
Blakeney Wlk. NG5: Arn ............2B 34
Blake Rd. NG2: West Br ............4B 58
NG9: Stap .........................5G 53
Blake St. DE7: Ilk ................6B 28
Blandford Av. NG10: Long E ........1D 72
Blandford Rd. NG9: Chil ...........6C 54
Bland La. NG14: Epp ...............6G 13
Blanford Gdns. NG2: West Br .......3C 32
Blankney St. NG5: Basf ............3C 32
Blants Cl. NG16: Kimb .............1H 29
Blantyre Av. NG5: Top V ...........4C 20
Blatherwick Cl. NG15: Huck ........3H 7
Blatherwick's Yd. NG5: Arn ........5B 22
Bleaberry Cl. NG2: West Br ........6E 59
Bleachers Yd. NG7: Basf ...........6C 32
Bleasby St. NG2: Nott .............5B 46
Bleasdale Cl. NG4: Ged ............5A 36
Blencathra Cl. NG2: West Br .......6E 59
BLENHEIM ...........................4F 19
Blenheim NG3: Nott ................2G 45
Blenheim Av. NG3: Mapp ............5E 35

Blenheim Cl.—Bridge Farm La.

Blenheim Cl. NG11: Rudd 6F 67
Blenheim Ct. NG6: Bulw 4E 19
NG10: Sand 1D 62
Blenheim Dr. NG9: Chil 6C 54
Blenheim Ind. Est. NG6: Bulw 5F 19
Blenheim La. NG6: Bulw 3D 18
Blenheim Pk. NG6: Bulw 4E 19
Blidworth Cl. NG8: Stre 5E 31
Blind La. DE72: Brea 5A 62
NG12: Key 5G 79
Bloomsbury Ct. *NG1: Nott* *3F 5*
*(off Beck St.)*
Bloomsbury Dr. NG16: Nuth 4E 31
Bloomsgrove Ind. Est. NG7: Radf 4D 44
Bloomsgrove Rd. DE7: Ilk 5B 28
Bloomsgrove St. NG7: Radf 4D 44
Bluebell Bank NG13: Bing 6D 50
Bluebell Cl. NG15: Huck 5C 6
Blue Bell Hill Rd. NG3: Nott 3A 46
Bluebell Way DE75: Hea 4F 15
Bluecoat Cl. NG1: Nott 1D 4 (3G 45)
Bluecoat Ho. NG1: Nott 1D 4 (3G 45)
Bluecoat St. NG1: Nott 1D 4 (3G 45)
Blundell Cl. NG3: Nott 1B 46
Blyth Gdns. NG3: Mapp 5A 34
Blyth St. NG3: Mapp 6A 34
Blyton Wlk. NG5: Bestw 6F 21
Boatmans Cl. DE7: Ilk 5B 28
Boatswain Dr. NG15: Huck 3H 7
Bobbers Mill NG8: H Grn 2C 44
Bobbers Mill Bri. NG7: H Grn 2B 44
NG8: H Grn 2B 44
Bobbers Mill Rd. NG7: H Grn 2C 44
Boden Dr. NG16: Nuth 1C 30
Boden St. NG7: Radf 4D 44
Bodill Gdns. NG15: Huck 5A 8
Bodmin Av. NG15: Huck 6C 6
Bodmin Dr. NG8: Aspl 5A 32
Body Rd. NG9: Chil 2B 64
BOGEND 3G 17
Bohem Rd. NG10: Long E 2E 63
Bold Cl. NG6: Bulw 5H 19
Bolero Cl. NG8: Woll 4E 43
Bolero Sq. NG1: Nott 4G 5
Bolingey Way NG15: Huck 6C 6
Bolsover St. NG15: Huck 4H 7
Bolton Av. NG9: Chil 1C 64
Bolton Cl. NG2: West Br 5C 58
Bolton Ter. NG12: Rad T 6F 49
Bond Ho. *NG5: Arn* *5A 22*
*(off Bond St.)*
Bonds Cl. DE7: Ilk 2B 28
Bond St. NG2: Nott 4H 5 (5A 46)
NG5: Arn 5A 22
Bonetti Cl. NG5: Arn 2D 34
Boniface Gdns. NG5: Top V 4E 21
Bonington Cl. NG6: Bulw 1G 31
Bonington Dr. NG5: Arn 6B 22
Bonington Gallery, The 1C 4
Bonington Rd. NG3: Mapp 3B 34
Bonington Theatre 5B 22
Bonner Hill NG14: Calv 5H 11
Bonner La. NG14: Calv 4A 12
Bonner's Rd. NG16: Aws 3E 29
Bonnington Cres. NG5: Sher 3G 33
Bonnymead NG12: Cotg 3E 71
Bonsall Ct. NG10: Long E 5G 63
Bonsall St. NG10: Long E 5G 63
Bonser Cl. NG4: Carl 2G 47
Bonser Hedge Ct. NG10: Long E 3D 72
Booth Cl. NG3: Nott 2F 5 (4H 45)
Booths Gdns. DE7: Ilk 3B 28
Boots Ct. NG10: Long E 6D 62
Borlace Cres. NG9: Stap 5G 53
Borman Cl. NG6: Bulw 2F 31
Borrowash By-Pass DE72: Dray, Ris 2A 62
Borrowdale Cl. NG2: Gam 5F 59
Borrowdale Ct. NG9: Chil 1B 64
Borrowdale Dr. NG10: Long E 1C 72
Boscawen Ct. DE7: Ilk 4B 28
Bosden Cl. NG8: Bilb 3C 42
Bosley Sq. NG9: Lent A 3G 55
Bostocks La. DE72: Ris 1B 62
NG10: Sand 2C 62
Boston M. NG5: Sher 4D 32
Boston St. NG1: Nott 3G 5 (4H 45)
Boswell St. NG7: Radf 4C 44
Bosworth Cl. NG12: Shel 1H 49
Bosworth Dr. NG16: Newth 2D 16
Bosworth Wlk. NG2: Nott 2F 57
Bosworth Way NG10: Long E 2F 73
Botany Av. NG3: Nott 2B 46
Botany Cl. NG2: West Br 2G 67
Botany M. NG3: Nott 2B 46
Bothe Cl. NG10: Long E 1E 73
Bottle La. NG1: Nott 4E 5 (5G 45)
Boulevard Ind. Pk. NG9: Bee 5H 55
Boundary Cres. NG9: Bee 2F 55
Boundary La. NG16: Lang M 2G 15
Boundary Rd. NG2: West Br 1A 68
NG9: Bee 2F 55
Bourne Cl. NG9: Bram 2D 54
Bourne Dr. NG16: Lang M 2F 15
Bourne M. NG4: Neth 3A 48
Bourne Sq. DE72: Brea 5A 62
Bourne St. NG4: Neth 3A 48
Bournmoor Av. NG11: Clif 4C 66
Bovill St. NG7: Radf 3D 44
Bowden Av. NG6: Bestw V 1C 20
Bowden Cl. NG5: Sher 4G 33
Bowden Dr. NG9: Bee 5H 55
Bowers Av. NG3: Mapp P 2H 45
Bowes Well Rd. DE7: Ilk 5A 28
Bowland Cl. NG3: Nott 2C 46
Bowland Rd. NG13: Bing 5C 50
Bowling Cl. DE7: Stant D 3A 52
Bowlwell Av. NG5: Top V 5D 20
Bowness Av. NG6: Basf 5A 32
Bowness Cl. NG2: Gam 4E 59
Bowscale Cl. NG2: West Br 6E 59
Boxley Dr. NG2: West Br 1G 67
Boxtree Av. NG15: Huck 5F 7
Boyce Gdns. NG3: Mapp 6B 34
Boycroft Av. NG3: Nott 1B 46
Boyd Cl. NG5: Arn 4D 22
Boynton Dr. NG3: Mapp 6B 34
Boythorpe Cl. DE7: Ilk 2B 28
Bracadale Rd. NG5: Top V 4D 20
Bracebridge Dr. NG8: Bilb 3D 42
Bracey Ri. NG2: West Br 2A 68
Bracken Cl. NG4: Carl 5F 35
NG8: Bilb 6F 31
NG10: Long E 4D 62
Brackendale Av. NG5: Arn 5B 22
Brackenfield Dr. NG16: Gilt 5D 16
Bracken Ho. NG6: Bulw 6H 19
Bracken Rd. NG10: Long E 4D 62
Bracknell Cres. NG8: Basf 6B 32
Bracton Dr. NG3: Nott 3B 46
Bradbourne Av. NG11: Wilf 6E 57
Bradbury Gdns. NG11: Rudd 6F 67
Bradbury/Midway Ind. Est. NG7: Lent 3C 56
Bradbury St. NG2: Nott 5C 46
Braddock Cl. NG7: Lent 5C 44
Braddon Av. NG9: Stap 2G 53
Bradfield Rd. NG8: Brox 6F 31
Bradford Ct. NG6: Bulw 1G 31
Bradford Way NG6: Bestw V 5F 9
Bradgate Cl. NG10: Sand 1D 62
Bradgate Rd. NG7: H Grn 1E 45
Bradley Ct. NG9: Bee 5G 55
Bradley St. NG10: Sand 6E 53
Bradleys Yd. NG12: Plum 6G 69
Bradley Wlk. NG11: Clif 5D 66
Bradman Gdns. NG5: Arn 1D 34
BRADMORE 4B 78
Bradmore Av. NG11: Rudd 5G 67
Bradmore Bus. Pk. NG11: Bunny 5A 78
Bradmore La. NG12: Plum 3E 79
Bradmore Ri. NG5: Sher 3G 33
Bradshaw St. NG10: Long E 2D 72
Bradstone Dr. NG3: Mapp 1F 35
Bradwell Cl. NG16: Gilt 5E 17
Bradwell Dr. NG5: Top V 5D 20
Braefell Cl. NG2: West Br 6F 59
Braefield Cl. DE7: Kirk H 4G 39
Braemar Av. NG16: Eastw 5B 16
Braemar Dr. NG4: Ged 6B 36
Braemar Rd. NG6: Bulw 6A 20
Braidwood Ct. NG7: H Grn 2D 44
Brailsford Rd. NG7: Lent 2C 56
Brailsford Way NG9: Chil 4C 64
Bramber Gro. NG11: Clif 6C 66
Bramble Cl. NG6: Basf 4B 32
NG9: Atten 3D 64
NG10: Long E 4D 62
Bramble Ct. NG4: Ged 6H 35
NG10: Sand 6E 53
Bramble Dr. NG3: Nott 2C 46
Bramble Gdns. NG8: Bilb 1G 43
Bramble Way NG12: Cotg 3G 71
BRAMCOTE 3A 54
Bramcote Av. NG9: Chil 5C 54
Bramcote Crematorium NG9: Bram 6A 42
Bramcote Dr. NG8: Woll 6D 42
NG9: Bee 4E 55
Bramcote Dr. W. NG9: Bee 5D 54
BRAMCOTE HILLS 2C 54
Bramcote La. NG8: Woll 1D 54
NG9: Chil 5C 54
Bramcote Leisure Cen. 2A 54
Bramcote Rd. NG9: Bee 4D 54
Bramcote St. NG7: Radf 4C 44
Bramcote Wlk. NG7: Radf 4C 44
Bramerton Rd. NG8: Bilb 3C 42
Bramhall Rd. NG8: Bilb 3C 42
Bramley Ct. NG16: Kimb 1H 29
Bramley Grn. NG8: Brox 6E 31
Bramley Rd. NG8: Brox 6E 31
NG10: Long E 2D 72
Brampton Av. DE75: Hea 3E 15
Brampton Cl. DE7: Ilk 2B 28
Brampton Dr. NG9: Stap 6H 53
Bramwell Dr. NG9: Bram 5C 54
Brancaster Cl. NG6: Cin 3H 31
Brandish Cres. NG11: Clif 4B 66
Brandreth Av. NG3: Nott 1B 46
Brandreth Dr. NG16: Gilt 5C 16
Brands Cl. DE7: Ilk 2B 28
Brand St. NG2: Nott 1B 58
Brangwen Ho. *NG7: Lent* *5C 44*
*(off Faraday Rd.)*
Branklene Cl. NG16: Kimb 6G 17
Branksome Wlk. NG2: Nott 1G 57
Bransdale Cl. NG10: Long E 1D 72
Bransdale Rd. NG11: Clif 4B 66
Branston Gdns. NG2: West Br 1H 67
Branston Wlk. NG5: Sher 3G 33
Brantford Av. NG11: Clif 4D 66
Brassington Cl. DE7: West H 1C 38
NG16: Gilt 6D 16
Bratton Dr. NG5: Bestw 2E 33
Braunton Cl. NG15: Huck 5D 6
Braunton Cres. NG3: Mapp 1F 35
Brayton Cres. NG6: Bulw 2B 32
Breach Ho. *NG7: Lent* *5C 44*
*(off Faraday Rd.)*
Breach Rd. DE75: Hea 5E 15
Breadsall Ct. DE7: Ilk 4B 28
BREASTON 5A 62
Breaston Ct. *NG5: Top V* *5E 21*
*(off Erewash Gdns.)*
Breaston La. DE72: Ris 2A 62
Brechin Cl. NG5: Arn 4D 22
Breckhill Rd. NG3: Mapp 2A 34
NG5: Woodt 2A 34
Brecknock Dr. NG10: Long E 6C 62
Breckswood Dr. NG11: Clif 6C 66
Brecon Cl. NG8: Cin 4G 31
NG10: Long E 5C 62
Breconshire Gdns. NG6: Basf 3C 32
Bredon Cl. NG10: Long E 5C 62
Breedon St. NG10: Long E 2D 62
Brendon Ct. NG9: Bram 3B 54
Brendon Dr. NG8: Woll 4G 43
NG16: Kimb 6H 17
Brendon Gdns. NG8: Woll 4G 43
Brendon Gro. NG13: Bing 4C 50
Brendon Lawrence Sports Hall 1H 45
Brendon Rd. NG8: Woll 4G 43
Brendon Way NG10: Long E 3C 62
Brentcliffe Av. NG3: Nott 2C 46
Brentnall Cl. NG10: Long E 6D 62
Brentnall Ct. NG9: Chil 2D 64
Bressingham Dr. NG2: West Br 2G 67
Brett Cl. NG15: Huck 6E 7
Brettsil Dr. NG11: Rudd 6F 67
Brewery St. NG16: Kimb 1H 29
Brewhouse Yd. NG1: Nott 6C 4 (6F 45)
Brewsters Cl. NG13: Bing 5E 51
Brewsters Rd. NG3: Nott 1A 46
Breydon Ind. Cen. NG10: Long E 6H 63
Brian Clough Way NG7: Lent, Nott 3A 4 (5D 44)
NG7: Nott 1H 55
NG9: Bram, Stap 5H 53
NG9: Stap 6F 53
Briar Av. NG10: Sand 2C 62
Briarbank Av. NG3: Nott 1C 46
Briarbank Wlk. NG3: Nott 2C 46
Briar Cl. NG9: Bram 2E 55
NG12: Key 3H 79
NG15: Huck 6D 6
Briar Ct. NG2: Nott 2F 57
Briar Gdns. NG14: Calv 3E 11
Briar Ga. NG10: Long E 3C 62
NG12: Cotg 3G 71
Briar Rd. NG16: Newth 5D 16
Briarwood Av. NG3: Nott 2C 46
Briarwood Ct. NG5: Sher 4A 34
Brickenell Rd. NG14: Calv 5H 11
Brickyard NG15: Huck 5A 8
Brickyard, The DE7: Stan C 6A 26
Brickyard Cotts. NG16: Newth 4C 16
Brickyard Dr. NG15: Huck 6A 8
Brickyard La. NG12: Rad T 6H 49
Brickyard Plantation Nature Reserve 1G 41
Bridge Av. NG9: Chil 6E 55
Bridge Ct. NG6: Bulw 4B 20
NG9: Bee 4H 55
NG15: Huck 5G 7
Bridge Farm La. NG11: Clif 3C 66

A-Z Nottingham 91

Bridge Grn. NG8: Brox . . . . . . . . . . . . . .6E 31
Bridge Grn. Wlk. NG8: Brox . . . . . . . . . .6E 31
Bridge Gro. NG2: West Br . . . . . . . . . . .3A 58
Bridgend Cl. NG9: Stap . . . . . . . . . . . . .6F 53
Bridge Rd. NG8: Woll . . . . . . . . . . . . . . .4D 42
Bridge St. DE7: Ilk . . . . . . . . . . . . . . . . .3B 28
  NG10: Long E . . . . . . . . . . . . . . . . .4E 63
  NG10: Sand . . . . . . . . . . . . . . . . . . .6E 53
  NG16: Lang M . . . . . . . . . . . . . . . . .2G 15
Bridgewater Ct. NG5: Woodt . . . . . . . .2H 33
Bridgeway Cen. NG2: Nott . . . . . . . . . .1G 57
Bridgeway Ct. NG2: Nott . . . . . . . . . . . .1H 57
Bridgford Rd. NG2: West Br . . . . . . . . .2A 58
Bridgnorth Dr. NG11: Clif . . . . . . . . . . . .3C 66
Bridgnorth Way NG9: Toton . . . . . . . . . .2G 63
Bridle Rd. NG9: Bram . . . . . . . . . . . . . . .2B 54
  NG14: Bur J . . . . . . . . . . . . . . . . . . .1D 36
Bridlesmith Ga. NG1: Nott . . . . .4E 5 (5H 45)
Bridlesmith Wlk. NG1: Nott . . . . . . . . . . .4E 5
Bridlington St. NG7: H Grn . . . . . . . . . .2C 44
Bridport Av. NG8: Radf . . . . . . . . . . . . . .4B 44
Brielen Ct. NG12: Rad T . . . . . . . . . . . . .6G 49
Brielen Rd. NG12: Rad T . . . . . . . . . . . .6G 49
Brierfield Av. NG11: Wilf . . . . . . . . . . . . .1F 67
Brierley Grn. NG4: Neth . . . . . . . . . . . . .2A 48
Brightmoor Ct. NG1: Nott . . . . . . . . . . . .4F 5
Brightmoor Pl. NG1: Nott . . . . . . . . . . . .4F 5
Brightmoor St. NG1: Nott . . . . .4F 5 (5H 45)
Bright St. DE7: Ilk . . . . . . . . . . . . . . . . . .4A 28
  NG7: Lent . . . . . . . . . . . . . . . . . . . .4C 44
  NG16: Kimb . . . . . . . . . . . . . . . . . . .1G 29
Brimington Cl. DE7: Ilk . . . . . . . . . . . . . .1B 28
Brindley Ct. NG5: Woodt . . . . . . . . . . . .3H 33
Brindley Rd. NG8: Bilb . . . . . . . . . . . . . .4C 42
Brinkhill Cres. NG11: Clif . . . . . . . . . . . .2D 66
Brinsley Cl. NG8: Aspl . . . . . . . . . . . . . .6G 31
Brisbane Dr. NG5: Top V . . . . . . . . . . . .5C 20
  NG9: Stap . . . . . . . . . . . . . . . . . . . .2H 53
Bristol Rd. DE7: Ilk . . . . . . . . . . . . . . . . .6A 28
Britannia Av. NG6: Basf . . . . . . . . . . . . .2C 32
Britannia Cl. NG16: Want . . . . . . . . . . . .6A 18
Britannia Ct. NG4: Neth . . . . . . . . . . . . .3A 48
Britannia Rd. NG10: Long E . . . . . . . . . .4F 63
British Geological Survey . . . . . . . . . . . .3A 80
Britten Gdns. NG3: Nott . . . . . . . . . . . . .3B 46
Brixham Rd. NG15: Huck . . . . . . . . . . . . .6D 6
Brixton Rd. NG7: Radf . . . . . . . . . . . . . .4C 44
B Road NG7: Nott . . . . . . . . . . . . . . . . . .5B 56
Broad Cl. NG14: Woodbo . . . . . . . . . . . .1C 24
Broad Eadow Rd. NG6: Bulw . . . . . . . . .6F 19
Broadfields NG14: Calv . . . . . . . . . . . . . .3H 11
Broadgate NG9: Bee . . . . . . . . . . . . . . .4G 55
Broadgate Av. NG9: Bee . . . . . . . . . . . .4G 55
Broadgate La. NG9: Bee . . . . . . . . . . . .4G 55
Broadgate Pk. NG9: Bee . . . . . . . . . . . .3G 55
Broadholme St. NG7: Lent . . . . . . . . . . .6D 44
Broadhurst Av. NG6: Basf . . . . . . . . . . . .5B 32
Broadlands NG10: Sand . . . . . . . . . . . . .2D 62
Broadleigh Cl. NG2: West Br . . . . . . . . .2G 67
Broad Marsh NG1: Nott . . . . .6E 5 (6G 45)
Broad Marsh Shop. Cen.
  NG1: Nott . . . . . . . . . . . .5E 5 (5G 45)
Broadmead NG14: Bur J . . . . . . . . . . . . .2F 37
Broadmeer NG12: Cotg . . . . . . . . . . . . . .2E 71
Broadmere Ct. NG5: Arn . . . . . . . . . . . . .4D 22
Broad Oak Cl. NG3: Nott . . . . . . . . . . . .2A 46
Broad Oak Dr. NG9: Stap . . . . . . . . . . . .5F 53
Broadstairs Rd. NG9: Toton . . . . . . . . . .3H 63
Broadstone Cl. NG2: West Br . . . . . . . . .6G 57
Broad St. NG1: Nott . . . . . . .3F 5 (4H 45)
  NG10: Long E . . . . . . . . . . . . . . . . .6F 63
Broad Valley Dr. NG6: Bestw V . . . . . . . .1C 20
Broad Wlk. NG6: Basf . . . . . . . . . . . . . . .4A 32
Broadway DE7: Ilk . . . . . . . . . . . . . . . . . .4A 28
  DE75: Hea . . . . . . . . . . . . . . . . . . . .4C 14
  NG1: Nott . . . . . . . . . . . . .5F 5 (5H 45)
Broadway Cinema . . . . . . . . . . . . . . . . . . .3F 5
Broadway E. NG4: Carl . . . . . . . . . . . . . .3F 47
Broadwood Ct. NG9: Bee . . . . . . . . . . . .3G 55
Broadwood Rd. NG5: Bestw . . . . . . . . . .5F 21
Brockdale Gdns. NG12: Key . . . . . . . . . .3G 79
Brockenhurst Gdns. NG3: Nott . . . . . . . .3B 46
Brockhall Ri. DE75: Hea . . . . . . . . . . . . .4E 15
Brockhole Cl. NG2: West Br . . . . . . . . . .6F 59
Brockley Rd. NG2: West Br . . . . . . . . . .4D 58
Brockwood Cres. NG12: Key . . . . . . . . .3G 79
Bromfield Cl. NG3: Nott . . . . . . . . . . . . . .2E 47
Bromley Cl. NG6: Bulw . . . . . . . . . . . . . .1H 31
Bromley Ct. DE7: Ilk . . . . . . . . . . . . . . . .2C 40
Bromley Pl. NG1: Nott . . . . . . .4C 4 (5F 45)
Bromley Rd. NG2: West Br . . . . . . . . . .5A 58
Brompton Cl. NG5: Arn . . . . . . . . . . . . . .3E 21
Brompton Way NG2: West Br . . . . . . . . .2G 67
Bronte Cl. NG10: Long E . . . . . . . . . . . .6C 62
Bronte Ct. NG7: Radf . . . . . . . . . . . . . . .3E 45
Brook Av. NG5: Arn . . . . . . . . . . . . . . . . .5D 22
Brook Chase Mdws. NG9: Chil . . . . . . . .6C 54

Brook Cl. NG6: Bulw . . . . . . . . . . . . . . . .1H 31
  NG10: Long E . . . . . . . . . . . . . . . . .2G 73
  NG16: Newth . . . . . . . . . . . . . . . . . .4D 16
Brook Cotts. DE7: Ilk . . . . . . . . . . . . . . .4B 28
Brook Ct. NG7: Radf . . . . . . . . . . . . . . . .3D 44
  NG16: Lang M . . . . . . . . . . . . . . . . .3F 15
Brookdale Ct. NG5: Sher . . . . . . . . . . . .2H 33
Brooke St. DE7: Ilk . . . . . . . . . . . . . . . . .3D 40
  NG10: Sand . . . . . . . . . . . . . . . . . . .6D 52
Brookfield Av. NG15: Huck . . . . . . . . . . . .6G 7
Brookfield Cl. NG12: Rad T . . . . . . . . . .6F 49
Brookfield Ct. NG2: Nott . . . . . . . . . . . . .1G 57
  NG5: Arn . . . . . . . . . . . . . . . . . . . . .6C 22
Brookfield Gdns. NG5: Arn . . . . . . . . . . .6C 22
Brookfield M. NG10: Sand . . . . . . . . . . . .5E 53
Brookfield Rd. NG5: Arn . . . . . . . . . . . . .6B 22
Brookfield Way DE75: Hea . . . . . . . . . . .4F 15
Brook Gdns. NG5: Arn . . . . . . . . . . . . . . .5C 22
BROOK HILL . . . . . . . . . . . . . . . . . . . . . . .5E 67
Brookhill Cres. NG8: Woll . . . . . . . . . . . .6E 43
Brookhill Dr. NG8: Woll . . . . . . . . . . . . . .6E 43
Brookhill Leys Rd. NG16: Eastw . . . . . . .4A 16
Brookhill St. NG9: Stap . . . . . . . . . . . . . .6E 53
Brookland Dr. NG9: Chil . . . . . . . . . . . . .6D 54
Brooklands Av. DE75: Hea . . . . . . . . . . .3D 14
Brooklands Bus. Cen. DE75: Los . . . . . .1B 14
Brooklands Cl. NG10: Long E . . . . . . . . .6F 63
Brooklands Cres. NG4: Ged . . . . . . . . . .6A 36
Brooklands Dr. NG4: Ged . . . . . . . . . . . .6A 36
Brooklands Rd. NG3: Nott . . . . . . . . . . . .2D 46
Brooklyn Av. NG14: Bur J . . . . . . . . . . . .2F 37
Brooklyn Cl. NG6: Bulw . . . . . . . . . . . . . .2B 32
Brooklyn Rd. NG6: Bulw . . . . . . . . . . . . .1B 32
Brooksby La. NG11: Clif . . . . . . . . . . . . .1D 66
Brooks Cotts. NG4: Carl . . . . . . . . . . . . .6E 35
Brookside NG15: Huck . . . . . . . . . . . . . . .6H 7
  NG16: Eastw . . . . . . . . . . . . . . . . . .1B 16
Brookside Av. NG8: Woll . . . . . . . . . . . . .1D 54
Brookside Cl. NG10: Long E . . . . . . . . . .5D 62
Brookside Cotts. NG14: Bur J . . . . . . . . .2E 37
Brookside Gdns. NG11: Rudd . . . . . . . . .5F 67
Brookside Ind. Units NG9: Stap . . . . . . . .3F 53
Brookside Rd. NG11: Rudd . . . . . . . . . . .5F 67
Brook St. DE75: Los . . . . . . . . . . . . . . . . .1A 14
  NG1: Nott . . . . . . . . . . . . .3F 5 (4H 45)
  NG15: Huck . . . . . . . . . . . . . . . . . . . .3G 7
Brookthorpe Way NG11: Wilf . . . . . . . . . .1E 67
Brookvale Rd. NG16: Lang M . . . . . . . . .3G 15
Brook Vw. Ct. NG12: Key . . . . . . . . . . . .5G 79
Brook Vw. Dr. NG12: Key . . . . . . . . . . . .5G 79
Brookwood Cres. NG4: Carl . . . . . . . . . .2E 47
Broom Cl. NG14: Calv . . . . . . . . . . . . . . .3H 11
Broomfield Cl. NG10: Sand . . . . . . . . . . .6C 52
BROOMHILL . . . . . . . . . . . . . . . . . . . . . . . .6A 8
Broomhill Av. DE7: Ilk . . . . . . . . . . . . . . .3C 40
                (not continuous)
Broomhill Cotts. NG15: Huck . . . . . . . . . .6A 8
Broomhill Pk. Vw. NG15: Huck . . . . . . . . .6A 8
Broomhill Rd. NG6: Bulw . . . . . . . . . . . .1A 32
  NG15: Huck . . . . . . . . . . . . . . . . . . . .6G 7
  NG16: Kimb . . . . . . . . . . . . . . . . . . .1A 30
Broom Rd. NG14: Calv . . . . . . . . . . . . . . .4H 11
Broom Wlk. NG3: Nott . . . . . . . . . . . . . . .1D 46
Brora Rd. NG6: Bulw . . . . . . . . . . . . . . . .6B 20
Broughton Cl. DE7: Ilk . . . . . . . . . . . . . . .4A 28
Broughton Dr. NG8: Woll . . . . . . . . . . . . .5A 44
Broughton St. NG9: Bee . . . . . . . . . . . . .4F 55
Brownes Rd. NG13: Bing . . . . . . . . . . . .4G 51
Browning Cl. NG5: Arn . . . . . . . . . . . . . .6H 21
Browning Ct. NG5: Sher . . . . . . . . . . . . .4F 33
Brown La. NG11: Bart F . . . . . . . . . . . . .1E 75
Browns Cft. NG6: Basf . . . . . . . . . . . . . .4B 32
Brown's Flats NG16: Kimb . . . . . . . . . . .6H 17
Browns La. NG12: Stant W . . . . . . . . . . .6B 80
Browns La. Bus. Pk. NG12: Stant W . . . .6C 80
Brown's Rd. NG10: Long E . . . . . . . . . . .5G 63
Brown St. NG7: H Grn . . . . . . . . . . . . . . .2D 44
Broxtowe Av. NG8: Aspl . . . . . . . . . . . . .5A 32
  NG16: Kimb . . . . . . . . . . . . . . . . . . .1F 29
BROXTOWE . . . . . . . . . . . . . . . . . . . . . . . .5G 31
Broxtowe Country Pk. . . . . . . . . . . . . . . .5E 31
Broxtowe Dr. NG15: Huck . . . . . . . . . . . . .2G 7
Broxtowe Hall Cl. NG8: Brox . . . . . . . . . .5G 31
Broxtowe La. NG8: Aspl, Brox . . . . . . . . .6F 31
Broxtowe Pk. Bus. Cen. NG8: Stre . . . . .5D 30
Broxtowe Ri. NG8: Cin . . . . . . . . . . . . . . .4H 31
Broxtowe St. NG5: Sher . . . . . . . . . . . . .5G 33
Bruce Cl. NG2: Nott . . . . . . . . . . . . . . . . .1H 57
Bruce Dr. NG2: West Br . . . . . . . . . . . . . .4H 57
Brunel Dr. NG16: Newth . . . . . . . . . . . . .1D 16
Brunel Ter. NG7: Nott . . . . . . . . . . . . . . . .4E 45
Brunswick Dr. NG9: Stap . . . . . . . . . . . . .6H 53
Brushfield St. NG7: H Grn . . . . . . . . . . . .2C 44
Brussells Ter. DE7: Ilk . . . . . . . . . . . . . . .6A 28
Brusty Pl. NG14: Bur J . . . . . . . . . . . . . . .2E 37

Bryan Ct. NG8: Aspl . . . . . . . . . . . . . . . . .1A 44
Buckfast Way NG2: West Br . . . . . . . . . .4C 58
Buckingham Av. NG15: Huck . . . . . . . . . .3H 7
Buckingham Ct. NG10: Sand . . . . . . . . . .2C 62
Buckingham Dr. DE75: Hea . . . . . . . . . .3A 14
Buckingham Rd. NG5: Woodt . . . . . . . . .2A 34
  NG10: Sand . . . . . . . . . . . . . . . . . . .1C 62
Buckingham Way NG16: Want . . . . . . . . .6B 18
Buckland Dr. NG14: Woodbo . . . . . . . . . .1C 24
Bucklee Dr. NG14: Calv . . . . . . . . . . . . . .4G 11
Bucklow Cl. NG8: Basf . . . . . . . . . . . . . . .6B 32
Buckminster Rd. DE7: Kirk H . . . . . . . . .5G 39
Budby Ri. NG15: Huck . . . . . . . . . . . . . . . .4H 7
Buildings, The NG11: Thru . . . . . . . . . . . .4C 74
BULCOTE . . . . . . . . . . . . . . . . . . . . . . . . . .1H 37
Bulcote Dr. NG14: Carl . . . . . . . . . . . . . .4D 36
Bulcote Ho. NG4: Carl . . . . . . . . . . . . . . .1G 47
              (off Garden City)
Bulcote Rd. NG11: Clif . . . . . . . . . . . . . . .2D 66
Bullace Rd. NG3: Nott . . . . . . . . . . . . . . .2B 46
Bull Cl. Rd. NG7: Lent . . . . . . . . . . . . . . .3C 56
Buller St. DE7: Ilk . . . . . . . . . . . . . . . . . . .3C 40
Buller Ter. NG5: Sher . . . . . . . . . . . . . . . .4H 33
Bullfinch Rd. NG6: Basf . . . . . . . . . . . . . .3B 32
Bullins Cl. NG5: Arn . . . . . . . . . . . . . . . . .4G 21
Bullivant St. NG3: Nott . . . . . . .1F 5 (3H 45)
BULWELL . . . . . . . . . . . . . . . . . . . . . . . . . .6A 20
Bulwell Bus. Cen. NG6: Bulw . . . . . . . . .6G 19
BULWELL FOREST . . . . . . . . . . . . . . . . . .5A 20
Bulwell Forest Golf Course . . . . . . . . . . .6C 20
Bulwell Forest Stop (NET) . . . . . . . . . . . .5A 20
Bulwell Hall Pk. . . . . . . . . . . . . . . . . . . . . .3H 19
Bulwell High Rd. NG6: Bulw . . . . . . . . . .1H 31
Bulwell La. NG6: Basf . . . . . . . . . . . . . . .3B 32
Bulwell Station (Rail) . . . . . . . . . . . . . . . .1A 32
Bulwell Stop (NET) . . . . . . . . . . . . . . . . . .1A 32
Bulwer Rd. NG7: Radf . . . . . . . . . . . . . . .4D 44
Bunbury St. NG2: Nott . . . . . . . . . . . . . . .2H 57
Bunny La. NG11: Bunny . . . . . . . . . . . . . .5D 78
  NG12: Key . . . . . . . . . . . . . . . . . . . .5D 78
Bunting Cl. DE7: Kirk H . . . . . . . . . . . . . .3G 39
Buntings La. NG4: Carl . . . . . . . . . . . . . .2E 47
Bunting St. NG7: Lent . . . . . . . . . . . . . . .2C 56
Burberry Av. NG15: Huck . . . . . . . . . . . .1A 20
Burcot Cl. DE7: West H . . . . . . . . . . . . . .1C 38
Burford Rd. NG7: H Grn . . . . . . . . . . . . .1D 44
Burford St. NG5: Arn . . . . . . . . . . . . . . . .5A 22
Burgass Rd. NG3: Nott . . . . . . . . . . . . . .2C 46
Burge Cl. NG2: Nott . . . . . . . . . . . . . . . . .1G 57
Burgh Hall Cl. NG9: Chil . . . . . . . . . . . . .3C 64
Burhill NG12: Cotg . . . . . . . . . . . . . . . . . .3G 71
Burke St. NG7: Radf . . . . . . . . .2A 4 (4E 45)
Burleigh Cl. NG4: Carl . . . . . . . . . . . . . . .2H 47
Burleigh Rd. NG2: West Br . . . . . . . . . . .5B 58
Burleigh Sq. NG9: Chil . . . . . . . . . . . . . . .1C 64
Burleigh St. DE7: Ilk . . . . . . . . . . . . . . . . .6B 28
Burlington Av. NG5: Sher . . . . . . . . . . . . .4F 33
Burlington Ct. NG5: Sher . . . . . . . . . . . . .4G 33
Burlington Rd. NG4: Carl . . . . . . . . . . . . .1G 47
  NG5: Sher . . . . . . . . . . . . . . . . . . . .4G 33
Burnaby St. NG6: Basf . . . . . . . . . . . . . . .3B 32
Burnbank Cl. NG2: West Br . . . . . . . . . . .6F 59
Burnbreck Gdns. NG8: Woll . . . . . . . . . .5E 43
Burncroft DE7: West H . . . . . . . . . . . . . . .2C 38
Burndale Wlk. NG5: Top V . . . . . . . . . . .5C 20
Burnham Av. NG9: Bee . . . . . . . . . . . . . .1F 65
Burnham Cl. DE7: West H . . . . . . . . . . . .1B 38
Burnham Lodge NG5: Top V . . . . . . . . . .4C 20
Burnham St. NG5: Sher . . . . . . . . . . . . . .5G 33
Burnham Way NG2: Nott . . . . . . . . . . . . .6G 45
Burnor Pool NG14: Calv . . . . . . . . . . . . . .4H 11
Burns Av. NG7: Radf . . . . . . . . .1A 4 (3E 45)
Burns Ct. NG5: Sher . . . . . . . . . . . . . . . . .4F 33
Burnside Dr. NG9: Bram . . . . . . . . . . . . .1C 54
Burnside Grn. NG8: Bilb . . . . . . . . . . . . .3D 42
Burnside Gro. NG12: Toll . . . . . . . . . . . . .4E 69
Burnside Rd. NG2: West Br . . . . . . . . . . .6A 58
  NG8: Bilb . . . . . . . . . . . . . . . . . . . . .3D 42
Burns St. DE7: Ilk . . . . . . . . . . . . . . . . . . .1A 40
  DE75: Hea . . . . . . . . . . . . . . . . . . . .3B 14
  NG7: Nott . . . . . . . . . . . . . .1A 4 (3E 45)
Burnt Oak Cl. NG16: Nuth . . . . . . . . . . . .4D 30
Burnthouse Rd. DE75: Hea . . . . . . . . . . .4B 14
Burntstump Country Pk. . . . . . . . . . . . . . . .1H 9
Burntstump Hill NG5: Arn . . . . . . . . . . . . .1G 9
Burnwood Dr. NG8: Woll . . . . . . . . . . . . .4D 42
Burr La. DE7: Ilk . . . . . . . . . . . . . . . . . . . .6B 28
Burrows Av. NG9: Bee . . . . . . . . . . . . . . .2F 55
Burrows Ct. NG3: Nott . . . . . . . . . . . . . . .4B 46
Burrows Cres. NG9: Bee . . . . . . . . . . . . .2F 55
Bursar Way NG10: Long E . . . . . . . . . . . .2E 63
Burtness Rd. NG11: Clif . . . . . . . . . . . . . .4C 66
Burton Av. NG4: Carl . . . . . . . . . . . . . . . .1C 48
Burton Cl. NG4: Carl . . . . . . . . . . . . . . . . .6A 36
Burton Dr. NG9: Chil . . . . . . . . . . . . . . . . .1C 64
BURTON JOYCE . . . . . . . . . . . . . . . . . . . .3F 37
Burton Joyce Station (Rail) . . . . . . . . . . . .4E 37

Burton Manderfield Ct. NG2: Nott . . . . . . . . . . .1G 57
Burton Rd. NG4: Carl, Ged . . . . . . . . . . . . . . . .2G 47
  NG14: Bur J . . . . . . . . . . . . . . . . . . . . . . . . . .5C 36
Burton St. DE75: Hea . . . . . . . . . . . . . . . . . . . . .3C 14
  NG1: Nott . . . . . . . . . . . . . . . . . .3D 4 (4G 45)
Burwell St. NG7: H Grn . . . . . . . . . . . . . . . . . . . .3D 44
Bush Cl. NG5: Top V . . . . . . . . . . . . . . . . . . . . . .5D 20
Bushy Cl. NG10: Long E . . . . . . . . . . . . . . . . . . .1C 72
Business Centre Beeston NG9: Bee . . . . . . . .6G 55
Bute Av. NG7: Lent . . . . . . . . . . . . . . . . . . . . . . .5D 44
Butler Av. NG12: Rad T . . . . . . . . . . . . . . . . . . . .5G 49
Butlers Cl. NG15: Huck . . . . . . . . . . . . . . . . . . . . .6A 8
BUTLER'S HILL . . . . . . . . . . . . . . . . . . . . . . . . . .5A 8
Butlers Hill Stop (NET) . . . . . . . . . . . . . . . . . . . .6B 8
Butterfield Ct. NG16: Want . . . . . . . . . . . . . . . . .6A 18
Butterley Cl. DE7: Ilk . . . . . . . . . . . . . . . . . . . . . .2B 28
Buttermead Cl. NG9: Trow . . . . . . . . . . . . . . . . . .1F 53
Buttermere Ct. NG2: Gam . . . . . . . . . . . . . . . . . .4F 59
  NG10: Long E . . . . . . . . . . . . . . . . . . . . . . . . .3C 62
Buttermere Dr. NG5: Sher . . . . . . . . . . . . . . . . . .5G 33
Buttermere Dr. NG9: Bram . . . . . . . . . . . . . . . . .3D 54
Butterton Cl. DE7: Ilk . . . . . . . . . . . . . . . . . . . . . .2C 40
Buttery Gdns. NG11: Rudd . . . . . . . . . . . . . . . . . .1G 77
Butt Houses NG7: Lent . . . . . . . . . . . . . . . . . . . .5C 44
Butt Rd. NG13: Bing . . . . . . . . . . . . . . . . . . . . . .5G 51
Butts Cl. DE7: Ilk . . . . . . . . . . . . . . . . . . . . . . . . .5C 40
Butt St. NG10: Sand . . . . . . . . . . . . . . . . . . . . . .6D 52
Buxton Av. DE75: Hea . . . . . . . . . . . . . . . . . . . . .5D 14
  NG4: Carl . . . . . . . . . . . . . . . . . . . . . . . . . . . .6F 35
Buxton Cl. NG5: Top V . . . . . . . . . . . . . . . . . . . . .5D 20
Buxton Grn. DE75: Hea . . . . . . . . . . . . . . . . . . . .5D 14
Byard La. NG1: Nott . . . . . . . . . .5E 5 (5G 45)
Bye Pass Rd. NG9: Chil . . . . . . . . . . . . . . . . . . . .3D 64
Byfield Cl. NG7: Radf . . . . . . . . . . . . . . . . . . . . . .3D 44
Byford Cl. NG3: Mapp . . . . . . . . . . . . . . . . . . . . .5A 34
Byley Rd. NG8: Bilb . . . . . . . . . . . . . . . . . . . . . . .4B 42
Byrne Ct. NG5: Arn . . . . . . . . . . . . . . . . . . . . . . .2D 34
Byron Av. NG10: Long E . . . . . . . . . . . . . . . . . . . .2D 62
Byron Bingo . . . . . . . . . . . . . . . . . . . . . . . . . . . .4H 7
Byron Centre, The NG15: Huck . . . . . . . . . . . . . .4G 7
Byron Ct. NG2: Nott . . . . . . . . .4H 5 (5A 46)
  NG9: Stap . . . . . . . . . . . . . . . . . . . . . . . . . . .2G 53
Byron Cres. NG16: Aws . . . . . . . . . . . . . . . . . . . .3E 29
Byron Gro. NG5: Sher . . . . . . . . . . . . . . . . . . . . .4G 33
Byron Ind. Est. NG5: Arn . . . . . . . . . . . . . . . . . . .6C 22
Byron Pl. NG7: Lent . . . . . . . . . . . . . . . . . . . . . . .4C 44
  (off Wragby Rd.)
Byron Rd. NG2: West Br . . . . . . . . . . . . . . . . . . . .4B 58
Byron Sq. NG15: Huck . . . . . . . . . . . . . . . . . . . . .4G 7
  (off Baker St.)
Byron St. DE7: Ilk . . . . . . . . . . . . . . . . . . . . . . . .6B 28
  NG5: Arn . . . . . . . . . . . . . . . . . . . . . . . . . . . .6H 21
  NG15: Huck . . . . . . . . . . . . . . . . . . . . . . . . . .5G 7

# C

Caddaw Av. NG15: Huck . . . . . . . . . . . . . . . . . . .5G 7
Cadlan Cl. NG5: Bestw . . . . . . . . . . . . . . . . . . . .6E 21
Cadlan Ct. NG5: Bestw . . . . . . . . . . . . . . . . . . . .6E 21
Caernarvon Pl. NG9: Chil . . . . . . . . . . . . . . . . . .1B 64
Caincross Rd. NG8: Bilb . . . . . . . . . . . . . . . . . . .2D 42
Cairngorm Dr. NG5: Arn . . . . . . . . . . . . . . . . . . .3F 21
Cairns Cl. NG5: Bestw . . . . . . . . . . . . . . . . . . . .2E 33
Cairnsmore Cl. NG10: Long E . . . . . . . . . . . . . . .4C 62
Cairns St. NG1: Nott . . . . . . . . . .2E 5 (4G 45)
Cairo St. NG7: Basf . . . . . . . . . . . . . . . . . . . . . . .6D 32
Caister Rd. NG11: Clif . . . . . . . . . . . . . . . . . . . . .5C 66
Caithness Ct. NG5: Sher . . . . . . . . . . . . . . . . . . .6F 33
Calcroft Cl. NG8: Aspl . . . . . . . . . . . . . . . . . . . . .5A 32
Caldbeck Cl. NG2: Gam . . . . . . . . . . . . . . . . . . .4E 59
Caldbeck Ct. NG9: Chil . . . . . . . . . . . . . . . . . . . .1B 64
Caldbeck Wlk. NG5: Bestw . . . . . . . . . . . . . . . . .6F 21
Calderdale NG8: Woll . . . . . . . . . . . . . . . . . . . . . .6B 42
Calderdale Dr. NG10: Long E . . . . . . . . . . . . . . . .1C 72
Calder Gdns. NG13: Bing . . . . . . . . . . . . . . . . . . .6D 50
Calderhall Gdns. NG5: Bestw . . . . . . . . . . . . . . .5G 21
Calder Wlk. NG6: Bulw . . . . . . . . . . . . . . . . . . . . .6H 19
Caldon Grn. NG6: Bulw . . . . . . . . . . . . . . . . . . . .3A 20
Caledon Rd. NG5: Sher . . . . . . . . . . . . . . . . . . . .4F 33
Calladine Cl. DE75: Hea . . . . . . . . . . . . . . . . . . .3B 14
Calladine Ct. NG6: Bulw . . . . . . . . . . . . . . . . . . .1G 31
Callaway Cl. NG8: Woll . . . . . . . . . . . . . . . . . . . .4E 43
Calley Av. DE7: Ilk . . . . . . . . . . . . . . . . . . . . . . . .1B 28
Calstock Rd. NG5: Woodt . . . . . . . . . . . . . . . . . .2A 34
Calveley Rd. NG8: Bilb . . . . . . . . . . . . . . . . . . . . .1E 43
Calver Cl. NG8: Woll . . . . . . . . . . . . . . . . . . . . . . .5A 44
Calvert Cl. NG9: Chil . . . . . . . . . . . . . . . . . . . . . .1D 64
  NG16: Lang M . . . . . . . . . . . . . . . . . . . . . . . .2F 15
CALVERTON . . . . . . . . . . . . . . . . . . . . . . . . . . . . .4H 11
Calverton Av. NG4: Carl . . . . . . . . . . . . . . . . . . . .6D 34
Calverton Bus. Pk. NG14: Calv . . . . . . . . . . . . . .2H 11
Calverton Cl. NG9: Toton . . . . . . . . . . . . . . . . . . .3A 64
Calverton Dr. NG8: Stre . . . . . . . . . . . . . . . . . . . .5D 30
Calverton Leisure Cen. . . . . . . . . . . . . . . . . . . . .3G 11
Calverton Rd. NG5: Arn . . . . . . . . . . . . . . . . . . . .4B 22
Camberley Ct. NG6: Bulw . . . . . . . . . . . . . . . . . .5G 19

Camberley Rd. NG6: Bulw . . . . . . . . . . . . . . . . . .5G 19
Camborne Dr. NG8: Aspl . . . . . . . . . . . . . . . . . . .5A 32
Cambria M. NG3: Nott . . . . . . . . . . . . . . . . . . . . .2G 45
Cambridge Cl. NG2: West Br . . . . . . . . . . . . . . . .3A 58
  NG7: Radf . . . . . . . . . . . . . . . . . . . . . . . . . . .3D 44
Cambridge Cres. NG9: Stap . . . . . . . . . . . . . . . . .1F 53
Cambridge Gdns. NG5: Woodt . . . . . . . . . . . . . .2D 34
Cambridge Rd. NG2: West Br . . . . . . . . . . . . . . . .4C 58
  NG8: Woll . . . . . . . . . . . . . . . . . . . . . . . . . . . .5G 43
Cambridge St. NG4: Carl . . . . . . . . . . . . . . . . . . .6G 35
Camdale Cl. NG9: Chil . . . . . . . . . . . . . . . . . . . . .5B 54
Camden Cl. NG2: Nott . . . . . . . . . .4H 5 (5A 46)
Camelia Av. NG11: Clif . . . . . . . . . . . . . . . . . . . .4A 66
Camelot Av. NG5: Sher . . . . . . . . . . . . . . . . . . . .5E 33
Camelot Cres. NG11: Rudd . . . . . . . . . . . . . . . . .5F 67
Camelot Rd. NG11: Rudd . . . . . . . . . . . . . . . . . . .5F 67
Cameo Cl. NG4: Colw . . . . . . . . . . . . . . . . . . . . . .3H 47
Camer Ct. NG9: Bee . . . . . . . . . . . . . . . . . . . . . . .5G 55
  (off Waverley Av.)
Cameron St. NG5: Sher . . . . . . . . . . . . . . . . . . . .5G 33
Camish Ho. NG10: Sand . . . . . . . . . . . . . . . . . . .6D 52
  (off Bennetts St.)
Camomile Cl. NG5: Top V . . . . . . . . . . . . . . . . . .6C 20
Camomile Gdns. NG7: H Grn . . . . . . . . . . . . . . . .2C 44
Campbell Cl. NG8: Brox . . . . . . . . . . . . . . . . . . . .6G 31
Campbell Dr. NG4: Carl . . . . . . . . . . . . . . . . . . . .1E 47
Campbell Gdns. NG5: Arn . . . . . . . . . . . . . . . . . .4E 23
Campbell Gro. NG3: Nott . . . . . . . . . .2G 5 (4H 45)
Campbell St. NG3: Nott . . . . . . . . . .2H 5 (4A 46)
  NG16: Lang M . . . . . . . . . . . . . . . . . . . . . . . .1G 15
Campden Grn. NG11: Clif . . . . . . . . . . . . . . . . . . .3C 66
Campion St. NG5: Arn . . . . . . . . . . . . . . . . . . . . .5A 22
Campion Way NG13: Bing . . . . . . . . . . . . . . . . . .5D 50
Camrose Cl. NG8: Bilb . . . . . . . . . . . . . . . . . . . . .1F 43
Canal Side DE7: Ilk . . . . . . . . . . . . . . . . . . . . . . .4B 28
  NG9: Bee . . . . . . . . . . . . . . . . . . . . . . . . . . . .2H 65
Canalside NG1: Nott . . . . . . . . . .6E 5 (6G 45)
Canalside Wlk. NG1: Nott . . . . . . . . . . . . . . . . . .6G 45
Canal St. DE7: Ilk . . . . . . . . . . . . . . . . . . . . . . . . .6C 28
  NG1: Nott . . . . . . . . . . . . . .6D 4 (6G 45)
  NG10: Long E . . . . . . . . . . . . . . . . . . . . . . . . .6D 62
  NG10: Sand . . . . . . . . . . . . . . . . . . . . . . . . . .6D 52
Canberra Cl. NG9: Stap . . . . . . . . . . . . . . . . . . . .2G 53
Canberra Cres. NG2: West Br . . . . . . . . . . . . . . . .1H 67
Canberra Gdns. NG2: West Br . . . . . . . . . . . . . . .2H 67
Candleby Cl. NG12: Cotg . . . . . . . . . . . . . . . . . . .2F 71
Candleby Ct. NG12: Cotg . . . . . . . . . . . . . . . . . . .2F 71
Candleby La. NG12: Cotg . . . . . . . . . . . . . . . . . . .2F 71
Candle Mdw. NG2: Colw . . . . . . . . . . . . . . . . . . . .5F 47
Canning Cir. NG7: Nott . . . . . . . . . .3A 4 (4E 45)
Canning Ter. NG7: Nott . . . . . . . . . .3A 4 (4E 45)
Cannock Way NG10: Long E . . . . . . . . . . . . . . . .6H 63
Cannon St. NG5: Sher . . . . . . . . . . . . . . . . . . . . .4G 33
Canonbie Cl. NG5: Arn . . . . . . . . . . . . . . . . . . . . .4D 22
Cantabury Av. NG7: H Grn . . . . . . . . . . . . . . . . . .1D 44
Cantelupe Gdns. NG16: Gilt . . . . . . . . . . . . . . . . .5E 17
Cantelupe Rd. DE7: Ilk . . . . . . . . . . . . . . . . . . . . .1B 40
Canterbury Cl. NG16: Nuth . . . . . . . . . . . . . . . . .3D 30
Canterbury Ct. NG1: Nott . . . . . . . . . .1C 4 (3F 45)
Canterbury Rd. NG8: Radf . . . . . . . . . . . . . . . . . .4B 44
Cantley Av. NG4: Ged . . . . . . . . . . . . . . . . . . . . . .5G 35
Cantrell Rd. NG6: Bulw . . . . . . . . . . . . . . . . . . . .1A 32
Canver Cl. NG8: Bilb . . . . . . . . . . . . . . . . . . . . . .3C 42
Canwick Cl. NG8: Bilb . . . . . . . . . . . . . . . . . . . . .3C 42
Capenwray Gdns. NG5: Bestw . . . . . . . . . . . . . .5G 21
Capital FM Arena . . . . . . . . . .4G 5 (5H 45)
Capitol Cl. NG8: Woll . . . . . . . . . . . . . . . . . . . . . .4G 43
Caporn Cl. NG6: Bulw . . . . . . . . . . . . . . . . . . . . .2H 31
Cardale Rd. NG3: Nott . . . . . . . . . . . . . . . . . . . . .3C 46
Cardiff St. NG3: Nott . . . . . . . . . . . . . . . . . . . . . .4B 46
Cardigan Cl. NG3: Nott . . . . . . . . . . . . . . . . . . . .2G 45
Cardigan St. NG3: Nott . . . . . . . . . . . . . . . . . . . .3A 46
Cardington Cl. NG5: Top V . . . . . . . . . . . . . . . . . .4C 20
Cardwell St. NG7: H Grn . . . . . . . . . . . . . . . . . . .1D 44
Carew Rd. NG11: Clif . . . . . . . . . . . . . . . . . . . . . .3C 66
Carey Rd. NG6: Bulw . . . . . . . . . . . . . . . . . . . . . .5A 20
Carisbrooke Av. NG3: Mapp P . . . . . . . . . . . . . . .6G 33
  NG4: Ged . . . . . . . . . . . . . . . . . . . . . . . . . . . .6B 36
  NG9: Bee . . . . . . . . . . . . . . . . . . . . . . . . . . . .1A 66
Carisbrooke Dr. NG3: Mapp P . . . . . . . . . . . . . . .6G 33
Carlight Gdns. Pk. Homes
  NG2: West Br . . . . . . . . . . . . . . . . . . . . . . . . .2D 58
Carlile Rd. NG4: Carl . . . . . . . . . . . . . . . . . . . . . .1G 47
Carlin Cl. DE72: Brea . . . . . . . . . . . . . . . . . . . . . .5A 62
Carlingford Rd. NG15: Huck . . . . . . . . . . . . . . . . .3G 7
Carlin St. NG6: Bulw . . . . . . . . . . . . . . . . . . . . . .6H 19
Carlisle Av. NG6: Bulw . . . . . . . . . . . . . . . . . . . . .6A 20
Carlswark Gdns. NG5: Top V . . . . . . . . . . . . . . . .4D 20
CARLTON . . . . . . . . . . . . . . . . . . . . . . . . . . . . . . .2H 47
Carlton Bus. Cen. NG4: Carl . . . . . . . . . . . . . . . .2H 47
Carlton Cl. DE75: Hea . . . . . . . . . . . . . . . . . . . . .2E 15
Carlton Fold NG2: Nott . . . . . . . . . . . . . . . . . . . .6B 46
Carlton Forum Leisure Cen. . . . . . . . . . . . . . . . . .6E 35
Carlton Hgts. NG4: Carl . . . . . . . . . . . . . . . . . . . .2E 47
Carlton Hill NG4: Carl . . . . . . . . . . . . . . . . . . . . . .2D 46
Carlton M. NG4: Carl . . . . . . . . . . . . . . . . . . . . . .2E 47

Carlton Rd. NG3: Nott . . . . . . . . . . .4H 5 (4A 46)
  NG10: Long E . . . . . . . . . . . . . . . . . . . . . . . . .2D 72
Carlton Sq. NG4: Carl . . . . . . . . . . . . . . . . . . . . . .2G 47
Carlton Station (Rail) . . . . . . . . . . . . . . . . . . . . . .2H 47
Carlton St. NG1: Nott . . . . . . . . . .4F 5 (5H 45)
Carlton Va. Cl. NG4: Carl . . . . . . . . . . . . . . . . . . .6F 35
Carlyle Pl. DE75: Hea . . . . . . . . . . . . . . . . . . . . . .2B 14
Carlyle Rd. NG2: West Br . . . . . . . . . . . . . . . . . . .4A 58
Carlyle St. DE75: Hea . . . . . . . . . . . . . . . . . . . . . .2B 14
Carman Cl. NG16: Want . . . . . . . . . . . . . . . . . . . .5A 18
Carmel Gdns. NG5: Arn . . . . . . . . . . . . . . . . . . . .1B 34
Carnarvon Cl. NG13: Bing . . . . . . . . . . . . . . . . . .4E 51
Carnarvon Dr. NG14: Bur J . . . . . . . . . . . . . . . . . .2F 37
Carnarvon Gro. NG4: Carl . . . . . . . . . . . . . . . . . .1F 47
  NG4: Ged . . . . . . . . . . . . . . . . . . . . . . . . . . . .6H 35
Carnarvon Pl. NG13: Bing . . . . . . . . . . . . . . . . . .5D 50
Carnarvon Rd. NG2: West Br . . . . . . . . . . . . . . . .5B 58
Carnarvon St. NG4: Neth . . . . . . . . . . . . . . . . . . .3A 48
Carnforth Cl. NG9: Stap . . . . . . . . . . . . . . . . . . . .6F 53
Carnforth Ct. NG5: Bestw . . . . . . . . . . . . . . . . . .5G 21
Carnwood Rd. NG5: Bestw . . . . . . . . . . . . . . . . . .1E 33
Caroline Ct. DE7: Ilk . . . . . . . . . . . . . . . . . . . . . . .3C 40
Caroline Wlk. NG3: Nott . . . . . . . . . . . . . . . . . . . .3H 45
Carradale Cl. NG5: Arn . . . . . . . . . . . . . . . . . . . . .5E 23
Carrfield Av. NG9: Toton . . . . . . . . . . . . . . . . . . . .4H 63
  NG10: Long E . . . . . . . . . . . . . . . . . . . . . . . . .5H 63
CARRINGTON . . . . . . . . . . . . . . . . . . . . . . . . . . . .5F 33
Carrington Ct. NG5: Sher . . . . . . . . . . . . . . . . . . .6G 33
Carrington La. NG14: Calv . . . . . . . . . . . . . . . . . .2H 11
Carrington St. NG1: Nott . . . . . . . . .6E 5 (6G 45)
  NG2: Nott . . . . . . . . . . . . . . . . . . . . . . . . . . . .6G 45
Carrock Av. DE75: Hea . . . . . . . . . . . . . . . . . . . . .4F 15
Carroll Gdns. NG2: Nott . . . . . . . . . . . . . . . . . . . .2G 57
Carr Rd. NG13: Bing . . . . . . . . . . . . . . . . . . . . . .4H 51
Cartbridge NG12: Cotg . . . . . . . . . . . . . . . . . . . . .3F 71
Carter Av. NG11: Rudd . . . . . . . . . . . . . . . . . . . . .1G 77
  NG12: Rad T . . . . . . . . . . . . . . . . . . . . . . . . .6H 49
Carter Cl. NG10: Long E . . . . . . . . . . . . . . . . . . . .1D 72
Carter Ga. NG1: Nott . . . . . . . . . .5G 5 (5H 45)
Carter Rd. NG9: Chil . . . . . . . . . . . . . . . . . . . . . . .3A 64
  (Swiney Way, not continuous)
  NG9: Chil . . . . . . . . . . . . . . . . . . . . . . . . . . . .2A 64
  (Whittaker Rd.)
Carterswood Dr. NG16: Nuth . . . . . . . . . . . . . . . .4F 31
Cartledge Dr. NG3: Arn . . . . . . . . . . . . . . . . . . . . .1E 35
Cartwright Way NG9: Bee . . . . . . . . . . . . . . . . . . .6F 55
Carver St. NG7: H Grn . . . . . . . . . . . . . . . . . . . . .1D 44
Carwood Rd. NG9: Bram . . . . . . . . . . . . . . . . . . .2D 54
Casper Ct. NG5: Top V . . . . . . . . . . . . . . . . . . . . .5E 21
  (off Birkdale Way)
Castellan Ri. NG5: Bestw . . . . . . . . . . . . . . . . . . .5G 21
Casterton Rd. NG5: Bestw . . . . . . . . . . . . . . . . . .5F 21
Castle Blvd. NG7: Lent, Nott . . . . . . . . .6A 4 (6D 44)
Castle Bri. Rd. NG7: Lent . . . . . . . . . . . . . . . . . . .6E 45
Castle Cl. DE75: Hea . . . . . . . . . . . . . . . . . . . . . .4F 11
  NG7: Nott . . . . . . . . . . . . . . . .6C 4 (6F 45)
Castle Exchange NG1: Nott . . . . . . . . . . . . . . . . . .3F 5
Castlefields NG2: Nott . . . . . . . . . . . . . . . . . . . . .1G 57
Castle Gdns. NG7: Lent . . . . . . . . . . . . . . . . . . . .6D 44
Castle Gate NG1: Nott . . . . . . . . . .5D 4 (5G 45)
Castle Gro. NG7: Nott . . . . . . . . . .5C 4 (5F 45)
Castle Ind. Pk. NG15: Huck . . . . . . . . . . . . . . . . . .6F 7
Castle Marina Pk. NG7: Lent . . . . . . . . . . . . . . . .6E 45
Castle Marina Rd. NG7: Lent . . . . . . . . . . . . . . . .1E 57
Castle Mdw. Retail Pk. NG7: Lent . . . . . . . . . . . .6F 45
Castle Mdw. Rd. NG2: Nott . . . . . . . . . . . . . . . . .6E 45
Castle M. NG7: Nott . . . . . . . . . .6A 4 (6E 45)
Castle Museum & Art Gallery
  Nottingham . . . . . . . . . .5C 4 (6F 45)
Castle Pk. NG2: Nott . . . . . . . . . . . . . . . . . . . . . .1F 57
Castle Pk. Ind. Est. NG2: Nott . . . . . . . . . . . . . . .2F 57
Castle Pl. NG1: Nott . . . . . . . . . .5C 4 (5F 45)
Castle Quay NG7: Nott . . . . . . . . . .6B 4 (6F 45)
Castle Quay Cl. NG7: Lent . . . . . . . . . . . . . . . . . .6E 45
Castle Retail Pk. NG7: Radf . . . . . . . . . . . . . . . . .3C 44
Castlerigg Cl. NG2: West Br . . . . . . . . . . . . . . . . .6E 59
Castle Rd. NG1: Nott . . . . . . . . . .5C 4 (5F 45)
Castle Rock NG7: Nott . . . . . . . . . .6C 4 (6F 45)
Castle St. NG2: Nott . . . . . . . . . . . . . . . . . . . . . . .5B 46
  NG16: Eastw . . . . . . . . . . . . . . . . . . . . . . . . . .4C 16
Castleton Av. DE7: Ilk . . . . . . . . . . . . . . . . . . . . . .2A 28
  NG4: Carl . . . . . . . . . . . . . . . . . . . . . . . . . . . .6G 35
  NG5: Arn . . . . . . . . . . . . . . . . . . . . . . . . . . . . .6B 22
Castleton Cl. NG2: Nott . . . . . . . . . . . . . . . . . . . .1F 57
  NG15: Huck . . . . . . . . . . . . . . . . . . . . . . . . . . .5D 6
Castleton Ct. NG6: Bulw . . . . . . . . . . . . . . . . . . . .1F 31
Castle Vw. NG2: West Br . . . . . . . . . . . . . . . . . . .5H 57
  NG9: Bee . . . . . . . . . . . . . . . . . . . . . . . . . . . .1E 15
Castle Vw. Cotts. NG9: Bee . . . . . . . . . . . . . . . . .5A 56
Castle Vs. NG2: Nott . . . . . . . . . . . . . . . . . . . . . . .5B 46
  (off Castle St.)
Castle Wlk. NG7: H Grn . . . . . . . . . . . . . . . . . . . . .2D 44
Castle Wharf NG1: Nott . . . . . . . . . .6D 4 (6G 45)
Cat & Fiddle La. DE7: West H . . . . . . . . . . . . . . . .3B 38
Cat & Fiddle Windmill . . . . . . . . . . . . . . . . . . . . .5D 38

Caterham Cl. NG8: Bilb .................2D 42
Catfoot La. NG4: Lamb ................5F 23
Catherine Av. DE7: Ilk ................3B 40
Catherine Cl. NG6: Bulw ...............6G 19
Catherine St. NG6: Bulw ...............6G 19
Catkin Dr. NG16: Gilt .................5E 17
Catlow Wlk. NG5: Bestw ...............5G 21
Cator Cl. NG4: Ged ....................4F 35
Cator La. NG9: Chil ...................5D 54
Cator La. Nth. NG9: Chil ..............5D 54
Catriona Cres. NG5: Arn ...............3C 22
Catt Cl. NG9: Chil ....................4B 64
Catterley Hill Rd. NG3: Nott ..........2C 46
Cattle Mkt. Rd. NG2: Nott .............1H 57
Catton Rd. NG5: Arn ...................5C 22
Caudale Ct. NG2: Gam ..................4E 59
Caulton St. NG7: H Grn ................3D 44
                    (not continuous)
Caunton Av. NG3: Nott .................6A 34
Causeway M. NG2: Nott .................1F 57
Cavan Ct. NG2: Nott ...................2G 57
Cavell Cl. NG11: Clif .................3B 66
Cavendish Av. NG4: Ged ................5F 35
  NG5: Sher ...........................4H 33
Cavendish Cl. NG15: Huck ..............6A 8
Cavendish Ct. NG3: Mapp ...............4B 34
  NG7: Nott .......................4A 4 (5E 45)
Cavendish Cres. NG4: Carl .............5E 35
  NG9: Stap ...........................1F 53
Cavendish Cres. Nth. NG7: Nott ...4A 4 (5E 45)
Cavendish Cres. Sth. NG7: Nott ...6A 4 (6E 45)
Cavendish Dr. NG4: Carl ...............1G 47
Cavendish Ho. NG4: Carl ...............1G 47
                    (off Garden City)
Cavendish M. NG7: Nott ............4A 4 (5E 45)
  NG12: Cotg ..........................3F 71
                    (off Daleside)
Cavendish Pl. NG7: Nott ...........6A 4 (6E 45)
  NG9: Bee ............................5F 55
Cavendish Rd. DE7: Ilk ................3B 40
  NG4: Carl ...........................5E 35
  NG10: Long E ........................3E 63
Cavendish Rd. E. NG7: Nott ........4A 4 (5E 45)
Cavendish Rd. W. NG7: Nott ............5E 45
Cavendish St. NG5: Arn ................5A 22
  NG7: Lent ...........................2C 56
                    (not continuous)
Cavendish Va. NG5: Sher ...............4H 33
Caversham Way DE7: West H .............1B 38
Cawdron Wlk. NG11: Clif ...............3C 66
Cawston Gdns. NG6: Bulw ...............5H 19
Caxmere Dr. NG8: Woll .................4F 43
Caxton Cl. NG4: Neth ..................2A 48
Caxton Rd. NG5: Sher ..................6F 33
Caythorpe Cres. NG5: Sher .............3G 33
Caythorpe Ri. NG5: Sher ...............3G 33
Cecil St. NG7: Lent ...................6D 44
Cedar Av. NG9: Bee ....................4G 55
  NG10: Long E ........................2E 73
  NG16: Nuth ..........................3F 31
Cedar Cl. NG10: Sand ..................4D 52
  NG13: Bing ..........................5G 51
Cedar Ct. NG9: Bee ....................4G 55
Cedar Dr. NG12: Key ...................5G 79
  NG8: Woll ...........................5F 43
  NG15: Huck ..........................6H 7
Cedarland Cres. NG16: Nuth ............3F 31
Cedar Lodge NG7: Nott .............4A 4 (5E 45)
Cedar Lodge Caravan Pk.
  NG12: Hol P .........................1C 60
Cedar Pk. DE7: Ilk ....................1A 40
Cedar Rd. NG7: H Grn ..................1E 45
  NG9: Chil ...........................6E 55
Cedars, The NG5: Sher .................3H 33
Cedar Tree Rd. NG5: Arn ...............4F 21
Celandine Cl. NG5: Top V ..............6C 20
Celandine Gdns. NG13: Bing ............5C 50
Celia Dr. NG4: Carl ...................2F 47
Cemetery Rd. NG9: Stap ................4G 53
Central Av. NG2: West Br ..............3B 58
  NG3: Mapp ...........................3D 34
  NG5: Arn ............................6B 22
  NG7: Basf ...........................6E 33
  NG9: Bee ............................2E 55
  NG9: Chil ...........................5D 54
  NG9: Stap ...........................3G 53
  NG10: Sand ..........................5D 52
  NG15: Huck ..........................5G 7
Central Av. Sth. NG5: Arn .............6B 22
Central Ct. NG7: Lent .................2D 56
Central St. NG3: Nott .................3A 46
Central Wlk. NG15: Huck ...............4G 7
Centre Way NG12: Rad T ................5E 49
Centurion Bus. Pk. NG6: Bulw ..........4E 19
Centurion Cl. NG15: Huck ..............3B 8
Centurion Way NG7: Nott ...............3E 57

Century Ct. NG1: Nott .................2F 45
                (off Nth. Sherwood St.)
Cernan Ct. NG6: Bulw ..................2F 31
Cerne Cl. NG11: Clif ..................5D 66
Chaceley Way NG11: Wilf ...............2E 67
Chadborn Av. NG11: Goth ...............6H 75
Chaddesden, The NG3: Mapp P ...........2G 45
Chad Gdns. NG5: Top V .................3E 21
Chadwick Rd. NG7: H Grn ...............2C 44
Chain La. NG7: Lent ...................2C 56
Chalfield Cl. NG11: Clif ..............4B 66
Chalons Cl. DE7: Ilk ..................6B 28
Chalons Way DE7: Ilk ..................6B 28
Chamberlain Cl. NG11: Clif ............4A 66
Chambers Av. DE7: Ilk .................2D 40
Champion Av. DE7: Ilk .................4G 27
Chancery, The NG9: Bram ...............4C 54
Chancery Ct. NG11: Wilf ...............5E 57
Chandos Av. NG4: Neth .................1A 48
Chandos St. NG3: Nott .................2A 46
  NG4: Neth ...........................2A 48
Chantrey Rd. NG2: West Br .............4A 58
Chantry Cl. NG9: Chil .................1D 64
  NG10: Long E ........................3C 72
  NG16: Kimb ..........................2A 30
Chapel Bar NG1: Nott ..............4C 4 (5F 45)
Chapel Cl. NG11: Goth .................6H 75
Chapel Ct. DE7: Ilk ...................3B 28
Chapel La. NG4: Lamb ..................6B 24
  NG5: Arn ............................5A 22
  NG12: Cotg ..........................2F 71
  NG13: Bing ..........................2D 50
  NG14: Epp ...........................5G 13
Chapel Mews Ct. NG9: Bram .............3B 54
Chapel Pl. NG16: Kimb .................1H 29
Chapel Quarter NG1: Nott ..........4C 4 (5F 45)
Chapel St. DE7: Ilk ...................6B 28
                    (not continuous)
  DE75: Hea ...........................5E 15
  NG7: Radf ...........................4E 45
  NG9: Bram ...........................3B 54
  NG10: Long E ........................6G 63
  NG11: Rudd ..........................1G 77
  NG15: Huck ..........................4G 7
  NG16: Kimb ..........................1H 29
Chapel Yd. NG12: Norm W ...............6A 70
Chapman Ct. NG8: Bilb .................2H 43
Chapmans Wlk. NG6: Bestw V .............5F 9
Chapter Dr. NG16: Kimb ................2A 30
Chardlace Wlk. NG1: Nott ...............5G 5
Chard St. NG7: Basf ...................5D 32
Chard Ter. NG7: Basf ..................5D 32
Charlbury Ct. NG9: Bram ...............5B 42
Charlbury Rd. NG8: Woll ...............3G 43
Charlecote Dr. NG8: Woll ..............6D 42
Charlecote Pk. Dr. NG2: West Br .......6D 42
Charles Av. NG9: Chil .................2C 64
  NG9: Lent A .........................2G 55
  NG9: Stap ...........................3H 53
  NG10: Sand ..........................5D 52
  NG16: Eastw .........................2A 16
  NG4: Ged ............................5H 35
Charles Cl. DE7: Ilk ..................3D 40
Charles Ct. NG15: Huck ................4G 7
Charles Ho. NG1: Nott .................5C 4
Charles St. NG5: Arn ..................6A 22
  NG10: Long E ........................1F 73
  NG11: Rudd ..........................6G 67
  NG15: Huck ..........................4G 7
Charles Way NG6: Bulw .................2H 31
Charles Way Bus. Pk. NG6: Bulw ........2A 32
Charlesworth Av. NG7: Basf ............1C 44
Charlock Cl. NG5: Top V ...............6C 20
Charlock Gdns. NG13: Bing .............6D 50
Charlotte Cl. NG5: Arn ................3A 22
Charlotte Ct. NG16: Eastw .............2B 16
Charlotte Gro. NG9: Bram ..............4C 54
Charlotte St. DE7: Ilk ................4A 28
Charlton Av. NG10: Long E .............4H 63
Charlton Gro. NG9: Bee ................1F 65
Charnock Av. NG8: Woll ................4H 43
Charnos St. DE7: Ilk ..................5C 40
Charnwood Av. NG9: Bee ................5D 54
  NG10: Long E ........................3D 72
  NG10: Sand ..........................1C 62
  NG12: Key ...........................5G 79
Charnwood Gdns. NG5: Sher .............6F 33
Charnwood Gro. NG2: West Br ...........4A 58
  NG13: Bing ..........................5D 50
  NG15: Huck ..........................4E 7
Charnwood La. NG5: Arn ................1C 34
Charnwood Way NG14: Woodbo ............1D 24
Charter Pk. DE7: Ilk ..................2A 40

Chartwell Av. NG11: Rudd ..............6F 67
Chartwell Gro. NG3: Mapp ..............2E 35
Chase Pk. NG2: Nott ...................6C 46
Chatham Cl. NG6: Bulw .................1A 32
Chatham St. NG1: Nott .................3G 45
Chatsworth Av. NG4: Carl ..............1G 47
  NG7: Basf ...........................5D 32
  NG9: Chil ...........................3C 64
  NG10: Long E ........................1A 74
  NG12: Rad T .........................5G 49
Chatsworth Cl. NG10: Sand .............1D 62
Chatsworth Ct. DE7: West H ............1C 38
  NG15: Huck ..........................5G 7
Chatsworth Dr. NG15: Huck .............5G 7
Chatsworth Pl. DE7: Kirk H ............4F 39
Chatsworth Rd. NG2: West Br ...........3D 58
Chatsworth Way DE75: Hea ..............3A 14
Chatterley Ct. NG7: Lent ..............4C 44
                    (off Wragby Rd.)
Chatterley Parkway NG8: Stre ..........5C 30
Chaucer St. DE7: Ilk ..................6B 28
  NG1: Nott .......................2C 4 (4F 45)
Chaworth Av. NG16: Want ...............4H 17
Chaworth Rd. NG2: West Br .............5A 58
  NG4: Colw ...........................3H 47
  NG13: Bing ..........................5D 50
Cheadle Cl. NG3: Mapp .................5D 34
  NG8: Bilb ...........................1D 43
Cheapside NG1: Nott ...............4E 5 (5G 45)
Cheddar Rd. NG11: Clif ................5C 66
Chedington Av. NG3: Mapp ..............1F 35
Chediston Va. NG5: Bestw ..............5F 21
Chedworth Cl. NG3: Nott ...............4B 46
Chelmsford Rd. NG7: Basf ..............5D 32
Chelmsford Ter. NG7: Basf .............5D 32
                    (off Zulu Rd.)
Chelsbury Ct. NG5: Arn ................6A 22
Chelsea Cl. NG16: Nuth ................4E 31
Chelsea St. NG7: Basf .................6D 32
Cheltenham Cl. NG9: Toton .............3H 63
Cheltenham St. NG6: Basf ..............3C 32
Chelwood Dr. NG3: Mapp ................4E 35
Chennel Nook NG12: Cotg ...............3G 71
Chepstow Rd. NG11: Clif ...............5C 66
Cherhill Cl. NG11: Clif ...............6B 66
Cheriton Dr. DE7: Ilk .................4G 27
Cherries, The NG11: Wilf ..............5F 57
Cherry Av. NG15: Huck .................6H 7
Cherry Cl. NG72: Brea .................5A 62
  NG2: West Br ........................2E 59
  NG5: Arn ............................5A 22
  NG5: Bestw ..........................1F 33
Cherry Hill NG12: Key .................4H 79
Cherry Orchard NG12: Cotg .............2F 71
Cherry Orchard Mt. NG5: Bestw .........1F 33
Cherry St. NG13: Bing .................5F 51
Cherry Tree Cl. DE7: Kirk H ...........3H 39
  DE72: Ris ...........................1B 62
  NG14: Calv ..........................4G 11
Cherrytree Cl. NG12: Rad T ............1F 61
Cherry Tree La. NG12: Edwal ...........2D 68
Cherry Tree Way NG16: Lang M ..........1G 15
Cherry Wood Dr. NG8: Aspl .............2H 43
Cherrywood Gdns. NG3: Nott ............1C 46
Chertsey Cl. NG3: Nott ................6B 34
Chertsey Ct. DE7: West H ..............1B 38
Cherwell Ct. NG6: Bulw ................1F 31
Cherwell Gdns. NG13: Bing .............6C 50
Chesham Dr. NG5: Sher .................5F 33
  NG9: Bram ...........................6B 42
Cheshire Ct. NG2: West Br .............6H 57
Chesil Av. NG8: Radf ..................4B 44
Chesil Cotts. NG8: Radf ...............4B 44
                    (off Chesil Av.)
Cheslyn Dr. NG8: Aspl .................1A 44
Chesnuts, The NG4: Ged ................6B 36
Chesterfield Av. NG4: Ged .............4F 35
  NG10: Long E ........................6H 63
  NG13: Bing ..........................5E 51
Chesterfield Ct. NG4: Ged .............4F 35
Chesterfield Dr. NG14: Bur J ..........2G 37
Chesterfield St. NG4: Carl ............2F 47
Chester Grn. NG9: Toton ...............3G 63
Chester Ho. NG3: Mapp P ...............1G 45
Chesterman Cl. NG16: Aws ..............3D 28
Chester Rd. NG3: Nott .................4E 47
Chestnut Av. NG3: Mapp ................5D 34
  NG9: Bee ............................5F 55
  NG13: Bing ..........................5E 51
Chestnut Bank DE75: Hea ...............4B 14
Chestnut Cl. NG12: Key ................4G 79
Chestnut Dr. NG16: Nuth ...............6B 18
Chestnut Gro. NG2: West Br ............4H 57
  NG3: Mapp P .........................2G 45
  NG4: Ged ............................6H 35
  NG5: Arn ............................4C 22
  NG10: Sand ..........................4C 52

**Chestnut Gro.** NG12: Rad T . . . . . . . . . . . . . .5F **49**
  NG14: Bur J . . . . . . . . . . . . . . . . .3F **37**
  NG15: Huck . . . . . . . . . . . . . . . . . .1H **19**
**Chestnut La.** NG11: Bart F . . . . . . . . . .1E **75**
**Chestnut M.** NG12: Toll . . . . . . . . . . . . .2H **69**
**Chestnut Rd.** NG16: Lang M . . . . . . . .2E **15**
**Chestnuts, The**
  NG3: Nott . . . . . . . . . . . . . . . . . . .6B **34**
  NG10: Long E . . . . . . . . . . . . . . . .5C **62**
  NG12: Rad T . . . . . . . . . . . . . . . . .6E **49**
**Chestnut Wlk.** NG5: Sher . . . . . . . . . .4A **34**
**Chettles Ind. Est.** NG7: Radf . . . . . . .4B **44**
**Chettles Trade Pk.** NG7: Radf . . . . . .4B **44**
**Chetwin Rd.** NG8: Bilb . . . . . . . . . . . . .4D **42**
**Chetwynd Bus. Pk.** NG9: Chil . . . . . . .3B **64**
**Chetwynd Rd.** NG9: Chil . . . . . . . . . . .2A **64**
  NG9: Toton . . . . . . . . . . . . . . . . . .3A **64**
**Chevin Gdns.** NG5: Top V . . . . . . . . . .4E **21**
**Cheviot Cl.** NG5: Arn . . . . . . . . . . . . . .3F **21**
**Cheviot Ct.** NG9: Chil . . . . . . . . . . . . . .2C **64**
**Cheviot Dr.** NG6: Bulw . . . . . . . . . . . . .5F **19**
**Cheviot Rd.** NG10: Long E . . . . . . . . .4C **62**
**Chewton Av.** NG16: Eastw . . . . . . . . .4C **16**
**Chewton St.** NG16: Eastw . . . . . . . . . .4B **16**
**Cheyne Wlk.** NG15: Huck . . . . . . . . . .3H **7**
**Cheyny Cl.** NG2: Nott . . . . . . . . . . . . . .2G **57**
**Chichester Cl.** DE7: Ilk . . . . . . . . . . . . .1C **40**
  NG5: Top V . . . . . . . . . . . . . . . . . .6C **20**
**Chichester Dr.** NG12: Cotg . . . . . . . . .1E **71**
**Chidlow Rd.** NG8: Bilb . . . . . . . . . . . . .2D **42**
**Chigwell Cl.** NG16: Nuth . . . . . . . . . . .4E **31**
**Chillon Way** NG15: Huck . . . . . . . . . . .5D **6**
**Chiltern Cl.** NG5: Arn . . . . . . . . . . . . . .3F **21**
**Chiltern Dr.** DE7: West H . . . . . . . . . .1C **38**
**Chiltern Gdns.**
  NG10: Long E . . . . . . . . . . . . . . . .4C **62**
**Chiltern Way** NG5: Bestw . . . . . . . . . .1F **33**
**Chilton Dr.** NG16: Want . . . . . . . . . . . .6A **18**
**Chilvers Cl.** NG5: Bestw . . . . . . . . . . .6E **21**
**CHILWELL** . . . . . . . . . . . . . . . . . . . . .5C **54**
**Chilwell Ct.** NG6: Bulw . . . . . . . . . . . .6B **20**
**Chilwell La.** NG9: Bram . . . . . . . . . . . .4B **54**
**Chilwell Manor Golf Course** . . . . . . . .1E **65**
**Chilwell Meadows Nature Reserve** . . .1D **64**
**Chilwell Olympia Leisure Cen.** . . . . . .2D **64**
**Chilwell Retail Pk.** NG9: Chil . . . . . . .4B **64**
**Chilwell Rd.** NG9: Bee . . . . . . . . . . . . .6F **55**
               (not continuous)
**Chilwell St.** NG7: Lent . . . . . . . . . . . . .6D **44**
**Chine Gdns.** NG2: West Br . . . . . . . . .6G **57**
**Chingford Rd.** NG8: Bilb . . . . . . . . . . .1E **43**
**Chipmunk Way** NG13: Newton . . . . . .2B **50**
**Chippendale St.** NG7: Lent . . . . . . . . .6D **44**
**Chippenham Rd.** NG5: Bestw . . . . . . .1F **33**
**Chisbury Grn.** NG11: Clif . . . . . . . . . . .6B **66**
**Chisholm Way** NG5: Bestw . . . . . . . . .1E **33**
**Chiswick St.** NG5: Sher . . . . . . . . . . . .4G **33**
**Christchurch Rd.** NG15: Huck . . . . . . .1D **19**
**Christina Av.** NG6: Cin . . . . . . . . . . . . .3A **32**
**Christina Cres.** NG6: Cin . . . . . . . . . . .3A **32**
**Christine Cl.** NG15: Huck . . . . . . . . . . .2A **8**
**Christine Ct.** NG3: Nott . . . . . . . . . . . .2C **46**
**Christopher Cl.** NG8: Woll . . . . . . . . . .3F **43**
**Christopher Cl.** NG15: Huck . . . . . . . . .1F **19**
**Chrysalis Way** NG16: Eastw . . . . . . . .2G **15**
**Church Av.** NG5: Arn . . . . . . . . . . . . . .6A **22**
  NG7: Lent . . . . . . . . . . . . . . . . . . .6D **44**
  NG10: Long E . . . . . . . . . . . . . . . .3C **72**
**Church Cl.** NG5: Arn . . . . . . . . . . . . . . .6H **21**
  NG9: Trow . . . . . . . . . . . . . . . . . . .5E **41**
  NG12: Rad T . . . . . . . . . . . . . . . . .6E **49**
  NG13: Bing . . . . . . . . . . . . . . . . . .4F **51**
**Church Ct.** NG12: Cotg . . . . . . . . . . . .2E **71**
**Church Cres.** NG5: Arn . . . . . . . . . . . .6H **21**
  NG9: Chil . . . . . . . . . . . . . . . . . . . .1A **64**
**Church Cft.** NG2: West Br . . . . . . . . . .3B **58**
**Churchdale Av.** NG9: Stap . . . . . . . . .2G **53**
**Church Dr.** DE7: Ilk . . . . . . . . . . . . . . .2H **27**
  NG2: West Br . . . . . . . . . . . . . . . .4B **58**
  NG5: Arn . . . . . . . . . . . . . . . . . . .6H **21**
  NG5: Sher . . . . . . . . . . . . . . . . . . .6F **33**
  NG10: Sand . . . . . . . . . . . . . . . . . .4D **52**
  NG12: Key . . . . . . . . . . . . . . . . . .4G **79**
  NG15: Huck . . . . . . . . . . . . . . . . . .4G **7**
**Church Dr. E.** NG5: Arn . . . . . . . . . . . .6A **22**
**Churchfield Ct.** NG5: Top V . . . . . . . . .4E **21**
**Churchfield La.** NG7: Radf . . . . . . . . .2C **44**
**Churchfield Ter.** NG6: Basf . . . . . . . . .5C **32**
**Churchfield Way** NG5: Top V . . . . . . .4E **21**
**Church Ga.** NG12: C'ton . . . . . . . . . . . .5C **70**
**Church Gro.** NG7: Lent . . . . . . . . . . . . .6C **44**
**Church Hill** NG12: Plum . . . . . . . . . . . .1G **79**
  NG16: Kimb . . . . . . . . . . . . . . . . . .1H **29**
**Churchill Cl.** NG5: Arn . . . . . . . . . . . . .1B **34**
**Churchill Dr.** NG9: Stap . . . . . . . . . . . .3G **53**
  NG11: Rudd . . . . . . . . . . . . . . . . . .6F **67**
**Churchill Pk.** NG4: Colw . . . . . . . . . . .4H **47**

**Church La.** DE7: Mapp . . . . . . . . . . . . .5C **26**
  DE7: Stant D . . . . . . . . . . . . . . . . .2B **52**
  NG5: Arn . . . . . . . . . . . . . . . . . . .4B **22**
  NG6: Bulw . . . . . . . . . . . . . . . . . . .6A **20**
  NG9: Atten . . . . . . . . . . . . . . . . . .4D **64**
  NG9: Stap . . . . . . . . . . . . . . . . . . .4F **53**
  NG11: Bart F . . . . . . . . . . . . . . . . .1E **75**
  NG11: Thru . . . . . . . . . . . . . . . . . .4B **74**
  NG12: Cotg . . . . . . . . . . . . . . . . . .2E **71**
  NG12: Plum . . . . . . . . . . . . . . . . . .6G **69**
  NG13: Bing . . . . . . . . . . . . . . . . . .5F **51**
  NG14: Epp . . . . . . . . . . . . . . . . . . .6D **26**
  NG15: Lin . . . . . . . . . . . . . . . . . . . .1G **7**
  NG16: Coss . . . . . . . . . . . . . . . . . .5E **29**
**Church Mdw.** NG14: Calv . . . . . . . . . .5H **11**
**Church M.** NG2: Nott . . . . . . . . . . . . . .2H **57**
**Churchmoor Ct.** NG5: Arn . . . . . . . . . .4A **22**
**Churchmoor La.** NG5: Arn . . . . . . . . . .4A **22**
**Church Rd.** NG3: Nott . . . . . . . . . . . . .2H **45**
  NG6: Bestw V . . . . . . . . . . . . . . . .1C **20**
  NG14: Bur J . . . . . . . . . . . . . . . . .3F **37**
  NG16: Grea, Want . . . . . . . . . . . . .2F **17**
**Churchside Gdns.** NG7: H Grn . . . . . .1C **44**
**Church Sq.** NG7: Lent . . . . . . . . . . . . .6D **44**
**Church St.** DE7: Ilk . . . . . . . . . . . . . . . .3H **27**
  DE75: Hea . . . . . . . . . . . . . . . . . . .4D **14**
  NG4: Carl . . . . . . . . . . . . . . . . . . . .2G **47**
  NG4: Lamb . . . . . . . . . . . . . . . . . .5C **24**
  NG5: Arn . . . . . . . . . . . . . . . . . . .5B **22**
  NG6: Basf . . . . . . . . . . . . . . . . . . .5C **32**
  NG7: Lent . . . . . . . . . . . . . . . . . . .6C **44**
  NG9: Bee . . . . . . . . . . . . . . . . . . .4F **55**
  NG9: Bram . . . . . . . . . . . . . . . . . .3B **54**
  NG9: Stap . . . . . . . . . . . . . . . . . . .4F **53**
  NG10: Sand . . . . . . . . . . . . . . . . . .4D **52**
  NG11: Goth . . . . . . . . . . . . . . . . . .6H **75**
  NG11: Rudd . . . . . . . . . . . . . . . . . .6G **67**
  NG12: Shel . . . . . . . . . . . . . . . . . .6H **37**
  NG13: Bing . . . . . . . . . . . . . . . . . .5F **51**
  NG16: Eastw . . . . . . . . . . . . . . . .3A **16**
**Church Vw.** DE7: Ilk . . . . . . . . . . . . . . .2A **40**
  DE72: Brea . . . . . . . . . . . . . . . . . .6A **62**
  DE75: Los . . . . . . . . . . . . . . . . . . .1A **14**
  NG4: Ged . . . . . . . . . . . . . . . . . . .6H **35**
**Church Vw. Cl.** NG5: Arn . . . . . . . . . .4F **21**
**Church Wlk.** NG4: Carl . . . . . . . . . . . . .2G **47**
  NG9: Stap . . . . . . . . . . . . . . . . . . .4G **53**
  NG14: Woodbo . . . . . . . . . . . . . . .1C **24**
  NG16: Eastw . . . . . . . . . . . . . . . .3B **16**
**Churnet Cl.** NG11: Clif . . . . . . . . . . . . .1C **66**
**Churston Ct.** NG9: Bee . . . . . . . . . . . .5G **55**
**Cider Orchard Pl.** NG16: Kimb . . . . . .1H **29**
**Cigar Factory, The** NG7: Nott . . . . . . . .3A **4**
              (off Derby Rd.)
**CINDERHILL** . . . . . . . . . . . . . . . . . . . .3H **31**
**Cinderhill Footway** NG6: Bulw . . . . . .3B **32**
**Cinderhill Gro.** NG4: Ged . . . . . . . . . . .5G **35**
**Cinderhill Gym** . . . . . . . . . . . . . . . . . . .4H **31**
**Cinderhill Rd.** NG6: Bulw, Cin . . . . . . .3H **31**
**Cinderhill Stop (NET)** . . . . . . . . . . . . .3H **31**
**Cinderhill Wlk.** NG6: Bulw . . . . . . . . . .1H **31**
**Cineworld Cinema**
  Nottingham . . . . . . . . . . . . . .3D **4** (4G **45**)
**Circuit Dr.** NG10: Long E . . . . . . . . . . .5H **63**
**Cirrus Dr.** NG16: Want . . . . . . . . . . . .6A **18**
**Citadel St.** NG7: Radf . . . . . . . . . . . . .4C **44**
**City, The** NG9: Bee . . . . . . . . . . . . . . .5G **55**
              (not continuous)
**City Bus. Pk.** NG4: Colw . . . . . . . . . . .3H **47**
**City Ground** . . . . . . . . . . . . . . . . . . . . .2A **58**
**CITY HOSPITAL (NOTTINGHAM UNIVERSITY)**
  . . . . . . . . . . . . . . . . . . . . . . . . . . .2F **33**
**City Link** NG2: Nott . . . . . . . . . .6G **5** (6H **45**)
**City of Caves** . . . . . . . . . . . . . . . . . . . .5E **5**
**City Point** NG1: Nott . . . . . . . . . .5C **4** (5F **45**)
**City Rd.** NG7: Nott . . . . . . . . . . . . . . . .2B **56**
  NG9: Bee . . . . . . . . . . . . . . . . . . .4G **55**
**City Vw.** NG3: Mapp . . . . . . . . . . . . . . .5B **34**
**Clandon Dr.** NG5: Sher . . . . . . . . . . . .5F **33**
**Clanfield Rd.** NG8: Bilb . . . . . . . . . . . .2E **43**
**Clapham St.** NG7: Radf . . . . . . . . . . . .4C **44**
**Claramount Rd.** DE75: Hea . . . . . . . . .4E **15**
**Clarborough Dr.** NG5: Arn . . . . . . . . . .1C **34**
**Clare Cl.** NG6: Basf . . . . . . . . . . . . . . . .3C **32**
**Clarehaven** NG9: Stap . . . . . . . . . . . . .6G **53**
**Claremont Av.** NG9: Bram . . . . . . . . . .3C **54**
  NG15: Huck . . . . . . . . . . . . . . . . . .6G **7**
**Claremont Dr.** NG2: West Br . . . . . . . .2G **67**
**Claremont Gdns.** NG5: Sher . . . . . . . .6F **33**
**Claremont Rd.** NG5: Sher . . . . . . . . . .6F **33**
**Clarence Ct.** NG3: Nott . . . . . .3H **5** (4A **46**)
**Clarence Rd.** NG9: Chil . . . . . . . . . . . .3D **64**
  NG10: Long E . . . . . . . . . . . . . . . .1E **73**
**Clarence St.** NG3: Nott . . . . . .2H **5** (4A **46**)
**Clarendon Chambers** NG1: Nott . .2B **4** (4F **45**)
**Clarendon Ct.** NG5: Sher . . . . . . . . . . .1F **45**

**Clarendon Ho.** NG1: Nott . . . . . . . .3B **4** (4F **45**)
**Clarendon Pk.** NG5: Sher . . . . . . . . . .1F **45**
**Clarendon St.** NG1: Nott . . . . . .2B **4** (4F **45**)
**Clare St.** NG1: Nott . . . . . . . . . .3E **5** (4G **45**)
**Clare Valley** NG7: Nott . . . . . . . .5B **4** (5F **45**)
**Clarewood Gro.** NG11: Clif . . . . . . . . . .6C **66**
**Clarges St.** NG6: Bulw . . . . . . . . . . . . .1A **32**
**Clarke Av.** DE75: Los . . . . . . . . . . . . . .3A **14**
  NG5: Arn . . . . . . . . . . . . . . . . . . .5B **22**
**Clarke Dr.** NG10: Long E . . . . . . . . . . .3C **72**
**Clarke Rd.** NG2: Nott . . . . . . . . . . . . . .1A **58**
**Clarke's La.** NG9: Chil . . . . . . . . . . . . .1D **64**
**Clarkson Dr.** NG9: Bee . . . . . . . . . . . .5H **55**
**Claude St.** NG7: Lent . . . . . . . . . . . . . .2C **56**
**Claxton St.** DE75: Hea . . . . . . . . . . . . .3B **14**
**Claxton Ter.** DE75: Hea . . . . . . . . . . . .3B **14**
**Clay Av.** NG3: Mapp . . . . . . . . . . . . . . .4C **34**
**Claye St.** NG10: Long E . . . . . . . . . . . .6G **63**
**Clayfield Cl.** NG6: Bulw . . . . . . . . . . . .1G **31**
**Claygate** NG3: Nott . . . . . . . . . . . . . . .2D **46**
**Clay La.** DE75: Hea . . . . . . . . . . . . . . . .3D **14**
**Claypit Wlk.** NG11: Wilf . . . . . . . . . . . .5E **57**
**Claypole Rd.** NG7: H Grn . . . . . . . . . .2D **44**
**Clayton Ct.** NG7: Radf . . . . . . . . . . . . .4D **44**
  NG9: Bee . . . . . . . . . . . . . . . . . . .6G **55**
**Clayton Gro.** DE75: Los . . . . . . . . . . . .1A **14**
**Claytons Dr.** NG7: Lent . . . . . . . . . . . .1C **56**
**Claytons Wharf** NG7: Lent . . . . . . . . . .1C **56**
**Clementine Dr.** NG3: Mapp . . . . . . . . .2E **35**
**Clether Rd.** NG8: Bilb . . . . . . . . . . . . . .3D **42**
**Cleve Av.** NG9: Toton . . . . . . . . . . . . . .2G **63**
**Clevedon Dr.** NG5: Arn . . . . . . . . . . . .4E **23**
**Cleveland Av.** NG10: Long E . . . . . . . .4H **63**
**Cleveland Cl.** NG7: Radf . . . . . . . . . . .4C **44**
**Cleveley's Rd.** NG9: Toton . . . . . . . . . .2G **63**
**Clevely Way** NG11: Clif . . . . . . . . . . . .2C **66**
**Cliff, The** NG6: Bulw . . . . . . . . . . . . . . .3H **31**
**Cliff Blvd.** NG16: Kimb . . . . . . . . . . . . .6H **17**
               (not continuous)
**Cliff Cres.** NG12: Rad T . . . . . . . . . . . .5F **49**
**Cliff Dr.** NG12: Rad T . . . . . . . . . . . . . .4G **49**
**Cliffe Hill Av.** NG9: Stap . . . . . . . . . . .4F **53**
**Cliffgrove Av.** NG9: Chil . . . . . . . . . . . .5D **54**
**Cliffmere Wlk.** NG11: Clif . . . . . . . . . . .4B **66**
               (not continuous)
**Clifford Av.** NG9: Bee . . . . . . . . . . . . . .3E **55**
**Clifford Cl.** NG10: Long E . . . . . . . . . . .3C **72**
  NG12: Key . . . . . . . . . . . . . . . . . .3H **79**
**Clifford Ct.** NG7: Radf . . . . . . . . . . . . .4D **44**
**Clifford St.** NG7: Radf . . . . . . . . . . . . .3D **44**
  NG10: Long E . . . . . . . . . . . . . . . .6C **63**
**Cliff Rd.** NG1: Nott . . . . . . . . . .5F **5** (5H **45**)
  NG4: Carl . . . . . . . . . . . . . . . . . . . .3F **47**
  NG12: Rad T . . . . . . . . . . . . . . . . .5E **49**
**Cliffs, The** NG12: Rad T . . . . . . . . . . . .4G **49**
**Cliff Way** NG12: Rad T . . . . . . . . . . . . .5F **49**
**CLIFTON** . . . . . . . . . . . . . . . . . . . . . . .4D **66**
**Clifton Av.** NG10: Long E . . . . . . . . . . .6A **64**
  NG11: Rudd . . . . . . . . . . . . . . . . . .5G **67**
**Clifton Blvd.** NG7: Lent, Nott . . . . . . . .1B **56**
  NG11: Rudd, Wilf . . . . . . . . . . . . . .1B **56**
**Clifton Cres.** NG9: Atten . . . . . . . . . . .2E **65**
**Clifton Grn.** NG11: Clif . . . . . . . . . . . . .3B **66**
**Clifton Gro.** NG4: Ged . . . . . . . . . . . . .5G **35**
**Clifton Hall Dr.** NG11: Clif . . . . . . . . . .3H **65**
**Clifton La.** NG11: Clif, Wilf . . . . . . . . . .5B **66**
  NG11: Rudd . . . . . . . . . . . . . . . . . .5E **67**
**Clifton Leisure Cen.** . . . . . . . . . . . . . . .4D **66**
**Clifton M.** NG7: Nott . . . . . . . . . .4A **4** (5E **45**)
**Clifton Pastures** NG11: Goth . . . . . . . .6A **66**
**Clifton Rd.** NG11: Rudd . . . . . . . . . . . .6F **67**
**Clifton St.** NG9: Bee . . . . . . . . . . . . . . .5G **55**
**Clifton Ter.** NG7: Nott . . . . . . . . .6A **4** (6E **45**)
**Clinton Av.** NG5: Sher . . . . . . . . . . . . .1F **45**
**Clinton Ct.** NG1: Nott . . . . . . . .2D **4** (4G **45**)
**Clinton St.** NG5: Arn . . . . . . . . . . . . . .6A **22**
  NG9: Bee . . . . . . . . . . . . . . . . . . .4E **55**
**Clinton St. E.** NG1: Nott . . . . . . .3E **5** (4G **45**)
**Clinton St. W.** NG1: Nott . . . . . . .3E **5** (4G **45**)
**Clinton Ter.** NG7: Nott . . . . . . . .3A **4** (4E **45**)
**CLIPSTON** . . . . . . . . . . . . . . . . . . . . . .4D **70**
**Clipstone Av.** NG1: Nott . . . . . . .1C **4** (3F **45**)
  NG3: Mapp . . . . . . . . . . . . . . . . . .3C **34**
**Clipstone Cl.** NG8: Stre . . . . . . . . . . . .5D **30**
**Clipston La.** NG12: Norm W . . . . . . . . .6H **69**
**Clive Cres.** NG16: Kimb . . . . . . . . . . . .2A **30**
**Cliveden Grn.** NG11: Clif . . . . . . . . . . .4B **66**
**Cloister Ho.** NG7: Lent . . . . . . . . . . . . .1C **56**
**Cloisters, The** NG9: Bee . . . . . . . . . . .3G **55**
**Cloister St.** NG7: Lent . . . . . . . . . . . . .1C **56**
**Close, The** NG5: Sher . . . . . . . . . . . . .4G **33**
  NG9: Chil . . . . . . . . . . . . . . . . . . . .1D **64**
**Close Quarters** NG9: Bram . . . . . . . . .3C **54**
**Cloud Av.** NG9: Stap . . . . . . . . . . . . . . .4H **53**
**Clouds Hill** NG11: Clif . . . . . . . . . . . . . .5C **66**
**Cloister Ct.** NG10: Sand . . . . . . . . . . . .4D **52**
**Cloudside Rd.** NG10: Sand . . . . . . . . . .4D **52**

Clough Ct. NG8: Bilb . . . . . . . . . . . . . . . .2H **43**
Clovelly Dr. NG3: Mapp . . . . . . . . . . . . . .2E **35**
Cloverdale NG12: Cotg . . . . . . . . . . . . . . .3G **71**
Clover Flds. NG14: Calv . . . . . . . . . . . . . .3A **12**
Clover Grn. NG6: Basf . . . . . . . . . . . . . . .4B **32**
Cloverlands NG2: West Br . . . . . . . . . . . .2G **67**
Cloverlands NG16: Want . . . . . . . . . . . . . .6A **18**
Cloverlands Dr. NG16: Want . . . . . . . . . . .6A **18**
Clover Ri. NG16: Newth . . . . . . . . . . . . . .4D **16**
Clumber Av. NG3: Mapp . . . . . . . . . . . . .3C **34**
  NG4: Neth . . . . . . . . . . . . . . . . . . . . . .2A **48**
  NG5: Sher . . . . . . . . . . . . . . . . . . . . . . .1F **45**
  NG9: Chil . . . . . . . . . . . . . . . . . . . . . . . .6D **54**
Clumber Ct. NG7: Nott . . . . . . . . .6A **4** (6E **45**)
Clumber Cres. Nth. NG7: Nott . . . .4A **4** (5E **45**)
Clumber Cres. Sth. NG7: Nott . . . .6A **4** (6E **45**)
Clumber Dr. NG12: Rad T . . . . . . . . . . . .4G **49**
Clumber Rd. NG2: West Br . . . . . . . . . . .4B **58**
Clumber Rd. E. NG7: Nott . . . . . . .5A **4** (5E **45**)
Clumber Rd. W. NG7: Nott . . . . . . .5A **4** (5E **45**)
Clumber St. NG1: Nott . . . . . . . . .3E **5** (4G **45**)
  NG10: Long E . . . . . . . . . . . . . . . . . . . .6F **63**
  NG15: Huck . . . . . . . . . . . . . . . . . . . . . . .5A **8**
Coach Dr. NG16: Eastw . . . . . . . . . . . . . .1B **16**
Coachmans Cft. NG8: Woll . . . . . . . . . . .4G **43**
Coachways DE7: Mapp . . . . . . . . . . . . . .4D **26**
Coates Av. NG15: Huck . . . . . . . . . . . . . . .2F **7**
Coatsby Rd. NG16: Kimb . . . . . . . . . . . . .6H **17**
Cobden Chambers NG1: Nott . . . . . . . . . .4E **5**
Cobden St. NG7: Lent . . . . . . . . . . . . . . .4C **44**
  NG10: Long E . . . . . . . . . . . . . . . . . . . .6F **63**
Cockayne Cl. NG10: Sand . . . . . . . . . . . .2D **62**
Cocker Beck NG4: Lamb . . . . . . . . . . . . .6C **24**
Cockerhouse Rd. NG16: Eastw . . . . . . . .1A **16**
Cockington Rd. NG8: Bilb . . . . . . . . . . . .4C **42**
Cockleys NG10: Long E . . . . . . . . . . . . . .1E **73**
Codrington Gdns. NG5: Bestw . . . . . . . . .5G **21**
Cogenhoe Wlk. NG5: Arn . . . . . . . . . . . .3B **22**
Cogley La. NG13: Bing . . . . . . . . . . . . . . .5G **51**
Cohen Cl. NG5: Arn . . . . . . . . . . . . . . . . .1D **34**
  NG9: Chil . . . . . . . . . . . . . . . . . . . . . . . .3B **64**
Cokefield Av. NG16: Nuth . . . . . . . . . . . .4F **31**
Colborn St. NG3: Nott . . . . . . . . . . . . . . .2B **46**
Colbrook Pl. NG4: Carl . . . . . . . . . . . . . . .2H **47**
Colchester Rd. NG8: Brox . . . . . . . . . . . .6E **31**
Coleby Av. NG7: Lent . . . . . . . . . . . . . . . .1C **56**
Coleby Rd. NG8: Brox . . . . . . . . . . . . . . . .5F **31**
Coledale NG2: West Br . . . . . . . . . . . . . .5E **59**
Coleridge Cres. NG5: Arn . . . . . . . . . . . .6H **21**
Coleridge St. NG7: Radf . . . . . . . . . . . . .3C **44**
Colesbourne Rd. NG11: Clif . . . . . . . . . .3D **66**
Colin Broughton Ct. NG6: Bulw . . . . . . . .6B **20**
Colindale Gdns. NG16: Nuth . . . . . . . . . .4E **31**
Colinwood Av. NG5: Top V . . . . . . . . . . .4C **20**
College Dr. NG11: Clif . . . . . . . . . . . . . . .3B **66**
  (not continuous)
College Rd. NG3: Mapp . . . . . . . . . . . . . .4E **35**
  NG9: Chil . . . . . . . . . . . . . . . . . . . . . . . .6E **55**
College St. NG1: Nott . . . . . . . .3B **4** (4F **45**)
  NG10: Long E . . . . . . . . . . . . . . . . . . . .2D **62**
College Way NG8: Bilb . . . . . . . . . . . . . .2C **42**
Colleymoor Leys La.
  NG11: Clif . . . . . . . . . . . . . . . . . . . . . . . .3D **66**
Colliers Bus. Pk. NG12: Cotg . . . . . . . . . .6G **61**
Colliers Way NG8: Cin . . . . . . . . . . . . . . .3G **31**
  NG12: Cotg . . . . . . . . . . . . . . . . . . . . . . .6G **61**
Colliery Cl. NG2: Nott . . . . . . . . . . . . . . . .2F **57**
Collin Av. NG10: Sand . . . . . . . . . . . . . . .1D **62**
Collin Grn. NG5: Sher . . . . . . . . . . . . . . .3H **33**
Collington St. NG9: Bee . . . . . . . . . . . . . .5E **55**
Collington Way NG2: West Br . . . . . . . . .6H **57**
Collingwood Cl. NG11: Clif . . . . . . . . . . .1C **66**
Collingwood Rd. NG10: Long E . . . . . . . .1F **73**
Collins Cl. NG6: Bulw . . . . . . . . . . . . . . . .2F **31**
Collins Homes NG9: Bee . . . . . . . . . . . . .2A **66**
Collin St. NG1: Nott . . . . . . . . . .6E **5** (6G **45**)
  NG9: Bee . . . . . . . . . . . . . . . . . . . . . . . .5F **55**
Collison St. NG7: H Grn . . . . . . . . . . . . . .3D **44**
Collyer Rd. NG14: Calv . . . . . . . . . . . . . .3E **11**
Colly Ga. NG16: Kimb . . . . . . . . . . . . . . .2A **30**
Collygate Rd. NG2: Nott . . . . . . . . . . . . .2H **57**
Colmon Cl. NG5: Bestw . . . . . . . . . . . . . .6E **21**
Colmon Wlk. NG5: Bestw . . . . . . . . . . . .6E **21**
Colonsay Cl. NG9: Trow . . . . . . . . . . . . . .6F **41**
Colston Cres. NG2: West Br . . . . . . . . . .1H **67**
Colston Ga.
  NG12: Cotg, Crop Bi . . . . . . . . . . . . . . .2F **71**
Colston Rd. NG6: Bulw . . . . . . . . . . . . . .5A **20**
Coltsfoot Cl. NG13: Bing . . . . . . . . . . . . .6C **50**
Colville Ct. NG1: Nott . . . . . . . . . . . . . . . .2F **45**
Colville St. NG1: Nott . . . . . . . . . . . . . . . .2F **45**
Colville Ter. NG1: Nott . . . . . . . . . . . . . . .3F **45**
Colville Vs. NG1: Nott . . . . . . . . . . . . . . . .2F **45**
COLWICK . . . . . . . . . . . . . . . . . . . . . . . .4G **47**
Colwick Bus. Pk. NG4: Colw . . . . . . . . . .4H **47**
Colwick Country Pk. . . . . . . . . . . . . . . . .6F **47**
Colwick Crossing NG2: Nott . . . . . . . . . .5C **46**

Colwick Ind. Est. NG4: Colw . . . . . . . . . .4H **47**
  (Private Rd. No. 2)
  NG4: Colw . . . . . . . . . . . . . . . . . . . . . . .4B **48**
  (Private Rd. No. 5)
  NG4: Colw . . . . . . . . . . . . . . . . . . . . . . .4G **47**
  (Private Rd. No. 8)
Colwick Lodge NG4: Carl . . . . . . . . . . . .3H **47**
Colwick Loop Rd. NG4: Carl, Colw, Neth . .1A **48**
Colwick Mnr. Farm NG4: Colw . . . . . . . .4G **47**
Colwick Pk. Cl. NG4: Colw . . . . . . . . . . .4G **47**
Colwick Quays Bus. Pk. NG4: Colw . . . . .4A **48**
Colwick Rd. NG2: Nott . . . . . . . . . . . . . . .6B **46**
  NG2: West Br . . . . . . . . . . . . . . . . . . . .2A **58**
COLWICK VALE . . . . . . . . . . . . . . . . . . .3G **47**
Comery Av. NG3: Nott . . . . . . . . . . . . . . .3C **46**
Comet Dr. NG16: Eastw . . . . . . . . . . . . .3C **16**
Comfrey Cl. NG5: Top V . . . . . . . . . . . . . .5D **20**
Commerce Sq. NG1: Nott . . . . . .5F **5** (5H **45**)
Commercial Av. NG9: Bee . . . . . . . . . . . .5F **55**
Commercial Rd. NG6: Bulw . . . . . . . . . . .6H **19**
  NG12: Key . . . . . . . . . . . . . . . . . . . . . . .5G **79**
Commodore Ct. NG8: Aspl . . . . . . . . . . .5A **32**
Commodore Gdns. NG8: Aspl . . . . . . . . .5A **32**
Common, The NG15: Huck . . . . . . . . . . . .5C **6**
Common La. DE7: Stan, Stan C . . . . . . . .4A **38**
  NG9: Bram . . . . . . . . . . . . . . . . . . . . . . .5A **54**
  NG15: Huck . . . . . . . . . . . . . . . . . . . . . . .5D **6**
  NG16: Want . . . . . . . . . . . . . . . . . . . . . .5A **18**
Commons Cl. NG16: Newth . . . . . . . . . . .5C **16**
COMMON SIDE . . . . . . . . . . . . . . . . . . .4B **14**
Compton Acres NG2: West Br . . . . . . . . .5F **57**
Compton Acres Shop. Cen.
  NG2: West Br . . . . . . . . . . . . . . . . . . . .6G **57**
Compton Rd. NG5: Sher . . . . . . . . . . . . . .4F **33**
Comyn Gdns. NG3: Nott . . . . . . .1F **5** (3H **45**)
Condor Rd. DE7: Ilk . . . . . . . . . . . . . . . . .5B **40**
Conduit Cl. NG2: Nott . . . . . . . . . . . . . . . .1G **57**
Coney Wlk. NG5: Top V . . . . . . . . . . . . . .5D **20**
Conifer Cres. NG11: Clif . . . . . . . . . . . . . .6C **66**
Conifer Wlk. NG3: Nott . . . . . . . . . . . . . .2C **46**
Coningsby Gdns. E. NG5: Woodt . . . . . . .3B **34**
Coningsby Rd. NG5: Woodt . . . . . . . . . . .2B **34**
Coningswath Rd. NG4: Carl . . . . . . . . . . .5E **35**
Conisborough Ter. NG2: Nott . . . . . . . . . .2G **57**
Conisbrough Av. NG4: Ged . . . . . . . . . . .6B **36**
Coniston Av. NG6: Basf . . . . . . . . . . . . . .5A **32**
Coniston Cl. NG2: Gam . . . . . . . . . . . . . .4E **59**
Coniston Dr. DE7: Kirk H . . . . . . . . . . . . .4H **39**
Coniston Rd. NG9: Bram . . . . . . . . . . . . .2D **54**
  NG10: Long E . . . . . . . . . . . . . . . . . . . .3C **62**
  NG15: Huck . . . . . . . . . . . . . . . . . . . . . . .3F **7**
Connelly Cl. NG5: Arn . . . . . . . . . . . . . . .1E **35**
Connelly Ct. NG6: Bulw . . . . . . . . . . . . . .1A **32**
Connery, The NG15: Huck . . . . . . . . . . . . .3H **7**
Connery M. NG9: Toton . . . . . . . . . . . . . .4B **64**
Conrad Ct. NG6: Bulw . . . . . . . . . . . . . . .2F **31**
Constance St. NG7: Basf . . . . . . . . . . . . .6E **33**
Convent, The NG1: Nott . . . . . . . . . . . . . .3B **4**
Convent St. NG1: Nott . . . . . . . .3F **5** (4H **45**)
Conway Av. NG4: Carl . . . . . . . . . . . . . . .2A **48**
Conway Cl. NG3: Nott . . . . . . . . . . . . . . .2G **45**
Conway Cres. NG4: Carl . . . . . . . . . . . . .1A **48**
Conway Gdns. NG5: Arn . . . . . . . . . . . . .1A **34**
Conway Rd. NG4: Carl . . . . . . . . . . . . . . .2H **47**
  NG15: Huck . . . . . . . . . . . . . . . . . . . . . .2D **18**
Conway St. NG10: Long E . . . . . . . . . . . .5G **63**
Conway Wlk. NG3: Nott . . . . . . . . . . . . . .2G **45**
Cook Dr. DE7: Ilk . . . . . . . . . . . . . . . . . . .3C **40**
Cooke Cl. NG10: Long E . . . . . . . . . . . . .1D **72**
Cookson Av. NG4: Ged . . . . . . . . . . . . . .5F **35**
Coombe Cl. NG8: Woll . . . . . . . . . . . . . . .6A **44**
Coombe Rd. NG16: Newth . . . . . . . . . . .1D **16**
Co-operative Av. NG15: Huck . . . . . . . . . .3H **7**
Co-operative St. NG10: Long E . . . . . . . .6G **63**
Cooper Cl. NG5: Arn . . . . . . . . . . . . . . . .1E **35**
Cooper Gdns. NG11: Rudd . . . . . . . . . . .6F **67**
Coopers Grn. NG8: Woll . . . . . . . . . . . . .4E **43**
Cooper St. NG4: Neth . . . . . . . . . . . . . . .3A **48**
Copeland Av. NG9: Stap . . . . . . . . . . . . .3G **53**
Copeland Gro. NG13: Bing . . . . . . . . . . .4C **50**
Copenhagen Ct. NG3: Nott . . . . . . . . . . .6H **33**
Copestake Cl. NG10: Long E . . . . . . . . . .6C **62**
Cope St. NG7: H Grn . . . . . . . . . . . . . . . .3D **44**
Coppice Av. DE7: Ilk . . . . . . . . . . . . . . . . .2H **27**
  NG15: Huck . . . . . . . . . . . . . . . . . . . . . . .6E **7**
Coppice Ct. DE75: Hea . . . . . . . . . . . . . .6D **14**
Coppice Dr. DE75: Hea . . . . . . . . . . . . . .6D **14**
  NG16: Eastw . . . . . . . . . . . . . . . . . . . . .2H **15**
Coppice Ga. NG15: Arn . . . . . . . . . . . . . .5B **22**
Coppice Gro. NG3: Mapp . . . . . . . . . . . .5B **34**
Coppice Lodge NG5: Arn . . . . . . . . . . . . .5C **22**
Coppice M. DE75: Hea . . . . . . . . . . . . . .6D **14**
Coppice Rd. NG5: Arn . . . . . . . . . . . . . . .5B **22**
Copplestone Dr. NG3: Mapp . . . . . . . . . .1E **35**

Copse, The DE7: Ilk . . . . . . . . . . . . . . . . .2H **27**
  NG9: Chil . . . . . . . . . . . . . . . . . . . . . . . .5C **54**
  NG15: Huck . . . . . . . . . . . . . . . . . . . . . . .5A **8**
Copse Cl. NG14: Bur J . . . . . . . . . . . . . . .2F **37**
Copseside Cl. NG10: Long E . . . . . . . . . .5C **62**
Copsey Cft. Ct. NG10: Long E . . . . . . . . .6H **63**
Corben Gdns. NG6: Bulw . . . . . . . . . . . . .6F **19**
Corbiere Av. NG16: Want . . . . . . . . . . . . .6A **18**
Corby Rd. NG3: Nott . . . . . . . . . . . . . . . .6A **34**
Corfield Av. DE75: Hea . . . . . . . . . . . . . .6D **14**
Coriander Dr. NG6: Basf . . . . . . . . . . . . .4B **32**
Corinthan Cl. NG15: Huck . . . . . . . . . . . . .2A **8**
Corinth Rd. NG11: Clif . . . . . . . . . . . . . . .3C **66**
Corke Ho. NG7: Lent . . . . . . . . . . . . . . . .5C **44**
  (off Faraday Rd.)
Corn Cl. NG12: Cotg . . . . . . . . . . . . . . . . .3E **71**
Corncrake Av. NG6: Basf . . . . . . . . . . . . .4B **32**
Corncrake Dr. NG5: Arn . . . . . . . . . . . . . .6E **23**
Corn Cft. NG11: Clif . . . . . . . . . . . . . . . . .4D **66**
Cornell Dr. NG5: Arn . . . . . . . . . . . . . . . .5D **22**
Cornfield Av. NG16: Kimb . . . . . . . . . . . .6G **17**
Cornfields, The NG5: Bestw . . . . . . . . . . .5F **21**
Cornhill Rd. NG4: Carl . . . . . . . . . . . . . . .1D **46**
Cornwall Av. NG9: Bee . . . . . . . . . . . . . . .1A **66**
Cornwallis Cl. NG10: Long E . . . . . . . . . .1F **73**
Cornwall Rd. NG5: Arn . . . . . . . . . . . . . . .6G **21**
Cornwall's Hill NG4: Lamb . . . . . . . . . . . .6D **24**
Coronation Av. NG10: Sand . . . . . . . . . . .4C **52**
  NG11: Wilf . . . . . . . . . . . . . . . . . . . . . . .3F **57**
Coronation Park . . . . . . . . . . . . . . . . . . .3C **16**
Coronation Rd. DE7: Ilk . . . . . . . . . . . . . .5C **28**
  DE7: Mapp . . . . . . . . . . . . . . . . . . . . . .4C **26**
  (not continuous)
  DE7: Stan . . . . . . . . . . . . . . . . . . . . . . .3A **38**
  NG3: Mapp . . . . . . . . . . . . . . . . . . . . . .4B **34**
  NG6: Bestw V . . . . . . . . . . . . . . . . . . . . .6C **8**
  NG15: Huck . . . . . . . . . . . . . . . . . . . . . . .3F **7**
  NG16: Coss . . . . . . . . . . . . . . . . . . . . . .5D **28**
  NG16: Nuth . . . . . . . . . . . . . . . . . . . . . .2B **30**
Coronation St. DE7: Ilk . . . . . . . . . . . . . .1B **40**
Coronation Wlk. NG4: Ged . . . . . . . . . . .6A **36**
Corporation Cotts. NG14: Bulc . . . . . . . . .2H **37**
Corporation Oaks NG3: Nott . . . . . . . . . .2G **45**
Corporation Rd. DE7: Ilk . . . . . . . . . . . . . .4C **40**
Corsham Gdns. NG3: Nott . . . . . . . . . . . .2C **46**
Corve Dale Wlk. NG2: West Br . . . . . . . . .6B **58**
Cosby Rd. NG2: Nott . . . . . . . . . . . . . . . .6B **46**
COSSALL . . . . . . . . . . . . . . . . . . . . . . . .6E **29**
Cossall Ind. Est. DE7: Ilk . . . . . . . . . . . . .5D **28**
COSSALL MARSH . . . . . . . . . . . . . . . . . .5E **29**
Cossall Rd. NG9: Trow . . . . . . . . . . . . . . .2E **41**
  NG16: Coss . . . . . . . . . . . . . . . . . . . . . .2E **41**
Costock Av. NG5: Sher . . . . . . . . . . . . . . .3F **33**
COTGRAVE . . . . . . . . . . . . . . . . . . . . . . .2F **71**
Cotgrave Av. NG4: Ged . . . . . . . . . . . . . .5H **35**
Cotgrave Cl. NG8: Stre . . . . . . . . . . . . . . .5E **31**
Cotgrave Country Pk. . . . . . . . . . . . . . . .5F **61**
Cotgrave La. NG12: Toll . . . . . . . . . . . . . .2H **69**
Cotgrave Leisure Cen. . . . . . . . . . . . . . .2G **71**
Cotgrave Place Golf Course . . . . . . . . . .4C **60**
Cotgrave Rd. NG12: Crop Bi, Owt . . . . . .5H **71**
  NG12: C'ton, Plum . . . . . . . . . . . . . . . .6H **69**
Cotgrave Shop. Cen. NG12: Cotg . . . . . . .2F **71**
COTMANHAY . . . . . . . . . . . . . . . . . . . . . .3A **28**
Cotmanhay Rd. DE7: Ilk . . . . . . . . . . . . . .4A **28**
Coton Cl. NG11: Wilf . . . . . . . . . . . . . . . . .2E **67**
Cotswold Cl. NG10: Long E . . . . . . . . . . .5D **62**
Cotswold Ct. NG9: Bram . . . . . . . . . . . . .2D **54**
Cotswold Rd. NG8: Stre . . . . . . . . . . . . . .6E **31**
Cottage Cl. DE7: Ilk . . . . . . . . . . . . . . . . .4H **27**
Cottage Gdn. La. DE75: Hea . . . . . . . . . .3B **14**
Cottage Grn. NG2: West Br . . . . . . . . . . .2E **59**
Cottage Mdw. NG4: Colw . . . . . . . . . . . .5H **47**
Cottage Ter. NG1: Nott . . . . . . . .3A **4** (4E **45**)
Cottage Wlk. NG4: Neth . . . . . . . . . . . . .4E **43**
Cottam Dr. NG5: Top V . . . . . . . . . . . . . .5D **20**
Cottam Gdns. NG5: Top V . . . . . . . . . . . .5E **21**
Cottesmore Rd. NG7: Lent . . . . . . . . . . . .5D **44**
Cotton Ho. NG7: Radf . . . . . . . . . . . . . . .3C **44**
  (off Radford Blvd.)
County Archives
  Nottingham . . . . . . . . . . . . . .6D **4** (6G **45**)
County Bus. Pk. NG2: Nott . . . . . . . . . . .1A **58**
County Cl. NG9: Bee . . . . . . . . . . . . . . . .6G **55**
County Court
  Nottingham . . . . . . . . . . . . . .6E **5** (6G **45**)
County Rd. NG2: Nott . . . . . . . . . . . . . . .1A **58**
  NG4: Ged . . . . . . . . . . . . . . . . . . . . . . .4E **35**
Coupe Gdns. NG15: Huck . . . . . . . . . . . . .5A **8**
Court, The NG9: Toton . . . . . . . . . . . . . . .3A **64**
Court Cres. NG8: Woll . . . . . . . . . . . . . . .5F **43**
Courtenay Gdns. NG3: Nott . . . . . . . . . .2H **45**
Court Gdns. NG2: West Br . . . . . . . . . . . .1F **67**
Courtleet Way NG6: Bulw . . . . . . . . . . . .2H **31**
Courtney Cl. NG8: Woll . . . . . . . . . . . . . .4E **43**
Court St. NG7: H Grn . . . . . . . . . . . . . . . .2D **44**
Court Vw. NG7: Nott . . . . . . . . . .4A **4** (5E **45**)

Court Yd. NG9: Bram . . . . . . . . . . . . . . . . . .3B 54
Courtyard, The NG16: Kimb . . . . . . . . . . .5G 17
Covedale Rd. NG5: Sher . . . . . . . . . . . . . .2G 33
Coventry Ct. NG6: Bulw . . . . . . . . . . . . . .2H 31
Coventry La. NG9: Bram . . . . . . . . . . . . . .2H 53
Coventry Rd. NG6: Bulw . . . . . . . . . . . . . .6H 19
                              (Gilead St.)
  NG6: Bulw . . . . . . . . . . . . . . . . . . . .1H 31
                              (Main St.)
  NG9: Bee . . . . . . . . . . . . . . . . . . . . .4G 55
Covers, The NG2: West Br . . . . . . . . . . . .2B 58
Covert Cl. NG12: Key . . . . . . . . . . . . . . . . .3H 79
  NG14: Bur J . . . . . . . . . . . . . . . . . . .2E 37
  NG15: Huck . . . . . . . . . . . . . . . . . . . .5A 8
Covert Cres. NG12: Rad T . . . . . . . . . . . .6H 49
Covert Rd. NG2: West Br . . . . . . . . . . . . .5D 58
Cowan St. NG1: Nott . . . . . . . . . .3F 5 (4H 45)
Cowdrey Gdns. NG5: Arn . . . . . . . . . . . . .1D 34
Cowlairs NG5: Top V . . . . . . . . . . . . . . . . .6C 20
Cow La. NG9: Bram . . . . . . . . . . . . . . . . .3B 54
Cowley Cl. DE7: Ilk . . . . . . . . . . . . . . . . . .2B 28
Cowley St. NG6: Basf . . . . . . . . . . . . . . . .2G 33
Cowper Rd. NG5: Woodt . . . . . . . . . . . . . .3A 34
  NG16: Newth . . . . . . . . . . . . . . . . . .5C 16
Cowslip Cl. NG13: Bing . . . . . . . . . . . . . . .5C 50
Coxmoor Cl. NG12: Edwal . . . . . . . . . . . . .1E 69
Coxmoor Ct. NG5: Top V . . . . . . . . . . . . . .4E 21
Crabapple Dr. NG16: Lang M . . . . . . . . . .1G 15
Crab Apple Gro. NG15: Huck . . . . . . . . . .1A 20
Crabtree Fld. NG2: Colw . . . . . . . . . . . . . .5F 47
Crabtree Rd. NG6: Bulw . . . . . . . . . . . . . .1G 31
Cragdale Rd. NG5: Sher . . . . . . . . . . . . . .2G 33
Cragmoor Rd. NG14: Bur J . . . . . . . . . . . .4E 37
Craig Moray NG12: Rad T . . . . . . . . . . . . .5G 49
Craig St. NG10: Long E . . . . . . . . . . . . . . .6G 63
Crammond Cl. NG2: Nott . . . . . . . . . . . . . .1F 57
Crampton Cl. NG5: Top V . . . . . . . . . . . . . .5E 21
Cramworth Gro. NG5: Sher . . . . . . . . . . . .4H 33
Cranberry Cl. NG2: West Br . . . . . . . . . . .5F 57
Cranborne Cl. NG9: Trow . . . . . . . . . . . . . .1F 53
Cranbourne Gro. NG15: Huck . . . . . . . . . . .4E 7
Cranbrook Ho. NG1: Nott . . . . . . . . . . . . . .4G 5
Cranbrook St. NG1: Nott . . . . . . . .3F 5 (4H 45)
Cranfield Wlk. NG11: Clif . . . . . . . . . . . . . .3D 66
               (off Southchurch Dr.)
Cranfleet Way NG10: Long E . . . . . . . . . . .6C 62
Cranford Gdns. NG2: West Br . . . . . . . . . .1G 67
Cranmer Gro. NG3: Nott . . . . . . . . . . . . . .2G 45
Cranmer St. DE7: Ilk . . . . . . . . . . . . . . . . .6B 28
  NG3: Nott . . . . . . . . . . . . . . . . . . . .2G 45
  NG10: Long E . . . . . . . . . . . . . . . . .5F 63
Cranmer Wlk. NG3: Nott . . . . . . . . . . . . . .2G 45
Cranmore Cl. NG5: Arn . . . . . . . . . . . . . . .3C 22
Cransley Av. NG8: Woll . . . . . . . . . . . . . . .1D 54
Cranston Av. NG5: Arn . . . . . . . . . . . . . . .4B 22
Cranston Rd. NG9: Bram . . . . . . . . . . . . . .2C 54
Cranthorne Dr. NG5: Arn . . . . . . . . . . . . . .3E 47
Crantock Gdns. NG12: Key . . . . . . . . . . . .4H 79
Cranwell Ct. NG6: Bulw . . . . . . . . . . . . . . .1F 31
Cranwell Rd. NG8: Stre . . . . . . . . . . . . . . .6D 30
Craster Dr. NG5: Arn . . . . . . . . . . . . . . . . .3C 22
  NG6: Bulw . . . . . . . . . . . . . . . . . . . .5F 19
Craven Rd. NG7: H Grn . . . . . . . . . . . . . . .2C 44
Crawford Av. NG9: Stap . . . . . . . . . . . . . . .3F 53
Crawford Cl. NG8: Woll . . . . . . . . . . . . . . .4E 43
Crawford Ri. NG5: Arn . . . . . . . . . . . . . . . .5E 23
Crawford Wlk. NG11: Clif . . . . . . . . . . . . . .3D 66
Creamery Cl. NG8: Bilb . . . . . . . . . . . . . . .2H 43
Creeton Grn. NG11: Clif . . . . . . . . . . . . . . .5D 66
Cremorne Dr. NG2: Nott . . . . . . . . . . . . . . .2F 57
Crescent, The DE7: Stan C . . . . . . . . . . . .1A 38
  DE72: Ris . . . . . . . . . . . . . . . . . . . . .2A 62
  NG3: Nott . . . . . . . . . . . . . . . . . . . .1H 45
  NG5: Woodt . . . . . . . . . . . . . . . . . . .3A 34
  NG9: Chil . . . . . . . . . . . . . . . . . . . . .2C 64
  NG9: Stap . . . . . . . . . . . . . . . . . . . .2G 53
  NG9: Toton . . . . . . . . . . . . . . . . . . . .3A 64
  NG12: Rad T . . . . . . . . . . . . . . . . . .6G 49
  NG16: Eastw . . . . . . . . . . . . . . . . . .2C 16
Crescent Av. NG4: Carl . . . . . . . . . . . . . . .6G 35
Cresswell Rd. NG9: Chil . . . . . . . . . . . . . . .6B 54
Cressy Rd. NG11: Clif . . . . . . . . . . . . . . . . .3D 66
Cresta Gdns. NG3: Mapp . . . . . . . . . . . . .5H 33
Crest Vw. NG5: Sher . . . . . . . . . . . . . . . . .4F 33
Crewe Cl. NG7: Radf . . . . . . . . . . . . . . . . .3D 44
Cribb Cl. NG11: Wilf . . . . . . . . . . . . . . . . . .4F 57
Crich Vw. NG5: Sher . . . . . . . . . . . . . . . . .5G 33
Cricketers Ct. NG2: West Br . . . . . . . . . . .2B 58
Criftin Ent. Cen. NG14: Epp . . . . . . . . . . . .3D 12
Criftin Rd. NG14: Bur J . . . . . . . . . . . . . . .3G 37
Cripps Hill NG7: Nott . . . . . . . . . . . . . . . . .1A 56
Critchley St. DE7: Ilk . . . . . . . . . . . . . . . . .6B 28
Critch's Flats NG16: Kimb . . . . . . . . . . . . .1H 29
Crocus Pl. NG2: Nott . . . . . . . . . . . . . . . . .6H 45
Crocus St. NG2: Nott . . . . . . . . . . . . . . . . .1G 57
Croft Av. NG15: Huck . . . . . . . . . . . . . . . . .6G 7
Croft Cres. NG16: Aws . . . . . . . . . . . . . . . .2E 29

Crofton Cl. NG8: Bilb . . . . . . . . . . . . . . . . .3H 43
  NG9: Chil . . . . . . . . . . . . . . . . . . . . .3D 64
Crofton Rd. NG9: Chil . . . . . . . . . . . . . . . . .2D 64
Croft Rd. NG5: Arn . . . . . . . . . . . . . . . . . .5B 22
  NG12: Edwal . . . . . . . . . . . . . . . . . .1C 68
  NG12: Key . . . . . . . . . . . . . . . . . . . .4F 79
Crofts, The NG13: Bing . . . . . . . . . . . . . . .5E 51
Cromdale Cl. NG5: Arn . . . . . . . . . . . . . . . .4E 23
Cromer Rd. NG3: Nott . . . . . . . . . . . . . . . .2A 46
Cromford Av. NG4: Carl . . . . . . . . . . . . . . .1F 47
Cromford Cl. NG10: Long E . . . . . . . . . . . .2C 72
  NG16: Lang M . . . . . . . . . . . . . . . . .1F 15
Cromford Rd. NG2: West Br . . . . . . . . . . . .5B 58
  NG16: Lang M . . . . . . . . . . . . . . . . .1D 14
                    (not continuous)
Cromford Rd. Ind. Est. NG16: Lang M . . . . .1F 15
Crompton Rd. DE7: Ilk, Stant D . . . . . . . . .1D 52
Crompton Rd. Ind. Est. DE7: Ilk . . . . . . . . .6C 40
Cromwell Av. DE7: Ilk . . . . . . . . . . . . . . . . .4C 40
Cromwell Rd. NG9: Bee . . . . . . . . . . . . . . .4E 55
Cromwell St. NG4: Carl . . . . . . . . . . . . . . .2G 47
  NG7: Radf . . . . . . . . . . . . . . .2A 4 (4E 45)
  NG16: Gilt . . . . . . . . . . . . . . . . . . . .5D 16
Cromwell Ter. DE7: Ilk . . . . . . . . . . . . . . . .4B 28
Crookdole La. NG14: Calv . . . . . . . . . . . . . .4H 11
Cropston Cl. NG2: West Br . . . . . . . . . . . . .1A 68
Cropton Cres. NG8: Bilb . . . . . . . . . . . . . . .3H 43
Cropton Gro. NG13: Bing . . . . . . . . . . . . . .5C 50
Cropwell Gdns. NG12: Rad T . . . . . . . . . . .1G 61
Cropwell Grn. NG3: Nott . . . . . . . . . . . . . .3B 46
Cropwell Rd. NG12: Rad T . . . . . . . . . . . . .6F 49
Crosby Rd. NG2: West Br . . . . . . . . . . . . . .2B 58
Cross, The NG12: Cotg . . . . . . . . . . . . . . .2E 71
Crossdale Dr. NG12: Key . . . . . . . . . . . . . .3G 79
Crossdale Wlk. NG5: Top V . . . . . . . . . . . .5C 20
Crossfield Ct. NG5: Top V . . . . . . . . . . . . . .5E 21
Crossfield Dr. NG5: Top V . . . . . . . . . . . . . .5E 21
Crossgate Dr. NG2: Nott . . . . . . . . . . . . . .3E 57
Crosshill NG12: Cotg . . . . . . . . . . . . . . . . .2G 71
Crosshill Dr. DE7: Kirk H . . . . . . . . . . . . . .4F 39
Crossland Rd. NG5: Bestw . . . . . . . . . . . . .2E 33
Crosslands Mdw. NG4: Colw . . . . . . . . . . .5H 47
Crossley St. NG5: Sher . . . . . . . . . . . . . . .5F 33
Crossman St. NG5: Sher . . . . . . . . . . . . . .5F 33
Cross St. NG4: Carl . . . . . . . . . . . . . . . . . .1F 47
  NG4: Neth . . . . . . . . . . . . . . . . . . . .5H 21
  NG5: Arn . . . . . . . . . . . . . . . . . . . . .5H 21
  NG9: Bee . . . . . . . . . . . . . . . . . . . . .4F 55
  NG10: Long E . . . . . . . . . . . . . . . . .5G 63
  NG10: Sand . . . . . . . . . . . . . . . . . . .5A 52
  NG16: Eastw . . . . . . . . . . . . . . . . . .3C 16
Crowborough Av. NG8: Woll . . . . . . . . . . . .1E 55
Crowcroft Way NG10: Long E . . . . . . . . . . .3D 62
Crow Ct. NG13: Bing . . . . . . . . . . . . . . . . .5G 51
Crow Hill Rd. NG4: Carl . . . . . . . . . . . . . . .2H 47
Crowley Cl. NG8: Bilb . . . . . . . . . . . . . . . . .3C 42
Crown Cl. NG10: Long E . . . . . . . . . . . . . . .6C 62
**Crown Court**
  **Nottingham** . . . . . . . . . . . . . . .6E 5 (6G 45)
Crown Hill Way DE7: Stan C . . . . . . . . . . .1A 38
Crown Way NG16: Lang M . . . . . . . . . . . . .1F 15
Crow Pk. Dr. NG14: Bur J . . . . . . . . . . . . . .4E 37
Crowthorne Cl. NG5: Top V . . . . . . . . . . . .4C 20
Crowthorne Gdns. NG5: Top V . . . . . . . . . .4C 20
Croxall Cl. NG11: Clif . . . . . . . . . . . . . . . . .1C 66
Croxley Gdns. NG16: Nuth . . . . . . . . . . . . .4D 30
Croydon Rd. NG7: Radf . . . . . . . . . . . . . . .4C 44
Crummock Cl. NG9: Bram . . . . . . . . . . . . .3C 54
Crusader Ct. NG11: Clif . . . . . . . . . . . . . . .4A 66
Crusader Ho. NG1: Nott . . . . . . . .3E 5 (5G 45)
Cudworth Dr. NG3: Mapp . . . . . . . . . . . . . .5B 34
Cuillin Cl. NG5: Top V . . . . . . . . . . . . . . . . .3D 20
  NG10: Long E . . . . . . . . . . . . . . . . .4C 62
Culbert Lodge NG7: Basf . . . . . . . . . . . . . .6D 32
Culbert Pl. NG7: Basf . . . . . . . . . . . . . . . . .6D 32
Cullens Ct. NG5: Sher . . . . . . . . . . . . . . . .5G 33
Cumberland Av. NG9: Bee . . . . . . . . . . . . .5D 54
Cumberland Cl. NG11: Rudd . . . . . . . . . . . .6H 67
Cumberland Pl. NG1: Nott . . . . . .4C 4 (5F 45)
Cumbria Grange NG2: Gam . . . . . . . . . . . .4E 59
Curie Ct. NG7: Nott . . . . . . . . . . . . . . . . . .1C 56
Curlew Cl. NG3: Nott . . . . . . . . . . . . . . . . .4E 47
Curlew Wharf NG7: Lent . . . . . . . . . . . . . . .1E 57
Cursley Way NG9: Chil . . . . . . . . . . . . . . . .3C 64
Curtis St. NG15: Huck . . . . . . . . . . . . . . . . .5G 7
Curzon Av. NG4: Carl . . . . . . . . . . . . . . . . .2D 46
Curzon Ct. NG3: Nott . . . . . . . . . .1G 5 (3H 45)
Curzon Gdns. NG3: Nott . . . . . . . .1G 5 (3H 45)
Curzon Pl. NG3: Nott . . . . . . . . . .2F 5 (4H 45)
Curzon St. NG3: Nott . . . . . . . . . .2F 5 (4H 45)
  NG4: Neth . . . . . . . . . . . . . . . . . . . .2A 48
  NG10: Long E . . . . . . . . . . . . . . . . .3D 62
  NG11: Goth . . . . . . . . . . . . . . . . . . .6H 75
Cuthrough La. NG7: Nott . . . . . . . . . . . . . .3H 55
Cutlers Ct. NG12: Rad T . . . . . . . . . . . . . . .6E 49
Cuxton Cl. NG8: Stre . . . . . . . . . . . . . . . . .6D 30

Cycle Rd. NG7: Lent . . . . . . . . . . . . . . . . . .5C 44
Cypress Ct. NG15: Huck . . . . . . . . . . . . . . .6C 6
Cyprus Av. NG9: Bee . . . . . . . . . . . . . . . . .4F 55
Cyprus Ct. NG3: Mapp P . . . . . . . . . . . . . .1G 45
Cyprus Dr. NG9: Bee . . . . . . . . . . . . . . . . .4F 55
Cyprus Rd. NG3: Mapp P . . . . . . . . . . . . . .1G 45
Cyril Av. NG8: Aspl . . . . . . . . . . . . . . . . . . .1B 44
  NG9: Bee . . . . . . . . . . . . . . . . . . . . .4E 55
  NG9: Stap . . . . . . . . . . . . . . . . . . . .4F 53
Cyril Cotts. NG8: Aspl . . . . . . . . . . . . . . . . .1B 44
Cyril Rd. NG2: West Br . . . . . . . . . . . . . . . .3C 58
Cyril's Nut Hut Indoor Play Cen. . . . . . . . . .1G 73

## D

Dabell Av. NG6: Bulw . . . . . . . . . . . . . . . . .5E 19
Dagmar Gro. NG3: Nott . . . . . . . . . . . . . . .6H 33
  NG9: Bee . . . . . . . . . . . . . . . . . . . . .5G 55
Dairy Sq. NG8: Bilb . . . . . . . . . . . . . . . . . .2H 43
Daisy Cl. NG12: Cotg . . . . . . . . . . . . . . . . .3E 71
Daisy Farm Rd. NG16: Newth . . . . . . . . . . .4D 16
Daisy Rd. NG3: Nott . . . . . . . . . . . . . . . . . .6C 34
Dakeyne St. NG3: Nott . . . . . . . . .3H 5 (4A 46)
Dalbeattie Cl. NG5: Arn . . . . . . . . . . . . . . .5D 22
Dalby Sq. NG8: Woll . . . . . . . . . . . . . . . . . .6A 44
DALE ABBEY . . . . . . . . . . . . . . . . . . . . . . .6D 38
Dale Av. NG3: Mapp . . . . . . . . . . . . . . . . . .5C 34
  NG4: Carl . . . . . . . . . . . . . . . . . . . . .2E 47
  NG10: Long E . . . . . . . . . . . . . . . . .4F 63
Dalebrook Cres. NG15: Huck . . . . . . . . . . . .5C 6
Dale Cl. DE72: Brea . . . . . . . . . . . . . . . . . .5A 62
  NG2: West Br . . . . . . . . . . . . . . . . . .4D 58
  NG15: Huck . . . . . . . . . . . . . . . . . . .5C 6
Dale Farm Av. NG3: Nott . . . . . . . . . . . . . .4C 46
Dale Gro. NG2: Nott . . . . . . . . . . . . . . . . . .5B 46
Dalehead Rd. NG11: Clif . . . . . . . . . . . . . . .3B 66
Dale La. DE7: D Ab . . . . . . . . . . . . . . . . . .6D 38
  NG9: Chil . . . . . . . . . . . . . . . . . . . . .5E 55
Dalemoor Gdns. NG8: Bilb . . . . . . . . . . . . .1H 43
Dale Rd. DE7: D Ab, Stant D . . . . . . . . . . .2A 52
  DE7: Stan . . . . . . . . . . . . . . . . . . . . .4A 38
  NG4: Carl . . . . . . . . . . . . . . . . . . . . .2E 47
  NG12: Key . . . . . . . . . . . . . . . . . . . .4G 79
  NG16: Kimb . . . . . . . . . . . . . . . . . . .2H 29
Dales, The DE7: West H . . . . . . . . . . . . . . .2C 38
Daleside NG12: Cotg . . . . . . . . . . . . . . . . .3E 71
Daleside Rd. NG2: Nott . . . . . . . . . . . . . . . .6B 46
Daleside Rd. E. NG2: Nott . . . . . . . . . . . . .5D 46
Dale St. DE7: Ilk . . . . . . . . . . . . . . . . . . . . .2B 40
  NG2: Nott . . . . . . . . . . . . . . . . . . . . .5A 46
Dale Ter. NG2: Nott . . . . . . . . . . . . . . . . . .5B 46
Dale Vw. DE7: Ilk . . . . . . . . . . . . . . . . . . . .3A 40
Dale Vw. Rd. NG3: Nott . . . . . . . . . . . . . . .2D 46
Dalkeith Ter. NG7: H Grn . . . . . . . . . . . . . .2D 44
Dallaglio M. NG9: Chil . . . . . . . . . . . . . . . . .3B 64
Dallas York Rd. NG9: Bee . . . . . . . . . . . . .5H 55
Dalley Cl. NG9: Stap . . . . . . . . . . . . . . . . . .4G 53
Dallimore Rd. DE7: Kirk H . . . . . . . . . . . . . .5H 39
Dallman Cl. NG15: Huck . . . . . . . . . . . . . . . .6G 7
Dalton Cl. NG9: Stap . . . . . . . . . . . . . . . . .6G 53
Daltons Cl. NG16: Lang M . . . . . . . . . . . . . .1E 15
Damson Wlk. NG3: Nott . . . . . . . . . . . . . . .1D 46
Danbury Mt. NG5: Sher . . . . . . . . . . . . . . .5H 33
Dane Cl. NG3: Nott . . . . . . . . . . . . . . . . . . .1F 5
Dane Ct. NG3: Nott . . . . . . . . . . . .1F 5 (3H 45)
Danehurst Dr. NG4: Ged . . . . . . . . . . . . . . .6A 36
Danes Cl. NG5: Arn . . . . . . . . . . . . . . . . . .5H 21
Danethorpe Va. NG5: Sher . . . . . . . . . . . . .3G 33
Daniel M. NG10: Sand . . . . . . . . . . . . . . . .6C 52
Daniels Cl. NG16: Eastw . . . . . . . . . . . . . . .4B 16
Daniels Way NG15: Huck . . . . . . . . . . . . . .1E 19
Dann Pl. NG11: Wilf . . . . . . . . . . . . . . . . . .3F 57
Darfield Dr. DE75: Hea . . . . . . . . . . . . . . . .3E 15
Darkey La. NG9: Stap . . . . . . . . . . . . . . . . .4G 53
                    (not continuous)
Darley Av. NG4: Carl . . . . . . . . . . . . . . . . . .6G 35
  NG7: H Grn . . . . . . . . . . . . . . . . . . . .2C 44
  NG9: Toton . . . . . . . . . . . . . . . . . . . .2G 63
Darley Dr. DE7: West H . . . . . . . . . . . . . . .1C 38
  NG10: Long E . . . . . . . . . . . . . . . . .2C 72
Darley Rd. NG7: H Grn . . . . . . . . . . . . . . . .2C 44
Darley Sq. DE7: Ilk . . . . . . . . . . . . . . . . . . .2A 28
Darlison St. NG15: Huck . . . . . . . . . . . . . . . .3G 7
                        (off Ogle St.)
Darlton Dr. NG5: Arn . . . . . . . . . . . . . . . . . .6C 22
Darnal Cl. NG5: Top V . . . . . . . . . . . . . . . . .6C 20
Darnhall Cres. NG8: Bilb . . . . . . . . . . . . . . .2D 42
Daron Gdns. NG5: Bestw . . . . . . . . . . . . . .6E 21
Dart Ct. NG13: Bing . . . . . . . . . . . . . . . . . .6D 50
Dartmeet Rd. NG7: Radf . . . . . . . . . . . . . . .2B 44
Dartmoor Cl. NG11: Clif . . . . . . . . . . . . . . .5B 66
Darvel Cl. NG8: Bilb . . . . . . . . . . . . . . . . . .3H 43
Darwin Av. DE7: Ilk . . . . . . . . . . . . . . . . . . .2A 40
Darwin Cl. NG5: Top V . . . . . . . . . . . . . . . .5C 20

Darwin Rd. NG10: Long E . . . . . . . . . . . . . . .2D 72
David Gro. NG9: Bram . . . . . . . . . . . . . . . . .2D 54
David La. NG6: Basf . . . . . . . . . . . . . . . . . . .4B 32
David Lane Stop (NET) . . . . . . . . . . . . . . . .4B 32
David Lloyd Leisure
 Nottingham . . . . . . . . . . . . . . . . . . . . . .2B 44
 West Bridgford . . . . . . . . . . . . . . . . . . . .5H 57
Davidson Cl. NG5: Arn . . . . . . . . . . . . . . . .6E 23
Davidson Gdns. NG11: Rudd . . . . . . . . . . . .6E 67
Davidson St. NG2: Nott . . . . . . . . . . . . . . . .6B 46
Davies Rd. NG2: West Br . . . . . . . . . . . . . .4B 58
Davies Way NG5: Bestw . . . . . . . . . . . . . . .2E 33
Davis Rd. NG9: Chil . . . . . . . . . . . . . . . . . .2B 64
Davy Cl. NG15: Lin . . . . . . . . . . . . . . . . . . .1H 7
Dawes Way NG7: Lent . . . . . . . . . . . . . . . .4C 44
Dawlish Cl. NG3: Mapp . . . . . . . . . . . . . . . .2E 35
 NG15: Huck . . . . . . . . . . . . . . . . . . . . . . .5D 6
Dawlish Ct. NG3: Mapp . . . . . . . . . . . . . . . .1F 35
 NG16: Eastw . . . . . . . . . . . . . . . . . . . . . .2H 15
Dawlish Dr. NG5: Bestw . . . . . . . . . . . . . . .2F 33
Dawn Cl. NG15: Huck . . . . . . . . . . . . . . . . . .2A 8
Dawn Vw. NG9: Trow . . . . . . . . . . . . . . . . .1F 53
Dawson Cl. NG16: Newth . . . . . . . . . . . . . .4C 16
Dawver Rd. NG16: Kimb . . . . . . . . . . . . . . .1H 29
DAYBROOK . . . . . . . . . . . . . . . . . . . . . . . .1A 34
Daybrook Av. NG5: Sher . . . . . . . . . . . . . . .4G 33
Daybrook Bus. Cen. NG5: Arn . . . . . . . . . . .1H 33
DAYBROOK SQUARE . . . . . . . . . . . . . . . . .1A 34
Daybrook St. NG5: Sher . . . . . . . . . . . . . . .4G 33
Deabill Ct. NG4: Neth . . . . . . . . . . . . . . . . .3A 48
Deabill St. NG4: Neth . . . . . . . . . . . . . . . . .3A 48
Dead La. NG16: Coss . . . . . . . . . . . . . . . . .6F 29
Deakins Pl. NG7: Radf . . . . . . . . . . . . . . . . .4C 44
Deal Gdns. NG6: Bulw . . . . . . . . . . . . . . . .6F 19
Dean Av. NG3: Mapp . . . . . . . . . . . . . . . . .4D 34
Dean Cl. NG8: Woll . . . . . . . . . . . . . . . . . . .4D 42
Deane Ct. NG11: Wilf . . . . . . . . . . . . . . . . .5E 57
Deane Rd. NG11: Wilf . . . . . . . . . . . . . . . . .5E 57
Dean Rd. NG5: Woodt . . . . . . . . . . . . . . . .2A 34
Deans Ct. NG12: Cotg . . . . . . . . . . . . . . . . .2G 71
Deans Cft. NG9: Bram . . . . . . . . . . . . . . . . .2B 54
Dean St. NG1: Nott . . . . . . . . . . . . . . .5G 5 (5H 45)
 NG16: Lang M . . . . . . . . . . . . . . . . . . . . .2G 15
Debdale La. NG12: Key . . . . . . . . . . . . . . . .4F 79
De Buseli Cl. NG4: Ged . . . . . . . . . . . . . . . .6A 36
Deddington La. NG9: Bram . . . . . . . . . . . . .1B 54
Deeley Cl. NG16: Want . . . . . . . . . . . . . . . .5A 18
Deepdale Av. NG9: Stap . . . . . . . . . . . . . . .5F 53
Deepdale Cl. NG2: Gam . . . . . . . . . . . . . . .4E 59
Deepdale Ct. DE75: Hea . . . . . . . . . . . . . . .4C 14
Deepdale Rd. NG8: Woll . . . . . . . . . . . . . . .5D 42
 NG10: Long E . . . . . . . . . . . . . . . . . . . . .1C 72
Deepdene Cl. NG8: Brox . . . . . . . . . . . . . . .5G 31
Deepdene Way NG8: Brox, Cin . . . . . . . . . .5G 31
Deep Furrow Av. NG4: Carl . . . . . . . . . . . . .1F 47
Deering Ct. NG2: Nott . . . . . . . . . . . . . . . . .1F 57
Deerleap Dr. NG5: Arn . . . . . . . . . . . . . . . . .6G 21
Deer Pk. NG8: Woll . . . . . . . . . . . . . . . . . . .5E 43
Deer Pk. Dr. NG5: Arn . . . . . . . . . . . . . . . . .5F 21
Delia Av. NG15: Huck . . . . . . . . . . . . . . . . . .2A 8
Dell Way NG11: Clif . . . . . . . . . . . . . . . . . .3D 66
Dellwood Cl. NG4: Carl . . . . . . . . . . . . . . . .5D 34
Delta Cl. NG1: Nott . . . . . . . . . . . . . . . . . . .3G 45
Delta St. NG7: Basf . . . . . . . . . . . . . . . . . . .6D 32
Deltic Cl. NG16: Want . . . . . . . . . . . . . . . . .6A 18
Delves Ct. NG5: Hea . . . . . . . . . . . . . . . . . .5C 14
Delves Rd. DE75: Hea . . . . . . . . . . . . . . . . .5B 14
Delville Av. NG12: Key . . . . . . . . . . . . . . . .3G 79
Denacre Av. NG10: Long E . . . . . . . . . . . . .4H 63
Denbury Ct. NG3: Mapp . . . . . . . . . . . . . . .2F 35
Denby Ct. NG4: Neth . . . . . . . . . . . . . . . . . .2A 48
Denby Hall Rd. DE7: Ilk . . . . . . . . . . . . . . . .1A 28
Denehurst Av. NG8: Aspl . . . . . . . . . . . . . . .6A 32
Denewood Av. NG9: Bram . . . . . . . . . . . . .1C 54
Denewood Cres. NG8: Bilb . . . . . . . . . . . . .1E 43
Denholme Rd. NG8: Bilb . . . . . . . . . . . . . . .4D 42
Denison Ct. NG7: Radf . . . . . . . . . . . . . . . .3D 44
Denison St. NG7: Radf . . . . . . . . . . . . . . . .3D 44
 NG9: Bee . . . . . . . . . . . . . . . . . . . . . . . .4E 55
Denman St. Central
 NG7: Radf . . . . . . . . . . . . . . . . . . . . . . .4C 44
Denman St. E. NG7: Radf . . . . . . . . . . . . . .4C 44
Denman St. W. NG7: Radf . . . . . . . . . . . . . .4C 44
Denmark Gro. NG3: Nott . . . . . . . . . . . . . . .6H 33
Dennett Cl. NG3: Nott . . . . . . . . . .1H 5 (3A 46)
Dennis Av. NG9: Bee . . . . . . . . . . . . . . . . . .3E 55
Dennis St. NG4: Neth . . . . . . . . . . . . . . . . .2A 48
Denstone Rd. NG3: Nott . . . . . . . . . . . . . . .4A 46
Dentdale Dr. NG8: Woll . . . . . . . . . . . . . . . .5B 42
Denton Av. NG10: Sand . . . . . . . . . . . . . . . .5C 52
Denton Dr. NG2: West Br . . . . . . . . . . . . . .1H 67
Denton Grn. NG8: Brox . . . . . . . . . . . . . . . .5F 31
Denver Ct. NG9: Stap . . . . . . . . . . . . . . . . .2G 53
Denz Childrens Play Cen. . . . . . . . . . . . . . . .5H 55
Depedale Av. DE7: Kirk H . . . . . . . . . . . . . .4H 39
Deptford Cres. NG6: Bulw . . . . . . . . . . . . . .1A 32
Derby Gro. NG7: Lent, Radf . . . . . . . . . . . . .4D 44

Derby Rd. DE7: Ilk . . . . . . . . . . . . . . . . . . . .2G 39
 DE7: Stan . . . . . . . . . . . . . . . . . . . . . . . .4A 38
 DE72: Ris . . . . . . . . . . . . . . . . . . . . . . . . .1A 62
 DE75: Hea . . . . . . . . . . . . . . . . . . . . . . . .4B 14
 (not continuous)
 NG1: Nott . . . . . . . . . . . . . . . . . . . .3A 4 (4E 45)
 NG7: Lent, Nott . . . . . . . . . . . . . . . . . . . .1B 56
 NG9: Bee, Bram, Nott . . . . . . . . . . .3A 4 (3A 54)
 NG9: Lent, Nott . . . . . . . . . . . . . . . . . . . .2F 55
 NG9: Stap . . . . . . . . . . . . . . . . . . . . . . . .6E 53
 NG10: Long E . . . . . . . . . . . . . . . . . . . . .5C 62
 NG10: Sand . . . . . . . . . . . . . . . . . . . . . .1A 62
 NG16: Eastw . . . . . . . . . . . . . . . . . . . . . .3H 15
 NG16: Lang M . . . . . . . . . . . . . . . . . . . . .2G 15
Derby Rd. Ind. Est. DE75: Hea . . . . . . . . . . .4B 14
 NG10: Sand . . . . . . . . . . . . . . . . . . . . . .6D 52
Derbyshire Av. DE7: West H . . . . . . . . . . . . .1C 38
 NG9: Trow . . . . . . . . . . . . . . . . . . . . . . . .5F 41
Derbyshire Cl. DE7: West H . . . . . . . . . . . . .1C 38
Derbyshire Cres. NG8: Woll . . . . . . . . . . . . .4G 43
Derbyshire Dr. DE7: Ilk . . . . . . . . . . . . . . . .3A 40
Derbyshire La. NG15: Huck . . . . . . . . . . . . . .4G 7
Derby St. DE7: Ilk . . . . . . . . . . . . . . . . . . . .1B 40
 NG1: Nott . . . . . . . . . . . . . . . . . . . .3B 4 (4F 45)
 NG5: Arn . . . . . . . . . . . . . . . . . . . . . . . .6B 22
 NG9: Bee . . . . . . . . . . . . . . . . . . . . . . . .4F 55
Derby Ter. NG7: Nott . . . . . . . . . . . . .3A 4 (4E 45)
Dereham Dr. NG5: Arn . . . . . . . . . . . . . . . .1B 34
Derry Dr. NG5: Arn . . . . . . . . . . . . . . . . . . .3B 22
Derry Hill Rd. NG5: Arn . . . . . . . . . . . . . . . .4A 22
Derry La. NG13: Bing . . . . . . . . . . . . . . . . .6H 51
Derwent Av. DE7: Ilk . . . . . . . . . . . . . . . . . .5H 27
 DE7: West H . . . . . . . . . . . . . . . . . . . . . .1C 38
Derwent Cl. NG2: Gam . . . . . . . . . . . . . . . .4E 59
 NG9: Atten . . . . . . . . . . . . . . . . . . . . . . .2E 65
Derwent Ct. NG7: Radf . . . . . . . . . . . . . . . .3E 45
Derwent Cres. NG5: Arn . . . . . . . . . . . . . . .1C 34
Derwent Dr. NG15: Huck . . . . . . . . . . . . . . .1G 19
Derwent St. NG10: Long E . . . . . . . . . . . . . .1E 73
Derwent St. Ind. Est. NG10: Long E . . . . . . .1E 73
Derwent Ter. NG5: Sher . . . . . . . . . . . . . . . .5G 33
Derwent Way NG7: Lent . . . . . . . . . . . . . . .5B 44
Desford Cl. NG5: Sher . . . . . . . . . . . . . . . . .3E 33
De Vere Gdns. NG5: Woodt . . . . . . . . . . . . .2B 34
Devitt Dr. NG15: Huck . . . . . . . . . . . . . . . . . .2A 8
Devon Cir. NG5: Redh . . . . . . . . . . . . . . . . .4H 21
Devon Cl. NG10: Sand . . . . . . . . . . . . . . . .6D 52
 NG16: Newth . . . . . . . . . . . . . . . . . . . . . .3D 16
Devon Dr. NG5: Sher . . . . . . . . . . . . . . . . .5F 33
 NG11: Rudd . . . . . . . . . . . . . . . . . . . . . .5H 67
Devonshire Av. NG9: Bee . . . . . . . . . . . . . .5F 55
 NG10: Long E . . . . . . . . . . . . . . . . . . . . .5A 64
Devonshire Cl. DE7: Ilk . . . . . . . . . . . . . . . .2A 28
Devonshire Cres. NG5: Sher . . . . . . . . . . . . .5F 33
Devonshire Dr. NG9: Stap . . . . . . . . . . . . . .1F 53
 NG16: Eastw . . . . . . . . . . . . . . . . . . . . . .3B 16
Devonshire Prom. NG7: Lent . . . . . . . . . . . .6C 44
Devonshire Rd. NG2: West Br . . . . . . . . . . .5A 58
 NG5: Sher . . . . . . . . . . . . . . . . . . . . . . . .5F 33
Devon St. DE7: Ilk . . . . . . . . . . . . . . . . . . .4C 40
 NG3: Nott . . . . . . . . . . . . . . . . . . . . . . . .4B 46
Dewberry La. NG12: Rad T . . . . . . . . . . . . .1H 61
Dexters Gro. NG15: Huck . . . . . . . . . . . . . . .4F 7
DH Lawrence Birthplace Mus. . . . . . . . . . .2B 16
DH Lawrence Craft Cen. . . . . . . . . . . . . . .2B 16
 (off Scargill Wlk.)
DH Lawrence 'Sons & Lovers' Cottage . . . . .2C 16
Dial, The NG2: Cotg . . . . . . . . . . . . . . . . . .4E 71
Diamond Cl. NG10: Long E . . . . . . . . . . . . .2C 72
Dickens Ct. NG16: Newth . . . . . . . . . . . . . .2D 16
Dicks La. NG16: Newth . . . . . . . . . . . . . . . .2E 17
Dickson Dr. NG11: Rudd . . . . . . . . . . . . . . .1H 77
Didcot Dr. NG8: Basf . . . . . . . . . . . . . . . . . .6B 32
Digby Av. NG3: Mapp . . . . . . . . . . . . . . . . .4D 34
Digby Ct. NG7: Lent . . . . . . . . . . . . . . . . . .6D 44
Digby Hall Dr. NG4: Ged . . . . . . . . . . . . . . .4E 35
Digby Ind. Est. NG16: Kimb . . . . . . . . . . . . .6F 17
Digby St. DE7: Ilk . . . . . . . . . . . . . . . . . . . .6C 28
 NG16: Kimb . . . . . . . . . . . . . . . . . . . . . . .1F 29
Dirac Cl. NG11: Clif . . . . . . . . . . . . . . . . . . .5A 66
Diseworth Gro. NG2: Nott . . . . . . . . . . . . . .2H 57
Disraeli Cres. DE7: Ilk . . . . . . . . . . . . . . . . .1B 40
Distillery St. NG11: Rudd . . . . . . . . . . . . . . .1G 77
Djanogly Community Leisure Cen. . . . . . . . .2E 45
DOBPARK . . . . . . . . . . . . . . . . . . . . . . . . . .3F 7
Dockholm Rd. NG10: Long E . . . . . . . . . . . .3E 63
Dodford Ct. DE75: Hea . . . . . . . . . . . . . . . .4E 15
Dogwood Av. NG6: Bulw . . . . . . . . . . . . . . .6F 19
Dolphin Ct. NG5: Top V . . . . . . . . . . . . . . . .5E 21
Donbas Cl. NG6: Bulw . . . . . . . . . . . . . . . . .3H 31
Doncaster Av. NG10: Sand . . . . . . . . . . . . .5D 52
Doncaster Gro. NG10: Long E . . . . . . . . . . .4H 63
Doncaster Ter. NG2: Nott . . . . . . . . . . . . . . .2G 57
Donington Rd. NG11: Clif . . . . . . . . . . . . . . .4C 66
Donkey La. NG11: Rudd . . . . . . . . . . . . . . .2A 78
Donner Cres. DE7: Ilk . . . . . . . . . . . . . . . . .2A 28

Dooland Dr. NG3: Nott . . . . . . . . . . . . . . . . .6B 34
Dorchester Gdns. NG2: West Br . . . . . . . . . .2A 68
Dorchester Rd. NG16: Kimb . . . . . . . . . . . . .6H 17
Doris Cl. NG9: Toton . . . . . . . . . . . . . . . . . .3A 64
Doris Rd. DE7: Ilk . . . . . . . . . . . . . . . . . . . .2C 40
Dorket Cl. NG5: Arn . . . . . . . . . . . . . . . . . .4C 22
Dorket Dr. NG8: Woll . . . . . . . . . . . . . . . . .6B 44
DORKET HEAD . . . . . . . . . . . . . . . . . . . . .2C 22
Dorket Ho. NG4: Carl . . . . . . . . . . . . . . . . . .1G 47
 (off Garden City)
Dorking Rd. NG7: Radf . . . . . . . . . . . . . . . .3C 44
Dormy Cl. NG9: Bram . . . . . . . . . . . . . . . . .4C 54
 NG12: Rad T . . . . . . . . . . . . . . . . . . . . . .6H 49
Dormy Ct. NG6: Bulw . . . . . . . . . . . . . . . . .6B 20
Dornoch Av. NG5: Sher . . . . . . . . . . . . . . . .5H 33
Dorothy Av. NG10: Sand . . . . . . . . . . . . . . .6D 52
 NG15: Huck . . . . . . . . . . . . . . . . . . . . . . . .2H 7
 NG16: Newth . . . . . . . . . . . . . . . . . . . . . .2C 16
Dorothy Boot Homes, The NG11: Wilf . . . . .3F 57
Dorothy Gro. NG8: Aspl . . . . . . . . . . . . . . . .3A 44
Dorset Gdns. NG2: West Br . . . . . . . . . . . . .6G 57
Dorset St. NG8: Radf . . . . . . . . . . . . . . . . .4B 44
Dorterry Cres. DE7: Ilk . . . . . . . . . . . . . . . .4C 40
Douglas Av. DE75: Hea . . . . . . . . . . . . . . . .3A 14
 NG4: Carl . . . . . . . . . . . . . . . . . . . . . . . .3F 47
 NG16: Aws . . . . . . . . . . . . . . . . . . . . . . .2E 29
Douglas Cl. NG12: Rad T . . . . . . . . . . . . . . .1F 61
Douglas Cres. NG4: Carl . . . . . . . . . . . . . . .3G 47
Douglas Rd. NG7: Lent, Radf . . . . . . . . . . . .4D 44
 NG10: Long E . . . . . . . . . . . . . . . . . . . . .3D 62
 NG13: Bing . . . . . . . . . . . . . . . . . . . . . . .5H 51
Douro Dr. NG5: Arn . . . . . . . . . . . . . . . . . . .4D 22
Dove Cl. NG13: Bing . . . . . . . . . . . . . . . . . .6F 51
Dovecote Dr. NG8: Woll . . . . . . . . . . . . . . . .5E 43
Dovecote La. NG9: Bee . . . . . . . . . . . . . . . .5F 55
Dovecote Rd. NG16: Eastw, Newth . . . . . . . .3D 16
Dovecotes, The NG9: Bee . . . . . . . . . . . . . .6F 55
Dovedale Av. NG10: Long E . . . . . . . . . . . . .1D 72
Dovedale Circ. DE7: Ilk . . . . . . . . . . . . . . . .2A 28
Dovedale Rd. NG10: Long E . . . . . . . . . . . . .1D 72
Dovedale Rd. NG2: West Br . . . . . . . . . . . . .6C 58
 NG3: Nott . . . . . . . . . . . . . . . . . . . . . . . .3E 47
Dove La. NG10: Long E . . . . . . . . . . . . . . . .5E 63
Dovenby Rd. NG11: Clif . . . . . . . . . . . . . . . .2D 66
Dover Beck Cl. NG14: Calv . . . . . . . . . . . . .4A 12
Doverbeck Dr. NG14: Woodbo . . . . . . . . . . .1C 24
Doveridge Av. NG4: Carl . . . . . . . . . . . . . . .1A 48
Doveridge Rd. NG4: Carl . . . . . . . . . . . . . . .1H 47
Dove St. NG6: Bulw . . . . . . . . . . . . . . . . . . .6H 19
Doveys Orchard NG14: Calv . . . . . . . . . . . . .4F 11
Downes Cl. NG6: Bulw . . . . . . . . . . . . . . . . .6G 19
Downham Cl. NG5: Arn . . . . . . . . . . . . . . . .1C 34
Downing Gdns. NG6: Bulw . . . . . . . . . . . . . .5H 19
Downing Rd. NG6: Bulw . . . . . . . . . . . . . . . .5H 19
Downs, The NG11: Wilf . . . . . . . . . . . . . . . .1E 67
Dowson Cl. NG12: Rad T . . . . . . . . . . . . . . .5H 49
Dowson St. NG3: Nott . . . . . . . . . . . . . . . . .3B 46
Doyne Ct. NG2: Nott . . . . . . . . . . . . . . . . . .2G 57
Drakemyre Cl. NG5: Arn . . . . . . . . . . . . . . . .4D 22
Drake Rd. NG4: Neth . . . . . . . . . . . . . . . . . .3B 48
Draycott Cl. DE75: Los . . . . . . . . . . . . . . . . .1A 14
Draycott Ct. DE7: Ilk . . . . . . . . . . . . . . . . . .4B 28
Draycott Rd. DE72: Brea . . . . . . . . . . . . . . .5A 62
 NG10: Long E . . . . . . . . . . . . . . . . . . . . .2B 72
Draymans Ct. NG7: Basf . . . . . . . . . . . . . . .6D 32
Drayton St. NG5: Sher . . . . . . . . . . . . . . . . .5G 33
Drewry Island NG8: Brox . . . . . . . . . . . . . . .6F 31
Drift, The NG11: Clif . . . . . . . . . . . . . . . . . .2C 66
 NG15: Huck . . . . . . . . . . . . . . . . . . . . . . . .2H 7
Drive, The NG9: Atten . . . . . . . . . . . . . . . . .2E 65
Dronfield Pl. DE7: Ilk . . . . . . . . . . . . . . . . . .2A 28
Drummond Av. NG4: Neth . . . . . . . . . . . . . .2B 48
Drummond Dr. NG16: Nuth . . . . . . . . . . . . . .3E 31
Drummond Rd. DE7: Ilk . . . . . . . . . . . . . . . .6A 28
Drury Cl. NG15: Huck . . . . . . . . . . . . . . . . . .6D 6
Drury Wlk. NG1: Nott . . . . . . . . . . . . .5E 5 (5G 45)
Dryden Ct. NG9: Stap . . . . . . . . . . . . . . . . .2G 53
Dryden St. NG1: Nott . . . . . . . . . . .1C 4 (3F 45)
Drysdale Cl. NG6: Bulw . . . . . . . . . . . . . . . . .2H 31
Duchess Gdns. NG6: Bulw . . . . . . . . . . . . . .5H 19
Duchess St. NG6: Bulw . . . . . . . . . . . . . . . .5H 19
Dudley Ct. NG9: Bram . . . . . . . . . . . . . . . . .3A 54
Duffield Cl. NG10: Long E . . . . . . . . . . . . . .2C 72
Duffield Cl. NG5: Top V . . . . . . . . . . . . . . . .5D 20
Duke Cl. NG6: Bulw . . . . . . . . . . . . . . . . . . .2F 31
Duke Cres. NG16: Gilt . . . . . . . . . . . . . . . . .4E 17
Dukes Ct. NG15: Huck . . . . . . . . . . . . . . . . . .4H 7
Dukes Pl. DE7: Ilk . . . . . . . . . . . . . . . . . . . .3A 28
 NG1: Nott . . . . . . . . . . . . . . . . . . .4G 5 (5H 45)
Duke St. DE7: Ilk . . . . . . . . . . . . . . . . . . . . .4B 28
 NG5: Arn . . . . . . . . . . . . . . . . . . . . . . . .6H 21
 NG6: Bulw . . . . . . . . . . . . . . . . . . . . . . . .6H 19
 NG7: Basf . . . . . . . . . . . . . . . . . . . . . . . .1D 44
 NG15: Huck . . . . . . . . . . . . . . . . . . . . . . . .4H 7
Duke St. E. NG15: Huck . . . . . . . . . . . . . . . . .4H 7
Dukes Wharf NG7: Nott . . . . . . . . . . .6C 4 (6F 45)

Duke William Mt.—Elton M.

Duke William Mt. NG7: Nott . . . . . . . . . .5A 4 (5E 45)
Dulverton Va. NG8: Cin . . . . . . . . . . . . . . . . . .4G 31
Dulwich Rd. NG7: Radf . . . . . . . . . . . . . . . . . .4C 44
Dumbles, The NG4: Lamb . . . . . . . . . . . . . . . .5B 24
Dumbles Cl. DE7: Kirk H . . . . . . . . . . . . . . . . .3G 39
Dunbar Cl. NG10: Long E . . . . . . . . . . . . . . . . .3G 73
Dunblane Rd. NG11: Rudd . . . . . . . . . . . . . . . .1G 77
Duncombe Cl. NG3: Nott . . . . . . . . . . . . . . . . .2A 46
Duncroft Av. NG4: Ged . . . . . . . . . . . . . . . . . .6H 35
Dundas Cl. NG1: Nott . . . . . . . . . . . . . . .1D 4 (3G 45)
Dunelm Dr. NG14: Calv . . . . . . . . . . . . . . . . . .4A 12
Dungannon Rd. NG11: Clif . . . . . . . . . . . . . . . .5C 66
Dunholme Cl. NG6: Bulw . . . . . . . . . . . . . . . . .5H 19
Dunkery Rd. NG11: Clif . . . . . . . . . . . . . . . . . .5D 66
DUNKIRK . . . . . . . . . . . . . . . . . . . . . . . . . . .1C 56
Dunkirk Pl. NG7: Lent . . . . . . . . . . . . . . . . . . .2C 56
Dunkirk Rd. NG7: Lent . . . . . . . . . . . . . . . . . .2C 56
(not continuous)
Dunlin Wharf NG7: Lent . . . . . . . . . . . . . . . . . .1E 57
Dunlop Av. NG7: Lent . . . . . . . . . . . . . . . . . . .5C 44
Dunn Dr. NG10: Long E . . . . . . . . . . . . . . . . . .6D 62
Dunoon Cl. NG5: Top V . . . . . . . . . . . . . . . . . .3C 20
Dunsby Cl. NG11: Clif . . . . . . . . . . . . . . . . . . .4C 66
Dunsford Dr. NG3: Mapp . . . . . . . . . . . . . . . . .1F 35
Dunsil Dr. NG2: Nott . . . . . . . . . . . . . . . . . . . .3E 57
Dunsil Rd. NG16: Newth . . . . . . . . . . . . . . . . .1D 16
Dunsmore Cl. NG9: Bee . . . . . . . . . . . . . . . . . .1H 65
Dunstan St. NG4: Neth . . . . . . . . . . . . . . . . . .2A 48
(not continuous)
Dunster Rd. NG2: West Br . . . . . . . . . . . . . . . .5C 58
NG16: Newth . . . . . . . . . . . . . . . . . . . . . . .3D 16
Dunston Cl. NG10: Long E . . . . . . . . . . . . . . . .6H 63
Dunvegan Dr. NG5: Top V . . . . . . . . . . . . . . . .3D 20
Durban House Heritage Cen. . . . . . . . . . . . . .2A 16
Durham Av. NG2: Nott . . . . . . . . . . . . . . . . . . .5B 46
Durham Chambers NG1: Nott . . . . . . . . . . . . . . .4E 5
Durham Cl. NG2: Nott . . . . . . . . . . . . . . . . . . .5B 46
Durham Cres. NG6: Bulw . . . . . . . . . . . . . . . . .1A 32
Durham Ho. NG3: Mapp P . . . . . . . . . . . . . . . .1G 45
Durham St. DE7: Ilk . . . . . . . . . . . . . . . . . . . .6B 28
Durlston Cl. NG2: West Br . . . . . . . . . . . . . . . .6F 57
Durnford St. NG7: Basf . . . . . . . . . . . . . . . . . .5D 32
Dursley Cl. NG6: Bulw . . . . . . . . . . . . . . . . . .2H 31
Dyce Cl. NG6: Bulw . . . . . . . . . . . . . . . . . . . . .6F 19
Dylan M. NG8: Bilb . . . . . . . . . . . . . . . . . . . . .1E 43
Dylan Thomas Rd. NG5: Bestw . . . . . . . . . . . . .5F 21

## E

Eagle Cl. NG5: Arn . . . . . . . . . . . . . . . . . . . . .6C 22
NG9: Bee . . . . . . . . . . . . . . . . . . . . . . . . .3D 54
Eagle Ct. NG6: Bulw . . . . . . . . . . . . . . . . . . . .6B 20
Eagle Rd. DE7: Ilk . . . . . . . . . . . . . . . . . . . . .5B 40
Ealing Av. NG6: Basf . . . . . . . . . . . . . . . . . . . .3B 32
Eames Cl. DE75: Hea . . . . . . . . . . . . . . . . . . .4B 14
Eardley Rd. NG5: Bestw . . . . . . . . . . . . . . . . .1C 32
Earl Cres. NG4: Ged . . . . . . . . . . . . . . . . . . . .4H 35
Earl Dr. NG16: Gilt . . . . . . . . . . . . . . . . . . . . .4E 17
Earlham Cl. DE7: Kirk H . . . . . . . . . . . . . . . . .3G 39
Earls Cl. NG8: Bilb . . . . . . . . . . . . . . . . . . . . .4C 42
Earlsfield Dr. NG5: Top V . . . . . . . . . . . . . . . .4B 20
Earlswood Dr. NG12: Edwal . . . . . . . . . . . . . . .1D 68
Easedale Cl. NG2: Gam . . . . . . . . . . . . . . . . . .4E 59
Easegill Ct. *NG5: Top V* . . . . . . . . . . . . . . . . .*5D 20*
*(off Aveline Cl.)*
East Acres NG12: Cotg . . . . . . . . . . . . . . . . . .2F 71
E. Bridgeford Rd. NG13: Newton . . . . . . . . . . . .1B 50
E. Circus St. NG1: Nott . . . . . . . . . . . . .4C 4 (5F 45)
Eastcliffe Av. NG4: Ged . . . . . . . . . . . . . . . . . .4F 35
East Cl. NG12: Key . . . . . . . . . . . . . . . . . . . . .5G 79
Eastcote Av. NG9: Bram . . . . . . . . . . . . . . . . .1B 54
East Cres. NG9: Bee . . . . . . . . . . . . . . . . . . . .6H 55
Eastdale Rd. NG3: Nott . . . . . . . . . . . . . . . . . .3E 47
East Dr. NG7: Nott . . . . . . . . . . . . . . . . . . . . .2A 56
Easter Pk. NG7: Lent . . . . . . . . . . . . . . . . . . .1D 56
Eastglade Rd. NG5: Bestw . . . . . . . . . . . . . . . .1D 32
East Gro. NG7: Basf . . . . . . . . . . . . . . . . . . . .1E 45
NG13: Bing . . . . . . . . . . . . . . . . . . . . . . . .5F 51
Eastham Cl. NG3: Nott . . . . . . . . . . . . . .1H 5 (3A 46)
Eastham Rd. NG5: Arn . . . . . . . . . . . . . . . . . .1D 34
Eastholme Cft. NG2: Colw . . . . . . . . . . . . . . . .4F 47
Easthorpe Cotts. NG11: Rudd . . . . . . . . . . . . .6H 67
Easthorpe St. NG11: Rudd . . . . . . . . . . . . . . . .6G 67
East Midlands Conference Cen. . . . . . . . . . . .2H 55
East Moor NG12: Cotg . . . . . . . . . . . . . . . . . .4G 71
Eastmoor Dr. NG4: Carl . . . . . . . . . . . . . . . . .1H 47
E. Nelson St. DE75: Hea . . . . . . . . . . . . . . . . .3C 14
East Rd. NG7: Nott . . . . . . . . . . . . . . . . . . . .1B 56
East St. DE7: Ilk . . . . . . . . . . . . . . . . . . . . . .1B 40
DE75: Hea . . . . . . . . . . . . . . . . . . . . . . . . .5E 15
NG1: Nott . . . . . . . . . . . . . . . . . . . .3F 5 (4H 45)
NG10: Long E . . . . . . . . . . . . . . . . . . . . . .5H 63
NG11: Goth . . . . . . . . . . . . . . . . . . . . . . .6H 75
NG13: Bing . . . . . . . . . . . . . . . . . . . . . . . .5F 51
East Vw. NG2: West Br . . . . . . . . . . . . . . . . . .5H 57
Eastview Ter. NG16: Lang M . . . . . . . . . . . . . . .2F 15
Eastwell Ct. *NG15: Huck* . . . . . . . . . . . . . . . . . .*3G 7*
*(off Annesley Rd.)*
Eastwell St. NG15: Huck . . . . . . . . . . . . . . . . . .3G 7
Eastwold NG12: Cotg . . . . . . . . . . . . . . . . . . .3G 71
EASTWOOD . . . . . . . . . . . . . . . . . . . . . . . . .3B 16
Eastwood Cl. NG15: Huck . . . . . . . . . . . . . . . .1E 19
Eastwood Community Sports Cen. . . . . . . . . .2A 16
Eastwood Rd. NG12: Rad T . . . . . . . . . . . . . . .6G 49
NG16: Kimb . . . . . . . . . . . . . . . . . . . . . . .6F 17
Eastwood St. NG6: Bulw . . . . . . . . . . . . . . . . .2A 32
Eastwood Town FC . . . . . . . . . . . . . . . . . . . .3C 16
Eaton Av. DE7: Kirk H . . . . . . . . . . . . . . . . . . .3H 39
NG5: Arn . . . . . . . . . . . . . . . . . . . . . . . . .6C 22
Eaton Cl. NG9: Bee . . . . . . . . . . . . . . . . . . . .5H 55
Eaton Grange Dr. NG10: Long E . . . . . . . . . . . .5C 62
Eaton Pl. NG13: Bing . . . . . . . . . . . . . . . . . . .5E 51
Eatons Rd. NG9: Stap . . . . . . . . . . . . . . . . . . .5F 53
Eaton St. NG3: Mapp . . . . . . . . . . . . . . . . . . .4B 34
Eaton Ter. NG3: Mapp . . . . . . . . . . . . . . . . . . .5B 34
Ebenezer St. DE7: Ilk . . . . . . . . . . . . . . . . . . .4B 28
NG16: Lang M . . . . . . . . . . . . . . . . . . . . . .2F 15
Ebers Gro. NG3: Mapp P . . . . . . . . . . . . . . . . .1G 45
Ebers Rd. NG3: Mapp P . . . . . . . . . . . . . . . . . .6G 33
Ebony Wlk. NG3: Nott . . . . . . . . . . . . . . . . . .1D 46
Ebury Rd. NG5: Sher . . . . . . . . . . . . . . . . . . .6F 33
Eccles Way NG3: Nott . . . . . . . . . . . . . . . . . .2B 46
Eckington Cl. DE7: West H . . . . . . . . . . . . . . .1C 38
Eckington Ter. NG2: Nott . . . . . . . . . . . . . . . .2G 57
Ecton Cl. NG5: Top V . . . . . . . . . . . . . . . . . . .4D 20
Edale Cl. NG10: Long E . . . . . . . . . . . . . . . . .1D 72
NG15: Huck . . . . . . . . . . . . . . . . . . . . . . . .5C 6
Edale Ri. NG9: Toton . . . . . . . . . . . . . . . . . . .2G 63
Edale Rd. NG2: Nott . . . . . . . . . . . . . . . . . . .4C 46
Edale Sq. DE7: Ilk . . . . . . . . . . . . . . . . . . . . .2A 28
Eddlestone Dr. NG11: Clif . . . . . . . . . . . . . . . .4D 66
Edenbridge Ct. NG8: Woll . . . . . . . . . . . . . . . .1D 54
Eden Cl. NG5: Arn . . . . . . . . . . . . . . . . . . . . .1C 34
NG15: Huck . . . . . . . . . . . . . . . . . . . . . . . .5C 6
Edenhall Gdns. NG11: Clif . . . . . . . . . . . . . . . .3D 66
Eden Wlk. NG13: Bing . . . . . . . . . . . . . . . . . .6D 50
Edern Cl. NG5: Bestw . . . . . . . . . . . . . . . . . . .6E 21
Edern Gdns. NG5: Bestw . . . . . . . . . . . . . . . . .6E 21
Edgbaston Gdns. NG8: Aspl . . . . . . . . . . . . . . .1B 44
Edgecote Way NG5: Bestw . . . . . . . . . . . . . . . .1E 33
Edge Hill Ct. NG10: Long E . . . . . . . . . . . . . . .3F 73
Edgeway NG8: Stre . . . . . . . . . . . . . . . . . . . .6D 30
Edgewood Dr. NG15: Huck . . . . . . . . . . . . . . . .6D 6
Edgewood Leisure Cen. . . . . . . . . . . . . . . . . .1D 18
Edgington Cl. NG12: Cotg . . . . . . . . . . . . . . . .3G 71
Edginton St. NG3: Nott . . . . . . . . . . . . . . . . . .2B 46
Edginton Ter. NG3: Nott . . . . . . . . . . . . . . . . .2B 46
Edgware Rd. NG6: Bulw . . . . . . . . . . . . . . . . .6B 20
Edgwood Rd. NG16: Kimb . . . . . . . . . . . . . . . .1H 29
Edinbane Cl. NG5: Top V . . . . . . . . . . . . . . . . .3D 20
Edinboro Row NG16: Kimb . . . . . . . . . . . . . . . .6G 17
Edinburgh Dr. NG13: Bing . . . . . . . . . . . . . . . .4D 50
Edingale Ct. NG9: Bram . . . . . . . . . . . . . . . . .5B 42
Edingley Av. NG5: Sher . . . . . . . . . . . . . . . . .3G 33
Edingley Sq. NG5: Sher . . . . . . . . . . . . . . . . .3F 33
Edison Village NG7: Nott . . . . . . . . . . . . . . . .2C 56
Edison Way NG5: Arn . . . . . . . . . . . . . . . . . . .6E 23
Edith Ter. *NG7: Radf* . . . . . . . . . . . . . . . . . . .*3C 44*
*(off Hartley Rd.)*
Edlington Dr. NG8: Woll . . . . . . . . . . . . . . . . .6C 42
Edmond Gro. NG15: Huck . . . . . . . . . . . . . . . . .3A 8
Edmonds Cl. NG5: Arn . . . . . . . . . . . . . . . . . .3E 21
Edmonstone Cres. NG5: Bestw . . . . . . . . . . . . .2D 32
Edmonton Ct. NG2: West Br . . . . . . . . . . . . . . .5H 57
Ednaston Rd. NG7: Nott . . . . . . . . . . . . . . . . .2B 56
Edwald Rd. NG12: Edwal . . . . . . . . . . . . . . . . .2D 68
EDWALTON . . . . . . . . . . . . . . . . . . . . . . . . .2D 68
Edwalton Av. NG2: West Br . . . . . . . . . . . . . . .4B 58
Edwalton Cl. NG12: Edwal . . . . . . . . . . . . . . . .2D 68
Edwalton Ct. NG6: Bulw . . . . . . . . . . . . . . . . .1C 32
Edwalton Golf Course . . . . . . . . . . . . . . . . . .2E 69
Edwalton Hall NG12: Edwal . . . . . . . . . . . . . . .2C 68
Edwalton Lodge Cl. NG12: Edwal . . . . . . . . . . .2C 68
Edward Av. NG8: Aspl . . . . . . . . . . . . . . . . . . .1B 44
Edward Cl. NG15: Huck . . . . . . . . . . . . . . . . . .1D 18
Edward Ct. NG2: West Br . . . . . . . . . . . . . . . .2B 58
Edward Rd. NG2: West Br . . . . . . . . . . . . . . . .2B 58
NG10: Long E . . . . . . . . . . . . . . . . . . . . . .5F 63
NG16: Eastw . . . . . . . . . . . . . . . . . . . . . . .3C 16
NG16: Nuth . . . . . . . . . . . . . . . . . . . . . . . .2C 30
Edwards Ct. NG5: Sher . . . . . . . . . . . . . . . . . .2F 33
Edwards La. NG5: Bestw, Sher . . . . . . . . . . . . .1F 33
(not continuous)
Edward St. NG9: Stap . . . . . . . . . . . . . . . . . . .4F 53
NG16: Lang M . . . . . . . . . . . . . . . . . . . . . .1F 15
Edwinstowe Av. NG2: West Br . . . . . . . . . . . . .4B 58
Edwinstowe Dr. NG5: Sher . . . . . . . . . . . . . . .3G 33
Edwin St. NG5: Arn . . . . . . . . . . . . . . . . . . . .1H 33
Eelwood Rd. NG15: Huck . . . . . . . . . . . . . . . . .1D 18
Egerton Dr. NG9: Stap . . . . . . . . . . . . . . . . . .1F 53
Egerton Rd. NG5: Woodt . . . . . . . . . . . . . . . . .3H 33
Egerton St. NG3: Nott . . . . . . . . . . . . . . . . . .2G 45
Egerton Wlk. NG3: Nott . . . . . . . . . . . . . . . . .2G 45
Egling Cft. NG4: Colw . . . . . . . . . . . . . . . . . . .5H 47
Egmont Ct. NG2: Nott . . . . . . . . . . . . . . . . . . .1G 57
Egreaves Av. DE75: Los . . . . . . . . . . . . . . . . .1A 14
Egypt Rd. NG7: Basf . . . . . . . . . . . . . . . . . . .6D 32
(not continuous)
Eighth Av. NG7: Nott . . . . . . . . . . . . . . . . . . .6A 56
Eileen Rd. NG9: Bee . . . . . . . . . . . . . . . . . . .2G 65
Eisele Cl. NG6: Bulw . . . . . . . . . . . . . . . . . . .1F 31
Ekowe St. NG7: Basf . . . . . . . . . . . . . . . . . . .5D 32
Eland St. NG7: Basf . . . . . . . . . . . . . . . . . . . .6D 32
Elder Cl. NG5: Arn . . . . . . . . . . . . . . . . . . . . .4C 22
Elder Gdns. NG5: Top V . . . . . . . . . . . . . . . . .5E 21
Elder Gro. NG15: Huck . . . . . . . . . . . . . . . . . .1H 19
Eldon Bus. Pk. NG9: Atten . . . . . . . . . . . . . . .4C 64
Eldon Chambers NG1: Nott . . . . . . . . . . .5D 4 (5G 45)
Eldon Rd. NG9: Atten . . . . . . . . . . . . . . . . . . .4C 64
Eldon Rd. Ind. Est. NG9: Atten . . . . . . . . . . . . .4C 64
Eldon Rd. Trad. Est. NG9: Chil . . . . . . . . . . . . .4C 64
Eleanor Av. DE7: Ilk . . . . . . . . . . . . . . . . . . . .4C 40
Eleanor Cres. NG9: Stap . . . . . . . . . . . . . . . . .4H 53
Electric Av. NG2: Nott . . . . . . . . . . . . . . . . . .4E 57
Eley Cl. DE7: Ilk . . . . . . . . . . . . . . . . . . . . . .5G 27
Elford Ri. NG3: Nott . . . . . . . . . . . . . . . . . . . .5B 46
Elgar Dr. NG10: Long E . . . . . . . . . . . . . . . . . .2D 72
Elgar Gdns. NG3: Nott . . . . . . . . . . . . . . . . . .3B 46
Eliot Cl. NG10: Long E . . . . . . . . . . . . . . . . . .2D 72
Eliot Dr. DE7: Kirk H . . . . . . . . . . . . . . . . . . .4H 39
Eliot Wlk. NG11: Clif . . . . . . . . . . . . . . . . . . .5A 66
Elizabeth Cl. DE7: West H . . . . . . . . . . . . . . . .1B 38
NG15: Huck . . . . . . . . . . . . . . . . . . . . . . . .6E 7
Elizabeth Ct. DE7: Ilk . . . . . . . . . . . . . . . . . . .6H 27
Elizabeth Gro. NG4: Ged . . . . . . . . . . . . . . . . .5G 35
Elizabeth Ho. NG5: Woodt . . . . . . . . . . . . . . . .2H 33
Ella Bank Rd. DE75: Hea . . . . . . . . . . . . . . . . .4E 15
Ella Rd. NG2: West Br . . . . . . . . . . . . . . . . . .2B 58
Ellastone Av. NG5: Bestw . . . . . . . . . . . . . . . .5G 21
Ellerby Av. NG11: Clif . . . . . . . . . . . . . . . . . .3C 66
Ellerslie Gro. NG10: Sand . . . . . . . . . . . . . . . .6C 52
Ellesmere Bus. Pk. NG5: Sher . . . . . . . . . . . . .5F 33
Ellesmere Cl. NG5: Arn . . . . . . . . . . . . . . . . . .6D 22
Ellesmere Cres. NG5: Sher . . . . . . . . . . . . . . .5F 33
Ellesmere Dr. NG9: Trow . . . . . . . . . . . . . . . . .4E 41
Ellesmere Rd. NG2: West Br . . . . . . . . . . . . . .1B 68
Ellington Rd. NG5: Arn . . . . . . . . . . . . . . . . . .3B 22
Elliot St. NG7: Nott . . . . . . . . . . . . . . . .3A 4 (4E 45)
Ellis Av. NG15: Huck . . . . . . . . . . . . . . . . . . . .5H 7
Ellis Cl. NG10: Long E . . . . . . . . . . . . . . . . . .1E 73
Ellis Ct. NG3: Nott . . . . . . . . . . . . . . . . . . . .3H 45
Ellis Gro. NG9: Bee . . . . . . . . . . . . . . . . . . . .6F 55
Ellsworth Ri. NG5: Bestw . . . . . . . . . . . . . . . .1D 32
Ellwood Cres. NG8: Woll . . . . . . . . . . . . . . . . .4G 43
Elm Av. NG3: Nott . . . . . . . . . . . . . . . . . . . . .2G 45
NG4: Carl . . . . . . . . . . . . . . . . . . . . . . . . .2H 47
NG9: Atten . . . . . . . . . . . . . . . . . . . . . . . .3D 64
NG9: Bee . . . . . . . . . . . . . . . . . . . . . . . . .5E 55
NG10: Long E . . . . . . . . . . . . . . . . . . . . . .4E 63
NG10: Sand . . . . . . . . . . . . . . . . . . . . . . . .4D 52
NG12: Key . . . . . . . . . . . . . . . . . . . . . . . . .5H 79
NG13: Bing . . . . . . . . . . . . . . . . . . . . . . . .5G 51
NG15: Huck . . . . . . . . . . . . . . . . . . . . . . . .6E 7
NG16: Nuth . . . . . . . . . . . . . . . . . . . . . . . .1B 30
Elm Bank NG3: Mapp P . . . . . . . . . . . . . . . . . .1G 45
Elm Bank Dr. NG3: Mapp P . . . . . . . . . . . . . . .1G 45
Elmbridge NG5: Bestw . . . . . . . . . . . . . . . . . .6F 21
Elm Cl. NG3: Mapp P . . . . . . . . . . . . . . . . . . .2G 45
NG12: Key . . . . . . . . . . . . . . . . . . . . . . . . .5H 79
Elmdale Gdns. NG8: Bilb . . . . . . . . . . . . . . . . .1H 43
Elm Dr. NG4: Carl . . . . . . . . . . . . . . . . . . . . .2H 47
Elm Gro. NG5: Arn . . . . . . . . . . . . . . . . . . . . .4C 22
Elmhurst Av. NG3: Mapp . . . . . . . . . . . . . . . . .5E 35
Elmore Ct. NG7: Radf . . . . . . . . . . . . . . . . . . .3E 45
Elms, The NG4: Colw . . . . . . . . . . . . . . . . . . .3H 47
NG16: Want . . . . . . . . . . . . . . . . . . . . . . . .6H 17
Elms Cl. NG11: Rudd . . . . . . . . . . . . . . . . . . .1H 77
Elmsdale Gdns. NG14: Bur J . . . . . . . . . . . . . . .3F 37
Elmsfield Av. DE75: Hea . . . . . . . . . . . . . . . . .3E 15
Elms Gdns. NG11: Rudd . . . . . . . . . . . . . . . . . .1G 77
Elmsham Av. NG5: Top V . . . . . . . . . . . . . . . . .4C 20
Elms Pk. NG11: Rudd . . . . . . . . . . . . . . . . . . .1H 77
Elmsthorpe Av. NG7: Lent . . . . . . . . . . . . . . . .5C 44
Elmswood Gdns. NG5: Sher . . . . . . . . . . . . . . .4H 33
Elm Tree Av. NG2: West Br . . . . . . . . . . . . . . .4H 57
Elmtree Rd. NG14: Calv . . . . . . . . . . . . . . . . .4F 11
Elm Vw. NG7: Radf . . . . . . . . . . . . . . . . . . . .3D 44
Elnor St. NG16: Lang M . . . . . . . . . . . . . . . . .3G 15
Elson St. NG7: Basf . . . . . . . . . . . . . . . . . . . .1D 44
Elston Gdns. NG11: Clif . . . . . . . . . . . . . . . . .1C 66
Elston M. NG3: Nott . . . . . . . . . . . . . . . . . . . .2D 46
Elstree Dr. NG8: Bilb . . . . . . . . . . . . . . . . . . .3G 43
Elswick Cl. NG5: Bestw . . . . . . . . . . . . . . . . . .5F 21
Elswick Dr. NG9: Bee . . . . . . . . . . . . . . . . . . .1H 65
Elterwater Dr. NG2: Gam . . . . . . . . . . . . . . . . .4E 59
Eltham Cl. NG8: Cin . . . . . . . . . . . . . . . . . . . .4F 31
Eltham Dr. NG8: Cin . . . . . . . . . . . . . . . . . . . .4F 31
Eltham Rd. NG2: West Br . . . . . . . . . . . . . . . .4B 58
Elton Cl. NG9: Stap . . . . . . . . . . . . . . . . . . . .3G 53
Elton M. NG5: Sher . . . . . . . . . . . . . . . . . . . .6F 33

| | |
|---|---|
| Elton Rd. Nth. NG5: Sher | .6F 33 |
| Elton Ter. NG7: H Grn | .2D 44 |
| Elvaston Ct. NG5: Bestw | .2D 32 |
| Elvaston Dr. NG10: Long E | .3B 72 |
| Elvaston Rd. NG8: Woll | .4G 43 |
| Elveden Dr. DE7: Ilk | .3G 27 |
| Elwes Lodge NG4: Carl | .3H 47 |
| Elwin Dr. NG9: Bram | .2C 54 |
| Embley Rd. NG5: Sher | .2E 33 |
| Emerys Rd. NG4: Ged, Neth | .1B 48 |
| Emmanuel Av. NG3: Mapp | .6C 34 |
| NG5: Arn | .4E 21 |
| Emneth Cl. NG3: Nott | .1B 46 |
| Emperor Cl. NG5: Sher | .6F 33 |
| Empingham Cl. NG9: Toton | .3B 64 |
| Empire Ct. DE75: Hea | .3C 14 |
| (off Fletcher St.) | |
| Emsworth Cl. DE7: Ilk | .4H 27 |
| Ena Av. NG2: Nott | .4B 46 |
| Enderby Gdns. NG5: Redh | .4A 22 |
| Enderby Sq. NG9: Lent A | .3F 55 |
| Endsleigh Gdns. NG9: Bee | .4F 55 |
| NG12: Edwal | .1C 68 |
| Enfield Chambers NG1: Nott | .5E 5 (5G 45) |
| Enfield St. NG9: Bee | .5E 55 |
| Engine La. NG16: Newth | .1D 16 |
| England Cres. DE75: Hea | .3E 15 |
| Ennerdale Cl. NG2: Gam | .4E 59 |
| Ennerdale Cl. NG10: Long E | .3D 62 |
| Ennerdale Rd. NG5: Sher | .2H 33 |
| NG10: Long E | .3D 62 |
| Ennismore Gdns. NG8: Aspl | .3A 44 |
| Ennismore M. NG2: West Br | .2G 67 |
| Enterprise Cl. DE7: Ilk | .6H 27 |
| Enterprise Way NG2: Nott | .1E 57 |
| NG16: Lang M | .2G 15 |
| Enthorpe St. NG8: Bilb | .3H 43 |
| EPPERSTONE | .5G 13 |
| Epperstone By-Pass NG14: Woodbo | .5E 13 |
| Epperstone Ct. NG2: West Br | .3A 58 |
| Epperstone Rd. NG2: West Br | .3A 58 |
| NG25: Oxt | .1B 12 |
| Epsom Rd. NG9: Toton | .2G 63 |
| Erdington Way NG9: Toton | .2G 63 |
| Erewash Ct. NG10: Long E | .4F 63 |
| Erewash Dr. DE7: Ilk | .3C 40 |
| Erewash Gdns. NG5: Top V | .5E 21 |
| Erewash Gro. NG9: Toton | .3H 63 |
| (not continuous) | |
| Erewash Indoor Bowling Club | .5A 64 |
| Erewash Mus. | .1B 40 |
| Erewash Sq. DE7: Ilk | .3D 40 |
| Erewash Valley Golf Course | .2D 52 |
| Eric Av. NG15: Huck | .2F 7 |
| Erith Cl. NG8: Stre | .6D 30 |
| Ernehale Ct. NG5: Arn | .5B 22 |
| Ernest Rd. NG4: Carl | .1D 46 |
| Erskine Rd. NG5: Sher | .6F 33 |
| Escape Family Entertaiment Cen. | .6E 17 |
| Esher Gro. NG3: Mapp P | .6G 33 |
| Eskdale Cl. NG10: Long E | .2D 72 |
| Eskdale Cl. NG2: Gam | .4E 59 |
| Eskdale Dr. NG8: Aspl | .1H 43 |
| NG9: Chil | .6A 54 |
| Essex St. DE7: Ilk | .6B 28 |
| Estwic Av. NG16: Eastw | .3B 16 |
| Estwic Av. NG16: Eastw | .2H 7 |
| Ethel Av. NG3: Mapp | .6C 34 |
| NG15: Huck | .2H 7 |
| Ethel Rd. NG2: West Br | .4B 58 |
| Eton Cl. DE7: West H | .1B 38 |
| Eton Gro. NG8: Woll | .5H 43 |
| Eton Pl. NG2: West Br | .6A 58 |
| Eton Rd. NG2: West Br | .5A 58 |
| NG5: Sher | .6F 33 |
| (off Claremont Av.) | |
| Eucalyptus Av. NG11: Clif | .4A 66 |
| Eugene Gdns. NG2: Nott | .1H 57 |
| Eugene St. NG2: Nott | .6H 45 |
| Europa Way NG2: West Br | .2G 67 |
| Evans Rd. NG6: Basf | .4B 32 |
| Evedon Wlk. NG5: Top V | .4E 21 |
| Evelyn St. NG2: Nott | .5H 5 (5A 46) |
| NG9: Bee | .4H 55 |
| Eversley Wlk. NG5: Bestw | .5F 21 |
| Evesham Ct. NG9: Toton | .4A 64 |
| Ewart Rd. NG7: H Grn | .1D 44 |
| Ewe Lamb Cl. NG9: Bram | .2H 53 |
| Ewe Lamb La. NG9: Bram | .2H 53 |
| Ewell Rd. NG8: Woll | .4E 43 |
| Exbourne Rd. NG8: Aspl | .6F 31 |
| Exbury Gdns. NG2: West Br | .1F 67 |
| Exchange Arc. NG1: Nott | .4E 5 |
| Exchange Rd. NG2: West Br | .4B 58 |
| Exchange Wlk. NG1: Nott | .4E 5 (5G 45) |
| Excise Chambers NG1: Nott | .4F 5 |

| | |
|---|---|
| Exeter Cl. NG4: Ged | .5H 35 |
| Exeter Rd. NG2: West Br | .5B 58 |
| NG7: H Grn | .1E 45 |
| Exton Rd. NG5: Sher | .4E 33 |
| Experian Way NG2: Nott | .1E 57 |
| Eyam Cl. NG9: Bram | .1C 54 |
| Eyre's Gdns. DE7: Ilk | .5B 28 |
| Eyre St. NG2: Nott | .4H 5 (5A 46) |

# F

| | |
|---|---|
| Fabis Dr. NG11: Clif | .1C 66 |
| Factory La. DE7: Ilk | .5A 28 |
| NG9: Chil | .6E 55 |
| Failsworth Cl. NG11: Clif | .4A 66 |
| Fairbank Cres. NG5: Sher | .5H 33 |
| Fairburn Cl. NG8: Woll | .5C 42 |
| Fairburn Way NG16: Want | .6A 18 |
| Faircroft Av. NG10: Sand | .6A 52 |
| Fairdale Dr. NG16: Newth | .3D 16 |
| Fairfax Cl. NG5: Basf | .5D 32 |
| Fairfield Cl. NG11: Wilf | .6F 57 |
| Fairfield Cres. NG10: Long E | .3C 72 |
| Fairfield St. NG13: Bing | .5E 51 |
| Fairham Av. NG11: Goth | .6H 75 |
| Fairham Brook Nature Reserve | .5D 66 |
| Fairham Cl. NG11: Rudd | .5F 67 |
| Fairham Cl. NG11: Wilf | .2E 67 |
| Fairham Dr. NG8: Woll | .5B 44 |
| Fairham Rd. NG12: Key | .4F 79 |
| Fairholm Ct. NG3: Nott | .1H 5 (3A 46) |
| Fairisle Cl. NG11: Clif | .4H 67 |
| Fairland Cres. NG2: West Br | .1H 67 |
| Fairlawn Pl. NG5: Sher | .5H 33 |
| Fair Lea Cl. NG10: Long E | .1F 73 |
| Fairlight Way NG5: Bestw | .6F 21 |
| Fairmaid Gro. NG11: Clif | .3C 66 |
| Fairmead Cl. NG3: Nott | .1C 46 |
| Fairney Rd. NG8: Bilb | .1D 42 |
| Fairview Ct. NG2: West Br | .3H 67 |
| Fairview Rd. NG5: Woodt | .3A 34 |
| Fairway NG12: Key | .4H 79 |
| Fairway, The NG4: Ged | .4G 35 |
| Fairway Cres. NG13: Newton | .1B 50 |
| Fairway Dr. NG4: Carl | .1E 47 |
| NG6: Bulw | .6B 20 |
| NG9: Chil | .5D 54 |
| Falcon Cl. NG7: Lent | .5C 44 |
| Falconers Wlk. NG5: Arn | .5G 21 |
| Falcon Gro. NG7: Basf | .6E 33 |
| Falcon St. NG7: Basf | .6E 33 |
| Falcon Way NG15: Huck | .2B 8 |
| Falconwood Gdns. NG11: Clif | .4A 66 |
| Fallow Cl. NG11: Clif | .3C 66 |
| Fall Rd. DE75: Hea | .2C 14 |
| Falstaff M. NG7: Basf | .6E 33 |
| Falston Rd. NG8: Bilb | .3G 43 |
| Faraday Bldg. NG7: Nott | .2B 56 |
| Faraday Ct. NG9: Stap | .2G 53 |
| Faraday Rd. NG7: Lent | .4C 44 |
| Far Dales Rd. DE7: Ilk | .5A 28 |
| Farfield Av. NG9: Bee | .3E 55 |
| Farfield Gro. NG9: Bee | .3E 55 |
| Farfield Rd. DE7: Ilk | .6C 28 |
| FARLEYS | .2H 19 |
| Farleys Gro. NG15: Huck | .6G 7 |
| Farleys La. NG15: Huck | .5G 7 |
| (not continuous) | |
| Farley St. NG6: Bulw | .6H 19 |
| Farm Av. NG15: Huck | .1D 18 |
| Farm Cl. DE7: Ilk | .1C 40 |
| NG10: Long E | .2G 73 |
| NG11: Clif | .3C 66 |
| Farmer St. NG11: Rudd | .4A 78 |
| Farm Rd. NG5: Arn | .6D 22 |
| NG9: Chil | .6C 54 |
| Farnborough Rd. NG11: Clif | .1D 66 |
| Farndale Cl. NG10: Long E | .2C 72 |
| Farndale Dr. NG8: Woll | .5B 42 |
| Farndon Dr. NG9: Toton | .2H 63 |
| Farndon Grn. NG8: Woll | .5A 44 |
| Farndon M. NG3: Nott | .1C 46 |
| Far New Cl. NG10: Sand | .6D 52 |
| Farnham Wlk. DE7: West H | .1B 38 |
| Farnsfield Av. NG14: Bur J | .2G 37 |
| Farnsworth Cl. NG16: Want | .4A 18 |
| Far Pastures Cl. NG12: Key | .5G 79 |
| Farriers Cft. DE7: Ilk | .4G 27 |
| Farriers Grn. NG11: Clif | .3A 66 |
| Farringdon Cl. NG16: Nuth | .4D 30 |
| Farrington Way NG16: Eastw | .3A 16 |
| Farr Row NG5: Bestw | .2E 33 |
| Far Rye NG8: Woll | .3F 43 |
| Far St. NG11: Rudd | .4A 78 |
| Farthing Ct. NG10: Long E | .6D 62 |
| Farthings, The NG7: Lent | .5C 44 |

| | |
|---|---|
| Farwells Cl. NG6: Basf | .4A 32 |
| Faulconbridge Cl. NG6: Bulw | .1H 31 |
| Fearn Chase NG4: Carl | .2G 47 |
| Fearn Cl. DE72: Brea | .6C 62 |
| Fearnleigh Dr. NG6: Basf | .5B 32 |
| Featherstone Cl. NG4: Ged | .4F 35 |
| Feignies Ct. NG12: Key | .4G 79 |
| Felen Cl. NG5: Bestw | .6E 21 |
| Fellbarrow Cl. NG2: West Br | .6E 59 |
| Felley Cl. NG15: Huck | .6E 7 |
| Fellows Rd. NG9: Bee | .4E 55 |
| Fellows Yd. NG12: Plum | .6G 69 |
| Fell Side NG5: Woodt | .2C 34 |
| Fellside Cl. NG2: Gam | .5E 59 |
| Felstead Ct. NG9: Bram | .2C 54 |
| Felstead Rd. NG8: Brox | .3G 43 |
| Felton Cl. NG9: Chil | .6B 54 |
| Felton Rd. NG2: Nott | .2H 57 |
| Fenchurch Cl. NG5: Arn | .4E 21 |
| Fenimore Ct. NG12: Rad T | .5H 49 |
| Fenroth Cl. NG6: Bulw | .5F 19 |
| Fenton Ct. NG5: Sher | .3D 32 |
| Fenton Dr. NG6: Bulw | .3A 20 |
| Fenton Rd. NG5: Sher | .3D 32 |
| Fenwick Cl. NG8: Brox | .5F 31 |
| Fenwick Cl. NG4: Neth | .2A 48 |
| Fenwick Rd. NG8: Brox | .5F 31 |
| Fergus Cl. NG11: Clif | .5D 66 |
| Ferguson Cl. NG9: Chil | .3C 64 |
| Fern Av. NG5: Sher | .6F 33 |
| Fern Cl. NG9: Bram | .4B 54 |
| Fern Cres. NG16: Eastw | .2A 16 |
| Ferndale Cl. NG9: Atten | .3D 64 |
| Ferndale Gro. NG3: Nott | .3D 46 |
| Ferndale Rd. NG3: Nott | .3D 46 |
| Ferndene Dr. NG10: Long E | .6C 62 |
| Ferngill Cl. NG2: Nott | .2F 57 |
| Fernilee Cl. DE7: West H | .1C 38 |
| Fern Lea Av. NG12: Cotg | .3E 71 |
| Fernleigh Av. NG3: Mapp | .5D 34 |
| Fernwood Commercial Workshops | |
| NG16: Want | .5A 18 |
| Fernwood Cres. NG8: Woll | .5C 42 |
| Fernwood Dr. NG12: Rad T | .5F 49 |
| NG16: Want | .5A 18 |
| Ferny Hollow Cl. NG5: Top V | .5C 20 |
| Ferrers Wlk. NG3: Nott | .2H 5 (4A 46) |
| Ferriby Ter. NG2: Nott | .2G 57 |
| Ferry Lodge NG4: Carl | .3G 47 |
| Ferryman Rd. NG11: Wilf | .5E 57 |
| Festival Cres. NG9: Trow | .5E 41 |
| Festival Rd. DE7: Kirk H | .4G 39 |
| Festus Cl. NG3: Nott | .3H 45 |
| Festus St. NG4: Neth | .2A 48 |
| Field, The DE7: Ship | .6E 15 |
| Field Av. NG15: Huck | .1D 18 |
| Field Cl. DE72: Brea | .6B 62 |
| NG2: West Br | .2E 59 |
| NG4: Ged | .5H 35 |
| NG9: Chil | .1A 64 |
| Fieldfare Cl. NG9: Bram | .5C 54 |
| Field Ho. Cl. NG8: Woll | .4D 42 |
| Field La. NG9: Chil | .1A 64 |
| NG14: Woodbo | .1C 24 |
| Field Maple Dr. NG7: H Grn | .1C 44 |
| Field Rd. DE7: Ilk | .2B 40 |
| Fields Av. NG11: Rudd | .2G 77 |
| Fields Farm Rd. NG10: Long E | .2E 73 |
| Fields Vw. NG12: Cotg | .1E 71 |
| Field Vw. NG12: Rad T | .5H 49 |
| Fieldway NG11: Wilf | .1F 67 |
| Fiennes Cres. NG7: Nott | .6A 4 (6E 45) |
| Fifth Av. NG7: Nott | .5A 56 |
| Filey St. NG6: Bulw | .5A 20 |
| Finch Cl. NG7: Lent | .3D 56 |
| Finchley Cl. NG11: Clif | .4A 66 |
| Findern Grn. NG3: Nott | .3C 46 |
| Fingal Cl. NG11: Clif | .4D 66 |
| Finsbury Av. NG2: Nott | .5B 46 |
| Finsbury Pk. Cl. NG2: West Br | .6G 57 |
| Finsbury Rd. NG5: Arn | .3E 21 |
| NG9: Bram | .6C 42 |
| Firbank Cl. NG9: Chil | .6B 54 |
| Firbeck Rd. NG5: Arn | .5C 22 |
| NG8: Woll | .5B 42 |
| Fir Cl. NG6: Bulw | .6F 19 |
| NG15: Huck | .1H 19 |
| Fircroft Av. NG8: Bilb | .1E 43 |
| Fircroft Dr. NG15: Huck | .6C 6 |
| Firdale NG12: Cotg | .2G 71 |
| Firecrest Way NG6: Basf | .3B 32 |
| Fire House, The NG5: Arn | .1A 34 |
| Firfield Av. DE72: Brea | .5A 62 |
| Firs, The NG5: Sher | .4H 33 |
| Firs Av. NG9: Bee | .4F 55 |
| Firsby Rd. NG8: Brox | .5F 31 |
| Firs Ho. NG5: Sher | .4H 33 |

Firs Rd. NG12: Edwal ......6D 58
Firs St. NG10: Long E ......3C 72
First Av. DE72: Ris ......6B 52
  NG4: Carl ......2E 47
  NG4: Colw ......4G 47
  NG4: Ged ......6H 35
  NG6: Bulw ......6H 19
  NG7: H Grn ......1F 45
  NG7: Nott ......5A 56
Firth Cl. NG5: Arn ......4E 23
Firth Dr. NG9: Chil ......3C 64
Firth Way NG6: Bulw ......5G 19
Fir Wlk. NG3: Nott ......2D 46
Fisher Av. NG5: Woodt ......2B 34
Fisher Ct. DE7: Ilk ......3B 28
Fisher Ga. NG1: Nott ......5G 5 (5H 45)
Fisher La. NG13: Bing ......5E 51
Fisher St. NG7: Basf ......1D 44
(not continuous)
Fishpond Dr. NG7: Nott ......6A 4 (6E 45)
Fitzgerald Ct. NG15: Huck ......5G 7
Five Acres NG11: Wilf ......1E 67
Flagholme NG12: Cotg ......3F 71
Flamingo Ct. NG7: Lent ......1E 57
Flamstead Av. DE75: Los ......1A 14
  NG4: Lamb ......6B 24
Flamstead Rd. DE7: Ilk ......6B 28
Flamsteed Rd. NG8: Stre ......6D 30
Flatts, The NG9: Chil ......6B 54
Flatts La. NG14: Calv ......1G 11
Flawborough Ri. NG2: West Br ......2G 67
Flawforth Av. NG11: Rudd ......6H 67
Flawforth La. NG11: Rudd ......6H 67
Flaxendale NG12: Cotg ......3G 71
Flaxton Way NG5: Top V ......6D 20
Fleam Rd. NG11: Clif ......1C 66
Fleeman Gro. NG2: West Br ......2C 58
Fleet Cl. NG7: Radf ......3B 44
Fleetway Cl. NG16: Newth ......4D 16
Fleetwith Cl. NG2: West Br ......6E 59
Fleming Cl. NG16: Want ......5A 18
Fleming Dr. NG4: Carl ......2E 47
Fleming Gdns. NG11: Clif ......4A 66
Fleming Ho. NG3: Mapp ......5B 34
Fletcher Ga. NG1: Nott ......4E 5 (5G 45)
Fletcher Rd. NG9: Bee ......4G 55
Fletcher St. DE75: Hea ......3C 14
  NG10: Long E ......5F 63
Fletcher Ter. NG3: Mapp ......5A 34
Fletton Cl. NG3: Nott ......2C 46
Flewitt Gdns. NG3: Nott ......1H 5 (3A 46)
Flinders Orchard NG12: Key ......5G 79
Flintham Dr. NG5: Sher ......3F 33
Flixton Rd. NG16: Kimb ......6H 17
Florence Av. NG10: Long E ......4H 63
Florence Boot Cl. NG7: Nott ......3H 55
Florence Ct. DE7: Ilk ......6B 28
Florence Cres. NG4: Ged ......1B 48
Florence Gro. NG3: Nott ......2C 46
Florence Rd. NG2: West Br ......3C 58
  NG3: Nott ......6C 34
  NG4: Ged ......6B 36
Florence St. NG15: Huck ......6G 7
Florey Wlk. NG11: Clif ......5A 66
Florimel Ct. NG5: Arn ......6G 21
Florin Gdns. NG10: Long E ......6C 62
Flowers Cl. NG5: Arn ......1D 34
Flying Horse Wlk. NG1: Nott ......4E 5 (5G 45)
Foljambe Ter. NG1: Nott ......2G 5 (4H 45)
Folkton Gdns. NG3: Mapp ......6B 34
Forbes Cl. NG10: Key ......2G 73
Forbes Hole Local Nature Reserve ......2G 73
Ford Av. DE75: Los ......1A 14
Fordham Grn. NG11: Clif ......5C 66
Ford St. NG7: Basf ......6E 33
Ford St. Nth. NG7: Basf ......6E 33
Foredrift Cl. NG11: Goth ......6G 75
Forest Cl. NG12: Cotg ......2E 71
Forest Cotts. NG6: Bulw ......4B 20
Forest Cl. NG7: Radf ......3E 45
Forester Cl. NG9: Chil ......1C 64
Forester Gro. NG4: Carl ......2F 47
Forester Rd. NG3: Nott ......1C 46
Forester St. NG4: Neth ......2A 48
FOREST FIELDS ......1E 45
Forest Gro. NG1: Nott ......2F 45
  NG7: Radf ......3E 45
Forest La. NG15: Pap ......1C 8
Forest Rd. NG13: Bing ......5C 50
  NG14: Calv ......3F 11
Forest Rd. E. NG1: Nott ......3E 45
Forest Rd. W. NG7: Radf ......1A 4 (3E 45)
Forest, The (Park & Ride) ......2E 45
Forest, The Stop (NET) ......2E 45
Forest Vw. Dr. NG15: Huck ......4E 7
Forge, The NG9: Trow ......4D 40

Forge Av. NG14: Calv ......3H 11
Forge Hill NG9: Chil ......1D 64
Forge Mill Gro. NG15: Huck ......6B 8
Forman Ho. NG5: Sher ......6F 33
Forman St. NG1: Nott ......3D 4 (4G 45)
Forster St. NG7: Radf ......3C 44
(not continuous)
Forsythia Gdns. NG7: Lent ......1C 56
Forum Rd. NG5: Bestw ......1C 32
Fosbrooke Dr. NG10: Long E ......2F 73
Fosse, The NG12: Cotg, Crop Bi, Owt ......6H 71
(not continuous)
Fosse Rd. NG13: Bing, Newton, Saxon ......5B 50
  NG13: Car C, East B ......1E 51
Fosse Wlk. NG12: Cotg ......3G 71
Fosse Way NG12: Crop Bu ......6A 50
  NG13: Bing ......6B 50
Foster Av. NG9: Bee ......5F 55
Foster Dr. NG5: Sher ......3H 33
Fosters La. NG13: Bing ......5F 51
Fothergill Ct. NG3: Mapp P ......2G 45
Fountain Dale Ct. NG3: Nott ......2H 45
Fountains Cl. NG2: West Br ......5D 58
Fountains Ct. NG9: Bee ......5G 55
Fourth Av. NG4: Carl ......1D 46
  NG7: H Grn ......1F 45
  NG7: Nott ......5A 56
Fowler M. NG16: Want ......6A 18
Fowler St. NG3: Mapp P ......1H 45
Fox Cl. NG10: Long E ......2F 73
Fox Covert NG4: Colw ......5H 47
Fox Covert La. NG11: Clif ......5H 65
Fox Covert Local Nature Reserve ......6F 63
Foxearth Av. NG11: Clif ......3E 67
Fox End NG5: Sher ......5H 33
Foxes Cl. NG7: Nott ......6A 4
Foxglove Cl. NG15: Huck ......1A 20
Foxglove Rd. NG16: Newth ......5D 16
Foxgloves, The NG13: Bing ......6D 50
Fox Gro. NG5: Basf ......4C 32
Fox Gro. Ct. NG5: Basf ......4C 32
Foxhall Rd. NG7: H Grn ......1E 45
Foxhill NG12: Cotg ......3E 71
Foxhill Ct. NG4: Carl ......1E 47
Foxhill Rd. NG4: Carl ......1E 47
  NG14: Bur J ......4D 37
Foxhill Rd. Central NG4: Carl ......1D 46
Foxhill Rd. E. NG4: Carl ......1F 47
Foxhill Rd. W. NG4: Carl ......1C 46
Foxhollies Gro. NG5: Sher ......4F 33
Foxley Rd. DE7: Ilk ......2B 28
Fox Mdw. NG15: Huck ......5F 7
Fox Rd. NG2: West Br ......2B 58
Foxton Cl. DE7: Ilk ......4G 27
Foxton Gdns. NG8: Bilb ......2G 43
Foxwood Gro. NG4: Carl ......4H 11
Foxwood La. NG14: Woodbo ......5H 11
Fradley Cl. NG6: Bulw ......3A 20
Frampton Rd. NG8: Bilb ......2G 43
Frances Gro. NG15: Huck ......2H 7
Francis Gro. NG6: Basf ......4C 32
Francis Mill NG9: Bee ......4F 55
Francis Rd. NG4: Carl ......1H 47
Francis St. NG7: Radf ......1A 4 (3E 45)
(not continuous)
Franklin Cl. NG5: Arn ......5G 21
Franklin Dr. NG12: Toll ......4F 69
Franklin Ho. NG3: Mapp ......5B 34
(off Ockbrook Dr.)
Franklyn Gdns. NG8: Aspl ......3A 44
  NG12: Key ......3G 79
Fraser Cres. NG4: Carl ......6D 34
Fraser Rd. NG2: Nott ......3H 57
  NG4: Carl ......1H 47
Fraser Sq. NG4: Carl ......6D 34
Frearson Farm Ct. NG16: Eastw ......1H 47
Freckingham St. NG1: Nott ......3H 5 (4H 45)
Freda Av. NG4: Ged ......5F 35
Freda Cl. NG4: Ged ......4F 35
Frederic Av. DE75: Hea ......6D 14
Frederick Av. DE7: Ilk ......4C 40
  NG4: Carl ......2D 46
Frederick Gro. NG7: Lent ......6D 44
Frederick Rd. NG9: Stap ......4F 53
Freeland Cl. NG10: Long E ......6H 63
Freeland Cl. NG9: Toton ......2H 63
Freemans Rd. NG4: Carl ......1A 48
Freemans Ter. NG4: Carl ......1H 47
Freemantle Wlk. NG5: Top V ......5C 20
Freeston Dr. NG6: Bulw ......5F 19
Freeth Cl. NG2: Nott ......1B 58
Freeth St. NG2: Nott ......1A 58
Freiston St. NG7: H Grn ......2C 44
Fremount Dr. NG8: Bilb ......3F 43
French St. DE7: Ilk ......3C 40
Fretwell St. NG7: H Grn ......2C 44

Friar La. NG1: Nott ......5C 4 (5F 45)
Friars Ct. DE7: Kirk H ......3G 39
  NG7: Nott ......6A 4 (6E 45)
Friar St. NG7: Lent ......1C 56
  NG10: Long E ......6F 63
Friar Wlk. NG13: Newton ......1C 50
Friary, The NG7: Lent ......1C 56
Friary Cl. NG7: Lent ......1C 56
Friday La. NG4: Ged ......5H 35
Friesland Dr. NG10: Sand ......6B 52
Frinton Rd. NG8: Brox ......6E 31
Frisby Av. NG10: Long E ......1G 73
Frobisher Gdns. NG5: Arn ......1H 33
Frogmore St. NG1: Nott ......1D 4 (3G 45)
Frome Gdns. NG13: Bing ......6D 50
Front St. NG5: Arn ......6B 22
Frost Av. NG16: Lang M ......1E 15
Fryar Rd. NG16: Eastw ......1B 16
Fulforth St. NG1: Nott ......1D 4 (3G 45)
Fuller St. NG11: Rudd ......1G 77
Fullwood Av. DE7: Ilk ......6A 28
Fullwood St. DE7: Ilk ......6A 28
Fulwood Cl. NG9: Chil ......1C 64
Fulwood Cres. NG8: Aspl ......6G 31
Fulwood Dr. NG10: Long E ......6C 62
Funky Pots ......5A 58
Furleys Cotts. NG14: Lowd ......2H 25
Furlong Av. NG5: Arn ......5A 22
Furlong Cl. NG9: Stap ......3F 53
Furlong Cl. NG5: Arn ......5A 22
Furlong St. NG5: Arn ......6A 22
Furnace La. DE75: Los ......1A 14
Furnace Rd. DE7: Ilk ......2D 40
Furness Rd. NG2: West Br ......4D 58
Furness Rd. NG6: Basf ......4A 32
Furzebrook Rd. NG4: Colw ......4G 47
Furze Gdns. NG3: Nott ......2H 45
Fylde Cl. NG9: Toton ......3G 63
Fylingdale Way NG8: Woll ......6B 42

# G

Gables, The NG3: Mapp ......3C 34
  NG7: Basf ......6E 33
Gabor Cl. NG11: Clif ......5A 66
Gabor Ct. NG11: Clif ......4A 66
Gabrielle Cl. NG6: Bulw ......3B 32
Gadd St. NG7: Radf ......3D 44
Gadsby Cl. DE7: Ilk ......5C 40
Gadwall Cres. NG7: Lent ......1E 57
Gainsborough Cl. NG9: Stap ......5G 53
  NG10: Long E ......2G 73
Gainsborough Ct. NG9: Bee ......4G 55
Gainsford Cl. NG5: Bestw ......2D 32
Gainsford Cres. NG5: Bestw ......2D 32
Gala Bingo
  Nottingham Castle ......3C 44
  Nottingham St Anns ......2F 5 (4H 45)
  Nottingham Top Valley ......1C 32
Gala Way NG5: Bestw ......1C 32
Galaxy Cinema
  Long Eaton ......5F 63
Gale Cl. NG9: Bee ......5H 55
Galena Dr. NG3: Nott ......2C 46
Gallery, The NG7: Nott ......6C 4 (6E 45)
GALLOWS INN ......3C 40
Gallows Inn Cl. DE7: Ilk ......3C 40
Gallows Inn Ind. Est. DE7: Ilk ......3D 40
Galway Rd. NG5: Arn ......5H 21
  NG7: Lent ......6D 44
Gamble St. NG7: Radf ......2A 4 (4H 45)
GAMSTON ......4E 59
Gamston Cres. NG5: Sher ......4G 33
Gamston District Cen. NG2: West Br ......5E 59
Gamston Lings Bar Rd.
  NG2: Gam ......4F 59
  NG12: Toll, Edwal ......4C 68
Gamston Lodge NG4: Carl ......3G 47
Ganton Cl. NG3: Mapp ......6B 34
Garden Av. DE7: Ilk ......4B 40
  NG4: Carl ......2F 47
Garden City NG4: Carl ......1G 47
Gardendale Av. NG11: Clif ......4B 66
Gardeners Cl. NG4: Carl ......6F 35
  NG13: Bing ......4D 50
  NG15: Huck ......4F 7
Gardeners Wlk. NG5: Sher ......3D 32
Gardenia Cl. NG9: Toton ......3A 64
Gardenia Cres. NG3: Mapp ......5D 34
Gardenia Gro. NG3: Mapp ......5D 34
Garden Rd. NG13: Bing ......5D 50
  NG15: Huck ......4F 7
  NG16: Eastw ......2B 16
Gardens, The DE75: Los ......1A 14
Gardens Ct. NG2: West Br ......4C 58
Garden St. NG7: Radf ......4D 44

Garfield Cl.—Grangewood Rd.


**Garfield Cl.** NG9: Stap 2G **53**
**Garfield Ct.** NG7: Radf 4D **44**
**Garfield Rd.** NG7: Radf 3C **44**
(not continuous)
**Garforth Cl.** NG8: Basf 1C **44**
**Garners Hill** NG1: Nott 5E **5** (5H **45**)
**Garnet Ct.** NG3: Nott 2H **5** (4A **46**)
**Garnet St.** NG4: Neth 2H **47**
**Garnett Av.** DE75: Hea 3D **14**
**Garrett Gro.** NG11: Clif 3A **66**
**Garsdale Cl.** NG2: Gam 5E **59**
**Garsdale Dr.** NG11: Wilf 2E **67**
**Garton Cl.** NG6: Bulw 2H **31**
NG9: Chil 6B **54**
**Gas St.** NG10: Sand 5E **53**
**Gatcombe Cl.** NG12: Rad T 6G **49**
**Gatcombe Gro.** NG10: Sand 2C **62**
**Gateford Cl.** NG9: Bram 1C **54**
**Gatehouse Ct.** NG9: Chil 6D **54**
**Gateside Rd.** NG2: Nott 2E **57**
**Gatling St.** NG7: Radf 4C **44**
**Gaul St.** NG6: Bulw 6H **19**
**Gauntley Ct.** NG7: Basf 1D **44**
**Gauntley St.** NG7: Basf 1C **44**
**Gautries Cl.** NG5: Top V 5E **21**
**Gavin M.** NG7: H Grn 1D **44**
**Gawthorne St.** NG7: Basf 6D **32**
**Gayhurst Grn.** NG6: Bulw 2C **32**
**Gayhurst Rd.** NG6: Bulw 2C **32**
**Gaynor Ct.** NG8: Bilb 3H **43**
**Gayrigg Ct.** NG9: Chil 6B **54**
**Gayton Cl.** NG8: Bilb 1D **42**
**Gayton Rd.** DE7: Ilk 1H **39**
**Gaywood Cl.** NG11: Clif 5D **66**
GEDLING 5H **35**
**Gedling Gro.** NG5: Arn 6B **22**
NG7: Radf 1A **4** (3E **45**)
**Gedling Rd.** NG4: Carl 1H **47**
NG5: Arn 6B **22**
**Gedling St.** NG1: Nott 4G **5** (5H **45**)
**Gedney Av.** NG3: Nott 1B **46**
**Gell Rd.** NG9: Chil 1A **64**
**Genesis Pk.** NG7: Radf 4B **44**
**George Av.** NG9: Bee 6F **55**
NG10: Long E 4H **63**
**George Grn. Ct.** *NG2: Nott 5B 46*
*(off Sneinton Blvd.)*
**George Grn. Way** NG7: Nott 3B **56**
**George Rd.** NG2: West Br 4A **58**
NG4: Carl 2G **47**
**George's La.** NG5: Woodbo 6D **10**
NG14: Calv 6D **10**
**George St.** NG1: Nott 3F **5** (4H **45**)
NG5: Arn 1A **34**
NG15: Huck 3G **7**
NG16: Lang M 2F **15**
**George St. Trad. Ho.** NG1: Nott 4F **5**
**Georgia Dr.** NG5: Arn 3A **22**
**Georgina Rd.** NG9: Bee 6F **55**
**Gerrard Cl.** NG5: Arn 3E **21**
**Gertrude Rd.** NG2: West Br 3C **58**
**Gervase Gdns.** NG11: Clif 3A **66**
**Ghost Ho. La.** NG9: Chil 6B **54**
(not continuous)
**Gibbons Av.** NG9: Stap 4F **53**
**Gibbons St.** NG7: Lent 3C **56**
**Gibb St.** NG10: Long E 6G **63**
**Gibson Rd.** NG7: H Grn 1E **45**
**Gifford Gdns.** NG2: Nott 1G **57**
**Gilbert Av.** NG11: Goth 6H **75**
**Gilbert Blvd.** NG5: Arn 6E **23**
**Gilbert Cl.** NG5: Bestw 2E **33**
**Gilbert Gdns.** NG3: Nott 3C **46**
**Gilbert St.** NG15: Huck 4G **7**
(not continuous)
**Gilead St.** NG6: Bulw 6H **19**
**Giles Av.** NG2: West Br 5H **57**
**Giles Ct.** NG2: West Br 4A **58**
**Gillercomb Cl.** NG2: West Br 6F **59**
**Gilliver La.** NG12: C'ton 4C **70**
**Gillotts Cl.** NG13: Bing 4E **51**
**Gillott St.** DE75: Hea 5E **15**
**Gill St.** NG1: Nott 1C **4** (3F **45**)
**Gilpet Av.** NG3: Nott 1B **46**
GILTBROOK 5E **17**
**Giltbrook Cres.** NG16: Gilt 5E **17**
**Giltbrook Ind. Est.** NG16: Gilt 6E **17**
**Giltbrook Retail Pk.** NG16: Gilt 6E **17**
**Gilt Hill** NG16: Kimb 6F **17**
**Giltway** NG16: Gilt 6E **17**
**Gimson Cl.** DE7: Ilk 4G **27**
**Gin Cl. Way** NG16: Aws 2E **29**
NG16: Gilt 1E **29**
**Gipsy La.** NG11: Clif 3A **66**
NG15: Huck 1D **6**
**Girton Rd.** NG5: Sher 4E **33**
**Gisburn Cl.** NG11: Wilf 1E **67**
**Glade, The** NG11: Clif 6C **66**
**Glade Av.** NG8: Woll 4A **44**
**Glade Bus. Centre, The** NG5: Bestw 1C **32**
**Gladehill Rd.** NG5: Arn, Bestw 6G **21**
**Glades, The** NG5: Top V 5D **20**
**Gladstone Av.** DE75: Hea 3C **14**
NG11: Goth 6H **75**
**Gladstone St.** DE7: Ilk 2B **40**
DE75: Hea 3C **14**
NG4: Carl 2F **47**
NG7: Basf, H Grn 1D **44**
(not continuous)
NG9: Bee 6E **55**
NG10: Long E 1F **73**
NG16: Lang M 2G **15**
**Gladys St.** NG7: Basf 6E **33**
**Glaisdale Dr. E.** NG8: Bilb 3D **42**
**Glaisdale Dr. W.** NG8: Bilb 4D **42**
**Glaisdale Pk. Ind. Est.** NG8: Bilb 3D **42**
**Glaisdale Parkway** NG8: Bilb 4D **42**
**Glamis Rd.** NG5: Sher 5E **33**
**Glanton Way** NG5: Arn 3C **22**
**Glapton La.** NG11: Clif 3B **66**
**Glapton Rd.** NG2: Nott 2G **57**
**Glaramara Cl.** NG2: Nott 2F **57**
**Glasshouse, The** NG3: Nott 2F **5** (4G **45**)
**Glasshouse St.** NG1: Nott 2E **5** (4G **45**)
**Glebe, The** NG16: Coss 3D **28**
**Glebe Cotts.** NG11: Wilf 3F **57**
**Glebe Cres.** DE7: Ilk 2C **40**
DE7: Stan 3A **38**
**Glebe Dr.** NG14: Bur J 4D **36**
**Glebe Farm Cl.** NG2: West Br 1G **67**
**Glebe Farm Vw.** NG4: Ged 4H **35**
**Glebe La.** NG12: Rad T 6F **49**
**Glebe Rd.** NG2: West Br 4B **58**
NG4: Carl 5E **35**
NG16: Nuth 1C **30**
**Glebe St.** NG9: Bee 5E **55**
NG15: Huck 3G **7**
**Glen, The** NG11: Clif 4C **66**
**Glen Av.** NG16: Eastw 4D **16**
**Glenbrook** NG12: Cotg 2G **71**
**Glenbrook Cres.** NG8: Bilb 2G **43**
**Glencairn Dr.** NG8: Bilb 1G **43**
**Glencairn M.** NG8: Bilb 1G **43**
**Glencoe Rd.** NG11: Clif 4E **67**
**Glencoyne Rd.** NG11: Clif 5C **66**
**Glencross Cl.** NG2: West Br 2E **59**
**Glendale Cl.** NG4: Carl 5F **35**
**Glendale Ct.** NG9: Chil 2E **65**
**Glendale Gdns.** NG5: Arn 6B **22**
**Glendoe Gro.** NG13: Bing 5C **50**
**Glendon Dr.** NG5: Sher 4E **33**
NG15: Huck 6G **7**
**Glendon Rd.** DE7: Kirk H 5G **39**
**Gleneagles Ct.** NG12: Edwal 2D **68**
**Gleneagles Dr.** NG5: Arn 4D **22**
**Glenfield Av.** NG16: Kimb 6F **17**
**Glenfield Rd.** NG10: Long E 2F **73**
**Glen Helen** NG4: Colw 3H **47**
**Glenlivet Gdns.** NG11: Clif 4D **66**
**Glenloch Dr.** NG11: Clif 5D **66**
**Glenmore Rd.** NG2: West Br 5D **58**
**Glenorchy Cres.** NG5: Top V 5C **20**
**Glen Parva Av.** NG5: Redh 4A **22**
**Glenridding Cl.** NG2: West Br 6F **59**
**Glen Rd.** NG14: Bur J 2E **37**
**Glensford Gdns.** NG5: Top V 3C **20**
**Glenside** NG5: Woodt 2D **34**
**Glenside Rd.** NG9: Bram 2C **54**
**Glenstone Ct.** NG7: H Grn 1D **44**
**Glentworth Rd.** NG7: Radf 3C **44**
**Glenwood Av.** NG8: Woll 5D **42**
**Glins Rd.** NG5: Top V 5D **20**
**Gloucester Av.** NG7: Lent 5C **44**
NG9: Bee 6F **55**
NG10: Sand 1C **62**
NG16: Nuth 4F **31**
**Glover Av.** NG8: Woll 5D **42**
**Glover Ho.** *NG5: Arn 1C 34*
*(off Derwent Cres.)*
**Glue La.** DE75: Los 3A **14**
**Goatchurch Ct.** NG5: Top V 5E **21**
**Goathland Cl.** NG5: Bestw 5F **21**
**Godber Cl.** NG16: Gilt 5C **16**
**Godber Rd.** NG15: Huck 6E **7**
**Goddard Ct.** NG3: Arn 1E **35**
**Godfrey Dr.** DE7: Kirk H 4G **39**
**Godfrey St.** DE75: Hea 4C **14**
(not continuous)
NG4: Neth 3A **48**
**Godkin Dr.** NG16: Lang M 1E **15**
**Goldcrest Cl.** NG13: Bing 6G **51**
**Goldcrest Rd.** NG6: Cin 4H **31**
**Goldenbrook Cl.** DE72: Brea 6A **62**
**Goldham Rd.** NG8: Stre 1D **42**
**Goldrill Cl.** NG2: Gam 4D **58**
**Goldsmith Ct.** NG1: Nott 2C **4**
**Goldsmith St.** NG1: Nott 2C **4** (4F **45**)
**Goldswong Ter.** NG3: Nott 2G **45**
**Golf Cl.** NG6: Bulw 3A **20**
**Golf Club Rd.** DE7: Stant D 2C **52**
**Golf Course Rd.** NG12: Stant W 5B **80**
**Golf Rd.** NG12: Rad T 6G **49**
**Gonalston La.** NG14: Epp 6H **13**
**Goodall Cres.** NG15: Huck 5A **8**
**Goodall St.** NG7: H Grn 2D **44**
**Goodliffe St.** NG7: H Grn 1D **44**
**Goodman Cl.** NG16: Gilt 5E **17**
**Goodwin Cl.** NG10: Sand 5C **52**
**Goodwin Dr.** NG16: Kimb 1G **29**
**Goodwin St.** NG7: Radf 1A **4** (3E **45**)
**Goodwood Av.** NG5: Arn 5A **22**
**Goodwood Cres.** DE7: Kirk H 5H **39**
**Goodwood Dr.** NG9: Toton 3H **63**
**Goodwood Rd.** NG8: Woll 5D **42**
**Goole Av.** DE7: Kirk H 4H **39**
**Goosedale La.** NG6: Bestw V 4C **8**
**Goose Ga.** NG1: Nott 4F **5** (5H **45**)
NG12: Cotg 2E **71**
**Gordon Cl.** NG9: Atten 3D **64**
**Gordon Gro.** NG7: Basf 6D **32**
**Gordon Ri.** NG3: Mapp 5A **34**
**Gordon Rd.** NG2: West Br 4B **58**
NG3: Nott 3A **46**
NG14: Bur J 2G **37**
**Gordon Sq.** NG2: West Br 4B **58**
**Gordon St.** DE7: Ilk 6B **28**
NG6: Basf 3B **32**
**Gorman Ct.** NG5: Arn 6D **22**
**Gorse Cl.** NG10: Long E 3D **62**
NG14: Calv 4F **11**
NG16: Newth 4D **16**
**Gorse Ct.** NG6: Bulw 2C **32**
**Gorse Rd.** NG12: Key 4F **79**
**Gorse Wlk.** NG3: Nott 2D **46**
**Gorsey Rd.** NG3: Mapp P 2H **45**
**Gosforth Av.** DE7: Ilk 1A **28**
**Gosforth Ct.** NG2: Nott 2H **57**
**Goshawk Rd.** DE7: Ilk 6C **40**
GOTHAM 6H **75**
**Gothic Cl.** NG6: Basf 3C **32**
**Gough Gro.** NG10: Long E 1E **73**
**Goverton Sq.** NG6: Bulw 2B **32**
**Gowan Cl.** NG9: Chil 3C **64**
**Goyden Cl.** NG5: Top V 5E **21**
**Grace Av.** NG9: Bee 5H **55**
**Grace Cres.** DE75: Hea 3D **14**
**Grace Dr.** NG8: Aspl 1B **44**
**Grafton Av.** NG5: Woodt 2A **34**
**Grafton Ct.** NG7: Radf 3A **4** (4E **45**)
**Graham St.** DE7: Ilk 2B **40**
NG7: Radf 4D **44**
**Grainger Av.** NG2: West Br 2A **68**
**Graingers Ter.** NG15: Huck 5H **7**
**Grainger St.** NG2: Nott 1A **58**
**Grampian Dr.** NG5: Arn 3F **21**
**Grampian Way** NG10: Long E 5C **62**
**Granby Ct.** NG13: Bing 5D **50**
**Granby St.** DE7: Ilk 5A **28**
**Granby Vs.** NG2: Nott 5B **46**
**Grandfield Av.** NG12: Rad T 5F **49**
**Grandfield Cres.** NG12: Rad T 5F **49**
**Grandfield St.** DE75: Los 1A **14**
**Grange, The** DE7: Smal 5A **14**
**Grange Av.** DE72: Brea 5A **62**
NG9: Bee 5F **55**
NG11: Rudd 5F **67**
**Grange Cl.** NG4: Lamb 6C **24**
NG11: Wilf 3F **57**
**Grange Ct.** NG11: Rudd 3G **67**
**Grange Cres.** NG4: Ged 4H **35**
**Grange Dr.** NG10: Long E 5H **63**
**Grange Est.** NG16: Coss 6F **29**
**Grange Farm** NG2: Gam 4E **59**
**Grange Farm Cl.** NG9: Toton 4A **64**
**Grange Farm Cotts.** NG14: Lowd 2F **25**
**Grange Gdns.** DE75: Los 2A **14**
**Grangelea Gdns.** NG9: Bram 3B **54**
**Grange M.** NG11: Rudd 3G **67**
**Grangemoor** NG15: Pap 2B **8**
GRANGE PARK 5A **64**
**Grange Pk.** NG2: West Br 6D **58**
NG10: Long E 5H **63**
**Grange Rd.** NG5: Woodt 3A **34**
NG6: Basf 4B **32**
NG10: Long E 5H **63**
NG12: Edwal 1C **68**
**Grange Vw.** NG16: Eastw 2B **16**
**Grange Vw. Rd.** NG4: Ged 5H **35**
**Grangewood Av.** DE7: Ilk 2B **40**
**Grangewood Ct.** NG8: Woll 6C **42**
**Grangewood Rd.** NG8: Woll 6C **42**

Grannis Dr. NG8: Bilb . . . . . . . . . . . . . . . .1G **43**
Grantham Cl. NG16: Gilt . . . . . . . . . . . .6E **17**
Grantham Rd. NG12: Rad T . . . . . . . . .1D **60**
  NG13: Bing . . . . . . . . . . . . . . . . . . . . .5F **51**
Grantleigh Cl. NG8: Woll . . . . . . . . . . .4F **43**
Granton Av. NG11: Clif . . . . . . . . . . . . .5D **66**
Grant St. NG7: Radf . . . . . . . . . . . . . . .4D **44**
Granville Av. NG10: Long E . . . . . . . . .4F **63**
Granville Ct. NG3: Nott . . . . . . . . . . . .4B **46**
Granville Cres. NG12: Rad T . . . . . . . .1E **61**
Granville Gro. NG3: Nott . . . . . . . . . . .4B **46**
Grasby Wlk. NG11: Clif . . . . . . . . . . . . .3B **66**
Grasmere Av. NG8: Aspl . . . . . . . . . . .5A **32**
Grasmere Cl. NG15: Huck . . . . . . . . . .3F **7**
Grasmere Ct. NG10: Long E . . . . . . . .3D **62**
Grasmere Gdns. NG11: Goth . . . . . . .5H **75**
Grasmere Rd. NG9: Bram . . . . . . . . . .3D **54**
  NG10: Long E . . . . . . . . . . . . . . . . . .3D **62**
Grasmere St. NG10: Sand . . . . . . . . . .6D **52**
Grasmoor Cl. NG3: Nott . . . . . . . . . . .1B **46**
Grassingdale Cl. NG4: Carl . . . . . . . . .5F **35**
Grassington Rd. NG8: Aspl . . . . . . . . .3B **44**
Grassmere NG12: Cotg . . . . . . . . . . . .2G **71**
Grass St. DE7: Ilk . . . . . . . . . . . . . . . . .4A **28**
Grassy La. NG9: Bee . . . . . . . . . . . . . .6G **55**
Gravelly Hollow NG14: Calv . . . . . . . .1B **10**
Graveney Gdns. NG5: Arn . . . . . . . . . .1D **34**
Graylands Rd. NG8: Bilb . . . . . . . . . . .2D **42**
Grayson M. NG9: Chil . . . . . . . . . . . . .3B **64**
Graystones Cl. NG2: West Br . . . . . . . .6E **59**
Grazingfield NG11: Wilf . . . . . . . . . . .1E **67**
GREASLEY . . . . . . . . . . . . . . . . . . . . . . .2G **17**
Greasley Av. NG16: Newth . . . . . . . . .3E **17**
Greasley Sports & Community Cen. . . .3D **16**
Greasley St. NG6: Bulw . . . . . . . . . . . .6H **19**
Great Central Railway
  Ruddington Station . . . . . . . . . . . . . .2G **77**
Gt. Freeman St. NG3: Nott . . . . . . . . .1E **5** (3G **45**)
Gt. Hoggett Dr. NG9: Chil . . . . . . . . . .5A **54**
Gt. Northern Cl. DE7: Ilk . . . . . . . . . . .5B **28**
Gt. Northern Close, The NG2: Nott . . .6G **5** (6H **45**)
Gt. Northern Cotts. NG15: Huck . . . . .2H **7**
Gt. Northern Rd. NG16: Eastw . . . . . . .3H **15**
Gt. Northern Way NG7: Neth . . . . . . . .3B **48**
Greaves Cl. NG5: Arn . . . . . . . . . . . . .2D **34**
  NG8: Stre . . . . . . . . . . . . . . . . . . . . . .6D **30**
Greek St. NG7: Radf . . . . . . . . . . . . . .4E **45**
Green, The DE72: Brea . . . . . . . . . . . .5A **62**
  NG4: Carl . . . . . . . . . . . . . . . . . . . . . .1E **47**
  NG9: Chil . . . . . . . . . . . . . . . . . . . . . .1E **65**
  NG11: Rudd . . . . . . . . . . . . . . . . . . . .1G **77**
  NG12: Rad T . . . . . . . . . . . . . . . . . . .6E **49**
  NG14: Lowd . . . . . . . . . . . . . . . . . . . .3F **25**
Green Acre NG8: Woll . . . . . . . . . . . . .4B **42**
Greenacre NG12: Edwal . . . . . . . . . . .1D **68**
  NG14: Bur J . . . . . . . . . . . . . . . . . . . .2E **37**
Greenacre Av. DE75: Hea . . . . . . . . . .2E **15**
Greenacres Cl. NG16: Newth . . . . . . . .3E **17**
Greenacres Pk. NG2: West Br . . . . . . . .2F **59**
Green App. NG4: Carl . . . . . . . . . . . . .1E **47**
Green Av. NG4: Neth . . . . . . . . . . . . . .2A **48**
Greenbank NG4: Carl . . . . . . . . . . . . .3F **47**
Greenbank Ct. NG5: Sher . . . . . . . . . .5G **33**
Greenbanks NG5: Woodt . . . . . . . . . .3A **34**
Greenburn Cl. NG2: Gam . . . . . . . . . .5F **59**
Green Cl. NG7: Nott . . . . . . . . . . . . . .1A **56**
  NG12: Key . . . . . . . . . . . . . . . . . . . . .3H **79**
  NG15: Huck . . . . . . . . . . . . . . . . . . . .6A **8**
Green Ct. NG13: Bing . . . . . . . . . . . . .4E **51**
Greencroft NG11: Clif . . . . . . . . . . . . .2D **66**
Greendale Gdns. NG8: Bilb . . . . . . . . .1H **43**
Greendale Rd. NG3: Nott . . . . . . . . . .3E **47**
  NG5: Arn . . . . . . . . . . . . . . . . . . . . . .1B **34**
Greenfield Gro. NG4: Carl . . . . . . . . . .1D **46**
Greenfields NG16: Lang M . . . . . . . . .1E **15**
Greenfields Dr. NG12: Cotg . . . . . . . .3F **71**
Greenfield St. NG7: Nott . . . . . . . . . . .2B **56**
Greenford Cl. NG16: Nuth . . . . . . . . . .4E **31**
Greengates Av. NG3: Mapp . . . . . . . .4B **34**
Greenhill Cres. NG4: Carl . . . . . . . . . .3G **47**
Greenhill Ri. NG4: Carl . . . . . . . . . . . .2G **47**
Greenhill Rd. NG4: Carl . . . . . . . . . . .3G **47**
Greenhills Av. NG16: Eastw . . . . . . . . .2C **16**
Greenhills Rd. NG16: Eastw . . . . . . . .2B **16**
Greenland Cres. NG9: Chil . . . . . . . . .1C **64**
Green La. DE7: Ilk . . . . . . . . . . . . . . . .2C **40**
  NG4: Lamb . . . . . . . . . . . . . . . . . . . .4B **24**
  NG11: Clif . . . . . . . . . . . . . . . . . . . . .3B **66**
Green Leys NG2: West Br . . . . . . . . . .1G **67**
Green Mews, The NG5: Bestw . . . . . . .2E **33**
Green Platt NG12: Cotg . . . . . . . . . . .2E **71**
Greens Farm La. NG4: Ged . . . . . . . . .5A **36**
Greenside Cl. NG10: Long E . . . . . . . .6G **63**
Greenside Wlk. NG3: Nott . . . . . . . . .3E **47**
Greens La. NG16: Kimb . . . . . . . . . . . .1H **29**
Green St. NG2: Nott . . . . . . . . . . . . . .2H **57**
  NG11: Bart F, Thru . . . . . . . . . . . . . . .3E **75**

Green's Windmill & Science Cen. . . . . . . . .5B **46**
Greenway, The NG10: Sand . . . . . . . . .5D **52**
Greenway Cl. NG12: Rad T . . . . . . . . .6E **49**
Greenwich Av. NG6: Basf . . . . . . . . . .3A **32**
Greenwich Pk. Cl. NG2: West Br . . . . . .6G **57**
Greenwood Av. DE7: Ilk . . . . . . . . . . .2C **40**
  NG3: Nott . . . . . . . . . . . . . . . . . . . . .4F **47**
  NG15: Huck . . . . . . . . . . . . . . . . . . . .3F **7**
Greenwood Bonsai Studio . . . . . . . . . . . .4A **10**
Greenwood Ct. NG9: Chil . . . . . . . . . .6D **54**
Greenwood Cres. NG4: Carl . . . . . . . .3G **47**
Greenwood Gdns. NG8: Bilb . . . . . . . .2C **42**
  NG11: Rudd . . . . . . . . . . . . . . . . . . . .1H **77**
Greenwood Rd. NG3: Nott . . . . . . . . .4C **46**
  NG4: Carl . . . . . . . . . . . . . . . . . . . . . .4E **47**
Greenwood Va. NG15: Huck . . . . . . . .3E **7**
Greet Ct. NG7: Radf . . . . . . . . . . . . . .2B **44**
Greetwell Cl. NG8: Bilb . . . . . . . . . . . .3G **43**
Gregg Av. DE75: Hea . . . . . . . . . . . . .3D **14**
Gregory Av. NG3: Mapp . . . . . . . . . . .5C **34**
  NG7: Lent . . . . . . . . . . . . . . . . . . . . . .6D **44**
  NG16: Lang M . . . . . . . . . . . . . . . . . .2E **15**
Gregory Blvd. NG7: H Grn . . . . . . . . . .2C **44**
Gregory Cl. NG9: Stap . . . . . . . . . . . .3H **53**
Gregory Ct. NG7: H Grn . . . . . . . . . . .1C **44**
  NG7: Lent . . . . . . . . . . . . . . . . . . . . . .6C **44**
  NG9: Chil . . . . . . . . . . . . . . . . . . . . . .1B **64**
Gregory St. DE7: Ilk . . . . . . . . . . . . . .1A **40**
  NG7: Lent . . . . . . . . . . . . . . . . . . . . . .6C **44**
Gregson Gdns. NG9: Toton . . . . . . . . .4B **64**
Gregson Rd. NG9: Chil . . . . . . . . . . . .2A **64**
Grenay Ct. NG11: Rudd . . . . . . . . . . .5F **67**
                  (not continuous)
Grenfell Ter. NG6: Basf . . . . . . . . . . . .3C **32**
Grenville Dr. DE7: Ilk . . . . . . . . . . . . . .4B **28**
  NG9: Stap . . . . . . . . . . . . . . . . . . . . .3G **53**
Grenville Ri. NG5: Arn . . . . . . . . . . . . .4B **22**
Grenville Rd. NG9: Bee . . . . . . . . . . . .1H **65**
Gresham Cl. NG2: West Br . . . . . . . . . .4G **57**
Gresham Gdns. NG2: West Br . . . . . . .4G **57**
  NG5: Woodt . . . . . . . . . . . . . . . . . . .2C **34**
Gresham Pk. Rd. NG2: West Br . . . . . .4G **57**
Gresley Dr. NG2: Nott . . . . . . . . . . . . .6B **46**
Gresley Rd. DE7: Ilk . . . . . . . . . . . . . .6B **28**
Gretton Rd. NG3: Mapp . . . . . . . . . . .3C **34**
Greyfriar Ga. NG1: Nott . . . . . . . . . .6D **4** (6G **45**)
Greyfriars Cl. DE75: Hea . . . . . . . . . . .4H **14**
Greyhound St. NG1: Nott . . . . . . . .4E **5** (5G **45**)
Grey Meadow Rd. DE7: Ilk . . . . . . . . .5A **28**
Greys Rd. NG5: Woodt . . . . . . . . . . . .3B **34**
Greystoke Dr. NG8: Bilb . . . . . . . . . . .2C **42**
Greythorn Dr. NG2: West Br . . . . . . . .1H **67**
Grierson Av. NG5: Bestw . . . . . . . . . .5F **21**
Griffiths Way NG15: Huck . . . . . . . . . .5H **7**
Griffon Ct. DE7: Ilk . . . . . . . . . . . . . . .5B **40**
Griffon Rd. DE7: Ilk . . . . . . . . . . . . . .5B **40**
Griffs Hollow NG4: Carl . . . . . . . . . . .2G **47**
Grimesmoor Rd. NG14: Calv . . . . . . . .3A **12**
Grimsby Ter. NG3: Nott . . . . . . . . .1E **5** (3G **45**)
Grimston Rd. NG7: Radf . . . . . . . . . . .3C **44**
Grindon Cres. NG6: Bulw . . . . . . . . . .3A **20**
Grindslow Av. DE7: West H . . . . . . . . .1C **38**
Grinsbrook Cl. NG7: Lent . . . . . . . . . .5C **44**
Gripps, The NG12: Cotg . . . . . . . . . . .3F **71**
            (off Owthorpe Rd.)
Gripps Comn. NG12: Cotg . . . . . . . . .3F **71**
Grisedale Ct. NG9: Chil . . . . . . . . . . . .1A **64**
Gritley M. NG2: Nott . . . . . . . . . . . . . .1F **57**
Grizedale Gro. NG13: Bing . . . . . . . . .5B **50**
Groome Av. DE75: Los . . . . . . . . . . . .1A **14**
Grosvenor Av. DE72: Brea . . . . . . . . . .5B **62**
  NG3: Mapp P . . . . . . . . . . . . . . . . . .6G **33**
  NG10: Long E . . . . . . . . . . . . . . . . . .3C **72**
Grosvenor Cl. NG3: Mapp P . . . . . . . .1G **45**
Grosvenor Rd. NG16: Eastw . . . . . . . .2B **16**
Grouville Dr. NG5: Woodt . . . . . . . . . .2C **34**
Grove, The DE72: Brea . . . . . . . . . . . .5B **62**
  NG5: Sher . . . . . . . . . . . . . . . . . . . . . .5F **33**
  NG7: Radf . . . . . . . . . . . . . . . . . . . . . .3D **44**
  NG14: Calv . . . . . . . . . . . . . . . . . . . .4A **12**
Grove Av. NG7: Radf . . . . . . . . . . . . . .3E **45**
  NG9: Chil . . . . . . . . . . . . . . . . . . . . . .5E **55**
Grove Cl. NG14: Bur J . . . . . . . . . . . . .2F **37**
Grove Ct. NG9: Chil . . . . . . . . . . . . . . .5D **54**
Grove M. NG16: Eastw . . . . . . . . . . . .4A **16**
Grover Av. NG3: Mapp . . . . . . . . . . . .4C **34**
Grove Rd. NG7: Lent . . . . . . . . . . . . . .6D **44**
  NG13: Bing . . . . . . . . . . . . . . . . . . . .4F **51**
Groveside Cres. NG11: Clif . . . . . . . . .2A **66**
Grove St. NG9: Bee . . . . . . . . . . . . . . .6G **55**
Grundy St. NG7: H Grn . . . . . . . . . . . .2B **44**
Guardian Ct. NG8: Aspl . . . . . . . . . . .1A **44**
Guinea Cl. NG10: Long E . . . . . . . . . .6C **62**
Gunn Cl. NG6: Bulw . . . . . . . . . . . . . .6G **19**
Gunnersbury Way NG16: Nuth . . . . . .4D **30**
Gunthorpe Cl. NG5: Sher . . . . . . . . . .4F **33**

Gunthorpe Dr. NG5: Sher . . . . . . . . . .4F **33**
Gunthorpe Rd. NG4: Ged . . . . . . . . . .4E **35**
Gutersloh Ct. NG9: Stap . . . . . . . . . . .3H **53**
Guy Cl. NG9: Stap . . . . . . . . . . . . . . . .5G **53**
Gwenbrook Av. NG9: Chil . . . . . . . . . .6E **55**
Gwenbrook Rd. NG9: Chil . . . . . . . . . .6E **55**
Gwndy Gdns. NG5: Bestw . . . . . . . . . .6E **21**
Gypsum La. NG11: Goth . . . . . . . . . . .6G **75**

## H

H2 Fitness . . . . . . . . . . . . . . . . . . . . .2E **5** (4G **45**)
Habitat, The NG1: Nott . . . . . . . . . . . .4F **5**
Hackworth Cl. NG16: Newth . . . . . . . .2D **16**
Hadbury Rd. NG5: Sher . . . . . . . . . . . .4D **32**
Hadden Ct. NG8: Bilb . . . . . . . . . . . . .4D **42**
Haddon Cl. DE7: West H . . . . . . . . . . .1C **38**
  DE75: Hea . . . . . . . . . . . . . . . . . . . . .3A **14**
  NG4: Carl . . . . . . . . . . . . . . . . . . . . . .5F **35**
  NG15: Huck . . . . . . . . . . . . . . . . . . . .5G **7**
Haddon Cres. NG9: Chil . . . . . . . . . . .2C **64**
Haddon Nurseries DE7: Ilk . . . . . . . . .4A **28**
Haddon Rd. NG2: West Br . . . . . . . . . .5B **58**
Haddon St. DE7: Ilk . . . . . . . . . . . . . .4A **28**
  NG5: Sher . . . . . . . . . . . . . . . . . . . . . .5F **33**
Haddon Way NG10: Long E . . . . . . . .3B **72**
  NG12: Rad T . . . . . . . . . . . . . . . . . . .5F **49**
Hadleigh Cl. NG9: Toton . . . . . . . . . . .3G **63**
Hadley St. DE7: Ilk . . . . . . . . . . . . . . .4C **40**
Hadrian Gdns. NG5: Top V . . . . . . . . .3E **21**
Hadstock Cl. NG10: Sand . . . . . . . . . .1D **62**
Hagg La. DE7: D Ab, West H . . . . . . . .4B **38**
  NG14: Epp . . . . . . . . . . . . . . . . . . . .6H **13**
Hagley Cl. NG3: Nott . . . . . . . . . . . . .3C **46**
Haileybury Cres. NG2: West Br . . . . . .6B **58**
Haileybury Rd. NG2: West Br . . . . . . . .6B **58**
Haise Ct. NG6: Bulw . . . . . . . . . . . . . .2F **31**
Halberton Dr. NG2: West Br . . . . . . . .1H **67**
Hales Cl. NG12: Cotg . . . . . . . . . . . . .2E **71**
Halfacre Gdns. DE7: Ilk . . . . . . . . . . . .5B **28**
Halfpenny Wlk. NG11: Wilf . . . . . . . . .5E **57**
Halifax Cl. NG8: Stre . . . . . . . . . . . . . .5D **30**
Halifax Pl. NG1: Nott . . . . . . . . . . .5F **5** (5H **45**)
Halina Ct. NG9: Bee . . . . . . . . . . . . . .4F **55**
Hallam Ct. DE7: Ilk . . . . . . . . . . . . . . .4B **28**
HALLAM FIELDS . . . . . . . . . . . . . . . . . .5C **40**
Hallam Flds. Rd. DE7: Ilk . . . . . . . . . . .5C **40**
Hallam Rd. NG3: Mapp . . . . . . . . . . .5C **34**
  NG9: Bee . . . . . . . . . . . . . . . . . . . . . .5F **55**
Hallams La. NG5: Arn . . . . . . . . . . . . .6B **22**
  NG9: Chil . . . . . . . . . . . . . . . . . . . . . .1C **64**
Hallam Way DE7: West H . . . . . . . . . .1B **38**
  NG16: Lang M . . . . . . . . . . . . . . . . . .2G **15**
Hall Cl. NG12: Rad T . . . . . . . . . . . . . .6E **49**
Hall Ct. DE7: West H . . . . . . . . . . . . . .2C **38**
Hall Cft. NG9: Bee . . . . . . . . . . . . . . . .6F **55**
Hallcroft DE7: Ilk . . . . . . . . . . . . . . . . .1B **40**
Hallcroft Rd. DE7: Ilk . . . . . . . . . . . . .1B **40**
Hall Dr. NG5: Arn . . . . . . . . . . . . . . . .5C **22**
  NG8: Woll . . . . . . . . . . . . . . . . . . . . .6E **43**
  NG9: Chil . . . . . . . . . . . . . . . . . . . . . .6C **54**
  NG10: Sand . . . . . . . . . . . . . . . . . . . .5D **52**
  NG11: Goth . . . . . . . . . . . . . . . . . . . .6G **75**
Hall Farm Cl. NG12: Toll . . . . . . . . . . .4F **69**
Hall Farm Ct. DE7: Stant D . . . . . . . . .3B **52**
  NG2: Gam . . . . . . . . . . . . . . . . . . . . .4E **59**
Hallfields NG12: Edwal . . . . . . . . . . . .2D **68**
Hall Gdns. NG9: Bram . . . . . . . . . . . .4B **54**
Hallington Dr. DE75: Hea . . . . . . . . . .4B **14**
Hallowell Dr. NG8: Woll . . . . . . . . . . .3F **43**
Hall Pk. Dr. NG12: Toll . . . . . . . . . . . .2A **16**
Hall Rd. NG16: Lang M . . . . . . . . . . . .1G **15**
Halls La. NG16: Newth . . . . . . . . . . . .5C **16**
Hall St. NG5: Sher . . . . . . . . . . . . . . . .4H **33**
Hall Vw. Dr. NG8: Bilb . . . . . . . . . . . . .3D **42**
Halstead Cl. NG8: Cin . . . . . . . . . . . . .4H **31**
  NG9: Chil . . . . . . . . . . . . . . . . . . . . . .1C **64**
Haltham Wlk. NG11: Clif . . . . . . . . . . .5B **66**
Hambledon Dr. NG8: Woll . . . . . . . . . .4H **43**
Hambleton Cl. NG10: Long E . . . . . . . .4C **62**
Hambling Cl. NG6: Bulw . . . . . . . . . . .6G **19**
Hamilton, The NG7: Lent . . . . . . . . . . .1C **56**
               (off Leen Ct.)
Hamilton Cl. NG5: Arn . . . . . . . . . . . .4E **23**
  NG9: Toton . . . . . . . . . . . . . . . . . . . .3H **63**
Hamilton Ct. NG7: Nott . . . . . . . . .6B **4** (6F **45**)
  NG11: Clif . . . . . . . . . . . . . . . . . . . . .2D **66**
Hamilton Dr. NG7: Nott . . . . . . . . .6B **4** (6F **45**)
  NG12: Rad T . . . . . . . . . . . . . . . . . . .5F **49**
Hamilton Gdns. NG5: Sher . . . . . . . . . .6F **33**
           (off Alexandra St.)
Hamilton Pl. NG2: Nott . . . . . . . . . . . .5B **46**
Hamilton Rd. NG5: Sher . . . . . . . . . . .1F **45**
  NG10: Long E . . . . . . . . . . . . . . . . . .4F **63**

Hamlet, The—Helmsley Dr.

**Hamlet, The** DE75: Hea 2C **14**
**Hammersmith Cl.** NG16: Nuth 3E **31**
**Hampden** NG1: Nott 1C **4** (3F **45**)
**Hampden Gro.** NG9: Bee 5E **55**
**Hampden Rd.** NG13: Newton 2B **50**
**Hampden St.** NG1: Nott 1C **4** (3F **45**)
NG16: Gilt 5D **16**
NG16: Lang M 2F **15**
**Hampshire Dr.** NG10: Sand 6D **52**
**Hampstead Ct.** *NG5: Sher* *4G 33*
*(off St Albans St.)*
**Hampstead Rd.** NG3: Nott 6A **34**
**Hampton Cl.** DE7: West H 1B **38**
NG9: Toton 2G **63**
**Hampton Ct.** DE75: Hea 3B **14**
**Hampton Rd.** NG2: West Br 5A **58**
**Handel St.** NG3: Nott 3H **5** (4A **46**)
**Hand's Rd.** DE75: Hea 4D **14**
**Hankin St.** NG15: Huck 5A **8**
**Hanley Av.** NG9: Bram 3B **54**
**Hanley St.** NG1: Nott 3C **4** (4F **45**)
**Hannah Cres.** NG11: Wilf 4F **57**
**Hanover Ct.** NG8: Bilb 3D **42**
**Hanselin Ct.** NG4: Ged 6A **36**
**Hanslope Cres.** NG8: Bilb 3D **42**
**Hanson Cres.** NG15: Huck 4G **7**
**Hanworth Gdns.** NG5: Arn 5H **21**
**Harberton Cl.** NG5: Redh 4A **22**
**Harby Dr.** NG8: Woll 5A **44**
**Harcourt Cl.** DE7: Ilk 6H **27**
**Harcourt Cres.** NG16: Nuth 4F **31**
**Harcourt Rd.** NG7: H Grn 1E **45**
**Harcourt St.** NG9: Bee 5E **55**
**Harcourt Ter.** NG3: Nott 2G **5** (4H **45**)
**Harden Ct.** NG11: Clif 5A **66**
**Hardstaff Almshouses** NG4: Ged 5G **35**
**Hardstaff Homes, The**
NG16: Gilt 5E **17**
**Hardstaff Rd.** NG2: Nott 4C **46**
**Hardwick Av.** DE7: West H 1C **38**
**Hardwick Ct.** NG10: Long E 3B **72**
**Hardwicke Rd.** NG9: Chil 2C **64**
**Hardwick Gro.** NG2: West Br 2B **58**
NG7: Nott 5E **45**
NG13: Bing 5D **50**
**Hardwick Pl.** DE7: Kirk H 4G **39**
**Hardwick Rd.** NG5: Sher 4G **33**
NG7: Nott 6A **4** (6E **45**)
**Hardwood Cl.** NG6: Bulw 6G **19**
**Hardy Barn** DE75: Ship 5E **15**
**Hardy Cl.** NG10: Long E 1F **73**
NG16: Kimb 6H **17**
**Hardy's Dr.** NG4: Ged 6H **35**
**Hardy St.** NG7: Radf 3E **45**
NG16: Kimb 6H **17**
**Harebell Gdns.** NG13: Bing 5C **50**
**Harewood Av.** NG6: Bulw 2B **32**
**Harewood Cl.** NG10: Sand 1C **62**
NG12: Rad T 6G **49**
**Hargreaves Ct.** DE7: Ilk 3C **40**
**Harkstead Rd.** NG5: Top V 4F **21**
**Harlaxton Dr.** NG7: Lent 5D **44**
(not continuous)
NG10: Long E 4A **64**
**Harlaxton Wlk.** NG3: Nott 1E **5** (3G **45**)
**Harlech Cl.** DE7: Ilk 4G **27**
**Harlech Ri.** NG9: Chil 1B **64**
HARLEQUIN 6H **49**
**Harlequin Cl.** NG12: Rad T 6H **49**
**Harlequin Ct.** NG16: Eastw 2H **15**
**Harlequin M.** NG12: Rad T 5H **49**
**Harley St.** NG7: Lent 6D **44**
**Harlow Ct.** DE7: West H 2B **38**
**Harlow Gro.** NG4: Ged 5G **35**
**Harmston Ri.** NG5: Sher 3D **32**
(not continuous)
**Harnett Cl.** NG1: Nott 5F **5** (5H **45**)
**Harold Av.** NG16: Lang M 1F **15**
**Harold Ct.** NG2: Nott 4H **5** (5A **46**)
**Harold St.** NG2: Nott 4H **5** (5A **46**)
**Harpenden Sq.** NG8: Cin 4G **31**
**Harpole Wlk.** NG5: Arn 3B **22**
**Harrier Gro.** NG15: Huck 1E **19**
**Harriett St.** NG9: Stap 4F **53**
**Harrimans Ct.** NG7: Lent 3C **56**
**Harrimans Dr.** DE72: Brea 5B **62**
**Harrimans La.** NG7: Lent 3B **56**
**Harrington Cl.** NG4: Ged 6B **36**
**Harrington Dr.** NG7: Lent 5D **44**
(not continuous)
**Harrington St.** NG10: Long E 2D **72**
**Harris Cl.** NG8: Woll 4F **43**
**Harrison Ct.** NG13: Bing 5C **50**
**Harrison Rd.** NG9: Stap 3F **53**
Harrison's Plantation Nature Reserve 4G **43**
**Harris Rd.** NG9: Chil 5D **54**
**Harrogate Rd.** NG3: Nott 4E **47**
**Harrogate St.** NG4: Neth 2H **47**
**Harrowby M.** NG7: Lent 5D **44**
**Harrowby Rd.** NG7: Lent 5D **44**
**Harrow Dr.** DE7: Ilk 5C **40**
**Harrow Gdns.** NG8: Woll 5A **44**
**Harrow Rd.** NG2: West Br 6A **58**
NG8: Woll 5G **43**
NG15: Huck 6D **6**
**Harry Peel Ct.** NG9: Bee 5G **55**
**Harston Gdns.** NG2: West Br 2F **67**
**Hart Av.** NG10: Sand 5C **52**
**Hartcroft Rd.** NG5: Bestw 1E **33**
**Hartford Cl.** NG2: Nott 1H **57**
**Hartill Cl.** NG9: Chil 3C **64**
**Hartington Av.** NG4: Carl 6F **35**
NG15: Huck 5C **6**
**Hartington Cl.** DE7: West H 1C **38**
**Hartington Pl.** DE7: Ilk 2A **28**
**Hartington Rd.** NG5: Sher 4G **33**
**Hart Lea** NG10: Sand 5D **52**
(Charles Av.)
NG10: Sand 5D **52**
(Hall Dr.)
**Hartley Ct.** NG7: Radf 3D **44**
**Hartley Dr.** NG9: Bee 5H **55**
**Hartley Rd.** NG7: Radf 3C **44**
**Hartness Rd.** NG11: Clif 4A **66**
**Hartshay Cl.** DE7: Ilk 2B **28**
**Hartside Cl.** NG2: Gam 4E **59**
**Hartside Gdns.** NG10: Long E 5C **62**
**Hartside Way** DE75: Hea 4F **15**
**Hart St.** NG7: Lent 6D **44**
**Hartwell St.** NG3: Nott 3H **45**
**Hartwood Dr.** NG9: Stap 2F **53**
**Harvest Cl.** NG5: Top V 5D **20**
NG13: Bing 5D **50**
**Harvey Cl.** NG11: Rudd 2H **77**
**Harvey Ct.** NG7: Nott 1C **56**
**Harvey Cft.** NG9: Trow 5E **41**
Harvey Hadden Sports Complex 2E **43**
Harvey Hadden Stadium 2F **43**
**Harvey Rd.** NG7: Nott 1B **56**
NG8: Bilb 2F **43**
**Harwich Cl.** NG6: Bulw 5G **19**
**Harwill Cres.** NG8: Aspl 5H **31**
**Harwood Cl.** NG5: Arn 5D **22**
**Haslam St.** NG7: Nott 6C **4** (6F **45**)
**Haslemere Rd.** NG8: Aspl 1B **44**
NG10: Long E 5D **62**
**Hassall Ct.** NG13: Bing 5F **51**
**Hassock La. Nth.** DE75: Ship 6F **15**
**Hassock La. Sth.** DE75: Ship 1G **27**
**Hassocks Cl.** NG9: Bee 4H **55**
**Hassocks La.** NG9: Bee 4H **55**
**Hastings St.** NG4: Carl 2E **47**
**Haswell Rd.** NG6: Bulw 2H **31**
**Hatfield Av.** NG10: Sand 1D **62**
**Hatfield Dr.** NG2: West Br 1G **67**
**Hatfield Rd.** NG3: Mapp P 6G **33**
**Hatherleigh Cl.** NG3: Mapp 1E **35**
**Hathern Cl.** NG10: Long E 2F **73**
**Hathern Grn.** NG9: Lent A 3G **55**
**Hathersage Av.** NG10: Long E 2B **72**
**Hathersage Cl.** NG5: Top V 5D **20**
**Hatley Cl.** NG2: Nott 2F **57**
**Hatton Cl.** NG5: Arn 3E **21**
**Hatton Crofts** NG10: Long E 1E **73**
**Hatton Gdns.** NG16: Nuth 4E **31**
**Havelock Gdns.**
NG3: Nott 1G **5** (3H **45**)
**Havelock St.** DE7: Ilk 2B **40**
**Haven Cl.** NG2: West Br 6H **57**
**Havenwood Ri.** NG11: Clif 5B **66**
**Haverhill Cres.** NG5: Top V 3B **20**
**Haversham Cl.** NG6: Basf 5B **32**
**Hawarden Ter.** NG7: H Grn 2D **44**
**Hawker Cl.** NG9: Chil 6B **54**
**Hawkhurst Dr.** NG8: Woll 1D **54**
**Hawkins Ct.** DE7: Ilk 3B **28**
**Hawkridge Gdns.**
NG3: Nott 2G **5** (4A **46**)
(not continuous)
**Hawkshead Cl.** NG2: West Br 6F **59**
**Hawksley Gdns.** NG11: Clif 3A **66**
**Hawksley Rd.** NG7: H Grn 2D **44**
**Hawkswood Cl.** NG9: Chil 1B **64**
**Hawksworth Av.** NG5: Sher 3H **33**
**Hawksworth Rd.** NG2: West Br 2B **58**
**Hawksworth St.** NG3: Nott 3H **5** (4A **46**)
**Hawley Mt.** NG5: Sher 4B **34**
**Haworth Ct.** NG11: Clif 4A **66**
**Hawthorn Av.** DE72: Brea 5B **62**
**Hawthorn Cl.** NG2: Nott 2F **57**
NG12: Edwal 1D **68**
NG12: Key 5G **79**
NG14: Woodbo 1C **24**
**Hawthorn Cres.** NG5: Arn 4C **22**
**Hawthorne Av.** NG9: Stap 5F **53**
NG10: Long E 1E **73**
NG12: Cotg 3F **71**
NG15: Huck 4F **7**
**Hawthorne Gro.** NG9: Bee 5H **55**
**Hawthorne Lodge** NG2: West Br 2D **58**
**Hawthorne Ri.** NG16: Aws 3D **28**
**Hawthorn Vw.** NG2: Nott 1F **57**
**Hawthorn Wlk.** NG3: Nott 2D **46**
**Hawton Cres.** NG8: Woll 5A **44**
**Hawton Spinney** NG8: Woll 5A **44**
**Hayden La.** NG15: Lin 1H **7**
**Haydn Av.** NG5: Sher 5F **33**
**Haydn Rd.** NG5: Sher 5E **33**
**Haydock Cl.** NG16: Kimb 6G **17**
**Hayes Cl.** DE7: West H 1C **38**
**Hayes Rd.** NG12: Key 4F **79**
**Hayles Cl.** NG5: Bestw 1F **33**
**Hayley Cl.** NG16: Kimb 1F **29**
**Hayling Cl.** DE7: Ilk 4G **27**
**Hayling Dr.** NG8: Basf 6B **32**
**Haynes Av.** NG9: Trow 4E **41**
**Haynes Cl.** NG11: Clif 2D **66**
**Hay's Cl.** DE7: Ilk 5H **27**
**Haywood Ct.** NG2: Nott 4H **5**
HAYWOOD HOUSE HOSPICE 3F **33**
**Haywood Rd.** NG3: Mapp 5B **34**
**Haywood St.** NG2: Nott 4H **5** (5A **46**)
**Hayworth Rd.** NG10: Sand 6D **52**
**Hazelbank Av.** NG3: Nott 6B **34**
**Hazel Cl.** DE75: Hea 4B **14**
NG2: West Br 2E **59**
NG13: Bing 5G **51**
**Hazel Dr.** NG16: Nuth 1B **30**
HAZELGROVE 1H **19**
**Hazel Gro.** NG3: Mapp 3C **34**
NG15: Huck 6G **7**
**Hazel Hill Cres.** NG5: Bestw 5F **21**
**Hazelhurst Gdns.** NG6: Bulw 6H **19**
**Hazel Mdws.** NG15: Huck 6G **7**
**Hazelmere Gro.** NG7: Lent 5C **44**
**Hazel St.** NG6: Bulw 5H **19**
(not continuous)
**Hazel Way** NG15: Lin 1H **7**
**Hazelwood** NG12: Cotg 2G **71**
**Hazelwood Cl.** NG16: Newth 3D **16**
**Hazelwood Dr.** NG15: Huck 5C **6**
**Hazelwood Rd.** NG7: H Grn 2C **44**
**Headingley Gdns.** NG8: Aspl 1B **44**
**Healey Cl.** NG2: Nott 1G **57**
HEANOR 4C **14**
Heanor & District Heritage Cen. 5D **14**
HEANOR GATE 5A **14**
**Heanor Ga.** DE75: Hea 4B **14**
**Heanor Ga. Ind. Est.** DE75: Hea 4B **14**
(not continuous)
**Heanor Ga. Rd.** DE75: Hea 4A **14**
HEANOR MEMORIAL HOSPITAL 4D **14**
**Heanor Retail Pk.** DE75: Hea 3C **14**
**Heanor Rd.** DE7: Ilk 2H **27**
DE7: Smal 5A **14**
DE75: Hea 5A **14**
DE75: Los 1A **14**
**Heanor Small Bus. Cen.** DE75: Hea 5A **14**
**Heard Cres.** NG9: Bee 3F **55**
**Heath, The** NG16: Gilt 5C **16**
**Heathcoat Bldg.** NG7: Nott 2B **56**
**Heathcoat Ho.** NG1: Nott 5F **5** (5H **45**)
**Heathcoat St.** NG1: Nott 4F **5** (5H **45**)
**Heather Cl.** NG3: Nott 2H **45**
NG16: Newth 4D **16**
**Heather Ct.** DE75: Hea 4F **15**
**Heather Cres.** DE72: Brea 5B **62**
**Heather Cft.** NG2: West Br 1G **67**
**Heatherington Gdns.** NG5: Top V 4E **21**
**Heatherley Dr.** NG6: Basf 3D **32**
**Heather Ri.** NG9: Bram 2E **55**
**Heather Rd.** NG4: Carl 6F **35**
**Heathervale** NG2: West Br 5F **57**
**Heathfield Av.** DE7: Ilk 1C **40**
**Heathfield Gro.** NG9: Chil 2C **64**
**Heathfield Rd.** NG5: Sher 3D **32**
**Heath Gdns.** DE72: Brea 5C **62**
**Heaton Cl.** NG3: Nott 6B **34**
**Heckington Dr.** NG8: Woll 4H **43**
**Hedderley Wlk.** NG3: Nott 1F **5** (3H **45**)
**Heddington Gdns.** NG5: Arn 5H **21**
**Hedges Dr.** DE7: Ilk 5B **40**
**Hedingham Cl.** DE7: Ilk 1H **39**
**Hedley St.** NG7: Basf 1E **45**
**Hedley Vs.** NG7: Basf 6E **33**
**Helen Cl.** NG9: Chil 5D **54**
**Hellebore Cl.** NG5: Top V 6C **20**
**Helm Cl.** NG6: Bulw 6F **19**
**Helmsdale Cl.** NG5: Arn 4D **22**
**Helmsdale Gdns.** NG5: Top V 4D **20**
**Helmsley Dr.** NG16: Eastw 2H **15**

Helston Dr.—Holly Lodge


Helston Dr. NG8: Stre 5D 30
Helvellyn Cl. NG2: Nott 1G 57
Helvellyn Way NG10: Long E 3D 62
Hemingway Cl. NG4: Carl 2E 47
NG16: Newth 4E 17
Hemlock Av. NG9: Stap 3G 53
NG10: Long E 4F 63
Hemlock Gdns. NG6: Bulw 1F 31
Hemlock La. DE7: Kirk H 4H 39
Hempshill Barns NG6: Bulw 2E 31
Hempshill La. NG6: Bulw 1H 31
(Lillington Rd.)
NG6: Bulw 1F 31
(Rochester Ct.)
HEMPSHILL VALE 2F 31
Hemsby Ct. NG5: Arn 1B 34
Hemsby Gdns. NG6: Bulw 5H 19
(not continuous)
Hemscott Cl. NG6: Bulw 5F 19
Hemswell Cl. NG3: Nott 4C 46
Hendon Ct. NG3: Nott 1B 46
Hendon Ri. NG3: Nott 1B 46
Hendre Gdns. NG5: Top V 6E 21
Henley Cl. NG4: Neth 3A 48
Henley Gdns. NG9: Stap 2G 53
Henley Ri. NG5: Sher 4E 33
Henley Way DE7: West H 1B 38
Hennessey Cl. NG9: Chil 3C 64
Henning Gdns. NG5: Top V 5E 21
Henrietta St. NG6: Bulw 1A 32
Henry Ct. NG2: Nott 1G 57
Henry Rd. NG2: West Br 3A 58
NG7: Lent 6D 44
NG9: Bee 5G 55
Henry St. NG2: Nott 4H 5 (5A 46)
NG5: Redh 3A 22
NG15: Huck 5H 7
Henshaw Av. DE7: Kirk H 4H 39
Henshaw Pl. DE7: Ilk 3A 28
Hensons Row NG6: Basf 5B 32
Hensons Sq. NG9: Bram 3B 54
(not continuous)
Hepple Dr. NG6: Bulw 6F 19
Herald Cl. NG9: Bee 4H 55
Herbert Buzzard Ct. *NG15: Huck* *5A 8*
*(off Hankin St.)*
Herbert Rd. NG5: Sher 6E 33
Hereford Rd. NG3: Nott 4D 46
NG4: Ged 4H 35
NG5: Woodt 2A 34
Hermitage Sq. NG2: Nott 5B 46
Hermitage Wlk. DE7: Ilk 4B 40
NG7: Nott 6A 4 (6E 45)
Hermon St. NG7: Nott 3A 4 (4E 45)
Heron Ct. DE7: Ilk 5B 40
Heron Dr. NG7: Lent 5C 44
Herons Ct. NG2: West Br 1E 69
Heron Wharf NG7: Lent 1D 56
Herrywell La. NG12: Owt 6H 71
Hertford M. NG4: Carl 1E 47
Hervey Grn. NG11: Clif 3C 66
Heskey Cl. NG3: Nott 3G 45
Heskey Wlk. NG3: Nott 3G 45
Heslington Av. NG8: Basf 1C 44
Hethbeth Ct. NG2: Nott 1G 57
Hethersett Gdns. NG6: Bulw 5H 19
Hetley Rd. NG9: Bee 3F 55
Hexham Av. DE7: Ilk 5C 40
Hexham Cl. NG2: West Br 5C 58
Hexham Gdns. NG5: Top V 3E 21
Heyford Ct. DE75: Hea 4E 15
Hey St. NG10: Long E 3D 72
Hicking Building, The NG2: Nott 6H 45
Hickings La. NG9: Stap 3G 53
Hickling Cl. NG10: Long E 2E 73
Hickling Rd. NG3: Mapp 5C 34
Hickling Way NG12: Cotg 4G 71
Hickton Dr. NG9: Chil 4B 64
Highbank Dr. NG11: Clif 5C 66
Highbury Av. NG6: Bulw 2A 32
Highbury Cl. NG16: Nuth 4D 30
HIGHBURY HOSPITAL 2A 32
Highbury Rd. NG6: Bulw 6A 20
NG12: Key 3G 79
HIGHBURY VALE 2B 32
Highbury Vale Stop (NET) 3B 32
Highbury Wlk. NG6: Bulw 1A 32
High Chu. St. NG7: Basf 6D 32
(not continuous)
Highclere Dr. NG4: Carl 1H 47
Highcliffe Rd. NG3: Nott 4C 46
Highcroft NG3: Mapp 3B 34
High Cft. Cl. NG10: Long E 2G 73
Highcroft Dr. NG8: Woll 4B 42
Highcross Ct. NG7: Radf 3D 44
High Cross Leys NG3: Nott 1E 5 (3G 45)
High Cross St. NG1: Nott 3F 5 (4H 45)
Highfield Ct. NG9: Bee 5F 55
Highfield Dr. DE7: Kirk H 4F 39
NG4: Carl 2D 46
NG16: Nuth 3F 31
Highfield Gro. NG2: West Br 4B 58
Highfield Rd. NG2: West Br 4B 58
NG7: Nott 2B 56
NG9: Chil 1A 64
NG12: Key 3G 79
NG16: Nuth 3E 31
Highfields Ct. NG15: Huck 5G 7
Highfield St. NG10: Long E 3E 63
Highgate Cl. NG4: Carl 5E 35
Highgate Dr. DE7: Ilk 4G 27
Highgrove Av. NG9: Chil 5D 54
Highgrove Cl. DE75: Hea 4A 14
Highgrove Gdns.
NG12: Edwal 1C 68
High Hazels Ct. NG16: Newth 1D 16
High Hazles Cl. NG4: Ged 4G 35
High Hazles Rd. NG12: Cotg 1G 71
High Holborn DE7: Ilk 4A 28
High Hurst NG14: Calv 4G 11
Highland Ct. NG5: Basf 5D 32
High La. Central DE7: West H 6D 26
High La. E. DE7: West H 6E 27
High La. W. DE7: West H 1A 38
High Leys Rd. NG15: Huck 5F 7
High Main Dr. NG6: Bestw V 1C 20
High Mdw. NG12: Toll 4F 69
High Pavement NG1: Nott 5F 5 (5H 45)
High Rd. NG9: Bee 5F 55
NG9: Chil 6E 55
NG9: Toton 3A 64
High School Stop (NET) 3E 45
High Spannia NG16: Kimb 6H 17
High St. DE7: Ilk 1B 40
DE75: Hea 3C 14
DE75: Los 1A 14
NG1: Nott 4E 5 (5G 45)
NG5: Arn 6A 22
NG9: Stap 4G 53
NG10: Long E 5G 63
NG11: Rudd 6G 67
NG15: Huck 4G 7
NG16: Kimb 1H 29
High St. Av. NG5: Arn 6A 22
High St. Pl. NG1: Nott 4E 5 (5G 45)
Highurst Ct. NG7: Radf 4E 45
Highurst St. NG7: Radf 4E 45
High Vw. Av. NG12: Key 4H 79
High Vw. Ct. NG3: Mapp P 1H 45
Highwood Av. NG8: Bilb 1F 43
Highwray Gro. NG11: Clif 4B 66
Hilary Cl. NG8: Woll 6D 42
Hilcot Dr. NG8: Aspl 6H 31
Hillary Pl. DE7: Kirk H 4F 39
Hillbeck Cres. NG8: Woll 5C 42
Hill Cl. NG2: West Br 5D 58
NG16: Newth 4E 17
Hillcrest Cl. NG16: Want 6A 18
Hillcrest Dr. NG15: Huck 5D 6
Hillcrest Gdns. NG14: Bur J 2E 37
Hillcrest Gro. NG5: Sher 4F 33
Hill Crest Pk. NG14: Calv 2H 11
Hillcrest Rd. NG12: Key 3G 79
Hillcrest Vw. NG4: Carl 6D 34
Hill Dr. NG13: Bing 4D 50
Hill Farm Ct. NG12: Edwal 3C 68
Hillfield Gdns. NG5: Top V 3C 20
Hillfield Rd. NG9: Stap 3H 53
Hillgrove Gdns. *NG5: Top V* *5E 21*
*(off Whitchurch Cl.)*
Hilliers Ct. NG5: Top V 5D 20
Hillingdon Av. NG16: Nuth 4D 30
Hillingdon Dr. DE7: Ilk 2C 40
Hillington Ri. NG5: Bestw 6G 21
Hill Ri. NG9: Trow 5E 41
Hill Rd. DE75: Hea 4B 14
NG6: Bestw V 1C 20
NG9: Chil 2B 64
Hillsford Cl. NG8: Woll 4G 43
Hillside NG7: Nott 6B 44
NG16: Lang M 2E 15
Hillside Av. NG3: Mapp 3C 34
Hillside Cres. NG9: Bram 3E 55
Hillside Dr. NG10: Long E 5D 62
NG14: Bur J 2F 37
Hillside Gro. NG10: Sand 5C 52
Hillside Rd. NG9: Bram 2C 54
NG9: Chil 2A 64
NG12: Rad T 6G 49
Hills Rd. NG5: Woodt 3A 34
Hill Syke NG14: Lowd 3G 25
HILL TOP 3D 16
Hilltop Ri. NG16: Eastw 3D 16
Hillview Av. NG3: Mapp 5H 33
Hillview Rd. NG4: Carl 6C 34
NG9: Toton 3A 64
Hilton Cl. NG10: Long E 3B 72
Hilton Ct. NG2: West Br 6D 58
Hilton Cres. NG2: West Br 6D 58
Hilton Rd. NG3: Mapp 5B 34
Hinchin Brook NG7: Lent 5C 44
Hine Hall NG3: Nott 6B 34
Hinshelwood Ct. NG11: Clif 4A 66
Hinsley Cl. NG5: Arn 5D 22
Hinsley Ct. NG8: Bilb 4C 42
Hirst Cl. NG5: Arn 3B 22
Hirst Ct. NG7: Radf 2A 4 (4E 45)
Hirst Cres. NG8: Woll 5F 43
Hitchen Rd. NG10: Long E 6D 62
HMP Lowdham Grange NG14: Lowd 3E 25
HMP Nottingham NG5: Sher 4F 33
Hobart Cl. NG2: Nott 2G 57
Hobart Dr. NG9: Stap 2H 53
Hobson Dr. DE7: Ilk 3A 40
Hockerwood NG11: Clif 1C 66
Hockley NG1: Nott 4G 5 (5H 45)
Hockley Ho. NG1: Nott 4G 5
Hodgkin Cl. NG11: Clif 4A 66
Hodgkinson St. NG4: Neth 3A 48
Hodson Ho. NG5: Sher 5G 33
Hoefield Cres. NG6: Bulw 1G 31
Hoe Hill Vw. NG12: Toll 4F 69
Hoewood Rd. NG6: Bulw 6G 19
Hogan Gdns. NG5: Top V 4E 21
Hogarth Cl. NG9: Stap 5G 53
Hogarth St. NG3: Nott 3B 46
Hoggbarn La. DE75: Los 1B 14
Hoggetts Cl. NG9: Chil 5B 54
Hogg La. NG12: Rad T 6E 49
(not continuous)
Hoggs Fld. NG16: Eastw 3B 16
Holbeck Rd. NG8: Aspl 3A 44
NG15: Huck 2H 7
Holborn Av. NG2: Nott 4B 46
Holborn Cl. NG16: Nuth 4D 30
Holborn Pl. NG6: Bulw 6A 20
Holbrook Ct. NG11: Clif 5C 66
Holbrook St. DE75: Hea 3E 15
Holby Cl. NG5: Top V 5D 20
Holcombe Cl. NG8: Aspl 5H 31
Holdale Rd. NG3: Nott 3D 46
Holden Ct. NG7: Radf 2A 4 (4E 45)
Holden Cres. NG16: Nuth 1C 30
Holden Gdns. NG9: Stap 5G 53
Holden Rd. NG9: Bee 4E 55
Holden St. NG7: Radf 2A 4 (4E 45)
Holgate NG11: Clif 3A 66
Holgate Rd. NG2: Nott 2G 57
Holgate Wlk. NG15: Huck 5E 7
Holkham Av. NG9: Chil 6C 54
Holkham Cl. DE7: Ilk 4G 27
NG5: Arn 1C 34
Holland Cl. NG11: Goth 6H 75
Holland Mdw. NG10: Long E 2F 73
Holland St. NG7: H Grn 2D 44
Holles Cres. NG7: Nott 6A 4 (6E 45)
Hollies, The NG10: Sand 6C 52
NG16: Eastw 3B 16
Hollies Dr. NG12: Edwal 1C 68
Hollington Rd. NG8: Bilb 3G 43
Hollingworth Av. NG10: Sand 2D 62
Hollins, The NG14: Calv 3A 12
Hollinwell Av. NG8: Woll 4H 43
Hollinwell Ct. NG12: Edwal 2D 68
Hollinwood La. NG14: Calv 4D 10
Hollis St. NG7: Basf 6E 33
Hollows, The NG10: Long E 5A 64
NG11: Wilf 1E 67
Hollowstone NG1: Nott 5G 5 (5H 45)
Holly Av. DE72: Brea 4B 62
NG3: Nott 2C 46
NG4: Carl 2F 47
NG11: Wilf 3F 57
Hollybrook Gro. NG16: Want 6B 18
Holly Cl. NG13: Bing 5G 51
NG15: Huck 6H 7
Holly Copse Nature Reserve 5H 29
Holly Ct. NG3: Nott 2B 46
NG9: Bram 3C 54
Hollycroft NG2: West Br 1C 68
Hollydale Rd. NG3: Nott 3D 46
Hollydene Cl. NG15: Huck 6C 6
Hollydene Cres. NG6: Cin 3H 31
Holly Farm Cotts. NG12: Key 6G 79
Holly Farm Ct. NG16: Newth 4E 17
Holly Gdns. NG3: Nott 2B 46
Hollygate Ind. Pk. NG12: Cotg 1G 71
Hollygate La. NG12: Cotg 2F 71
Holly La. NG9: Chil 6E 55
Holly Leaf Rd. NG15: Huck 1A 20
Holly Lodge NG2: West Br 2D 58


*A-Z Nottingham 105*

Holly Rd. NG16: Want . . . . . . . . . . . . . . . .6H 17
Hollythorpe Pl. NG15: Huck . . . . . . . . . . . .6C 6
Holme Cl. DE7: Ilk . . . . . . . . . . . . . . . . . .5H 27
   NG14: Woodbo . . . . . . . . . . . . . . . . . .1D 24
Holme Cft. DE7: West H . . . . . . . . . . . . . .2C 38
Holmefield Cres. DE7: Ilk . . . . . . . . . . . . .1C 40
Holme Gro. NG2: West Br . . . . . . . . . . . . .1D 58
Holme La. NG12: Hol P, Rad T . . . . . . . . .6B 48
   NG12: Rad T . . . . . . . . . . . . . . . . . . . .3H 59
Holme Lea NG10: Sand . . . . . . . . . . . . . . .5D 52
Holme Lodge NG4: Carl . . . . . . . . . . . . . .3G 47
HOLME PIERREPONT . . . . . . . . . . . . . . .6A 48
Holme Pierrepont Country Pk. . . . . . . . . .6A 48
Holme Pierrepont Hall . . . . . . . . . . . . . . .6B 48
Holme Rd. NG2: West Br . . . . . . . . . . . . .2B 58
   NG13: Bing . . . . . . . . . . . . . . . . . . . . . .5F 51
Holmes Cl. NG16: Lang M . . . . . . . . . . . . .2E 15
Holmesfield Dr. DE75: Hea . . . . . . . . . . . .3B 14
Holmes Rd. DE72: Brea . . . . . . . . . . . . . .5A 62
Holmes St. DE75: Hea . . . . . . . . . . . . . . .3B 14
Holme St. NG2: Nott . . . . . . . . . . . . . . . .1A 58
Holmewood Av. DE7: Ilk . . . . . . . . . . . . . .2B 28
Holmewood Cres. NG5: Bestw . . . . . . . . . .1E 33
Holmewood Dr. NG16: Gilt . . . . . . . . . . . .5D 16
Holmfield Rd. NG9: Chil . . . . . . . . . . . . . .2C 64
Holmsfield NG12: Key . . . . . . . . . . . . . . .5G 79
Holroyd Av. NG9: Bram . . . . . . . . . . . . . .5B 46
Holt Gro. NG14: Calv . . . . . . . . . . . . . . . .3H 11
Holwood Ct. NG6: Bulw . . . . . . . . . . . . . .1G 31
Holyoake Dr. NG10: Long E . . . . . . . . . . .6H 63
Holyoake Rd. NG3: Mapp . . . . . . . . . . . . .4E 35
Holyoake Vs. NG4: Colw . . . . . . . . . . . . . .3H 47
Holywell Rd. DE7: Ilk . . . . . . . . . . . . . . . .4G 27
Home Cl. NG5: Arn . . . . . . . . . . . . . . . . .5H 21
Home Croft, The NG9: Bram . . . . . . . . . . .4B 54
Home Farm Cl. NG11: Goth . . . . . . . . . . . .6G 75
Homefield Av. NG5: Arn . . . . . . . . . . . . . .3C 22
Homefield Rd. NG8: Aspl . . . . . . . . . . . . .2B 44
Homestead NG16: Lang M . . . . . . . . . . . .1E 15
Homewell Wlk. NG11: Clif . . . . . . . . . . . . .2D 66
Honeysuckle Cl. NG6: Brox . . . . . . . . . . . .6E 31
Honeysuckle Gro. NG6: Cin . . . . . . . . . . . .3H 31
   NG13: Bing . . . . . . . . . . . . . . . . . . . . . .6D 50
Honeywood Ct. NG3: Nott . . . . . . . . . . . . .2C 46
Honeywood Dr. NG3: Nott . . . . . . . . . . . . .2C 46
Honingham Cl. NG5: Arn . . . . . . . . . . . . . .2B 34
Honingham Rd. DE7: Ilk . . . . . . . . . . . . . .4G 27
Honister Cl. NG2: Gam . . . . . . . . . . . . . . .4E 59
   NG11: Clif . . . . . . . . . . . . . . . . . . . . . . .6B 66
Honiton Cl. NG9: Toton . . . . . . . . . . . . . . .3A 64
Honiton Rd. NG8: Brox . . . . . . . . . . . . . . .6E 31
Hood Cotts. NG5: Sher . . . . . . . . . . . . . . .5H 33
Hood St. NG5: Sher . . . . . . . . . . . . . . . . .5H 33
Hook Cl. NG9: Bram . . . . . . . . . . . . . . . . .3C 64
Hooley Cl. NG10: Long E . . . . . . . . . . . . .1D 72
Hooley Pl. NG5: Sher . . . . . . . . . . . . . . . .4H 33
Hoopers Wlk. NG2: Nott . . . . . . . . . . . . . .1G 57
Hooton Rd. NG4: Carl . . . . . . . . . . . . . . . .2E 47
Hooton St. NG3: Nott . . . . . . . . . . . . . . . .4B 46
Hope Cl. NG2: Nott . . . . . . . . . . . . . . . . .1F 57
Hopedale Cl. NG7: Radf . . . . . . . . . . . . . .4C 44
Hope Dr. NG7: Nott . . . . . . . . . .6B 4 (6F 45)
Hope St. DE7: Ilk . . . . . . . . . . . . . . . . . . .2B 40
   NG9: Bee . . . . . . . . . . . . . . . . . . . . . . .4E 55
Hopewell Cl. NG12: Rad T . . . . . . . . . . . . .4G 49
Hopkin Ct. NG3: Mapp . . . . . . . . . . . . . . .1E 35
Hopkins Ct. NG16: Eastw . . . . . . . . . . . . .2B 16
Hopkinson Ct. NG6: Bestw V . . . . . . . . . .2C 20
Horace Av. NG9: Stap . . . . . . . . . . . . . . .4E 53
Horizon Pl. NG8: Stre . . . . . . . . . . . . . . . .5C 30
Hornbeam Cl. DE7: Ilk . . . . . . . . . . . . . . .2D 40
Hornbeam Gdns. NG6: Bulw . . . . . . . . . . .6F 19
Hornbuckle Ct. NG7: Radf . . . . . . . . . . . . .4D 44
Hornchurch Rd. NG8: Bilb . . . . . . . . . . . . .1D 42
Hornsby Wlk. NG5: Top V . . . . . . . . . . . . .5C 20
Horridge St. DE7: Ilk . . . . . . . . . . . . . . . .3B 28
Horsecroft Cl. DE7: Ilk . . . . . . . . . . . . . . .5G 27
Horsendale Av. NG9: Nuth . . . . . . . . . . . . .3E 31
Horsham Dr. NG5: Top V . . . . . . . . . . . . .5D 20
Horsley Cres. NG16: Lang M . . . . . . . . . . .2E 15
Hoselett Fld. Rd. NG10: Long E . . . . . . . . .2G 73
Hoten Rd. NG2: Nott . . . . . . . . . . . . . . . .6B 46
Hotspur Cl. NG6: Basf . . . . . . . . . . . . . . .2C 32
Hotspur Dr. NG4: Colw . . . . . . . . . . . . . . .3G 47
Houghton Av. DE7: Ilk . . . . . . . . . . . . . . .4G 27
Houghton Cl. NG16: Nuth . . . . . . . . . . . . .3E 31
Houldsworth Ri. NG5: Arn . . . . . . . . . . . . .3A 22
Hound Rd. NG2: West Br . . . . . . . . . . . . .3A 58
Hounds Gate NG1: Nott . . . . . .5C 4 (5G 45)
   (not continuous)
Houseman Gdns. NG2: Nott . . . . . . . . . . . .1G 57
Houston Cl. NG5: Top V . . . . . . . . . . . . . .4C 20
Hovenden Gdns. NG7: H Grn . . . . . . . . . . .2C 44
Hove Rd. NG5: Bestw . . . . . . . . . . . . . . . .2C 32
Howard Cl. NG10: Long E . . . . . . . . . . . . .4G 63
Howard St. NG1: Nott . . . . . . . . .2F 5 (4G 45)

Howarth Cl. NG10: Long E . . . . . . . . . . . .6C 62
Howbeck Rd. NG5: Arn . . . . . . . . . . . . . . .4D 22
Howden Rd. NG6: Bulw . . . . . . . . . . . . . . .3A 20
Howell Jones Rd. NG9: Chil . . . . . . . . . . .2B 64
Howells Cl. NG5: Arn . . . . . . . . . . . . . . . .5G 21
Howick Dr. NG6: Bulw . . . . . . . . . . . . . . .6F 19
Howieson Cl. NG3: Mapp . . . . . . . . . . . . .2D 34
Howitt St. DE75: Hea . . . . . . . . . . . . . . . .3D 14
   NG10: Long E . . . . . . . . . . . . . . . . . . .6G 63
Hoylake Cres. NG8: Bilb . . . . . . . . . . . . . .2D 42
Hoyland Av. NG7: Lent . . . . . . . . . . . . . . .1C 56
Hoyle Rd. NG14: Calv . . . . . . . . . . . . . . . .2H 11
Hubert Ct. NG7: H Grn . . . . . . . . . . . . . . .3D 44
Hubert St. NG7: H Grn . . . . . . . . . . . . . . .3D 44
Huckerby Rd. DE7: Ilk . . . . . . . . . . . . . . .5G 27
Huckerbys Fld. NG4: Carl . . . . . . . . . . . . .6E 35
HUCKNALL . . . . . . . . . . . . . . . . . . . . . . .4G 7
Hucknall (Park & Ride) . . . . . . . . . . . . . . .4A 8
Hucknall By-Pass NG15: Huck . . . . . . . . . .4E 7
Hucknall Cl. NG8: Stre . . . . . . . . . . . . . . .5D 30
Hucknall Cres. NG4: Ged . . . . . . . . . . . . .5G 35
Hucknall Golf Course . . . . . . . . . . . . . . . . .4A 8
Hucknall Ind. Pk. NG15: Huck . . . . . . . . . .1F 19
Hucknall La. NG6: Bulw . . . . . . . . . . . . . .5A 20
Hucknall Leisure Cen. . . . . . . . . . . . . . . . .3H 7
Hucknall Rd.
   NG5: Bestw, Sher, Top V . . . . . . . . . . .4B 20
   NG6: Bulw . . . . . . . . . . . . . . . . . . . . . .4B 20
Hucknall Station (Rail & NET) . . . . . . . . . . .4A 8
Hucknall Town FC . . . . . . . . . . . . . . . . . . .6F 7
Hudson St. NG3: Nott . . . . . . . . . . . . . . . .3B 46
Hudson Way NG12: Rad T . . . . . . . . . . . .5H 49
Hufton's Ct. DE75: Hea . . . . . . . . . . . . . . .6E 15
Hufton's Dr. DE75: Hea . . . . . . . . . . . . . . .6D 14
Hugessen Av. NG15: Huck . . . . . . . . . . . . .3A 8
Huggett Gdns. NG5: Top V . . . . . . . . . . . .5E 21
Humber Cl. NG2: Nott . . . . . . . . . . . . . . . .1G 57
Humber Lodge NG9: Bee . . . . . . . . . . . . . .4G 55
Humber Rd. NG9: Bee . . . . . . . . . . . . . . . .4G 55
   (not continuous)
   NG10: Long E . . . . . . . . . . . . . . . . . . .4E 63
Humber Rd. Sth. NG9: Bee . . . . . . . . . . . .5H 55
Humberston Rd. NG8: Woll . . . . . . . . . . . .6C 42
HUNGERHILL GARDENS . . . . . . . . . . . . .2H 45
Hungerhill La. NG14: Woodbo . . . . . . . . . .3H 23
Hungerhill Rd. NG3: Nott . . . . . . . . . . . . . .2H 45
Hungerton St. NG7: Lent . . . . . . . . . . . . . .6D 44
Hunston Cl. NG8: Bilb . . . . . . . . . . . . . . . .2G 43
Hunt Av. DE75: Hea . . . . . . . . . . . . . . . . .4D 14
Hunt Cl. NG12: Rad T . . . . . . . . . . . . . . . .6F 49
Hunter Rd. NG5: Arn . . . . . . . . . . . . . . . . .1E 35
Hunters Cl. NG11: Wilf . . . . . . . . . . . . . . .5E 57
Hunter St. NG2: Nott . . . . . . . . . . . . . . . .1H 57
Huntingdon Dr. NG7: Nott . . . . .5B 4 (5F 45)
Huntingdon St. NG1: Nott . . . . . .1D 4 (3G 45)
Huntingdon Wlk. NG10: Sand . . . . . . . . . . .6D 52
Huntingdon Way NG9: Toton . . . . . . . . . . .3H 63
Huntly Cl. NG11: Clif . . . . . . . . . . . . . . . . .4E 67
Hurcomb St. NG3: Nott . . . . . . . . . . . . . . .2B 46
Hurley Ct. DE7: West H . . . . . . . . . . . . . .1C 38
Hurst Dr. DE7: Stan . . . . . . . . . . . . . . . . .3A 38
Hurts Cft. NG9: Chil . . . . . . . . . . . . . . . . .1D 64
Hurt's Yd. NG1: Nott . . . . . . . . .3D 4 (4G 45)
Huss's La. NG10: Long E . . . . . . . . . . . . .2H 63
Hutchinson Grn. NG3: Nott . . . . .1F 5 (3H 45)
Hutton Cl. NG9: Bram . . . . . . . . . . . . . . . .2D 54
Hutton St. NG2: Nott . . . . . . . . . . . . . . . .6B 46
Huxley Cl. NG8: Bilb . . . . . . . . . . . . . . . . .2D 42
Hyde Cl. NG11: Clif . . . . . . . . . . . . . . . . .1D 66
Hyde Pk. Cl. NG2: West Br . . . . . . . . . . . .6G 57
Hyson Cl. NG7: H Grn . . . . . . . . . . . . . . . .2D 44
HYSON GREEN . . . . . . . . . . . . . . . . . . . .2D 44
Hyson Green Market Stop (NET) . . . . . . . . .2D 44
Hyson St. NG7: H Grn . . . . . . . . . . . . . . . .2D 44

Imperial Av. NG4: Ged . . . . . . . . . . . . . . .6G 35
   NG9: Bee . . . . . . . . . . . . . . . . . . . . . . .5E 55
Imperial Rd. NG6: Bulw . . . . . . . . . . . . . . .1B 32
   NG9: Bee . . . . . . . . . . . . . . . . . . . . . . .5E 55
Incher M. NG4: Carl . . . . . . . . . . . . . . . . .6E 35
Inchwood Cl. NG9: Toton . . . . . . . . . . . . . .3H 63
Incinerator Rd. NG2: Nott . . . . . . . . . . . . .1A 58
Independent St. NG7: Radf . . . . . . . . . . . .3D 44
Ingham Gro. NG7: Lent . . . . . . . . . . . . . . .6C 44
Ingham Rd. NG10: Long E . . . . . . . . . . . . .3E 63
Ingleborough Gdns. NG10: Long E . . . . . . .5C 62
Ingleby Cl. NG8: Woll . . . . . . . . . . . . . . . .5B 42
   NG12: Cotg . . . . . . . . . . . . . . . . . . . . .3E 71
Ingleby Rd. NG10: Long E . . . . . . . . . . . . .3B 72
Inglefield Cl. DE7: Ilk . . . . . . . . . . . . . . . .3B 40
Inglewood Rd. NG11: Clif . . . . . . . . . . . . .4C 66
Ingram Rd. NG6: Bulw . . . . . . . . . . . . . . .1A 32
Ingram Ter. NG6: Bulw . . . . . . . . . . . . . . .1B 32
Inham Cir. NG9: Chil . . . . . . . . . . . . . . . . .5C 54
Inham Cl. NG9: Chil . . . . . . . . . . . . . . . . .6A 54
Inham Rd. NG9: Chil . . . . . . . . . . . . . . . . .6A 54
Inkerman Cl. DE7: Ilk . . . . . . . . . . . . . . . .2A 28
Innes Cl. NG4: Carl . . . . . . . . . . . . . . . . .2E 47
Innovation Pk. NG7: Lent . . . . . . . . . . . . .5B 44
Instow Ri. NG3: Nott . . . . . . . . . .1G 5 (3H 45)
Intake Rd. NG12: Key . . . . . . . . . . . . . . . .4F 79
Interchange 25 Bus. Pk. NG10: Sand . . . . .1C 62
Invaders Cl. NG10: Long E . . . . . . . . . . . .5H 63
Iona Dr. NG9: Trow . . . . . . . . . . . . . . . . . .6F 41
Iona Gdns. NG5: Top V . . . . . . . . . . . . . . .4E 21
Ipswich Cir. NG3: Nott . . . . . . . . . . . . . . .4C 46
Ireland Av. NG9: Bee . . . . . . . . . . . . . . . . .6G 55
Ireland Cl. NG9: Bee . . . . . . . . . . . . . . . . .6G 55
Iremonger Rd. NG2: Nott . . . . . . . . . . . . . .1H 57
Irene Ter. NG7: Basf . . . . . . . . . . . . . . . . .5D 32
Ireton Gro. NG9: Atten . . . . . . . . . . . . . . .3D 64
Ireton St. NG7: Radf . . . . . . . . .2A 4 (4E 45)
   NG9: Bee . . . . . . . . . . . . . . . . . . . . . . .5E 55
Irwin Dr. NG6: Bulw . . . . . . . . . . . . . . . . .2F 31
Isaac Newton Cen. NG7: Nott . . . . . . . . . .2B 56
Isaacs La. NG9: Stap . . . . . . . . . . . . . . . .4F 53
Isabella St. NG1: Nott . . . . . . . . .6D 4 (6G 45)
Isandula Rd. NG7: Basf . . . . . . . . . . . . . . .5D 32
Island, The NG16: Eastw . . . . . . . . . . . . . .4B 16
Island La. NG12: Rad T . . . . . . . . . . . . . . .5D 48
Islay Cl. NG5: Arn . . . . . . . . . . . . . . . . . . .4B 22
   NG9: Trow . . . . . . . . . . . . . . . . . . . . . .6F 41
Ivatt Dr. NG2: Nott . . . . . . . . . . . . . . . . . .6B 46
Ives Cl. NG2: West Br . . . . . . . . . . . . . . . .1G 67
Ivy Cl. NG16: Want . . . . . . . . . . . . . . . . . .4H 17
Ivy Gro. NG4: Carl . . . . . . . . . . . . . . . . . .2F 47
   NG7: Basf . . . . . . . . . . . . . . . . . . . . . . .1E 45
Ivy La. NG16: Eastw . . . . . . . . . . . . . . . . .3A 16

                 J

Jacklin Gdns. NG5: Top V . . . . . . . . . . . . .4E 21
Jackson Av. DE7: Ilk . . . . . . . . . . . . . . . . .6A 28
   NG10: Sand . . . . . . . . . . . . . . . . . . . .5C 52
Jackson Dr. NG5: Bestw . . . . . . . . . . . . . .2E 33
Jake Rd. NG9: Bee . . . . . . . . . . . . . . . . . .2G 65
James Dr. NG14: Calv . . . . . . . . . . . . . . . .2G 11
James St. NG5: Arn . . . . . . . . . . . . . . . . .5A 22
   NG16: Kimb . . . . . . . . . . . . . . . . . . . . .1H 29
Japonica Dr. NG5: Bestw . . . . . . . . . . . . . .3H 31
Jardines, The NG9: Bram . . . . . . . . . . . . .2C 54
Jarrow Gdns. NG5: Top V . . . . . . . . . . . . .3D 20
Jarvis Av. NG3: Nott . . . . . . . . . . . . . . . . .3D 46
Jasmine Cl. NG8: Brox . . . . . . . . . . . . . . .6E 31
   NG9: Bram . . . . . . . . . . . . . . . . . . . . .2D 54
   NG11: Clif . . . . . . . . . . . . . . . . . . . . . . .4A 66
Jasmine Ct. DE75: Hea . . . . . . . . . . . . . . .4G 15
Jasmine Rd. NG5: Basf . . . . . . . . . . . . . . .4C 32
Jasper Cl. NG12: Rad T . . . . . . . . . . . . . . .1E 61
Jayne Cl. NG4: Ged . . . . . . . . . . . . . . . . .5A 36
   NG8: Woll . . . . . . . . . . . . . . . . . . . . . . .3E 43
Jebb's La. NG13: Bing . . . . . . . . . . . . . . . .5F 51
Jedburgh Cl. NG3: Nott . . . . . . .1G 5 (3H 45)
   NG16: Kimb . . . . . . . . . . . . . . . . . . . . .6G 17
Jedburgh Wlk. NG3: Nott . . . . . .1G 5 (3H 45)
Jeffries Cl. DE7: Ilk . . . . . . . . . . . . . . . . . .3H 27
Jenned Rd. NG5: Arn . . . . . . . . . . . . . . . .3C 22
Jenner Ho. NG3: Mapp . . . . . . . . . . . . . . .5B 34
Jenner St. NG5: Sher . . . . . . . . . . . . . . . .6F 33
Jenness Av. NG5: Top V . . . . . . . . . . . . . .4C 20
Jennison St. NG6: Bulw . . . . . . . . . . . . . . .6A 20
Jenny Burton Way NG15: Huck . . . . . . . . . .6A 8
Jensen Way NG5: Sher . . . . . . . . . . . . . . .6F 33
Jermyn Dr. NG5: Arn . . . . . . . . . . . . . . . . .4E 21
Jersey Gdns. NG3: Nott . . . . . . . . . . . . . . .3A 46
Jervis Ct. DE7: Ilk . . . . . . . . . . . . . . . . . . .4B 28
Jesmond Rd. NG6: Bulw . . . . . . . . . . . . . .1B 32
Jessamine Ct. NG9: Bee . . . . . . . . . . . . . .5G 55
Jesse Boot Av. NG7: Nott . . . . . . . . . . . . .2B 56
Jessops La. NG4: Ged . . . . . . . . . . . . . . . .4H 35
Jewitt Way NG11: Rudd . . . . . . . . . . . . . . .6F 67

**Jill-Iain Ct.** NG9: Stap . . . . . . . . . . . . . . . .5G 53
**Joan Av.** DE75: Hea . . . . . . . . . . . . . . . . . . .3C 14
**John & Eliza Jelley Homes**
  NG7: Nott . . . . . . . . . . . . . . . . . . . . . .6B 44
**John Carroll Cl.** NG3: Nott . . . . . . . . . . . . .3B 46
**John Carroll Leisure Cen.** . . . . . . . . . . . . .4D 44
**John Quinn Ct.** NG7: Basf . . . . . . . . . . . . . .6D 32
**Johnson Av.** NG15: Huck . . . . . . . . . . . . . . . .6H 7
**Johnson Cl.** NG16: Want . . . . . . . . . . . . . . .6A 18
**Johnson Dr.** DE75: Hea . . . . . . . . . . . . . . . .3D 14
**Johnson Rd.** NG7: Lent . . . . . . . . . . . . . . . .5C 44
**Johnson Way** NG9: Chil . . . . . . . . . . . . . . . .3B 64
**Johns Rd.** NG9: Bee . . . . . . . . . . . . . . . . . .2G 65
**Johnstone Way** NG6: Bestw V . . . . . . . . . . . .5F 9
**John St.** DE7: Ilk . . . . . . . . . . . . . . . . . . . .6B 28
  DE75: Hea . . . . . . . . . . . . . . . . . . . . . .3B 14
  NG7: Basf . . . . . . . . . . . . . . . . . . . . . .6D 32
**John Wright Cl.** NG6: Bulw . . . . . . . . . . . . . .4B 20
**Joseph Ct.** DE7: Ilk . . . . . . . . . . . . . . . . . .4A 28
**Joshua Bus. Pk.** NG16: Lang M . . . . . . . . . . .2G 15
**Joyce Av.** NG5: Sher . . . . . . . . . . . . . . . . . .3H 33
  NG9: Toton . . . . . . . . . . . . . . . . . . . . .2H 63
**Joyce Cl.** NG5: Sher . . . . . . . . . . . . . . . . . .3H 33
**Jubilee Ct.** DE7: West H . . . . . . . . . . . . . . .1A 38
  NG8: Stre . . . . . . . . . . . . . . . . . . . . . .6D 30
  NG15: Huck . . . . . . . . . . . . . . . . . . . . .6E 7
**Jubilee Rd.** NG5: Arn . . . . . . . . . . . . . . . . .1A 34
**Jubilee St.** NG2: Nott . . . . . . . . . . . . . . . . .5B 46
  NG16: Kimb . . . . . . . . . . . . . . . . . . . . .6G 17
**Judson Av.** NG9: Stap . . . . . . . . . . . . . . . . .5H 53
**Julian Cl.** DE7: Ilk . . . . . . . . . . . . . . . . . . .3D 40
**Julian Rd.** NG2: West Br . . . . . . . . . . . . . . .3D 58
**Julie Av.** DE75: Hea . . . . . . . . . . . . . . . . . .4E 15
**Julius Cl.** NG16: Lang M . . . . . . . . . . . . . . .1F 15
**Jumelles Dr.** NG14: Calv . . . . . . . . . . . . . . .4F 11
**Junction, The** NG15: Huck . . . . . . . . . . . . . . .4H 7
**Junction Rd.** NG10: Long E . . . . . . . . . . . . .1A 74
**Jungletastic Play Cen.** . . . . . . . . . . . . . . . .3F 31
**Juniper Cl.** NG11: Clif . . . . . . . . . . . . . . . . .4A 66
**Juniper Ct.** NG7: Radf . . . . . . . . . . . . . . . . .3E 45
              *(off Waterloo Prom.)*
  NG16: Gilt . . . . . . . . . . . . . . . . . . . . . .5E 17
**Juniper Gdns.** NG13: Bing . . . . . . . . . . . . . .5G 51
**Justnian Cl.** NG15: Huck . . . . . . . . . . . . . . . .3A 8

## K

**Kappler Cl.** NG4: Neth . . . . . . . . . . . . . . . . .2A 48
**Karen Gdns.** NG9: Chil . . . . . . . . . . . . . . . .1D 64
**Karen Ri.** NG5: Arn . . . . . . . . . . . . . . . . . . .4C 22
**Katherine Dr.** NG9: Toton . . . . . . . . . . . . . .1H 63
**Kayes Ct.** NG9: Stap . . . . . . . . . . . . . . . . . .4F 53
**Kayes Wlk.** NG1: Nott . . . . . . . . . .5F 5 (5H 45)
**Kay's Mdw.** NG9: Bee . . . . . . . . . . . . . . . . .4G 55
**Keats Cl.** NG5: Arn . . . . . . . . . . . . . . . . . . .6H 21
  NG10: Long E . . . . . . . . . . . . . . . . . . .2D 72
  NG16: Nuth . . . . . . . . . . . . . . . . . . . . .1B 30
**Keats Dr.** NG15: Huck . . . . . . . . . . . . . . . . .5D 6
**Keble Cl.** DE75: Hea . . . . . . . . . . . . . . . . . .5C 14
**Kedleston Cl.** NG9: Chil . . . . . . . . . . . . . . . .6C 54
  NG10: Long E . . . . . . . . . . . . . . . . . . .2C 72
**Kedleston Dr.** DE7: Ilk . . . . . . . . . . . . . . . . .4H 27
  DE75: Hea . . . . . . . . . . . . . . . . . . . . . .3A 14
**Kedleston Dr. Sth.** DE7: Ilk . . . . . . . . . . . . .4A 28
**Keeling Cl.** NG16: Newth . . . . . . . . . . . . . . .4D 16
**Keepers Cl.** NG6: Bestw V . . . . . . . . . . . . . .1C 20
**Kegworth Rd.** NG11: Goth . . . . . . . . . . . . . .6F 75
**Keighton Dr.** NG7: Nott . . . . . . . . . . . . . . . .2A 56
**Kelfield Cl.** NG6: Bulw . . . . . . . . . . . . . . . . .2C 32
**Kelham Dr.** NG5: Sher . . . . . . . . . . . . . . . . .5E 33
**Kelham Grn.** NG3: Nott . . . . . . . . . . . . . . . .3B 46
**Kelham M.** NG3: Nott . . . . . . . . . . . . . . . . . .1D 46
**Kelham Way** NG16: Eastw . . . . . . . . . . . . . .2A 16
**Kelling Cl.** NG5: Bestw . . . . . . . . . . . . . . . . .1E 33
**Kelly Wlk.** NG11: Wilf . . . . . . . . . . . . . . . . .4F 57
**Kelsey Cl.** NG5: Atten . . . . . . . . . . . . . . . . .2E 65
**Kelso Gdns.** NG2: Nott . . . . . . . . . . . . . . . .1F 57
**Kelstern Cl.** NG8: Cin . . . . . . . . . . . . . . . . .4H 31
**Kelvedon Gdns.**
  NG3: Nott . . . . . . . . . . . . .1H 5 (3A 46)
**Kelvin Cl.** NG9: Stap . . . . . . . . . . . . . . . . . .6E 53
**Kelvin Rd.** NG3: Nott . . . . . . . . . . . . . . . . . .2C 46
**Kemmel Rd.** NG6: Bulw . . . . . . . . . . . . . . . .2B 32
**Kempsey Cl.** NG5: Top V . . . . . . . . . . . . . . .5C 20
**Kempson St.** NG11: Rudd . . . . . . . . . . . . . . .6G 67
**Kempton Cl.** NG16: Kimb . . . . . . . . . . . . . . .6G 17
**Kempton Dr.** NG5: Arn . . . . . . . . . . . . . . . . .4C 22
**Kenbrook Rd.** NG15: Huck, Pap . . . . . . . . . . .2A 8
**Kendal Cl.** NG15: Huck . . . . . . . . . . . . . . . . .3F 7
**Kendal Ct.** NG2: West Br . . . . . . . . . . . . . . .3D 58
**Kendal Dr.** NG9: Bram . . . . . . . . . . . . . . . . .3D 54
**Kendale Ct.** NG3: Nott . . . . . . . . . . . . . . . . .6B 34
**Kendrew Ct.** NG11: Clif . . . . . . . . . . . . . . . .4A 66
**Kenia Cl.** NG4: Carl . . . . . . . . . . . . . . . . . . .1F 47

**Kenilworth Ct.** NG7: Nott . . . . . . . .6B 4 (6F 45)
  NG9: Bee . . . . . . . . . . . . . . . . . . . . . .3G 55
**Kenilworth Dr.** DE7: Kirk H . . . . . . . . . . . . .4G 39
**Kenilworth Rd.** NG7: Nott . . . . . . .6B 4 (6F 45)
  NG9: Bee . . . . . . . . . . . . . . . . . . . . . .4G 55
**Ken Martin Leisure Cen.** . . . . . . . . . . . . . . .4A 20
**Kenmore Gdns.** NG3: Nott . . . . . .1G 5 (3H 45)
**Kennedy Av.** NG10: Long E . . . . . . . . . . . . .2E 73
**Kennedy Cl.** NG5: Arn . . . . . . . . . . . . . . . . .6H 21
**Kennedy Dr.** NG9: Stap . . . . . . . . . . . . . . . .2G 53
**Kennel La.** NG5: Arn . . . . . . . . . . . . . . . . . .2A 6
**Kenneth Rd.** NG5: Arn . . . . . . . . . . . . . . . . .3B 22
**Kennington Rd.** NG8: Radf . . . . . . . . . . . . . .4B 44
**Ken Reid Gdns.** NG6: Bulw . . . . . . . . . . . . .5A 20
                  *(off Ragdale Rd.)*
**Kenrick Rd.** NG3: Mapp . . . . . . . . . . . . . . . .6C 34
**Kenrick St.** NG4: Neth . . . . . . . . . . . . . . . . .2A 48
**Kensal Ct.** NG2: West Br . . . . . . . . . . . . . . .3A 58
**Kensington Av.** DE75: Hea . . . . . . . . . . . . . .4A 14
**Kensington Cl.** NG9: Toton . . . . . . . . . . . . . .4A 64
**Kensington Ct.** NG5: Sher . . . . . . . . . . . . . . .4G 33
                 *(off St Albans St.)*
**Kensington Gdns.** DE7: Ilk . . . . . . . . . . . . . .2C 40
  NG4: Carl . . . . . . . . . . . . . . . . . . . . . .2G 47
**Kensington Pk. Cl.** NG2: West Br . . . . . . . . .6G 57
**Kensington Rd.** NG10: Sand . . . . . . . . . . . . .1C 62
**Kensington St.** DE7: Ilk . . . . . . . . . . . . . . . .3B 40
**Kenslow Av.** NG7: H Grn . . . . . . . . . . . . . . .2C 44
**Kenton Av.** NG9: Bee . . . . . . . . . . . . . . . . . .1F 65
**Kentmere Cl.** NG2: Gam . . . . . . . . . . . . . . . .4E 59
**Kenton Av.** NG16: Nuth . . . . . . . . . . . . . . . .4D 30
**Kenton Ct.** NG2: Nott . . . . . . . . . . . . . . . . .2H 57
**Kent Rd.** NG3: Mapp . . . . . . . . . . . . . . . . . .5B 34
  NG16: Gilt . . . . . . . . . . . . . . . . . . . . . .4E 17
**Kent St.** NG1: Nott . . . . . . . . . . . .3F 5 (4H 45)
**Kentwood Rd.** NG2: Nott . . . . . . . . . . . . . . .5B 46
**Kenyon Rd.** NG7: Lent . . . . . . . . . . . . . . . . .6B 44
**Keppel Ct.** DE7: Ilk . . . . . . . . . . . . . . . . . . .4B 28
**Kersall Ct.** NG6: Bulw . . . . . . . . . . . . . . . . .2B 32
**Kersall Dr.** NG6: Bulw . . . . . . . . . . . . . . . . .2B 32
**Kersall Gdns.** NG15: Huck . . . . . . . . . . . . . . .4H 7
**Kestrel Cl.** DE7: Ilk . . . . . . . . . . . . . . . . . . .5B 40
  NG4: Carl . . . . . . . . . . . . . . . . . . . . . .6D 34
**Kestrel Dr.** NG13: Bing . . . . . . . . . . . . . . . . .6F 51
**Kestrel Gro.** NG15: Huck . . . . . . . . . . . . . . . .5F 7
**Keswick Cl.** DE7: Kirk H . . . . . . . . . . . . . . . .4H 39
  NG2: Gam . . . . . . . . . . . . . . . . . . . . . .4E 59
  NG9: Bram . . . . . . . . . . . . . . . . . . . . .3D 54
**Keswick Cl.** NG2: Nott . . . . . . . . . .4H 5 (5A 46)
  NG10: Long E . . . . . . . . . . . . . . . . . . .3D 62
**Keswick St.** NG2: Nott . . . . . . . . . .4H 5 (5A 46)
**Kett St.** NG6: Bulw . . . . . . . . . . . . . . . . . . .6H 19
**Keverne Cl.** NG8: Aspl . . . . . . . . . . . . . . . . .4A 32
                  *(not continuous)*
**Kevin Rd.** NG8: Woll . . . . . . . . . . . . . . . . . .1D 54
**Kew Cl.** NG2: West Br . . . . . . . . . . . . . . . . .2G 67
**Kew Cres.** DE75: Hea . . . . . . . . . . . . . . . . .4F 15
**Kew Gdns.** NG16: Nuth . . . . . . . . . . . . . . . .4E 31
**Key VI Fitness** . . . . . . . . . . . . . . . . . . . . . .5G 79
**Keys Cl.** NG6: Bulw . . . . . . . . . . . . . . . . . . .6G 19
**Key St.** NG3: Nott . . . . . . . . . . . . . . . . . . . .4B 46
**KEYWORTH** . . . . . . . . . . . . . . . . . . . . . . . .5G 79
**Keyworth La.** NG11: Bunny . . . . . . . . . . . . . .6B 78
**Keyworth Leisure Cen.** . . . . . . . . . . . . . . . .4H 79
**Keyworth Rd.** NG4: Ged . . . . . . . . . . . . . . . .4F 35
**Kibworth Cl.** NG5: Sher . . . . . . . . . . . . . . . .3D 32
**Kiddier Av.** NG5: Arn . . . . . . . . . . . . . . . . . .6D 22
**Kielder Dr.** NG13: Bing . . . . . . . . . . . . . . . . .5C 50
**Kilbourne Rd.** NG5: Arn . . . . . . . . . . . . . . . .4D 22
**Kilburn St.** NG5: Sher . . . . . . . . . . . . . . . . .3G 45
**Kilburn Cl.** NG9: Bram . . . . . . . . . . . . . . . . .1B 54
**Kilburn Dr.** DE7: Ilk . . . . . . . . . . . . . . . . . .4H 27
**Kilby Av.** NG3: Nott . . . . . . . . . . . . . . . . . . .3C 46
**Kilby Ho.** NG10: Long E . . . . . . . . . . . . . . . .6F 63
**Kildare Rd.** NG3: Nott . . . . . . . . . . . . . . . . .1B 46
**Kildonan Cl.** NG8: Stre . . . . . . . . . . . . . . . .5D 30
**Killarney Pk.** NG6: Bestw V . . . . . . . . . . . . .5F 9
**Killerton Grn.** NG11: Clif . . . . . . . . . . . . . . .6D 66
**Killerton Pk. Dr.** NG2: West Br . . . . . . . . . . .1F 67
**Killisick Cl.** NG5: Arn . . . . . . . . . . . . . . . . . .3D 22
**Killisick Rd.** NG5: Arn . . . . . . . . . . . . . . . . .5C 22
**Kilnbrook Av.** NG5: Arn . . . . . . . . . . . . . . . .4D 22
**Kiln Cl.** DE7: West H . . . . . . . . . . . . . . . . . .6C 26
**Kilnwood Cl.** NG3: Nott . . . . . . . . . . . . . . . .2C 46
**Kilsby Rd.** NG11: Clif . . . . . . . . . . . . . . . . . .3A 66
**Kilverston Rd.** NG10: Sand . . . . . . . . . . . . . .5C 52
**Kilverton Cl.** NG8: Woll . . . . . . . . . . . . . . . .5A 44
**Kilvington Rd.** NG5: Arn . . . . . . . . . . . . . . . .6D 22
**Kimber Cl.** NG8: Bilb . . . . . . . . . . . . . . . . . .3D 42
**KIMBERLEY** . . . . . . . . . . . . . . . . . . . . . . . .1H 29
**Kimberley Cl.** NG16: Kimb . . . . . . . . . . . . . .2H 29
**Kimberley Eastwood By-Pass** NG8: Cin . . . . .3E 31
  NG16: Eastw, Gilt, Kimb, Newth, Nuth
                      . . . .3H 15
**Kimberley Leisure Cen.** . . . . . . . . . . . . . . . .1A 30
**Kimberley Rd.** NG16: Nuth . . . . . . . . . . . . . .2B 30
**Kimberley St.** NG2: Nott . . . . . . . . . . . . . . . .5C 46

**Kimbolton Av.** NG7: Lent, Radf . . . . . . . . . . .4D 44
**Kindlewood Dr.** NG9: Toton . . . . . . . . . . . . .3B 64
**King Charles St.** NG1: Nott . . . . . . .5C 4 (5F 45)
**King Edward Ct.** NG1: Nott . . . . . . . .3F 5 (4H 45)
**King Edward Gdns.** NG10: Sand . . . . . . . . . .5D 52
**King Edward St.** NG1: Nott . . . . . . .3F 5 (4H 45)
  NG10: Sand . . . . . . . . . . . . . . . . . . . .5D 52
  NG15: Huck . . . . . . . . . . . . . . . . . . . . .5G 7
**Kingfisher Cl.** NG6: Basf . . . . . . . . . . . . . . . .3B 32
  NG9: Bee . . . . . . . . . . . . . . . . . . . . . .6H 55
**Kingfishers Ct.** NG2: West Br . . . . . . . . . . . .1E 69
**Kingfisher Wharf** NG7: Lent . . . . . . . . . . . . .1E 57
**King George Av.** DE7: Ilk . . . . . . . . . . . . . . .1A 40
**King John's Arc.** NG1: Nott . . . . . . . . . . . . . .4E 5
**King John's Chambers** NG1: Nott . . . . . . . . .4E 5
**Kinglake Pl.** NG2: Nott . . . . . . . . . . . . . . . . .1G 57
**Kingrove Av.** NG9: Chil . . . . . . . . . . . . . . . . .5D 54
**Kings Av.** NG4: Ged . . . . . . . . . . . . . . . . . . .5G 35
**Kingsbridge Av.** NG3: Mapp . . . . . . . . . . . . .1E 35
**Kingsbridge Way** NG9: Bram . . . . . . . . . . . .5G 53
**Kingsbury Dr.** NG8: Bilb . . . . . . . . . . . . . . . .1G 43
**Kings Cl.** DE75: Hea . . . . . . . . . . . . . . . . . . .4A 14
**Kingsdale Cl.** NG10: Long E . . . . . . . . . . . . .2C 72
**Kingsdown Mt.** NG8: Woll . . . . . . . . . . . . . .1E 55
**Kingsford Av.** NG7: Radf . . . . . . . . . . . . . . . .3C 44
**Kingsley Cres.** NG10: Long E . . . . . . . . . . . .3D 72
**Kingsley Dr.** NG4: Neth . . . . . . . . . . . . . . . .3A 48
**Kingsley Rd.** NG2: Nott . . . . . . . . . . . . . . . .5C 46
**Kingsmead Av.** NG9: Trow . . . . . . . . . . . . . .1F 53
**Kingsmoor Cl.** NG5: Top V . . . . . . . . . . . . . .6C 20
**King's Pl.** NG1: Nott . . . . . . . . . . .4F 5 (5H 45)
**Kings Rd.** NG10: Sand . . . . . . . . . . . . . . . . .5D 52
**Kingsthorpe Cl.** NG3: Nott . . . . . . . . . . . . . .6B 34
**Kingston Av.** DE7: Ilk . . . . . . . . . . . . . . . . . .5C 40
**Kingston Ct.** DE7: West H . . . . . . . . . . . . . . .1B 38
  NG2: Nott . . . . . . . . . . . . . .4H 5 (5A 46)
  NG12: Rad T . . . . . . . . . . . . . . . . . . . .6F 49
                *(off Bingham Rd.)*
**Kingston Dr.** NG12: Cotg . . . . . . . . . . . . . . . .4F 71
**Kingston Rd.** NG2: West Br . . . . . . . . . . . . . .5A 58
**King St.** DE7: Ilk . . . . . . . . . . . . . . . . . . . . .6B 28
  NG1: Nott . . . . . . . . . . . . . .3D 4 (5G 45)
  NG9: Bee . . . . . . . . . . . . . . . . . . . . . .5G 55
  NG10: Long E . . . . . . . . . . . . . . . . . . .5F 63
  NG16: Eastw . . . . . . . . . . . . . . . . . . . .3B 16
**Kings Wlk.** NG1: Nott . . . . . . . . . .3D 4 (4G 45)
**Kingsway** DE7: Ilk . . . . . . . . . . . . . . . . . . . .4B 40
  DE75: Hea . . . . . . . . . . . . . . . . . . . . . .3B 14
  NG12: Rad T . . . . . . . . . . . . . . . . . . . .1E 61
**Kingsway Gdns.** NG15: Huck . . . . . . . . . . . . .1E 19
**Kingsway Rd.** NG15: Huck . . . . . . . . . . . . . .1E 19
**Kingswell Av.** NG5: Arn . . . . . . . . . . . . . . . .6B 22
**Kingswell Rd.** NG5: Arn . . . . . . . . . . . . . . . .6B 22
**Kingswood Cl.** NG2: West Br . . . . . . . . . . . . .6H 57
**Kingswood Rd.** NG2: West Br . . . . . . . . . . . .6H 57
  NG8: Woll . . . . . . . . . . . . . . . . . . . . . .4H 43
**Kinlet Rd.** NG5: Bestw . . . . . . . . . . . . . . . . .1E 33
**Kinoulton La.** NG12: Kin . . . . . . . . . . . . . . . .6H 81
**KINOULTON WOLDS** . . . . . . . . . . . . . . . . . .6H 81
**Kinross Cres.** NG8: Bilb . . . . . . . . . . . . . . . .3G 43
**Kinsale Wlk.** NG11: Clif . . . . . . . . . . . . . . . .3C 66
**Kipling Cl.** NG11: Clif . . . . . . . . . . . . . . . . . .5A 66
**Kipps St.** NG1: Nott . . . . . . . . . . .3F 5 (4H 45)
**Kirby Cl.** NG16: Newth . . . . . . . . . . . . . . . . .2C 16
**Kirby Rd.** NG16: Newth . . . . . . . . . . . . . . . .2C 16
**Kirkbride Ct.** NG9: Chil . . . . . . . . . . . . . . . . .1B 64
**Kirkby Av.** DE7: Ilk . . . . . . . . . . . . . . . . . . .3B 40
**Kirkby Gdns.** NG2: Nott . . . . . . . . . . . . . . . .5B 46
**Kirk Cl.** NG9: Chil . . . . . . . . . . . . . . . . . . . .1D 64
**Kirkdale Cl.** NG8: Woll . . . . . . . . . . . . . . . . .5B 42
**Kirkdale Gdns.** NG10: Long E . . . . . . . . . . . .1D 72
**Kirkdale Rd.** NG3: Nott . . . . . . . . . . . . . . . .3D 46
  NG10: Long E . . . . . . . . . . . . . . . . . . .2D 72
**Kirkewhite Ct.** NG2: Nott . . . . . . . . . . . . . . .1H 57
**Kirkewhite St. W.** NG2: Nott . . . . . . . . . . . . .1G 57
**Kirkewhite Wlk.** NG2: Nott . . . . . . . . . . . . . .1G 57
**Kirkfell Cl.** NG2: West Br . . . . . . . . . . . . . . .6E 59
**Kirkfield Dr.** DE72: Brea . . . . . . . . . . . . . . . .5A 62
**KIRK HALLAM** . . . . . . . . . . . . . . . . . . . . . .4H 39
**Kirkham Cl.** DE75: Hea . . . . . . . . . . . . . . . . .4B 14
**Kirkham Dr.** NG9: Toton . . . . . . . . . . . . . . . .3H 63
**Kirkhill** NG13: Bing . . . . . . . . . . . . . . . . . . .4E 51
**Kirkland Dr.** NG9: Chil . . . . . . . . . . . . . . . . .3C 64
**Kirk La.** NG11: Rudd . . . . . . . . . . . . . . . . . . .6G 67
**Kirkley Dr.** DE7: Ilk . . . . . . . . . . . . . . . . . . .4A 14
**Kirkley Gdns.** NG5: Arn . . . . . . . . . . . . . . . .5C 22
**Kirkman Rd.** DE75: Los . . . . . . . . . . . . . . . . .1A 14
**Kirk Rd.** NG3: Mapp . . . . . . . . . . . . . . . . . . .5C 34
**Kirk's Bldgs.** NG4: Carl . . . . . . . . . . . . . . . . .2F 47
**Kirkstead Gdns.** NG7: H Grn . . . . . . . . . . . . .1H 29
**Kirkstead St.** NG7: H Grn . . . . . . . . . . . . . . .2D 44
**Kirkstone Ct.** NG10: Long E . . . . . . . . . . . . .3D 62
**Kirkstone Dr.** NG2: Gam . . . . . . . . . . . . . . . .4E 59
**Kirkwhite Av.** NG10: Long E . . . . . . . . . . . . .6F 63
**Kirkwhite Ho.** NG10: Long E . . . . . . . . . . . . .6F 63
                *(off Kirkwhite Av.)*

Kirtle Cl. NG8: Aspl .................1H 43
Kirtley Cl. NG16: Want ...............5A 18
Kirtley Dr. NG7: Lent ................1E 57
Kirtling Cl. NG5: Bestw ..............5G 21
Kirton Av. NG10: Long E ..............6F 63
Kittiwake M. NG7: Lent ...............5C 44
Kiwi Cl. NG15: Huck ..................6D 6
KK Sports & Leisure Cen. ............3C 46
Knapp Av. NG16: Eastw ...............4B 16
Kneesall Gro. NG15: Huck .............4H 7
Kneeton Cl. NG4: Ged .................3F 35
  NG5: Sher .........................3G 33
Kneeton Va. NG5: Sher ...............3G 33
Knighton Av. NG7: Radf ..............3C 44
Knighton Rd. NG5: Woodt .............2H 33
Knightsbridge Ct. NG5: Sher ..........4G 33
                 (off St Albans St.)
Knightsbridge Dr. NG2: West Br .......1G 67
  NG16: Nuth .......................4E 31
Knightsbridge Gdns. NG15: Huck .......1F 7
Knightsbridge Way NG15: Huck .........2F 7
Knights Cl. NG2: West Br .............2G 67
  NG5: Top V ........................5D 20
  NG9: Toton ........................3H 63
Knight St. NG4: Neth .................3H 47
Knightsyard Ct. NG10: Long E .........2E 73
Knightwood Dr. NG5: Bestw V ..........6F 9
Kniveton Pk. DE7: Ilk ................2H 39
Knole Rd. NG8: Woll ..................4E 43
Knoll Av. NG15: Huck .................6D 6
Knowle Hill NG16: Kimb ...............2A 30
Knowle La. NG16: Kimb ................3A 30
Knowle Pk. NG16: Kimb ................2A 30
Knowles Wlk. NG5: Arn ................5H 21
Kozi Kots NG4: Neth ..................2H 47
Krebs Cl. NG11: Clif .................4A 66
Kyle Vw. NG5: Top V ..................4E 21
Kyme St. NG7: Radf ...................4D 44
Kynance Gdns. NG11: Wilf .............6F 57

Labray Rd. NG14: Calv ................3G 11
Laburnum Av. NG12: Key ...............5A 80
Laburnum Cl. NG10: Sand ..............4D 52
Laburnum Gdns. NG6: Bulw .............2C 32
Laburnum Gro. NG9: Bee ...............6H 55
  NG15: Huck ........................6H 7
Laburnum St. NG3: Nott ...............2H 45
Lace Cl. NG10: Long E ................4E 63
LACE MARKET .........................5F 5 (5H 45)
Lace Mkt. Sq. NG1: Nott ..............4F 5
Lace Market Stop (NET) ..............4E 5 (5G 45)
Lace Market Theatre .................5F 5 (5H 45)
Lace Mill Ct. NG6: Basf ..............4B 32
Lace Rd. NG9: Bee ....................4F 55
Lace St. NG7: Nott, Lent .............2B 56
Lace Way NG1: Nott ...................5H 5 (5A 46)
  NG2: Nott .........................5H 5 (5A 46)
Lacey Av. NG15: Huck .................6G 7
Lacey Cl. DE7: Ilk ...................4G 27
Laceyfields Rd. DE75: Hea ............4E 15
Ladbrooke Cres. NG6: Basf ...........4A 32
Lady Bay Av. NG2: West Br ............2B 58
Lady Bay Bri. NG2: Nott, West Br .....1A 58
Lady Bay Ct. NG2: West Br ............2C 58
Lady Bay Rd. NG2: West Br ............2C 58
Ladybay Workshops NG2: West Br .......2D 58
                 (off Lady Bay Av.)
Ladybridge Cl. NG9: Atten ...........2E 63
Ladycroft Av. NG15: Huck .............4G 7
Ladylea Rd. NG10: Long E .............3C 72
Ladysmith St. NG2: Nott ..............5C 46
Ladysmock Gdns. NG2: Nott ............1H 57
Ladywood Rd. DE7: D Ab, Kirk H .......4F 39
Lake Av. DE75: Los ...................1A 14
Lake Gdns. DE75: Los .................1A 14
Lakehead Ho. NG11: Clif ..............4C 66
Lakeland Av. NG15: Huck ..............6A 8
Lakeland Rd. NG14: Calv ..............5C 12
Lakeside Adventure Base .............1G 59
Lakeside Arts Cen. ..................2A 56
Lakeside Av. NG10: Long E ............3E 73
Lakeside Bus. Cen. DE75: Ship ........1E 27
Lakeside Cres. NG10: Long E ..........2F 73
Lake St. NG7: Radf ...................4G 44
Lamartine St. NG3: Nott .............2G 5 (4H 45)
Lamb Cl. Dr. NG16: Eastw, Newth ......1C 16
Lambert Gdns. NG8: Aspl ..............1A 44
Lambert Hill NG15: Huck ..............4F 7
Lambert St. NG7: H Grn ...............2C 44
Lambeth Ct. NG9: Bee .................4H 55
Lambeth Rd. NG5: Arn .................3E 21
Lambie Cl. NG8: Woll .................4A 44
LAMBLEY .............................6C 24

Lambley Almshouses NG3: Nott .........1H 45
Lambley Av. NG3: Mapp ................4D 34
Lambley Bridle Rd. NG14: Bur J .......1D 36
Lambley Ct. NG3: Mapp ................4B 34
Lambley La. NG4: Ged .................4G 35
  NG14: Bur J .......................2D 36
Lambley Rd. NG14: Lowd ...............5G 25
Lambourne Cl. NG9: Bram ..............3C 54
Lambourne Dr. NG8: Woll ..............4F 43
Lambourne Gdns. NG5: Woodt ...........2C 34
Lambton Cl. DE7: Ilk .................4A 28
Lamcote Gdns. NG12: Rad T ............6E 49
Lamcote Gro. NG2: Nott ...............2H 57
Lamcote M. NG12: Rad T ...............6E 49
Lamcote St. NG2: Nott ................2H 57
Laming Gap La. NG12: Cotg, Stant W ...3C 80
Lamins La. NG6: Bestw V ..............6F 9
Lammas Gdns. NG2: Nott ...............1H 57
Lamorna Gro. NG11: Wilf ..............5F 57
Lamplands NG12: Cotg .................2E 71
Lamp Wood Cl. NG14: Calv .............4G 11
Lanark Cl. NG8: Woll .................6A 44
Lancaster Av. NG9: Stap ..............5G 53
  NG10: Sand ........................1C 62
Lancaster Rd. NG3: Nott ..............2D 46
  NG6: Bestw V ......................1C 20
  NG15: Huck ........................1D 18
Lancaster Way NG8: Stre ..............5D 30
Lancelot Dr. NG16: Want ..............4H 17
Lancelyn Gdns. NG2: West Br ..........1A 68
Landcroft Cres. NG5: Bestw ...........1E 33
Landmere Cl. DE7: Ilk ................4G 27
Landmere Gdns. NG3: Nott .............6B 34
Landmere La. NG2: West Br ............2F 67
  NG11: Rudd ........................3H 67
  NG12: Edwal .......................4B 68
Landsdown Gro. NG10: Long E ..........4H 63
Landseer Cl. NG7: Radf ...............3C 44
Lane, The NG16: Aws ..................3E 29
Laneham Av. NG5: Arn .................6C 22
Laneside Av. NG9: Toton ..............3G 63
Laneward Cl. DE7: Ilk ................3H 27
Langar Cl. NG5: Sher .................3G 33
Langar Rd. NG13: Bing ................6E 51
Langbank Av. NG5: Top V ..............4C 20
Langdale Dr. NG10: Long E ............1C 72
Langdale Gro. NG13: Bing .............5B 50
Langdale Rd. NG3: Nott ...............4D 46
Langdon Cl. NG5: Sher ................5E 33
  NG10: Long E ......................4C 62
Langen Ct. NG10: Long E ..............1G 73
Langford Rd. NG5: Arn ................6D 22
Langham Av. NG3: Nott ................3C 46
Langham Dr. NG14: Bur J ..............2F 37
Langham Pk. DE7: Stant D .............2D 52
LANGLEY .............................4F 15
Langley Av. DE7: Ilk .................2H 27
  NG5: Arn ..........................1B 34
Langley Bus. Pk. NG16: Lang M ........3F 15
Langley Cl. NG6: Bestw V .............1C 20
Langley Farm Cl. DE75: Hea ...........4F 15
LANGLEY MILL ........................2G 15
Langley Mill By-Pass
  NG16: Lang M ...........1E 15 & 1G 15
Langley Mill Station (Rail) ..........2F 15
Langley Pk. NG16: Lang M .............2F 15
Langstrath Dr. NG2: West Br ..........1E 69
Langstrath Rd. NG11: Clif ............4C 66
Langton Cl. NG4: Colw ................3G 47
Langtry Gdns. NG13: Bing .............4F 51
Langtry Gro. NG7: Basf ...............6E 33
Langwith Cl. DE7: Ilk ................2B 28
Lanky Bills Fun Shack ...............1F 15
Lansdown Cl. NG9: Chil ...............1B 64
Lansdowne Dr. NG2: West Br ...........1H 67
Lansdowne Rd. NG6: Basf ..............3C 32
Lansing Cl. NG11: Clif ...............5D 66
Lanthwaite Cl. NG11: Clif ............4C 66
Lanthwaite Rd. NG11: Clif ............4C 66
Lapford Cl. NG3: Mapp ................1F 35
Larch Cl. NG2: West Br ...............2E 59
  NG5: Arn ..........................5G 21
  NG13: Bing ........................5B 51
  NG15: Huck ........................6H 7
Larch Cres. NG9: Bee .................4E 55
  NG16: Eastw .......................3A 16
Larchdene Av. NG8: Woll ..............6D 42
Larch Dr. NG10: Sand .................4D 52
Larch Gdns. NG6: Bulw ................6G 19
Larch Ho. NG5: Sher ..................4H 33
Larch Way NG12: Key ..................5A 80
Largs Cl. NG5: Top V .................3C 20
Lark Cl. NG9: Chil ...................6A 54
Larkdale St. NG7: Radf ..........1A 4 (3E 45)
Larkfield Rd. NG16: Nuth .............2B 30

LARKFIELDS ..........................2B 30
Lark Hill Village NG11: Clif .........5A 66
LARKLANDS ...........................2C 40
Larkland's Av. DE7: Ilk ..............2C 40
Larkspur Av. NG5: Redh ...............3A 22
Larkwood Cl. NG8: Bilb ...............1G 43
Larwood Gro. NG5: Sher ...............3G 33
Lascelles Av. NG4: Ged ...............5F 35
Latham St. NG6: Bulw .................6H 19
Lathkill Av. DE7: Ilk ................2A 28
Lathkill Cl. DE7: West H .............1C 38
  NG6: Bulw .........................1A 32
Lathkilldale Cres. NG10: Long E ......2C 72
Latimer Cl. NG6: Bulw ................1A 32
Latimer Dr. NG9: Bram ................6B 42
Latin Gro. NG15: Huck ................3A 8
Laughton Av. NG2: West Br ............1G 67
Laughton Cres. NG15: Huck ............1E 19
Launceston Cres. NG11: Wilf ..........1E 67
Launder St. NG2: Nott ................1G 57
Laurel Av. NG12: Key .................5H 79
Laurel Cres. NG10: Long E ............1E 73
  NG16: Nuth ........................6B 18
Laurel Rd. NG4: Carl .................1F 47
Lauren Gro. NG9: Toton ...............3H 63
Laurie Av. NG7: H Grn ................1E 45
Laurie Cl. NG7: H Grn ................1E 45
Lauriston Dr. NG6: Bulw ..............3B 32
Lavelle Cl. NG8: Woll ................3C 64
Lavender Cl. NG8: Brox ...............6E 31
Lavender Cres. NG4: Carl .............6F 35
Lavender Gdns. DE75: Hea .............4F 15
Lavender Gro. NG9: Bee ...............6H 55
Lavender Wlk. NG3: Nott ..............2H 45
Laver Cl. NG5: Arn ...................6D 22
Laverock Cl. NG16: Kimb ..............1H 29
Lawdon Rd. NG5: Arn ..................4C 22
Lawley Av. NG5: Lent A ...............2G 55
Lawn Cl. DE75: Hea ...................3D 14
Lawn Gro. NG4: Carl, Ged .............6A 36
Lawn Mill Rd. NG16: Kimb .............6G 17
Lawn Mills NG16: Kimb ................6G 17
Lawrence Av. DE72: Brea ..............5A 62
  NG4: Colw .........................4G 47
  NG16: Aws .........................3E 29
  NG16: Eastw .......................3B 16
Lawrence Cl. NG12: Cotg ..............2F 71
Lawrence Dr. NG8: Stre ...............5C 30
Lawrence M. NG12: Cotg ...............2F 71
Lawrence St. NG9: Stap ...............5F 53
  NG10: Long E ......................5F 63
  NG10: Sand ........................4D 52
Lawrence Way NG7: Lent ...............1E 57
Lawson Av. NG10: Long E ..............1G 63
Lawson St. NG7: Radf .................3E 45
Lawton Dr. NG6: Bulw .................4A 20
Laxton Av. NG6: Bulw .................2B 32
Laxton Dr. NG15: Huck ................5E 7
Leabrook Cl. NG11: Clif ..............2A 66
Leabrook Gdns. NG15: Huck ............3A 8
Leacroft Rd. NG8: Aspl ...............2B 44
Leadale Av. NG15: Huck ...............3A 8
Leaf Cl. NG15: Huck ..................2H 7
Leafe Cl. NG9: Chil ..................3C 64
Leafield Grn. NG11: Clif .............3C 66
Leafy La. DE75: Hea ..................4D 14
Leahurst Gdns. NG2: West Br ..........6D 58
Leahurst Rd. NG2: West Br ............6C 58
Leahy Gdns. NG5: Bestw ...............1D 32
Leake Rd. NG11: Goth .................6H 75
Leamington Dr. NG9: Chil .............1C 64
Leander Cl. NG11: Wilf ...............5F 57
Leas, The NG14: Bulc .................2H 37
Lechlade Cl. DE7: West H .............1B 38
Lechlade Rd. NG5: Bestw ..............1D 32
Ledbury Va. NG8: Aspl ................1H 43
Ledger Wlk. NG5: Sher ................6F 33
                 (off Jensen Way)
Leech Ct. NG16: Gilt .................6D 16
Lee Cres. DE7: Ilk ...................1D 40
Lee La. DE75: Hea ....................4F 15
Leen Cl. NG6: Bestw V ................1D 20
  NG15: Huck ........................3A 8
Leen Ct. NG7: Lent ...................1C 56
Leen Dr. NG6: Bulw ...................4A 20
  NG15: Huck ........................2H 7
Leen Ga. NG7: Lent, Nott .............1B 56
Leen Mills La. NG15: Huck ............2H 7
Leen Pl. NG7: Radf ...................4C 44
Leen Valley Country Pk. .............6B 8
Leen Valley Way NG15: Huck ...........6A 8
Lee Rd. NG14: Bur J ..................2G 37
  NG14: Calv ........................3F 11
Lees Barn Rd. NG12: Rad T ............1D 60
Lees Hill Footpath NG2: Nott .........6A 46
Lees Hill St. NG2: Nott ..............5A 46
Lees Rd. NG3: Mapp ...................6C 34

Lee Westwood Sports Cen. . . . . . . . . . . . .2B 66
Leicester Ho. NG9: Bram . . . . . . . . . . . . .3H 53
Leicester St. NG10: Long E . . . . . . . . . . . .1G 73
Leigh Cl. NG2: West Br . . . . . . . . . . . . . . .5G 57
Leigh Rd. NG9: Toton . . . . . . . . . . . . . . . .2H 63
Leighton St. NG3: Nott . . . . . . . . . . . . . . .3B 46
Leiston Gdns. NG5: Top V . . . . . . . . . . . . .5E 21
Leivers Av. NG5: Arn . . . . . . . . . . . . . . . . .5B 22
Leivers Ho. *NG5: Arn* . . . . . . . . . . . . . . .1C 34
*(off Derwent Cres.)*
Lema Cl. NG6: Bulw . . . . . . . . . . . . . . . . . .5B 20
Lendal Ct. NG7: Radf . . . . . . . . . .2A 4 (4E 45)
Lendrum Ct. NG14: Bur J . . . . . . . . . . . . .3F 37
Leniscar Av. DE75: Los . . . . . . . . . . . . . . .1A 14
Len Maynard Ct. NG3: Nott . . . . . . . . . . .3C 46
Lennox St. NG1: Nott . . . . . . .3G 5 (4H 45)
LENTON ABBEY . . . . . . . . . . . . . . . . . . . .2G 55
Lenton Av. NG7: Nott . . . . . . . . . . . . . . . .5E 45
NG12: Toll . . . . . . . . . . . . . . . . . . . . . .4E 69
Lenton Blvd. NG7: Lent . . . . . . . . . . . . . . .4D 44
Lenton Bus. Pk. NG7: Lent . . . . . . . . . . . .5C 44
Lenton Centre, The . . . . . . . . . . . . . . . . . .6D 44
Lenton Cir. NG12: Toll . . . . . . . . . . . . . . . .4E 69
Lenton Ct. NG7: Lent . . . . . . . . . . . . . . . .5D 44
NG7: Nott . . . . . . . . . . . . . . .6A 4 (6E 45)
Lenton Hall Dr. NG7: Nott . . . . . . . . . . . .1A 56
Lenton Ind. Est. E. NG7: Lent . . . . . . . . . .4E 57
Lenton Ind. Est. W. NG7: Lent . . . . . . . . .3D 56
Lenton La. NG7: Lent . . . . . . . . . . . . . . . .1D 56
Lenton Rd. NG7: Nott . . . . . . . .6A 4 (6E 45)
Lenton St. NG10: Sand . . . . . . . . . . . . . . .5E 53
Leonard Av. NG5: Sher . . . . . . . . . . . . . . .5F 33
Leonard Cheshire Cl.
DE75: Hea . . . . . . . . . . . . . . . . . . . . . .4F 15
Leonard M. NG9: Chil . . . . . . . . . . . . . . . .3B 64
Leonard St. NG6: Bulw . . . . . . . . . . . . . . .2H 31
Leopold St. NG10: Long E . . . . . . . . . . . .5F 63
Le Page Ct. NG8: Bilb . . . . . . . . . . . . . . . .1G 43
Leroy Wallace Av. NG7: Radf . . . . . . . . . .3D 44
Lerwick Cl. NG11: Clif . . . . . . . . . . . . . . . .4E 67
Leslie Av. NG7: H Grn . . . . . . . . . . . . . . . .1E 45
NG9: Bee . . . . . . . . . . . . . . . . . . . . . .6F 55
NG16: Kimb . . . . . . . . . . . . . . . . . . . .2H 29
Leslie Gro. NG14: Calv . . . . . . . . . . . . . . .4H 11
Leslie Rd. NG7: H Grn . . . . . . . . . . . . . . .1E 45
*(not continuous)*
Letchworth Cres. NG9: Chil . . . . . . . . . . .1C 64
Letcombe Rd. NG11: Clif . . . . . . . . . . . . . .2C 66
Levens Cl. NG2: West Br . . . . . . . . . . . . . .5G 57
Leverton Ct. NG2: West Br . . . . . . . . . . . .6B 58
Leverton Grn. NG11: Clif . . . . . . . . . . . . .3C 66
Levertons Pl. NG15: Huck . . . . . . . . . . . .1H 19
Leverton Wlk. NG5: Arn . . . . . . . . . . . . . .5C 22
Levick Ct. NG2: Nott . . . . . . . . . . . . . . . . .1G 57
Lewcote La. DE7: West H . . . . . . . . . . . . .6E 27
Lewindon Dr. NG5: Woodt . . . . . . . . . . . .3A 34
Lewis Cl. NG3: Nott . . . . . . . . . .1F 5 (3H 45)
Lewis Way NG6: Bestw V . . . . . . . . . . . . . .6F 9
Lewsey Cl. NG9: Chil . . . . . . . . . . . . . . . . .3B 64
Lexington Gdns. NG5: Sher . . . . . . . . . . .3H 33
Lexington Pl. NG1: Nott . . . . . . . . . . . . . . .4G 5
Leybourne Dr. NG5: Bestw . . . . . . . . . . . .1C 32
Leyland Cl. NG9: Toton . . . . . . . . . . . . . . .3H 63
Leys, The NG11: Clif . . . . . . . . . . . . . . . . .4A 66
NG12: Norm W . . . . . . . . . . . . . . . . . .6H 69
Leys Ct. NG11: Rudd . . . . . . . . . . . . . . . . .1G 77
Leys Rd. NG11: Rudd . . . . . . . . . . . . . . . . .1G 77
Ley St. NG4: Neth . . . . . . . . . . . . . . . . . . .2A 48
Leyton Cres. NG9: Bee . . . . . . . . . . . . . . .6H 55
Library Rd. NG7: Nott . . . . . . . . . . . . . . . .2A 56
Lichfield Cl. NG9: Toton . . . . . . . . . . . . . .2G 63
NG10: Long E . . . . . . . . . . . . . . . . . . .6H 63
Lichfield Rd. NG2: Nott . . . . . . . . . . . . . . .5C 46
Liddell Gro. NG8: Woll . . . . . . . . . . . . . . .4F 43
Liddington St. NG7: Basf . . . . . . . . . . . . .6D 32
Lido Cl. NG6: Bulw . . . . . . . . . . . . . . . . . .4A 20
Lilac Av. NG4: Carl . . . . . . . . . . . . . . . . . .1E 47
Lilac Cl. NG8: Brox . . . . . . . . . . . . . . . . . .6E 31
NG12: Key . . . . . . . . . . . . . . . . . . . . . .5A 80
Lilac Cl. NG11: Clif . . . . . . . . . . . . . . . . . .4A 66
Lilac Cres. NG9: Bee . . . . . . . . . . . . . . . . .6H 55
Lilac Gro. DE75: Hea . . . . . . . . . . . . . . . . .4C 14
NG9: Bee . . . . . . . . . . . . . . . . . . . . . . .6H 55
Lilac M. DE7: Ilk . . . . . . . . . . . . . . . . . . . .4H 27
Lilac Rd. NG15: Huck . . . . . . . . . . . . . . . . .6H 7
Lilacs, The NG9: Bee . . . . . . . . . . . . . . . . .5F 55
Lilian Hind Ct. NG6: Bulw . . . . . . . . . . . . .5F 19
Lilleker Ri. NG5: Arn . . . . . . . . . . . . . . . . .4A 22
Lillie Ter. NG7: Arn . . . . . . . . . . . . . . . . . .5B 46
Lillington Rd. NG6: Bulw . . . . . . . . . . . . . .6H 19
Lily Av. NG4: Neth . . . . . . . . . . . . . . . . . . .2A 48
Lily Gro. NG9: Bee . . . . . . . . . . . . . . . . . .6H 55
Lime Av. NG16: Lang M . . . . . . . . . . . . . . .3G 15
Lime Cl. NG12: Rad T . . . . . . . . . . . . . . . .6F 49
NG16: Nuth . . . . . . . . . . . . . . . . . . . .1A 30
Limefield Ct. NG2: West Br . . . . . . . . . . . .2C 58

Lime Gro. NG9: Stap . . . . . . . . . . . . . . . . .6F 53
NG10: Long E . . . . . . . . . . . . . . . . . . .5F 63
NG10: Sand . . . . . . . . . . . . . . . . . . . . .5D 52
Lime Gro. Av. NG9: Chil . . . . . . . . . . . . . .6E 55
Limekiln Ct. NG6: Bulw . . . . . . . . . . . . . . .5G 19
Lime La. NG5: Arn . . . . . . . . . . . . . . . . . . .6A 10
Limes, The DE7: Mapp . . . . . . . . . . . . . . .4C 26
NG11: Bart F . . . . . . . . . . . . . . . . . . . .1E 75
Limes Cl. NG16: Lang M . . . . . . . . . . . . . .1G 15
Lime St. DE7: Ilk . . . . . . . . . . . . . . . . . . . .2B 40
NG6: Bulw . . . . . . . . . . . . . . . . . . . . . .6H 19
Lime Ter. NG10: Long E . . . . . . . . . . . . . .5F 63
Lime Tree Av. NG8: Cin . . . . . . . . . . . . . . .4H 31
NG8: Woll . . . . . . . . . . . . . . . . . . . . . . .6H 43
Limetree Cl. NG12: Key . . . . . . . . . . . . . . .5H 79
Lime Tree Ct. NG9: Nott . . . . . . . . . . . . . .2G 55
Lime Tree Ri. DE7: Kirk H . . . . . . . . . . . . .3G 39
Lime Tree Rd. NG15: Huck . . . . . . . . . . . .1H 19
Limmen Gdns. NG3: Nott . . . . . . .1H 5 (3A 46)
Limpenny St. NG7: Radf . . . . . . . . . . . . . .3D 44
LINBY . . . . . . . . . . . . . . . . . . . . . . . . . . . . .1H 7
Linby Av. NG15: Huck . . . . . . . . . . . . . . . . .4H 7
Linby Cl. NG4: Ged . . . . . . . . . . . . . . . . . .5G 35
NG5: Sher . . . . . . . . . . . . . . . . . . . . . .2H 33
Linby Dr. NG8: Stre . . . . . . . . . . . . . . . . . .5D 30
Linby Gro. NG15: Huck . . . . . . . . . . . . . . . .3H 7
Linby Ho. NG15: Lin . . . . . . . . . . . . . . . . . .1H 7
Linby La. NG15: Lin, Pap . . . . . . . . . . . . . . .1A 8
Linby Rd. NG15: Huck . . . . . . . . . . . . . . . . .3H 7
Linby St. NG6: Bulw . . . . . . . . . . . . . . . . . .5A 20
Linby Wlk. NG15: Huck . . . . . . . . . . . . . . . .3G 7
Lincoln Av. NG10: Sand . . . . . . . . . . . . . . .1C 62
Lincoln Cir. NG7: Nott . . . . . . . . .5A 4 (5E 45)
Lincoln Cl. NG9: Stap . . . . . . . . . . . . . . . .2G 53
Lincoln Ct. NG8: Bilb . . . . . . . . . . . . . . . . .2D 42
Lincoln Gro. NG12: Rad T . . . . . . . . . . . . .6F 49
Lincoln Ho. NG3: Mapp P . . . . . . . . . . . . .1H 45
Lincoln St. NG1: Nott . . . . . . . . .3E 5 (4G 45)
NG6: Basf . . . . . . . . . . . . . . . . . . . . . .4C 32
Lindale Cl. NG2: Gam . . . . . . . . . . . . . . . . .5E 59
Lindbridge Rd. NG8: Brox . . . . . . . . . . . . .5F 31
Linden Av. NG11: Clif . . . . . . . . . . . . . . . . .4A 66
Linden Ct. NG9: Bee . . . . . . . . . . . . . . . . .6G 55
Linden Gro. NG4: Ged . . . . . . . . . . . . . . . .6B 36
NG9: Bee . . . . . . . . . . . . . . . . . . . . . .6G 55
NG9: Stap . . . . . . . . . . . . . . . . . . . . . .5G 53
NG10: Sand . . . . . . . . . . . . . . . . . . . . .4C 52
Linden Pl. NG3: Mapp . . . . . . . . . . . . . . . .1E 35
Linden St. NG3: Nott . . . . . . . . . . . . . . . . .2H 45
Lindfield Cl. NG8: Brox . . . . . . . . . . . . . . .5G 31
Lindfield Rd. NG8: Brox . . . . . . . . . . . . . . .5F 31
Lindisfarne Gdns. NG5: Top V . . . . . . . . . .4E 21
Lindley Ter. NG7: H Grn . . . . . . . . . . . . . . .2C 44
Lindrick Cl. NG12: Edwal . . . . . . . . . . . . . .1E 69
Lindsay St. NG7: H Grn . . . . . . . . . . . . . . .2C 44
Lindum Gro. NG2: Nott . . . . . . . . . . . . . . .6B 46
Lindum Rd. NG6: Basf . . . . . . . . . . . . . . . .4C 32
Linen Ho. *NG7: Radf* . . . . . . . . . . . . . . . .3C 44
*(off Hartley Rd.)*
Linette Cl. NG5: Sher . . . . . . . . . . . . . . . . .5E 33
Linford Ct. NG9: Bram . . . . . . . . . . . . . . . .5B 42
Ling Cres. NG11: Rudd . . . . . . . . . . . . . . .5G 67
Lingfield Ct. NG8: Woll . . . . . . . . . . . . . . .6D 42
Lingford NG12: Cotg . . . . . . . . . . . . . . . . .2G 71
Lingford St. NG15: Huck . . . . . . . . . . . . . .5H 7
Lingmell Cl. NG2: West Br . . . . . . . . . . . . .5E 59
LINGS BAR HOSPITAL . . . . . . . . . . . . . . . .5F 59
Lings Bar Rd. *NG2: Gam* . . . . . . . . . . . .5F 59
*(off Ambleside)*
Lings Cl. DE7: Ilk . . . . . . . . . . . . . . . . . . . .2B 28
Lings La. NG12: Key . . . . . . . . . . . . . . . . .6G 79
Linkin Rd. NG9: Chil . . . . . . . . . . . . . . . . .5C 54
Linkmel Cl. NG2: Nott . . . . . . . . . . . . . . . .2E 57
Linkmead Rd. NG16: Eastw . . . . . . . . . . . .2G 15
Linksfield Ct. NG2: West Br . . . . . . . . . . . .3G 67
Linley Ct. *NG13: Bing* . . . . . . . . . . . . . . .5E 51
*(off Long Acre)*
Linnell St. NG3: Nott . . . . . . . . . . . . . . . . .3B 46
Linnet Way NG15: Huck . . . . . . . . . . . . . . .4F 7
Linsdale Cl. NG8: Bilb . . . . . . . . . . . . . . . .4B 42
Linsdale Gdns. NG4: Ged . . . . . . . . . . . . .3F 35
Linton Ri. NG3: Nott . . . . . . . . . . . . . . . . .3C 46
Linwood Cres. NG16: Eastw . . . . . . . . . . .4B 16
Lion Cl. NG8: Aspl . . . . . . . . . . . . . . . . . . .5A 32
Lismore Cl. NG7: Radf . . . . . . . . . . . . . . . .4C 44
Lissett Av. DE7: Ilk . . . . . . . . . . . . . . . . . . .2A 40
Lister Ga. NG1: Nott . . . . . . . . . .5E 5 (5G 45)
Listergate Sq. NG1: Nott . . . . . . .5E 5 (5G 45)
Lister Ho. NG3: Mapp . . . . . . . . . . . . . . . .5B 34
Lister Rd. NG7: Nott . . . . . . . . . . . . . . . . .1C 56
Listowel Cres. NG11: Clif . . . . . . . . . . . . .5B 28
Litchen Cl. DE7: Ilk . . . . . . . . . . . . . . . . . .5B 28
Litchfield Ri. NG5: Arn . . . . . . . . . . . . . . . .3A 22
Litmus Building, The NG1: Nott . . . . . . . . .2F 5

Little Bounds NG2: West Br . . . . . . . . . . . .4H 57
Little Drivers Soft Play Cen. . . . . . . . . . . .5F 53
Littlegreen Rd. NG5: Woodt . . . . . . . . . . .3A 34
LITTLE HALLAM . . . . . . . . . . . . . . . . . . . . .3B 40
Lit. Hallam Hill DE7: Ilk . . . . . . . . . . . . . . .4A 40
Lit. Hallam La. DE7: Ilk . . . . . . . . . . . . . . .3B 40
Little Hayes NG2: West Br . . . . . . . . . . . . .1G 67
Lit. Holland Gdns. NG16: Nuth . . . . . . . . .1B 30
Lit. John Wlk. NG3: Nott . . . . . . . . . . . . . .2H 45
Little La. NG12: Toll . . . . . . . . . . . . . . . . . .2G 69
NG14: Calv . . . . . . . . . . . . . . . . . . . . . .4F 11
NG16: Kimb . . . . . . . . . . . . . . . . . . . .2H 29
Lit. Lime La. NG5: Arn . . . . . . . . . . . . . . . .6A 10
Little Lunnon NG11: Bart F . . . . . . . . . . . .1E 75
Little Meadow NG12: Cotg . . . . . . . . . . . .3G 71
Lit. Meadow Cl. DE7: Ilk . . . . . . . . . . . . . .5A 28
Littlemoor La. NG11: Rudd . . . . . . . . . . . .4A 78
Lit. Oakwood Dr. NG5: Top V . . . . . . . . . .3B 20
Little Ox NG4: Colw . . . . . . . . . . . . . . . . . .5H 47
Lit. Tennis St. NG2: Nott . . . . . . . . . . . . . .6C 46
Lit. Tennis St. Sth. NG2: Nott . . . . . . . . . .1C 58
Littlewell La. DE7: Stant D . . . . . . . . . . . .1B 52
Lit. Wood Cl. NG15: Huck . . . . . . . . . . . . . .6E 7
Littlewoods Gdns. NG8: Bilb . . . . . . . . . . .4C 42
Litton Cl. DE7: Ilk . . . . . . . . . . . . . . . . . . . .3A 28
NG5: Woodt . . . . . . . . . . . . . . . . . . . .3A 34
Liverpool St. NG3: Nott . . . . . . . .3H 5 (4A 46)
LivingWell Health Club
Nottingham . . . . . . . . . . . . . .3E 5 (4G 45)
Llanberis Gro. NG8: Aspl . . . . . . . . . . . . . .5A 32
Lloyd St. NG5: Sher . . . . . . . . . . . . . . . . . .5G 33
Loach Ct. NG8: Woll . . . . . . . . . . . . . . . . . .4A 44
Lobelia Cl. NG3: Nott . . . . . . . . . . . . . . . . .2H 45
Lock Cl. DE7: Kirk H . . . . . . . . . . . . . . . . . .3G 39
NG9: Bee . . . . . . . . . . . . . . . . . . . . . . .2G 65
Lockerbie St. NG4: Colw . . . . . . . . . . . . . .3H 47
Lock La. NG10: Long E . . . . . . . . . . . . . . . .3D 72
NG10: Sand . . . . . . . . . . . . . . . . . . . . .6D 52
Locksley Ho. NG3: Nott . . . . . . . . . . . . . . .3H 45
Locksley La. NG11: Clif . . . . . . . . . . . . . . .1C 66
Lockton Av. DE75: Hea . . . . . . . . . . . . . . .5C 14
Lockwood Cl. NG5: Top V . . . . . . . . . . . . .4E 21
NG9: Bee . . . . . . . . . . . . . . . . . . . . . .1H 65
Lodge Cl. NG5: Redh . . . . . . . . . . . . . . . . .3A 22
NG8: Aspl . . . . . . . . . . . . . . . . . . . . . .1B 44
Lodge Farm La. NG5: Arn . . . . . . . . . . . . .4A 22
Lodge Rd. DE7: Mapp . . . . . . . . . . . . . . . .4D 26
NG10: Long E . . . . . . . . . . . . . . . . . . .2F 73
NG16: Newth . . . . . . . . . . . . . . . . . . .5C 16
Lodge Row DE7: Mapp . . . . . . . . . . . . . . .4C 26
Lodgewood Cl. NG6: Bulw . . . . . . . . . . . .1G 31
Lodore Cl. NG2: West Br . . . . . . . . . . . . . .5E 59
Logan Sq. NG6: Basf . . . . . . . . . . . . . . . . .2C 32
Logan St. NG6: Bulw . . . . . . . . . . . . . . . . .1A 32
Lois Av. NG7: Lent . . . . . . . . . . . . . . . . . . .6D 44
Lombard Cl. NG7: Lent . . . . . . . . . . . . . . . .5D 44
Lombardy Lodge NG9: Toton . . . . . . . . . . .4A 64
London Rd. NG2: Nott . . . . . . . . .5G 5 (5H 45)
NG15: Huck . . . . . . . . . . . . . . . . . . . .4D 6
Longacre NG5: Woodt . . . . . . . . . . . . . . . .3B 34
Long Acre E. NG13: Bing . . . . . . . . . . . . . .5F 51
Longbeck Av. NG3: Nott . . . . . . . . . . . . . .6C 34
Longbridge La. DE75: Los . . . . . . . . . . . . .2B 14
Longclose Ct. NG6: Bulw . . . . . . . . . . . . .1G 31
Longcroft Av. DE7: Ilk . . . . . . . . . . . . . . . .2A 28
Longdale Rd. NG5: Arn . . . . . . . . . . . . . . .1H 33
Longden Cl. NG9: Bram . . . . . . . . . . . . . . .1H 53
Longden Mill NG3: Nott . . . . . . . . . . . . . . .3H 5
Longden St. NG3: Nott . . . . . . . . .3H 5 (4A 46)
LONG EATON . . . . . . . . . . . . . . . . . . . . . . .5G 63
Long Eaton Station (Rail) . . . . . . . . . . . . .2E 73
Longfellows Cl. NG5: Bestw . . . . . . . . . . .5F 21
Longfield Av. NG8: Bilb . . . . . . . . . . . . . . .2C 42
Longfield Cres. DE7: Ilk . . . . . . . . . . . . . . .4B 40
Longfield La. DE7: Ilk . . . . . . . . . . . . . . . . .4B 40
Longford Cres. NG6: Bulw . . . . . . . . . . . . .3A 20
Long Hill Ri. NG15: Huck . . . . . . . . . . . . . . .5F 7
Longhurst Dr. NG5: Arn . . . . . . . . . . . . . . .3B 22
Longlands Cl. NG9: Bee . . . . . . . . . . . . . . .1H 65
Longlands Dr. NG2: West Br . . . . . . . . . . .6F 59
Longlands Rd. NG9: Bee . . . . . . . . . . . . . .1H 65
Long La. DE7: Ship . . . . . . . . . . . . . . . . . . .6H 15
NG9: Atten . . . . . . . . . . . . . . . . . . . . .3D 64
NG16: Want . . . . . . . . . . . . . . . . . . . .4A 18
Longleat Cres. NG9: Chil . . . . . . . . . . . . . .6C 54
Longmead Cl. NG5: Bestw . . . . . . . . . . . . .1G 33
Longmead Dr. NG5: Bestw . . . . . . . . . . . . .1G 33
Long Mdw. Hill NG14: Lowd . . . . . . . . . . .3F 25
Longmoor Gdns. NG10: Long E . . . . . . . . .3C 62
Longmoor La. DE72: Brea . . . . . . . . . . . . .4A 62
NG10: Sand . . . . . . . . . . . . . . . . . . . . .6D 52
Longmoor Rd. NG10: Long E, Sand . . . . . .3C 62
Longore Sq. NG8: Woll . . . . . . . . . . . . . . .5B 44
Longridge Rd. NG5: Woodt . . . . . . . . . . . .3B 34
Long Row NG1: Nott . . . . . . . . . .4D 4 (5G 45)
*(not continuous)*

Long Row W. NG1: Nott . . . . . . . . . . . .4D **4** (5G **45**)
Long Stairs NG1: Nott . . . . . . . . . . . . . .5G **5**
Longthorpe Ct. NG5: Arn . . . . . . . . . . . .6B **22**
Longue Dr. NG14: Calv . . . . . . . . . . . . .4F **11**
Longwall Av. NG2: Nott . . . . . . . . . . . . .2E **57**
Long West Cft. NG14: Calv . . . . . . . . . .4E **11**
Longwood Ct. NG5: Top V . . . . . . . . . . .5D **20**
Lonscale Cl. NG2: West Br . . . . . . . . . .6E **59**
Lonsdale Dr. NG9: Toton . . . . . . . . . . . .3G **63**
Lonsdale Rd. NG7: Radf . . . . . . . . . . . .3C **44**
Lord Haddon Rd. DE7: Ilk . . . . . . . . . . .6A **28**
Lord Nelson St. NG2: Nott . . . . . . . . . . .5B **46**
Lord St. NG2: Nott . . . . . . . . . . . . . . . . .5B **46**
Lorimer Av. NG4: Ged . . . . . . . . . . . . . .4H **35**
Lorna Ct. NG3: Nott . . . . . . . . . . . . . . . .6H **33**
Lorne Gro. NG12: Rad T . . . . . . . . . . . . .6F **49**
Lorne Wlk. NG3: Nott . . . . . . . . . . . . . . .2G **45**
Lortas Rd. NG5: Sher . . . . . . . . . . . . . . .5D **32**
LOSCOE . . . . . . . . . . . . . . . . . . . . . . . . . .1A **14**
Loscoe-Denby La. DE75: Los . . . . . . . . .1A **14**
Loscoe Gdns. NG5: Sher . . . . . . . . . . . .6F **33**
Loscoe Grange DE75: Los . . . . . . . . . . .2A **14**
Loscoe Mt. Rd. NG5: Sher . . . . . . . . . . .5G **33**
Loscoe Rd. DE75: Hea . . . . . . . . . . . . . .2B **14**
   NG5: Sher . . . . . . . . . . . . . . . . . . . .6G **33**
Lothian Rd. NG12: Toll . . . . . . . . . . . . . .4E **69**
Lothmore Ct. NG2: Nott . . . . . . . . . . . . .1F **57**
Lotus Cl. NG3: Nott . . . . . . . . . . . . . . . . .2A **46**
Loughborough Av. NG2: Nott . . . . . . . . .5B **46**
Loughborough Rd. NG2: West Br . . . . . .5A **58**
   NG11: Bunny, Rudd . . . . . . . . . . . . .3H **67**
Loughrigg Cl. NG2: Nott . . . . . . . . . . . . .2F **57**
Louis Av. NG9: Bee . . . . . . . . . . . . . . . . .4E **55**
Louise Av. NG4: Neth . . . . . . . . . . . . . . .1A **48**
Lovelace Wlk. NG15: Huck . . . . . . . . . . .3H **7**
Lovell Cl. NG6: Bulw . . . . . . . . . . . . . . . .2F **31**
Lowater Pl. NG4: Carl . . . . . . . . . . . . . . .2D **46**
Lowater St. NG4: Carl . . . . . . . . . . . . . . .2D **46**
Lowcroft NG5: Woodt . . . . . . . . . . . . . . .3B **34**
Lowdham La. NG14: Woodbo . . . . . . . . .1D **24**
Lowdham Rd. NG4: Ged . . . . . . . . . . . . .4E **35**
   NG14: Epp . . . . . . . . . . . . . . . . . . . . .1g **25**
Lowdham St. NG3: Nott . . . . . . . .3H **5** (4A **46**)
LOWER BEAUVALE . . . . . . . . . . . . . . . .2C **16**
Lower Beauvale NG16: Newth . . . . . . . . .2C **16**
Lwr. Bloomsgrove Rd. DE7: Ilk . . . . . . . .5B **28**
Lwr. Brook St. NG10: Long E . . . . . . . . .6G **63**
Lower Canaan NG11: Rudd . . . . . . . . . . .5H **67**
Lwr. Chapel St. DE7: Ilk . . . . . . . . . . . . .6B **28**
Lwr. Claramount Rd. DE75: Hea . . . . . .4E **15**
Lower Ct. NG9: Bee . . . . . . . . . . . . . . . . .4G **55**
Lwr. Dunstead Rd. NG16: Lang M . . . . . .2E **15**
Lwr. Eldon St. NG2: Nott . . . . . . . .5H **5** (5A **46**)
Lwr. Gladstone St. DE75: Hea . . . . . . . .3C **14**
Lwr. Granby St. DE7: Ilk . . . . . . . . . . . . .5B **28**
Lower Maples DE75: Ship . . . . . . . . . . . .5E **15**
Lwr. Middleton St. DE7: Ilk . . . . . . . . . . .6C **28**
Lwr. Orchard St. NG9: Stap . . . . . . . . . .4G **53**
Lwr. Park St. NG9: Stap . . . . . . . . . . . . .5E **53**
Lwr. Parliament St. NG1: Nott . . . . .3E **5** (4G **45**)
Lwr. Regent St. NG9: Bee . . . . . . . . . . . .5G **55**
Lower Rd. NG9: Bee . . . . . . . . . . . . . . . . .4H **55**
Lwr. Stanton Rd. DE7: Ilk . . . . . . . . . . . .3B **40**
Lwr. Whitworth Rd. DE7: Ilk . . . . . . . . . .3B **40**
Loweswater Ct. NG2: Gam . . . . . . . . . . .4E **59**
Lowlands Dr. NG12: Key . . . . . . . . . . . . .3H **79**
Lowlands Lea DE75: Hea . . . . . . . . . . . .3D **14**
Low Pavement NG1: Nott . . . . . . . .5E **5** (5G **45**)
Low Wood Rd. NG6: Bulw . . . . . . . . . . . .2E **31**
Loxley Cl. NG15: Huck . . . . . . . . . . . . . . .6E **7**
Loxley Mdw. NG14: Bur J . . . . . . . . . . . .3E **37**
Lucerne Cl. NG11: Wilf . . . . . . . . . . . . . .5F **57**
Lucknow Av. NG3: Mapp P . . . . . . . . . . .1H **45**
Lucknow Ct. NG3: Mapp P . . . . . . . . . . .6H **33**
Lucknow Dr. NG3: Mapp P . . . . . . . . . . .1H **45**
Lucknow Rd. NG3: Mapp P . . . . . . . . . . .1H **45**
Ludford Cl. NG10: Long E . . . . . . . . . . . .3G **73**
Ludford Rd. NG6: Bulw . . . . . . . . . . . . . .5A **20**
Ludgate Cl. NG5: Arn . . . . . . . . . . . . . . .3E **21**
Ludham Av. NG6: Bulw . . . . . . . . . . . . . .5H **19**
Ludlam Av. NG16: Gilt . . . . . . . . . . . . . . .6C **16**
Ludlow Av. NG2: West Br . . . . . . . . . . . .4B **58**
Ludlow Cl. NG9: Bram . . . . . . . . . . . . . . .2D **54**
Ludlow Hill Rd. NG2: West Br . . . . . . . . .6B **58**
Lulworth Cl. NG2: West Br . . . . . . . . . . .6G **57**
Lulworth Ct. NG16: Kimb . . . . . . . . . . . . .6H **17**
Lune Cl. NG9: Atten . . . . . . . . . . . . . . . . .2E **65**
Lune Way NG13: Bing . . . . . . . . . . . . . . .6D **50**
Lupin Cl. NG3: Nott . . . . . . . . . . . . . . . . .2H **45**
Luther Cl. NG3: Nott . . . . . . . . . . . . . . . .2A **46**
Luton Cl. NG8: Aspl . . . . . . . . . . . . . . . . .6B **32**
Lutterell Ct. NG2: West Br . . . . . . . . . . . .6H **57**
Lutterell Way NG2: West Br . . . . . . . . . .6D **58**
Lybster M. NG2: Nott . . . . . . . . . . . . . . . .1F **57**
Lychgate Ct. NG16: Want . . . . . . . . . . . .5H **17**
Lydia Gdns. NG16: Eastw . . . . . . . . . . . .4A **16**

Lydney Pk. NG2: West Br . . . . . . . . . . . .5F **57**
Lyle Cl. NG16: Kimb . . . . . . . . . . . . . . . . .6G **17**
Lyme Pk. NG2: West Br . . . . . . . . . . . . . .6F **57**
Lymington Gdns. NG3: Nott . . . . . . . . . .3C **46**
Lymn Av. NG4: Ged . . . . . . . . . . . . . . . . .5H **35**
Lynam Ct. NG6: Bulw . . . . . . . . . . . . . . . .6H **19**
Lyncombe Gdns. NG12: Key . . . . . . . . . .3H **79**
Lyndale Rd. NG9: Bram . . . . . . . . . . . . . .3A **54**
Lynden Av. NG10: Long E . . . . . . . . . . . .1F **73**
Lyndhurst Gdns. NG2: West Br . . . . . . . .1H **67**
Lyndhurst Rd. NG2: Nott . . . . . . . . . . . . .5B **46**
Lynemouth Ct. NG5: Arn . . . . . . . . . . . . .3C **22**
Lyn Gilzean Ct. NG3: Nott . . . . . . .1G **5** (3H **45**)
Lynmoor Ct. NG5: Huck . . . . . . . . . . . . . .2A **8**
Lynmouth Cres. NG7: Radf . . . . . . . . . . .2C **44**
Lynmouth Dr. DE7: Ilk . . . . . . . . . . . . . . .4H **27**
Lynncroft NG16: Eastw . . . . . . . . . . . . . .2C **16**
Lynstead Dr. NG15: Huck . . . . . . . . . . . .6C **6**
Lynton Cl. NG3: Nott . . . . . . . . . . . . . . . .2B **46**
Lynton Gdns. NG5: Arn . . . . . . . . . . . . . .5C **22**
Lynton Rd. NG9: Chil . . . . . . . . . . . . . . . .5C **54**
Lyons Cl. NG11: Rudd . . . . . . . . . . . . . . .5F **67**
Lytham Dr. NG12: Edwal . . . . . . . . . . . . .2E **69**
Lytham Gdns. NG5: Top V . . . . . . . . . . . .4E **21**
Lythe Cl. NG11: Wilf . . . . . . . . . . . . . . . . .6E **57**
Lytton Cl. NG3: Nott . . . . . . . . . . .2H **5** (4A **46**)

# M

Mabel Gro. NG2: West Br . . . . . . . . . . . .3C **58**
Mabel St. NG2: Nott . . . . . . . . . . . . . . . . .1H **57**
Macaulay Gro. NG16: Nuth . . . . . . . . . . .1B **30**
McClelland Av. NG6: Bestw V . . . . . . . . .6F **9**
Macdonald Sq. DE7: Kirk H . . . . . . . . . .4G **39**
Machins La. NG12: Edwal . . . . . . . . . . . .2C **68**
McIntosh Rd. NG4: Ged . . . . . . . . . . . . . .4F **35**
Mackinley Av. NG9: Stap . . . . . . . . . . . . .2G **53**
Maclaren Gdns. NG11: Rudd . . . . . . . . . .1H **77**
Maclean Rd. NG4: Carl . . . . . . . . . . . . . .2E **47**
Macmillan Cl. NG3: Mapp . . . . . . . . . . . .5B **34**
Madden Cl. NG5: Bestw . . . . . . . . . . . . . .2D **32**
Madford Bus. Pk. NG5: Arn . . . . . . . . . . .1H **33**
Madison Ct. NG7: Lent . . . . . . . . . . . . . . .5B **44**
Madryn Wlk. NG5: Bestw . . . . . . . . . . . . .6E **21**
Mafeking St. NG2: Nott . . . . . . . . . . . . . .5C **46**
Magdala Rd. NG3: Mapp P . . . . . . . . . . .1g **45**
Magdalene Way NG15: Huck . . . . . . . . . .3G **7**
Magistrates' Court
   Nottingham . . . . . . . . . . . . . . . .6E **5** (6G **45**)
Magnolia Cl. NG8: Brox . . . . . . . . . . . . . .6E **31**
Magnolia Gdns. NG9: Bram . . . . . . . . . . .2D **54**
Magnolia Gro. NG15: Huck . . . . . . . . . . .1H **19**
Magnus Ct. NG9: Bee . . . . . . . . . . . . . . . .5G **55**
Magnus Rd. NG5: Sher . . . . . . . . . . . . . .4G **33**
Magson Cl. NG3: Nott . . . . . . . . . . . . . . .4A **46**
Maiden La. NG1: Nott . . . . . . . . . . .4G **5** (5H **45**)
Maidens Dale NG5: Arn . . . . . . . . . . . . . .5H **21**
Maid Marian Way NG1: Nott . . . . .4C **4** (5F **45**)
Maidstone Dr. NG8: Woll . . . . . . . . . . . . .1D **54**
Main Rd. NG4: Ged . . . . . . . . . . . . . . . . .6H **35**
   NG7: Nott . . . . . . . . . . . . . . . . . . . . . .5A **56**
   NG11: Wilf . . . . . . . . . . . . . . . . . . . . . .5F **57**
   NG12: Cotg, Rad T . . . . . . . . . . . . . . .4D **60**
   NG12: Plum . . . . . . . . . . . . . . . . . . . .5G **69**
   NG12: Rad T . . . . . . . . . . . . . . . . . . . .6F **49**
   NG12: Shel . . . . . . . . . . . . . . . . . . . . .1H **49**
   NG14: Bulc, Lowd . . . . . . . . . . . . . . . .2G **37**
   NG16: Want . . . . . . . . . . . . . . . . . . . . .4H **17**
Main St. DE7: Mapp . . . . . . . . . . . . . . . . .4C **26**
   DE7: Stant D . . . . . . . . . . . . . . . . . . . .3B **52**
   DE72: Brea . . . . . . . . . . . . . . . . . . . . .5A **62**
   NG2: Gam . . . . . . . . . . . . . . . . . . . . . .4E **59**
   NG4: Lamb . . . . . . . . . . . . . . . . . . . . .6B **24**
   NG6: Bulw . . . . . . . . . . . . . . . . . . . . . .1H **31**
   (not continuous)
   NG8: Stre . . . . . . . . . . . . . . . . . . . . . .6B **30**
   NG10: Long E . . . . . . . . . . . . . . . . . . .6G **63**
   NG11: Rudd . . . . . . . . . . . . . . . . . . . . .4A **78**
   NG12: Key . . . . . . . . . . . . . . . . . . . . . .6G **79**
   NG13: Newton . . . . . . . . . . . . . . . . . .3C **50**
   NG14: Bur J . . . . . . . . . . . . . . . . . . . . .3F **37**
   NG14: Calv . . . . . . . . . . . . . . . . . . . . .3D **10**
   NG14: Epp . . . . . . . . . . . . . . . . . . . . .5E **13**
   NG14: Woodbo . . . . . . . . . . . . . . . . .1B **24**
   NG15: Lin . . . . . . . . . . . . . . . . . . . . . . .1G **7**
   NG15: Pap . . . . . . . . . . . . . . . . . . . . . .1B **8**
   NG16: Aws . . . . . . . . . . . . . . . . . . . . . .2E **29**
   NG16: Eastw . . . . . . . . . . . . . . . . . . . .4B **16**
   NG16: Kimb . . . . . . . . . . . . . . . . . . . . .5C **62**
   NG16: Newth . . . . . . . . . . . . . . . . . . . .3E **17**
   NG16: Oxt . . . . . . . . . . . . . . . . . . . . . . .1B **12**
Maitland Av. NG5: Woodt . . . . . . . . . . . . .3B **34**
Maitland Rd. NG5: Woodt . . . . . . . . . . . .3B **34**
Major St. NG1: Nott . . . . . . . . . . .2D **4** (4G **45**)
Malbon Cl. NG3: Nott . . . . . . . . . . . . . . . .1B **46**
Malcolm Cl. NG3: Mapp P . . . . . . . . . . . .2G **45**

Maldon Cl. NG9: Chil . . . . . . . . . . . . . . . .1C **64**
   NG10: Long E . . . . . . . . . . . . . . . . . . .2G **73**
Malik Way DE75: Hea . . . . . . . . . . . . . . .5D **14**
Malin Cl. NG5: Arn . . . . . . . . . . . . . . . . . .5D **22**
Malin Hill NG1: Nott . . . . . . . . . . . . . . . . .5F **5**
Malkin Av. NG12: Rad T . . . . . . . . . . . . . .5G **49**
Mallard Cl. NG6: Basf . . . . . . . . . . . . . . .3D **32**
   NG13: Bing . . . . . . . . . . . . . . . . . . . . .6G **51**
Mallard Ct. NG9: Bee . . . . . . . . . . . . . . . .6G **55**
Mallard Rd. NG4: Neth . . . . . . . . . . . . . . .3B **48**
Mallow Way NG13: Bing . . . . . . . . . . . . . .5C **50**
Malmesbury Rd. NG3: Mapp . . . . . . . . . .3C **34**
Maltby Cl. NG8: Aspl . . . . . . . . . . . . . . . .5H **31**
Maltby Rd. NG3: Mapp . . . . . . . . . . . . . . .3C **34**
Malt Cotts. NG7: Basf . . . . . . . . . . . . . . .6D **32**
Malt Cross Gallery, The . . . . . . . . . . . . . .4D **4**
Malthouse Cl. NG16: Eastw . . . . . . . . . .4B **16**
Malthouse Rd. DE7: Ilk . . . . . . . . . . . . . .4B **40**
Malting Cl. NG11: Rudd . . . . . . . . . . . . . .1G **77**
Maltings, The NG3: Nott . . . . . . . . . . . . .2B **46**
   NG6: Basf . . . . . . . . . . . . . . . . . . . . . .5C **32**
Maltmill La. NG1: Nott . . . . . . . . . .5F **5** (5H **45**)
Malton Rd. NG5: Sher . . . . . . . . . . . . . . .5D **32**
Malt St. NG11: Goth . . . . . . . . . . . . . . . . .6H **75**
Malvern Cl. NG3: Nott . . . . . . . . . . . . . . .6A **34**
   NG9: Bee . . . . . . . . . . . . . . . . . . . . . . .5H **55**
Malvern Ct. NG3: Mapp P . . . . . . . . . . . .2G **45**
   NG9: Bee . . . . . . . . . . . . . . . . . . . . . . .5H **55**
Malvern Cres. NG2: West Br . . . . . . . . . .6B **58**
Malvern Gdns. NG10: Long E . . . . . . . . .5C **62**
Malvern Rd. NG2: West Br . . . . . . . . . . . .6A **58**
   NG3: Nott . . . . . . . . . . . . . . . . . . . . . .6A **34**
Manchester St. NG10: Long E . . . . . . . . .1F **73**
Mandalay St. NG6: Basf . . . . . . . . . . . . .3B **32**
Manesty Cres. NG11: Clif . . . . . . . . . . . .6C **66**
Manifold Gdns. NG2: Nott . . . . . . . . . . . .1G **57**
Manly Cl. NG5: Top V . . . . . . . . . . . . . . . .5C **20**
Manners Av. DE7: Ilk . . . . . . . . . . . . . . . .6H **27**
Manners Ind. Est. DE7: Ilk . . . . . . . . . . .6H **27**
Manners Rd. DE7: Ilk . . . . . . . . . . . . . . . .6A **28**
Manners St. DE7: Ilk . . . . . . . . . . . . . . . .3C **40**
Manning St. NG3: Nott . . . . . . . . . . . . . . .2H **45**
Manning Vw. DE7: Ilk . . . . . . . . . . . . . . . .5B **28**
Mannion Cres. NG10: Long E . . . . . . . . .2D **72**
Manns Leys NG12: Cotg . . . . . . . . . . . . .3E **71**
Mann St. NG7: Basf . . . . . . . . . . . . . . . . .1D **44**
Manor Av. NG2: Nott . . . . . . . . . . . . . . . .5A **46**
   NG9: Atten . . . . . . . . . . . . . . . . . . . . .2E **65**
   NG9: Bee . . . . . . . . . . . . . . . . . . . . . . .5F **55**
   NG9: Stap . . . . . . . . . . . . . . . . . . . . . .3F **53**
Manor Cl. NG12: Edwal . . . . . . . . . . . . . .2D **68**
Manor Ct. DE72: Brea . . . . . . . . . . . . . . .5A **62**
   NG4: Carl . . . . . . . . . . . . . . . . . . . . . .2H **47**
   NG9: Bram . . . . . . . . . . . . . . . . . . . . . .4C **54**
Manor Cres. NG4: Carl . . . . . . . . . . . . . . .1H **47**
Manor Cft. NG6: Basf . . . . . . . . . . . . . . . .4C **32**
Mnr. Farm Caravan & Camping Site
   NG15: Thru . . . . . . . . . . . . . . . . . . . . .4D **74**
Mnr. Farm Cl. NG11: Rudd . . . . . . . . . . .4A **78**
Mnr. Farm La. NG11: Clif . . . . . . . . . . . . .3C **66**
Manor Flds. Dr. DE7: Ilk . . . . . . . . . . . . .2H **39**
Manor Grn. NG4: Carl . . . . . . . . . . . . . . .1H **47**
Manor Grn. Wlk. NG4: Carl . . . . . . . . . . .1H **47**
Manor Health & Racquets Club, The . . . .6A **28**
Manor Ho. Cl. NG11: Wilf . . . . . . . . . . . . .3F **57**
Manor Ho. Rd. NG10: Long E . . . . . . . . .1H **73**
Manorleigh DE72: Brea . . . . . . . . . . . . . .5A **62**
Manor Pk. NG11: Rudd . . . . . . . . . . . . . .6F **67**
Manor Pk. La. NG14: Epp . . . . . . . . . . . .6G **13**
Manor Rd. DE7: Ilk . . . . . . . . . . . . . . . . . .6A **28**
   NG4: Carl . . . . . . . . . . . . . . . . . . . . . .1H **47**
   NG11: Bart F . . . . . . . . . . . . . . . . . . . .1E **75**
   NG12: Key . . . . . . . . . . . . . . . . . . . . . .4G **79**
   NG13: Bing . . . . . . . . . . . . . . . . . . . . .5F **51**
   NG14: Calv . . . . . . . . . . . . . . . . . . . . .4G **11**
   NG16: Eastw . . . . . . . . . . . . . . . . . . . .4B **16**
Manor St. NG2: Nott . . . . . . . . . . . . . . . . .5A **46**
Manor Wlk. NG14: Epp . . . . . . . . . . . . . . .6G **13**
Manorwood Rd. NG12: Cotg . . . . . . . . . .3F **71**
Mansell Cl. NG16: Eastw . . . . . . . . . . . . .4D **16**
Mansfield Gro. NG1: Nott . . . . . . . .1C **4** (3F **45**)
Mansfield La. NG14: Calv . . . . . . . . . . . .2H **11**
Mansfield Rd. DE75: Hea . . . . . . . . . . . .3D **14**
   NG1: Nott . . . . . . . . . . . . . . . . .1D **4** (2F **45**)
   NG5: Arn, Redh, Sher . . . . . . . . . . . . .2G **9**
   NG15: Pap . . . . . . . . . . . . . . . . . . . . . .1F **9**
   NG16: Brins, Eastw . . . . . . . . . . . . . . .1A **16**
Mansfield St. NG5: Sher . . . . . . . . . . . . .5G **33**
Manston M. NG7: Radf . . . . . . . . . . . . . . .3D **44**
Manthorpe Cres. NG5: Sher . . . . . . . . . .4B **34**
Manton Cres. NG9: Lent A . . . . . . . . . . . .3F **55**
Manvers Bus. Pk. NG12: Cotg . . . . . . . .1G **71**
Manvers Ct. NG2: Nott . . . . . . . . . .4H **5** (5A **46**)
Manvers Gro. NG12: Rad T . . . . . . . . . . .6F **49**
Manvers Rd. NG2: West Br . . . . . . . . . . .5B **58**
Manvers St. NG2: Nott . . . . . . . . . .4H **5** (5A **46**)
   NG4: Neth . . . . . . . . . . . . . . . . . . . . . .3A **48**

**Manville Cl.** NG8: Aspl . . . . . . . . . . . . . . . .3A **44**
  NG9: Bram . . . . . . . . . . . . . . . . . . . . .6B **42**
**Maori Av.** NG15: Huck . . . . . . . . . . . . . . . .6D **6**
**Maple Av.** NG9: Bee . . . . . . . . . . . . . . . . .6H **55**
  NG10: Sand . . . . . . . . . . . . . . . . . . . .4D **52**
**Maplebeck Rd.** NG5: Arn . . . . . . . . . . . . . .6C **22**
**Maple Cl.** NG12: Key . . . . . . . . . . . . . . . . .5A **80**
  NG12: Rad T . . . . . . . . . . . . . . . . . . .1F **61**
  NG13: Bing . . . . . . . . . . . . . . . . . . . .5G **51**
  NG14: Calv . . . . . . . . . . . . . . . . . . . . .4F **11**
**Maple Ct.** NG7: Lent . . . . . . . . . . . . . . . . .6D **44**
  NG16: Kimb . . . . . . . . . . . . . . . . . . . .1H **29**
**Mapledene Cres.** NG8: Woll . . . . . . . . . . . .6C **42**
**Maple Dr.** NG4: Ged . . . . . . . . . . . . . . . . .5B **36**
  NG15: Huck . . . . . . . . . . . . . . . . . . . . .6E **7**
  NG16: Nuth . . . . . . . . . . . . . . . . . . . . .1B **30**
**Maple Gdns.** DE75: Hea . . . . . . . . . . . . . .4B **14**
  NG16: Lang M . . . . . . . . . . . . . . . . . . .2F **15**
**Maple Gro.** DE72: Brea . . . . . . . . . . . . . . .5B **62**
**Maple Leaf Way** NG15: Huck . . . . . . . . . . .1A **20**
**Maples, The** DE75: Ship . . . . . . . . . . . . . .5E **15**
**Maples St.** NG7: H Grn . . . . . . . . . . . . . . .2D **44**
**Maplestead Av.** NG11: Wilf . . . . . . . . . . . . .5F **57**
**Mapletree Cl.** NG5: Bestw . . . . . . . . . . . . .6F **21**
**Maple Vw.** NG11: Wilf . . . . . . . . . . . . . . . .1F **67**
**Maple Way** NG2: West Br . . . . . . . . . . . . . .1A **68**
**MAPPERLEY**
  DE7 . . . . . . . . . . . . . . . . . . . . . . . . . .5C **26**
  NG5 . . . . . . . . . . . . . . . . . . . . . . . . . .4B **34**
**Mapperley Brook** DE7: Mapp . . . . . . . . . . .5E **27**
**Mapperley Cres.** NG3: Mapp . . . . . . . . . . .5A **34**
*Mapperley Golf Course* . . . . . . . . . . . . . . . .3D **34**
**Mapperley Hall Dr.** NG3: Mapp P . . . . . . . .6G **33**
**Mapperley Hall Gdns.** NG3: Mapp P . . . . . .6H **33**
**Mapperley Hgts.** NG5: Woodt . . . . . . . . . . .2D **34**
**Mapperley La.** DE7: Mapp . . . . . . . . . . . . .5C **26**
**Mapperley Orchard** NG5: Arn . . . . . . . . . . .6D **22**
**MAPPERLEY PARK**
  DE7 . . . . . . . . . . . . . . . . . . . . . . . . . .4B **26**
  NG3 . . . . . . . . . . . . . . . . . . . . . . . . . .6G **33**
**Mapperley Pk. Dr.** NG3: Mapp P . . . . . . . . .1G **45**
**Mapperley Plains** NG3: Mapp . . . . . . . . . . .2D **34**
**Mapperley Ri.** NG3: Mapp . . . . . . . . . . . . .5A **34**
**Mapperley Rd.** NG3: Mapp P . . . . . . . . . . .2G **45**
*Mapperley Sports Village* . . . . . . . . . . . . . . .6A **34**
**Mapperley St.** NG5: Sher . . . . . . . . . . . . . .5G **33**
*Mapperley Wood Local Nature Reserve* . . . . .4D **26**
**March Cl.** NG5: Top V . . . . . . . . . . . . . . . .6C **20**
**Marchesi Cl.** NG15: Huck . . . . . . . . . . . . . .1E **19**
**Marchwood Cl.** NG8: Radf . . . . . . . . . . . . .4B **44**
**Marco Island** NG1: Nott . . . . . . . . . . . . . . .3G **5**
**Mardale Cl.** NG2: West Br . . . . . . . . . . . . .6E **59**
**Mardling Av.** NG5: Bestw . . . . . . . . . . . . . .2E **33**
**Margaret Av.** DE7: Ilk . . . . . . . . . . . . . . . .1B **40**
  NG10: Long E . . . . . . . . . . . . . . . . . . .4H **63**
  NG10: Sand . . . . . . . . . . . . . . . . . . . .1D **62**
**Margaret Cres.** NG4: Ged . . . . . . . . . . . . . .5G **35**
**Margaret Pl.** NG13: Bing . . . . . . . . . . . . . .4D **50**
**Margarets Ct.** NG9: Bram . . . . . . . . . . . . . .3A **54**
**Marham Cl.** NG2: Nott . . . . . . . . . . . . . . . .6A **46**
**Marhill Rd.** NG4: Carl . . . . . . . . . . . . . . . .2H **47**
**Maria Ct.** NG7: Nott . . . . . . . . . . . .6A **4** (6E **45**)
**Marie Gdns.** NG15: Huck . . . . . . . . . . . . . .6G **7**
**Marina Av.** NG9: Bee . . . . . . . . . . . . . . . . .6F **55**
**Marina Rd.** DE7: Smal . . . . . . . . . . . . . . . .5A **14**
**Mariner Ct.** NG6: Bulw . . . . . . . . . . . . . . . .1G **31**
**Marion Av.** NG15: Huck . . . . . . . . . . . . . . . .2A **8**
**Marion Murdoch Ct.** NG4: Ged . . . . . . . . . .5G **35**
**Maris Cl.** NG11: Clif . . . . . . . . . . . . . . . . . .3A **66**
**Maris Dr.** NG14: Bur J . . . . . . . . . . . . . . . .3E **37**
**Market Pl.** DE7: Ilk . . . . . . . . . . . . . . . . . .1A **40**
  *DE75: Hea* . . . . . . . . . . . . . . . . . . . .4C **14**
              *(off Market St.)*
  NG5: Arn . . . . . . . . . . . . . . . . . . . . . .6B **22**
  NG6: Bulw . . . . . . . . . . . . . . . . . . . . .6H **19**
  NG10: Long E . . . . . . . . . . . . . . . . . . .5G **63**
  NG13: Bing . . . . . . . . . . . . . . . . . . . .5E **51**
  NG15: Huck . . . . . . . . . . . . . . . . . . . . .4G **7**
**Market Side** NG6: Bulw . . . . . . . . . . . . . . .6H **19**
              *(off Duke St.)*
**Market St.** DE7: Ilk . . . . . . . . . . . . . . . . . .1B **40**
  DE75: Hea . . . . . . . . . . . . . . . . . . . . .3C **14**
  NG1: Nott . . . . . . . . . . . . . . .3D **4** (4G **45**)
  NG13: Bing . . . . . . . . . . . . . . . . . . . .5E **51**
**Markham Cres.** NG5: Sher . . . . . . . . . . . . .3G **33**
**Markham Rd.** NG9: Bram . . . . . . . . . . . . . .2D **54**
**Mark St.** NG10: Sand . . . . . . . . . . . . . . . . .6E **53**
**Marlborough, The** NG3: Nott . . . . . . . . . . . .2G **45**
**Marlborough Rd.** NG2: West Br . . . . . . . . . .4B **58**
  NG9: Bee . . . . . . . . . . . . . . . . . . . . . .3F **55**
**Marlborough Rd.** NG5: Woodt . . . . . . . . . . .2H **33**
  NG9: Bee . . . . . . . . . . . . . . . . . . . . . .3F **55**
  NG10: Long E . . . . . . . . . . . . . . . . . . .4H **63**
**Marlborough St.** NG7: Lent . . . . . . . . . . . . .2C **56**
**Marldon Cl.** NG8: Bilb . . . . . . . . . . . . . . . . .4B **42**
**Marlow Av.** NG6: Basf . . . . . . . . . . . . . . . .5C **32**
**Marlow Cres.** DE7: West H . . . . . . . . . . . . .1B **38**

**MARLPOOL** . . . . . . . . . . . . . . . . . . . . . .6D **14**
**Marl Rd.** NG12: Rad T . . . . . . . . . . . . . . . .6H **49**
**Marlwood** NG12: Cotg . . . . . . . . . . . . . . . . .4G **71**
**Marmion Ct.** NG3: Nott . . . . . . . . . . . . . . . .3B **46**
**Marmion Rd.** NG3: Nott . . . . . . . . . . . . . . .2C **46**
**Marnham Dr.** NG3: Nott . . . . . . . . . . . . . . .6A **34**
**Marriott Av.** NG9: Chil . . . . . . . . . . . . . . . .6A **54**
**Marriott Cl.** NG9: Chil . . . . . . . . . . . . . . . .6A **54**
**Marsant Cl.** NG8: Woll . . . . . . . . . . . . . . . .4A **44**
**Marsden Cl.** NG6: Bulw . . . . . . . . . . . . . . .2C **32**
**Marshall Cl.** NG14: Calv . . . . . . . . . . . . . . .3F **11**
**Marshall Dr.** NG9: Bram . . . . . . . . . . . . . . .3H **53**
**Marshall Hill Dr.** NG3: Mapp . . . . . . . . . . . .6C **34**
**Marshall Rd.** NG3: Mapp . . . . . . . . . . . . . .6C **34**
**Marshall St.** DE75: Hea . . . . . . . . . . . . . . .3D **14**
  NG5: Sher . . . . . . . . . . . . . . . . . . . . .5G **33**
**Marshall Way** DE7: Kirk H . . . . . . . . . . . . .3G **39**
**Marsham Dr.** NG5: Arn . . . . . . . . . . . . . . . .1B **34**
**Marsh Av.** DE7: Ilk . . . . . . . . . . . . . . . . . .2A **28**
**Marston Rd.** NG3: Nott . . . . . . . . . . . . . . .2D **46**
**Martell Ct.** NG9: Chil . . . . . . . . . . . . . . . . .2C **64**
**Martin Cl.** NG6: Bulw . . . . . . . . . . . . . . . . .6A **20**
**Martin Ct.** NG6: Bulw . . . . . . . . . . . . . . . . .5G **19**
**Martin Cres.** NG11: Rudd . . . . . . . . . . . . . .6F **67**
**Martindale Cl.** NG2: Gam . . . . . . . . . . . . . .4E **59**
**Martinmass Cl.** NG7: Lent . . . . . . . . . . . . .6C **44**
**Martin's Hill** NG4: Carl . . . . . . . . . . . . . . . .2G **47**
*Martin's Pond Nature Reserve* . . . . . . . . . . . .4E **43**
**Marton Rd.** NG6: Bulw . . . . . . . . . . . . . . . .4A **20**
  NG9: Chil . . . . . . . . . . . . . . . . . . . . . .2C **64**
**Marvin Rd.** NG9: Bee . . . . . . . . . . . . . . . . .5F **55**
**Marvyn Cl.** NG6: Bulw . . . . . . . . . . . . . . . .1C **32**
**Marwood Cres.** NG4: Carl . . . . . . . . . . . . . .5E **35**
**Marwood Rd.** NG4: Carl . . . . . . . . . . . . . . .6E **35**
**Mary Ct.** NG3: Nott . . . . . . . . . . . . . . . . . .6A **34**
**Maryland Ct.** NG9: Stap . . . . . . . . . . . . . . .2G **53**
**Mary Rd.** NG16: Eastw . . . . . . . . . . . . . . . .4D **16**
**Masonic Pl.** NG1: Nott . . . . . . . . .3C **4** (4F **45**)
**Mason Rd.** DE7: Ilk . . . . . . . . . . . . . . . . . .5H **27**
**Massey Cl.** NG14: Bur J . . . . . . . . . . . . . . .4E **37**
**Massey Gdns.** NG3: Nott . . . . . . . . . . . . . .3A **46**
**Masson Ct.** NG5: Top V . . . . . . . . . . . . . . .4E **21**
**Matlock Ct.** NG1: Nott . . . . . . . . .2D **4** (4G **45**)
  NG10: Long E . . . . . . . . . . . . . . . . . . .2B **72**
**Matlock St.** NG4: Neth . . . . . . . . . . . . . . . .2H **47**
**Matthews Ct.** NG9: Stap . . . . . . . . . . . . . . .1H **53**
**Matthew Thomas Ct.** NG9: Bee . . . . . . . . . .5G **55**
**Mattingly Rd.** NG6: Bulw . . . . . . . . . . . . . . .1G **31**
**Maud St.** NG7: Basf . . . . . . . . . . . . . . . . . .6E **33**
**Maun Av.** NG7: Radf . . . . . . . . . . . . . . . . .3B **44**
**Maun Gdns.** NG7: Radf . . . . . . . . . . . . . . .3B **44**
**Maurice Dr.** NG3: Mapp . . . . . . . . . . . . . . .4B **34**
**Maws La.** NG16: Kimb . . . . . . . . . . . . . . . .6G **17**
**Maxtoke Rd.** NG7: Nott . . . . . . . . .6A **4** (6E **45**)
**Maxwell Cl.** NG7: Lent . . . . . . . . . . . . . . . .6D **44**
**Maxwell St.** DE72: Brea . . . . . . . . . . . . . . .5B **62**
  NG10: Long E . . . . . . . . . . . . . . . . . . .6G **63**
**May Av.** NG8: Woll . . . . . . . . . . . . . . . . . . .5E **43**
**May Ct.** NG5: Sher . . . . . . . . . . . . . . . . . .6F **33**
**Maycroft Gdns.** NG3: Nott . . . . . . . . . . . . .2C **46**
**Maydene Cl.** NG11: Clif . . . . . . . . . . . . . . . .4B **66**
**Mayes Ri.** NG6: Bestw V . . . . . . . . . . . . . . .1C **20**
**Mayfair Gdns.** NG5: Sher . . . . . . . . . . . . . .2D **32**
**Mayfield Av.** DE75: Hea . . . . . . . . . . . . . . .4C **14**
  NG14: Bur J . . . . . . . . . . . . . . . . . . . .2F **37**
**Mayfield Ct.** NG2: Nott . . . . . . . . . . . . . . . .1G **57**
**Mayfield Dr.** NG9: Stap . . . . . . . . . . . . . . .1H **53**
**Mayfield Gro.** NG10: Long E . . . . . . . . . . . .4G **63**
**Mayfield Rd.** NG4: Carl . . . . . . . . . . . . . . . .2D **46**
**Mayflower Cl.** NG2: West Br . . . . . . . . . . . .4C **58**
**Mayflower Rd.** NG16: Newth . . . . . . . . . . . .5D **16**
**Mayland Cl.** NG8: Bilb . . . . . . . . . . . . . . . .3C **42**
**Maylands Av.** DE72: Brea . . . . . . . . . . . . . .5A **62**
**Mayo Rd.** NG5: Sher . . . . . . . . . . . . . . . . .6F **33**
**Maypole** NG11: Clif . . . . . . . . . . . . . . . . . .2C **66**
**Maypole Yd.** NG1: Nott . . . . . . . . .3E **5** (4G **45**)
**May's Av.** NG4: Carl . . . . . . . . . . . . . . . . . .3E **47**
**Mays Cl.** NG4: Carl . . . . . . . . . . . . . . . . . .3E **47**
**May St.** DE7: Ilk . . . . . . . . . . . . . . . . . . . .3A **28**
**Maythorn Cl.** NG2: West Br . . . . . . . . . . . . .2G **67**
**Maythorne Wlk.** NG5: Bestw . . . . . . . . . . . .5G **21**
*Maywood Golf Course* . . . . . . . . . . . . . . . . .5A **52**
**Meadowbank Ct.** NG16: Eastw . . . . . . . . . .2H **15**
**Meadowbank Way** NG16: Eastw . . . . . . . . .2H **15**
**Meadow Brown Rd.** NG7: H Grn . . . . . . . . .1C **44**
**Meadow Cl.** DE72: Brea . . . . . . . . . . . . . . .6A **62**
  NG2: Nott . . . . . . . . . . . . . . . . . . . . .1B **58**
  NG15: Huck . . . . . . . . . . . . . . . . . . . . .6D **6**
  NG16: Eastw . . . . . . . . . . . . . . . . . . .1B **16**
**Meadow Cotts.** NG4: Neth . . . . . . . . . . . . . .2H **47**
**Meadow Ct.** NG2: Nott . . . . . . . . . . . . . . . .1B **58**
**Meadow Cft. Gdns.** NG15: Huck . . . . . . . . . .6F **7**
**Meadow Dr.** NG12: Key . . . . . . . . . . . . . . . .4A **80**
**Meadow End** NG11: Goth . . . . . . . . . . . . . .6H **75**
  NG12: Rad T . . . . . . . . . . . . . . . . . . .6H **49**
**Meadow Gdns.** DE75: Hea . . . . . . . . . . . . .4F **15**
  NG9: Chil . . . . . . . . . . . . . . . . . . . . . .1E **65**

**Meadow Gro.** NG2: Nott . . . . . . . . . . . . . . .1A **58**
**Meadow Lane** . . . . . . . . . . . . . . . . . . . . .1A **58**
**Meadow La.** NG2: Nott . . . . . . . . . . . . . . . .1A **58**
              *(not continuous)*
  NG9: Chil . . . . . . . . . . . . . . . . . . . . . .6E **55**
  NG10: Long E . . . . . . . . . . . . . . . . . . .6H **63**
              *(not continuous)*
  NG14: Bur J . . . . . . . . . . . . . . . . . . . .3F **37**
**Meadow Rise** NG6: Bulw . . . . . . . . . . . . . . .1F **31**
**Meadow Rd.** NG4: Neth . . . . . . . . . . . . . . .3H **47**
  NG9: Bee . . . . . . . . . . . . . . . . . . . . . .6G **55**
  NG16: Aws . . . . . . . . . . . . . . . . . . . . .2E **29**
**MEADOWS** . . . . . . . . . . . . . . . . . . . . . . .1G **57**
**Meadows, The** DE75: Hea . . . . . . . . . . . . .4C **14**
  NG14: Woodbo . . . . . . . . . . . . . . . . . .1B **24**
  NG16: Aws . . . . . . . . . . . . . . . . . . . . .2E **29**
**Meadow St.** DE7: Ilk . . . . . . . . . . . . . . . . .6B **28**
**Meadows Way** NG2: Nott . . . . . . . . . . . . . .2F **57**
**Meadowsweet Hill** NG13: Bing . . . . . . . . . . .5C **50**
**Meadow Trad. Est.** NG2: Nott . . . . . . . . . . .6A **46**
**Meadowvale Cres.** NG11: Clif . . . . . . . . . . .4C **66**
**Meadow Vw.** NG9: Stap . . . . . . . . . . . . . . .3F **53**
**Meadow Vw. Ct.** DE72: Ris . . . . . . . . . . . . .1B **62**
**Medawar Cl.** NG11: Clif . . . . . . . . . . . . . . .4A **66**
**Medbank Ct.** NG11: Wilf . . . . . . . . . . . . . . .6E **57**
**Meden Cl.** NG11: Clif . . . . . . . . . . . . . . . . .2C **66**
**Meden Gdns.** NG7: H Grn . . . . . . . . . . . . . .2B **44**
**Medina Dr.** NG12: Toll . . . . . . . . . . . . . . . .4F **69**
**Medway Cl.** NG9: Chil . . . . . . . . . . . . . . . . .6C **54**
**Medway Dr.** NG13: Bing . . . . . . . . . . . . . . .6C **50**
**Medway St.** NG8: Radf . . . . . . . . . . . . . . . .4B **44**
**Meeks Rd.** NG5: Arn . . . . . . . . . . . . . . . . . .5D **22**
**Meerbrook Pl.** DE7: Kirk H . . . . . . . . . . . . .4G **39**
**Meer Rd.** NG9: Chil . . . . . . . . . . . . . . . . . .6A **54**
**Melbourne Ct.** NG8: Aspl . . . . . . . . . . . . . .6A **32**
  NG10: Long E . . . . . . . . . . . . . . . . . . .3B **72**
**Melbourne Rd.** NG2: West Br . . . . . . . . . . . .2B **58**
  NG8: Aspl . . . . . . . . . . . . . . . . . . . . .1H **43**
  NG9: Stap . . . . . . . . . . . . . . . . . . . . .1G **53**
**Melbury Rd.** NG5: Woodt . . . . . . . . . . . . . .3B **34**
  NG8: Bilb . . . . . . . . . . . . . . . . . . . . . .1D **42**
**Meldreth Rd.** NG8: Bilb . . . . . . . . . . . . . . . .3E **43**
**Melford Hall Dr.** NG2: West Br . . . . . . . . . . .1G **67**
**Melford Rd.** NG8: Bilb . . . . . . . . . . . . . . . . .1D **42**
**Melksham Rd.** NG5: Bestw . . . . . . . . . . . . .5G **21**
**Mellbreak Cl.** NG2: West Br . . . . . . . . . . . . .5E **59**
**Mellers Ct.** NG3: Nott . . . . . . . . . . . . . . . . .2C **46**
*Mellish Sports Cen.* . . . . . . . . . . . . . . . . . . .2B **32**
**Mellors Rd.** NG2: West Br . . . . . . . . . . . . . .6B **58**
  NG5: Arn . . . . . . . . . . . . . . . . . . . . . .4B **22**
**Mellors Way** NG8: Stre . . . . . . . . . . . . . . . .5C **30**
**Melrose Av.** NG5: Sher . . . . . . . . . . . . . . . .4G **33**
  NG9: Bee . . . . . . . . . . . . . . . . . . . . . .6G **55**
**Melrose Gdns.** NG2: West Br . . . . . . . . . . . .1H **67**
**Melrose St.** NG5: Sher . . . . . . . . . . . . . . . .4G **33**
**Melton Ct.** NG10: Sand . . . . . . . . . . . . . . . .6C **52**
**Melton Gdns.** NG12: Edwal . . . . . . . . . . . . .1C **68**
**Melton Gro.** NG2: West Br . . . . . . . . . . . . . .4A **58**
**Melton Hall** NG8: Woll . . . . . . . . . . . . . . . .5A **44**
**Melton Rd.** NG2: West Br . . . . . . . . . . . . . .4A **58**
  NG12: Edwal, Key, Plum, Stant W . . . . . .4C **68**
**Melville Ct.** NG3: Mapp P . . . . . . . . . . . . . .1G **45**
**Melville Gdns.** NG3: Nott . . . . . . . .1H **5** (3A **46**)
**Melville St.** NG1: Nott . . . . . . . . . .6E **5** (6G **45**)
**Melvyn Dr.** NG13: Bing . . . . . . . . . . . . . . . .5E **51**
**Mendip Cl.** NG10: Long E . . . . . . . . . . . . . .4C **62**
**Mendip Ct.** NG5: Top V . . . . . . . . . . . . . . . .5D **20**
**Mensing Av.** NG12: Cotg . . . . . . . . . . . . . . .2E **71**
**Merchant St.** NG6: Bulw . . . . . . . . . . . . . . .5H **19**
              *(not continuous)*
**Mercia Cl.** NG16: Gilt . . . . . . . . . . . . . . . . .5C **16**
**Mercian Cl.** DE7: Ilk . . . . . . . . . . . . . . . . . .6A **28**
**Mercury Cl.** NG6: Basf . . . . . . . . . . . . . . . .2C **32**
**Mere Av.** NG14: Calv . . . . . . . . . . . . . . . . .4H **11**
**Mere Cl.** NG14: Calv . . . . . . . . . . . . . . . . .4H **11**
**Meredith Cl.** NG2: Nott . . . . . . . . . . . . . . . .2F **57**
**Meredith Ct.** NG9: Stap . . . . . . . . . . . . . . . .1G **53**
**Meregill Cl.** NG5: Top V . . . . . . . . . . . . . . . .4D **20**
**Merevale Av.** NG11: Clif . . . . . . . . . . . . . . .1D **66**
**Mere Way** NG11: Rudd . . . . . . . . . . . . . . . .3H **77**
**Meriac Cl.** NG5: Top V . . . . . . . . . . . . . . . .5D **20**
**Meriden Av.** NG9: Lent A . . . . . . . . . . . . . . .3G **55**
**Meridian Cl.** DE7: Ilk . . . . . . . . . . . . . . . . .3A **28**
**Meridian Ct.** NG5: Sher . . . . . . . . . . . . . . . .5E **33**
**Merlin Cl.** NG11: Clif . . . . . . . . . . . . . . . . .3C **66**
**Merlin Dr.** NG15: Huck . . . . . . . . . . . . . . . .1E **19**
**Merlin Way** DE7: Ilk . . . . . . . . . . . . . . . . . .5B **40**
**Merrivale Ct.** NG3: Mapp P . . . . . . . . . . . . .1G **45**
**Mersey St.** NG6: Bulw . . . . . . . . . . . . . . . . .6H **19**
**Merton Cl.** DE75: Hea . . . . . . . . . . . . . . . . .4D **14**
  NG5: Arn . . . . . . . . . . . . . . . . . . . . . .4D **22**
**Merton Ct.** NG9: Stap . . . . . . . . . . . . . . . . .2G **53**
**Metcalf Rd.** NG16: Newth . . . . . . . . . . . . . .2D **16**
**Meteor Ct.** NG3: Newton . . . . . . . . . . . . . . .2B **50**
**Mettham St.** NG7: Lent . . . . . . . . . . . . . . . .6D **44**
**Mevell Ct.** NG7: Nott . . . . . . . . . . .5A **4** (5E **45**)
**Mews, The** NG7: Basf . . . . . . . . . . . . . . . . .1E **45**

**Mews La.** NG14: Calv ....................4G **11**
**Meynell Gro.** NG7: Basf ..................6E **33**
**Meynell Rd.** NG10: Long E .............2F **73**
**Miall Ct.** NG7: Lent ......................4C **44**
**Miall St.** NG7: Lent ......................4C **44**
**Michael Gdns.** NG5: Sher ...............6F **33**
**Michael Rayner Ct.** NG6: Basf ........4B **32**
**Mickleborough Av.** NG3: Nott ..........1B **46**
**Mickleborough Way** NG2: West Br ...2G **67**
**Mickledon Cl.** NG2: Nott ...............1G **57**
   NG10: Long E ........................5D **62**
**Micklemoor La.** NG13: Car C ..........1H **51**
**Middle Av.** NG4: Carl ....................1E **47**
**Middlebeck Av.** NG5: Arn ..............5E **23**
**Middlebeck Dr.** NG5: Arn ...............5D **22**
**Middledale Rd.** NG4: Carl ..............3E **47**
**Middlefell Way** NG11: Clif ..............4B **66**
**Middle Furlong Gdns.** NG2: Nott .....1F **57**
**Middle Furlong M.** NG2: Nott .........1F **57**
**Middle Hill** NG1: Nott ..........5E **5** (5G **45**)
**Middle La.** NG9: Chil ....................6E **55**
**Middle Nook** *NG8: Woll* ................*4E 43*
             *(off Cottage Wlk.)*
**Middle Orchard St.** NG9: Stap .......4F **53**
**Middle Pavement** NG1: Nott ..5E **5** (5G **45**)
**Middle St.** NG9: Bee ....................5F **55**
**Middleton Blvd.** NG8: Woll ............5A **44**
**Middleton Cl.** NG16: Nuth .............1C **30**
**Middleton Ct.** NG8: Bilb ...............4D **42**
**Middleton Cres.** NG9: Bee ............2E **55**
**Middleton Rd.** DE7: Ilk .................4C **40**
**Middleton St.** DE7: Ilk .................6C **28**
   NG7: Lent ...........................4C **44**
   NG9: Bee ...........................4E **55**
   NG16: Aws ..........................3E **29**
**Midhurst Cl.** NG9: Chil ..................1C **64**
**Midhurst Way** NG11: Clif ..............3C **66**
**Midlame Gdns.** NG6: Bulw ............6F **19**
**Midland Av.** NG4: Neth .................2A **48**
   NG7: Lent ...........................6C **44**
   NG9: Stap ...........................6E **53**
**Midland Cotts.** NG2: West Br ........4B **58**
**Midland Ct.** NG7: Radf .................3B **44**
**Midland Cres.** NG4: Carl ..............2H **47**
**Midland Gro.** NG4: Neth ...............1A **48**
**Midland Rd.** DE75: Hea .................3C **14**
   NG4: Carl ...........................2H **47**
   NG16: Eastw .......................3B **16**
**Midland St.** NG10: Long E .............5G **63**
**Midland Way** NG7: Radf ................3B **44**
**Midway, The** NG7: Lent ................3C **56**
**Mikado Rd.** NG10: Long E ..............2E **73**
**Milburn Gro.** NG13: Bing ..............5C **50**
**Mildenhall Cres.** NG5: Bestw .........5G **21**
**Mile End Rd.** NG4: Colw ...............4G **47**
**Milford Av.** NG10: Long E ..............2D **62**
**Milford Cl.** NG6: Bulw ...................5G **19**
**Milford Ct.** NG5: Arn ....................1H **33**
**Milford Dr.** DE7: Ilk .....................4H **27**
   NG3: Nott ...........................2E **47**
**Mill Acre Cl.** DE7: Ilk ...................5H **27**
**Millbank** DE75: Hea ......................4E **15**
**Millbank Cl.** DE7: Ilk .....................4H **27**
**Millbank Ct.** NG6: Bulw .................1G **31**
**Millbank Pl.** NG6: Bestw V .............2B **20**
**Millbeck Av.** NG8: Woll .................5C **42**
**Millbeck Cl.** NG2: Gam .................5E **59**
**Millbrook Dr.** NG4: Carl ................6E **35**
**Mill Close, The** NG6: Basf .............4C **32**
**Mill Ct.** NG10: Long E ....................6G **63**
**Mill Cres.** NG5: Arn ......................5A **22**
**Milldale Cl.** NG11: Clif ...................3A **66**
**Milldale Rd.** NG10: Long E .............1D **72**
**Millennium Cl.** DE7: Ilk ..................4A **28**
**Millennium Ct.** NG6: Bulw ..............2B **32**
**Millennium Way** NG8: Cin ..............3G **31**
**Millennium Way E.** NG8: Cin ..........3G **31**
**Millennium Way W.** NG8: Cin .........3G **31**
**Miller Hives Cl.** NG12: Cotg ...........2E **71**
**Millers Bri.** NG12: Cotg .................3E **71**
**Millers Ct.** NG7: Radf ....................3C **44**
**Millersdale Av.** DE7: Ilk .................2A **28**
**Millers Grn.** NG2: Nott ..................5C **46**
**Millership Way** DE7: Ilk .................5B **28**
**Mill Fld. Cl.** NG14: Bur J ...............4E **37**
**Millfield Cl.** DE7: Ilk ......................3G **27**
**Millfield Rd.** DE7: Ilk .....................2C **40**
   NG16: Kimb .........................6G **17**
**Mill Hill La.** DE72: Brea .................4A **62**
**Mill Hill Rd.** NG13: Bing ................6D **50**
**Millicent Gro.** NG2: West Br ..........3B **58**
**Millicent Rd.** NG2: West Br ...........3A **58**
**Millidge Cl.** NG5: Bestw ................2D **32**
**Mill Lakes Country Pk.** .................1B **20**
**Mill La.** NG4: Lamb .......................6B **24**
   NG5: Arn ............................5A **22**
   NG6: Bestw V .......................2B **20**

**Mill La.** NG10: Sand ......................5E **53**
   NG11: Rudd ..........................3B **78**
   NG12: Cotg ...........................1E **71**
   NG12: C'ton, Cotg ..................4D **70**
   NG16: Coss ...........................1D **40**
**Mill Rd.** DE75: Hea ......................5E **15**
   NG9: Stap .............................3F **53**
   NG16: Newth ..........................2C **16**
**Mills Bldgs.** NG1: Nott ...................5G **5**
**Mill St.** DE7: Ilk ...........................6B **28**
   NG6: Basf .............................4B **32**
**Mill Vw. Cl.** NG2: Nott ...................5B **46**
**Millview Ct.** NG2: Nott ........5H **5** (5A **46**)
**Mill Yd.** NG15: Huck ......................4G **7**
**Milner Rd.** NG5: Sher .....................5G **33**
   NG10: Long E .........................5F **63**
**Milnhay Rd.** DE75: Hea ..................4G **15**
**Milton Av.** DE7: Ilk .......................3A **28**
**Milton Ct.** NG5: Arn .....................6D **22**
   NG5: Sher ............................4F **33**
**Milton Cres.** NG9: Atten .................3D **64**
**Milton Ho.** NG1: Nott ..........3E **5** (4G **45**)
**Milton Ri.** NG15: Huck ....................6D **6**
**Milton Rd.** DE7: Ilk .......................3A **28**
**Milton St.** DE7: Ilk ........................3A **28**
   NG1: Nott ................2E **5** (4G **45**)
   NG10: Long E .........................6F **63**
**Milton Ter.** NG10: Long E ...............6F **63**
**Milverton Rd.** NG5: Bestw ..............5G **21**
**Milward Rd.** DE75: Los ..................3B **14**
**Mimosa Cl.** NG11: Clif ...................4A **66**
**Minerva Gro.** NG15: Huck ...............3A **8**
**Minerva St.** NG6: Bulw ..................5H **19**
             *(not continuous)*
**Mint Gro.** NG10: Long E ................6C **62**
**Minton Cl.** NG9: Chil ....................4B **64**
**Minver Cres.** NG8: Aspl ..................6G **31**
**Mirberry M.** NG7: Lent ...................6C **44**
**Miriam Ct.** NG2: West Br ...............4A **58**
**Misk Hollows** NG15: Huck ...............3F **7**
**Misk Vw.** NG16: Eastw ..................3D **16**
**Mission St.** NG3: Mapp ..................5A **34**
**Mitchell Av.** NG16: Lang M .............1E **15**
**Mitchell Cl.** NG6: Bulw ..................1G **31**
**Mitchell St.** NG10: Long E ..............6G **63**
**Mitchell Ter.** DE7: Ilk ....................4C **40**
**Mitford Dr.** NG5: Arn .....................3B **22**
**Moffat Cl.** NG3: Nott ....................2B **46**
**Mohan Bus. Cen.** NG10: Long E ......4F **63**
**Monarch Way** DE75: Hea ...............3B **14**
**Mona Rd.** NG2: West Br .................2C **58**
**Mona St.** NG9: Bee ......................5G **55**
**Monks Cl.** DE7: Ilk .......................1C **40**
**Monk's La.** NG11: Goth ..................6H **75**
**Monksway** NG11: Wilf ....................1E **67**
**Monkton Cl.** DE7: Ilk ....................4H **27**
**Monkton Dr.** NG8: Bilb ..................2E **43**
**Monmouth Cl.** NG8: Woll ...............5B **42**
**Monroe Wlk.** NG5: Bestw ...............6E **21**
**Monsaldale Cl.** NG10: Long E ..........1D **72**
**Monsall Av.** DE7: Ilk .....................2A **28**
**Monsall St.** NG7: Basf ...................6D **32**
**Monsell Dr.** NG5: Redh ..................4A **22**
**Montague Rd.** NG15: Huck ..............3G **7**
**Montague St.** NG6: Bulw ................6A **20**
   NG9: Bee .............................4E **55**
**Montfort Cres.** NG5: Sher ..............3H **33**
**Montfort St.** NG7: Radf .................4E **45**
**Montgomery Cl.** NG9: Chil .............3C **64**
**Montgomery St.** NG7: Radf ...1A **4** (3E **45**)
**Montpelier Rd.** NG7: Lent ..............2C **56**
**Montrose Ct.** NG9: Stap ................1B **54**
**Monyash Cl.** DE7: Ilk .....................4A **28**
**Moody Cl.** NG9: Chil .....................3B **64**
**Moon Cres.** NG16: Eastw ...............4A **16**
**Moor, The** DE7: D Ab ....................6E **39**
   NG9: Trow ............................3A **42**
**Moor Bridge (Park & Ride)** ...........3B **20**
**Moorbridge Caravan Pk.** NG6: Bulw ..3B **20**
**Moorbridge Cotts.** NG6: Bulw .........3B **20**
**Moorbridge Ct.** NG13: Bing ............4E **51**
**Moorbridge La.** NG9: Stap ..............2F **53**
**Moorbridge Rd.** NG13: Bing ............4E **51**
**Moorbridge Rd. E.** NG13: Bing ........4E **51**
**Moor Bridge Stop (NET)** ...............3B **20**
**Moore Cl.** NG2: West Br .................2D **58**
**Moore Ga.** NG9: Bee .....................5F **55**
**Moore Rd.** NG3: Mapp ..................5C **34**

**Moores Av.** NG10: Sand .................4E **53**
**Moores Pl.** NG5: Sher ....................5E **33**
**Moore St.** NG6: Bulw .....................2A **32**
**Moor Farm Holiday & Home Pk.** NG14: Calv ..5C **12**
**Moor Farm Inn La.** NG9: Bram ........1A **54**
**Moorfield Ct.** NG9: Stap .................2G **53**
**Moorfield Cres.** NG10: Sand ............6D **52**
**Moorfields Av.** NG16: Eastw ............2B **16**
**Moorgate St.** NG7: Radf .......2A **4** (4E **45**)
**MOORGREEN** ..............................2F **17**
**Moorgreen** NG16: Newth ................1E **17**
**Moorgreen Dr.** NG8: Stre ...............5D **30**
**Moorgreen Ind. Pk.** NG16: Newth .....1D **16**
**Moorhouse Rd.** NG8: Bilb ..............3E **43**
**Moorings, The** NG7: Lent ...............1D **56**
**Moorland Av.** NG9: Stap .................5F **53**
**Moorlands Cl.** NG10: Long E ...........3D **62**
**Moor La.** DE7: D Ab .......................6D **38**
   NG9: Bram ...........................1B **54**
   NG11: Bunny .........................6G **77**
   NG11: Goth, Rudd ..................6H **75**
   NG11: Rudd ..........................6H **75**
               *(Leys Ct.)*
   NG11: Rudd ..........................5H **77**
            *(Littlemoor La.)*
   NG13: Bing ...........................4E **51**
   NG14: Calv, Epp ....................5C **12**
**Moor Rd.** NG6: Bestw V ..................2B **20**
   NG8: Stre ............................6D **30**
   NG14: Calv ..........................4A **12**
   NG15: Pap ............................1B **8**
**Moorsholm Dr.** NG8: Woll ..............5C **42**
**Moor St.** NG4: Neth ......................2H **47**
**Moray Ct.** NG16: Kimb ...................6H **17**
**Morden Cl.** NG8: Bilb .....................1D **42**
**Morden Rd.** NG16: Gilt ...................5E **17**
**Moreland Ct.** NG2: Nott ..................6B **46**
   NG4: Carl ............................2E **47**
**Moreland Pl.** NG2: Nott ..................6B **46**
**Moreland St.** NG2: Nott ..................6B **46**
**Morel Ho.** *NG7: Lent* .....................*4C 44*
            *(off Faraday Rd.)*
**Morello Av.** NG4: Carl ....................2H **47**
**Moreton Rd.** NG11: Clif ..................6C **66**
**Morgan M.** NG11: Clif .....................3B **66**
**Morkinshire Cres.** NG12: Cotg .........1F **71**
**Morkinshire La.** NG12: Cotg .............1E **71**
**Morley Av.** NG3: Mapp ...................5A **34**
**Morley Ct.** NG2: Nott .....................3H **5**
**Morley Dr.** DE7: Ilk .......................4H **27**
**Morley Gdns.** NG5: Sher .................6F **33**
**Morley Rd.** NG3: Nott .....................6C **34**
**Morley St.** NG5: Arn ......................1H **33**
**Mornington Cl.** NG10: Sand .............5E **53**
**Mornington Cres.** NG8: Nuth ...........4D **30**
**Morrell Bank** NG5: Bestw ...............1D **32**
**Morris Av.** NG9: Chil ......................4B **64**
**Morris Cl.** NG4: Colw ......................4A **48**
**Morris Rd.** NG8: Stre ......................6D **30**
**Morris St.** NG4: Neth ......................2A **48**
**Morton Av.** DE7: Ilk .......................2B **28**
**Morton Gdns.** NG12: Rad T .............6H **49**
**Morval Rd.** NG8: Bilb .....................2E **43**
**Morven Av.** NG15: Huck ...................5H **7**
**Mosley St.** NG7: Basf .....................1D **44**
   NG15: Huck ...........................5G **7**
**Moss Cl.** NG5: Arn .........................5G **21**
**Mosscroft Av.** NG11: Clif .................4B **66**
**Mossdale Rd.** NG5: Sher .................2G **33**
**Moss Dr.** NG9: Bram ......................4B **54**
**Moss Ri.** NG3: Mapp .......................5D **34**
**Moss Rd.** DE7: Ilk .........................2A **40**
   NG15: Huck ...........................4F **7**
**Moss Side** NG11: Wilf .....................2E **67**
**Mosswood Cres.** ...........................
   NG5: Bestw ..........................6F **21**
**Mottram Rd.** NG9: Chil ...................5C **54**
**Mount, The** NG3: Mapp ..................5E **35**
   NG5: Redh ...........................4H **21**
   NG6: Bestw V .......................1C **20**
   NG8: Stre ............................6E **31**
   NG9: Stap ...........................5F **53**
**Mountbatten Ct.** DE7: Ilk ...............4B **28**
**Mountbatten Gro.** NG4: Ged ...........5G **35**
**Mountbatten Way** NG9: Chil ............3B **64**
**Mountfield Av.** NG10: Sand .............1C **62**
**Mountfield Dr.** NG5: Bestw .............6E **21**
**Mount Hgts.** NG7: Basf ..................6E **33**
**Mount Hooton** NG1: Nott ...............3E **45**
**Mt. Hooton Rd.** NG7: Radf .............2E **45**
**Mt. Pleasant** DE7: Ilk ....................3A **28**
   NG4: Carl ...........................2G **47**
   NG6: Basf ............................5B **32**
   NG12: Key ............................4H **79**
   NG12: Rad T .........................6E **49**
**Mountsorrel Dr.** NG2: West Br .........5D **58**

Mount St. DE72: Brea . . . . . . . . . . . . . . . .6B 62
  DE75: Hea . . . . . . . . . . . . . . . . . . . . . . .4C 14
  NG1: Nott . . . . . . . . . . . . . . . . . . . .4C 4 (5F 45)
     (not continuous)
  NG7: Basf . . . . . . . . . . . . . . . . . . . . . . .6D 32
  NG9: Stap . . . . . . . . . . . . . . . . . . . . . . .4G 53
Mount St. Arc. NG1: Nott . . . . . . . . . . . . . .4C 4
Mowbray Ct. NG3: Nott . . . . . . . . .2G 5 (4H 45)
Mowbray Gdns. NG2: West Br . . . . . . . . .6B 58
Mowbray Ri. NG5: Arn . . . . . . . . . . . . . . .4B 22
Moyra Dr. NG5: Arn . . . . . . . . . . . . . . . . .6G 21
Moyra Ho. NG5: Arn . . . . . . . . . . . . . . . .6A 22
Mozart Cl. NG7: Radf . . . . . . . . . . . . . . . .4C 44
Mudpie La. NG2: West Br . . . . . . . . . . . . .2D 58
Muir Av. NG12: Toll . . . . . . . . . . . . . . . . .5F 69
Muirfield Rd. NG5: Arn, Top V . . . . . . . . .4D 20
Mulberry Cl. NG2: West Br . . . . . . . . . . .6F 57
Mulberry Gdns. NG6: Bulw . . . . . . . . . . .5G 19
Mulberry Gro. NG15: Huck . . . . . . . . . . .1H 19
Mundella Rd. NG2: Nott . . . . . . . . . . . . .2H 57
Mundy's Dr. DE75: Hea . . . . . . . . . . . . . .5D 14
Mundy St. DE7: Ilk . . . . . . . . . . . . . . . . .5B 28
  DE75: Hea . . . . . . . . . . . . . . . . . . . . . . .4C 14
Munford Cir. NG8: Cin . . . . . . . . . . . . . . .4G 31
Munks Av. NG15: Huck . . . . . . . . . . . . . . . .4F 7
Murby Cres. NG6: Bulw . . . . . . . . . . . . . .5H 19
Murden Way NG9: Bee . . . . . . . . . . . . . .5H 55
Muriel Gdns. NG6: Bulw . . . . . . . . . . . . .6H 19
Muriel Rd. NG9: Bee . . . . . . . . . . . . . . . .4F 55
Muriel St. NG6: Bulw . . . . . . . . . . . . . . .6H 19
Murray Cl. NG5: Bestw . . . . . . . . . . . . . .2D 32
Museum of Nottingham Life at Brewhouse Yard
  . . . . . . . . . . . . . . . . . . . . . . . .6C 4 (6F 45)
Mushroom Farm Ct. NG16: Eastw . . . . . .2H 15
Muskham Av. DE7: Ilk . . . . . . . . . . . . . . .4B 28
Muskham St. NG2: Nott . . . . . . . . . . . . .2H 57
Musters Ct. NG2: West Br . . . . . . . . . . . .3A 58
  NG15: Huck . . . . . . . . . . . . . . . . . . . . . . .5A 8
Musters Cres. NG2: West Br . . . . . . . . . . .6B 58
Musters Cft. NG4: Colw . . . . . . . . . . . . .6H 47
Musters Rd. NG2: West Br . . . . . . . . . . . .3A 58
  NG11: Rudd . . . . . . . . . . . . . . . . . . . . . .1F 77
  NG13: Bing . . . . . . . . . . . . . . . . . . . . . .5D 50
Musters Wlk. NG6: Bulw . . . . . . . . . . . . .6G 19
Muston Cl. NG3: Mapp . . . . . . . . . . . . . .6B 34
Myrtle Av. NG7: H Grn . . . . . . . . . . . . . . .1F 45
  NG9: Stap . . . . . . . . . . . . . . . . . . . . . . .5G 53
  NG10: Long E . . . . . . . . . . . . . . . . . . . .2E 63
Myrtle Gro. NG9: Bee . . . . . . . . . . . . . . .4G 55
Myrtle Rd. NG4: Carl . . . . . . . . . . . . . . . .1F 47
Myrtus Cl. NG11: Clif . . . . . . . . . . . . . . .3A 66
Mytholme Cl. NG10: Long E . . . . . . . . . .3E 63

## N

Nabarro Ct. NG14: Calv . . . . . . . . . . . . . .4G 11
Nabbs La. NG15: Huck . . . . . . . . . . . . . . .5D 6
Naburn Ct. NG8: Basf . . . . . . . . . . . . . . .6B 32
Nairn Cl. NG5: Arn . . . . . . . . . . . . . . . . .4D 22
Nairn M. NG4: Carl . . . . . . . . . . . . . . . . .2G 47
Nansen Gdns. NG5: Bestw . . . . . . . . . . . .1D 32
Nansen St. NG6: Bulw . . . . . . . . . . . . . . .1A 32
Naomi Ct. NG6: Bulw . . . . . . . . . . . . . . .4A 20
Naomi Cres. NG6: Bulw . . . . . . . . . . . . . .4A 20
Naranjan M. NG7: Radf . . . . . . . . .1A 4 (3E 45)
Narrow La. NG16: Want . . . . . . . . . . . . . .4H 17
Naseby Cl. NG5: Sher . . . . . . . . . . . . . . .3D 32
Naseby Dr. NG10: Long E . . . . . . . . . . . .2G 73
Nathaniel Rd. NG10: Long E . . . . . . . . . .6H 63
Nathans La. NG12: Rad T . . . . . . . . . . . .4A 60
National Ice Centre, The . . . . . . .4G 5 (5H 45)
National Water Sports Cen. . . . . . . . . . .1G 59
National Water Sports Cen.
  Holme Pierrepont Caravan & Camping Pk.
  NG2: West Br . . . . . . . . . . . . . . . . . . . .2F 59
Natural History Mus. . . . . . . . . . . . . . . .6G 43
Navdeep Ct. NG2: West Br . . . . . . . . . . . .4A 58
Navenby Wlk. NG11: Clif . . . . . . . . . . . . .3C 66
Naworth Cl. NG6: Bulw . . . . . . . . . . . . . .2C 32
Naylor Av. NG11: Goth . . . . . . . . . . . . . .6H 75
Naylor Ho. NG5: Arn . . . . . . . . . . . . . . . .1C 34
    (off Derwent Cres.)
Nazareth Ct. NG7: Lent . . . . . . . . . . . . . .1C 56
Nazareth Rd. NG7: Lent . . . . . . . . . . . . . .1C 56
Neal Ct. NG16: Lang M . . . . . . . . . . . . . .2E 15
Neale St. NG10: Long E . . . . . . . . . . . . . .6G 63
Near Mdw. NG10: Long E . . . . . . . . . . . .2G 73
Nearsby Dr. NG2: West Br . . . . . . . . . . . .5D 58
Needham Rd. NG5: Arn . . . . . . . . . . . . . .5C 22
Needham St. NG13: Bing . . . . . . . . . . . . .5E 51
Needwood Av. NG9: Trow . . . . . . . . . . . .1F 53
Neeps Cft. NG14: Epp . . . . . . . . . . . . . . .5G 13
Negus Ct. NG4: Lamb . . . . . . . . . . . . . . .6B 24
Neighwood Cl. NG9: Toton . . . . . . . . . . .3G 63
Nell Gwyn Cres. NG5: Arn . . . . . . . . . . . .4G 21
Nelper Cres. DE7: Ilk . . . . . . . . . . . . . . . .4C 40

Nelson Rd. NG5: Arn . . . . . . . . . . . . . . . .6A 22
  NG6: Bulw . . . . . . . . . . . . . . . . . . . . . . .6A 20
  NG9: Bee . . . . . . . . . . . . . . . . . . . . . . . .1G 65
Nelson St. DE7: Ilk . . . . . . . . . . . . . . . . .3B 28
  DE75: Hea . . . . . . . . . . . . . . . . . . . . . . .3B 14
  NG1: Nott . . . . . . . . . . . . . . . . . .4G 5 (5H 45)
  NG10: Long E . . . . . . . . . . . . . . . . . . . .1F 73
Nene Cl. NG15: Huck . . . . . . . . . . . . . . . .2E 19
Nesfield Ct. DE7: Ilk . . . . . . . . . . . . . . . .6A 28
Nesfield Rd. DE7: Ilk . . . . . . . . . . . . . . . .6A 28
Neston Dr. NG6: Cin . . . . . . . . . . . . . . . .3H 31
Nether Cl. NG3: Nott . . . . . . . . . . . . . . . .3C 46
  NG5: Eastw . . . . . . . . . . . . . . . . . . . . . .1B 16
NETHERFIELD . . . . . . . . . . . . . . . . . . . . .3H 47
Netherfield Rd. NG10: Long E . . . . . . . . .3D 72
  NG10: Sand . . . . . . . . . . . . . . . . . . . . . .6D 52
Netherfields La. DE72: Shar . . . . . . . . . . .6B 72
Netherfield Station (Rail) . . . . . . . . . . . .3H 47
Nethergate NG11: Clif . . . . . . . . . . . . . . .3A 66
NETHER GREEN . . . . . . . . . . . . . . . . . . . .1B 16
Nether Grn. NG16: Eastw . . . . . . . . . . . .2B 16
Nether Pasture NG4: Neth . . . . . . . . . . . .3A 48
Nether Slade Rd. DE7: Ilk . . . . . . . . . . . .5A 28
Nether St. NG9: Bee . . . . . . . . . . . . . . . .5G 55
Nettlecliff Wlk. NG5: Top V . . . . . . . . . . .5C 20
Neville Rd. NG14: Calv . . . . . . . . . . . . . .5H 11
Neville Sadler Ct. NG9: Bee . . . . . . . . . . .4G 55
New Alexandra Court, The NG3: Nott . . . .1H 45
Newall Dr. NG9: Chil . . . . . . . . . . . . . . . .3C 64
Newark Av. NG2: Nott . . . . . . . . . . . . . . .5A 46
Newark Cres. NG2: Nott . . . . . . . . .5H 5 (5A 46)
Newark Hall NG8: Woll . . . . . . . . . . . . . .5B 44
Newark St. NG2: Nott . . . . . . . . . . .5H 5 (5A 46)
New Art Exchange . . . . . . . . . . . . . . . . .2D 44
NEW BASFORD . . . . . . . . . . . . . . . . . . . . .6D 32
New Basford Bus. Area NG7: Basf . . . . . .6D 32
    (off Palm St.)
Newbery Av. NG10: Long E . . . . . . . . . . .1H 73
Newbridge Cl. DE7: West H . . . . . . . . . . .1B 38
New Brook Ho. NG7: Radf . . . . . . . . . . . .3D 44
Newbury Cl. NG3: Mapp . . . . . . . . . . . . .3C 34
Newbury Dr. NG5: Sher . . . . . . . . . . . . . .1F 45
Newbury Dr. NG16: Nuth . . . . . . . . . . . .4D 30
Newcastle Av. NG4: Ged . . . . . . . . . . . . .6G 35
  NG9: Bee . . . . . . . . . . . . . . . . . . . . . . . .5F 55
Newcastle Chambers NG1: Nott . . . .4D 4 (5G 45)
Newcastle Cir. NG7: Nott . . . . . . . .5A 4 (5E 45)
Newcastle Ct. NG7: Nott . . . . . . . . .5A 4 (5E 45)
Newcastle Dr. NG7: Nott . . . . . . . . .3A 4 (5E 45)
Newcastle Farm Dr. NG8: Aspl . . . . . . . . .6A 32
Newcastle St. NG6: Bulw . . . . . . . . . . . . .5A 20
Newcastle Ter. NG7: Nott . . . . . . . .3A 4 (4E 45)
  NG8: Aspl . . . . . . . . . . . . . . . . . . . . . . .6B 32
Newcombe Dr. NG5: Arn . . . . . . . . . . . . .6E 23
New Ct. NG1: Nott . . . . . . . . . . . . . . . . . .4F 5
New Derby Rd. NG16: Eastw . . . . . . . . . .2H 15
Newdigate Rd. NG16: Want . . . . . . . . . . .6A 18
Newdigate St. DE7: Ilk . . . . . . . . . . . . . .3C 40
  DE7: West H . . . . . . . . . . . . . . . . . . . . .1A 38
  NG7: Radf . . . . . . . . . . . . . . . . . .2A 4 (4E 45)
  NG16: Kimb . . . . . . . . . . . . . . . . . . . . . .1H 29
Newdigate Vs. NG7: Radf . . . . . . . .2A 4 (4E 45)
NEW EASTWOOD . . . . . . . . . . . . . . . . . . .4B 16
New Eaton Rd. NG9: Stap . . . . . . . . . . . .5F 53
New Farm La. NG16: Nuth . . . . . . . . . . . .1C 30
Newfield Rd. NG5: Sher . . . . . . . . . . . . . .4D 32
Newgate Cl. NG4: Carl . . . . . . . . . . . . . .2G 47
Newgate Ct. NG7: Lent . . . . . . . . . . . . . .5D 44
Newgate St. NG13: Bing . . . . . . . . . . . . .4E 51
Newhall Gro. NG2: West Br . . . . . . . . . . .2B 58
Newham Cl. DE75: Hea . . . . . . . . . . . . . .4E 15
Newholm Dr. NG11: Wilf . . . . . . . . . . . . .6E 57
Newland Cl. NG8: Aspl . . . . . . . . . . . . . .4A 44
  NG9: Toton . . . . . . . . . . . . . . . . . . . . . .3A 64
NEWLANDS . . . . . . . . . . . . . . . . . . . . . . .3E 15
Newlands Cl. NG12: Edwal . . . . . . . . . . .1E 69
Newlands Dr. DE75: Hea . . . . . . . . . . . . .2C 14
  NG4: Ged . . . . . . . . . . . . . . . . . . . . . . .6H 35
New Lawn Rd. DE7: Ilk . . . . . . . . . . . . . .1A 40
NEW LENTON . . . . . . . . . . . . . . . . . . . . . .6D 44
Newlyn Dr. NG8: Aspl . . . . . . . . . . . . . . .1B 44
Newlyn Gdns. NG8: Aspl . . . . . . . . . . . . .1B 44
Newmanleys Rd. NG16: Eastw . . . . . . . . .5A 16
Newmanleys Rd. Sth.
  NG16: Eastw . . . . . . . . . . . . . . . . . . . . .4A 16
New Manor Ground . . . . . . . . . . . . . . . .4C 28
Newman Rd. NG14: Calv . . . . . . . . . . . . .3G 11
Newmarket Rd. NG6: Bulw . . . . . . . . . . .1H 31
Newmarket Way NG9: Toton . . . . . . . . . .4H 63
NEW NUTHALL . . . . . . . . . . . . . . . . . . . . .1C 30
Newport Dr. NG8: Basf . . . . . . . . . . . . . .6B 32
Newquay Av. NG7: Radf . . . . . . . . . . . . . .2C 44
New Ri. NG11: Clif . . . . . . . . . . . . . . . . . .5A 66
New Rd. NG7: Radf . . . . . . . . . . . . . . . . .3B 44
  NG9: Stap . . . . . . . . . . . . . . . . . . . . . . .2F 53
  NG11: Bart F . . . . . . . . . . . . . . . . . . . . .1E 75

New Rd. NG12: Rad T . . . . . . . . . . . . . . .6F 49
  NG16: Newth, Want . . . . . . . . . .5A 6 & 1F 17
New Row NG4: Carl . . . . . . . . . . . . . . . . .2F 47
  NG14: Woodbo . . . . . . . . . . . . . . . . . . .1C 24
NEW SAWLEY . . . . . . . . . . . . . . . . . . . . . .2D 72
NEW STANTON . . . . . . . . . . . . . . . . . . . . .6A 40
NEW STAPLEFORD . . . . . . . . . . . . . . . . . .2G 53
Newstead Av. NG3: Mapp . . . . . . . . . . . .5D 34
  NG12: Rad T . . . . . . . . . . . . . . . . . . . . .5G 49
Newstead Ct. NG5: Woodt . . . . . . . . . . . .2C 34
Newstead Dr. NG2: West Br . . . . . . . . . . .4D 58
Newstead Gro. NG1: Nott . . . . . . . .1C 4 (3F 45)
  NG13: Bing . . . . . . . . . . . . . . . . . . . . . .5C 50
Newstead Ind. Est. NG5: Arn . . . . . . . . . .6C 22
Newstead Rd. NG10: Long E . . . . . . . . . .2E 63
Newstead Rd. Nth. DE7: Ilk . . . . . . . . . . .4H 27
Newstead Rd. Sth. DE7: Ilk . . . . . . . . . . .4H 27
Newstead St. NG5: Sher . . . . . . . . . . . . . .4G 33
Newstead Ter. NG15: Huck . . . . . . . . . . . .3G 7
Newstead Way NG8: Stre . . . . . . . . . . . . .5D 30
New St. DE7: Stan . . . . . . . . . . . . . . . . . .3A 38
  NG5: Redh . . . . . . . . . . . . . . . . . . . . . . .4A 22
  NG5: Sher . . . . . . . . . . . . . . . . . . . . . . .6F 33
  NG10: Long E . . . . . . . . . . . . . . . . . . . .5G 63
New Ter. NG10: Sand . . . . . . . . . . . . . . . .5D 52
NEWTHORPE . . . . . . . . . . . . . . . . . . . . . . .4E 17
NEWTHORPE COMMON . . . . . . . . . . . . . .5D 16
Newthorpe Comn.
  NG16: Newth . . . . . . . . . . . . . . . . . . . .4C 16
Newthorpe St. NG2: Nott . . . . . . . . . . . .1H 57
NEWTON . . . . . . . . . . . . . . . . . . . . . . . . .1B 50
Newton Av. NG12: Rad T . . . . . . . . . . . . .5G 49
  NG13: Bing . . . . . . . . . . . . . . . . . . . . . .5D 50
    (not continuous)
Newton Cl. NG5: Arn . . . . . . . . . . . . . . . .1D 34
Newtondale Cl. NG8: Aspl . . . . . . . . . . . .6B 32
Newton Dr. NG2: West Br . . . . . . . . . . . .1G 67
  NG9: Stap . . . . . . . . . . . . . . . . . . . . . . .5G 53
Newton Gdns. NG13: Newton . . . . . . . . .3C 50
    (not continuous)
Newton Rd. NG4: Ged . . . . . . . . . . . . . . .4F 35
Newton's La. NG16: Coss . . . . . . . . . . . . .4C 28
    (not continuous)
Newton St. NG7: Lent . . . . . . . . . . . . . . .3C 56
  NG9: Bee . . . . . . . . . . . . . . . . . . . . . . . .5E 55
New Tythe St. NG10: Long E . . . . . . . . . .6H 63
New Vale Rd. NG4: Colw . . . . . . . . . . . . .4F 47
New Windmill Ct. NG2: Nott . . . . . . . . . .5B 46
New Works Cotts.
  NG14: Stoke B . . . . . . . . . . . . . . . . . . . .1C 48
ng2 Bus. Pk. NG2: Nott . . . . . . . . . . . . . .1E 57
NHS WALK-IN CENTRE
  Nottingham, City Link . . . . . . . .6G 5 (6H 45)
  Nottingham, Upper Parliament Street . . . .3D 4
Nicholas Rd. NG9: Bram . . . . . . . . . . . . .2D 54
Nicker Hill NG12: Key . . . . . . . . . . . . . . .3H 79
Nicklaus Ct. NG5: Top V . . . . . . . . . . . . .5E 21
    (off Crossfield Dr.)
Nidderdale NG8: Woll . . . . . . . . . . . . . . .5C 42
Nidderdale Cl. NG8: Woll . . . . . . . . . . . .6C 42
Nightingale Cl. NG7: Nott . . . . . . . . . . . .2G 55
  NG16: Nuth . . . . . . . . . . . . . . . . . . . . . .1D 30
Nightingale Ho. NG3: Mapp . . . . . . . . . .5B 34
Nightingale Way NG13: Bing . . . . . . . . . .6G 51
Nile St. NG1: Nott . . . . . . . . . . . . .3G 5 (4H 45)
Nilsson Rd. NG9: Chil . . . . . . . . . . . . . . .2B 64
Nimbus Way NG16: Want . . . . . . . . . . . .6H 17
Nine Acre Gdns. NG6: Bulw . . . . . . . . . . .6F 19
Nine Corners NG16: Kimb . . . . . . . . . . . .1H 29
Nixon Ri. NG15: Huck . . . . . . . . . . . . . . . .6D 6
Nobel Rd. NG11: Clif . . . . . . . . . . . . . . . .5A 66
Noel St. NG7: Basf, H Grn . . . . . . . . . . . .1D 44
    (not continuous)
  NG16: Kimb . . . . . . . . . . . . . . . . . . . . . .1A 30
Noel Street Stop (NET) . . . . . . . . . . . . . .2D 44
No Man's La. DE72: Ris . . . . . . . . . . . . . .4A 52
  NG10: Sand . . . . . . . . . . . . . . . . . . . . . .4A 52
Nook, The DE75: Los . . . . . . . . . . . . . . . .1A 14
  NG8: Woll . . . . . . . . . . . . . . . . . . . . . . .5E 43
  NG9: Bee . . . . . . . . . . . . . . . . . . . . . . . .4G 55
  NG9: Chil . . . . . . . . . . . . . . . . . . . . . . . .1E 65
  NG14: Calv . . . . . . . . . . . . . . . . . . . . . .4H 11
  NG16: Nuth . . . . . . . . . . . . . . . . . . . . . .2A 30
Nook End Rd. DE75: Hea . . . . . . . . . . . . .4B 14
Norbett Cl. NG9: Chil . . . . . . . . . . . . . . .2C 64
Norbett Ct. NG5: Arn . . . . . . . . . . . . . . .4C 22
Norbett Rd. NG5: Arn . . . . . . . . . . . . . . .5C 22
Norbreck Cl. NG8: Cin . . . . . . . . . . . . . . .4H 31
Norburn Cres. NG6: Basf . . . . . . . . . . . . .4D 32
Norbury Way NG10: Sand . . . . . . . . . . . .5C 52
Nordean Rd. NG5: Woodt . . . . . . . . . . . .2C 34
Norfolk Av. NG9: Toton . . . . . . . . . . . . . .4A 64
Norfolk Cl. NG15: Huck . . . . . . . . . . . . . .6D 6
Norfolk Pk. NG5: Arn . . . . . . . . . . . . . . . .2D 34
Norfolk Pl. NG1: Nott . . . . . . . . . .3D 4 (4G 45)
Norfolk Rd. NG10: Long E . . . . . . . . . . . .4H 63
Norfolk Wlk. NG10: Sand . . . . . . . . . . . .6D 52

| | |
|---|---|
| Norland Cl. NG3: Nott | .2A **46** |
| | (not continuous) |
| Normanby Rd. NG8: Woll | .6C **42** |
| Norman Cl. NG3: Nott | .1E **5** (3G **45**) |
| NG9: Chil | .6C **54** |
| Norman Cres. DE7: Ilk | .4A **28** |
| Norman Dr. NG15: Huck | .1E **19** |
| NG16: Eastw | .3D **16** |
| Norman Rd. NG3: Nott | .1C **46** |
| Norman St. DE7: Ilk | .3A **28** |
| NG4: Neth | .3A **48** |
| NG16: Kimb | .6H **17** |
| Normanton La. NG12: Key | .4H **79** |
| NORMANTON-ON-THE-WOLDS | .1A **80** |
| Norris Homes NG7: H Grn | .1F **45** |
| Northall Av. NG6: Bulw | .1H **31** |
| Northampton St. NG3: Nott | .3A **46** |
| North Av. NG10: Sand | .5D **52** |
| Nth. Church St. NG1: Nott | .2D **4** (4G **45**) |
| Nth. Circus St. NG1: Nott | .3B **4** (5F **45**) |
| Northcliffe Av. NG3: Mapp | .5C **34** |
| Northcote St. NG10: Long E | .6D **63** |
| Northcote Way NG6: Bulw | .2A **32** |
| Northdale Rd. NG3: Nott | .2D **46** |
| Northdown Dr. NG9: Chil | .1C **64** |
| Northdown Rd. NG8: Aspl | .3B **44** |
| North Dr. NG9: Chil | .5E **55** |
| Northern Ct. NG6: Basf | .3B **32** |
| Northern Dr. NG9: Bestw V | .1D **20** |
| NG9: Trow | .6F **41** |
| Northern Rd. DE75: Hea | .3B **14** |
| Northfield Av. DE7: Ilk | .5A **28** |
| NG10: Long E | .3D **72** |
| NG12: Rad T | .5H **49** |
| Northfield Cres. NG9: Chil | .1H **63** |
| Northfield Rd. NG9: Chil | .1A **64** |
| Northfields NG10: Long E | .3D **72** |
| North Gate NG7: Basf | .6D **32** |
| North Ga. Pl. *NG7: Basf* | .6D **32** |
| | (off High Chu. St.) |
| Northgate St. DE7: Ilk | .6A **28** |
| North Grn. NG14: Calv | .2E **11** |
| North Hill Av. NG15: Huck | .4F **7** |
| North Hill Cres. NG15: Huck | .4F **7** |
| Northolme Av. NG6: Bulw | .6A **20** |
| Northolt Dr. NG16: Nuth | .4D **30** |
| North Rd. NG2: West Br | .5A **58** |
| NG5: Sher | .3E **33** |
| | (not continuous) |
| NG7: Nott | .1B **56** |
| | (West Rd.) |
| NG7: Nott | .4A **4** (5E **45**) |
| | (Western Ter.) |
| NG10: Long E | .1E **73** |
| NG11: Rudd | .5F **67** |
| Nth. Sherwood St. NG1: Nott | .1D **4** (2F **45**) |
| Northside Wlk. NG5: Arn | .3B **22** |
| North St. DE7: Ilk | .6B **28** |
| NG2: Nott | .4H **5** |
| NG9: Bee | .5E **55** |
| NG16: Kimb | .2A **30** |
| NG16: Lang M | .2F **15** |
| NG16: Newth | .3E **17** |
| Northumberland Cl. NG3: Nott | .1F **5** (3H **45**) |
| Northville Ct. NG3: Nott | .2H **45** |
| Northwold Av. NG2: West Br | .5H **57** |
| Northwood Cres. NG5: Bestw | .1G **33** |
| Northwood Rd. NG5: Bestw | .1G **33** |
| Northwood St. NG9: Stap | .3F **53** |
| Norton Cl. NG7: Radf | .3C **44** |
| Norton St. NG7: Radf | .3C **44** |
| Norwich Gdns. NG6: Bulw | .4H **19** |
| Norwood Cl. DE7: Ilk | .2B **28** |
| Norwood Rd. NG7: Radf | .4C **44** |
| Noskwith St. DE7: Ilk | .4C **40** |
| Notintone Pl. NG2: Nott | .5A **46** |
| Notintone St. NG2: Nott | .5A **46** |
| NOTTINGHAM | .4E **5** (5G **45**) |
| NOTTINGHAM AIRPORT | .6H **59** |
| Nottingham Arts Theatre | .4F **5** (5H **45**) |
| Nottingham Bus. Pk. NG2: Nott | .6H **5** (6A **46**) |
| NG8: Stre | .5C **30** |
| Nottingham Castle | .6C **4** (5F **45**) |
| Nottingham Castle Caves | .6C **4** |
| Nottingham City Golf Course | .3G **19** |
| Nottingham Climbing Cen. | .1D **44** |
| Nottingham Contemporary | .5E **5** (5H **45**) |
| Nottingham Forest FC | .2A **58** |
| Nottingham Forest Football Academy | .4H **57** |
| Nottingham Greyhound Stadium | .5D **46** |
| Nottingham Indoor Bowls Cen. | .2G **43** |
| Nottingham Industrial Mus. | .6F **43** |
| Nottingham Intl. Clothing Cen. | |
| NG15: Huck | .1E **7** |
| NOTTINGHAM NHS TREATMENT CENTRE | .1C **56** |
| Nottingham Playhouse | .4C **4** (5F **45**) |
| Nottingham Racecourse | .6E **47** |

| | |
|---|---|
| Nottingham Rd. DE7: Ilk | .2B **40** |
| DE72: Dray, Ris | .1A **62** |
| NG5: Arn | .1A **34** |
| NG6: Basf | .4C **32** |
| | (not continuous) |
| NG7: Basf | .5D **32** |
| NG8: Cin | .3E **31** |
| NG9: Chil, Toton | .5G **63** |
| NG9: Stap | .4F **53** |
| NG9: Trow | .5E **41** |
| NG10: Long E | .5G **63** |
| NG11: Goth | .6H **75** |
| NG12: Key | .5G **79** |
| NG12: Rad T | .1D **60** |
| NG13: Bing | .5B **50** |
| NG14: Bur J | .4D **36** |
| NG14: Woodbo | .3F **23** |
| NG15: Huck | .6A **8** |
| NG16: Cin, Nuth | .2D **30** |
| NG16: Eastw | .3B **16** |
| NG16: Gilt, Newth | .4D **16** |
| NG16: Kimb | .1A **30** |
| NG25: Oxt | .1B **12** |
| Nottingham Rd. E. NG16: Eastw, Gilt, Newth | .4D **16** |
| Nottingham Sailing Club | .1E **59** |
| Nottingham Science & Technology Pk. | |
| NG7: Nott | .2B **56** |
| Nottinghamshire County Cricket Ground | .2A **58** |
| NOTTINGHAMSHIRE HOSPICE | .1H **45** |
| Nottingham Sth. & Wilford Ind. Est. | |
| NG11: Wilf | .1F **67** |
| Nottingham Station (Rail) | .6F **5** (6H **45**) |
| Nottingham Tennis Cen. | .3B **56** |
| Nottingham Transport Heritage Cen. | .2G **77** |
| Nottingham Trent University | |
| City Campus | .2C **4** (4F **45**) |
| Clifton Campus | .2B **66** |
| Union Rd. | .2E **5** (4G **45**) |
| Waverley St. | .1B **4** (3F **45**) |
| York St. | .2E **5** (4G **45**) |
| Nottingham Trent University Stop (NET) | |
| | .2C **4** (4F **45**) |
| Nottingham Wildcats Arena | .4D **46** |
| NOTTINGHAM WOODTHORPE HOSPITAL | .2H **33** |
| Notts County FC | .1A **58** |
| Nuart Rd. NG9: Bee | .5F **55** |
| Nuffield Health Club | |
| Nottingham | .3D **34** |
| Nugent Gdns. NG3: Nott | .1H **5** (3A **46**) |
| Nurseries, The NG16: Eastw | .3C **16** |
| Nursery Av. DE7: West H | .2C **38** |
| NG9: Chil | .6C **54** |
| NG10: Sand | .6B **52** |
| Nursery Cl. NG12: Rad T | .6H **49** |
| NG15: Huck | .1G **19** |
| Nursery Dr. NG4: Carl | .1F **47** |
| Nursery Hollow DE7: Ilk | .3A **40** |
| Nursery La. NG6: Basf | .3C **32** |
| Nursery Rd. NG5: Arn | .6B **22** |
| NG12: Rad T | .6H **49** |
| NG13: Bing | .5H **51** |
| Nutbrook Cres. DE7: Kirk H | .5H **39** |
| NUTHALL | .2D **30** |
| Nuthall Circ. DE7: Kirk H | .5G **39** |
| Nuthall Gdns. NG8: Aspl | .1B **44** |
| Nuthall Rd. NG8: Aspl, Cin | .4H **31** |

**O**

| | |
|---|---|
| Oak Acres NG9: Chil | .6A **54** |
| Oak Apple Cres. DE7: Ilk | .3A **40** |
| Oakash Ct. NG16: Nuth | .1B **30** |
| Oak Av. NG10: Sand | .4C **52** |
| NG12: Rad T | .5E **49** |
| NG13: Bing | .5G **51** |
| NG16: Lang M | .1F **15** |
| Oakdale Dr. NG9: Chil | .1C **64** |
| Oakdale Rd. NG3: Nott | .3D **46** |
| NG4: Carl | .3F **47** |
| NG5: Arn | .5D **22** |
| NG16: Nuth | .1B **30** |
| Oak Dr. NG16: Eastw | .3A **16** |
| Oakenhall Av. NG15: Huck | .4A **8** |
| Oakfield NG12: Rad T | .5G **49** |
| Oakfield Cl. NG8: Woll | .6C **42** |
| NG12: Rad T | .6H **49** |
| Oakfield Dr. NG10: Sand | .2D **62** |
| Oakfield Rd. NG8: Woll | .6C **42** |
| NG9: Stap | .4F **53** |
| NG15: Huck | .5H **7** |
| Oakfields Rd. NG2: West Br | .2C **58** |
| Oak Flatt NG9: Chil | .5A **54** |
| Oakford Cl. NG8: Brox | .5G **31** |
| Oak Gro. NG15: Huck | .1H **19** |
| Oakham Cl. NG5: Top V | .6D **20** |
| Oakham Rd. NG11: Rudd | .3H **67** |

| | |
|---|---|
| Oakham Way DE7: Ilk | .4H **27** |
| Oakington Cl. NG5: Bestw | .2F **33** |
| Oakland Av. NG10: Long E | .2E **73** |
| Oakland Ct. NG9: Bram | .2A **54** |
| Oakland Gro. NG14: Calv | .4H **11** |
| Oaklands Av. DE75: Hea | .3E **15** |
| Oakland St. NG7: H Grn | .2C **44** |
| Oakland Ter. NG10: Long E | .2E **73** |
| Oakland Way NG8: Woll | .1D **42** |
| Oakleigh Av. NG3: Mapp | .5E **35** |
| Oakleigh St. NG6: Bulw | .3B **32** |
| Oakley M. NG6: Bulw | .1F **31** |
| Oakley's Rd. NG10: Long E | .6G **63** |
| Oakley's Rd. W. NG10: Long E | .1F **73** |
| Oak Lodge NG13: Bing | .5G **51** |
| Oak Lodge Dr. NG16: Kimb | .6H **17** |
| Oakmead Av. NG8: Bilb | .1F **43** |
| Oakmere Cl. NG12: Edwal | .1E **69** |
| Oaks, The NG3: Nott | .2H **5** (4H **45**) |
| Oak St. NG5: Sher | .6F **33** |
| Oak Tree Av. NG12: Rad T | .5F **49** |
| Oak Tree Cl. NG2: West Br | .3C **58** |
| NG15: Huck | .1D **18** |
| Oak Tree Dr. NG4: Ged | .5A **36** |
| Oak Vw. NG7: Radf | .3D **44** |
| Oakwell Cres. DE7: Ilk | .1A **40** |
| Oakwell Dr. DE7: Ilk | .1A **40** |
| Oakwood Dr. NG8: Aspl | .2A **44** |
| Oakwood Gdns. NG16: Nuth | .4D **30** |
| Oban Rd. NG9: Chil | .5C **54** |
| Occupation Rd. NG6: Bulw | .2H **31** |
| NG15: Huck | .6G **7** |
| Oceans of Fun | .4G **7** |
| Ockbrook Ct. DE7: Ilk | .4B **28** |
| Ockbrook Dr. NG3: Mapp | .5B **34** |
| Ockerby St. NG6: Bulw | .1A **32** |
| Odesa Dr. NG6: Bulw | .3H **31** |
| Odin Ct. NG4: Carl | .1H **47** |
| Ogdon Ct. NG3: Nott | .3B **46** |
| Ogle Dr. NG7: Nott | .6B **4** (6F **45**) |
| Ogle St. NG15: Huck | .4G **7** |
| Okehampton Cres. NG3: Mapp | .1E **35** |
| Oldacres NG14: Woodbo | .1D **24** |
| Old Bank Ct. NG6: Basf | .5B **32** |
| OLD BASFORD | .3C **32** |
| Old Brickyard NG3: Nott | .2C **46** |
| Oldbury Cl. NG11: Clif | .6B **66** |
| Old Church St. NG7: Lent | .1C **56** |
| Old Coach Rd. NG8: Bilb, Woll | .3E **43** |
| | (not continuous) |
| Old Coppice Side DE75: Hea | .5C **14** |
| | (Roper Av.) |
| DE75: Hea | .5D **14** |
| | (Sunningdale Av.) |
| Old Derby Rd. NG16: Eastw | .2H **15** |
| Old Dr. NG9: Bee | .3D **54** |
| Old Epperstone Rd. NG14: Lowd | .1G **25** |
| Old Farm Ct. NG11: Bart F | .1E **75** |
| Old Farm Rd. NG5: Top V | .5D **20** |
| Old Hall Cl. NG14: Calv | .4G **11** |
| Old Hall Dr. NG3: Mapp P | .6H **33** |
| Oldham Ct. NG9: Chil | .1C **64** |
| Old Kiln La. NG16: Eastw | .4C **16** |
| Oldknow St. NG7: H Grn | .3D **44** |
| OLD LENTON | .6C **44** |
| Old Lenton St. NG1: Nott | .3F **5** (4H **45**) |
| Old Lodge Dr. NG5: Sher | .3H **33** |
| Old Main Rd. NG14: Bulc | .2G **37** |
| Old Manor Cl. NG14: Woodbo | .1D **24** |
| Old Market Square Stop (NET) | .4D **4** (5G **45**) |
| Old Melton Rd. NG12: Plum | .6G **69** |
| Old Mill Cl. NG6: Bestw V | .2B **20** |
| NG7: Radf | .4D **44** |
| NG9: Toton | .3A **64** |
| Old Mill Ct. NG13: Bing | .4E **51** |
| Old Mission Forge Wlk. | |
| NG16: Newth | .3E **17** |
| Oldmoor Wood Nature Reserve | .1H **41** |
| Old Oak Rd. NG11: Clif | .3E **67** |
| Old Park, The NG12: Cotg | .1F **71** |
| Old Park Cl. NG8: Bilb | .2E **43** |
| Old Pond, The DE75: Hea | .5E **15** |
| OLD RADFORD | .3B **44** |
| Old Rd. NG11: Rudd | .4H **67** |
| Old School Cl. NG11: Clif | .5C **66** |
| Old School La. NG16: Aws | .2E **29** |
| Old Station Dr. NG11: Rudd | .6F **67** |
| Old St. NG1: Nott | .2E **5** (4G **45**) |
| Old Tollerton Rd. NG2: Gam | .4E **59** |
| Olga Ct. NG3: Nott | .3B **46** |
| Olga Rd. NG3: Nott | .3B **46** |
| Olive Av. NG10: Long E | .4F **63** |
| Olive Gro. NG14: Bur J | .2F **37** |
| Oliver Cl. DE75: Hea | .3F **15** |
| NG7: Radf | .1A **4** (3E **45**) |
| Oliver Rd. DE7: Kirk H | .4G **39** |
| Oliver St. NG7: Radf | .1A **4** (3E **45**) |

Ollerton Rd. NG5: Arn . . . . . . . . . . . . . . . . . .1A 22
(not continuous)
NG14: Calv . . . . . . . . . . . . . . . . . . . . . . . . .1A 22
Olton Av. NG9: Lent A . . . . . . . . . . . . . . . . . .2F 55
Olympus Ct. NG15: Huck . . . . . . . . . . . . . . . .2D 18
Omer Ct. NG16: Want . . . . . . . . . . . . . . . . . .6A 18
Onchan Av. NG4: Carl . . . . . . . . . . . . . . . . . .3G 47
Onchan Dr. NG4: Carl . . . . . . . . . . . . . . . . . .3G 47
Open University, The
Nottingham . . . . . . . . . . . . . . . . . . . . . . . .1F 45
Orange Gdns. NG2: Nott . . . . . . . . . . . . . . . .1H 57
Orby Cl. NG3: Nott . . . . . . . . . . . . . . . . . . . .3B 46
Orby Wlk. NG3: Nott . . . . . . . . . . . . . . . . . . .4B 46
Orchard, The DE7: Stant D . . . . . . . . . . . . . .3B 52
Orchard Av. NG4: Carl . . . . . . . . . . . . . . . . . .2G 47
NG13: Bing . . . . . . . . . . . . . . . . . . . . . . . .5D 50
Orchard Bus. Pk. DE7: Ilk . . . . . . . . . . . . . . .6H 27
Orchard Cl. DE7: West H . . . . . . . . . . . . . . . .2C 38
DE72: Brea . . . . . . . . . . . . . . . . . . . . . . . .5B 62
NG11: Clif . . . . . . . . . . . . . . . . . . . . . . . . .3A 66
NG12: Rad T . . . . . . . . . . . . . . . . . . . . . . .6E 49
NG12: Toll . . . . . . . . . . . . . . . . . . . . . . . . .5F 69
NG14: Bur J . . . . . . . . . . . . . . . . . . . . . . . .2F 37
Orchard Ct. NG4: Carl . . . . . . . . . . . . . . . . . .2G 47
NG4: Ged . . . . . . . . . . . . . . . . . . . . . . . . .5F 35
NG8: Basf . . . . . . . . . . . . . . . . . . . . . . . . .1C 44
NG15: Huck . . . . . . . . . . . . . . . . . . . . . . . .5G 7
NG16: Lang M . . . . . . . . . . . . . . . . . . . . . .2F 15
Orchard Cres. NG9: Chil . . . . . . . . . . . . . . . .6C 54
Orchard Dr. NG14: Calv . . . . . . . . . . . . . . . .4A 12
Orchard Gro. NG5: Arn . . . . . . . . . . . . . . . . .1G 33
Orchard Pk. NG3: Mapp . . . . . . . . . . . . . . . .1E 35
Orchard Pk. Ind. Est. NG10: Sand . . . . . . . . .5E 53
Orchard Pl. NG8: Stre . . . . . . . . . . . . . . . . . .5C 30
Orchard Ri. DE75: Hea . . . . . . . . . . . . . . . . .3D 14
NG4: Lamb . . . . . . . . . . . . . . . . . . . . . . . .6C 24
Orchards, The NG4: Ged . . . . . . . . . . . . . . . .6A 36
Orchard St. DE7: Ilk . . . . . . . . . . . . . . . . . . .2B 40
NG10: Long E . . . . . . . . . . . . . . . . . . . . . .6G 63
NG11: Goth . . . . . . . . . . . . . . . . . . . . . . . .6H 75
NG15: Huck . . . . . . . . . . . . . . . . . . . . . . . .5G 7
NG16: Kimb . . . . . . . . . . . . . . . . . . . . . . . .1H 29
NG16: Lang M . . . . . . . . . . . . . . . . . . . . . .2F 15
NG16: Newth . . . . . . . . . . . . . . . . . . . . . . .4C 16
Orchard Way NG10: Sand . . . . . . . . . . . . . . .2C 62
Orchid Cl. NG2: West Br . . . . . . . . . . . . . . . .1G 67
Orchid Cft. NG15: Huck . . . . . . . . . . . . . . . .1A 20
Orchil St. NG16: Gilt . . . . . . . . . . . . . . . . . . .5D 16
Ordnance Ct. NG9: Chil . . . . . . . . . . . . . . . .2C 64
Orford Av. NG11: Clif . . . . . . . . . . . . . . . . . .1D 66
NG12: Rad T . . . . . . . . . . . . . . . . . . . . . . .1E 61
Orient M. NG16: Want . . . . . . . . . . . . . . . . .6A 18
Orion Cl. NG8: Bilb . . . . . . . . . . . . . . . . . . . .2E 43
Orion Dr. NG8: Bilb . . . . . . . . . . . . . . . . . . .2E 43
Orlando Dr. NG4: Carl . . . . . . . . . . . . . . . . . .1H 47
Orlock Wlk. NG5: Bestw . . . . . . . . . . . . . . . .2F 33
Ormonde St. NG16: Lang M . . . . . . . . . . . . .1F 15
Ormonde Ter. NG5: Sher . . . . . . . . . . . . . . . .5G 33
NG16: Lang M . . . . . . . . . . . . . . . . . . . . . .1F 15
Ornsay Cl. NG5: Top V . . . . . . . . . . . . . . . . .4C 20
Orpean Way NG9: Toton . . . . . . . . . . . . . . . .3G 63
Orston Av. NG5: Arn . . . . . . . . . . . . . . . . . . .6C 22
Orston Dr. NG8: Woll . . . . . . . . . . . . . . . . . .5A 44
Orston Grn. NG8: Woll . . . . . . . . . . . . . . . . .6B 44
Orston Rd. E. NG2: West Br . . . . . . . . . . . . .2B 58
Orston Rd. W. NG2: West Br . . . . . . . . . . . . .2A 58
Orton Av. NG9: Bram . . . . . . . . . . . . . . . . . .5C 54
Orton Flds. NG9: Bram . . . . . . . . . . . . . . . . .5B 54
Ortzen Ct. NG7: Radf . . . . . . . . . . . . . . . . . .3D 44
Ortzen St. NG7: Radf . . . . . . . . . . . . . . . . . .3D 44
Orville Rd. NG5: Bestw . . . . . . . . . . . . . . . . .2C 32
Osborne Av. NG5: Sher . . . . . . . . . . . . . . . . .4G 33
Osborne Cl. NG10: Sand . . . . . . . . . . . . . . . .1D 62
Osborne Gro. NG5: Sher . . . . . . . . . . . . . . . .4A 34
Osborne St. NG7: Radf . . . . . . . . . . . . . . . . .3C 44
Osbourne Cl. NG16: Want . . . . . . . . . . . . . . .6B 18
Osgood Rd. NG5: Arn . . . . . . . . . . . . . . . . . .2E 35
Osier Rd. NG2: Nott . . . . . . . . . . . . . . . . . . .2G 57
Osman Cl. NG2: Nott . . . . . . . . . . . . . . . . . .2F 57
Osmaston Cl. NG10: Long E . . . . . . . . . . . . .2B 72
Osmaston St. NG7: Lent . . . . . . . . . . . . . . . .6D 44
NG10: Sand . . . . . . . . . . . . . . . . . . . . . . .6E 53
Osprey Cl. NG11: Clif . . . . . . . . . . . . . . . . . .4A 66
NG13: Bing . . . . . . . . . . . . . . . . . . . . . . . .6F 51
Osprey Gro. NG15: Huck . . . . . . . . . . . . . . . .2B 8
Ossington Cl. NG1: Nott . . . . . . . . . .1D 4 (3G 45)
Ossington St. NG7: Radf . . . . . . . . . . . . . . . .3D 44
Osterley Gro. NG16: Nuth . . . . . . . . . . . . . . .4D 30
Oulton Cl. NG5: Arn . . . . . . . . . . . . . . . . . . .1B 34
Oulton Lodge NG5: Top V . . . . . . . . . . . . . . .4B 20
Oundle Dr. DE7: Ilk . . . . . . . . . . . . . . . . . . . .2D 40
NG8: Woll . . . . . . . . . . . . . . . . . . . . . . . . .6A 44
Ousebridge Cres. NG4: Carl . . . . . . . . . . . . .1A 48
Ousebridge Dr. NG4: Carl . . . . . . . . . . . . . . .1A 48
Out Track, The DE7: Mapp . . . . . . . . . . . . . .5C 26
(off Church La.)
Oval Gdns. NG8: Aspl . . . . . . . . . . . . . . . . . .1B 44

Overdale Cl. NG10: Long E . . . . . . . . . . . . . .1B 72
Overdale Rd. NG6: Basf . . . . . . . . . . . . . . . .5A 32
Overstrand Cl. NG5: Arn . . . . . . . . . . . . . . . .1B 34
Owen Av. NG10: Long E . . . . . . . . . . . . . . . .1A 74
Owers Av. DE75: Hea . . . . . . . . . . . . . . . . . .6D 14
Owlston Cl. NG16: Eastw . . . . . . . . . . . . . . . .2B 16
Owsthorpe Cl. NG5: Top V . . . . . . . . . . . . . .5E 21
Owthorpe Gro. NG5: Sher . . . . . . . . . . . . . . .5F 33
Owthorpe Rd. NG12: Cotg . . . . . . . . . . . . . .3F 71
Oxborough Rd. NG5: Arn . . . . . . . . . . . . . . . .6G 21
Oxbow Cl. NG2: Nott . . . . . . . . . . . . . . . . . .2G 57
Oxbury Rd. NG16: Want . . . . . . . . . . . . . . . .5H 17
Oxclose La. NG5: Arn . . . . . . . . . . . . . . . . . .1F 33
Oxendale Cl. NG2: West Br . . . . . . . . . . . . . .5E 59
Oxengate NG5: Arn . . . . . . . . . . . . . . . . . . . .1G 33
Oxford Rd. NG2: West Br . . . . . . . . . . . . . . . .4C 58
Oxford St. DE7: Ilk . . . . . . . . . . . . . . . . . . . .2B 40
NG1: Nott . . . . . . . . . . . . . . . . . .4B 4 (5F 45)
NG4: Carl . . . . . . . . . . . . . . . . . . . . . . . . .6G 35
NG10: Long E . . . . . . . . . . . . . . . . . . . . . .5F 63
NG16: Eastw . . . . . . . . . . . . . . . . . . . . . . .3B 16
Oxton Av. NG5: Sher . . . . . . . . . . . . . . . . . .3G 33
Oxton By-Pass NG25: Oxt . . . . . . . . . . . . . . .1B 12
Oxton Rd. NG5: Arn . . . . . . . . . . . . . . . . . . .4B 10
NG14: Calv . . . . . . . . . . . . . . . . . . . . . . . .2F 11
NG14: Epp . . . . . . . . . . . . . . . . . . . . . . . . .1B 12
NG25: Oxt . . . . . . . . . . . . . . . . . . . . . . . . .1B 12
Ozier Holt NG4: Colw . . . . . . . . . . . . . . . . . .5G 47
NG10: Long E . . . . . . . . . . . . . . . . . . . . . .1E 73

# P

Packham Ct. NG6: Basf . . . . . . . . . . . . . . . . .3C 32
Packman Dr. NG11: Rudd . . . . . . . . . . . . . . .5H 67
Paddington M. NG3: Nott . . . . . . . . . . . . . . .2C 46
Paddock, The NG9: Atten . . . . . . . . . . . . . . .3D 64
NG13: Bing . . . . . . . . . . . . . . . . . . . . . . . .5E 51
Paddock Cl. NG6: Bulw . . . . . . . . . . . . . . . . .2H 31
NG12: Rad T . . . . . . . . . . . . . . . . . . . . . . .1E 61
NG14: Calv . . . . . . . . . . . . . . . . . . . . . . . .4H 11
Paddock Farm Cotts. NG14: Epp . . . . . . . . . .6G 13
Paddocks, The NG10: Sand . . . . . . . . . . . . . .6C 52
NG12: Edwal . . . . . . . . . . . . . . . . . . . . . . .2D 68
NG16: Nuth . . . . . . . . . . . . . . . . . . . . . . . .2B 30
Paddocks Vw. NG10: Long E . . . . . . . . . . . . .1H 73
Padge Rd. NG9: Bee . . . . . . . . . . . . . . . . . . .5H 55
Padgham Ct. NG5: Top V . . . . . . . . . . . . . . . .5E 21
Padley Cl. NG6: Bulw . . . . . . . . . . . . . . . . . .1G 31
Padleys La. NG14: Bur J . . . . . . . . . . . . . . . .2E 37
Padstow Rd. NG5: Bestw . . . . . . . . . . . . . . . .1D 32
Page Av. NG5: Bestw . . . . . . . . . . . . . . . . . .2E 33
Paget Cres. NG11: Rudd . . . . . . . . . . . . . . . .5G 67
Pagett Cl. NG15: Huck . . . . . . . . . . . . . . . . .5A 8
Paige Gdns. NG10: Sand . . . . . . . . . . . . . . . .6C 52
Paignton Cl. NG8: Aspl . . . . . . . . . . . . . . . . .5H 31
Paisley Gro. NG9: Chil . . . . . . . . . . . . . . . . .4C 64
Palatine St. NG7: Nott . . . . . . . . . . . .6B 4 (6F 45)
Palin Ct. NG7: H Grn . . . . . . . . . . . . . . . . . . .2D 44
Palin Gdns. NG12: Rad T . . . . . . . . . . . . . . . .6G 49
Palin St. NG7: H Grn . . . . . . . . . . . . . . . . . . .3D 44
Palm Cotts. NG5: Sher . . . . . . . . . . . . . . . . .4H 33
Palm Ct. NG7: Basf . . . . . . . . . . . . . . . . . . . .6D 32
Palmer Av. NG15: Huck . . . . . . . . . . . . . . . . .3G 7
Palmer Bus. Ct. NG10: Long E . . . . . . . . . . .1H 73
Palmer Cres. NG4: Carl . . . . . . . . . . . . . . . . .2F 47
Palmer Dr. NG9: Stap . . . . . . . . . . . . . . . . . .6F 53
Palmerston Gdns. NG3: Nott . . . . . . . .1E 5 (3G 45)
(not continuous)
Palmerston Rd. DE7: Ilk . . . . . . . . . . . . . . . . .1B 40
Palm St. NG7: Basf . . . . . . . . . . . . . . . . . . . .6D 32
Palmwood Ct. NG6: Bulw . . . . . . . . . . . . . . .2A 32
PAPPLEWICK . . . . . . . . . . . . . . . . . . . . . . . .1B 8
Papplewick Grange NG15: Pap . . . . . . . . . . . .2B 8
Papplewick La. NG15: Huck . . . . . . . . . . . . . .4H 7
Parchment M. NG5: Sher . . . . . . . . . . . . . . . .6F 33
PARK, THE . . . . . . . . . . . . . . . . . . . .4B 4 (5F 45)
Park, The NG12: Cotg . . . . . . . . . . . . . . . . . .1F 71
Park & Ride
Hucknall . . . . . . . . . . . . . . . . . . . . . . . . . .4A 8
Moor Bridge . . . . . . . . . . . . . . . . . . . . . . .3B 20
Phoenix Park . . . . . . . . . . . . . . . . . . . . . . .3G 31
Queen's Drive . . . . . . . . . . . . . . . . . . . . . .4E 57
Racecourse . . . . . . . . . . . . . . . . . . . . . . . .6D 46
The Forest . . . . . . . . . . . . . . . . . . . . . . . . .2E 45
Wilkinson Street . . . . . . . . . . . . . . . . . . . .1C 44
Park Av. DE7: Ilk . . . . . . . . . . . . . . . . . . . . .1B 40
DE7: Stan . . . . . . . . . . . . . . . . . . . . . . . . .3A 38
NG2: West Br . . . . . . . . . . . . . . . . . . . . . . .3B 58
NG3: Mapp P . . . . . . . . . . . . . . . . . . . . . . .1G 45
NG4: Carl . . . . . . . . . . . . . . . . . . . . . . . . .1H 47
NG5: Woodt . . . . . . . . . . . . . . . . . . . . . . . .2A 34
NG12: Key . . . . . . . . . . . . . . . . . . . . . . . . .4F 79
(Croft Rd.)
NG12: Key . . . . . . . . . . . . . . . . . . . . . . . . .3H 79
(Park Rd.)
NG14: Bur J . . . . . . . . . . . . . . . . . . . . . . . .3F 37

Park Av. NG14: Woodbo . . . . . . . . . . . . . . . .1B 24
NG15: Huck . . . . . . . . . . . . . . . . . . . . . . . .4F 7
NG16: Aws . . . . . . . . . . . . . . . . . . . . . . . . .2D 28
NG16: Eastw . . . . . . . . . . . . . . . . . . . . . . .2A 16
NG16: Kimb . . . . . . . . . . . . . . . . . . . . . . . .3A 30
Park Av. E. NG12: Key . . . . . . . . . . . . . . . . . .4F 79
Park Av. W. NG12: Key . . . . . . . . . . . . . . . . .4F 79
PARK BMI HOSPITAL . . . . . . . . . . . . . . . . . .1H 9
Park Chase NG6: Bulw . . . . . . . . . . . . . . . . .2H 31
Park Cl. DE7: Stant D . . . . . . . . . . . . . . . . . .3B 52
NG3: Mapp . . . . . . . . . . . . . . . . . . . . . . . .5A 34
Park Ct. DE75: Hea . . . . . . . . . . . . . . . . . . . .4D 14
NG7: Lent . . . . . . . . . . . . . . . . . . . . . . . . .2C 56
Park Cres. DE7: Ilk . . . . . . . . . . . . . . . . . . . .1C 40
NG8: Woll . . . . . . . . . . . . . . . . . . . . . . . . .5C 42
NG16: Eastw . . . . . . . . . . . . . . . . . . . . . . .1B 16
Parkcroft Rd. NG2: West Br . . . . . . . . . . . . . .5B 58
Parkdale Rd. NG3: Nott . . . . . . . . . . . . . . . . .3D 46
NG4: Carl . . . . . . . . . . . . . . . . . . . . . . . . .3D 46
Park Dr. DE7: Ilk . . . . . . . . . . . . . . . . . . . . .2B 40
NG7: Nott . . . . . . . . . . . . . . . . . . . .5A 4 (5E 45)
NG10: Sand . . . . . . . . . . . . . . . . . . . . . . .2C 62
NG15: Huck . . . . . . . . . . . . . . . . . . . . . . . .6G 7
Parker Cl. NG5: Arn . . . . . . . . . . . . . . . . . . .5E 23
Parker Gdns. NG9: Stap . . . . . . . . . . . . . . . .3H 53
Parker St. NG15: Huck . . . . . . . . . . . . . . . . .4H 7
Parkes Bldg. NG9: Bee . . . . . . . . . . . . . . . . .4F 55
Parkgate NG15: Huck . . . . . . . . . . . . . . . . . .2H 7
Park Hall DE7: Mapp . . . . . . . . . . . . . . . . . .4B 26
Park Hall La.
DE7: Mapp, West H . . . . . . . . . . . . . . . . .5B 26
Parkham Rd. NG16: Kimb . . . . . . . . . . . . . . .6H 17
Park Hgts. NG7: Nott . . . . . . . . . . . . .6A 4 (6E 45)
Park Hill NG7: Nott . . . . . . . . . . . . . .3A 4 (4E 45)
NG16: Aws . . . . . . . . . . . . . . . . . . . . . . . . .2D 28
Park Ho. Gates NG3: Mapp P . . . . . . . . . . . .6H 33
Parkland Cl. NG11: Clif . . . . . . . . . . . . . . . . .2A 66
Parkland M. NG10: Long E . . . . . . . . . . . . . .5F 63
(off Derby Rd.)
Parklands Cl. NG5: Top V . . . . . . . . . . . . . . . .4F 21
Park La. NG4: Lamb . . . . . . . . . . . . . . . . . . .6C 24
NG6: Basf, Bulw . . . . . . . . . . . . . . . . . . . . .3C 32
NG14: Epp . . . . . . . . . . . . . . . . . . . . . . . . .6G 13
Park La. Bus. Cen. NG6: Bulw . . . . . . . . . . . .2C 32
Park Lodge Rd. NG16: Newth . . . . . . . . . . . .6C 16
Park M. NG3: Mapp P . . . . . . . . . . . . . . . . . .1G 45
Park Ravine NG7: Nott . . . . . . . . . . . .6A 4 (6E 45)
Park Rd. DE7: Ilk . . . . . . . . . . . . . . . . . . . . .2B 40
NG4: Carl . . . . . . . . . . . . . . . . . . . . . . . . .2H 47
NG5: Woodt . . . . . . . . . . . . . . . . . . . . . . . .2A 34
NG6: Bestw V . . . . . . . . . . . . . . . . . . . . . .1C 20
NG7: Lent . . . . . . . . . . . . . . . . . . . . . . . . .6D 44
NG9: Bram . . . . . . . . . . . . . . . . . . . . . . . .3H 53
NG9: Chil . . . . . . . . . . . . . . . . . . . . . . . . . .5E 55
NG12: Key . . . . . . . . . . . . . . . . . . . . . . . . .3H 79
NG12: Rad T . . . . . . . . . . . . . . . . . . . . . . .5F 49
NG14: Calv . . . . . . . . . . . . . . . . . . . . . . . .3F 11
NG15: Huck . . . . . . . . . . . . . . . . . . . . . . . .4F 7
Park Rd. E. NG14: Woodbo . . . . . . . . . . . . . .3H 11
Park Rd. Nth. NG9: Chil . . . . . . . . . . . . . . . . .5E 55
Park Rock NG7: Lent . . . . . . . . . . . . . .6A 4 (6E 45)
Park Row NG1: Nott . . . . . . . . . . . . . .5C 4 (5F 45)
Parkside NG8: Woll . . . . . . . . . . . . . . . . . . . .6E 43
NG12: Key . . . . . . . . . . . . . . . . . . . . . . . . .3H 79
Parkside Av. NG10: Long E . . . . . . . . . . . . . .5D 62
Parkside Dr. NG10: Long E . . . . . . . . . . . . . .5D 62
Parkside Gdns. NG8: Woll . . . . . . . . . . . . . . .6E 43
Parkside Ri. NG8: Woll . . . . . . . . . . . . . . . . . .1E 55
Parkstone Cl. NG2: West Br . . . . . . . . . . . . . .6G 57
Park St. DE72: Brea . . . . . . . . . . . . . . . . . . . .5B 62
DE75: Hea . . . . . . . . . . . . . . . . . . . . . . . . .3B 14
NG7: Lent . . . . . . . . . . . . . . . . . . . . . . . . .5D 44
NG9: Bee . . . . . . . . . . . . . . . . . . . . . . . . . .5E 55
NG9: Stap . . . . . . . . . . . . . . . . . . . . . . . . .5E 53
NG10: Long E . . . . . . . . . . . . . . . . . . . . . .4E 63
Park Ter. NG1: Nott . . . . . . . . . . . . . .4B 4 (5F 45)
NG12: Key . . . . . . . . . . . . . . . . . . . . . . . . .2H 79
Park Valley NG7: Nott . . . . . . . . . . . .5B 4 (5F 45)
Park Vw. DE75: Hea . . . . . . . . . . . . . . . . . . .4B 14
NG3: Mapp . . . . . . . . . . . . . . . . . . . . . . . .5A 34
NG15: Huck . . . . . . . . . . . . . . . . . . . . . . . .5H 7
NG16: Eastw . . . . . . . . . . . . . . . . . . . . . . .4B 16
Park Vw. Ct. NG1: Nott . . . . . . . . . . . .3G 5 (4H 45)
NG9: Chil . . . . . . . . . . . . . . . . . . . . . . . . . .5D 54
Parkview Dr. NG5: Bestw . . . . . . . . . . . . . . . .6E 21
Parkway NG8: Bilb . . . . . . . . . . . . . . . . . . . . .4D 42
Park W. NG7: Nott . . . . . . . . . . . . . . . . . . . . .3A 4
Park Wharf
NG7: Nott . . . . . . . . . . . . . . . . . . . .6C 4 (6F 45)
Parkwood Ct. NG6: Bulw . . . . . . . . . . . . . . . .2C 32
Parkwood Cres. NG5: Sher . . . . . . . . . . . . . .4A 34
Park Yacht Club . . . . . . . . . . . . . . . . . . . . . .1C 58
Parkyn Rd. NG5: Arn . . . . . . . . . . . . . . . . . . .1H 33
Parkyns St. NG11: Rudd . . . . . . . . . . . . . . . .6G 67
Parliament Ter. NG1: Nott . . . . . . . . . .3C 4 (4F 45)
Parr Ct. NG12: Rad T . . . . . . . . . . . . . . . . . .6F 49
Parr Gate NG9: Chil . . . . . . . . . . . . . . . . . . .6A 54

Parrs, The—Porchester


Parrs, The NG9: Bee .5H 55
Parry Ct. NG3: Mapp .3C 34
NG3: Nott .3C 46
Parry Way NG5: Arn .5D 22
Parsons Mdw. NG4: Colw .5G 47
Partridge Cl. NG13: Bing .6F 51
Pasteur Ho. NG3: Mapp .5B 34
Pasture Cl. NG2: Colw .5G 47
Pasture La. NG10: Long E .1A 74
NG11: Rudd .1D 76
Pasture Rd. NG9: Stap .2F 53
Pastures, The NG8: Bilb .2H 43
NG14: Calv .4F 11
NG16: Gilt .5D 16
Pastures Av. NG11: Clif .5B 66
Patchings Art Cen. .3D 10
Pateley Rd. NG3: Mapp .3C 34
Paton Ct. NG14: Calv .2G 11
Paton Rd. NG5: Bestw .2C 32
Patricia Dr. NG5: Arn .4C 22
Patrick Rd. NG2: West Br .3A 58
Patriot Cl. NG16: Want .6A 18
Patterdale Cl. NG2: Gam .4E 59
Patterdale Ct. NG9: Chil .6A 54
Patterdale Rd. NG5: Woodt .2B 34
Patterson Rd. NG7: H Grn .2D 44
Pavilion, The NG7: H Grn .2E 45
Pavilion Cl. NG2: Nott .2H 57
Pavilion Ct. DE7: West H .2B 38
Pavilion Rd. NG2: West Br .2A 58
NG5: Arn .4F 21
Pavior Rd. NG5: Bestw .2D 32
Paxton Gdns. NG3: Nott .2H 5 (4A 46)
(not continuous)
Payne Rd. NG9: Chil .2A 64
Peache Way NG9: Bram .4B 54
Peachey St. NG1: Nott .2D 4 (4G 45)
Peach St. DE75: Hea .4B 14
Peacock Cl. NG11: Rudd .1F 77
Peacock Cres. NG11: Clif .3C 66
Peacock Pl. DE7: Ilk .3H 27
Peakdale Cl. NG10: Long E .1C 72
Pearce Dr. NG8: Bilb .2H 43
Pearmain Dr. NG3: Nott .2B 46
Pearson Av. NG9: Chil .6B 54
Pearson Cl. NG9: Chil .6B 54
Pearson Ct. NG5: Arn .6A 22
NG9: Bram .3B 54
Pearson St. NG4: Neth .3A 48
NG7: Basf .5D 32
Pear Tree Ct. NG6: Basf .3C 32
Peartree Orchard NG11: Rudd .6G 67
Pear Tree Yd. NG10: Sand .5D 52
Peary Cl. NG5: Bestw .1D 32
Peashill La. NG12: Cotg .6C 60
Peas Hill Rd. NG3: Nott .3H 45
Peatburn Av. DE75: Hea .3A 14
Peatfield Ct. NG9: Stap .2F 53
Peatfield Rd. NG9: Stap .2F 53
Peck La. NG1: Nott .4E 5 (5G 45)
Pedley St. DE7: Ilk .2B 40
Pedmore Valley NG5: Bestw .6E 21
Peel St. NG1: Nott .1C 4 (3F 45)
NG10: Long E .5G 63
NG16: Lang M .2F 15
Peel Vs. NG3: Mapp .5A 34
Pegswood Dr. NG5: Arn .3C 22
Pelham Av. DE7: Ilk .6A 28
NG5: Sher .1F 45
Pelham Cotts. NG7: Nott .5D 44
(off Pelham Cres.)
Pelham Ct. NG5: Sher .5G 33
(off Private Rd.)
Pelham Cres. NG7: Nott .5D 44
NG9: Bee .4H 55
Pelham Rd. NG5: Sher .1F 45
Pelham St. DE7: Ilk .6A 28
NG1: Nott .4E 5 (5G 45)
Pellham Ct. NG5: Sher .1F 45
Pemberton St. NG1: Nott .5G 5 (5H 45)
Pembrey Cl. NG9: Trow .1F 53
Pembridge Cl. NG6: Basf .5B 32
Pembroke Dr. NG3: Mapp P .6G 33
Pembury Rd. NG8: Woll .4E 43
Penarth Gdns. NG5: Sher .4A 34
Penarth Ri. NG5: Sher .4A 34
Pendennis Cl. NG4: Ged .6B 36
Pendine Cl. NG5: Redh .4H 21
Pendle Cres. NG3: Nott .6B 34
Pendock La. NG11: Rudd .5B 78
Penhale Dr. NG15: Huck .6C 6
Penhurst Cl. NG11: Wilf .1E 67
Penllech Cl. NG5: Bestw .6E 21
Penllech Wlk. NG5: Bestw .6E 21
Pen Moor Cl. NG10: Long E .1C 72
Pennant Rd. NG6: Basf .5B 32
Pennard Wlk. NG11: Clif .5B 66
Penn Av. NG7: Lent .6C 44
Pennhome Almshouses NG5: Sher .5G 33
(off Haydn Rd.)
Pennhome Av. NG5: Sher .5G 33
Pennie Cl. NG10: Long E .3F 73
Pennine Cl. NG5: Arn .4F 21
NG10: Long E .4C 62
Pennyfields Blvd. NG10: Long E .6C 62
Pennyfoot St. NG1: Nott .5H 5 (5A 46)
Penrhyn Cl. NG3: Nott .1F 5
Penrhyn Cres. NG9: Chil .1B 64
Penrith Av. NG12: Rad T .5G 49
Penrith Cres. NG8: Aspl .5A 32
Penshore Cl. NG11: Clif .4B 66
Pentland Dr. NG5: Arn .3F 21
Pentland Gdns. NG10: Long E .4C 62
Pentrich Rd. NG16: Gilt .6E 17
Pentridge Dr. DE7: Ilk .4G 27
Pentwood Av. NG5: Arn .3B 22
Peoples Hall Cotts. NG1: Nott .4F 5
Peppercorn Gdns. NG8: Woll .3A 44
Pepper La. DE7: Stant D .3A 52
Pepper Rd. NG14: Calv .3G 11
Pepper St. NG1: Nott .5E 5 (5G 45)
Percival Rd. NG5: Sher .5F 33
Percy St. DE7: Ilk .2B 40
NG6: Basf .4B 32
NG16: Eastw .3C 16
Peregrine Cl. NG7: Lent .5C 44
Peregrine Rd. NG15: Huck .2B 8
Perivale Cl. NG16: Nuth .4D 30
Perlethorpe Av. NG2: Nott .5B 46
NG4: Ged .5F 35
Perlethorpe Cl. NG4: Ged .5G 35
Perlethorpe Cres. NG4: Ged .5G 35
Perlethorpe Dr. NG4: Ged .5F 35
NG15: Huck .4H 7
Perry Gro. NG13: Bing .5F 51
Perry Rd. NG5: Sher .5D 32
Perth Dr. NG9: Stap .2G 53
Perth St. NG1: Nott .2E 5 (4G 45)
Peters Cl. NG5: Arn .1E 35
NG16: Newth .3E 17
Petersfield Cl. NG5: Top V .6D 20
Petersgate NG10: Long E .4C 62
Petersgate Cl. NG10: Long E .3C 62
Petersham Ct. NG10: Long E .3D 62
Petersham M. NG7: Lent .6D 44
Petersham Rd. NG10: Long E .3C 62
Petworth Av. NG9: Toton .2H 63
Petworth Dr. NG5: Sher .3D 32
Peverell Hall NG11: Clif .2B 66
Peveril Ct. NG2: West Br .4A 58
Peveril Cres. DE7: West H .1C 38
NG10: Long E .2B 72
Peveril Dr. DE7: Ilk .5H 27
NG2: West Br .2A 68
NG7: Nott .6B 4 (6F 45)
Peveril M. NG7: Nott .5A 4
Peveril Rd. NG9: Bee .3F 55
Peveril St. NG7: Radf .3D 44
NG15: Huck .3G 7
Pewit Golf Course .1H 39
Philip Av. NG16: Eastw .4C 16
NG16: Nuth .1C 30
Philip Gro. NG4: Ged .5G 35
Phoenix Av. NG4: Ged .5G 35
Phoenix Cen. NG8: Cin .3G 31
Phoenix Cl. NG2: Nott .1F 57
Phoenix Ct. NG7: Lent .3D 56
NG16: Eastw .3C 16
Phoenix Park (Park & Ride) .3G 31
Phoenix Park Stop (NET) .3G 31
Phoenix Pl. NG8: Cin .3H 31
Phoenix Rd. NG16: Newth .1D 16
Phyllis Cl. NG15: Huck .2F 7
Phyllis Gro. NG10: Long E .6H 63
Piccadilly NG6: Bulw .1B 32
Pickering Av. NG16: Eastw .3B 16
Pieris Dr. NG11: Clif .4A 66
Pierrepont Av. NG4: Ged .6G 35
Pierrepont Ct. NG2: West Br .2D 58
Pierrepont Rd. NG2: West Br .3C 58
Pilcher Ga. NG1: Nott .4E 5 (5H 45)
Pilkington Rd. NG3: Mapp .6C 34
Pilkington St. NG6: Bulw .6H 19
Pimlico DE7: Ilk .1A 40
Pimlico Av. NG9: Bram .6B 42
Pine Av. NG16: Lang M .2E 15
Pine Gro. NG15: Huck .1H 19
Pine Hill Cl. NG5: Top V .4D 20
Pinehurst Av. NG15: Huck .6C 6
Pines, The NG9: Bram .3C 54
Pines Ct. NG5: Sher .3H 33
Pine Tree Wlk. NG16: Eastw .3A 16
Pine Vw. NG7: Radf .3D 44
Pinewood Av. NG5: Arn .4D 22
Pinewood Gdns. NG11: Clif .5B 66
Pinfold NG13: Bing .5F 51
Pinfold Cl. NG12: Cotg .1F 71
NG14: Woodbo .1C 24
Pinfold Cres. NG14: Woodbo .1C 24
Pinfold La. NG9: Stap .4F 53
NG11: Wilf .5F 57
NG12: Plum .6H 69
Pinfold Rd. NG16: Gilt .4E 17
Pinfold Trad. Est. NG9: Stap .4G 53
Pingle, The NG10: Long E .4F 63
Pingle Cres. NG5: Top V .5D 20
Pintail Cl. NG4: Neth .3B 48
Pioneer Meadows Local Nature Reserve .5G 39
Piper Cl. NG15: Huck .2H 7
Pippin Cl. NG3: Nott .2B 46
Pitcairn Cl. NG2: Nott .2G 57
Pitch Cl. NG4: Carl .1E 47
NG16: Gilt .5E 17
Pit La. DE7: Ilk .1F 27
DE75: Ship .1F 27
Plackett Cl. DE72: Brea .5A 62
NG9: Stap .3H 53
Plains Farm Cl. NG3: Mapp .2E 35
Plains Gro. NG3: Mapp .3C 34
Plains Rd. NG3: Mapp .4B 34
Plane Cl. NG6: Bulw .6F 19
Plane Tree Ct. NG15: Huck .6H 7
Plantagenet Ct. NG3: Nott .1G 5 (4H 45)
Plantagenet St. NG3: Nott .2G 5 (4H 45)
Plantation Cl. NG5: Arn .4F 21
Plantation Cotts. NG14: Epp .5F 13
Plantation Rd. NG8: Woll .5C 42
NG12: Key .4F 79
Plantations, The NG10: Long E .5C 62
Plantation Side NG7: H Grn .2C 44
Plantin Rd. NG5: Sher .6F 33
Plant La. NG10: Long E .3C 72
Platt La. NG12: Key, Norm W .3H 79
Platts Av. DE75: Hea .4A 14
Player Ct. NG7: Radf .3C 44
Player St. NG7: Radf .3C 44
Plaza Gdns. NG6: Basf .3C 32
Pleasant Ct. NG7: H Grn .2D 44
Pleasant Row NG7: H Grn .2D 44
Plimsoll St. NG7: H Grn .1C 44
Plough La. NG1: Nott .5H 5 (5A 46)
Ploughman Av. NG14: Woodbo .1D 24
Plover Wharf NG7: Lent .1E 57
Plowman Ct. NG9: Stap .5F 53
Plowright Ct. NG3: Nott .2H 45
Plowright St. NG3: Nott .2H 45
Plumb Rd. NG15: Huck .4F 7
Plumptre Cl. NG16: Eastw .4B 16
Plumptre Gdns. NG16: Eastw .3B 16
Plumptre Pl. NG1: Nott .5F 5 (5H 45)
Plumptre Rd. NG16: Lang M .1F 15
Plumptre Sq. NG1: Nott .5G 5 (5H 45)
Plumptre St. NG1: Nott .5F 5 (5H 45)
Plumptre Way NG16: Eastw .4B 16
PLUMTREE .6G 69
Plumtree Ct. NG12: Plum .6G 69
Plumtree Gdns. NG14: Calv .4H 11
PLUMTREE PARK .3H 79
Plumtree Rd. NG12: Cotg .3D 70
Plungar Cl. NG8: Bilb .3H 43
Podder La. NG3: Mapp .1E 35
Point, The NG1: Nott .5G 5
NG2: West Br .4A 58
(off Loughborough Rd.)
NG3: Mapp P .1H 45
Pointers Ct. NG3: Nott .2C 46
Pollard Ct. NG9: Bee .4F 55
Polperro Way NG15: Huck .6C 6
Pond Hills La. NG5: Arn .5B 22
Pool Mdw. NG4: Colw .5H 47
Popham Ct. NG1: Nott .5F 5 (5H 45)
Popham St. NG1: Nott .5F 5 (5H 45)
Poplar Av. NG5: Sher .5E 33
NG10: Sand .4C 52
Poplar Cl. NG4: Carl .3F 47
NG13: Bing .5G 51
Poplar Cres. NG16: Nuth .1A 30
Poplar Rd. DE72: Brea .4B 62
Poplars, The NG2: West Br .4B 58
NG7: H Grn .1C 44
NG9: Bee .4F 55
NG12: Plum .1G 79
Poplars Av. NG14: Bur J .2G 37
Poplars Cl. NG12: Key .3H 79
Poplars Ct. NG7: Lent .1D 56
Poplars Rd. NG7: Lent .1D 56
Poplar St. NG1: Nott .5G 5 (5H 45)
(not continuous)
Poplar Way DE7: Kirk H .4H 39
Poppy M. NG15: Huck .1B 20
PORCHESTER .5D 34

Porchester Cl. NG15: Huck . . . . . . . . . . . . . .4A 8
Porchester Ct. NG3: Nott . . . . . . . . . . . . . . .1C 46
Porchester Rd. NG3: Mapp, Nott . . . . . . . . .5B 34
  NG13: Bing . . . . . . . . . . . . . . . . . . . . . . .5D 50
Porlock Cl. NG10: Long E . . . . . . . . . . . . . .5C 62
Portage Cl. NG12: Rad T . . . . . . . . . . . . . . .1E 61
Port Arthur Rd. NG2: Nott . . . . . . . . . . . . . .5B 46
Porter Cl. NG11: Clif . . . . . . . . . . . . . . . . . .5A 66
Porters Wlk. NG3: Nott . . . . . . . . . . . . . . . .2C 46
Portinscale Cl. NG2: West Br . . . . . . . . . . . .6E 59
Portland Cl. NG5: Bestw . . . . . . . . . . . . . . .2F 33
Portland Cres. NG9: Stap . . . . . . . . . . . . . .5G 53
Portland Gdns. NG15: Huck . . . . . . . . . . . . .4F 7
Portland Grange NG15: Huck . . . . . . . . . . . .4E 7
Portland Hill NG7: Nott . . . . . . . . . . . . . . . .2A 56
Portland Leisure Cen. . . . . . . . . . . . . . . . . .2H 57
Portland Pk. Cl. NG15: Huck . . . . . . . . . . . .4F 7
Portland Rd. DE7: Ilk . . . . . . . . . . . . . . . . .4B 28
  NG2: West Br . . . . . . . . . . . . . . . . . . . . .5B 58
  NG4: Carl . . . . . . . . . . . . . . . . . . . . . . . .5E 35
  NG7: Radf . . . . . . . . . . . . . . . . . .2A 4 (4E 45)
  NG9: Toton . . . . . . . . . . . . . . . . . . . . . . .4H 63
  NG10: Long E . . . . . . . . . . . . . . . . . . . .3C 72
  NG15: Huck . . . . . . . . . . . . . . . . . . . . . .4H 7
  NG16: Gilt . . . . . . . . . . . . . . . . . . . . . . .5D 16
Portland Sq. NG7: Radf . . . . . . . . . .2A 4 (4E 45)
Portland St. NG5: Arn . . . . . . . . . . . . . . . . .1H 33
  NG9: Bee . . . . . . . . . . . . . . . . . . . . . . . .4G 55
Portree Dr. NG5: Top V . . . . . . . . . . . . . . . .4D 20
Port Said Vs. NG7: Basf . . . . . . . . . . . . . . .6D 32
Postern St. NG1: Nott . . . . . . . . . .4C 4 (5F 45)
Pot 'n' Kettle (Ceramic Cafe) . . . . . . . . . . .4G 55
(off High Rd.)
Potomac M. NG7: Nott . . . . . . . . . .5A 4 (5E 45)
Potters Cl. NG5: Top V . . . . . . . . . . . . . . . .6E 21
Potters Ct. NG9: Bram . . . . . . . . . . . . . . . .2D 54
Potters Hollow NG6: Bulw . . . . . . . . . . . . . .2A 32
Potters Way DE7: Ilk . . . . . . . . . . . . . . . . .1C 40
Pottery Cl. NG6: Bulw . . . . . . . . . . . . . . . .6G 19
Pottery Way NG6: Bulw . . . . . . . . . . . . . . .6G 19
Poulter Cl. NG7: Radf . . . . . . . . . . . . . . . . .2B 44
Poulton Dr. NG2: Nott . . . . . . . . . . . . . . . .6B 46
Poultry NG1: Nott . . . . . . . . . . . . .4E 5 (5G 45)
Poultry Arc. NG1: Nott . . . . . . . . . . . . . . . .4E 5
Powerleague
  Nottingham . . . . . . . . . . . . . . . . . . . . . .5C 56
Powis St. NG6: Bulw . . . . . . . . . . . . . . . . .6H 19
Powtrell Pl. DE7: Ilk . . . . . . . . . . . . . . . . .3D 40
Poynter Cl. DE75: Hea . . . . . . . . . . . . . . . .4A 14
Poynton St. NG1: Nott . . . . . . . . . .3C 4 (4F 45)
Poyser Cl. NG7: Basf . . . . . . . . . . . . . . . . .6E 33
Premier Rd. NG7: H Grn . . . . . . . . . . . . . . .1E 45
Prendwick Gdns. NG5: Bestw . . . . . . . . . . .5F 21
Prestwick Cl. NG8: Stre . . . . . . . . . . . . . . .5D 30
Prestwood Dr. NG8: Aspl . . . . . . . . . . . . . .2H 43
Pretoria Vs. NG8: Aspl . . . . . . . . . . . . . . . .5A 32
Previn Gdns. NG3: Nott . . . . . . . . . . . . . . .3B 46
Primrose Bank NG13: Bing . . . . . . . . . . . . .5D 50
Primrose Cl. NG3: Nott . . . . . . . . . . . . . . .2H 45
Primrose Cotts. DE72: Ris . . . . . . . . . . . . . .2A 62
Primrose Cres. NG4: Carl . . . . . . . . . . . . . .2H 47
Primrose Gdns. NG15: Huck . . . . . . . . . . . .1B 20
Primrose Hill DE7: Ilk . . . . . . . . . . . . . . . .4A 28
Primrose Ri. NG16: Newth . . . . . . . . . . . . .5C 16
Primrose St. DE7: Ilk . . . . . . . . . . . . . . . .2H 27
  NG4: Carl . . . . . . . . . . . . . . . . . . . . . . .2H 47
Primula Cl. NG11: Clif . . . . . . . . . . . . . . . .3A 66
Prince Edward Cres. NG12: Rad T . . . . . . . .1D 60
Princess Av. NG9: Bee . . . . . . . . . . . . . . . .5G 55
Princess Cl. DE75: Hea . . . . . . . . . . . . . . .3B 14
  NG4: Ged . . . . . . . . . . . . . . . . . . . . . . .5G 35
Princess Dr. NG10: Sand . . . . . . . . . . . . . .1D 62
Princess St. NG10: Long E . . . . . . . . . . . . .5F 63
Princes St. NG16: Eastw . . . . . . . . . . . . . .2B 16
Prince St. DE7: Ilk . . . . . . . . . . . . . . . . . .3A 28
  NG10: Long E . . . . . . . . . . . . . . . . . . . .5F 63
Prioridge NG12: Cotg . . . . . . . . . . . . . . . . .3G 71
Prior Rd. NG5: Arn . . . . . . . . . . . . . . . . . .1H 33
Priors Cl. NG13: Bing . . . . . . . . . . . . . . . .4G 51
Priory Av. NG12: Toll . . . . . . . . . . . . . . . . .4E 69
Priory Cir. NG12: Toll . . . . . . . . . . . . . . . . .4E 69
Priory Cl. DE7: Kirk H . . . . . . . . . . . . . . . . .3G 39
Priory Ct. NG3: Mapp . . . . . . . . . . . . . . . . .6A 34
  NG4: Ged . . . . . . . . . . . . . . . . . . . . . . .6H 35
  NG7: Lent . . . . . . . . . . . . . . . . . . . . . . .6C 44
Priory Cres. NG4: Ged . . . . . . . . . . . . . . . .6H 35
Priory M. NG7: Lent . . . . . . . . . . . . . . . . .1C 56
Priory Rd. NG2: West Br . . . . . . . . . . . . . . .3B 58
  NG4: Ged . . . . . . . . . . . . . . . . . . . . . . .6H 35
  NG15: Huck . . . . . . . . . . . . . . . . . . . . . .4E 7
  NG16: Eastw . . . . . . . . . . . . . . . . . . . . .4B 16
Priory St. NG7: Lent . . . . . . . . . . . . . . . . .1C 56
Pritchard Dr. NG9: Stap . . . . . . . . . . . . . . .5G 53
Private Rd. NG3: Mapp . . . . . . . . . . . . . . .5G 33
  NG5: Sher . . . . . . . . . . . . . . . . . . . . . . .5G 33
  NG14: Woodbo . . . . . . . . . . . . . . . . . . .6B 12
  NG15: Huck . . . . . . . . . . . . . . . . . . . . . .4E 7

Private Rd. No. 1 NG4: Colw . . . . . . . . . . . .3H 47
Private Rd. No. 2 NG4: Colw . . . . . . . . . . . .4H 47
Private Rd. No. 3 NG4: Colw . . . . . . . . . . . .4A 48
Private Rd. No. 4 NG4: Colw . . . . . . . . . . . .4B 48
Private Rd. No. 5 NG4: Colw . . . . . . . . . . . .4B 48
Private Rd. No. 7 NG4: Colw . . . . . . . . . . . .3H 47
Private Rd. No. 8 NG4: Colw . . . . . . . . . . . .4H 47
Prize Cl. NG11: Clif . . . . . . . . . . . . . . . . . .4A 66
Promenade NG3: Nott . . . . . . . . . .2G 5 (4H 45)
Prospect Ct. NG4: Carl . . . . . . . . . . . . . . . .6C 34
Prospect Pl. NG7: Lent . . . . . . . . . . . . . . . .6D 44
Prospect Rd. DE75: Hea . . . . . . . . . . . . . . .5E 15
  NG4: Carl . . . . . . . . . . . . . . . . . . . . . . .6C 34
Prospect St. NG7: Radf . . . . . . . . . . . . . . .3C 44
Prospect Ter. NG7: Radf . . . . . . . . . . . . . . .3C 44
Providence Pl. DE7: Ilk . . . . . . . . . . . . . . . .6A 28
Provident Works NG7: Radf . . . . . . . . . . . . .2A 4
Prudhoe Cl. NG2: Nott . . . . . . . . . . . . . . . .2H 57
Pulborough Cl. NG5: Sher . . . . . . . . . . . . . .3D 32
Pullman Rd. NG2: Nott . . . . . . . . . . . . . . . .1H 31
Purbeck Cl. NG10: Long E . . . . . . . . . . . . . .5C 62
Purbeck Dr. NG2: West Br . . . . . . . . . . . . . .6G 57
Purchase Av. DE75: Los . . . . . . . . . . . . . . .3A 14
Purdy Mdw. NG10: Long E . . . . . . . . . . . . . .6A 72
Pyatt St. NG2: Nott . . . . . . . . . . . . . . . . . .2H 57
Pygall Av. NG11: Goth . . . . . . . . . . . . . . . .6G 75
Pym Leys NG10: Long E . . . . . . . . . . . . . . .2B 72
Pym St. NG3: Nott . . . . . . . . . . . . . . . . . . .3B 46
Pym Wlk. NG3: Nott . . . . . . . . . . . .1H 5 (3A 46)

# Q

Quantock Cl. NG5: Arn . . . . . . . . . . . . . . . .3F 21
Quantock Gro. NG13: Bing . . . . . . . . . . . . .5C 50
Quantock Rd. NG10: Long E . . . . . . . . . . . .4C 62
Quarry Av. NG6: Bulw . . . . . . . . . . . . . . . .1H 31
Quarrydale NG15: Huck . . . . . . . . . . . . . . . .2F 7
Quarry Hill DE7: Stant D . . . . . . . . . . . . . . .3B 52
Quarry Hill Ind. Est. DE7: Ilk . . . . . . . . . . . .5B 40
Quarry Hill Rd. DE7: Ilk . . . . . . . . . . . . . . .4B 40
Quays, The NG7: Lent . . . . . . . . . . . . . . . . .6E 45
Quayside Cl. NG2: Nott . . . . . . . . . . . . . . . .2A 58
Queen Elizabeth Rd. NG9: Chil . . . . . . . . . .1A 64
Queen Elizabeth Way DE7: Kirk H . . . . . . . .4G 39
Queens Av. DE7: Ilk . . . . . . . . . . . . . . . . . .5H 27
  DE7: Stan . . . . . . . . . . . . . . . . . . . . . . .3A 38
  DE75: Hea . . . . . . . . . . . . . . . . . . . . . . .3B 14
  NG4: Ged . . . . . . . . . . . . . . . . . . . . . . .5G 35
Queensberry St. NG6: Basf . . . . . . . . . . . . .3C 32
Queens Bri. Rd. NG2: Nott . . . . . . . . . . . . .6G 45
Queensbury Av. NG2: West Br . . . . . . . . . . .2G 67
Queens Ct. NG2: Nott . . . . . . . . . . . . . . . . .4E 57
  NG13: Bing . . . . . . . . . . . . . . . . . . . . . .4D 50
Queens Dr. DE7: Ilk . . . . . . . . . . . . . . . . . .1A 40
  NG2: Nott . . . . . . . . . . . . . . . . . . . . . . .4E 57
  NG9: Bee . . . . . . . . . . . . . . . . . . . . . . . .5G 55
  NG10: Sand . . . . . . . . . . . . . . . . . . . . .1D 62
  NG16: Nuth . . . . . . . . . . . . . . . . . . . . . .1C 30
Queen's Drive (Park & Ride) . . . . . . . . . . . .4E 57
Queens Dr. Ind. Est. NG2: Nott . . . . . . . . . .2E 57
Queens Gro. NG2: Nott . . . . . . . . . . . . . . . .6G 45
QUEEN'S MEDICAL CENTRE
  UNIVERSITY HOSPITAL . . . . . . . . . . . . . .1B 56
Queens Rd. NG2: Nott . . . . . . . . . . . . . . . .6G 45
  NG9: Bee . . . . . . . . . . . . . . . . . . . . . . . .6G 55
  NG12: Rad T . . . . . . . . . . . . . . . . . . . . .5F 49
Queen's Rd. E. NG9: Bee . . . . . . . . . . . . . .4H 55
Queens Rd. Nth. NG16: Eastw . . . . . . . . . . .3B 16
Queens Rd. Sth. NG16: Eastw . . . . . . . . . . .4B 16
Queen's Rd. W. NG9: Bee, Chil . . . . . . . . . .1D 64
Queen's Sq. NG16: Eastw . . . . . . . . . . . . . .3B 16
Queen St. DE7: Ilk . . . . . . . . . . . . . . . . . . .1A 40
  NG1: Nott . . . . . . . . . . . . . . . .3D 4 (4G 45)
  NG5: Arn . . . . . . . . . . . . . . . . . . . . . . . .4B 22
  NG10: Long E . . . . . . . . . . . . . . . . . . . .6G 63
  NG15: Huck . . . . . . . . . . . . . . . . . . . . . . .3F 7
  NG16: Lang M . . . . . . . . . . . . . . . . . . . .2G 15
Queen's Wlk. NG2: Nott . . . . . . . . . . . . . . .2F 57
(not continuous)
Queen Ter. DE7: Ilk . . . . . . . . . . . . . . . . . .1A 40
Querneby Av. NG3: Mapp . . . . . . . . . . . . . .5A 34
Querneby Rd. NG3: Mapp . . . . . . . . . . . . . .5A 34
Quinton Cl. NG11: Wilf . . . . . . . . . . . . . . . .6E 57
Quorn Cl. NG9: Atten . . . . . . . . . . . . . . . . .2E 65
Quorndon Cres. NG10: Long E . . . . . . . . . . .2F 73
Quorn Gro. NG5: Sher . . . . . . . . . . . . . . . .4E 33
Quorn Rd. NG5: Sher . . . . . . . . . . . . . . . . .4E 33

# R

Racecourse (Park & Ride) . . . . . . . . . . . . . .6D 46
Racecourse Rd. NG2: Colw, Nott . . . . . . . . .5D 46
Radbourne Rd. NG2: Nott . . . . . . . . . . . . . .6B 46
Radburn Ct. NG9: Stap . . . . . . . . . . . . . . . .2G 53

Radcliffe Gdns. NG4: Carl . . . . . . . . . . . . . .1F 47
Radcliffe Lodge NG12: Rad T . . . . . . . . . . . .6E 49
Radcliffe Mt. NG2: West Br . . . . . . . . . . . . .2B 58
RADCLIFFE ON TRENT . . . . . . . . . . . . . . . .6F 49
Radcliffe on Trent Golf Course . . . . . . . . . . .1H 61
Radcliffe Rd.
  NG2: Gam, West Br . . . . . . . . . . . . . . . .2A 58
  NG12: Hol P . . . . . . . . . . . . . . . . . . . . .3F 59
Radcliffe Station (Rail) . . . . . . . . . . . . . . . .6F 49
Radcliffe St. NG2: Nott . . . . . . . . . . . . . . . .2H 57
RADFORD . . . . . . . . . . . . . . . . . . . . . . . . .4D 44
Radford Blvd. NG7: Radf . . . . . . . . . . . . . . .3C 44
Radford Bri. Rd. NG8: Aspl, Woll . . . . . . . . .3A 44
Radford Ct. NG7: Basf . . . . . . . . . . . . . . . .5D 32
(off Radford Rd.)
  NG7: Radf . . . . . . . . . . . . . . . . . . . . . . .4D 44
Radford Ct. Ind. Est. NG7: Radf . . . . . . . . . .4D 44
Radford Cres. NG4: Ged . . . . . . . . . . . . . . .5G 35
Radford Gro. La. NG7: Radf . . . . . . . . . . . .3C 44
Radford Rd. NG7: Basf, H Grn . . . . . . . . . . .5D 32
Radford Road Stop (NET) . . . . . . . . . . . . . .1D 44
Radham Ct. NG5: Sher . . . . . . . . . . . . . . . .5G 33
Radley Sq. NG6: Bulw . . . . . . . . . . . . . . . .2B 32
Radmarsh Rd. NG7: Lent . . . . . . . . . . . . . . .6C 44
Rad Mdws. NG10: Long E . . . . . . . . . . . . . .1E 73
Radnor Gro. NG13: Bing . . . . . . . . . . . . . . .5C 50
Radstock Rd. NG3: Nott . . . . . . . . . . . . . . .2C 46
Radway Dr. NG11: Wilf . . . . . . . . . . . . . . . .6E 57
Raeburn Dr. NG9: Toton . . . . . . . . . . . . . . .3G 63
Rafters, The NG7: Basf . . . . . . . . . . . . . . . .5D 32
Ragdale Rd. NG6: Bulw . . . . . . . . . . . . . . .5H 19
(not continuous)
Raglan Cl. NG3: Nott . . . . . . . . . . . . . . . . .2H 45
Raglan Ct. NG9: Lent A . . . . . . . . . . . . . . . .2G 55
Raglan Dr. NG4: Ged . . . . . . . . . . . . . . . . .6B 36
Raglan St. NG16: Eastw . . . . . . . . . . . . . . .4C 16
Raibank Gdns. NG5: Woodt . . . . . . . . . . . . .2A 34
Railway Cotts. NG16: Kimb . . . . . . . . . . . . .1H 29
Rainham Gdns. NG11: Rudd . . . . . . . . . . . .1G 77
Raithby Cl. NG5: Bestw . . . . . . . . . . . . . . .1E 33
Raleigh Cl. DE7: Ilk . . . . . . . . . . . . . . . . . .4B 28
  NG11: Clif . . . . . . . . . . . . . . . . . . . . . . .4A 66
Raleigh Ct. NG7: Radf . . . . . . . . . . .1A 4 (3E 45)
Raleigh Pk. NG7: Lent . . . . . . . . . . . . . . . .6C 44
Raleigh Sq. NG7: Radf . . . . . . . . . . .2A 4 (4E 45)
Raleigh St. NG7: Radf . . . . . . . . . . .2A 4 (4E 45)
Ralf Cl. NG2: West Br . . . . . . . . . . . . . . . . .1A 68
Ralph Way NG5: Sher . . . . . . . . . . . . . . . . .2G 33
Ramblers Cl. NG4: Colw . . . . . . . . . . . . . . .4G 47
Ramsdale Av. NG14: Calv . . . . . . . . . . . . . .3F 11
Ramsdale Cres. NG5: Sher . . . . . . . . . . . . .4H 33
Ramsdale Pk. NG5: Arn . . . . . . . . . . . . . . . .5D 10
Ramsdale Park Golf Cen. . . . . . . . . . . . . . .4D 10
Ramsdale Rd. NG4: Carl . . . . . . . . . . . . . . .6G 35
Ramsey Cl. NG9: Stap . . . . . . . . . . . . . . . .1G 53
Ramsey Ct. NG5: Sher . . . . . . . . . . . . . . . .6F 33
Ramsey Dr. NG5: Arn . . . . . . . . . . . . . . . . .1D 34
Ranby Wlk. NG3: Nott . . . . . . . . . . . . . . . . .3B 46
Rancliffe Av. NG12: Key . . . . . . . . . . . . . . .3F 79
Randal Gdns. NG7: H Grn . . . . . . . . . . . . . .2D 44
Randal St. NG7: H Grn . . . . . . . . . . . . . . . .2C 44
(not continuous)
Ranelagh Gro. NG8: Woll . . . . . . . . . . . . . .4G 43
Rani Dr. NG5: Basf . . . . . . . . . . . . . . . . . . .3D 32
Ranmere Rd. NG8: Bilb . . . . . . . . . . . . . . . .2G 43
Ranmoor Rd. NG4: Ged . . . . . . . . . . . . . . .6H 35
Ranmore Cl. NG9: Bram . . . . . . . . . . . . . . .1B 54
Rannerdale Cl. NG2: West Br . . . . . . . . . . . .5D 58
Rannoch Ri. NG5: Arn . . . . . . . . . . . . . . . . .4B 22
Rannock Gdns. NG12: Key . . . . . . . . . . . . .4H 79
Ranskill Gdns. NG5: Top V . . . . . . . . . . . . .5E 21
Ransom Dr. NG3: Mapp . . . . . . . . . . . . . . . .6A 34
Ransom Rd. NG3: Nott . . . . . . . . . . . . . . . .6A 34
Ranson Rd. NG9: Chil . . . . . . . . . . . . . . . . .4B 64
Ratcliffe Rd. NG16: Eastw . . . . . . . . . . . . . .3B 16
Rathgar Cl. NG8: Woll . . . . . . . . . . . . . . . . .5D 42
Rathmines Cl. NG7: Lent . . . . . . . . . . . . . . .6C 44
Rathvale Cl. NG9: Chil . . . . . . . . . . . . . . . . .1A 64
Raven Av. NG5: Sher . . . . . . . . . . . . . . . . .3F 33
Raven Ct. DE75: Hea . . . . . . . . . . . . . . . . .3C 14
Ravenhill Cl. NG9: Chil . . . . . . . . . . . . . . . .1B 64
Ravens Ct. NG5: Bestw . . . . . . . . . . . . . . . .2F 33
Ravensdale Av. NG10: Long E . . . . . . . . . . .3D 62
Ravensdale Dr. NG8: Woll . . . . . . . . . . . . . .6C 42
Ravensdene Ct. NG3: Mapp P . . . . . . . . . . .1G 45
Ravensmore Rd. NG5: Sher . . . . . . . . . . . . .5F 33
Ravenstone Ct. NG15: Huck . . . . . . . . . . . .2D 18
Ravenswood Rd. NG5: Arn . . . . . . . . . . . . .6B 22
Ravensworth Rd. NG6: Bulw . . . . . . . . . . . .5H 19
Rawson St. NG7: Basf . . . . . . . . . . . . . . . . .6D 32
Raymede Cl. NG5: Bestw . . . . . . . . . . . . . .1D 32
Raymede Dr. NG5: Bestw . . . . . . . . . . . . . .1C 32
Raymond Dr. NG13: Bing . . . . . . . . . . . . . .5G 51
Raynham Rd. DE7: Ilk . . . . . . . . . . . . . . . . .3G 27
Rayner Ct. NG7: Lent . . . . . . . . . . . . . . . . .4D 44
Raynford Av. NG9: Chil . . . . . . . . . . . . . . . .1D 64
Raynham Lodge NG5: Top V . . . . . . . . . . . .4B 20

Rays Av. DE75: Hea .....4C 14
Ray St. DE75: Hea .....4B 14
Read Av. NG9: Bee .....5G 55
Read Lodge NG9: Bee .....5G 55
Readman Rd. NG9: Chil .....2A 64
Rearsby Cl. NG8: Bilb .....4D 42
Recreation Rd. NG10: Sand .....5D 52
Recreation St. NG10: Long E .....5H 63
Recreation Ter. NG9: Stap .....5F 53
Rectory Av. NG8: Woll .....5E 43
Rectory Ct. NG2: West Br .....4B 58
Rectory Dr. NG4: Ged .....5H 35
  NG11: Wilf .....3F 57
Rectory Gdns. NG8: Woll .....5F 43
Rectory Pl. NG11: Bart F .....1E 75
Rectory Rd. DE72: Brea .....5A 62
  NG2: West Br .....4A 58
  NG4: Colw .....4G 47
  NG12: Cotg .....2E 71
Redbourne Dr. NG8: Aspl .....3A 44
Redbridge Cl. DE7: Ilk .....2C 40
Redbridge Dr. NG16: Nuth .....4D 30
Redcar Cl. NG4: Ged .....5G 35
Redcliffe Gdns. NG3: Mapp P .....1G 45
Redcliffe Rd. NG3: Mapp P .....1F 45
Redens, The NG10: Long E .....3D 72
Redfield Rd. NG7: Lent .....3C 56
Redfield Way NG7: Lent .....2C 56
Redgates Ct. NG14: Calv .....4F 11
REDHILL .....4A 22
Redhill Leisure Cen. .....4A 22
Redhill Lodge Dr. NG5: Redh .....4H 21
Redhill Rd. NG5: Arn .....4A 22
Red Kite Cl. NG15: Huck .....3B 8
Redland Av. NG4: Carl .....1H 47
Redland Cl. DE7: Ilk .....4B 28
  NG9: Chil .....1C 64
Redland Dr. NG9: Chil .....2C 64
Redland Gro. NG4: Carl .....1G 47
Red Lion Sq. DE75: Hea .....3C 14
Red Lion Yd. NG15: Huck .....4G 7
  *(off High St.)*
Redmays Dr. NG14: Bulc .....1H 37
Redmile Rd. NG8: Aspl .....5A 32
Redoubt St. NG7: Radf .....4C 44
Redruth Cl. NG8: Bilb .....3C 42
Redwood NG2: West Br .....5F 57
Redwood Av. NG8: Woll .....6D 42
Redwood Cl. NG8: Bilb .....2D 42
Redwood Ct. *NG7: Lent* .....5C 44
  *(off Faraday Rd.)*
  NG15: Huck .....3F 7
Redwood Cres. NG9: Bee .....6G 55
Reeders Cft. NG9: Chil .....2D 64
Reedham Wlk. NG5: Bestw .....5F 21
Reedman Rd. NG10: Long E .....3D 72
Rees Gdns. NG5: Top V .....4E 21
Regan Way NG9: Chil .....3B 64
Regatta Way NG2: West Br .....3E 59
Regency Ct. NG9: Bee .....4G 55
Regency Point NG2: West Br .....3B 58
Regent M. NG1: Nott .....3B 4 (4F 45)
Regents Pk. Cl. NG2: West Br .....6G 57
Regents Pl. NG11: Wilf .....5F 57
Regent St. DE7: Ilk .....2B 40
  NG1: Nott .....4B 4 (4F 45)
  NG7: Basf .....6E 33
  NG9: Bee .....4G 55
  NG10: Long E .....5F 63
  NG10: Sand .....6E 53
  NG16: Kimb .....1H 29
  NG16: Lang M .....2F 15
Regina Cl. NG12: Rad T .....1E 61
Reid Gdns. NG16: Want .....1B 30
Reigate Cl. NG9: Atten .....3E 65
Reigate Dr. NG9: Atten .....3E 65
Reigate Rd. NG7: Basf .....5D 32
Rempstone Dr. NG6: Bulw .....2B 32
Renals Way NG14: Calv .....5H 11
Renfrew Dr. NG8: Woll .....5E 43
Rennie Hogg Rd. NG2: Nott .....2D 56
Repton Dr. DE7: Ilk .....2D 40
Repton Rd. NG2: West Br .....6A 58
  NG6: Bulw .....1B 32
  NG10: Long E .....3B 72
Retford Rd. NG5: Sher .....4E 33
Retlaw Ct. NG9: Chil .....6D 54
Revelstoke Av. NG5: Top V .....4B 20
Revelstoke Way NG5: Top V .....4B 20
Revena Cl. NG4: Colw .....3G 47
Revesby Gdns. NG8: Aspl .....2A 44
Revesby Rd. NG5: Woodt .....2B 34
Revill Cl. DE7: Ilk .....5G 27
Revill Cres. NG9: Stap .....3H 53
Reydon Dr. NG8: Basf .....6B 32
Reynolds Dr. NG8: Woll .....4F 43
Rhodes Way NG5: Bestw V .....5F 9

Rhyl Cres. NG4: Ged .....5H 35
Ribblesdale DE7: Kirk H .....4G 39
Ribblesdale Ct. NG9: Chil .....1A 64
Ribblesdale Rd. NG5: Sher .....2G 33
  NG10: Long E .....2C 72
Riber Cl. DE7: West H .....1C 38
Riber Cres. NG5: Bestw .....2D 32
Richard Herrod Cen. .....1E 47
Richardson Cl. NG11: Clif .....4A 66
Richborough Pl. NG8: Woll .....1D 54
Richey Cl. NG5: Arn .....6D 22
Richmond Av. DE7: Ilk .....3B 28
  DE72: Brea .....5C 62
  NG3: Nott .....2B 46
  NG10: Sand .....1C 62
  NG14: Calv .....3A 12
  NG16: Newth .....3D 16
Richmond Cl. DE7: West H .....1B 38
Richmond Ct. NG9: Chil .....6E 55
Richmond Dr. NG3: Mapp P .....5H 33
  NG9: Chil .....6E 55
  NG12: Rad T .....5F 49
Richmond Gdns. NG5: Redh .....4A 22
Richmond Rd. NG2: West Br .....2B 58
Richmond Ter. NG12: Rad T .....6F 49
Ricklow Ct. *NG5: Top V* .....5E 21
  *(off Gautries Cl.)*
Rick St. NG1: Nott .....3F 5 (4H 45)
Riddings, The *NG4: Neth* .....2A 48
  *(off Morris St.)*
Ridding Ter. NG3: Nott .....1E 5 (3G 45)
Riddles Ct. NG16: Want .....5A 18
Ridge La. NG12: Rad T .....4G 49
Ridgeway DE75: Hea .....5D 14
  NG5: Top V .....6C 20
Ridgeway Dr. DE7: Kirk H .....4F 39
Ridgeway Wlk. NG5: Top V .....5E 21
Ridgewood Dr. NG9: Chil .....1C 64
Ridgmont Wlk. NG11: Clif .....5B 66
  *(not continuous)*
Ridgway Cl. NG2: West Br .....6E 59
Ridgway St. NG3: Nott .....3A 46
Ridings, The NG12: Key .....4A 80
  NG14: Bulc .....2G 37
Ridsdale Rd. NG5: Sher .....2G 33
Rifle St. NG7: Radf .....4C 44
Rigg La. NG5: Arn .....1A 10
Rigley Av. DE7: Ilk .....6B 28
Rigley Dr. NG5: Top V .....6C 20
Ring Leas NG12: Cotg .....3F 71
Ringstead Cl. NG2: West Br .....6G 57
Ringstead Wlk. NG5: Bestw .....5F 21
Ringwood Cres. NG8: Woll .....4A 44
Ringwood Rd. NG13: Bing .....5C 50
Ripon Rd. NG3: Nott .....4D 46
Rise, The NG5: Sher .....4H 33
Riseborough Wlk. NG6: Bulw .....4H 19
  *(not continuous)*
Rise Ct. NG5: Sher .....1F 45
Risegate NG12: Cotg .....2F 71
Risegate Gdns. NG12: Cotg .....2F 71
Riseholme Av. NG8: Woll .....6C 42
RISE PARK .....4C 20
Rise Pk. Rd. NG5: Top V .....4B 20
Rise Pk. Shop. Cen. NG5: Top V .....4C 20
RISLEY .....1A 62
Risley Ct. DE7: Ilk .....4B 28
Risley Dr. NG2: Nott .....1F 57
Risley La. DE72: Brea, Ris .....2A 62
Riste's Pl. NG1: Nott .....4F 5 (5H 45)
Ritchie Cl. NG12: Cotg .....3G 71
Ritson Cl. NG3: Nott .....1G 5 (3H 45)
River Cres. NG2: Nott .....1C 58
Riverdale Rd. NG9: Chil .....3D 64
Rivergreen NG11: Clif .....2C 66
Rivergreen Cl. NG9: Bram .....1C 54
Rivergreen Cres. NG9: Bram .....1C 54
Rivermead NG2: West Br .....4H 57
  NG12: Cotg .....2F 71
River Rd. NG4: Colw .....5G 47
Riverside NG14: Stoke B .....1F 49
Riverside Cl. NG9: Bee .....2H 65
Riverside Golf Cen. .....5D 56
Riverside Golf Course .....5D 56
Riverside Point NG7: Lent .....6C 44
Riverside Retail Pk. NG2: Nott .....3E 57
Riverside Rd. NG9: Bee .....2G 65
Riverside Way NG2: Nott .....2F 57
River Vw. NG2: Nott .....2H 57
  NG10: Long E .....4C 72
Riverway Gdns. NG2: Nott .....1H 57
Rivington Rd. NG9: Toton .....3G 63
Robbie Burns Rd. NG5: Bestw .....5G 21
Robbinetts La. NG8: Stre .....6H 29
  NG16: Babb, Coss .....6F 29
  *(not continuous)*

Roberts La. NG15: Huck .....4F 7
Roberts St. DE7: Ilk .....3C 40
  NG2: Nott .....5A 46
Roberts Yd. NG9: Bee .....4G 55
Robert Wilkinson Smith Homes
  NG3: Mapp P .....2G 45
Robey Cl. NG15: Lin .....2H 7
Robey Dr. NG16: Eastw .....2B 16
Robey Ter. NG7: H Grn .....2D 44
Robina Dr. NG16: Gilt .....5E 17
Robin Bailey Way NG15: Huck .....5A 8
Robinet Rd. NG9: Bee .....6F 55
Robin Hood Chase NG3: Nott .....2H 45
Robin Hood Cl. NG16: Eastw .....4B 16
Robin Hood Dr. NG15: Huck .....1E 19
Robin Hood Ind. Est. NG3: Nott .....2H 5 (4A 46)
Robin Hood Rd. NG5: Arn .....4G 21
Robin Hood Statue .....5C 4
Robin Hood St. NG3: Nott .....3H 5 (4A 46)
Robin Hood Ter. NG3: Nott .....2G 5 (4H 45)
Robin Hood Way NG2: Nott .....2F 57
Robinia Cl. NG2: West Br .....6C 58
Robinson Ct. NG9: Chil .....3B 64
Robinson Gdns. NG11: Clif .....4A 66
Robinson Rd. NG3: Mapp .....4B 34
Robinsons Hill NG6: Bulw .....6H 19
Robin's Row NG15: Huck .....6E 7
  *(off Knoll Av.)*
Robins Wood House .....2H 43
Robins Wood Rd. NG8: Aspl .....3H 43
Rob Roy Av. NG7: Lent .....6D 44
Roche Cl. NG5: Arn .....6E 23
Rochester Av. NG4: Neth .....2A 48
Rochester Cl. NG10: Long E .....6C 62
Rochester Ct. NG6: Bulw .....1F 31
Rochester Wlk. NG11: Clif .....4D 66
Rochford Ct. NG12: Edwal .....2E 69
Rock City .....3C 4
Rock Ct. NG6: Basf .....4B 32
Rock Dr. NG7: Nott .....6A 4 (6E 45)
Rocket Cl. NG16: Want .....6A 18
Rockford Ct. NG9: Stap .....2G 53
Rockford Rd. NG5: Sher .....4D 32
Rockingham Gro. NG13: Bing .....5C 50
Rockley Av. NG12: Rad T .....5F 49
  NG16: Newth .....4C 16
Rockley Cl. NG15: Huck .....5C 6
Rockleys Vw. NG14: Lowd .....3G 25
Rock Side NG16: Kimb .....1H 29
  *(off Edgwood Rd.)*
Rockside Gdns. NG15: Huck .....4E 7
Rock St. NG6: Bulw .....5G 19
Rockwell Ct. NG9: Stap .....4G 53
Rockwood Cres. NG15: Huck .....5D 6
Rockwood Wlk. NG15: Huck .....5C 7
Rodel Ct. NG3: Nott .....1F 5 (3H 45)
Roden St. NG3: Nott .....3H 5 (4A 46)
Roderick St. NG6: Basf .....3B 32
Rodice Ct. NG7: Lent .....4C 44
Rodney Rd. NG2: West Br .....5C 58
Rodney Way DE7: Ilk .....4B 28
Rodwell Cl. NG8: Aspl .....3A 44
Roebuck Cl. NG5: Arn .....5F 21
Roecliffe NG2: West Br .....1A 68
Roe Gdns. NG11: Rudd .....6F 67
Roehampton Dr. NG9: Trow .....1F 53
Roe Hill NG14: Woodbo .....5C 12
Roe La. NG14: Woodbo .....1C 24
Roes La. NG14: Calv .....4A 12
Roker Cl. NG8: Aspl .....6G 31
Roland Av. NG11: Wilf .....4F 57
  NG6: Nuth .....3E 31
Rolleston Cl. NG15: Huck .....6D 6
Rolleston Cres. NG16: Want .....4H 17
Rolleston Dr. NG5: Arn .....6C 22
  NG7: Lent .....5D 44
  NG16: Newth .....5C 16
Roman Cres. NG15: Huck .....3B 8
Roman Dr. NG6: Basf .....3C 32
Romans Ct. NG6: Basf .....5C 32
Romilay Cl. NG9: Lent A .....3G 55
Romney Av. NG8: Woll .....1D 55
Romorantin Pl. NG10: Long E .....6G 63
Rona Ct. NG6: Bulw .....2C 32
Ronald St. NG7: Radf .....4D 44
Rookery Gdns. NG5: Arn .....5B 22
Rookwood Cl. NG9: Bee .....5E 55
Roosa Cl. NG6: Bulw .....2F 31
Roosevelt Av. NG10: Long E .....2E 73
Roper Av. DE75: Hea .....5C 14
Ropewalk, The DE7: Ilk .....6C 28
  DE7: Stan C .....6A 26
  DE75: Hea .....5D 14
  NG1: Nott .....3A 4 (4E 45)
Ropewalk Ind. Est. DE7: Ilk .....6C 28
Ropsley Cres. NG2: West Br .....2C 58

Rosa Ct.—St Mary's Cres.

**Rosa Ct.** NG4: Ged 6A **36**
**Roscoe Av.** NG5: Redh 3A **22**
**Roseacre** NG9: Bee 6G **55**
**Rose Ash La.** NG5: Bestw 5F **21**
**Rose Av.** DE7: Ilk 5A **28**
**Rosebank Dr.** NG5: Arn 4D **22**
**Rosebay Av.** NG7: H Grn 1C **44**
**Roseberry Gdns.** NG15: Huck 5A **8**
**Rosebery Av.** NG2: West Br 2A **58**
**Rosebery St.** NG6: Basf 3C **32**
**Rose Cl.** NG3: Nott 2H **45**
**Rose Cotts.** NG14: Bur J 2E **37**
**Rose Ct.** NG10: Long E 4D **62**
**Rosecroft Dr.** NG5: Bestw 1G **33**
**Rosedale Cl.** NG10: Long E 1D **72**
**Rosedale Dr.** NG8: Woll 5B **42**
**Rosedale Rd.** NG3: Nott 3E **47**
**Rose Flower Gro.** NG15: Huck 1A **20**
**Rosegarth Wlk.** NG6: Basf 3B **32**
**Rose Gro.** NG9: Bee 6H **55**
NG12: Key 3H **79**
**Rosegrove Av.** NG5: Arn 4B **22**
**Rose Hill** NG12: Key 4G **79**
**Roseland Cl.** NG12: Key 5G **79**
**Roseleigh Av.** NG3: Mapp 5D **34**
**Rosemary Cl.** NG8: Brox 6E **31**
**Rose M.** NG3: Nott 2H **45**
**Roseneath Av.** NG5: Top V 4C **20**
**Rosetta Rd.** NG7: Basf 6D **32**
(not continuous)
**Rosewall Ct.** NG5: Arn 6D **22**
**Rosewood Cres.** DE75: Hea 3F **15**
**Rosewood Gdns.** NG2: West Br 2G **67**
NG6: Bulw 6F **19**
**Roslyn Av.** NG4: Ged 5G **35**
**Roslyn Ct.** NG14: Bur J 2F **37**
**Rossell Dr.** NG9: Stap 6G **53**
**Rossendale** DE7: Ilk 3A **28**
**Rossett Cl.** NG2: Gam 5F **59**
**Rossington Rd.** NG2: Nott 4B **46**
**Ross La.** NG4: Lamb 6C **24**
**Rosslyn Dr.** NG8: Aspl 5G **31**
NG15: Huck 3A **8**
**Rosthwaite Cl.** NG2: West Br 6E **59**
**Rothbury Av.** NG9: Trow 1F **53**
**Rothbury Gro.** NG13: Bing 4C **50**
**Rothesay Av.** NG7: Lent 4D **44**
**Rothley Av.** NG3: Nott 4B **46**
**Rothwell Cl.** NG11: Wilf 1E **67**
**Roughs Wood La.** NG15: Huck 1D **18**
**Roundwood Rd.** NG5: Arn 6G **21**
**Rowan Av.** NG9: Stap 1G **53**
**Rowan Cl.** DE7: Ilk 4B **40**
NG13: Bing 5G **51**
NG14: Calv 4F **11**
**Rowan Ct.** NG16: Nuth 1B **30**
**Rowan Dr.** NG11: Wilf 1E **67**
NG12: Key 5A **80**
**Rowan Gdns.** NG6: Bulw 6F **19**
**Rowans Cres.** NG6: Cin 3H **31**
**Rowan Wlk.** NG3: Nott 1C **46**
**Rowe Ct.** NG10: Long E 6G **63**
**Rowe Gdns.** NG6: Bulw 1B **32**
**Rowland Av.** NG3: Mapp 5C **34**
**Rowland M.** NG3: Nott 2A **46**
**Rowley Ct.** NG5: Sher 5E **33**
**Rowley Dr.** NG5: Sher 5E **33**
**Rowsley Av.** NG10: Long E 2C **72**
**Roxby Ho.** NG5: Arn 1C **34**
**Roxley Ct.** NG9: Bee 4E **55**
**Roxton Ct.** NG16: Kimb 6H **17**
**Royal Albert Ct.** *NG7: Radf 3E 45*
*(off Russell St.)*
**Royal Av.** NG10: Long E 4F **63**
**Royal Cen.** NG1: Nott 3D **4**
Royal Centre Stop (NET) 3D **4** (4F **45**)
Royal Concert Hall 3D **4** (4G **45**)
**Royal Ct.** *NG5: Sher 5G 33*
*(off Haydn Rd.)*
**Royal M.** NG9: Chil 2C **64**
**Royal Standard Ho.** NG1: Nott 5C **4** (5F **45**)
**Royal Standard Pl.** NG1: Nott 5C **4**
**Royal Victoria Ct.** NG7: Radf 1A **4** (3E **45**)
**Roy Av.** NG9: Bee 1H **65**
**Royce Av.** NG15: Huck 1E **19**
**Royston Cl.** NG2: Nott 2F **57**
**Royston Ct.** NG4: Carl 1E **47**
**Ruby Paddocks** NG16: Kimb 2H **29**
RUDDINGTON 6G **67**
**Ruddington Flds. Bus. Pk.** NG11: Rudd 2H **77**
Ruddington Framework Knitters Mus. 1G **77**
Ruddington Grange Golf Course 3G **67**
**Ruddington La.** NG11: Wilf 5F **57**
Ruddington Station
Great Central Railway 2G **77**
Ruddington Village Mus. 6G **67**
**Rudge Cl.** NG8: Woll 4F **43**
**Ruffles Av.** NG5: Arn 2D **34**
**Rufford Av.** NG4: Ged 5F **35**
NG9: Bram 3A **54**
**Rufford Cl.** NG15: Huck 5A **8**
**Rufford Gro.** NG13: Bing 5D **50**
**Rufford Hall** NG2: Nott 1C **58**
**Rufford Rd.** NG5: Sher 4G **33**
NG10: Long E 3D **72**
NG11: Rudd 6H **67**
**Rufford Wlk.** NG6: Bulw 6H **19**
NG11: Rudd 6H **67**
**Rufford Way** NG2: West Br 5D **58**
RUFFS 6E **7**
**Ruffs Dr.** NG15: Huck 6E **7**
**Rugby Cl.** NG5: Top V 6C **20**
**Rugby Ct.** NG2: West Br 6A **58**
**Rugby Rd.** NG2: West Br 6G **57**
**Rugby Ter.** NG7: H Grn 2D **44**
**Rugeley Av.** NG10: Long E 6H **63**
**Ruislip Cl.** NG16: Kimb 6G **17**
**Runcie Cl.** NG12: Cotg 3F **71**
**Runnymede Ct.** NG7: Radf 2A **4** (4E **45**)
*NG9: Bee 6G 55*
*(off Grove St.)*
*Run Riot 5H 57*
*(within Rushcliffe Arena)*
**Runswick Dr.** NG5: Arn 5B **22**
NG8: Woll 4G **43**
**Runton Dr.** NG6: Basf 3D **32**
**Rupert Rd.** NG13: Bing 5D **50**
**Rupert St.** DE7: Ilk 6C **28**
**Ruscombe Pl.** NG3: Nott 3H **45**
Rushcliffe Arena 5H **57**
**Rushcliffe Av.** NG4: Carl 1F **47**
NG12: Rad T 6F **49**
Rushcliffe Country Pk. 2G **77**
**Rushcliffe Ct.** NG6: Bulw 1B **32**
Rushcliffe Leisure Cen. 1B **68**
**Rushcliffe Ri.** NG5: Sher 2H **33**
**Rushcliffe Rd.** NG15: Huck 6E **7**
**Rushes, The** NG11: Goth 6H **75**
**Rushes Cl.** NG9: Bee 5G **55**
**Rushford Dr.** NG8: Woll 5C **42**
**Rush Leys** NG10: Long E 2F **73**
**Rushmere Wlk.** NG5: Woodt 2B **34**
**Rushton Gdns.** NG3: Nott 2A **46**
**Rushworth Av.** NG2: West Br 3A **58**
**Rushworth Cl.** NG3: Nott 2A **46**
**Rushworth Ct.** NG2: West Br 3A **58**
**Rushy Cl.** NG8: Bilb 4D **42**
**Rushy La.** DE72: Ris 6A **52**
NG10: Sand 5A **52**
**Ruskin Av.** NG9: Chil 1D **64**
NG10: Long E 2D **72**
**Ruskin Cl.** NG5: Arn 6H **21**
**Ruskin St.** NG7: Radf 4C **44**
**Russell Av.** NG8: Woll 4F **43**
**Russell Ct.** NG10: Long E 4F **63**
**Russell Cres.** NG8: Woll 4F **43**
**Russell Dr.** NG8: Woll 4E **43**
**Russell Farm Cl.** NG12: Toll 4F **69**
**Russell Gdns.** NG9: Chil 3C **64**
**Russell Pl.** NG1: Nott 3C **4** (4F **45**)
**Russell Rd.** NG7: H Grn 1D **44**
**Russell St.** NG7: Radf 1A **4** (3E **45**)
(not continuous)
NG10: Long E 4F **63**
**Russet Av.** NG4: Carl 2G **47**
**Russley Rd.** NG9: Bram 3A **54**
**Ruth Dr.** NG5: Arn 4C **22**
**Rutherford Ho.** NG7: Nott 2B **56**
**Ruthwell Gdns.** NG5: Top V 3E **21**
**Rutland Av.** NG9: Toton 3A **64**
**Rutland Gro.** NG10: Sand 6E **53**
**Rutland Rd.** NG2: West Br 2B **58**
NG4: Ged 4F **35**
NG13: Bing 5F **51**
**Rutland St.** DE7: Ilk 5B **28**
NG1: Nott 5C **4** (5F **45**)
**Rutland Ter.** DE7: Ilk 5B **28**
**Rutland Vs.** NG2: Nott 5B **46**
**Ryan Way** NG9: Bee 2G **65**
**Rydal Av.** NG10: Long E 3D **62**
**Rydal Dr.** NG9: Bram 3D **54**
NG15: Huck 3F **7**
**Rydale Rd.** NG5: Sher 2G **33**
**Rydal Gdns.** NG2: West Br 6C **58**
**Rydal Gro.** NG6: Basf 4C **32**
**Ryder St.** NG6: Basf 3B **32**
**Ryecroft St.** NG9: Stap 2G **53**
**Ryefield Av.** DE7: Ilk 2B **28**
**Ryehill Cl.** NG2: Nott 1H **57**
**Ryehill St.** NG2: Nott 1H **57**
**Ryeland Gdns.** NG2: Nott 1G **57**
**Ryemere Cl.** NG16: Eastw 3A **16**
**Ryemere Ct.** *NG16: Eastw 3A 16*
*(off Bailey Gro. Rd.)*
**Rye St.** NG7: Basf 6D **32**
**Ryknield Rd.** NG15: Huck 3B **8**
RYLANDS 6H **55**
**Rylands Cl.** NG9: Bee 1H **65**
**Rylands Ct.** NG9: Bee 6G **55**
**Ryton Ct.** NG2: Nott 2H **57**
**Ryton Sq.** NG8: Aspl 6H **31**

## S

**Saco Ho.** NG1: Nott 4B **4** (5F **45**)
**Saddlers Ga.** NG12: Rad T 6F **49**
**Saddlers Yd.** NG12: Plum 6G **69**
**Saddleworth Ct.** NG3: Nott 2G **45**
**Saffron Gdns.** NG2: Nott 1F **57**
**St Agnes Cl.** NG8: Bilb 1D **42**
**St Aidans Ct.** NG6: Basf 3C **32**
**St Albans Cl.** NG10: Long E 2G **73**
**St Albans M.** NG6: Bulw 1B **32**
**St Albans Rd.** NG5: Arn 6H **21**
NG6: Bestw V 1C **20**
NG6: Bulw 5A **20**
**St Albans St.** NG5: Sher 4G **33**
**St Andrew Cl.** NG11: Goth 6H **75**
**St Andrews Cl.** NG6: Bulw 6A **20**
NG15: Huck 3F **7**
**St Andrews Ct.** NG6: Bulw 6B **20**
**St Andrew's Dr.** DE7: Ilk 1A **40**
**St Andrews Ho.** NG3: Mapp 4E **35**
**St Andrews M.** DE7: Stan 4A **38**
**St Andrew's Rd.** NG3: Mapp P 2F **45**
ST ANN'S 3H **45**
**St Ann's Gdns.** NG3: Nott 2A **46**
**St Ann's Hill** NG3: Nott 2G **45**
**St Ann's Hill Rd.** NG3: Nott 2G **45**
**St Ann's St.** NG1: Nott 2E **5** (4G **45**)
**St Ann's Valley** NG3: Nott 3A **46**
**St Ann's Way** NG3: Nott 1E **5** (3G **45**)
**St Ann's Well Rd.** NG3: Nott 2F **5** (4H **45**)
**St Anthony Ct.** NG7: Lent 1C **56**
**St Augustines Cl.** NG7: Basf 6E **33**
**St Austell Dr.** NG11: Wilf 6F **57**
**St Austins Ct.** NG4: Carl 1H **47**
**St Austins Dr.** NG4: Carl 1H **47**
St Barnabas' RC Cathedral 3B **4** (5F **45**)
**St Bartholomews Ct.** NG3: Nott 2B **46**
**St Bartholomew's Rd.** NG3: Nott 2B **46**
**St Catherines St.** NG12: Rad T 1E **61**
**St Cecilia Gdns.** NG3: Nott 3H **45**
**St Chads** NG4: Carl 2H **47**
**St Chad's Rd.** NG3: Nott 4A **46**
**St Christopher St.** NG2: Nott 5B **46**
**St Cuthbert's Rd.** NG3: Nott 4A **46**
**St Emmanuel Vw.** NG5: Arn 4F **21**
**St Ervan Rd.** NG11: Wilf 5F **57**
**St Georges Dr.** NG2: Nott 1G **57**
NG9: Toton 3H **63**
**St Helens Cres.** NG9: Trow 5E **41**
NG14: Bur J 3F **37**
**St Helen's Gro.** NG14: Bur J 4E **37**
**St Helens Rd.** NG2: West Br 5B **58**
**St Helen's St.** NG7: Nott 3A **4** (4E **45**)
**St Helier** NG7: Nott 5A **4** (5E **45**)
**St James Av.** DE7: Ilk 2C **40**
**St James Ct.** NG3: Mapp 5D **34**
NG10: Sand 2D **62**
**St James's St.** NG1: Nott 5C **4** (5F **45**)
**St James's Ter.** NG1: Nott 5C **4** (5F **45**)
**St James St.** NG9: Stap 5E **53**
**St James Ter.** NG9: Stap 5E **53**
**St John's Ct.** NG4: Carl 2F **47**
**St John's Cres.** NG15: Huck 6A **8**
**St John's Rd.** DE7: Ilk 2C **40**
NG11: Rudd 6G **67**
**St Johns St.** NG10: Long E 6F **63**
**St Jude's Av.** NG3: Mapp 5H **33**
**St Laurence Ct.** NG10: Long E 1G **73**
**St Lawrence Blvd.** NG12: Rad T 1D **60**
**St Lawrence Cl.** DE75: Hea 3D **14**
**St Leonard's Dr.** NG8: Woll 5F **43**
**St Leven Cl.** NG8: Bilb 1D **42**
**St Lukes Cl.** NG2: West Br 6D **58**
**St Luke's St.** NG3: Nott 3H **5** (4A **46**)
**St Lukes Way** NG14: Stoke B 1F **49**
**St Margaret's Av.** NG8: Aspl 1A **44**
**St Mark's St.** NG3: Nott 2F **5** (4H **45**)
**St Martins Cl.** NG8: Stre 1E **43**
**St Martin's Gdns.** NG8: Stre 1D **42**
**St Martin's Rd.** NG8: Stre 1E **43**
**St Mary Ct.** *DE7: Ilk 1A 40*
*(off St Mary St.)*
**St Mary's Av.** NG4: Ged 5G **35**
St Mary's Church 5F **5**
**St Mary's Cl.** NG5: Arn 4B **22**
NG9: Atten 4D **64**
**St Mary's Cres.** NG11: Rudd 6G **67**

St Mary's Ga. NG1: Nott . . . . . . . . . . . . .4F 5 (5H 45)
St Mary's Pl. NG1: Nott . . . . . . . . . . . . .4F 5 (5H 45)
St Marys Rd. NG13: Bing . . . . . . . . . . . . . .4F 51
St Mary St. DE7: Ilk . . . . . . . . . . . . . . . . .1A 40
St Marys Vw. NG15: Huck . . . . . . . . . . . . . .4G 7
(off Ogle St.)
St Marys Way NG15: Huck . . . . . . . . . . . . . .3F 7
St Matthias Rd. NG3: Nott . . . . . . . . . . . . .3A 46
St Mawes Av. NG11: Wilf . . . . . . . . . . . . . .5F 57
St Michael's Av. NG4: Ged . . . . . . . . . . . . .5G 35
NG8: Bilb . . . . . . . . . . . . . . . . .1D 42
St Michaels Sq. NG9: Bram . . . . . . . . . . . .3B 54
St Michaels Vw. NG15: Huck . . . . . . . . . . . .2H 7
St Nicholas Cl. NG5: Arn . . . . . . . . . . . . . .6A 22
St Nicholas St. NG1: Nott . . . . . . .5D 4 (5G 45)
St Norbert Dr. DE7: Kirk H . . . . . . . . . . . .4G 39
St Patrick's Rd. NG15: Huck . . . . . . . . . . . . .4F 7
NG16: Nuth . . . . . . . . . . . . . . . .1B 30
St Paul's Av. NG7: H Grn . . . . . . . . . . . . . .2D 44
St Pauls Ct. NG16: Kimb . . . . . . . . . . . . . .1H 29
St Paul's St. NG8: Radf . . . . . . . . . . . . . .4B 44
St Paul's Ter. NG7: H Grn . . . . . . . . . . . . .2D 44
St Peters Chambers NG1: Nott . . . . . . . . . . . .4E 5
(off Bank Pl.)
St Peter's Chu. Wlk. NG1: Nott . . .4E 5 (5G 45)
St Peters Ct. NG7: Radf . . . . . . . . . . . . . .4B 44
St Peters Cres. NG11: Rudd . . . . . . . . . . . . .6G 67
St Peter's Ga. NG1: Nott . . . . . .4E 5 (5G 45)
St Peter's Sq. NG1: Nott . . . . . . . . . . . . . .4E 5
St Peter's St. NG7: Radf . . . . . . . . . . . . . .4C 44
St Saviours Gdns. NG2: Nott . . . . . . . . . . . .1H 57
St Stephen's Av. NG2: Nott . . . . . . . . . . . .5B 46
St Stephen's Rd. NG2: Nott . . . . . . . . . . . .5A 46
St Vincent Cl. NG10: Long E . . . . . . . . . . . .1G 73
St Wilfrids Chu. Dr. NG11: Wilf . . . . . . . . . .3F 57
St Wilfrid's Rd. DE7: West H . . . . . . . . . . . .2C 38
St Wilfrid's Sq. NG14: Calv . . . . . . . . . . . .4H 11
Salamander Cl. NG4: Carl . . . . . . . . . . . . .5F 35
Salcey Dr. NG9: Trow . . . . . . . . . . . . . . . .1F 53
Salcombe Cir. NG5: Redh . . . . . . . . . . . . .4H 21
Salcombe Cl. NG16: Newth . . . . . . . . . . . . .4E 17
Salcombe Cres. NG11: Rudd . . . . . . . . . . . .5H 67
Salcombe Dr. NG5: Redh . . . . . . . . . . . . .4H 21
Salcombe Rd. NG5: Sher . . . . . . . . . . . . . .4D 32
Salford Gdns. NG3: Nott . . . . . . . . . .2G 5 (4H 45)
(not continuous)
Salisbury Ct. NG3: Mapp . . . . . . . . . . . . . .5A 34
Salisbury Sq. NG7: Lent . . . . . . . . . . . . . .5C 44
Salisbury St. NG7: Lent . . . . . . . . . . . . . .4C 44
NG9: Bee . . . . . . . . . . . . . . . . .4G 55
NG10: Long E . . . . . . . . . . . . . . .6G 63
Salmon Cl. NG6: Bulw . . . . . . . . . . . . . . .6F 19
Salop St. NG5: Arn . . . . . . . . . . . . . . . . .6H 21
Saltburn Rd. NG8: Bilb . . . . . . . . . . . . . .3G 43
Saltby Grn. NG2: West Br . . . . . . . . . . . . .2F 67
Salterford Av. NG14: Calv . . . . . . . . . . . . .3H 11
Salterford Rd. NG15: Huck . . . . . . . . . . . . .6E 7
Saltford Cl. NG4: Ged . . . . . . . . . . . . . . .5H 35
Salthouse Cl. NG9: Bee . . . . . . . . . . . . . .3G 55
Salthouse Ct. NG9: Bee . . . . . . . . . . . . . .3G 55
Salthouse La. NG9: Bee . . . . . . . . . . . . . .3G 55
Saltney Way NG11: Wilf . . . . . . . . . . . . . .2E 67
Samson Ct. NG11: Rudd . . . . . . . . . . . . . .5F 67
Sandale Cl. NG2: Gam . . . . . . . . . . . . . . .5E 59
Sandays Cl. NG2: Nott . . . . . . . . . . . . . . .2G 57
Sandby NG1: Nott . . . . . . . . . . . . . . . . . . .2C 4
Sandby Ct. NG9: Chil . . . . . . . . . . . . . . . .6C 54
Sanders Cl. DE7: Ilk . . . . . . . . . . . . . . . .5G 27
Sanderson Dr. NG3: Mapp . . . . . . . . . . . . .1F 35
Sandfield Ct. NG6: Bulw . . . . . . . . . . . . . .1G 31
Sandfield Rd. NG5: Arn . . . . . . . . . . . . . .1B 34
NG7: Lent . . . . . . . . . . . . . . . . .5D 44
NG9: Toton . . . . . . . . . . . . . . . .3G 63
Sandford Av. NG10: Long E . . . . . . . . . . . .6G 63
Sandford Rd. NG3: Mapp . . . . . . . . . . . . .5B 34
Sandgate NG9: Bram . . . . . . . . . . . . . . . .2D 54
Sandham Wlk. NG11: Clif . . . . . . . . . . . . . .2C 66
Sandhurst Dr. NG9: Chil . . . . . . . . . . . . . .3C 64
NG11: Rudd . . . . . . . . . . . . . . . .1F 77
Sandhurst Rd. NG6: Bulw . . . . . . . . . . . . .4H 19
SANDIACRE . . . . . . . . . . . . . . . . . . . . .6D 52
Sandiacre Friesland Sports Cen. . . . . . . . .6B 52
Sandiacre Rd. NG9: Stap . . . . . . . . . . . . . .5E 53
Sandon St. NG7: Basf . . . . . . . . . . . . . . .6E 33
Sandown Rd. NG9: Toton . . . . . . . . . . . . . .2H 63
Sandpiper Cl. NG13: Bing . . . . . . . . . . . . . .6F 51
Sandpiper Way NG7: Lent . . . . . . . . . . . . .5C 44
Sandringham Av.
NG2: West Br . . . . . . . . . . . . . . .3A 58
Sandringham Cres. NG8: Woll . . . . . . . . . . .4C 42
Sandringham Dr. DE75: Hea . . . . . . . . . . . .3A 14
NG9: Bram . . . . . . . . . . . . . . . .2C 54
Sandringham Pl. DE7: Kirk H . . . . . . . . . . .4H 39
NG15: Huck . . . . . . . . . . . . . . . .3H 7
Sandringham Rd. NG2: Nott . . . . . . . . . . . .5B 46
NG10: Sand . . . . . . . . . . . . . . . .2D 62

Sands Cl. NG4: Colw . . . . . . . . . . . . . . . .4G 47
Sandside NG12: Cotg . . . . . . . . . . . . . . . .3F 71
Sandstone Ct. NG6: Bulw . . . . . . . . . . . . .5G 19
Sandwell Cl. NG10: Long E . . . . . . . . . . . .1C 72
Sandyford Cl. NG6: Basf . . . . . . . . . . . . . .4A 32
Sandy La. NG9: Bram . . . . . . . . . . . . . . . .1D 54
NG12: Hol P . . . . . . . . . . . . . . . .1B 60
NG15: Huck . . . . . . . . . . . . . . . . .4G 7
Sanger Cl. NG11: Clif . . . . . . . . . . . . . . . .5A 66
Sanger Gdns. NG11: Clif . . . . . . . . . . . . . .5A 66
Sankey Dr. NG6: Bulw . . . . . . . . . . . . . . .6G 19
Sapele Cl. NG4: Ged . . . . . . . . . . . . . . . .5A 36
Sarah Av. NG5: Sher . . . . . . . . . . . . . . . .5E 33
Sargent Gdns. NG3: Nott . . . . . . . . . . . . . .3B 46
Sasakatoon Cl. NG12: Rad T . . . . . . . . . . . .1E 61
Saunby Cl. NG5: Arn . . . . . . . . . . . . . . . .6D 22
Saunton Cl. NG12: Edwal . . . . . . . . . . . . . .1E 69
Savages Rd. NG11: Rudd . . . . . . . . . . . . . .4G 67
Savages Row NG11: Rudd . . . . . . . . . . . . .5G 67
Saville Cl. NG9: Stap . . . . . . . . . . . . . . . .3G 53
Saville Rd. NG5: Woodt . . . . . . . . . . . . . . .2B 34
Savoy Cinema
Nottingham . . . . . . . . . . . . . . . .5D 44
Savoy Workshops NG7: Lent . . . . . . . . . . . .6D 44
SAWLEY . . . . . . . . . . . . . . . . . . . . . . .3C 72
Sawley Rd. DE72: Brea, Dray . . . . . . . . . . .6A 62
DE72: Dray . . . . . . . . . . . . . . . .2A 72
Sawmand Cl. NG10: Long E . . . . . . . . . . . .1E 73
Sawmills Ind. Pk. DE75: Los . . . . . . . . . . . .2B 14
Saxby Ct. NG11: Rudd . . . . . . . . . . . . . . .6H 67
Saxelby Gdns. NG6: Bulw . . . . . . . . . . . . .5H 19
SAXONDALE . . . . . . . . . . . . . . . . . . . .5A 50
Saxondale Ct. NG6: Bulw . . . . . . . . . . . . . .4A 20
Saxondale Dr. NG6: Bulw . . . . . . . . . . . . . .2B 32
Saxon Grn. NG7: Lent . . . . . . . . . . . . . . .6C 44
Saxon Way NG12: Cotg . . . . . . . . . . . . . . .4F 71
Saxton Av. DE75: Hea . . . . . . . . . . . . . . .3D 14
Saxton Cl. NG9: Bee . . . . . . . . . . . . . . . .4H 55
Saxton Ct. NG5: Arn . . . . . . . . . . . . . . . .6E 23
Saxton Cl. NG2: West Br . . . . . . . . . . . . . .6H 57
Scafell Cl. NG9: Clif . . . . . . . . . . . . . . . .6B 66
Scala Cinema
Ilkeston . . . . . . . . . . . . . . . . . .1A 40
Scalby Cl. NG16: Eastw . . . . . . . . . . . . . . .3H 15
Scalford Dr. NG8: Woll . . . . . . . . . . . . . . .5A 44
Scarborough Av. DE7: Ilk . . . . . . . . . . . . . .1H 39
Scarborough St.
NG3: Nott . . . . . . . . . . . . .2G 5 (4H 45)
Scarf Wlk. NG11: Wilf . . . . . . . . . . . . . . . .4F 57
Scargill Av. NG16: Newth . . . . . . . . . . . . . .4D 16
Scargill Cl. NG16: Newth . . . . . . . . . . . . . .4D 16
Scargill Rd. DE7: West H . . . . . . . . . . . . . .1C 38
Scargill Wlk. NG16: Eastw . . . . . . . . . . . . .2B 16
Scarrington Rd. NG2: West Br . . . . . . . . . . .2B 58
Sceptre St. NG5: Sher . . . . . . . . . . . . . . .5G 33
School Av. NG15: Huck . . . . . . . . . . . . . . .1D 18
School Cl. NG2: Nott . . . . . . . . . . . . . . . .2H 57
School Gdns. NG25: Oxt . . . . . . . . . . . . . .1B 12
School La. DE7: Stant D . . . . . . . . . . . . . .4B 52
NG9: Chil . . . . . . . . . . . . . . . . .1C 64
NG13: Bing . . . . . . . . . . . . . . . .4E 51
School Sq. DE7: West H . . . . . . . . . . . . . .2C 38
School Wlk. NG6: Bestw V . . . . . . . . . . . . .1C 20
School Way NG2: Nott . . . . . . . . . . . . . . .2H 57
School Woods Cl. DE75: Ship . . . . . . . . . . .1E 27
Science Rd. NG7: Nott . . . . . . . . . . . . . . .2B 56
Scotholme Av. NG7: H Grn . . . . . . . . . . . . .1D 44
Scotland Bank NG12: Cotg . . . . . . . . . . . . .2F 71
Scotland Rd. NG5: Basf . . . . . . . . . . . . . . .4D 32
Scott Av. NG9: Bee . . . . . . . . . . . . . . . . .5F 55
Scott Cl. NG6: Bulw . . . . . . . . . . . . . . . . .2F 31
Scrimshire La. NG12: Cotg . . . . . . . . . . . . .2E 71
Script Dr. NG6: Basf . . . . . . . . . . . . . . . .3C 32
Scrivelsby Gdns. NG9: Chil . . . . . . . . . . . .1D 64
Scrooby Row NG5: Top V . . . . . . . . . . . . . .5E 21
Seaburn Rd. NG9: Toton . . . . . . . . . . . . . .2G 63
Seaford Av. NG8: Woll . . . . . . . . . . . . . . .4H 43
Seagrave Cl. NG5: Arn . . . . . . . . . . . . . . .6A 22
NG8: Stre . . . . . . . . . . . . . . . . .6D 30
Seagrave Rd. NG8: Stre . . . . . . . . . . . . . .6D 30
Seamer Rd. NG16: Kimb . . . . . . . . . . . . . .6H 17
Seathwaite Cl. NG2: West Br . . . . . . . . . . . .1E 69
Seatoller Cl. NG2: West Br . . . . . . . . . . . . .6E 59
Seaton Cres. NG8: Aspl . . . . . . . . . . . . . . .6G 31
Second Av. DE72: Ris . . . . . . . . . . . . . . . .1B 62
NG4: Carl . . . . . . . . . . . . . . . . .2E 47
NG4: Ged . . . . . . . . . . . . . . . . .6H 35
NG6: Bulw . . . . . . . . . . . . . . . . .6H 19
NG7: H Grn . . . . . . . . . . . . . . . .1F 45
NG14: Bur J . . . . . . . . . . . . . . . .3A 56
Sedgebrook Cl. NG6: Basf . . . . . . . . . . . . .4A 32
Sedgemoor Rd. NG10: Long E . . . . . . . . . . .2G 73
Sedgewood Gro. NG11: Clif . . . . . . . . . . . .2C 66
Sedgley Av. NG2: Nott . . . . . . . . . . . . . . .4B 46
Sedgley Rd. NG12: Toll . . . . . . . . . . . . . . .5F 69

Sedgwick St. NG16: Lang M . . . . . . . . . . . .2F 15
Sedley Av. NG16: Nuth . . . . . . . . . . . . . . .1C 30
Seeley Ho. NG1: Nott . . . . . . . . . . . . . . . . .5G 5
(off Malin Hill)
Seely Av. NG14: Calv . . . . . . . . . . . . . . . .3F 11
Seely Rd. NG7: Lent, Radf . . . . . . . . . . . . .4D 44
Sefton Av. NG9: Stap . . . . . . . . . . . . . . . .3G 53
Sefton Dr. NG3: Mapp P . . . . . . . . . . . . . .6H 33
Selby Cl. NG9: Toton . . . . . . . . . . . . . . . .2G 63
Selby La. NG12: Key . . . . . . . . . . . . . . . .5G 79
Selby Rd. NG2: West Br . . . . . . . . . . . . . . .5B 58
Selhurst Ct. NG7: H Grn . . . . . . . . . . . . . .2D 44
Selhurst St. NG7: H Grn . . . . . . . . . . . . . .2D 44
Selkirk Way NG5: Sher . . . . . . . . . . . . . . .6F 33
Sellars Av. NG11: Rudd . . . . . . . . . . . . . . .1G 77
Sellers Wood Dr. NG6: Bulw . . . . . . . . . . . .5F 19
Sellers Wood Dr. W. NG6: Bulw . . . . . . . . . .6E 19
Seller's Wood Nature Reserve . . . . . . . . . . .6E 19
Selside Ct. NG9: Chil . . . . . . . . . . . . . . . .1A 64
Selston Dr. NG8: Woll . . . . . . . . . . . . . . . .6A 44
Selwyn Cl. NG6: Bulw . . . . . . . . . . . . . . . .2C 32
Senso Ct. NG4: Ged . . . . . . . . . . . . . . . . .6B 36
Serif Cl. NG5: Sher . . . . . . . . . . . . . . . . .6F 33
Serina Ct. NG2: West Br . . . . . . . . . . . . . .4A 58
NG9: Bee . . . . . . . . . . . . . . . . .4H 55
Serlby Ri. NG3: Nott . . . . . . . . . . . . . . . .3B 46
Serlby Rd. NG16: Newth . . . . . . . . . . . . . .2C 16
Seven Oaks Cres. NG9: Bram . . . . . . . . . . .2B 54
Seven Oaks Rd. DE7: Stant D . . . . . . . . . . .2C 52
Seventh Av. NG7: Nott . . . . . . . . . . . . . . .6A 56
Severals NG9: Stap . . . . . . . . . . . . . . . . .4H 53
Severn St. NG6: Bulw . . . . . . . . . . . . . . . .6H 19
Seymour Cl. DE7: Ilk . . . . . . . . . . . . . . . .2B 28
Seymour Ct. NG7: Radf . . . . . . . . . .1A 4 (3E 45)
Seymour Pl. NG2: West Br . . . . . . . . . . . . .2D 58
Seymour Rd. NG2: West Br . . . . . . . . . . . . .3D 58
NG15: Huck . . . . . . . . . . . . . . . . .6E 7
NG16: Eastw . . . . . . . . . . . . . . .4B 16
Seymour St. NG3: Nott . . . . . . . . . . . . . . .4A 46
Shackleton Cl. NG8: Stre . . . . . . . . . . . . . .5D 30
Shacklock Cl. NG5: Arn . . . . . . . . . . . . . . .3E 21
Shadwell Gro. NG12: Rad T . . . . . . . . . . . .6E 49
Shady La. NG9: Atten . . . . . . . . . . . . . . . .3D 64
Shaftesbury Av. NG10: Long E . . . . . . . . . . .3D 72
NG10: Sand . . . . . . . . . . . . . . . .6C 52
NG14: Bur J . . . . . . . . . . . . . . . .2G 37
Shaftesbury St. NG7: Basf . . . . . . . . . . . . .6E 33
Shakespeare Cl. NG4: Colw . . . . . . . . . . . .4G 47
Shakespeare Ho. NG1: Nott . . . . . . .2E 5 (4G 45)
Shakespeare Rd. NG16: Aws . . . . . . . . . . . .2E 29
Shakespeare St. NG1: Nott . . . . . . .2C 4 (4F 45)
NG10: Long E . . . . . . . . . . . . . . .4E 63
Shakespeare Vs. NG1: Nott . . . . . . .2D 4 (4G 45)
Shakir Cl. NG7: Basf . . . . . . . . . . . . . . . . .
Shaldon Cl. NG5: Top V . . . . . . . . . . . . . . .4D 20
Shandwick Cl. NG5: Arn . . . . . . . . . . . . . .4D 22
Shanklin Dr. NG9: Stap . . . . . . . . . . . . . . .4F 53
Shanwell Cl. NG8: Stre . . . . . . . . . . . . . . .5D 30
Shardale Gdns. NG6: Basf . . . . . . . . . . . . .3B 32
Sharnford Way NG9: Bram . . . . . . . . . . . . .5B 42
Sharp Cl. DE7: Kirk H . . . . . . . . . . . . . . . .3G 39
NG10: Long E . . . . . . . . . . . . . . .1E 73
Sharpes Way NG6: Bestw V . . . . . . . . . . . . .6F 9
Sharphill Rd. NG12: Edwal . . . . . . . . . . . . .1D 68
Shaw Cres. NG15: Huck . . . . . . . . . . . . . . .1E 19
Shaw Gdns. NG4: Ged . . . . . . . . . . . . . . .1B 48
NG11: Clif . . . . . . . . . . . . . . . . .5A 66
Shaw Rd. NG9: Chil . . . . . . . . . . . . . . . . .3B 64
Shaw St. NG11: Rudd . . . . . . . . . . . . . . . .6G 67
Shaw St. E. DE7: Ilk . . . . . . . . . . . . . . . . .3C 40
Shaw St. W. DE7: Ilk . . . . . . . . . . . . . . . .3C 40
Shearing Cl. NG4: Ged . . . . . . . . . . . . . . .4A 36
Shearing Hill NG4: Ged . . . . . . . . . . . . . . .6A 36
Sheepfold La. NG11: Rudd . . . . . . . . . . . . .1G 77
Sheets Stores Ind. Est. NG10: Long E . . . . . .2F 73
Shelby Cl. NG7: Lent . . . . . . . . . . . . . . . . .5C 44
Sheldon Cl. NG10: Long E . . . . . . . . . . . . .2D 62
Sheldon Rd. DE75: Los . . . . . . . . . . . . . . .1A 14
SHELFORD . . . . . . . . . . . . . . . . . . . . . .6H 37
Shelford Cl. NG9: Chil . . . . . . . . . . . . . . . .1D 64
NG12: Rad T . . . . . . . . . . . . . . . .5G 49
Shelford Cres. NG14: Bur J . . . . . . . . . . . . .3D 36
Shelford Dr. NG13: Bing . . . . . . . . . . . . . .5D 50
Shelford Ri. NG3: Nott . . . . . . . . . . . . . . .3C 46
Shelford Rd. NG4: Ged . . . . . . . . . . . . . . .4E 35
NG12: Rad T, Shel . . . . . . . . . . . . .6F 49
NG13: Newton . . . . . . . . . . . . . .1A 50
Shellburne Cl. NG5: Top V . . . . . . . . . . . . .5C 20
Shelley Av. NG11: Clif . . . . . . . . . . . . . . . .2C 66
Shelley Cl. NG15: Huck . . . . . . . . . . . . . . .5D 6
NG16: Nuth . . . . . . . . . . . . . . . .1B 30
Shelley Rd. NG5: Arn . . . . . . . . . . . . . . . .6H 21
Shelt Hill NG14: Woodbo . . . . . . . . . . . . . .1D 24
Shelton Av. NG15: Huck . . . . . . . . . . . . . . .1A 20
Shelton Gdns. NG11: Rudd . . . . . . . . . . . . .6F 67
Shelton St. NG3: Nott . . . . . . . . . . .1E 5 (3G 45)

Shenfield Gdns. NG5: Top V . . . . . . . . . . . . . . .4B 20
Shepard Cl. NG6: Bulw . . . . . . . . . . . . . . . . . .1F 31
Shepherd Ct. NG15: Huck . . . . . . . . . . . . . . . .1D 18
Shepherd Ho. NG5: Bestw . . . . . . . . . . . . . . . .2E 33
Shepherds Cl. NG8: Bilb . . . . . . . . . . . . . . . . .2G 43
Shepherds Wood Dr. NG8: Aspl . . . . . . . . . . . .2A 44
Shepton Cl. DE7: Ilk . . . . . . . . . . . . . . . . . . . .4H 27
Shepton Cres. NG8: Aspl . . . . . . . . . . . . . . . . .5H 31
Sheraton Dr. NG8: Woll . . . . . . . . . . . . . . . . . .6E 43
Sherborne Rd. NG2: West Br . . . . . . . . . . . . . .6B 58
  NG8: Aspl . . . . . . . . . . . . . . . . . . . . . . . . . .6G 31
Sherbrook Av. NG5: Arn . . . . . . . . . . . . . . . . . .1H 33
Sherbrook Bus. Cen. NG5: Arn . . . . . . . . . . . . .1H 33
Sherbrooke Cl. NG14: Calv . . . . . . . . . . . . . . . .3G 11
Sherbrooke Rd. NG5: Sher . . . . . . . . . . . . . . . .6F 33
Sherbrooke Ter. NG5: Sher . . . . . . . . . . . . . . . .6F 33
Sherbrook Rd. NG5: Arn . . . . . . . . . . . . . . . . . .1G 33
Sherbrook Ter. NG5: Arn . . . . . . . . . . . . . . . . .1H 33
Sheridan Ct. NG1: Nott . . . . . . . . . . . . . . . . . . .1D 4
  NG9: Stap . . . . . . . . . . . . . . . . . . . . . . . . . .2H 53
Sheridan Way NG5: Sher . . . . . . . . . . . . . . . . .4E 33
  NG15: Huck . . . . . . . . . . . . . . . . . . . . . . . . .6G 7
Sheriffs Lea NG9: Toton . . . . . . . . . . . . . . . . . .3G 63
Sheriffs Way NG2: Nott . . . . . . . . . . . . . . . . . .6G 45
Sheringham Cl. NG5: Arn . . . . . . . . . . . . . . . . .1B 34
Sherman Dr. NG9: Chil . . . . . . . . . . . . . . . . . . .3C 64
Sherrington Cl. NG11: Clif . . . . . . . . . . . . . . . . .4A 66
Sherwin Gro. NG7: Lent . . . . . . . . . . . . . . . . . .6C 44
Sherwin Rd. NG7: Lent . . . . . . . . . . . . . . . . . . .6C 44
  NG9: Stap . . . . . . . . . . . . . . . . . . . . . . . . . .2H 53
Sherwin Wlk. NG3: Nott . . . . . . . . . . . .1D 4 (3G 45)
SHERWOOD . . . . . . . . . . . . . . . . . . . . . . . . .4E 33
Sherwood Av. NG5: Sher . . . . . . . . . . . . . . . . .4H 33
  NG14: Calv . . . . . . . . . . . . . . . . . . . . . . . . . .3F 11
Sherwood Ct. NG9: Chil . . . . . . . . . . . . . . . . . .2C 64
  NG14: Calv . . . . . . . . . . . . . . . . . . . . . . . . . .3H 11
Sherwood Gro. NG13: Bing . . . . . . . . . . . . . . . .5D 50
  NG14: Calv . . . . . . . . . . . . . . . . . . . . . . . . . .3H 11
Sherwood Lodge Dr. NG5: Arn . . . . . . . . . . . . .1G 9
SHERWOOD RISE . . . . . . . . . . . . . . . . . . . . .1F 45
Sherwood Ri. NG7: Sher . . . . . . . . . . . . . . . . . .6E 33
  NG16: Eastw . . . . . . . . . . . . . . . . . . . . . . . .4B 16
Sherwood St. NG15: Huck . . . . . . . . . . . . . . . . .5A 8
Sherwood Va. NG5: Sher . . . . . . . . . . . . . . . . .4A 34
Sherwood Wlk. NG15: Lin . . . . . . . . . . . . . . . . .1G 7
Shilling Way NG10: Long E . . . . . . . . . . . . . . . .6C 62
Shilo Way NG16: Aws . . . . . . . . . . . . . . . . . . .3D 28
SHIPLEY . . . . . . . . . . . . . . . . . . . . . . . . . . . .1F 27
SHIPLEY COMMON . . . . . . . . . . . . . . . . . . . .4G 27
Shipley Comn. La. DE7: Ilk . . . . . . . . . . . . . . . .3G 27
Shipley Country Pk. . . . . . . . . . . . . . . . . . . . . .3D 26
Shipley Country Pk. Vis. Cen. . . . . . . . . . . . . . .6C 14
Shipley Ct. DE75: Hea . . . . . . . . . . . . . . . . . . .5B 14
Shipley Ga. NG16: Eastw . . . . . . . . . . . . . . . . .6A 16
Shipley La. DE75: Hea, Ship . . . . . . . . . . . . . . .2D 26
Shipley Ri. NG4: Carl . . . . . . . . . . . . . . . . . . . .2G 47
Shipley Rd. NG8: Brox . . . . . . . . . . . . . . . . . . .5F 31
Shipstones Bus. Cen. NG7: Basf . . . . . . . . . . . .6D 32
Shipstone Street Stop (NET) . . . . . . . . . . . . . . .1D 44
Shipstones St. NG7: Basf . . . . . . . . . . . . . . . . .1D 44
Shipstones Yd. NG6: Bulw . . . . . . . . . . . . . . . .5A 20
Shirebrook Cl. DE7: Ilk . . . . . . . . . . . . . . . . . . .1B 28
Shirebrooke Cl. NG6: Basf . . . . . . . . . . . . . . . .4A 32
Shire Hall & Galleries of Justice Mus.
  . . . . . . . . . . . . . . . . . . . . . . . . . . . . .5F 5 (5H 45)
Shires Dr. NG3: Mapp . . . . . . . . . . . . . . . . . . .5A 34
Shirland Cl. DE7: Ilk . . . . . . . . . . . . . . . . . . . . .2B 28
Shirley Ct. NG9: Toton . . . . . . . . . . . . . . . . . . .3A 64
Shirley Cres. DE72: Brea . . . . . . . . . . . . . . . . .5A 62
Shirley Dr. NG5: Arn . . . . . . . . . . . . . . . . . . . .6D 22
Shirley Rd. NG3: Mapp P . . . . . . . . . . . . . . . . .1G 45
Shirley St. NG10: Long E . . . . . . . . . . . . . . . . .3C 72
Shoreswood Cl. NG5: Bestw . . . . . . . . . . . . . . .5F 21
Shortcross Av. NG3: Mapp . . . . . . . . . . . . . . . .3B 34
Short Hill NG1: Nott . . . . . . . . . . . . . . .5G 5 (5H 45)
Short Stairs NG1: Nott . . . . . . . . . . . . . . . . . . . .5G 5
Shortwood Av. NG15: Huck . . . . . . . . . . . . . . . .6F 7
Shortwood Cl. NG1: Nott . . . . . . . . . .5F 5 (5H 45)
Shorwell Rd. NG3: Nott . . . . . . . . . . . . . . . . . . .2E 47
Shotton Dr. NG5: Arn . . . . . . . . . . . . . . . . . . . .3C 22
Showcase Cinema
  Nottingham . . . . . . . . . . . . . . . . . . . . . . . . .3C 56
Shrewsbury Rd. NG2: Nott . . . . . . . . . . . . . . . .5C 46
Shrimpton Ct. NG11: Rudd . . . . . . . . . . . . . . . .1H 77
Sibson Wlk. NG5: Arn . . . . . . . . . . . . . . . . . . . .3B 22
Sidings, The NG16: Kimb . . . . . . . . . . . . . . . . .1H 29
Sidings La. NG9: Bram . . . . . . . . . . . . . . . . . . .6A 42
Sidlaw Ri. NG5: Arn . . . . . . . . . . . . . . . . . . . . .3F 21
Sidmouth Cl. NG12: Key . . . . . . . . . . . . . . . . . .3G 79
Sidney Rd. NG9: Bee . . . . . . . . . . . . . . . . . . . .4E 55
Sidney St. NG10: Long E . . . . . . . . . . . . . . . . .1F 73
  NG16: Kimb . . . . . . . . . . . . . . . . . . . . . . . . .1H 29
Silbury Cl. NG11: Clif . . . . . . . . . . . . . . . . . . . .6B 66
Sillitoe Ct. NG7: Lent . . . . . . . . . . . . . . . . . . . .4B 44
Sillitoe Way NG7: Lent . . . . . . . . . . . . . . . . . . .5B 44
Silver Birch Cl. NG6: Cin . . . . . . . . . . . . . . . . . .3H 31

SILVERDALE . . . . . . . . . . . . . . . . . . . . . . . . .1E 67
Silverdale NG9: Stap . . . . . . . . . . . . . . . . . . . .6G 53
Silverdale Rd. NG7: Basf . . . . . . . . . . . . . . . . .5D 32
Silverdale Wlk. NG11: Clif, Wilf . . . . . . . . . . . .2E 67
Silverhill Cl. NG8: Stre . . . . . . . . . . . . . . . . . . .5D 30
Silverhow Cl. NG2: West Br . . . . . . . . . . . . . . .6E 59
Silverwood Rd. NG9: Bee . . . . . . . . . . . . . . . . .5E 55
Simkin Av. NG3: Mapp . . . . . . . . . . . . . . . . . . .6C 34
Simkin Wlk. NG10: Long E . . . . . . . . . . . . . . . .6D 62
Simone Gdns. NG11: Clif . . . . . . . . . . . . . . . . .3C 66
Simons Ct. NG9: Bram . . . . . . . . . . . . . . . . . . .2D 54
Sinclair Cl. DE75: Hea . . . . . . . . . . . . . . . . . . . .5B 14
Sir John Robinson Way NG5: Arn . . . . . . . . . . .6H 21
Siskin Cl. NG9: Bram . . . . . . . . . . . . . . . . . . . .5C 54
Sisley Av. NG9: Stap . . . . . . . . . . . . . . . . . . . .5G 53
Sixth Av. NG7: Nott . . . . . . . . . . . . . . . . . . . . .6A 56
Skeavingtons La. DE7: Ilk . . . . . . . . . . . . . . . . .2A 28
Skelwith Cl. NG2: West Br . . . . . . . . . . . . . . . .6E 59
Sketchley Ct. NG6: Bulw . . . . . . . . . . . . . . . . . .6G 19
Sketchley St. NG3: Nott . . . . . . . . . . . . . . . . . .3B 46
Skiddaw Cl. NG2: West Br . . . . . . . . . . . . . . . .6E 59
Skipton Cir. NG3: Nott . . . . . . . . . . . . . . . . . . .3C 46
Skipton Cl. DE7: Ilk . . . . . . . . . . . . . . . . . . . . . .4H 27
Skylark Cl. NG13: Bing . . . . . . . . . . . . . . . . . . .6F 51
Skylark Dr. NG6: Basf . . . . . . . . . . . . . . . . . . . .3B 32
Slack La. DE75: Hea . . . . . . . . . . . . . . . . . . . . .5C 14
Slack Rd. DE7: Mapp . . . . . . . . . . . . . . . . . . . .4D 26
Slade Cl. DE7: Ilk . . . . . . . . . . . . . . . . . . . . . . .4C 40
Slade Rd. NG9: Bee . . . . . . . . . . . . . . . . . . . . .5C 54
Slaidburn Av. NG11: Wilf . . . . . . . . . . . . . . . . .6E 57
Slalom Run NG4: Carl . . . . . . . . . . . . . . . . . . . .6E 35
Slaters Way NG5: Bestw . . . . . . . . . . . . . . . . .2D 32
Sloan Dr. NG9: Bram . . . . . . . . . . . . . . . . . . . .6B 42
Sloane Ct. NG2: West Br . . . . . . . . . . . . . . . . .2G 67
Sloethorne Gdns. NG5: Arn . . . . . . . . . . . . . . . .5H 21
Small's Cft. NG14: Woodbo . . . . . . . . . . . . . . .1C 24
Smedley Av. DE7: Ilk . . . . . . . . . . . . . . . . . . . . .2C 40
Smedley Cl. NG8: Aspl . . . . . . . . . . . . . . . . . . .5H 31
Smedley's Av. NG10: Sand . . . . . . . . . . . . . . . .6D 52
Smeeton St. DE75: Hea . . . . . . . . . . . . . . . . . .4F 15
Smite Ct. NG7: Radf . . . . . . . . . . . . . . . . . . . . .2B 44
Smith Dr. NG16: Lang M . . . . . . . . . . . . . . . . . .2E 15
Smithfield Av. NG9: Trow . . . . . . . . . . . . . . . . .5F 41
Smithurst Rd. NG16: Gilt . . . . . . . . . . . . . . . . . .5C 16
Smithy Cl. NG11: Clif . . . . . . . . . . . . . . . . . . . .3B 66
  NG14: Woodbo . . . . . . . . . . . . . . . . . . . . . . .2C 24
Smithy Cres. NG5: Arn . . . . . . . . . . . . . . . . . . .5B 22
Smithy Row NG1: Nott . . . . . . . . . . . .4E 5 (5G 45)
Smithy Vw. NG6: Bestw V . . . . . . . . . . . . . . . . .6F 9
  NG14: Calv . . . . . . . . . . . . . . . . . . . . . . . . . .4G 11
Smythson Dr. NG8: Woll . . . . . . . . . . . . . . . . . .5E 43
Snape Nook Ct. NG6: Bulw . . . . . . . . . . . . . . . .6F 19
Snape Wood Rd. NG6: Bulw . . . . . . . . . . . . . . . .6F 19
Snead Ct. NG5: Top V . . . . . . . . . . . . . . . . . . . .4E 21
SNEINTON . . . . . . . . . . . . . . . . . . . . . . . . . . .5B 46
Sneinton Blvd. NG2: Nott . . . . . . . . . . . . . . . . .5B 46
Sneinton Dale NG2: Nott . . . . . . . . . . . . . . . . .5B 46
  NG3: Nott . . . . . . . . . . . . . . . . . . . . . . . . . .4C 46
Sneinton Hermitage NG2: Nott . . . . . . . .6H 5 (6A 46)
Sneinton Hollows NG2: Nott . . . . . . . . . . . . . . .5B 46
Sneinton Mkt. Sq. NG1: Nott . . . . . . . . . . . . . . .4A 46
  (off Bath St.)
Sneinton Rd. NG2: Nott . . . . . . . . . . . .4H 5 (5A 46)
Snowdon Cl. NG5: Top V . . . . . . . . . . . . . . . . .4F 21
Snowdrop Cl. NG15: Huck . . . . . . . . . . . . . . . . .1A 20
Soarbank Cl. NG16: Kimb . . . . . . . . . . . . . . . . .6G 17
Sobers Gdns. NG5: Arn . . . . . . . . . . . . . . . . . .1D 34
Softwood Cl. NG6: Bulw . . . . . . . . . . . . . . . . . .6F 19
Soloman Pk. DE7: Ilk . . . . . . . . . . . . . . . . . . . .5D 28
Soloman Rd. DE7: Ilk . . . . . . . . . . . . . . . . . . . .5D 28
Solway Cl. NG9: Chil . . . . . . . . . . . . . . . . . . . .6E 55
Somerby Ct. NG9: Bram . . . . . . . . . . . . . . . . . .5B 42
Somerleyton Dr. DE7: Ilk . . . . . . . . . . . . . . . . .5C 40
Somersby Rd. NG3: Mapp . . . . . . . . . . . . . . . .2B 34
  NG5: Woodt . . . . . . . . . . . . . . . . . . . . . . . . .2B 34
Somerset Cl. NG10: Long E . . . . . . . . . . . . . . .5A 64
Somerton Av. NG11: Wilf . . . . . . . . . . . . . . . . .1E 67
Songthrush Av. NG6: Basf . . . . . . . . . . . . . . . .3B 32
Sophie Rd. NG7: H Grn . . . . . . . . . . . . . . . . . . .3D 44
Sorrel Dr. NG13: Bing . . . . . . . . . . . . . . . . . . . .5C 50
Soudan Dr. NG2: Nott . . . . . . . . . . . . . . . . . . . .2F 57
Southampton St. NG3: Nott . . . . . . . . . . . . . . .3A 46
South Av. NG12: Rad T . . . . . . . . . . . . . . . . . . .5H 49
Southchurch Ct. NG11: Clif . . . . . . . . . . . . . . . .2D 66
Southchurch Dr. NG11: Clif . . . . . . . . . . . . . . . .5C 66
Southcliffe Rd. NG4: Carl . . . . . . . . . . . . . . . . .2F 47
South Ct. NG9: Bee . . . . . . . . . . . . . . . . . . . . .1H 65
Southdale Dr. NG4: Carl . . . . . . . . . . . . . . . . . .2F 47
Southdale Rd. NG4: Carl . . . . . . . . . . . . . . . . . .2F 47
Sth. Devon Av. NG3: Mapp . . . . . . . . . . . . . . . .5D 34
Southey St. NG7: Radf . . . . . . . . . . . . . . . . . . .3D 44
Southfield Rd. NG8: Aspl . . . . . . . . . . . . . . . . . .3B 44
Southfields NG10: Long E . . . . . . . . . . . . . . . . .6G 63
Southfields Cl. NG9: Chil . . . . . . . . . . . . . . . . . .5B 54
Southglade Food Pk. NG5: Bestw . . . . . . . . . . .1C 32
Southglade Leisure Cen. . . . . . . . . . . . . . . . . . .6D 20

Southglade Rd. NG5: Bestw . . . . . . . . . . . . . . . .1C 32
Southlea Rd. NG4: Carl . . . . . . . . . . . . . . . . . . .2F 47
South Pde. NG1: Nott . . . . . . . . . . . . . .4D 4 (5G 45)
Southport Ter. NG7: H Grn . . . . . . . . . . . . . . . .2C 44
Southreef 1,2,3 & 4 NG1: Nott . . . . . . . .6F 5 (6H 45)
South Rd. NG2: West Br . . . . . . . . . . . . . . . . . .5A 58
  NG5: Sher . . . . . . . . . . . . . . . . . . . . . . . . . . .3F 33
  NG7: Nott . . . . . . . . . . . . . . . . . . . . .5A 4 (6E 45)
  (Newcastle Cir.)
  NG7: Nott . . . . . . . . . . . . . . . . . . . . . . . . . . .1B 56
  (West Rd.)
  NG9: Bee . . . . . . . . . . . . . . . . . . . . . . . . . . .1G 66
Sth. Sherwood St. NG1: Nott . . . . . . . . .2D 4 (4G 45)
Southside NG5: Arn . . . . . . . . . . . . . . . . . . . . .5E 23
Sth. Snape Cl. NG6: Bulw . . . . . . . . . . . . . . . . .6F 19
South St. DE7: Ilk . . . . . . . . . . . . . . . . . . . . . . .1A 40
  NG10: Long E . . . . . . . . . . . . . . . . . . . . . . . .6G 63
  NG15: Huck . . . . . . . . . . . . . . . . . . . . . . . . . .4G 7
  NG16: Eastw . . . . . . . . . . . . . . . . . . . . . . . . .3A 16
  NG16: Gilt . . . . . . . . . . . . . . . . . . . . . . . . . . .5E 17
South Vw. Rd. NG4: Carl . . . . . . . . . . . . . . . . . .5F 35
Southwark St. NG6: Basf . . . . . . . . . . . . . . . . .4C 32
Southwell Hall NG8: Woll . . . . . . . . . . . . . . . . .5B 44
Southwell Ri. NG16: Gilt . . . . . . . . . . . . . . . . . .6D 16
Southwell Rd. NG1: Nott . . . . . . . . . . .4H 5 (5H 45)
  NG25: Oxt, Sout . . . . . . . . . . . . . . . . . . . . . . .1C 12
Southwold Dr. NG8: Aspl . . . . . . . . . . . . . . . . .4A 44
Sovereign Cl. NG9: Bee . . . . . . . . . . . . . . . . . .6G 55
Sovereign Gro. NG10: Long E . . . . . . . . . . . . . .6D 62
Sovereign Way DE75: Hea . . . . . . . . . . . . . . . .4B 14
Sowbrook La.
  DE7: D Ab, Stant D . . . . . . . . . . . . . . . . . . . .5H 39
Spalding Rd. NG3: Nott . . . . . . . . . . . . . . . . . . .4A 46
Spaniel Row NG1: Nott . . . . . . . . . . . .5D 4 (5G 45)
Sparrow Cl. DE7: Ilk . . . . . . . . . . . . . . . . . . . . .4C 40
Spean Ct. NG8: Woll . . . . . . . . . . . . . . . . . . . . .4G 43
Spean Dr. NG8: Aspl . . . . . . . . . . . . . . . . . . . . .2H 43
Speedway Cl. NG10: Long E . . . . . . . . . . . . . . .5H 63
Speedwell Cl. NG13: Bing . . . . . . . . . . . . . . . . .5C 50
Speedwell La. NG16: Kimb . . . . . . . . . . . . . . . .1G 29
Spencer Av. NG3: Mapp . . . . . . . . . . . . . . . . . .2E 35
  NG10: Sand . . . . . . . . . . . . . . . . . . . . . . . . .4D 52
Spencer Cl. NG11: Rudd . . . . . . . . . . . . . . . . . .6F 67
Spencer Ct. NG7: H Grn . . . . . . . . . . . . . . . . . .1F 45
Spencer Cres. NG9: Stap . . . . . . . . . . . . . . . . .3H 53
Spencer Dr. NG16: Nuth . . . . . . . . . . . . . . . . . .1C 30
Spey Cl. NG15: Huck . . . . . . . . . . . . . . . . . . . .2D 18
Spicer Cl. NG9: Chil . . . . . . . . . . . . . . . . . . . . .3C 64
Spindle Gdns. NG6: Bulw . . . . . . . . . . . . . . . . .6G 19
Spindle La. NG14: Woodbo . . . . . . . . . . . . . . . .6E 11
Spindle Vw. NG14: Calv . . . . . . . . . . . . . . . . . .5H 11
Spinney, The DE7: Ilk . . . . . . . . . . . . . . . . . . . .3A 40
  DE7: Stant D . . . . . . . . . . . . . . . . . . . . . . . . .3B 52
  NG5: Woodt . . . . . . . . . . . . . . . . . . . . . . . . .3A 34
  NG6: Bestw V . . . . . . . . . . . . . . . . . . . . . . . . .6C 8
  NG14: Bulc . . . . . . . . . . . . . . . . . . . . . . . . . .2H 37
  NG16: Nuth . . . . . . . . . . . . . . . . . . . . . . . . . .4F 31
  (Harcourt Cres.)
  NG16: Nuth . . . . . . . . . . . . . . . . . . . . . . . . . .1B 30
  (Keats Cl.)
Spinney Cl. NG2: West Br . . . . . . . . . . . . . . . . .1D 68
  NG12: Cotg . . . . . . . . . . . . . . . . . . . . . . . . . .3F 71
Spinney Cres. NG9: Toton . . . . . . . . . . . . . . . . .2H 63
Spinney Dr. NG10: Long E . . . . . . . . . . . . . . . . .3E 63
Spinney Hill NG2: West Br . . . . . . . . . . . . . . . . .3H 67
Spinney Ri. NG9: Toton . . . . . . . . . . . . . . . . . . .2G 63
Spinney Rd. DE7: Ilk . . . . . . . . . . . . . . . . . . . . .3A 40
  NG10: Long E . . . . . . . . . . . . . . . . . . . . . . . .3E 63
  NG12: Key . . . . . . . . . . . . . . . . . . . . . . . . . . .4F 79
  NG13: Bing . . . . . . . . . . . . . . . . . . . . . . . . . .5D 50
Spinney Way NG11: Wilf . . . . . . . . . . . . . . . . . .1E 67
Spinningdale NG5: Arn . . . . . . . . . . . . . . . . . . .4D 22
Spire Vw. NG10: Long E . . . . . . . . . . . . . . . . . .3D 72
Spondon Rd. DE7: D Ab . . . . . . . . . . . . . . . . . .6B 38
Spondon St. NG5: Sher . . . . . . . . . . . . . . . . . . .5G 33
Spray Cl. NG4: Colw . . . . . . . . . . . . . . . . . . . . .4G 47
Spridgeon Cl. NG10: Long E . . . . . . . . . . . . . . .3D 62
Spring, The NG10: Long E . . . . . . . . . . . . . . . . .2F 73
Spring Cl. NG16: Want . . . . . . . . . . . . . . . . . . .6A 18
Spring Ct. NG2: West Br . . . . . . . . . . . . . . . . . .3D 58
  NG9: Stap . . . . . . . . . . . . . . . . . . . . . . . . . . .4G 53
Springdale Gdns. NG9: Trow . . . . . . . . . . . . . . .1F 53
Springfield Av. NG10: Long E . . . . . . . . . . . . . .5H 63
  NG10: Sand . . . . . . . . . . . . . . . . . . . . . . . . .2C 62
  NG16: Eastw . . . . . . . . . . . . . . . . . . . . . . . . .3C 16
Springfield Dr. NG6: Bulw . . . . . . . . . . . . . . . . .1F 31
Springfield Gdns. DE7: Ilk . . . . . . . . . . . . . . . . .5B 28
Springfield Mill NG10: Sand . . . . . . . . . . . . . . .5D 52
SPRINGFIELD PARK . . . . . . . . . . . . . . . . . . . .2D 62
Springfield Retail Pk.
  NG6: Bulw . . . . . . . . . . . . . . . . . . . . . . . . . .5A 20
Springfield Rd. NG5: Redh . . . . . . . . . . . . . . . . .4A 22
  NG15: Huck . . . . . . . . . . . . . . . . . . . . . . . . . .5D 6
Springfields NG2: West Br . . . . . . . . . . . . . . . . .5H 57
Springfield St. NG7: Basf . . . . . . . . . . . . . . . . .6D 32

| | | |
|---|---|---|
| Spring Gdns. NG8: Bilb | ....2C 42 | |
| Spring Garden Ter. DE7: Ilk | ....5B 28 | |
| Spring Grn. NG11: Clif | ....6C 66 | |
| Springhead Ct. NG6: Bulw | ....1G 31 | |
| Spring Hill NG16: Nuth | ....2H 29 | |
| Springhill Cl. NG6: Bulw | ....4H 19 | |
| Springland Farm Cotts. | | |
|   NG16: Nuth | ....1D 30 | |
|   (off Watnall Rd.) | | |
| Spring La. DE75: Hea | ....4C 14 | |
|   NG3: Mapp | ....1E 35 | |
|   NG4: Lamb | ....1E 35 | |
| Spring Mdw. NG12: Cotg | ....2G 71 | |
| Spring Moor NG2: Colw | ....4F 47 | |
| Spring Rd. NG6: Bulw | ....6A 20 | |
| Spring St. NG15: Huck | ....3G 7 | |
| Spring Ter. NG16: Nuth | ....2D 30 | |
| Spring Ter. Gdns. NG16: Nuth | ....1D 30 | |
| Springwater Golf Course | ....5C 12 | |
| Springwood Cl. NG14: Calv | ....4A 12 | |
| Springwood Gdns. NG5: Woodt | ....4B 34 | |
| Spruce Gdns. NG6: Bulw | ....6G 19 | |
| Spruce Gro. NG15: Huck | ....6H 7 | |
| Sprydon Wlk. NG11: Clif | ....6D 66 | |
| Square, The NG6: Bestw V | ....1C 20 | |
|   NG8: Woll | ....5E 43 | |
|   NG9: Bee | ....5F 55 | |
|   NG11: Goth | ....6H 75 | |
|   NG12: Key | ....5G 79 | |
| Squires Av. NG6: Bulw | ....4H 19 | |
| Squires Dr. NG6: Bestw V | ....5F 9 | |
| Squires Way NG2: West Br | ....5H 57 | |
| Stacey Av. NG5: Top V | ....6D 20 | |
| Stadium Ind. Pk. NG10: Long E | ....5H 63 | |
| Stafford Av. NG6: Bulw | ....1H 31 | |
| Stafford Ct. NG6: Bulw | ....2F 31 | |
| Staffords Ct. NG4: Neth | ....2A 48 | |
| Stafford St. NG10: Long E | ....5H 63 | |
| Stagsden Cres. NG8: Bilb | ....4C 42 | |
| Staindale Ct. NG8: Aspl | ....6A 32 | |
| Staindale Dr. NG8: Aspl | ....6A 32 | |
| Stainmore Gro. NG13: Bing | ....5C 50 | |
| Stainsborough Rd. NG15: Huck | ....5C 6 | |
| Stainsby Av. DE75: Hea | ....4C 14 | |
| Stakeford Ct. NG5: Arn | ....3B 22 | |
| Stamford Cl. NG10: Long E | ....3G 73 | |
| Stamford Cl. DE75: Hea | ....3C 14 | |
|   (off Nelson St.) | | |
|   NG5: Bestw | ....5F 21 | |
| Stamford Rd. NG2: West Br | ....6B 58 | |
| Stamford St. DE7: Ilk | ....6A 28 | |
|   DE75: Hea | ....3C 14 | |
|   NG16: Aws | ....3E 29 | |
|   NG16: Newth | ....4E 17 | |
| Stancliffe Av. NG6: Bulw | ....6A 20 | |
| Standard Ct. NG1: Nott | ....5C 4 (5F 45) | |
| STANDARD HILL | ....5C 4 (5F 45) | |
| Standard Hill NG1: Nott | ....5C 4 (5F 45) | |
| Standhill Av. NG4: Carl | ....1D 46 | |
| Standhill Rd. NG4: Carl | ....6C 34 | |
| Stanesby Ri. NG11: Clif | ....4C 66 | |
| Stanford Gdns. NG12: Rad T | ....5F 49 | |
| Stanford St. NG1: Nott | ....5D 4 (5G 45) | |
| Stanhome Ct. NG2: West Br | ....1H 67 | |
| Stanhome Dr. NG2: West Br | ....1H 67 | |
| Stanhome Sq. NG2: West Br | ....1H 67 | |
| Stanhope Av. NG5: Sher | ....6F 33 | |
| Stanhope Cres. NG5: Arn | ....5A 22 | |
|   NG14: Stoke B | ....2F 49 | |
| Stanhope Rd. NG4: Ged | ....3F 35 | |
|   NG5: Arn | ....5A 22 | |
| Stanhope St. DE7: Ilk | ....3C 40 | |
|   DE7: Stant D | ....3B 52 | |
|   NG1: Nott | ....4G 5 (5H 45) | |
|   NG10: Long E | ....5F 63 | |
| Stanhope Way NG13: Bing | ....5E 51 | |
| Staniland Cl. NG9: Chil | ....3C 64 | |
| STANLEY | ....3A 38 | |
| Stanley Av. NG7: H Grn | ....1E 45 | |
| Stanley Cl. DE7: Ilk | ....2A 40 | |
| STANLEY COMMON | ....6A 26 | |
| Stanley Ct. NG16: Eastw | ....4B 16 | |
| Stanley Dr. NG9: Bram | ....3A 54 | |
| Stanley M. NG16: Kimb | ....6F 17 | |
| Stanley Pl. NG1: Nott | ....3C 4 (4F 45) | |
| Stanley Rd. NG2: West Br | ....5B 58 | |
|   NG3: Mapp | ....5C 34 | |
|   NG7: H Grn | ....1E 45 | |
|   (not continuous) | | |
| Stanley St. DE7: Ilk | ....2B 40 | |
|   NG10: Long E | ....6G 63 | |
| Stanmore Cl. NG16: Nuth | ....4E 31 | |
| Stanmore Gdns. NG5: Arn | ....1A 34 | |
|   (not continuous) | | |
| Stannier Way NG16: Want | ....6A 18 | |
| Stansfield St. NG7: Lent | ....4C 44 | |
| Stanstead Av. NG5: Top V | ....5B 20 | |
|   NG12: Toll | ....5F 69 | |
| Stanthorne Cl. NG11: Wilf | ....1E 67 | |
| STANTON-BY-DALE | ....3B 52 | |
| STANTON GATE | ....2E 53 | |
| Stanton Ga. DE7: Stant D | ....2E 53 | |
| Stanton La. NG12: Stant W | ....5B 80 | |
| Stanton M. NG12: Stant W | ....5C 80 | |
| STANTON-ON-THE-WOLDS | ....6B 80 | |
| Stanton-on-the-Wolds Golf Course | ....5B 80 | |
| Stanton Rd. DE7: Ilk | ....3B 40 | |
|   NG10: Sand | ....4B 52 | |
| Stanway Cl. NG3: Nott | ....3E 47 | |
| Stanwick Cl. NG8: Bilb | ....1E 43 | |
| STAPLEFORD | ....4F 53 | |
| Stapleford By-Pass | | |
|   NG10: Sand | ....1C 62 | |
| Stapleford La. NG9: Toton | ....1H 63 | |
| Stapleford Rd. NG9: Trow | ....5E 41 | |
| Staplehurst Dr. NG5: Sher | ....3E 33 | |
| Stapleton Rd. DE7: Ilk | ....3A 28 | |
| Starch La. NG10: Sand | ....4D 52 | |
| Starthe Bank DE75: Hea | ....3D 14 | |
| Starth Wood Rd. NG15: Huck | ....1D 18 | |
| Stathern Wlk. NG5: Bestw | ....6F 21 | |
| Station Av. NG4: Ged | ....6A 36 | |
| Station Ct. DE7: Ilk | ....6A 28 | |
|   (off Bath Rd.) | | |
| Station Rd. DE7: Ilk | ....6B 28 | |
|   DE7: Stan, West H | ....1A 38 | |
|   NG4: Carl | ....2G 47 | |
|   NG6: Bulw | ....1A 32 | |
|   NG9: Bee | ....5F 55 | |
|   (not continuous) | | |
|   NG10: Long E | ....5H 63 | |
|   NG10: Sand | ....6E 53 | |
|   NG12: Key, Plum | ....1G 79 | |
|   NG14: Bur J | ....4F 37 | |
|   NG15: Huck | ....4H 7 | |
|   NG16: Aws | ....2E 29 | |
|   NG16: Kimb | ....1H 29 | |
|   NG16: Lang M | ....3E 15 | |
| Station St. DE7: Ilk | ....5C 28 | |
|   NG2: Nott | ....6E 5 (6G 45) | |
|   NG10: Long E | ....6G 63 | |
|   NG13: Bing | ....4F 51 | |
| Station Street Stop (NET) | ....6F 5 (6H 45) | |
| Station Ter. NG12: Rad T | ....2F 49 | |
|   NG15: Huck | ....4H 7 | |
| Station Vs. NG9: Bee | ....6G 55 | |
| Staunton Dr. NG5: Sher | ....3G 33 | |
| Stavely Way NG2: Gam | ....4E 59 | |
| Staverton Rd. NG8: Bilb | ....3D 42 | |
| Steadfold Cl. NG6: Bulw | ....1H 31 | |
| Steads Cl. NG4: Carl | ....2H 47 | |
| Steedman Av. NG3: Mapp | ....3C 34 | |
| Steeles Way NG4: Lamb | ....6B 24 | |
| Steinbeck Rd. NG4: Carl | ....2E 47 | |
| Stella Av. NG12: Toll | ....5F 69 | |
| Stella Gro. NG12: Toll | ....5F 69 | |
| Stepney Ct. NG8: Brox | ....6F 31 | |
| Sterndale Rd. NG10: Long E | ....1D 72 | |
| Steven Cl. NG9: Toton | ....1H 63 | |
| Stevenholme Cres. | | |
|   NG5: Bestw | ....1E 33 | |
| Steven's La. DE72: Brea | ....4A 62 | |
| Stevenson Gdns. | | |
|   NG11: Rudd | ....1H 77 | |
| Stevens Rd. NG10: Sand | ....6C 52 | |
| Stewarton Cl. NG5: Arn | ....4D 22 | |
| Stiles Rd. NG5: Arn | ....1E 35 | |
| Stinsford Cl. NG5: Bestw | ....5G 21 | |
| Stirling Gdns. NG9: Chil | ....3B 64 | |
| Stirling Gro. NG11: Clif | ....5D 66 | |
|   NG16: Kimb | ....6G 17 | |
| Stockdale Cl. NG5: Arn | ....3E 21 | |
| Stockgill Cl. NG2: West Br | ....5E 59 | |
| Stockhill Cir. NG6: Basf | ....4A 32 | |
| Stockhill La. NG6: Basf | ....4A 32 | |
| Stocks Rd. NG16: Kimb | ....6G 17 | |
| Stockton St. NG6: Bulw | ....6H 19 | |
| Stock Well NG6: Bulw | ....1H 31 | |
| Stoddard Dr. DE75: Hea | ....3D 14 | |
| STOKE BARDOLPH | ....1F 49 | |
| Stoke Ferry La. | | |
|   NG12: Shel | ....6F 37 | |
| Stoke La. NG4: Ged | ....6B 36 | |
|   NG14: Stoke B | ....1D 48 | |
|   (not continuous) | | |
| Stokesay Wlk. NG2: West Br | ....6B 58 | |
| Stolle Cl. NG5: Arn | ....6E 23 | |
| Stoneacre NG5: Bestw | ....5F 21 | |
| Stonebridge City Farm | ....2H 5 (4A 46) | |
| Stonebridge Ct. NG3: Nott | ....2H 5 (4A 46) | |
| Stonebridge Rd. NG3: Nott | ....2H 5 (4A 46) | |
| Stonehaven Cl. NG5: Arn | ....4D 22 | |
| Stoneleigh Cl. NG9: Chil | ....6C 54 | |
| Stoneleigh St. NG7: Radf | ....2A 4 (4E 45) | |
| Stone Mdws. NG10: Long E | ....2G 73 | |
| Stonepit Cl. NG3: Nott | ....6B 34 | |
| Stonesby Va. NG2: West Br | ....2F 67 | |
| Stoneycroft Rd. NG6: Bulw | ....2C 32 | |
| Stoney Houghton Gdns. NG6: Bulw | ....5F 19 | |
| Stoney La. NG9: Trow | ....3D 40 | |
| Stoney St. NG1: Nott | ....4F 5 (5H 45) | |
|   NG9: Bee | ....4F 55 | |
| Stony Clouds Local Nature Reserve | ....3D 52 | |
| Stoppard Cl. DE7: Ilk | ....5H 27 | |
| Storey Av. NG4: Ged | ....5G 35 | |
| Stornoway Cl. NG9: Bee | ....6G 55 | |
| Storth Av. NG15: Huck | ....5G 7 | |
| Story Gdns. NG15: Huck | ....6A 8 | |
| Stotfield Rd. NG8: Bilb | ....4B 42 | |
| Stourdale Cl. NG10: Long E | ....1C 72 | |
| Stowe Av. NG2: West Br | ....6H 57 | |
| STRAGGLETHORPE | ....4G 61 | |
| Stragglethorpe La. NG12: Rad T | ....2C 60 | |
| Strand, The NG9: Atten | ....4D 64 | |
| Stratford Cl. NG4: Colw | ....4G 47 | |
| Stratford Rd. NG2: West Br | ....4B 58 | |
| Stratford St. DE7: Ilk | ....3B 28 | |
| Strathglen Cl. NG16: Kimb | ....6G 17 | |
| Strathmore Cl. NG15: Huck | ....6E 7 | |
| Strathmore Rd. NG5: Arn | ....4D 22 | |
| STRELLEY | ....1D 42 | |
| Strelley La. NG8: Stre | ....1B 42 | |
| Strelley Rd. NG8: Bilb, Stre | ....1C 42 | |
| Strelley St. NG6: Bulw | ....6H 19 | |
| Stretton St. NG3: Nott | ....1F 5 (3H 45) | |
| Striding Edge Cl. NG10: Long E | ....3D 62 | |
| Stripes Vw. NG14: Calv | ....5H 11 | |
| Strome Cl. NG2: Nott | ....1G 57 | |
| Strome Ct. NG2: Nott | ....1G 57 | |
| Stuart Cl. NG5: Arn | ....5D 22 | |
| Studio Theatre, The | ....5D 58 | |
| Studland Way NG2: West Br | ....6G 57 | |
| Sturgeon Av. NG11: Clif | ....1D 66 | |
| Sturton St. NG7: H Grn | ....1E 45 | |
| Styring St. NG9: Bee | ....5F 55 | |
| Sudbury Av. DE7: Ilk | ....2C 40 | |
|   NG10: Sand | ....4C 52 | |
| Sudbury Ct. NG10: Long E | ....3B 72 | |
| Sudbury M. NG16: Eastw | ....4A 16 | |
| Suez St. NG7: Basf | ....6D 32 | |
| Suffolk Av. NG9: Bee | ....1A 66 | |
|   NG15: Huck | ....6C 6 | |
| Sullivan Cl. NG3: Nott | ....2B 46 | |
| Sullivan St. NG7: Radf | ....4C 44 | |
| Sumburgh Rd. NG11: Clif | ....4E 67 | |
| Summerfields Way DE7: Ilk | ....3G 71 | |
| Summerfields Way Sth. DE7: Ilk | ....5H 27 | |
| Summer Leys Rd. NG2: Nott | ....6H 45 | |
| Summer Way NG12: Rad T | ....5E 49 | |
| Summerwood La. NG11: Clif | ....5B 66 | |
| Sunbourne Ct. NG7: Radf | ....3E 45 | |
| Sunbury Gdns. NG5: Arn | ....4C 22 | |
| Sunderland Gro. NG8: Stre | ....5D 30 | |
| Sundridge Pk. Cl. NG2: West Br | ....6G 57 | |
| Sunlea Cres. NG9: Stap | ....6H 53 | |
| Sunningdale Dr. NG12: Toll | ....4F 69 | |
| Sunningdale Av. DE75: Hea | ....5D 14 | |
| Sunningdale Dr. DE7: Kirk H | ....4F 39 | |
|   NG14: Woodbo | ....6C 12 | |
| Sunningdale Rd. NG6: Bulw | ....1B 32 | |
| Sunninghill Cl. DE7: West H | ....1B 38 | |
| Sunninghill Dr. NG11: Clif | ....2C 66 | |
| Sunninghill Ri. NG5: Arn | ....4C 22 | |
| Sunnydale Rd. NG3: Nott | ....3D 46 | |
| Sunny Row NG8: Woll | ....4E 43 | |
| Sunnyside Rd. NG9: Chil | ....5C 54 | |
| Sunridge Ct. NG3: Mapp P | ....1G 45 | |
| Sunrise Av. NG5: Bestw | ....2D 32 | |
|   NG6: Bestw | ....6G 9 | |
| Surbiton Ct. DE7: West H | ....1B 38 | |
|   NG3: Mapp | ....6A 34 | |
| Surbiton Sq. NG8: Cin | ....4H 31 | |
| Surfleet Cl. NG8: Woll | ....6C 42 | |
| Surgey's La. NG5: Arn | ....4B 22 | |
| Surrey Ct. NG3: Mapp | ....6A 34 | |
| Susan Cl. NG15: Huck | ....2H 7 | |
| Susan Dr. NG6: Bulw | ....3B 32 | |
| Sussex Cl. NG16: Gilt | ....5C 16 | |
| Sussex St. NG1: Nott | ....5E 5 (5G 45) | |
| Sussex Way NG10: Sand | ....6D 52 | |
| Sutherland Dr. NG2: West Br | ....1C 68 | |
| Sutherland Rd. NG3: Nott | ....2D 46 | |
| Sutton Cl. NG16: Eastw | ....3B 16 | |
| Sutton Gdns. NG11: Rudd | ....1G 77 | |
| Sutton Gro. NG9: Chil | ....5D 54 | |
| Sutton Passeys Cres. NG8: Woll | ....5H 43 | |
| Sutton Rd. NG5: Arn | ....3B 22 | |

Swain's Av.—Todd Cl.

**Swain's Av.** NG3: Nott 3C **46**
**Swale Cl.** NG6: Bulw 6B **20**
**Swaledale Cl.** NG8: Aspl 6B **32**
**Swale Gro.** NG13: Bing 6D **50**
**Swallow Cl.** NG6: Basf 3B **32**
**Swallow Dr.** NG13: Bing 6F **51**
**Swallow Gdns.** NG4: Carl 6D **34**
**Swan Mdw.** NG4: Colw 5G **47**
**Swansdowne Dr.** NG11: Clif 3D **66**
**Swanwick Rd.** DE7: Ilk 2B **28**
**Sweeney Ct.** NG5: Top V 5E **21**
**Sweet Leys Rd.** NG2: Nott 2G **57**
**Swenson Av.** NG7: Lent 6C **44**
**Swift Ct.** NG16: Eastw 3B **16**
**Swigert Cl.** NG6: Bulw 2F **31**
**Swildon Wlk.** NG5: Top V 5D **20**
**Swinburne St.** NG3: Nott 3B **46**
**Swinburne Way** NG5: Arn 6G **21**
**Swindale Cl.** NG2: Gam 4D **58**
**Swindell Cl.** NG3: Mapp 2D **34**
**Swindon Cl.** NG16: Gilt 6E **17**
**Swiney Way** NG9: Chil, Toton 3H **63**
**SWINGATE** 2A **30**
**Swingate** NG16: Kimb 2A **30**
**Swinscoe Gdns.** NG5: Top V 5D **20**
**Swinstead Cl.** NG8: Bilb 3F **43**
**Swithland Dr.** NG2: West Br 1A **68**
**Sycamore Cl.** DE7: Mapp 4D **26**
NG11: Rudd 6H **67**
NG12: Rad T 1F **61**
NG13: Bing 5G **51**
NG15: Huck 6E **7**
**Sycamore Ct.** NG9: Bee 4G **55**
**Sycamore Cres.** NG10: Sand 4C **52**
**Sycamore Dr.** DE7: Ilk 2D **40**
**Sycamore Gdns.** DE75: Hea 4B **14**
**Sycamore Pl.** NG3: Mapp P 1G **45**
**Sycamore Ri.** NG6: Cin 3H **31**
**Sycamore Rd.** NG10: Long E 2E **73**
NG16: Aws 2D **28**
**Sycamores, The** NG16: Eastw 4A **16**
**Syderstone Wlk.** NG5: Arn 2B **34**
**Sydney Gro.** NG12: Rad T 6E **49**
**Sydney Rd.** NG8: Woll 4H **43**
**Syke Rd.** NG5: Top V 5D **20**
**Synge Cl.** NG11: Clif 5A **66**
**Syon Pk. Cl.** NG2: West Br 6G **57**

## T

**Taft Av.** NG10: Sand 5D **52**
**Talbot Ct.** NG12: Rad T 6E **49**
**Talbot Dr.** NG9: Stap 1F **53**
**Talbot St.** NG1: Nott 3B **4** (4F **45**)
**Tamarix Cl.** NG4: Ged 5A **36**
**Tambling Cl.** NG5: Arn 1D **34**
**Tame Cl.** NG11: Clif 1C **66**
**Tamworth Gro.** NG11: Clif 3D **66**
**Tamworth Rd.** DE72: Shar 6A **72**
NG10: Long E 4C **72**
(not continuous)
**Tangmere Cres.** NG8: Stre 6E **31**
**Tanners Wlk.** NG1: Nott 5E **5** (5G **45**)
**Tannery Rd.** NG16: Gilt 6E **17**
**Tannin Cres.** NG6: Bulw 2A **32**
**Tansy Way** NG13: Bing 6C **50**
**Tantum Av.** DE75: Los 1A **14**
**Tanwood Rd.** NG9: Toton 4B **64**
**Tarbert Cl.** NG2: Nott 1F **57**
**Target St.** NG7: Radf 4C **44**
**Tarn Cl.** NG16: Lang M 1F **15**
**Tatham's La.** DE7: Ilk 5A **28**
**Tattershall Dr.** NG7: Nott 4A **4** (5E **45**)
NG9: Bee 4H **55**
**Taunton Rd.** NG2: West Br 5B **58**
**Taupo Dr.** NG15: Huck 6C **6**
**Tavern Av.** NG8: Aspl 5A **32**
**Tavistock Av.** NG3: Mapp P 6G **33**
**Tavistock Cl.** NG15: Huck 6D **6**
**Tavistock Ct.** NG5: Sher 6G **33**
**Tavistock Dr.** NG3: Mapp P 6G **33**
**Tavistock Rd.** NG2: West Br 5B **58**
**Taylor Cl.** NG2: Nott 5C **46**
**Taylor Cres.** NG9: Stap 3H **53**
**Taylor La.** DE75: Los 2B **14**
**Taylor La. Ind. Est.** DE75: Los 2B **14**
**Taylors Cft.** NG14: Woodbo 1B **24**
**Taylor St.** DE7: Ilk 6B **28**
**TDG Pinnacle (Storage Park)** DE7: West H 3C **38**
**Teak Cl.** NG3: Nott 2H **45**
**Tealby Cl.** NG6: Bulw 6F **19**
**Teal Cl.** NG4: Neth 2B **48**
**Teal Wharf** NG7: Lent 1E **57**
**Teasels, The** NG13: Bing 6D **50**
**Technology Dr.** NG9: Bee 6G **55**
**Teesbrook Dr.** NG8: Woll 5B **42**
**Tees Ct.** NG13: Bing 6D **50**
**Teesdale Ct.** NG9: Chil 1A **64**
**Teesdale Rd.** NG5: Sher 5E **33**
NG10: Long E 1C **72**
**Telford Dr.** NG16: Newth 2D **16**
**Teme Ct.** NG2: West Br 6B **58**
**Templar Lodge** NG9: Bee 5H **55**
**Templar Rd.** NG9: Bee 5H **55**
**Templars Ct.** *NG7: Radf* *3B 44*
*(off New Rd.)*
**Temple Cres.** NG16: Nuth 3D **30**
**Temple Dr.** NG16: Nuth 3E **31**
**Templeman Cl.** NG11: Rudd 5F **67**
**Templeoak Dr.** NG8: Woll 6C **42**
**Tenants Hall Cl.** NG9: Lent A 2G **55**
**Tenbury Cres.** NG8: Aspl 6H **31**
**Tene Cl.** NG5: Arn 3B **22**
**Tennis Ct. Ind. Est.** NG2: Nott 6C **46**
**Tennis Dr.** NG7: Nott 4A **4** (5E **45**)
**Tennis M.** NG7: Nott 4A **4** (5E **45**)
**Tennis Vw.** NG7: Nott 4A **4** (5E **45**)
**Tennyson Av.** NG4: Ged 6H **35**
**Tennyson Ct.** NG5: Sher 4F **33**
NG15: Huck 5D **6**
**Tennyson Dr.** NG9: Atten 3D **64**
**Tennyson Grange** NG4: Ged 6A **36**
**Tennyson Rd.** NG5: Woodt 3A **34**
**Tennyson Sq.** NG16: Aws 3E **29**
**Tennyson St.** DE7: Ilk 4A **28**
NG7: Radf 1A **4** (3E **45**)
(not continuous)
**Tenpin**
**Nottingham** 2C **56**
**Tenter Cl.** NG5: Top V 5D **20**
NG10: Long E 2F **73**
**Terrace St.** NG7: H Grn 2D **44**
**Terrian Cres.** NG2: West Br 4B **58**
**Terton Rd.** NG5: Top V 5D **20**
**Tether Art Gallery** 3G **45**
**Tetney Wlk.** NG8: Bilb 2G **43**
**Tettenbury Rd.** NG5: Sher 4D **32**
**Teversal Av.** NG7: Lent 5D **44**
**Tevery Cl.** NG9: Stap 3G **53**
**Teviot Rd.** NG5: Bestw 2D **32**
**Tewkesbury Cl.** NG2: West Br 5C **58**
**Tewkesbury Dr.** NG6: Basf 3C **32**
NG16: Kimb 6G **17**
**Tewkesbury Rd.** NG10: Long E 3G **73**
**Thackeray's La.** NG5: Woodt 2H **33**
**Thackeray St.** NG7: Radf 4D **44**
**Thales Dr.** NG5: Arn 6E **23**
**Thames St.** NG6: Bulw 6H **19**
**Thane Rd.** NG7: Lent, Nott 5B **56**
**Thatchmarsh Cl.** DE7: Ilk 1B **28**
**Thaxted Cl.** NG8: Bilb 3D **42**
**The .......**
Names prefixed with 'The' for example 'The Aerodrome' are indexed under the main name such as 'Aerodrome, The'
**Theatre Royal**
**Nottingham** 3D **4** (4G **45**)
**Theatre Sq.** NG1: Nott 3D **4**
**Thelda Av.** NG12: Key 4G **79**
**Thetford Cl.** NG5: Arn 1C **34**
**Third Av.** NG4: Carl 1D **46**
(not continuous)
NG4: Ged 6H **35**
NG6: Bulw 6H **19**
NG7: H Grn 1F **45**
NG7: Nott 5A **56**
**Thirlmere** NG2: West Br 6E **59**
**Thirlmere Cl.** NG3: Nott 2B **46**
NG10: Long E 3D **62**
**Thirlmere Rd.** NG10: Long E 3D **62**
**Thirston Cl.** NG6: Bulw 6F **19**
**Thistle Cl.** NG16: Newth 5D **16**
**Thistledown Rd.** NG11: Clif 6C **66**
**Thistlegreen Cl.** DE75: Hea 4F **15**
**Thistle Rd.** DE7: Ilk 5C **40**
**Thomas Av.** NG12: Rad T 5H **49**
**Thomas Cl.** NG3: Nott 1G **5** (3H **45**)
**Thomas Forman Ct.** NG5: Sher 6F **33**
**Thompson Cl.** NG9: Chil 2C **64**
**Thompson Ct.** NG9: Chil 4B **64**
**Thompson Gdns.** NG5: Top V 4E **21**
**Thompson St.** NG16: Lang M 2F **15**
**Thoresby Av.** NG2: Nott 6B **46**
NG4: Ged 5F **35**
**Thoresby Cl.** NG12: Rad T 5G **49**
**Thoresby Ct.** NG3: Mapp P 1H **45**
**Thoresby Dale** NG15: Huck 4H **7**
**Thoresby Rd.** NG9: Bram 2C **54**
NG10: Long E 1D **72**
NG13: Bing 5C **50**
**Thoresby St.** NG1: Nott 5H **5** (5A **46**)
**Thor Gdns.** NG5: Top V 4D **20**
**Thornbury Way** NG5: Top V 6D **20**
**Thorncliffe Ho.** NG5: Top V 5C **20**
**Thorncliffe Ri.** NG3: Mapp P 1G **45**
**Thorncliffe Rd.** NG3: Mapp P 1G **45**
**Thorndale Rd.** NG6: Basf 5A **32**
NG14: Calv 4H **11**
**Thorn Dr.** NG16: Newth 5D **16**
**Thorndyke Cl.** NG9: Bee 1H **65**
**Thorner Cl.** NG6: Bulw 2C **32**
**Thorney Hill** NG3: Nott 2B **46**
**THORNEYWOOD** 1C **46**
**Thorneywood Mt.** NG3: Nott 2B **46**
**Thorneywood Ri.** NG3: Nott 2B **46**
**Thorneywood Rd.** NG10: Long E 5H **63**
**Thornfield Ind. Est.** NG3: Nott 4B **46**
**Thornfield Sq.** NG10: Long E 5H **63**
**Thorn Gro.** NG15: Huck 1H **19**
**Thornhill Cl.** NG9: Bram 1B **54**
**Thornley St.** NG7: H Grn 2C **44**
**Thornthwaite Cl.** NG2: West Br 5E **59**
**Thornton Av.** NG5: Redh 4H **21**
**Thornton Cl.** NG8: Woll 5E **43**
**Thorntons Cl.** NG12: Cotg 2G **71**
**Thornton's Holt Camping Pk.** NG12: Rad T 3D **60**
**Thorntree Cl.** DE72: Brea 4B **62**
**Thorn Tree Gdns.** NG16: Eastw 1B **16**
**Thorold Cl.** NG11: Clif 3C **66**
**Thoroton Rd.** NG2: West Br 2B **58**
**Thoroton St.** NG7: Radf 4E **45**
**Thorpe Cl.** NG5: Top V 5D **20**
NG9: Stap 4E **53**
**Thorpe Cres.** NG3: Mapp 5D **34**
**Thorpe Hill Dr.** DE75: Hea 6C **14**
**Thorpe Leys** NG10: Long E 2F **73**
**Thorpe Rd.** NG16: Eastw 1B **16**
**Thorpe's Rd.** DE75: Hea 4B **14**
**Thorpes Rd. Ind. Est.** DE75: Hea 5B **14**
**Thorpe St.** DE7: Ilk 4A **28**
**Thrapston Av.** NG5: Arn 3B **22**
**Thraves Yd.** NG12: Rad T 6E **49**
**Threeleys Cl.** DE7: Ilk 4B **40**
**Three Tuns Rd.** NG16: Eastw 3C **16**
**Threlkeld Cl.** NG2: West Br 5E **59**
**THRUMPTON** 4B **74**
**Thrumpton Av.** NG10: Long E 6H **63**
**Thrumpton Dr.** NG2: Nott 2F **57**
**Thrumpton La.** NG11: Bart F 3F **75**
**Thurgarton Av.** NG2: Nott 5B **46**
**Thurgarton St.** NG2: Nott 5B **46**
**Thurland St.** NG1: Nott 4E **5** (5G **45**)
**Thurlbeck** NG12: Cotg 4G **71**
**Thurlby La.** NG12: Stant W 6B **80**
**Thurlestone Dr.** NG3: Mapp 1E **35**
**Thurloe Ct.** NG2: West Br 2G **67**
**Thurman Dr.** NG12: Cotg 2F **71**
**Thurman St.** DE7: Ilk 3C **40**
NG7: H Grn 3D **44**
**Thursby Rd.** NG11: Clif 2C **66**
**Thymus Wlk.** NG11: Clif 4A **66**
**Thyra Ct.** NG3: Nott 6A **34**
**Thyra Gro.** NG3: Nott 6H **33**
NG9: Bee 5G **55**
**Tidworth Cl.** NG8: Bilb 3G **43**
**Tilberthwaite Cl.** NG2: Gam 5E **59**
**Tilbury Ri.** NG8: Cin 4G **31**
**Tilford Gdns.** NG9: Stap 5G **53**
**Tilstock Ct.** NG16: Want 5A **18**
**Tilton Gro.** DE7: Kirk H 4G **39**
**Tim La.** NG14: Bur J 3F **37**
**Tindall Cl.** NG9: Chil 3B **64**
**Tinker Cft.** DE7: Ilk 2A **40**
**Tinkers Way** NG7: Lent 6F **45**
**Tinsley Rd.** NG16: Eastw 4A **16**
**Tintagel Grn.** NG11: Clif 4C **66**
**Tintern Dr.** NG8: Basf 5B **32**
**Tippett Ct.** NG3: Nott 3B **46**
**Tip Tree Cl.** NG16: Kimb 6H **17**
**Tiree Cl.** NG9: Trow 1F **53**
**Tishbite St.** NG6: Bulw 6H **19**
**Tissington Cl.** NG7: H Grn 1E **45**
NG9: Chil 4C **64**
**Tissington Rd.** NG7: H Grn 1E **45**
**Titchfield Ct.** NG15: Huck 5G **7**
**Titchfield St.** NG15: Huck 4H **7**
**Titchfield Ter.** NG15: Huck 4H **7**
**Tithby Dr.** NG5: Sher 3H **33**
**Tithby Rd.** NG13: Bing 6E **51**
(not continuous)
**Tithe Gdns.** NG5: Top V 4E **21**
**Tithe La.** NG14: Calv 4H **11**
**Tiverton Cl.** NG8: Aspl 5H **31**
NG15: Huck 6D **6**
**Toad La.** NG14: Epp 6G **13**
**Tobias Cl.** NG5: Top V 5D **20**
**Todd Cl.** NG11: Clif 5A **66**

*A-Z Nottingham 123*

Todd Ct. NG11: Clif . . . . . . . . . . . . . . . . . .5A 66
Toft Cl. NG12: Cotg . . . . . . . . . . . . . . . . . .3E 71
Toft Rd. NG9: Chil . . . . . . . . . . . . . . . . . .2A 64
Token Ho. Yd. NG1: Nott . . . . . . . . . . . . . .4E 5
TOLLERTON . . . . . . . . . . . . . . . . . . . . . .4F 69
Tollerton Grn. NG6: Bulw . . . . . . . . . . . . . .2B 32
Tollerton La. NG12: Toll . . . . . . . . . . . . . .5F 69
Tollerton Pk. Caravan Pk. NG12: Toll . . . .5G 59
Tollerton Rd. NG12: Toll . . . . . . . . . . . . . .5F 59
Tollhouse Hill NG1: Nott . . . . . . . . .3C 4 (4F 45)
Tom Blower Cl. NG8: Woll . . . . . . . . . . . . . .4G 43
Tomlinson Av. NG1: Goth . . . . . . . . . . . . . .6G 75
Tonbridge Mt. NG8: Woll . . . . . . . . . . . . . .1D 54
Tonnelier Rd. NG7: Lent . . . . . . . . . . . . . .2C 56
Topliff Rd. NG9: Chil . . . . . . . . . . . . . . . . .3C 64
Top Rd. NG11: Rudd . . . . . . . . . . . . . . . . . .1G 77
Top Row NG14: Stoke B . . . . . . . . . . . . . . . .2D 48
TOP VALLEY . . . . . . . . . . . . . . . . . . . . . .5C 20
Top Valley Dr. NG5: Top V . . . . . . . . . . . . .5C 20
Top Valley Way NG5: Top V . . . . . . . . . . . .6C 20
Torbay Cres. NG5: Bestw . . . . . . . . . . . . . .1F 33
Torkard Ct. NG15: Huck . . . . . . . . . . . . . . . .6G 7
Torkard Dr. NG5: Top V . . . . . . . . . . . . . . .5D 20
Torrington Ct. NG5: Sher . . . . . . . . . . . . . .5H 33
Torvill Dr. NG8: Woll . . . . . . . . . . . . . . . . .4E 43
Torvill Hgts. NG8: Woll . . . . . . . . . . . . . . .4E 43
Toston Dr. NG8: Woll . . . . . . . . . . . . . . . . .5A 44
Totland Dr. NG8: Basf . . . . . . . . . . . . . . . .5B 32
Totland Rd. NG9: Bram . . . . . . . . . . . . . . .1C 54
Totley Cl. NG6: Bulw . . . . . . . . . . . . . . . . .3A 20
Totnes Cl. NG15: Huck . . . . . . . . . . . . . . . .5D 6
Totnes Rd. NG3: Nott . . . . . . . . . . . . . . . . .4D 46
TOTON . . . . . . . . . . . . . . . . . . . . . . . . . . .3A 64
Toton Cl. NG6: Bulw . . . . . . . . . . . . . . . . . .2B 32
Toton La. NG9: Stap . . . . . . . . . . . . . . . . .4F 53
Toton Sidings NG9: Toton . . . . . . . . . . . . .2F 63
Tottle Gdns. NG7: Radf . . . . . . . . . . . . . . .3B 44
Tottle Rd. NG2: Nott . . . . . . . . . . . . . . . . .3E 57
Tourist Info. Cen.
    Nottingham . . . . . . . . . . . . . . . . .4E 5 (5G 45)
Tower Cres. NG16: Kimb . . . . . . . . . . . . . . .3A 30
Towe's Mt. NG4: Carl . . . . . . . . . . . . . . . . .2G 47
Towle St. NG10: Long E . . . . . . . . . . . . . . .3C 72
Towlson Ct. NG9: Chil . . . . . . . . . . . . . . . .2D 64
Towlsons Cft. NG6: Basf . . . . . . . . . . . . . .4B 32
Town End Cotts. NG12: Plum . . . . . . . . . . .6G 69
Townsend Ct. NG5: Top V . . . . . . . . . . . . .4E 21
Townside Cl. NG10: Long E . . . . . . . . . . . .3D 72
Town St. NG9: Bram . . . . . . . . . . . . . . . . . .3B 54
    NG10: Sand . . . . . . . . . . . . . . . . . . . .6D 52
Town Vw. NG16: Kimb . . . . . . . . . . . . . . . .6H 15
Towson Av. NG16: Lang M . . . . . . . . . . . . .3G 15
Towyn Ct. NG5: Bestw . . . . . . . . . . . . . . . .6E 21
Tracy Cl. NG9: Bram . . . . . . . . . . . . . . . . . .2E 55
Trafalgar Cl. NG7: Radf . . . . . . . . . . . . . . .3D 44
Trafalgar Rd. NG9: Bee . . . . . . . . . . . . . . .1G 65
    NG10: Long E . . . . . . . . . . . . . . . . . . .1F 73
Trafalgar Sq. NG10: Long E . . . . . . . . . . . .6H 63
Trafalgar Ter. NG10: Long E . . . . . . . . . . .6G 63
Traffic St. NG2: Nott . . . . . . . . . . . . . . . . .6G 45
Trafford Gdns. NG8: Aspl . . . . . . . . . . . . . .2B 44
Tranby Gdns. NG8: Woll . . . . . . . . . . . . . . .5F 43
Travers Rd. NG10: Sand . . . . . . . . . . . . . . .5C 52
Treegarth Sq. NG5: Top V . . . . . . . . . . . . .4F 21
TREETOPS HOSPICE . . . . . . . . . . . . . . . . .1A 62
Tree Vw. Cl. NG5: Arn . . . . . . . . . . . . . . . . .4G 21
Trefan Gdns. NG5: Bestw . . . . . . . . . . . . . .6E 21
Trefoil Cl. NG13: Bing . . . . . . . . . . . . . . . . .6D 50
Trelawn Cl. NG5: Sher . . . . . . . . . . . . . . . . .5H 33
Tremadoc Ct. NG5: Sher . . . . . . . . . . . . . . .1F 45
Tremayne Rd. NG8: Bilb . . . . . . . . . . . . . . .3C 42
Trenchard Cl. NG13: Newton . . . . . . . . . . .2B 50
Trent Av. NG11: Rudd . . . . . . . . . . . . . . . . .5G 67
Trent Blvd. NG2: West Br . . . . . . . . . . . . . .2B 58
Trent Bridge . . . . . . . . . . . . . . . . . . . . . . .2A 58
Trent Bri. NG2: Nott, West Br . . . . . . . . . . .2A 58
Trent Bri. Bldgs. NG2: West Br . . . . . . . . . .2A 58
Trent Bus. Cen.
    NG10: Long E . . . . . . . . . . . . . . . . . . .3E 63
Trent Cotts. NG10: Long E . . . . . . . . . . . . .1H 73
Trent Ct. NG2: West Br . . . . . . . . . . . . . . . .2C 58
Trent Cres. NG9: Atten . . . . . . . . . . . . . . . .2E 65
Trentdale Rd. NG4: Carl . . . . . . . . . . . . . . .3F 47
Trent Dr. NG15: Huck . . . . . . . . . . . . . . . . .2D 18
Trent Gdns. NG14: Bur J . . . . . . . . . . . . . . .3G 37
Trentham Dr. NG8: Aspl . . . . . . . . . . . . . . .2A 44
Trentham Gdns. NG8: Aspl . . . . . . . . . . . . .2A 44
    NG14: Bur J . . . . . . . . . . . . . . . . . . . .4D 36
Trent Ho. NG10: Long E . . . . . . . . . . . . . . .3C 72
Trent La. NG2: Nott . . . . . . . . . . . . . . . . . .6B 46
    NG10: Long E . . . . . . . . . . . . . . . . . . .3G 73
    NG14: Bur J . . . . . . . . . . . . . . . . . . . .3G 37
TRENTLOCK . . . . . . . . . . . . . . . . . . . . . . .4G 73
Trent Lock Golf Course . . . . . . . . . . . . . . .3F 73
Trenton Cl. NG9: Bram . . . . . . . . . . . . . . . .2A 54
Trenton Dr. NG10: Long E . . . . . . . . . . . . .5A 64

Trent Rd. DE7: Kirk H . . . . . . . . . . . . . . . . .5H 39
    NG2: Nott . . . . . . . . . . . . . . . . . . . . . .5B 46
    NG9: Bee . . . . . . . . . . . . . . . . . . . . . . .1G 65
Trentside NG2: West Br . . . . . . . . . . . . . . .3A 58
    NG9: Bee . . . . . . . . . . . . . . . . . . . . . . .2G 65
                                        (off Riverside Rd.)
Trentside Nth. NG2: West Br . . . . . . . . . . . .2A 58
Trent Sth. Ind. Pk. NG2: Nott . . . . . . . . . . .6C 46
Trent St. NG2: Nott . . . . . . . . . . .6F 5 (6H 45)
    NG10: Long E . . . . . . . . . . . . . . . . . . .5G 63
Trent Vale Rd. NG9: Bee . . . . . . . . . . . . . . .1G 65
Trent Valley Rd. NG4: Ged, Neth . . . . . . . . .2B 48
    NG14: Bur J . . . . . . . . . . . . . . . . . . . .2B 48
Trent Valley Sailing Club . . . . . . . . . . . . .4G 73
Trent Valley Vw. NG3: Mapp . . . . . . . . . . .6C 34
                                        (off Hickling Rd.)
Trentview Ct. NG2: Nott . . . . . . . . . . . . . . .1B 58
Trent Vw. Gdns. NG12: Rad T . . . . . . . . . . .4G 49
Tressall Cl. DE7: Ilk . . . . . . . . . . . . . . . . . .1C 40
Trevelyan Rd. NG2: West Br . . . . . . . . . . . .2B 58
Trevino Gdns. NG5: Top V . . . . . . . . . . . . .4E 21
Trevone Av. NG9: Stap . . . . . . . . . . . . . . . .5G 53
Trevor Rd. NG2: West Br . . . . . . . . . . . . . . .3B 58
    NG9: Bee . . . . . . . . . . . . . . . . . . . . . . .6F 55
Trevose Gdns. NG5: Sher . . . . . . . . . . . . . .4H 33
Treyford Cl. NG11: Wilf . . . . . . . . . . . . . . . .1E 67
Triangle, The DE7: Ilk . . . . . . . . . . . . . . . . .3C 40
    NG2: Nott . . . . . . . . . . . . . . . . . . . . . .1E 57
Tricornia Dr. NG6: Cin . . . . . . . . . . . . . . . . .3H 31
Tring Va. NG5: Sher . . . . . . . . . . . . . . . . . .3E 33
Trinity Av. NG7: Lent . . . . . . . . . . . . . . . . .6C 44
Trinity Cl. DE7: Ilk . . . . . . . . . . . . . . . . . . .4A 28
Trinity Cres. NG4: Lamb . . . . . . . . . . . . . . .6C 24
Trinity Row NG1: Nott . . . . . . . . . .3D 4 (4G 45)
Trinity Sq. NG1: Nott . . . . . . . . . . .3D 4 (4G 45)
Trinity Wlk. NG1: Nott . . . . . . . . . . .3E 5 (4G 45)
Trinity Vw. NG10: Long E . . . . . . . . . . . . . .5G 63
Trinity Wlk. NG1: Nott . . . . . . . . . . .3E 5 (4G 45)
Trinity Way DE75: Hea . . . . . . . . . . . . . . . .5C 14
Trinstead Way NG5: Bestw . . . . . . . . . . . . .6G 21
Triumph Rd. NG7: Lent . . . . . . . . . . . . . . . .5B 44
Trivett Sq. NG1: Nott . . . . . . . . . . . . . . . . .5G 5
Troon Cl. NG16: Kimb . . . . . . . . . . . . . . . . .6G 17
Trough La. NG16: Want . . . . . . . . . . . . . . . .5H 17
Trough Rd. NG16: Want . . . . . . . . . . . . . . .5H 17
Troutbeck NG12: Cotg . . . . . . . . . . . . . . . . .2G 71
Troutbeck Cres. NG9: Bram . . . . . . . . . . . .3C 54
TROWELL . . . . . . . . . . . . . . . . . . . . . . . . .5E 41
Trowell Av. DE7: Ilk . . . . . . . . . . . . . . . . . .4C 40
    NG8: Woll . . . . . . . . . . . . . . . . . . . . . .4B 42
Trowell Gdns. NG8: Bilb . . . . . . . . . . . . . . .4C 42
Trowell Gro. NG9: Trow . . . . . . . . . . . . . . . .6F 41
    NG10: Long E . . . . . . . . . . . . . . . . . . .3D 62
TROWELL MOOR . . . . . . . . . . . . . . . . . . . .4B 42
Trowell Pk. Dr. NG9: Trow . . . . . . . . . . . . . .1F 53
Trowell Rd. NG8: Woll . . . . . . . . . . . . . . . . .5B 42
    NG9: Stap . . . . . . . . . . . . . . . . . . . . . .1G 53
TROWELL SERVICE AREA . . . . . . . . . . . . . .3G 41
Trueman Gdns. NG5: Arn . . . . . . . . . . . . . . .1D 34
Trueman St. DE7: Ilk . . . . . . . . . . . . . . . . . .3B 28
Truman Cl. NG3: Nott . . . . . . . . . . .1F 5 (3H 45)
Truman Dr. NG15: Huck . . . . . . . . . . . . . . . .5G 7
Trumans Rd. NG2: Nott . . . . . . . . . . . . . . . .2H 57
Truman St. NG16: Kimb . . . . . . . . . . . . . . . .6F 17
Truro Cres. NG7: Radf . . . . . . . . . . . . . . . . .2C 44
Tudor Cl. NG4: Colw . . . . . . . . . . . . . . . . . .4G 47
    NG10: Long E . . . . . . . . . . . . . . . . . . .4G 63
Tudor Ct. NG9: Stap . . . . . . . . . . . . . . . . . .6F 53
    NG15: Huck . . . . . . . . . . . . . . . . . . . .6C 6
Tudor Falls DE75: Hea . . . . . . . . . . . . . . . . .2C 14
Tudor Gro. NG1: Nott . . . . . . . . . . . . . . . . .2F 45
Tudor Pl. DE7: Kirk H . . . . . . . . . . . . . . . . .4G 39
Tudor Rd. NG2: West Br . . . . . . . . . . . . . . .4B 58
Tudor Sq. NG2: West Br . . . . . . . . . . . . . . .4B 58
Tudwal Cl. NG5: Bestw . . . . . . . . . . . . . . . .6E 21
Tudwal Wlk. NG5: Bestw . . . . . . . . . . . . . . .6E 21
Tulip Av. NG3: Nott . . . . . . . . . . . . . . . . . . .2H 45
Tulip Rd. NG16: Aws . . . . . . . . . . . . . . . . . .2D 28
Tumble Town Play Cen. . . . . . . . . . . . . . . .5A 22
Tunnel Rd. NG7: Nott . . . . . . . . . . .5A 4 (5E 45)
Tunnicliffe Ct. DE7: Ilk . . . . . . . . . . . . . . . .3B 28
Tunstall Cres. NG8: Aspl . . . . . . . . . . . . . . .6G 31
Tunstall Dr. NG5: Sher . . . . . . . . . . . . . . . .3D 32
Tunstall Rd. NG5: Woodt . . . . . . . . . . . . . .3B 34
Turnberry Cl. DE7: Ilk . . . . . . . . . . . . . . . . .5G 27
    NG9: Bram . . . . . . . . . . . . . . . . . . . . .1H 55
Turnberry Ct. NG12: Edwal . . . . . . . . . . . . .2E 69
Turnberry Rd. NG6: Bulw . . . . . . . . . . . . . .1B 32
Turner Av. NG16: Lang M . . . . . . . . . . . . . .2E 15
Turner Cl. NG5: Sher . . . . . . . . . . . . . . . . . .2F 33
    NG9: Stap . . . . . . . . . . . . . . . . . . . . . .5G 53
Turner Dr. NG16: Gilt . . . . . . . . . . . . . . . . .6D 16
Turner Rd. NG10: Long E . . . . . . . . . . . . . . .3E 73
Turner St. NG15: Huck . . . . . . . . . . . . . . . . .4G 7
Turneys Ct. NG2: Nott . . . . . . . . . . . . . . . .2A 58
Turney St. NG2: Nott . . . . . . . . . . . . . . . . .2H 57
Turnoak Av. DE7: Ilk . . . . . . . . . . . . . . . . . .2B 28

Turnpike La. NG9: Bee . . . . . . . . . . . . . . . . .3G 55
Turnpike Village NG9: Bee . . . . . . . . . . . . .3G 55
Turnstone Wharf NG7: Lent . . . . . . . . . . . .1D 56
Turpin Av. NG4: Ged . . . . . . . . . . . . . . . . . .4F 35
Turton Cl. NG16: Lang M . . . . . . . . . . . . . . .2E 15
Turton Dr. NG5: Arn . . . . . . . . . . . . . . . . . .6A 22
Tuxford Wlk. NG3: Nott . . . . . . . . . . . . . . . .3B 46
Twells Cl. NG3: Nott . . . . . . . . . . . . . . . . . .2B 46
Twelve Houses DE7: Stant D . . . . . . . . . . . .6A 40
Twitchell, The NG9: Chil . . . . . . . . . . . . . . .1E 65
Twycross Rd. NG5: Bestw . . . . . . . . . . . . . .6F 21
Twyford Cl. DE7: West H . . . . . . . . . . . . . . .1B 38
    DE75: Hea . . . . . . . . . . . . . . . . . . . . . .5A 14
Twyford Gdns. NG11: Clif . . . . . . . . . . . . . .1C 66
Twyford Rd. NG10: Long E . . . . . . . . . . . . .3B 72
Tyburn Cl. NG5: Arn . . . . . . . . . . . . . . . . . .4E 21
Tyne Cl. NG8: Aspl . . . . . . . . . . . . . . . . . . .5A 32
Tynedale Cl. NG8: Aspl . . . . . . . . . . . . . . . .6B 32
    NG10: Long E . . . . . . . . . . . . . . . . . . .1C 72
Tyne Gdns. NG15: Huck . . . . . . . . . . . . . . . .2D 18
Tyrian St. NG16: Gilt . . . . . . . . . . . . . . . . . .5D 16

# U

Ulldale Ct. NG9: Chil . . . . . . . . . . . . . . . . . .1B 64
Ullscarf Cl. NG2: West Br . . . . . . . . . . . . . .6E 59
Ullswater Cl. NG2: Gam . . . . . . . . . . . . . . .5F 59
    NG4: Ged . . . . . . . . . . . . . . . . . . . . . .5H 35
Ullswater Cres. NG9: Bram . . . . . . . . . . . . .2C 54
Ullswater Dr. NG15: Huck . . . . . . . . . . . . . .4F 7
Union Cl. NG15: Lin . . . . . . . . . . . . . . . . . . .1G 7
Union Rd. DE7: Ilk . . . . . . . . . . . . . . . . . . . .2A 40
    NG1: Nott . . . . . . . . . . . . . . . . .2E 5 (4G 45)
    NG3: Nott . . . . . . . . . . . . . . . . .2F 5 (4H 45)
Union St. NG9: Bee . . . . . . . . . . . . . . . . . . .5F 55
    NG10: Long E . . . . . . . . . . . . . . . . . . .5G 63
    NG13: Bing . . . . . . . . . . . . . . . . . . . . .5E 51
Unity Cres. NG3: Mapp . . . . . . . . . . . . . . . .5E 35
University Blvd. NG7: Nott . . . . . . . . . . . . . .3H 55
    NG9: Bee . . . . . . . . . . . . . . . . . . . . . . .3H 55
University of Nottingham, The
    Jubilee Campus . . . . . . . . . . . . . . . . .5B 44
    King's Meadow Campus . . . . . . . . . . .2D 56
    University Pk. Campus . . . . . . . . . . . .1A 56
University Pk. NG7: Nott . . . . . . . . . . . . . . .2H 55
Uplands Ct. NG8: Woll . . . . . . . . . . . . . . . . .3F 43
Upminster Dr. NG5: Arn . . . . . . . . . . . . . . .4B 22
    NG16: Nuth . . . . . . . . . . . . . . . . . . . .3D 30
Up. Barn Cl. DE75: Hea . . . . . . . . . . . . . . . .3D 14
Upper Canaan NG11: Rudd . . . . . . . . . . . . .5H 67
Up. College St.
    NG1: Nott . . . . . . . . . . . . . . . . .3B 4 (4F 45)
Up. Dunstead Rd. NG16: Lang M . . . . . . . .2F 15
Up. Eldon St. NG2: Nott . . . . . . . .4H 5 (5A 46)
Up. Orchard St. NG9: Stap . . . . . . . . . . . . .4D 54
Up. Parliament St.
    NG1: Nott . . . . . . . . . . . . . . . . .3C 4 (4F 45)
Up. Wellington St. NG10: Long E . . . . . . . . .4E 63
Uppingham Cres. NG2: West Br . . . . . . . . . .6H 57
Uppingham Gdns. NG2: Nott . . . . . . . . . . . .1H 57
Upton Cl. DE75: Hea . . . . . . . . . . . . . . . . . .4E 15
Upton Dr. NG5: Sher . . . . . . . . . . . . . . . . . .2H 33
Upton M. NG3: Nott . . . . . . . . . . . . . . . . . .1D 46
Utile Gdns. NG6: Bulw . . . . . . . . . . . . . . . . .6G 19

# V

Vale, The DE7: Ilk . . . . . . . . . . . . . . . . . . . .4A 28
Valebrook Rd. NG5: Sher . . . . . . . . . . . . . . .2G 33
Vale Cl. NG16: Eastw . . . . . . . . . . . . . . . . . .3D 16
Vale Cres. Nth. NG8: Aspl . . . . . . . . . . . . . .3B 44
Vale Cres. Sth. NG8: Aspl . . . . . . . . . . . . . .3B 44
Vale Gdns. NG4: Colw . . . . . . . . . . . . . . . . .4F 47
Valerian Way NG13: Bing . . . . . . . . . . . . . . .5C 50
Vale Rd. NG4: Colw . . . . . . . . . . . . . . . . . . .4G 47
Valeside Gdns. NG4: Colw . . . . . . . . . . . . . .4G 47
Valetta Rd. NG5: Arn . . . . . . . . . . . . . . . . . .6D 22
Valeview Ho. NG12: Cotg . . . . . . . . . . . . . .2F 71
Valley Cl. NG4: Carl . . . . . . . . . . . . . . . . . . .6D 34
    NG5: Sher . . . . . . . . . . . . . . . . . . . . . .2H 33
Valley Dr. NG16: Newth . . . . . . . . . . . . . . . .3D 16
Valley Farm Ct. NG5: Top V . . . . . . . . . . . . .5E 21
Valley Gdns. NG2: West Br . . . . . . . . . . . . .6E 59
Valley Ho. NG1: Nott . . . . . . . . . . . . . . . . . .5C 4
Valley Rd. DE7: Kirk H . . . . . . . . . . . . . . . . .4A 40
    NG2: West Br . . . . . . . . . . . . . . . . . . .6C 58
    NG4: Carl . . . . . . . . . . . . . . . . . . . . . .6D 34
    NG5: Basf, Sher . . . . . . . . . . . . . . . . .5D 32
    NG6: Carl . . . . . . . . . . . . . . . . . . . . . .6A 54
    NG12: Rad T . . . . . . . . . . . . . . . . . . .4G 49
    NG16: Kimb . . . . . . . . . . . . . . . . . . . .6F 17
Valley Vw. DE7: Kirk H . . . . . . . . . . . . . . . .4A 40
Valmont Rd. NG5: Sher . . . . . . . . . . . . . . . .4E 33
    NG9: Bram . . . . . . . . . . . . . . . . . . . . .3A 54

Vancouver Av. NG12: Rad T .....1E 61
Vanguard Rd. NG10: Long E .....2F 73
Vantage, The NG7: H Grn .....1F 45
Varden Av. NG9: Lent A .....2G 55
Varney Rd. NG11: Clif .....2D 66
Vaughan Av. NG15: Huck .....2A 8
Vaughan Rd. NG9: Chil .....1A 64
Vedonis Pk. NG15: Huck .....6G 7
Venn Ct. NG9: Bee .....5F 55
Ventnor Ri. NG5: Sher .....3D 32
Ventura Dr. NG6: Bulw .....4A 20
Venus Cl. NG6: Basf .....2C 32
Verbena Cl. NG3: Nott .....2H 45
Verder Gro. NG5: Top V .....5C 20
Vere St. NG6: Bulw .....6H 19
Verne Cl. NG4: Carl .....2E 47
Vernon Av. NG4: Carl .....1H 47
   NG6: Basf .....4C 32
   NG9: Bee .....5F 55
   NG11: Wilf .....3F 57
Vernon Ct. NG12: Rad T .....6F 49
   NG16: Nuth .....4F 31
Vernon Dr. NG16: Nuth .....4F 31
Vernon Pk. Dr. NG6: Basf .....4C 32
Vernon Pk. Trad. Est.
   NG6: Basf .....4C 32
Vernon Pl. NG6: Basf .....3B 32
Vernon Rd. NG6: Basf .....3B 32
Vernon St. DE7: Ilk .....3B 28
   NG1: Nott .....3B 4 (4F 45)
Vernon Works NG6: Basf .....4C 32
Verona Av. NG4: Colw .....3H 47
Veronica St. NG4: Carl .....6F 35
   NG16: Gilt .....5E 17
Veronica Wlk. NG11: Clif .....4A 66
Versailles Gdns. NG15: Huck .....6G 7
Vicarage Av. DE7: Ilk .....3H 27
Vicarage Cl. NG5: Sher .....4D 32
Vicarage Dr. NG14: Bur J .....3E 37
Vicarage Gdns. DE75: Hea .....4D 14
Vicarage Grn. NG12: Edwal .....2D 68
Vicarage La. NG11: Rudd .....6G 67
   NG12: Rad T .....6E 49
Vicarage St. DE7: Ilk .....3H 27
   NG9: Bee .....5E 55
Vickers St. NG3: Mapp P .....1H 45
Vickery Way NG9: Chil .....3B 64
Victor, The NG7: Lent .....1C 56
   (off Leen Ct.)
Victor Cres. NG10: Sand .....1E 63
Victoria Av. DE75: Hea .....4B 14
   NG2: Nott .....5B 46
Victoria Bus. Pk. NG4: Neth .....3B 48
Victoria Cen. NG1: Nott .....2E 5 (4G 45)
Victoria Cen. Sth. NG1: Nott .....3E 5
   (off Clinton St. E.)
Victoria Cl. NG5: Arn .....3B 22
Victoria Cl. DE7: Ilk .....6A 28
   NG10: Long E .....5G 63
Victoria Cres. NG5: Sher .....5H 33
Victoria Emb. NG2: Nott .....2G 57
Victoria Gdns. NG16: Want .....4A 18
Victoria Gro. NG15: Lin .....1H 7
Victoria Hall NG3: Nott .....2F 5 (4H 45)
   (not continuous)
Victoria Leisure Cen. .....3G 5 (4H 45)
Victoria Mkt. NG1: Nott .....3E 5 (4G 45)
Victoria Pk. NG11: Rudd .....6G 67
Victoria Park Leisure Cen. .....6A 28
Victoria Pk. Way NG4: Neth .....3B 48
Victoria Rd. NG2: West Br .....4A 58
   NG4: Neth .....2H 47
   NG5: Sher .....4F 33
   NG10: Sand .....6D 52
   NG11: Bunny .....6A 78
   NG13: Bing .....4G 51
Victoria St. DE7: Ilk .....6A 28
   NG1: Nott .....4E 5 (5G 45)
   NG4: Ged .....6H 35
   NG9: Stap .....4F 53
   NG10: Long E .....2D 72
   NG12: Rad T .....6F 49
   NG15: Huck .....3F 7
   NG16: Eastw .....2B 16
   NG16: Kimb .....1A 30
   NG16: Lang M .....2G 15
Victoria Ter. NG2: Nott .....5A 46
Victor Ter. NG5: Sher .....5G 33
Victory Cl. NG10: Long E .....2F 73
Victory Rd. NG9: Bee .....1G 65
View, The NG9: Bram .....4B 54
Village, The DE7: D Ab .....6D 38
   DE7: West H .....2C 38
Village Cl. NG12: Edwal .....2D 68
Village Rd. NG11: Clif .....3A 66
Village St. NG12: Edwal .....2C 68

Villa Rd. NG3: Mapp P .....2G 45
   NG12: Key .....3H 79
Villa St. NG9: Bee .....4F 55
Villiers Rd. NG2: West Br .....5C 58
   NG5: Woodt .....3H 33
Vincent Av. DE7: Ilk .....1B 40
   NG9: Bee .....6F 55
Vincent Gdns. NG7: H Grn .....2C 44
Vine Cres. NG10: Sand .....5D 52
Vine Farm Cl. DE7: Kirk H .....3H 39
   NG12: Cotg .....2E 71
Vines Cross NG8: Woll .....1E 55
Vine Ter. NG15: Huck .....4H 7
Violet Av. NG16: Newth .....5D 16
Violet Cl. NG6: Basf .....4B 32
Violet Gro. NG15: Huck .....4A 8
Violet Rd. NG2: West Br .....3C 58
   NG4: Carl .....5F 35
Virgin Active
   Nottingham .....6G 5 (6H 45)
Vision Bus. Cen. NG6: Bulw .....4G 19
Vista, The NG9: Stap .....6G 53
Vivian Av. NG5: Sher .....1F 45
Vivian Ct. NG5: Sher .....1F 45
Viyella Gdns. NG15: Huck .....6G 7
Viyella M. NG15: Huck .....5G 7
Voce Gdns. NG15: Huck .....5A 8
Vulcan Cl. NG6: Basf .....3C 32
Vyse Dr. NG10: Long E .....1D 72

## W

Waddington Dr. NG2: West Br .....6H 57
Wade Av. DE7: Ilk .....2C 40
Wades Av. NG7: H Grn .....1C 44
Wades Way NG13: Bing .....6G 51
Wadham Rd. NG5: Woodt .....2A 34
Wadhurst Gdns. NG3: Nott .....1G 5 (3H 45)
Wadhurst Gro. NG8: Woll .....1D 54
Wadsworth Rd. NG9: Stap .....3H 53
Wainfleet Cl. DE7: Ilk .....4G 27
Wainfleet Ct. NG5: Arn .....3C 22
Waingrove NG11: Wilf .....2E 67
Wakefield Av. NG12: Rad T .....5G 49
Wakefield Cl. NG11: Wilf .....6E 57
Wakefield Cft. DE7: Ilk .....4G 27
Walbrook Cl. NG8: Cin .....4G 31
Walcote Dr. NG2: West Br .....6H 57
Walcott Grn. NG11: Clif .....4B 66
Waldeck Rd. NG5: Sher .....4G 33
Waldemar Gro. NG9: Bee .....5G 55
Waldron Cl. NG2: Nott .....1H 57
Walesby Cres. NG8: Aspl .....3A 44
Walgrave Wlk. NG5: Bestw .....6F 21
Walker Cl. DE7: Ilk .....5C 40
Walker Gro. NG9: Stap .....5G 53
Walkers Cl. NG13: Bing .....5E 51
Walker St. NG2: Nott .....3H 5 (5A 46)
   NG16: Eastw .....3C 16
Walker's Yd. NG12: Rad T .....6F 49
Walk Mill Dr. NG15: Huck .....2H 7
Wallace Av. NG4: Carl .....2H 47
Wallace Gdns. NG9: Toton .....3H 63
Wallace St. NG11: Goth .....5H 75
Wallan St. NG7: Radf .....3C 44
Wallet St. NG2: Nott .....1H 57
   NG4: Neth .....2A 48
Wallett Av. NG9: Bee .....3F 55
Wallis St. NG6: Basf .....3C 32
Walnut Cl. DE7: Ilk .....2C 40
   NG2: West Br .....2E 59
Walnut Ct. NG12: Rad T .....6F 49
   (off Walnut Gro.)
Walnut Dr. NG9: Bram .....3B 54
Walnut Gro. NG12: Cotg .....2F 71
   NG12: Rad T .....6F 49
   NG14: Calv .....3H 11
Walnut Tree Gdns. NG6: Bulw .....6F 19
Walsham Cl. NG9: Chil .....3C 64
Walsingham Rd. NG5: Woodt .....2C 34
Walter St. NG7: Radf .....1A 4 (3E 45)
Waltham Cl. NG2: West Br .....5D 58
Walton Av. NG3: Nott .....4B 46
Walton Cl. DE7: West H .....1B 38
   NG4: Carl .....2G 47
   NG12: Key .....4H 79
Walton Cres. NG4: Carl .....2G 47
Walton Dr. NG12: Key .....4H 79
Walton M. NG3: Nott .....2B 46
Walton Rd. NG5: Arn .....4C 22
Walton St. NG10: Long E .....5F 63
Wansbeck Cl. NG7: Radf .....4E 45
Wansford Av. NG5: Arn .....3B 22
Wanstead Way NG5: Top V .....4C 20

Warburton Ct. NG15: Huck .....5H 7
Ward Av. NG3: Mapp .....4D 34
   NG15: Huck .....2F 7
Wardle Gro. NG5: Arn .....5C 22
Wardlow Rd. DE7: Ilk .....4A 28
Ward's La. DE72: Brea .....5A 62
Ward St. NG7: Basf .....1D 44
Wareham Cl. NG2: West Br .....6G 57
   NG8: Cin .....4G 31
Warehouse, The NG1: Nott .....5F 5
Warkton Cl. NG9: Chil .....6C 54
Warner St. NG7: Radf .....4C 44
Warren, The NG12: Cotg .....3F 71
Warren Av. NG5: Sher .....5E 33
   NG9: Stap .....4F 53
Warren Ct. NG9: Stap .....4F 53
Warrender Cl. NG9: Bram .....2C 54
Warrener Gro. NG5: Top V .....5C 20
Warren Hill Cl. NG5: Arn .....6G 21
Warren La. DE74: Lock .....5C 72
   NG10: Long E .....5C 72
Warren Rd. NG15: Huck .....6D 6
Warrington Rd. NG6: Bulw .....6A 20
Warser Ga. NG1: Nott .....4F 5 (5H 45)
Warsop Cl. NG8: Stre .....5D 30
Warton Av. NG3: Nott .....1B 46
Warwick Av. NG5: Woodt .....2A 34
   NG9: Bee .....3F 55
Warwick Dr. DE7: Ilk .....4G 27
Warwick Gdns. NG12: Cotg .....4F 71
Warwick Rd. NG3: Mapp P .....5H 33
   NG10: Long E .....6H 63
Warwick St. NG7: Lent .....1C 56
Wasdale Cl. NG2: West Br .....6E 59
Washdyke La. NG15: Huck .....2E 7
Washington Cl. NG5: Arn .....6B 22
Washington Dr. NG9: Stap .....2H 53
Wasnidge Cl. NG3: Nott .....2G 5 (4H 45)
Wasnidge Wlk. NG3: Nott .....1G 5
Watchwood Gro. NG14: Calv .....3H 11
Watcombe Cir. NG5: Sher .....5F 33
Watcombe Rd. NG5: Sher .....6G 33
Watendlath Cl. NG2: West Br .....6E 59
Waterdown Rd. NG11: Clif .....4B 66
Waterford St. NG6: Basf .....4C 32
Waterfront Plaza NG7: Nott .....6G 5 (6H 45)
Waterhouse La. NG4: Ged .....5A 36
Water La. NG12: Rad T .....6E 49
   NG25: Oxt .....1B 12
Waterloo Cres. NG7: Radf .....3E 45
Waterloo La. NG9: Trow .....3G 41
Waterloo Prom. NG7: Radf .....3E 45
   (not continuous)
Waterloo Rd. NG7: Radf .....3E 45
   NG9: Bee .....6G 55
   NG15: Lin .....1G 7
Watermark Cl. NG5: Sher .....5F 33
Watermark Ho. NG5: Sher .....5F 33
Watermeadows, The NG10: Long E .....5C 62
Water Orton Cl. NG9: Toton .....2G 63
Waters Edge NG11: Wilf .....4F 57
Waterside Cl. NG2: Gam .....5E 59
   NG10: Sand .....2D 62
Waterside Gdns. NG7: Lent .....2C 56
Waterside Retail Pk. DE7: Ilk .....6C 28
Waterside Way NG2: Colw, Nott .....1C 58
Waterway, The NG10: Sand .....1E 63
Waterway St. NG2: Nott .....1H 57
   (Newthorpe St.)
   NG2: Nott .....1H 57
   (Wallet St.)
Waterway St. W. NG2: Nott .....1G 57
Watford Rd. NG8: Aspl .....5H 31
Watkinson St. DE75: Hea .....3B 14
Watkin St. NG3: Nott .....1E 5 (3G 45)
WATNALL .....5A 18
WATNALL CANTELUPE .....5H 17
WATNALL CHAWORTH .....4A 18
Watnall Rd. NG15: Huck .....3D 18
   NG16: Nuth .....1C 30
Watnall Rd. Factory Units NG15: Huck .....6F 7
Watson Av. DE75: Hea .....3D 14
   NG3: Nott .....3D 46
Watson Rd. DE7: Ilk .....5G 27
Waveney Cl. NG5: Arn .....1C 34
Waverley Av. NG4: Ged .....6A 36
   NG9: Bee .....5G 55
Waverley Mt. NG7: Nott .....3E 45
Waverley St. NG1: Nott .....1A 4 (3E 45)
   NG7: Nott .....1A 4 (3E 45)
   NG10: Long E .....5G 63
Waverley Ter. NG1: Nott .....2C 4 (4F 45)
Wayford Wlk. NG6: Bulw .....5H 19
Wayne Cl. NG11: Clif .....4C 66
Wayte Ct. NG11: Rudd .....4A 68
Weardale Rd. NG5: Sher .....5E 33

Wearmouth Gdns. NG5: Top V .............4E 21
Weave Cl. NG6: Basf .............3C 32
Weaver Row DE7: Ilk .............1B 40
Weaverthorpe Rd. NG5: Woodt .............2C 34
Webb Rd. NG8: Bilb .............2H 43
Webster Av. NG16: Eastw .............4B 16
Weedon Cl. NG3: Nott .............4B 16
Weekday Cross NG1: Nott .............5E 5 (5G 45)
Weetman Gdns. NG5: Top V .............5E 21
Weightman Dr. NG16: Gilt .............6D 16
Welbeck Av. DE7: Kirk H .............4H 39
 NG4: Ged .............5F 35
Welbeck Cl. NG5: Woodt .............3C 34
Welbeck Gdns. NG5: Woodt .............3C 34
 NG9: Toton .............2H 63
Welbeck Gro. NG13: Bing .............5C 50
Welbeck Rd. NG2: West Br .............3A 58
 NG10: Long E .............2D 62
 NG12: Rad T .............5G 49
Welbeck Wlk. NG3: Nott .............3G 45
Welbeck Workshops NG3: Nott .............3G 45
 (off Alfred Cl.)
Welby Av. NG7: Lent .............5D 44
Welch Av. NG9: Stap .............3H 53
Weldbank Cl. NG9: Chil .............1B 64
Welham Cres. NG5: Arn .............6C 22
Welland Cl. NG3: Nott .............3B 46
Welland Gdns. NG13: Bing .............6D 50
Wellesley Cres. NG8: Stre .............5D 30
Wellin Cl. NG12: Edwal .............2D 68
Wellin Ct. NG12: Edwal .............2D 68
Wellington Cir.
 NG1: Nott .............4B 4 (5F 45)
Wellington Ct. NG1: Nott .............4C 4
 NG16: Eastw .............3B 16
Wellington Cres. NG2: West Br .............4B 58
Wellington Pl. NG16: Eastw .............3B 16
Wellington Rd. NG2: Bur J .............2G 37
Wellington Sq. NG7: Nott .............3A 4 (4E 45)
Wellington St. DE75: Hea .............3B 14
 NG3: Nott .............1E 5 (3G 45)
 NG9: Stap .............5E 53
 NG10: Long E .............2E 63
 NG16: Eastw .............2B 16
Wellington Ter. NG7: Radf .............4E 45
Wellington Vs. NG7: Lent .............4E 45
Wellin La. NG12: Edwal .............2D 68
Wells Gdns. NG3: Nott .............1B 46
Wellspring Dale NG9: Stap .............6G 53
Wells Road, The NG3: Mapp, Nott .............5A 34
Welstead Av. NG8: Aspl .............5G 31
Welton Gdns. NG6: Bulw .............5G 19
Welwyn Rd. NG8: Woll .............4E 43
Wembley Gdns. NG9: Bram .............1B 54
Wembley Rd. NG5: Arn .............2D 34
Wemyss Gdns. NG8: Woll .............6B 44
Wendling Gdns. NG5: Bestw .............6F 21
Wendover Dr. NG8: Aspl .............5H 31
Wenlock Cl. NG16: Gilt .............5E 17
Wenlock Dr. NG2: West Br .............6B 58
Wensleydale Cl. NG8: Aspl .............6B 32
Wensleydale Rd. NG10: Long E .............1D 72
Wensley Rd. NG5: Woodt .............2A 34
Wensor Av. NG9: Lent A .............3F 55
Wentworth Ct. NG16: Kimb .............1G 29
Wentworth Cft. DE75: Hea .............2E 15
Wentworth Rd. NG5: Sher .............5F 33
 NG9: Chil .............5C 54
Wentworth St. DE7: Ilk .............5C 28
Wentworth Way NG12: Edwal .............2D 68
Wesleyan Chapel Wlk. NG9: Stap .............4F 53
Wesley Ct. NG5: Sher .............5G 33
 (off Drayton St.)
Wesley Gro. NG5: Sher .............6F 33
Wesley Pl. NG9: Stap .............3G 53
Wesley St. DE7: Ilk .............3A 28
 NG5: Sher .............6F 33
 NG16: Lang M .............2F 15
Wesley Way NG11: Rudd .............1H 77
Wessex Dr. NG16: Gilt .............5C 16
West Av. NG2: West Br .............4A 58
 NG9: Stap .............3G 53
 NG10: Sand .............5C 52
Westbourne Ct. NG9: Bram .............2H 53
WEST BRIDGFORD .............5A 58
Westbury Cl. NG9: Chil .............1C 64
Westbury Rd. NG5: Sher .............5D 32
Westby La. NG16: Babb, Coss .............3E 29
Westcliffe Av. NG4: Ged .............4F 35
 NG12: Rad T .............5G 49
Westcliffe Ct. NG12: Rad T .............5G 49
West Cl. NG12: Key .............5G 79
West Cres. NG9: Bee .............1H 65
W. Cross Av. NG9: Stap .............3G 53
Westdale Cl. NG10: Long E .............2C 72
Westdale Ct. NG4: Carl .............5F 35

Westdale Cres. NG4: Carl .............6G 35
Westdale La. E. NG4: Carl .............5E 35
Westdale La. W. NG3: Mapp .............4C 34
West Dr. NG7: Nott .............3H 55
West End NG9: Bee .............6F 55
 NG14: Calv .............3E 11
West End Arc. NG1: Nott .............4C 4 (5F 45)
West End Cres. DE7: Ilk .............1H 39
West End Dr. DE7: Ilk .............1H 39
West End St. NG9: Stap .............5E 53
West End Vs. NG12: Rad T .............6E 49
 (off Main Rd.)
 NG14: Lowd .............2H 25
Westerfield Way NG11: Wilf .............1E 67
Westerham Cl. NG8: Bilb .............2D 42
Westerham Rd. NG11: Rudd .............1F 77
Westerhope Cl. NG12: Edwal .............1E 69
Westerlands NG9: Stap .............5G 53
Western Av. NG13: Bing .............4D 50
Western Blvd. NG8: Aspl, Basf .............1A 44
Western Dr. DE75: Hea .............5D 14
Western Flds. NG11: Rudd .............1F 77
Western Gdns. NG8: Aspl .............1B 44
Western St. NG1: Nott .............3F 5 (4H 45)
Western Ter. NG7: Nott .............4A 4 (5E 45)
Westfield Av. DE75: Hea .............5D 14
Westfield Cl. DE7: Kirk H .............3G 39
Westfield Dr. DE7: Ilk .............5H 27
Westfield La. NG14: Woodbo .............1A 24
Westfield Rd. NG13: Bing .............5D 50
West Furlong NG12: Cotg .............3G 71
West Gate NG10: Long E .............6G 63
Westgate Ct. NG9: Chil .............6E 55
Westgate St. NG3: Nott .............3A 46
WEST HALLAM .............1B 38
WEST HALLAM COMMON .............1A 38
Westhay Ct. NG8: Woll .............4A 44
Westholme Gdns. NG8: Aspl .............3A 44
Westhorpe Av. NG3: Nott .............4B 46
Westhorpe Dr. NG10: Long E .............5E 63
Westland Av. NG15: Huck .............1D 18
W. Leake La. NG11: King .............6C 74
Westleigh Rd. NG8: Brox .............5E 31
Westmaner Ct. NG9: Chil .............6D 54
West Mnr. Pk. NG14: Epp .............5F 13
Westminster Av. NG10: Sand .............6E 53
Westminster Cl. NG3: Nott .............2A 46
West Moor NG2: Colw .............5F 47
Westmoore Cl. NG3: Mapp .............4D 34
Westmoore Ct. NG3: Mapp .............4D 34
Westmoreland Ct. NG5: Sher .............6F 33
 (off Ebury Rd.)
Weston Av. NG7: Radf .............3E 45
Weston Cl. NG5: Woodt .............3A 34
Weston Cotts. NG7: Radf .............3C 44
Weston Cres. NG10: Long E .............3B 72
Weston St. DE75: Hea .............5E 15
Weston Ter. NG5: Sher .............4G 33
West Pk. Ct. NG10: Long E .............6F 63
West Park Leisure Cen. .............6D 62
Westpoint NG2: West Br .............4H 57
Westray Cl. NG9: Bram .............6B 42
West Rd. NG7: Nott .............1B 56
West St. DE7: Ilk .............2A 40
 DE75: Hea .............3B 14
 NG2: Nott .............4H 5 (5A 46)
 NG5: Arn .............6A 22
 NG12: Shel .............6H 37
 NG15: Huck .............4G 7
 NG16: Kimb .............3A 30
 NG16: Lang M .............2F 15
West Ter. DE7: Ilk .............6B 28
 NG15: Huck .............4G 7
West Vw. NG2: West Br .............6H 57
Westview Ct. NG4: Carl .............1H 47
West Vw. Rd. NG4: Carl .............1H 47
WESTVILLE .............1D 18
Westville Dr. NG2: West Br .............5A 58
Westville Dr. NG15: Huck .............2E 19
Westville Gdns. NG3: Nott .............2H 45
West Wlk. NG2: Nott .............4H 5 (5A 46)
Westward Av. NG9: Bee .............5G 55
Westway NG12: Cotg .............3F 71
Westwick Rd. NG8: Bilb .............3C 42
Westwick St. DE7: Ilk .............3C 40
Westwood Rd. NG2: Nott .............5B 46
Wetherby Cl. NG8: Aspl .............6H 31
 NG16: Kimb .............6G 17
Wetherlam Cl. NG2: Nott .............1G 57
Weybridge Cl. DE7: West H .............1B 38
Wharfedale NG8: Woll .............6B 42
Wharfedale Rd. NG10: Long E .............1C 72
Wharf Gdns. NG13: Bing .............6C 50
Wharf La. NG12: Rad T .............6E 49
Wharf Rd. NG7: Nott .............6C 4 (6F 45)
Wharncliffe Rd. DE7: Ilk .............1A 40

Wharton Cres. NG9: Bee .............1F 65
Whatton Dr. NG2: West Br .............2F 67
Whatton Ri. NG5: Sher .............3F 33
Wheatacre Rd. NG11: Clif .............4D 66
Wheat Cl. NG8: Bilb .............4D 42
Wheatcroft Vw. NG2: West Br .............2G 67
Wheatfields Rd. NG3: Nott .............2C 46
Wheatgrass Rd. NG9: Chil .............6B 54
Wheatley Cl. NG11: Rudd .............2G 77
Wheatley Dr. NG4: Carl .............2E 47
Wheatley Gro. NG9: Chil .............1F 65
Wheatsheaf Cl. NG14: Bur J .............3F 37
Wheeldale Cl. NG8: Woll .............5B 42
Wheeldon Cl. DE7: Ilk .............1B 28
Wheeldon Ct. NG7: Basf .............6D 32
Wheeler Av. NG16: Eastw .............4D 16
Wheeler Ga. NG1: Nott .............4D 4 (5G 45)
Wheldon Av. NG4: Carl .............5E 35
Whernside Rd. NG5: Woodt .............2A 34
Whetstone Cl. NG16: Nuth .............5D 30
Whickham Ct. NG2: Nott .............2H 57
Whilton Cres. DE7: West H .............1B 38
Whimsey Pk. NG4: Carl .............3H 47
Whinbush La. NG14: Calv .............1G 11
Whinfell Cl. NG11: Clif .............3D 66
Whinlatter Dr. NG5: Top V .............5E 59
Whiston Cl. NG5: Bestw .............1E 33
Whitbread St. NG7: Basf .............1D 44
Whitburn Rd. NG9: Toton .............2G 63
Whitby Cl. NG8: Woll .............5B 42
Whitby Cres. NG5: Woodt .............2C 34
Whitby Rd. NG16: Newth .............2C 16
Whitchurch Cl. NG5: Top V .............5D 20
Whitcliffe Gdns. NG2: West Br .............6B 58
Whitcombe Gdns. NG5: Top V .............5E 21
Whiteacre NG14: Bur J .............2E 37
Whitebeam Gdns. NG6: Bulw .............6F 19
Whitechapel St. NG6: Basf .............5B 32
White City Trad. Est.
 NG2: Nott .............6C 46
White Furrows NG12: Cotg .............3E 71
Whitegate Va. NG11: Clif .............4B 66
Whitehead Cl. DE7: Ilk .............5H 27
Whitelands NG12: Cotg .............3G 71
White Lodge Gdns. NG8: Bilb .............2D 42
Whitely Av. DE7: Ilk .............2B 28
Whitely Cl. NG9: Stap .............3G 53
WHITEMOOR .............1B 44
Whitemoor Av. NG8: Aspl, Basf .............1B 44
Whitemoor Ct. NG8: Aspl .............1B 44
Whitemoor Ct. Ind. Est.
 NG8: Aspl .............1B 44
Whitemoor Rd. NG6: Basf .............5B 32
Whitemoss Cl. NG8: Woll .............6E 43
White Rd. NG5: Basf .............4C 32
White's Av. NG3: Nott .............3D 46
Whites Cft. NG14: Woodbo .............1B 24
Whiteways Ct. NG11: Clif .............4C 66
Whitfield Cl. NG11: Wilf .............5F 57
Whiting Av. NG9: Toton .............3H 63
Whittaker Rd. NG9: Chil .............2A 64
Whittier Rd. NG2: Nott .............6C 46
Whittingham Ct. NG3: Mapp .............4C 34
Whittingham Rd. NG3: Mapp .............4C 34
Whitton Cl. NG5: Top V .............4F 21
 NG9: Chil .............3C 64
Whitwell Cl. DE7: Ilk .............1A 28
 NG8: Brox .............6F 31
Whitwell Rd. NG8: Brox .............6E 31
Whitworth Dr. NG12: Rad T .............1E 61
 NG14: Bur J .............5C 36
Whitworth Ri. NG5: Top V .............5D 20
Whitworth Rd. DE7: Ilk .............3B 40
Whyatt Cl. NG5: Arn .............1H 33
Whyburn La. NG15: Huck .............4C 6
Whyburn Pct. NG15: Huck .............6E 7
Whyburn St. NG15: Huck .............5A 8
Whysall Rd. NG10: Long E .............6D 62
Whysall St. DE75: Hea .............3C 14
Whyston Ct. NG15: Huck .............6C 6
Whytehall Ct. NG10: Long E .............2E 73
Wibberley Dr. NG11: Rudd .............6F 67
Wichal Cl. NG5: Bestw .............2G 33
Wichnor Cl. NG11: Clif .............1C 66
Wickens Wlk. NG3: Nott .............3A 46
 (not continuous)
Wicker Cl. NG6: Basf .............3C 32
Wicket Gro. NG7: Lent .............5C 44
Wickets, The NG2: West Br .............2B 58
Wickstead Cl. NG5: Woodt .............4B 34
Widdowson Cl. NG6: Bulw .............5F 19
Widdowson Rd. NG10: Long E .............2D 72
Widdowson's Row
 NG11: Rudd .............6G 67
 (off Easthorpe St.)
Widecombe La. NG11: Clif .............5B 66

Widmerpool La. NG12: Key, Widm . . . . . . . . . .5A **80**
WIGHAY . . . . . . . . . . . . . . . . . . . . . . . . . . . . . .2F **7**
Wighay Rd. NG15: Huck . . . . . . . . . . . . . . . . . .2F **7**
Wigley Cl. NG3: Nott . . . . . . . . . . . . . . . . . . . .3A **46**
Wigman Ct. NG15: Huck . . . . . . . . . . . . . . . . . .5B **8**
Wigman Rd. NG8: Bilb . . . . . . . . . . . . . . . . . . .1D **42**
Wigwam Gro. NG15: Huck . . . . . . . . . . . . . . . . .4A **8**
Wigwam La. NG15: Huck . . . . . . . . . . . . . . . . . .4A **8**
Wilberforce Rd. NG11: Wilf . . . . . . . . . . . . . . . .6E **57**
Wilcocksons Yd. *NG15: Huck* . . . . . . . . . . . . . .*4G **7***
　　　　　　　　　　　　　　　　　　　*(off Baker St.)*
Wilden Cres. NG11: Clif . . . . . . . . . . . . . . . . . .2C **66**
Wildman St. NG7: Radf . . . . . . . . . .1A **4** (3E **45**)
WILFORD . . . . . . . . . . . . . . . . . . . . . . . . . . . .5F **57**
Wilford Cres. NG11: Rudd . . . . . . . . . . . . . . . .5G **67**
Wilford Cres. E. NG2: Nott . . . . . . . . . . . . . . . .2H **57**
Wilford Cres. W. NG2: Nott . . . . . . . . . . . . . . .1G **57**
Wilford Gro. NG2: Nott . . . . . . . . . . . . . . . . . .1G **57**
　　　　　　　　　　　　　　　　　　　*(not continuous)*
WILFORD HILL . . . . . . . . . . . . . . . . . . . . . . . .1A **68**
Wilford Hill Crematorium NG2: West Br . . . . .2H **67**
　　NG11: West Br, Wilf . . . . . . . . . . . . . . . . .5F **57**
Wilford La. NG2: West Br . . . . . . . . . . . . . . . . .5F **57**
Wilford Rd. NG2: Nott . . . . . . . . . . .6D **4** (1F **57**)
　　　　　　　　　　　　　　　　　　　*(not continuous)*
　　NG11: Rudd . . . . . . . . . . . . . . . . . . . . . . .2F **67**
Wilford St. NG2: Nott . . . . . . . . . . .6D **4** (6G **45**)
Wilfrid Gro. NG2: West Br . . . . . . . . . . . . . . . .2A **68**
Wilkins Gdns. NG11: Clif . . . . . . . . . . . . . . . . .4A **66**
Wilkinson Av. NG9: Bee . . . . . . . . . . . . . . . . . .5F **55**
Wilkinson Cl. NG9: Chil . . . . . . . . . . . . . . . . . .3B **64**
Wilkinson St. NG7: Basf . . . . . . . . . . . . . . . . . .6B **32**
　　NG8: Basf . . . . . . . . . . . . . . . . . . . . . . . .6B **32**
Wilkinson Street (Park & Ride) . . . . . . . . . . . .1C **44**
Wilkinson Street Stop (NET) . . . . . . . . . . . . .1C **44**
Willaston Cl. NG6: Cin . . . . . . . . . . . . . . . . . . .3A **32**
Willbert Rd. NG5: Arn . . . . . . . . . . . . . . . . . . .5C **22**
Willerby Rd. NG5: Woodt . . . . . . . . . . . . . . . . .2C **34**
Willersley Dr. NG2: Nott . . . . . . . . . . . . . . . . .1G **57**
Willesden Grn. NG16: Nuth . . . . . . . . . . . . . . .4D **30**
William Av. NG16: Eastw . . . . . . . . . . . . . . . . .3B **16**
William Bancroft Bldg. NG3: Nott . . . . . . . . . .2H **5**
William Booth Birthplace Mus. . . . . . . . . . . . .5A **46**
William Booth Rd. NG2: Nott . . . . . . . . . . . . . .5C **46**
William Cl. NG4: Ged . . . . . . . . . . . . . . . . . . .1B **48**
William Gregg VC Leisure Cen. . . . . . . . . . . . .4D **14**
William Lee Bldgs. NG7: Nott . . . . . . . . . . . . . .3B **56**
William Olds Ct. NG8: Woll . . . . . . . . . . . . . . . .4G **43**
William Rd. NG2: West Br . . . . . . . . . . . . . . . .3A **58**
　　NG9: Stap . . . . . . . . . . . . . . . . . . . . . . . .4F **53**
Williams Dr. NG14: Calv . . . . . . . . . . . . . . . . .2G **11**
Williamson Gdns.
　　NG16: Lang M . . . . . . . . . . . . . . . . . . . . .2E **15**
Williamson Row *NG5: Bestw* . . . . . . . . . . . . .*2E **33***
　　　　　　　　　　　　　　　　　　　*(off Arnold Rd.)*
Williams Rd. NG9: Chil . . . . . . . . . . . . . . . . . .2A **64**
William St. NG10: Long E . . . . . . . . . . . . . . . . .3E **63**
　　NG15: Huck . . . . . . . . . . . . . . . . . . . . . . .4G **7**
Willoughby Av. NG7: Lent . . . . . . . . . . . . . . . .5D **44**
　　NG10: Long E . . . . . . . . . . . . . . . . . . . . . .3E **63**
Willoughby Cl. DE72: Brea . . . . . . . . . . . . . . . .5B **62**
　　NG7: Nott . . . . . . . . . . . . . . . . . . . . . . . .3H **55**
Willoughby Ct. NG7: Lent . . . . . . . . . . . . . . . .6D **44**
Willoughby Rd. NG2: West Br . . . . . . . . . . . . . .5B **58**
Willoughby St. NG7: Lent . . . . . . . . . . . . . . . .6D **44**
　　NG9: Bee . . . . . . . . . . . . . . . . . . . . . . . . .4F **55**
Willow Av. NG4: Carl . . . . . . . . . . . . . . . . . . .1A **48**
　　NG9: Stap . . . . . . . . . . . . . . . . . . . . . . . .5F **53**
　　NG10: Long E . . . . . . . . . . . . . . . . . . . . . .4F **63**
　　NG15: Huck . . . . . . . . . . . . . . . . . . . . . . .1D **18**
Willow Brook NG12: Key . . . . . . . . . . . . . . . . .5A **80**
Willowbrook Ct. NG2: Nott . . . . . . . . . . . . . . .2G **57**
Willow Cl. NG2: West Br . . . . . . . . . . . . . . . . .2F **59**
　　NG12: Rad T . . . . . . . . . . . . . . . . . . . . . .1F **61**
　　NG14: Bur J . . . . . . . . . . . . . . . . . . . . . . .2F **37**
　　NG16: Lang M . . . . . . . . . . . . . . . . . . . . .2F **15**
Willow Cotts. NG8: Bilb . . . . . . . . . . . . . . . . . .2G **43**
Willow Ct. NG2: West Br . . . . . . . . . . . . . . . . .6H **57**
Willow Cres. NG4: Ged . . . . . . . . . . . . . . . . . .5A **36**
　　NG4: Lamb . . . . . . . . . . . . . . . . . . . . . . . .6B **24**
Willowdene NG12: Cotg . . . . . . . . . . . . . . . . . .2G **71**
Willow Hill Cl. NG6: Bulw . . . . . . . . . . . . . . . .1G **31**
Willow La. NG4: Ged . . . . . . . . . . . . . . . . . . . .5H **35**
Willow Ri. NG10: Sand . . . . . . . . . . . . . . . . . . .6D **52**
Willow Rd. NG2: West Br . . . . . . . . . . . . . . . . .1A **68**
　　NG4: Carl . . . . . . . . . . . . . . . . . . . . . . . .1A **48**
　　NG7: Lent . . . . . . . . . . . . . . . . . . . . . . . .2C **56**
　　NG13: Bing . . . . . . . . . . . . . . . . . . . . . . . .5G **51**
Willows, The NG8: Bilb . . . . . . . . . . . . . . . . . .2G **43**
　　NG9: Bee . . . . . . . . . . . . . . . . . . . . . . . . .5F **55**
Willow Vw. NG7: Radf . . . . . . . . . . . . . . . . . . .3D **44**
Willow Wong NG14: Bur J . . . . . . . . . . . . . . . .2F **37**
Willow Wong Cotts. NG14: Bur J . . . . . . . . . . .2F **37**
Willwell Dr. NG2: West Br . . . . . . . . . . . . . . . .2G **67**
Wilmington Gdns. NG5: Arn . . . . . . . . . . . . . . .1H **33**
Wilmore Cl. NG9: Chil . . . . . . . . . . . . . . . . . . .1D **64**

Wilmot La. NG9: Bee . . . . . . . . . . . . . . . . . . . .6F **55**
Wilmot St. DE7: Ilk . . . . . . . . . . . . . . . . . . . . .6A **28**
　　DE75: Hea . . . . . . . . . . . . . . . . . . . . . . . .4C **14**
　　NG10: Long E . . . . . . . . . . . . . . . . . . . . . .2C **72**
Wilne Av. NG10: Long E . . . . . . . . . . . . . . . . . .3C **72**
Wilne Cl. NG10: Long E . . . . . . . . . . . . . . . . . .3B **72**
Wilne La. DE72: Dray . . . . . . . . . . . . . . . . . . . .3A **72**
　　NG10: Long E . . . . . . . . . . . . . . . . . . . . . .3A **72**
Wilne Rd. NG10: Long E . . . . . . . . . . . . . . . . . .3B **72**
Wilson Av. DE75: Los . . . . . . . . . . . . . . . . . . .1A **14**
Wilson Cl. NG5: Arn . . . . . . . . . . . . . . . . . . . .1D **34**
Wilson Rd. NG16: Eastw . . . . . . . . . . . . . . . . .4B **16**
Wilsons Ct. NG11: Rudd . . . . . . . . . . . . . . . . . .6G **67**
WILSTHORPE . . . . . . . . . . . . . . . . . . . . . . . . .5D **62**
Wilsthorpe Rd. DE72: Brea . . . . . . . . . . . . . . . .5A **62**
　　NG10: Long E . . . . . . . . . . . . . . . . . . . . . .5D **62**
Wilton Pl. DE7: Ilk . . . . . . . . . . . . . . . . . . . . .6B **28**
Wilton Rd. NG7: Radf . . . . . . . . . . . . . . . . . . .3C **44**
Wilton St. DE7: Ilk . . . . . . . . . . . . . . . . . . . . .6B **28**
　　NG6: Basf . . . . . . . . . . . . . . . . . . . . . . . .3C **32**
Wilton Ter. NG6: Basf . . . . . . . . . . . . . . . . . . .3C **32**
Wimbledon Dr. NG16: Nuth . . . . . . . . . . . . . . .4E **31**
Wimbledon Rd. NG5: Sher . . . . . . . . . . . . . . . .4E **33**
Wimborne Cl. NG2: West Br . . . . . . . . . . . . . . .6G **57**
Wimbourne Rd. NG7: Radf . . . . . . . . . . . . . . . .3D **44**
Wimpole Rd. NG9: Bram . . . . . . . . . . . . . . . . . .2D **54**
Winchester Av. NG9: Bee . . . . . . . . . . . . . . . . .3E **55**
Winchester Ct. NG5: Sher . . . . . . . . . . . . . . . . .4A **34**
Winchester Cres. DE7: Ilk . . . . . . . . . . . . . . . . .1C **40**
Winchester St. NG5: Sher . . . . . . . . . . . . . . . . .4G **33**
Winchester Ter. NG5: Sher . . . . . . . . . . . . . . . .4G **33**
Windermere Av. DE7: Kirk H . . . . . . . . . . . . . . .4G **39**
Windermere Cl. NG2: Gam . . . . . . . . . . . . . . . .4F **59**
　　NG4: Ged . . . . . . . . . . . . . . . . . . . . . . . . .5H **35**
Windermere Gdns. NG10: Long E . . . . . . . . . . . .3D **62**
Windermere Rd. NG7: H Grn . . . . . . . . . . . . . . .1E **45**
　　NG9: Bram . . . . . . . . . . . . . . . . . . . . . . . .2D **54**
　　NG10: Long E . . . . . . . . . . . . . . . . . . . . . .3C **62**
　　NG15: Huck . . . . . . . . . . . . . . . . . . . . . . .4F **7**
Windings, The *NG4: Carl* . . . . . . . . . . . . . . . .*2F **47***
　　　　　　　　　　　　　　　　　　*(off Chesterfield St.)*
Windles Sq. NG14: Calv . . . . . . . . . . . . . . . . . .4A **12**
Windley Dr. DE7: Ilk . . . . . . . . . . . . . . . . . . . .4H **27**
Windmill Av. NG15: Huck . . . . . . . . . . . . . . . . .5G **7**
Windmill Cl. NG3: Nott . . . . . . . . . . . . . . . . . .4B **46**
　　NG11: Goth . . . . . . . . . . . . . . . . . . . . . . . .6H **75**
Windmill Ct. NG12: Key . . . . . . . . . . . . . . . . . .5H **79**
Windmill Gro. NG15: Huck . . . . . . . . . . . . . . . .4G **7**
Windmill La. NG2: Nott . . . . . . . . . . . . . . . . . .5A **46**
　　NG3: Nott . . . . . . . . . . . . . . . . . . . . . . . .5A **46**
Windmill Vw. NG2: Nott . . . . . . . . . . . . . . . . . .5C **46**
Windrush Cl. NG9: Bram . . . . . . . . . . . . . . . . . .2D **54**
Windsor Cl. DE75: Hea . . . . . . . . . . . . . . . . . . .2C **14**
　　NG9: Trow . . . . . . . . . . . . . . . . . . . . . . . .4D **40**
　　NG15: Huck . . . . . . . . . . . . . . . . . . . . . . .3H **7**
Windsor Ct. DE7: West H . . . . . . . . . . . . . . . . .1B **38**
　　NG10: Long E . . . . . . . . . . . . . . . . . . . . . .6G **63**
　　NG10: Sand . . . . . . . . . . . . . . . . . . . . . . .1D **62**
　　NG13: Bing . . . . . . . . . . . . . . . . . . . . . . . .5C **50**
Windsor Cres. DE7: Kirk H . . . . . . . . . . . . . . . .4H **39**
　　NG5: Woodt . . . . . . . . . . . . . . . . . . . . . . .1C **34**
　　NG9: Stap . . . . . . . . . . . . . . . . . . . . . . . .4G **53**
Windsor Ho. NG3: Mapp P . . . . . . . . . . . . . . . .1G **45**
Windsor St. NG9: Bee . . . . . . . . . . . . . . . . . . . .5G **55**
　　NG9: Stap . . . . . . . . . . . . . . . . . . . . . . . .4G **53**
Wing All. NG1: Nott . . . . . . . . . . . .4F **5** (5H **45**)
Wingate Cl. NG8: Bilb . . . . . . . . . . . . . . . . . . .3F **43**
Wingbourne Wlk. NG6: Bulw . . . . . . . . . . . . . . .4A **20**
　　　　　　　　　　　　　　　　　　　*(not continuous)*
Wingfield Dr. DE7: Ilk . . . . . . . . . . . . . . . . . . .4H **27**
Wings Dr. NG15: Huck . . . . . . . . . . . . . . . . . . .1D **18**
Winfield Cl. NG11: Wilf . . . . . . . . . . . . . . . . . . .5E **57**
Winifred Cres. NG14: Bur J . . . . . . . . . . . . . . . .3F **37**
Winifred St. NG15: Huck . . . . . . . . . . . . . . . . . .5H **7**
Winrow Gdns. NG6: Basf . . . . . . . . . . . . . . . . .4A **32**
Winscale Av. NG5: Top V . . . . . . . . . . . . . . . . .5E **21**
Winscale Gdns. NG5: Top V . . . . . . . . . . . . . . . .5E **21**
Winscombe Mt. NG11: Clif . . . . . . . . . . . . . . . .5B **66**
Winsford Cl. NG8: Aspl . . . . . . . . . . . . . . . . . .5H **31**
Winster Av. NG4: Carl . . . . . . . . . . . . . . . . . . .6F **35**
Winster Cl. NG9: Lent A . . . . . . . . . . . . . . . . . .2F **55**
Winster Pk. DE7: Ilk . . . . . . . . . . . . . . . . . . . .4C **40**
Winster Way NG10: Long E . . . . . . . . . . . . . . . .3B **72**
Winston Cl. NG3: Mapp . . . . . . . . . . . . . . . . . .2E **35**
　　NG9: Stap . . . . . . . . . . . . . . . . . . . . . . . .3G **53**
Winterbourne Dr. NG9: Stap . . . . . . . . . . . . . . .2G **53**
Winterton Cl. NG5: Arn . . . . . . . . . . . . . . . . . .1B **34**
Winterton Ri. NG5: Bestw . . . . . . . . . . . . . . . . .6F **21**
Winthorpe Rd. NG5: Arn . . . . . . . . . . . . . . . . . .6C **22**
Wintringham Cres. NG5: Woodt . . . . . . . . . . . .2C **34**
Wirksworth Rd. DE7: Kirk H . . . . . . . . . . . . . . .4F **39**
Wisa Ter. NG5: Sher . . . . . . . . . . . . . . . . . . . .4H **33**
Wishford Av. NG7: Lent . . . . . . . . . . . . . . . . . .6C **44**
Wisley Cl. NG2: West Br . . . . . . . . . . . . . . . . . .2G **67**
Wistow Cl. NG8: Basf . . . . . . . . . . . . . . . . . . .1C **44**

Withern Rd. NG8: Brox . . . . . . . . . . . . . . . . . . .6F **31**
Witney Cl. NG5: Top V . . . . . . . . . . . . . . . . . . .5C **20**
Wittering Cl. NG10: Long E . . . . . . . . . . . . . . . .2G **73**
Wiverton Rd. NG7: H Grn . . . . . . . . . . . . . . . . .1E **45**
　　NG13: Bing . . . . . . . . . . . . . . . . . . . . . . . .5E **51**
Woburn Cl. NG12: Edwal . . . . . . . . . . . . . . . . .1E **69**
Woburn Cft. NG10: Sand . . . . . . . . . . . . . . . . .1C **62**
Woburn Ri. NG5: Woodt . . . . . . . . . . . . . . . . . .2D **34**
Wodehouse Av. NG11: Goth . . . . . . . . . . . . . . .5H **75**
Wolds Dr. NG12: Key . . . . . . . . . . . . . . . . . . . .5H **79**
Wolds Farm Cotts. NG12: Stant W . . . . . . . . . .2D **80**
Wolds La. NG12: C'ton . . . . . . . . . . . . . . . . . . .5D **70**
　　NG12: Key . . . . . . . . . . . . . . . . . . . . . . . .6G **79**
　　NG12: Norm W . . . . . . . . . . . . . . . . . . . . .6B **70**
Wolds Ri. NG12: Key . . . . . . . . . . . . . . . . . . . .4H **79**
Woldsview Ho. NG12: Cotg . . . . . . . . . . . . . . . .2F **71**
WOLLATON . . . . . . . . . . . . . . . . . . . . . . . . . . .6D **42**
Wollaton Av. NG4: Ged . . . . . . . . . . . . . . . . . . .4F **35**
Wollaton Ct. NG6: Bulw . . . . . . . . . . . . . . . . . .1C **32**
Wollaton Cres. NG9: Bee . . . . . . . . . . . . . . . . .3E **55**
Wollaton Hall . . . . . . . . . . . . . . . . . . . . . . . . .6G **43**
Wollaton Hall Dr. NG8: Woll . . . . . . . . . . . . . . .6B **44**
Wollaton Paddocks NG8: Woll . . . . . . . . . . . . . .5C **42**
Wollaton Pk. Golf Course . . . . . . . . . . . . . . . . .6H **43**
Wollaton Ri. NG8: Woll . . . . . . . . . . . . . . . . . . .1E **55**
Wollaton Rd. NG8: Radf, Woll . . . . . . . . . . . . . .5E **43**
　　NG9: Bee . . . . . . . . . . . . . . . . . . . . . . . . .1C **54**
Wollaton St. NG1: Nott . . . . . . . . . . .3B **4** (4F **45**)
　　NG15: Huck . . . . . . . . . . . . . . . . . . . . . . .4H **7**
Wollaton Va. NG8: Woll . . . . . . . . . . . . . . . . . .5B **42**
Wolsey Av. NG7: Radf . . . . . . . . . . . . . . . . . . .4D **44**
Wood Av. NG10: Sand . . . . . . . . . . . . . . . . . . .5C **52**
Woodbank Dr. NG8: Woll . . . . . . . . . . . . . . . . .1D **54**
WOODBOROUGH . . . . . . . . . . . . . . . . . . . . . . .1C **24**
Woodborough La. NG3: Mapp . . . . . . . . . . . . . .2D **22**
　　NG5: Arn . . . . . . . . . . . . . . . . . . . . . . . . .2D **22**
Woodborough Rd. NG1: Nott . . . . . . . .1E **5** (3G **45**)
　　NG3: Mapp, Nott . . . . . . . . . . . . .1E **5** (3G **45**)
Woodbridge Av. NG11: Clif . . . . . . . . . . . . . . . .2C **66**
Woodbridge Cl. DE75: Hea . . . . . . . . . . . . . . . .4F **15**
Woodbridge Ct. *NG7: H Grn* . . . . . . . . . . . . . .*2D **44***
　　　　　　　　　　　　　　　　　　　*(off St Paul's Av.)*
Woodchurch Rd. NG5: Arn . . . . . . . . . . . . . . . . .4F **21**
Wood End Rd. DE75: Hea . . . . . . . . . . . . . . . . .3C **14**
Wood Farm Ct. NG5: Thru . . . . . . . . . . . . . . . . .5C **74**
Woodfield Rd. NG8: Brox . . . . . . . . . . . . . . . . .6E **31**
Woodford Cl. NG5: Top V . . . . . . . . . . . . . . . . .4C **20**
Woodford Rd. NG5: Woodt . . . . . . . . . . . . . . . .2C **34**
　　NG15: Huck . . . . . . . . . . . . . . . . . . . . . . .5H **7**
Woodgate Cl. NG12: Cotg . . . . . . . . . . . . . . . . .2E **71**
Woodgate Ct. NG7: Radf . . . . . . . . . .3A **4** (4E **45**)
Woodgate La. NG12: Cotg . . . . . . . . . . . . . . . . .1D **70**
Wood Gro. NG14: Calv . . . . . . . . . . . . . . . . . . .3H **11**
Woodhall Rd. NG8: Woll . . . . . . . . . . . . . . . . . .4H **43**
Woodhedge Dr. NG3: Nott . . . . . . . . . . . . . . . . .1C **46**
Woodhouse Gdns. NG11: Rudd . . . . . . . . . . . . .5F **67**
Woodhouse St. NG3: Nott . . . . . . . . . . . . . . . . .4B **46**
Woodhouse Way NG8: Stre . . . . . . . . . . . . . . . .1D **42**
　　NG16: Nuth . . . . . . . . . . . . . . . . . . . . . . .1D **42**
Woodkirk Rd. NG11: Clif . . . . . . . . . . . . . . . . . .3D **66**
Woodland Av. DE7: Ilk . . . . . . . . . . . . . . . . . . .3H **27**
　　DE72: Brea . . . . . . . . . . . . . . . . . . . . . . . .5B **62**
　　NG6: Bulw . . . . . . . . . . . . . . . . . . . . . . . .2A **32**
Woodland Cl. NG12: Cotg . . . . . . . . . . . . . . . . .3F **71**
　　NG12: Rad T . . . . . . . . . . . . . . . . . . . . . .6H **49**
　　NG16: Want . . . . . . . . . . . . . . . . . . . . . . .6A **18**
Woodland Ct. NG9: Bee . . . . . . . . . . . . . . . . . .4G **55**
Woodland Dr. NG3: Mapp P . . . . . . . . . . . . . . .6H **33**
　　NG16: Nuth . . . . . . . . . . . . . . . . . . . . . . .3F **31**
Woodland Gro. NG4: Colw . . . . . . . . . . . . . . . . .3H **47**
　　NG5: Sher . . . . . . . . . . . . . . . . . . . . . . . .3H **33**
　　NG9: Chil . . . . . . . . . . . . . . . . . . . . . . . . .6D **54**
Woodland Rd. NG2: West Br . . . . . . . . . . . . . . .2B **58**
Woodlands, The NG12: Rad T . . . . . . . . . . . . . .6E **49**
Woodlands Farm Cl.
　　NG15: Huck . . . . . . . . . . . . . . . . . . . . . . .1D **18**
Woodlands Gro. NG15: Huck . . . . . . . . . . . . . . .1D **18**
Woodland Way NG16: Eastw . . . . . . . . . . . . . . .3A **16**
Wood La. NG4: Ged . . . . . . . . . . . . . . . . . . . . .6A **36**
　　NG15: Huck . . . . . . . . . . . . . . . . . . . . . . .4E **7**
Woodlane Gdns. NG3: Nott . . . . . . . . . . . . . . . .2B **46**
Woodlark Ho. NG3: Nott . . . . . . . . . . . . . . . . . .2B **46**
Woodleigh NG12: Key . . . . . . . . . . . . . . . . . . . .5G **79**
Woodleigh Gdns. NG3: Mapp . . . . . . . . . . . . . .5D **34**
Wood Leys NG3: Nott . . . . . . . . . . . . . . . . . . . .2C **46**
Woodley Sq. NG6: Bulw . . . . . . . . . . . . . . . . . .3A **20**
Woodley St. NG11: Rudd . . . . . . . . . . . . . . . . . .6G **67**
Wood Link NG6: Bulw . . . . . . . . . . . . . . . . . . . .6E **19**
Woodpecker Cl. NG13: Bing . . . . . . . . . . . . . . . .6F **51**
Woodpecker Hill DE7: D Ab . . . . . . . . . . . . . . . .6E **39**
Woodrow Av. NG8: Bilb . . . . . . . . . . . . . . . . . . .1G **43**
Woodsend Cl. NG14: Bur J . . . . . . . . . . . . . . . .3F **37**
Woodsford Gro. NG11: Clif . . . . . . . . . . . . . . . .3C **66**
Woodside NG16: Eastw . . . . . . . . . . . . . . . . . . .3A **16**
Woodside Av. NG12: Rad T . . . . . . . . . . . . . . . .6H **49**
　　NG16: Nuth . . . . . . . . . . . . . . . . . . . . . . .1B **30**

Woodside Cres. DE7: Ilk . . . . . . . . . . . . . . . . . . . . .2H 27
　NG10: Long E . . . . . . . . . . . . . . . . . . . . . . . .5D 62
Woodside Dr. NG5: Arn . . . . . . . . . . . . . . . . . . . .5H 21
Woodside Rd. NG9: Bee, Lent A . . . . . . . . . . . . .2F 55
　NG9: Chil . . . . . . . . . . . . . . . . . . . . . . . . . . .1A 64
　NG10: Sand . . . . . . . . . . . . . . . . . . . . . . . . .6C 52
　NG12: Rad T . . . . . . . . . . . . . . . . . . . . . . . . .6H 49
　NG14: Bur J . . . . . . . . . . . . . . . . . . . . . . . . .4D 36
Woods La. NG14: Calv . . . . . . . . . . . . . . . . . . . . .4G 11
Woodstock Av. NG7: Radf . . . . . . . . . . . . . . . . . .3C 44
Woodstock Rd. NG9: Toton . . . . . . . . . . . . . . . . .2G 63
Woodstock St. NG15: Huck . . . . . . . . . . . . . . . . .5H 7
Woodstock St. W. NG15: Huck . . . . . . . . . . . . . . .4H 7
Woodston Wlk. NG5: Arn . . . . . . . . . . . . . . . . . . .3C 22
Wood St. DE7: Ilk . . . . . . . . . . . . . . . . . . . . . . . . .6B 28
　NG5: Arn . . . . . . . . . . . . . . . . . . . . . . . . . . .5H 21
　NG7: Radf . . . . . . . . . . . . . . . . . . . .3A 44 (4E 45)
　NG16: Eastw . . . . . . . . . . . . . . . . . . . . . . . . .3B 16
WOODTHORPE . . . . . . . . . . . . . . . . . . . . . . . . . . .2B 34
Woodthorpe Av. NG5: Woodt . . . . . . . . . . . . . . . .3A 34
Woodthorpe Ct. NG5: Sher . . . . . . . . . . . . . . . . . .4A 34
Woodthorpe Dr. NG3: Mapp . . . . . . . . . . . . . . . . .3A 34
　NG5: Woodt . . . . . . . . . . . . . . . . . . . . . . . . .3H 33
Woodthorpe Gdns. NG5: Sher . . . . . . . . . . . . . . .4B 34
Woodthorpe Grange NG5: Woodt . . . . . . . . . . . .4A 34
Woodthorpe M. NG5: Woodt . . . . . . . . . . . . . . . .3H 33
Woodthorpe Rd. NG3: Mapp . . . . . . . . . . . . . . . . .4B 34
Woodvale NG8: Woll . . . . . . . . . . . . . . . . . . . . . . .5B 42
Woodview NG12: Cotg . . . . . . . . . . . . . . . . . . . . .2G 71
　NG12: Edwal . . . . . . . . . . . . . . . . . . . . . . . .2D 68
Woodview Bus. Cen. NG5: Top V . . . . . . . . . . . . .4E 21
Woodview St. NG3: Nott . . . . . . . . . . . . . . . . . . . .4E 47
Woodville Cl. NG9: Chil . . . . . . . . . . . . . . . . . . . . .5C 54
Woodville Dr. NG5: Sher . . . . . . . . . . . . . . . . . . . .4G 33
Woodville Rd. NG5: Sher . . . . . . . . . . . . . . . . . . .5G 33
Woodward Av. NG9: Chil . . . . . . . . . . . . . . . . . . . .3B 64
Woodward St. NG2: Nott . . . . . . . . . . . . . . . . . . . .2H 57
Woodyard La. NG8: Woll . . . . . . . . . . . . . . . . . . . .4G 43
　　　　　　　　　　　　　　　　(Coachmans Cft.)
　NG8: Woll . . . . . . . . . . . . . . . . . . . . . . . . . . .4G 43
　　　　　　　　　　　　　　　　(Tom Blower Cl.)
Woolacombe Cl. NG3: Mapp . . . . . . . . . . . . . . . . .2F 35
Wooliscroft Cl. DE7: Ilk . . . . . . . . . . . . . . . . . . . . .5G 27
Woolmer Rd. NG2: Nott . . . . . . . . . . . . . . . . . . . .2G 57
Woolpack La. NG1: Nott . . . . . . . . . . .4F 5 (5H 45)
Woolsington Cl. NG8: Stre . . . . . . . . . . . . . . . . . .5D 30
Woolsthorpe Cl. NG8: Bilb . . . . . . . . . . . . . . . . . . .3F 43
Woolsthorpe Cres. DE7: Kirk H . . . . . . . . . . . . . . .5H 39
Wootton Cl. NG8: Bilb . . . . . . . . . . . . . . . . . . . . . .2D 42

Worcester Gdns. NG5: Woodt . . . . . . . . . . . . . . . .1A 34
Worcester Rd. NG5: Woodt . . . . . . . . . . . . . . . . . .2A 34
Wordsworth Av. NG15: Huck . . . . . . . . . . . . . . . . .5D 6
Wordsworth Rd. NG2: West Br . . . . . . . . . . . . . . .5A 58
　NG5: Arn . . . . . . . . . . . . . . . . . . . . . . . . . . .6H 21
　NG7: Radf . . . . . . . . . . . . . . . . . . . . . . . . . . .3C 44
　NG16: Aws . . . . . . . . . . . . . . . . . . . . . . . . . .2E 29
Worksop Rd. NG3: Nott . . . . . . . . . . . . . . . . . . . . .4B 46
Worrall Av. NG5: Arn . . . . . . . . . . . . . . . . . . . . . . .6B 22
　NG10: Long E . . . . . . . . . . . . . . . . . . . . . . . .4G 63
Worth St. NG4: Carl . . . . . . . . . . . . . . . . . . . . . . .1G 47
Worthy Row NG5: Bestw . . . . . . . . . . . . . . . . . . .2E 33
　　　　　　　　　　　　　　　　　(off Arnold Rd.)
Wortley Av. NG9: Trow . . . . . . . . . . . . . . . . . . . . . .6F 41
Wortley Cl. DE7: Ilk . . . . . . . . . . . . . . . . . . . . . . . .1C 40
Wortley Hall Cl. NG7: Nott . . . . . . . . . . . . . . . . . . .1A 56
Worwood Dr. NG2: West Br . . . . . . . . . . . . . . . . . .1G 67
Woulds Fld. NG12: Cotg . . . . . . . . . . . . . . . . . . . . .4F 71
Wragby Rd. NG7: Lent . . . . . . . . . . . . . . . . . . . . . .4C 44
Wray Cl. NG3: Nott . . . . . . . . . . . . . . . . . . . . . . . .4A 46
Wren Cl. NG10: Long E . . . . . . . . . . . . . . . . . . . . .3C 72
Wren Dr. NG6: Bestw V . . . . . . . . . . . . . . . . . . . . .2C 20
Wrenthorpe Va. NG11: Clif . . . . . . . . . . . . . . . . . . .4C 66
Wrights Orchard NG12: Key . . . . . . . . . . . . . . . . .5G 79
Wright St. NG4: Neth . . . . . . . . . . . . . . . . . . . . . . .2A 48
Wroughton Ct. NG16: Eastw . . . . . . . . . . . . . . . . .3C 16
Wroxham Dr. NG8: Woll . . . . . . . . . . . . . . . . . . . . .6D 42
Wychwood Dr. NG9: Trow . . . . . . . . . . . . . . . . . . .1F 53
Wychwood Rd. NG13: Bing . . . . . . . . . . . . . . . . . .5C 50
Wycliffe Gro. NG3: Mapp . . . . . . . . . . . . . . . . . . . .5A 34
Wycliffe St. NG7: Basf . . . . . . . . . . . . . . . . . . . . . .6D 32
Wycombe Cl. NG11: Clif . . . . . . . . . . . . . . . . . . . . .5B 66
Wye Gdns. NG7: Radf . . . . . . . . . . . . . . . . . . . . . .3B 44
Wykeham Rd. NG5: Woodt . . . . . . . . . . . . . . . . . .2C 34
Wykes Av. NG4: Ged . . . . . . . . . . . . . . . . . . . . . . .5H 35
Wymondham Cl. NG5: Arn . . . . . . . . . . . . . . . . . .1C 34
Wynbreck Dr. NG12: Key . . . . . . . . . . . . . . . . . . . .4H 79
Wyndale Dr. DE7: Kirk H . . . . . . . . . . . . . . . . . . . .3G 39
Wyndham Ct. NG9: Chil . . . . . . . . . . . . . . . . . . . . .1B 64
Wyndham M. NG3: Mapp P . . . . . . . . . . . . . . . . . .2F 45
Wyndings, The NG5: Woodt . . . . . . . . . . . . . . . . .3B 34
Wynhill Ct. NG13: Bing . . . . . . . . . . . . . . . . . . . . .4C 50
Wynndale Dr. NG5: Sher . . . . . . . . . . . . . . . . . . . .4E 33
Wynwood Cl. NG9: Toton . . . . . . . . . . . . . . . . . . . .3B 64
Wynwood Rd. NG9: Toton . . . . . . . . . . . . . . . . . . .3B 64
Wynyard Cl. DE7: Ilk . . . . . . . . . . . . . . . . . . . . . . .4G 27
Wyrale Dr. NG8: Stre . . . . . . . . . . . . . . . . . . . . . . .6E 31
Wysall La. NG11: Bunny . . . . . . . . . . . . . . . . . . . .6D 78
　NG12: Key . . . . . . . . . . . . . . . . . . . . . . . . . . .6G 79

Wyton Cl. NG5: Bestw . . . . . . . . . . . . . . . . . . . . . .2E 33
Wyvern Av. NG10: Long E . . . . . . . . . . . . . . . . . . .1F 73
Wyvern Cl. NG16: Newth . . . . . . . . . . . . . . . . . . . .5C 16
Wyville Cl. NG7: Radf . . . . . . . . . . . . . . . . . . . . . . .4C 44

## Y

Yalding Dr. NG8: Woll . . . . . . . . . . . . . . . . . . . . . .5C 42
Yalding Gdns. NG8: Woll . . . . . . . . . . . . . . . . . . . .5C 42
Yard, The NG7: H Grn . . . . . . . . . . . . . . . . . . . . . . .3D 44
　　　　　　　　　　　　　　　　(off Sophie Rd.)
Yard Gallery, The . . . . . . . . . . . . . . . . . . . . . . . . .6G 43
Yarwell Cl. NG3: Nott . . . . . . . . . . . . . . . . . . . . . . .2E 47
Yatesbury Cres. NG8: Stre . . . . . . . . . . . . . . . . . .1E 43
Yates Gdns. NG5: Top V . . . . . . . . . . . . . . . . . . . .5E 21
Ye Olde Trip To Jerusalem Inn . . . . . . . . . . . . . . . .6D 4
　　　　　　　　　　　　　　　　(off Castle Rd.)
Yeoman Av. NG6: Bestw V . . . . . . . . . . . . . . . . . . .1D 20
Yeomans Pde. NG4: Carl . . . . . . . . . . . . . . . . . . . .2H 47
Yewbarrow Cl. NG2: West Br . . . . . . . . . . . . . . . . .6E 59
Yew Cl. NG5: Sher . . . . . . . . . . . . . . . . . . . . . . . . .5H 33
Yewdale Cl. NG2: West Br . . . . . . . . . . . . . . . . . . .6E 59
　NG11: Clif . . . . . . . . . . . . . . . . . . . . . . . . . . .5B 66
Yew Tree Av. NG5: Sher . . . . . . . . . . . . . . . . . . . .6G 33
Yew Tree Cl. NG12: Rad T . . . . . . . . . . . . . . . . . . .6D 48
Yew Tree Ct. NG5: Sher . . . . . . . . . . . . . . . . . . . .6G 33
　NG9: Bee . . . . . . . . . . . . . . . . . . . . . . . . . . .5G 55
Yew Tree La. NG4: Ged . . . . . . . . . . . . . . . . . . . . .5A 36
　NG11: Clif . . . . . . . . . . . . . . . . . . . . . . . . . . .3A 66
Yew Tree Rd. NG15: Huck . . . . . . . . . . . . . . . . . . .6H 7
Yonge Cl. NG12: Rad T . . . . . . . . . . . . . . . . . . . . .1E 61
York Av. NG9: Bee . . . . . . . . . . . . . . . . . . . . . . . . .1F 65
　NG10: Sand . . . . . . . . . . . . . . . . . . . . . . . . . .6C 52
York Cl. NG4: Ged . . . . . . . . . . . . . . . . . . . . . . . . .5H 35
York Dr. NG8: Stre . . . . . . . . . . . . . . . . . . . . . . . . .5D 30
Yorke St. NG15: Huck . . . . . . . . . . . . . . . . . . . . . . .4G 7
York Rd. NG10: Long E . . . . . . . . . . . . . . . . . . . . .4E 63
York St. NG1: Nott . . . . . . . . . . . . . . . . . .1E 5 (3G 45)
　NG4: Neth . . . . . . . . . . . . . . . . . . . . . . . . . . .2A 48
Young Cl. NG6: Bulw . . . . . . . . . . . . . . . . . . . . . . .2F 31
Yvonne Cres. NG4: Carl . . . . . . . . . . . . . . . . . . . . .2H 47

## Z

Zone, The NG1: Nott . . . . . . . . . . . . . . . . . . . . . . . .3F 5
Zulla Rd. NG3: Mapp P . . . . . . . . . . . . . . . . . . . . .1G 45
Zulu Rd. NG7: Basf . . . . . . . . . . . . . . . . . . . . . . . .5D 32

### SAFETY CAMERA INFORMATION

PocketGPSWorld.com's CamerAlert is a self-contained speed and red light camera warning system for SatNavs and Android or Apple iOS smartphones/tablets. Visit www.cameralert.co.uk to download.

Safety camera locations are publicised by the Safer Roads Partnership which operates them in order to encourage drivers to observe with speed limits at these sites. It is the driver's absolute responsibility to be aware of and to adhere to speed limits at all times.

By showing this safety camera information it is the intention of Geographers' A-Z Map Company Ltd., to encourage safe driving and greater awareness of speed limits and vehicle speed. Data accurate at time of printing.